PORNOGRAPHY AND SEXUAL REPRESENTATION

VOLUME II

Recent Titles in
American Popular Culture

American Popular Music: A Reference Guide
Mark W. Booth

American Popular Illustration: A Reference Guide
James J. Best

Recreational Vehicles and Travel: A Resource Guide
Bernard Mergen

Magic: A Reference Guide
Earle J. Coleman

Newspapers: A Reference Guide
Richard A. Schwarzlose

Radio: A Reference Guide
Thomas Allen Greenfield

Popular American Housing: A Reference Guide
Ruth Brent and Benyamin Schwarz, editors

Fashion and Costume in American Popular Culture: A Reference Guide
Valerie Burnham Oliver

Editorial Cartooning and Caricature: A Reference Guide
Paul P. Somers, Jr.

American Mystery and Detective Novels: A Reference Guide
Larry Landrum

Self-Help and Popular Religion in Early American Culture: An Interpretive Guide
Roy M. Anker

Self-Help and Popular Religion in Modern American Culture: An Interpretive Guide
Roy M. Anker

PORNOGRAPHY AND SEXUAL REPRESENTATION

A Reference Guide

VOLUME II

Joseph W. Slade

American Popular Culture
M. Thomas Inge, Series Editor

GREENWOOD PRESS
Westport, Connecticut • London

Library of Congress Cataloging-in-Publication Data

Slade, Joseph W.
    Pornography and sexual representation : a reference guide / by Joseph W. Slade.
      p. cm.—(American popular culture, ISSN 0193–6859)
    Includes bibliographical references and index.
    ISBN 0–313–27568–8 (set : alk. paper)—ISBN 0–313–31519–1 (vol. I : alk. paper)—
ISBN 0–313–31520–5 (vol. II : alk. paper)—ISBN 0–313–31521–3 (vol. III : alk. paper)
    1. Pornography—United States—Bibliography. 2. Pornography—United States. I. Title.
II. Series.
Z7164.P84S56   2001
[HQ472.U6]
016.3634'7—dc21   99–085695

British Library Cataloguing in Publication Data is available.

An on-line version of *Pornography and Sexual Representation:
A Reference Guide* is available from Greenwood Press,
an imprint of Greenwood Publishing Group, Inc.
(ISBN 0–313–31536–1)

Library of Congress Catalog Card Number: 99–085695
ISBN: 0–313–27568–8 (set)
       0–313–31519–1 (Volume I)
       0–313–31520–5 (Volume II)
       0–313–31521–3 (Volume III)
ISSN: 0193–6859

First published in 2001

Greenwood Press, 88 Post Road West, Westport, CT 06881
An imprint of Greenwood Publishing Group, Inc.
www.greenwood.com

Printed in the United States of America

The paper used in this book complies with the
Permanent Paper Standard issued by the National
Information Standards Organization (Z39.48–1984).

10 9 8 7 6 5 4 3 2 1

Copyright Acknowledgments

The author and the publisher gratefully acknowledge permission for use of the following material:

Excerpts from David Aaron Clark, "Madonna Exposed," *Gauntlet*, 5 (1993): 18–23. Reprinted with permission from *Gauntlet*.

Excerpts from David Aaron Clark, "Interview with Annie Sprinkle," *Gauntlet*, 1:5 (1993): 123–130. Reprinted with permission from *Gauntlet*.

Excerpts from Nina Hartley, "Pornography at the Millennium," *Gauntlet*, 14 (1997): 20–24. Reprinted with permission from *Gauntlet*.

Excerpts from Nina Hartley, "Reflections of a Feminist Porn Star," *Gauntlet*, 5 (1993): 62–68. Reprinted with permission from *Gauntlet*.

Excerpts from Rhonda Nettles, "Let Me Tell Ya 'bout Suffering," *Gauntlet*, 5 (1993): 69–70.

Every reasonable effort has been made to trace the owners of copyright materials in this book, but in some instances this has proven impossible. The author and publisher will be glad to receive information leading to more complete acknowledgments in subsequent printings of the book and in the meantime extend their apologies for any omissions.

For

Judith, Joey, and Marya

Contents

VOLUME III

Preface

This *Reference Guide* is structured around two premises. The first is that re-gardless of how one may feel about pornography, sexual expression, and rep-resentation, it has profoundly enriched American culture. Rather than try to "prove" this assertion, I allow the sources cited to speak for themselves. At the very least, gathering materials together indicates the degree to which pornog-raphy has permeated the social, economic, and political life of America, and I am confident that readers of this *Guide* will be just as astonished as I am by the evidence from so many quarters. As members of a culture, we think about pornography in many different ways. The diversity of opinion is a reminder that far from encapsulating dominant or hegemonic ideas and attitudes—as some critics hold—pornography does not compel assent to a particular agenda. Rather, it invites a constant reevaluation that has so far not tapped the secret of its marginality. Sexual expression somehow continuously refreshes itself, so that it *remains* taboo and thus, in a version of cultural thermodynamics, continuously energizes mainstream social and political expression. *How* pornography remains forever at the edge is not always clear; that it does so is manifest in the debate that it engenders.

The second premise is that pornography and what we say about pornography constitute our principal ways of speaking about sex, one reason that many re-searchers prefer the neutral term *sexual materials* to the more charged word *pornography*. Traced far enough, all such materials, all such forms of speaking, are rooted in the oral genres of folklore. "All folklore is erotic," said the late folklorist Gershon Legman, who had in mind the speech of the unwashed. But, in a larger sense, pornography and the comment that it generates, some of it sophisticated, much of it carried by advanced communication conduits, are con-temporary versions of the same ancient narratives, jokes, and legends that Legman studied. Calling pornography sexual folklore helps to explain its pervasiveness and also its humanity. Pornography can demystify and secularize sexuality and thus weaken the barriers that divide genders and classes of people; it can also betray and shame our erotic longing and thus reinforce those barriers. The sexual discourse of "others" can seem demeaning, dehumanizing, cheap, tawdry, inauthentic, dangerous, commercial, pathetic, or political, while our own seems inspirational, natural, objective, "real," dignified, safe, and spiritual. Agreeing to disagree about sexual expression will probably bring no more permanent peace than agreeing to disagree about religion, politics, or other things we think important, and this *Guide* does not argue that we should.

Comment on pornography—and eroticism—is, without exception, biased along gender, class, racial, religious, aesthetic, and/or ideological lines. My own biases, easily visible, are of the type traditionally called liberal. Moreover, to pretend that my interest is solely academic would be dishonest. Few academics choose to study materials they abhor. The sheer volume of materials I have canvassed has left me largely unaroused, though I do believe that seeking arousal is a perfectly legitimate goal. Every now and then, fortunately, I run across some passage or image that I do find erotic—or, if you will, pornographic— and hope of stimulation can always spring anew. And yes, I am just as often repulsed by what I see and hear and read.

One final observation. When the South African photojournalist Kevin Carter won the Pulitzer Prize in 1993 for his shot of a vulture patiently waiting near a tiny Sudanese child only seconds away from death by starvation, one of my students asked me how a human being who had taken such a photograph could go on living. She received her answer in mid-1994, when Carter committed suicide. Over the years, I have seen in excess of 5,000 pornographic films or videos, and I have looked at perhaps 150,000 pornographic photos in which bodies have been frozen in states of false passion by entirely unrepentant photographers. Not even the most extreme of these have come remotely close to the inhumanity of the scene captured by Carter. The point, made before, though not often enough, is that as Americans we lack a sense of proportion. We are affronted by a picture of an erect penis or a bare breast, but we glance thoughtlessly every day at obscenities that by rights should stop our hearts.

ACKNOWLEDGMENTS

Many people who assisted me in finding material wish to remain anonymous, but I want to thank them anyway. They include writers and fellow academics, casual and professional correspondents, theater owners, bookshop staffs, photographers and publishers, producers and directors, performers and sex workers, and especially collectors; the latter have given me information about, and often access to, some remarkable archives. Of those friends and correspondents I can name, Joe Amato, Bob and Jean Ashton, Bob Barr, Kenneth Bernard, Ruth Bradley, Joan Brewer, Bill Brigman, Joani Blank, Ray Browne, Vern Bullough,

James Card, Greg Crosbie, Bill Dellenback, Paul Gebhard, Jay Gertzman, Larry Gross, Martha Harsanyi, Christie Hefner, Gary Hunt, Tom Inge, Cathy Janes, Walter Kendrick, George Korn, Raoul Kulberg, Gershon Legman, Terence Malley, Ted McIlvenna, J. B. Rund, C. J. Scheiner, Ivan Stormgart, Joan Templeton, and Joseph Vasta all gave generous amounts of encouragement, information, criticism, or time. Graduate assistants Anthony Bush, Usha Zacharias, and Sharon Zechowski have meticulously traced sources and copied articles. Librarians at many institutions here and abroad have been gracious and patient, especially those at the Kinsey Institute for Research in Sex, Gender, and Reproduction; British Film Archives; Long Island University; New York Public Library; George Eastman House; New York University; Ohio University; and University of Texas. I am grateful to three editors at Greenwood Press, Alicia Merritt, Pamela St. Clair, and M. Thomas Inge, the latter the editor for the series of which this *Guide* is a part, for their help and forbearance. Any mistakes in this *Guide* are mine, of course, not theirs.

The influence of two mentors, perhaps visible only to me, has strongly shaped this project. A quarter century ago, long before writing about pornography was commonplace among academics, my first published article on the subject was reprinted in one of those office magazines compiled for doctors by a drug company. In its pages, next to mine, was an article by Margaret Mead (1901–1978), who, to my enormous surprise and pleasure, invited me to tea. A compilation of comment on pornography, she suggested, would be an anthropological treasure. About the same time, my dean at Long Island University, Felice Flanery Lewis, author of *Literature, Obscenity, and the Law* (still one of the best books on literary censorship), shielded me from attacks on my research into sexual expression. That I was granted tenure was due, in large measure, to her principled defenses of faculty. To these two, then, the first an intrepid voyager of cultures, the second a steadfast guardian of intellectual freedom, I owe major debts.

Because immersing one's self in pornography for so long stimulates a sense of the transgressive, I am conscious of having finished this *Guide* with time stolen from my wife and children. I cannot give that time back, but I hope I can repay the affection with which they allowed me to take it.

How to Use This Guide

Organizing the vast comment on pornography and ancillary, but related, representations of sexuality and gender is difficult. The best scheme begins with historical, bibliographic, and broad theoretical approaches, moves to comment on specific genres arranged by communication media, and concludes with overviews of research and policy. Though I hope the merits of this structure will be evident, some redundancy has been inevitable, in part because historians and commentators often make forays into different genres and periods. To assist the reader I have placed "See Also" notations to other chapters where I think they might help.

The *Guide* has been divided into twenty-one chapters arranged in three volumes, with complete table of contents reproduced in each volume. The sequence is roughly from general to specific, with the first volume offering the broadest view. Chapter 1 is a chronology of significant dates in the history of American pornography. Leaving aside a brief introduction and a reflection on the nature of pornography, the first volume begins with a history of American pornography that discusses pornographic media as they become popular: books, art, and magazines precede photography, film, dance, and the Internet. Should you not find what you are looking for at first glance, look further in Chapter 3, **A Brief History of American Pornography**. Bibliographies, indexes, and encyclopedias (Chapter 4) are broken down into categories for convenience, on the assumption that the reader may wish to locate a starting point for research. As Chapter 5 makes clear, context is important; here are other starting points, located in historical commentaries on various issues and sectors of culture. Chapter 6 outlines major theoretical positions (e.g., aesthetic, technological) on the subject of sexual representation.

The remaining sections in volume I are intended as fairly quick references.

Chapter 7 provides information on famous collectors and collections of porno-graphic materials, on major research libraries, and on important subcollections and archives broken down, when possible, by genres or media. Chapter 8 covers child pornography, a category that our culture has legally and conceptually sep-arated from other forms of erotic expression, even though conservatives try to conflate them. Despite the dangers that Michel Foucault thought inherent in classifications of sexuality and gender, categorizing types of erotic expression counters the American tendency to lump all such expression together and makes exploration possible.

The other two volumes treat specific categories. The first chapter of volume II addresses scholarship on beauty, bodies, clothing, fetishes, genitalia, mastur-bation, and appliances. The remaining chapters of the volume explore comment on pornographic expression in dramatic, visual, and electronic media. Here are to be found citations to works dealing with performance, art, photography, mo-tion pictures and videotapes, and electronic media such as the Internet. Volume III outlines criticism on oral, print, and journalistic media by treating folklore, books, newspapers, magazines, advertising, and comic books. Also in the final volume are chapters on research into the nature and effects of pornography, law and censorship, and, finally, economics.

If your subject is exploitation films, for instance, you might begin in volume I with chapter 3 **A Brief History of American Pornography**, look next in film bibliographies in Chapter 4, check Chapter 1 (**Chronology**) for useful dates, and then move to Chapter 13 in volume II for the section on **Exploitation Films**, and go from there to Chapter 19 (**Research on Pornography in the Medical and Social Sciences**) of volume III for studies of effects or to Chapter 20 on **Censorship of Film and Video**. Conversely, you might begin with discussion of the films themselves (Chapter 13) and then backtrack to the broader chapters. The table of contents is detailed enough to suggest links. Almost always, finding material on topics requires looking at several chapters. Comment on *Playboy* magazine, for example, appears in chapters on magazines (17, **Playboy and Its Imitators**), on photography (12, **Female Pinups, Centerfolds, and Magazine Pictorials** and **Models and Techniques**), on research, and on economics, as well as in **A Brief History of American Pornography** (volume I, Chapter 3). As another example, a book of photographic studies of striptease dancers is more likely to be covered in the section on photography (12, **Documentary Photographs**) unless it contains significant textual comment, in which case it would appear in the chapter on performance (10, **Erotic Dance**).

Because this *Guide* deals only with American pornography, I have omitted many excellent works (e.g., Graham Greene's *Lord Rochester's Monkey*, a study of John Wilmot, one of the great British pornographers) that deal with artifacts of other nationalities. It hardly needs saying, I hope, that most of the citations here are to materials designed to shed light on pornography, not to titillate in themselves. Referring to a particular artifact in the larger context of the continuing discussion of sexual representation does not imply that the example is itself pornographic, let alone obscene. Even so, the desire to be as comprehensive as possible has led me to include citations to works that someone, somewhere, has called pornographic. It is silly to speak about pornography without providing examples.

The cutoff point for sources gathered here is late 1998, when the *Guide* started on its way to editors and printers, though as it moved along I added a few in the early part of 1999. Those disappointed not to find up-to-date sources must forgive the lengthy time necessary to make ready so large a work.

Introduction: Performing Sex and Gender

A gob of spit in the face of Art.
> —Henry Miller, speaking of *Tropic of Cancer* (1934)

For Americans today, "pornography" usually refers to visual and electronic depictions of sexuality, to performances such as striptease, to paintings, photographs, and movies, or to images transmitted by Internet rather than to older oral and print genres. The second volume of the *Guide* addresses comment on those categories, after first reviewing American attitudes toward beauty, nudity, cross-dressing, body modification, popular fetishes, masturbation, sex toys, and genitalia in chapter 9, **The Landscape of the Body**. Pornography foregrounds the body and can tell us a great deal about the body's essential aesthetic, moral, and sexual configurations at the same time that it exposes the influence of fashion and style on desire. Here, in fact, pornography's significance becomes obvious. Arbiters of American tastes from Puritans to radical feminists have attempted to denigrate beauty as a snare and a delusion. The naked bodies in pornographic genres are clothed in beauty that triggers biological arousal; beauty—the kind that Santayana wrote about, not fashion—is crucial to survival. In this respect as in others, pornography affirms what we secretly know to be true.

That Americans these days pay a lot of attention to bodies—theirs and others—is clear enough. One school holds that the proliferation of sexy images is a source of dehumanization, a rank form of objectification, especially of women. A second insists on the reverse: that eroticizing everything is an attempt to counter the dehumanization inherent in complex technological social and economic systems, to remind us of our animal natures, and to vent biological energies that artifice cannot entirely dissipate. A third believes that sexual representation serves a corporate ethos that commodifies in order to control. Still others argue that pornography is part of a larger trend of converting all experience—sexual, social, religious, political—into superficiality or—and to such critics it may come down to the same thing—into dessicated data streams, the currency of an information age. In any case, sexual representations reflect and perhaps help determine fashions in bodies, in clothing, in obsessions. Pornography has come to the middle class: Bloomingdale's now sells Tom of Finland shirts and trousers, housewives celebrate their birthdays by piercing their genitals, college students dance naked instead of waiting tables to pay their tuition, and middle-level managers schedule a session with a dominatrix in their favorite dungeon after a game of racquetball at their regular health club. But in the welter of tastes and roles that Americans embrace one might also detect the resolve of individuals determined to take charge of their erotic lives.

Performance studies, which foreground action, depart from quasi-behaviorist poststructuralist theories predicated on the notion that events are static texts and that humans are passively determined. According to theories of performance, events take place in time, involve motion and energy, and result from action and motivation, not merely tropistic responses to behavioral stimuli. Agency and choice generate meaning, and sex *dramatizes* human experience. The effect can be to glamorize the ordinary, as when a waitress demonstrates enough style and skill to become a porn star, or to hype the merely entertaining, as when rock stars simulate intercourse in huge auditoriums, or to socialize the sinister, as when artists warn that unprotected sex can lead to HIV. One performs, say the theorists, in order to be.

One effect of performance theories has been to move discussion away from sterile notions of objectification, a term with almost no meaning in an economy that objectifies and commodifies everything. Given the rewards of pornography, some of which trickle down to performers, women and men line up to model or perform. Exploitation occurs in every industry, may even occur at higher rates in adult businesses than in other enterprises, but women do not have to be drugged or drunk to perform, as one popular myth holds, nor, with so many willing candidates, is there any reason for physical coercion. So many strippers now dance in so many cities that the economics of exotic clubs affect local elections.[1] Every spring break, the nation's youth migrate to beaches and clubs to display their bodies and to mate. The *New York Times* runs ads for "penile enlargement."[2] Playwrights slip swearwords into the mouths of Broadway actors, strip them of their clothing, and pile them in beds together, as often as not to rave reviews. For many Americans, women as well as men, watching pornographic videotapes is as entertaining as watching football on television: both trigger libidos or adrenaline and, in aficionados, appreciation of finer points of ritual.

Or so it seems. Despite decades of media criticism, we know almost nothing about how audiences process messages. Whether one subscribes to the "male gaze" thesis—the notion that masculinity is so dominant as to force everyone to see the world through male eyes—or adopts some other equally beguiling explanation, it is obvious that dramatic and visual representations of sexuality have become an essential component of contemporary American culture. Avoiding such images—as displayed on surfaces as random as billboards, magazine and record album covers, and the catalogs of academic presses—is simply not possible. The trend moves sexual representation beyond low-level genital buzz to a kind of trash synthesis, a recognition by turns exhilarating and oppressive that so many messages mimic erotic tropes. Like all other messages, these program the citizens of a culture, but whether in the main they foster homogeneity or rebellion, emulation or contempt, we do not know. We can dismiss sexual scripts as the flotsam of a culture shipwrecked by its own commerce or eroticized beyond all reason, or we can see in their proliferation a scaling of the world in human terms or a longing for the exotic, but no one interpretation will convince more than a few.

As Chapter 11 (**Erotic and Pornographic Art**) indicates, critics still argue over the place of sexual representation even in works of art so "serious" that they should be hallowed by custom. At the same time, newer generations of Americans raised on romantic clichés are better prepared to deal with the artist's need to find intimations of humanity in folds of flesh. Every now and then, artistic institutions rehabilitate a dirty old man by at last figuring out what he was trying to do. The National Academy recently hung *Men without Women*, a show of notorious canvases, some dating from the 1930s, by the homoerotic painter Paul Cadmus. "My penis is not the most important organ in my body," says the ninety-four-year-old Cadmus, whose explicit paintings have been pulled off walls in the best galleries in America; "My eyes are."[3] Indeed. As Giorgio de Chirico famously observed, the real challenge for the artist is "to make the banal strange." Accomplishing that goal is harder than one would think, and choosing bodies as subjects may or may not do it. What seems most shocking may illuminate not at all, while the cheesy sketch of today might become the masterpiece of tomorrow. Where painting and the plastic arts are concerned, past generations were accustomed to verdicts delivered in the future. Modern marketplaces being what they are, artists, vendors, and consumers are less inclined to wait. Measured against the artifacts of mass reproduction, objets d'art are unique, and their worth can be validated by the prices they command. If *Art in America* takes notice of a painting of intercourse, a sculpture of a penis, or a collage of breasts, then by definition they are not pornographic works but investments. Both a commerce awed at the prices a trendy artist can fetch and a bourgeois conviction that romantic madness drives painters toward obscenity give license to a Larry Rivers or an Andy Warhol but not to a striptease dancer or a porn video producer.

Mass media are, of course, déclassé. Historians easily demonstrate that sexual representation drives each new communication technology, from printing press to Internet, accelerating both the pace of innovations and their diffusion throughout society. Capitalists associate the increased speed and volume of production, distribution, and consumption with the steady march of democratization, but the very cheapness and ubiquity of sexual texts and images seem most problematic to conservatives. With each new technology, access to erotica becomes more available to more Americans in more places, not just to individuals the culture has vetted in venues the culture has set aside. Will pornography circulated without restriction incite the lower classes to commit crimes against their betters or inspire fantasies of mating with those in more privileged sectors of the gene pool, as Anthony Comstock once believed? Can the poor handle sexuality any more intelligently than they vote? Can a society still ask such questions?

Photographs for a time threatened to destroy aesthetics altogether in a blitz of endless reproduction. Americans still worry about the implications of a technology cheaper and more demotic than ever, especially since photographs can still circulate in secret as pocket prints and almost as covertly as images on the Internet. They see corporations issue ever sexier advertisements for products, see collectors trade nude images as obsessively as baseball cards, see magazines such as *Penthouse* issue bolder centerfolds to recapture subscribers lost to videotape viewing. Those same Americans take millions of amateur photographs of each other naked, bedecked in lingerie or fetish garb, or engaged in intercourse, using every kind of camera, from ten-dollar, cardboard, one-use gadgets, to thousand-dollar, fully digitalized Nikons, to immortalize their own erotic moments. Did the invention of the camera turn us into a nation of voyeurs? Hardly. One of Stefan George's memoirs recalled that every woman's bathhouse in mid-nineteenth-century Vienna was riddled with holes drilled there so that men could peep at them. Americans of the past also peeped and spied just as eagerly as their descendants do. Did the camera stabilize the postures considered seductive by a modern culture? Perhaps. After all, how many poses are possible when one is trying to conceal and reveal a body to the fixed focal-length of an unmoving lens? Not to worry: one moving set of eyes peering directly into another moving set still conveys more sexual information than any frozen image. Photography did give Americans portable pictures, however, to study in private.

And that cost the powers-that-be another bit of control. A Foucauldian would immediately say that the culture "disciplines" audiences in other ways, precisely by prescribing the shapes and limits of desire—through internalized standards of beauty, codes of gender, fetishes of one sort or another (big breasts, small male hips), sanctioned positions of intercourse, or those poses of seduction mentioned earlier—and eliciting predictable responses to such stimuli. But who knows what lurks in the sexual consciousness of Americans in the privacy of their homes?

When the managers of video rental stores try to guess, they find that they are wrong at least part of the time. Doubtless mindful of what opinion-makers say they are supposed to think, Americans lie about their sexual preferences to journalists, to surveyors of sex habits, and probably to their mates. They do not lie with their pocketbooks. They rent videotapes with an astonishing array of sexual practices to watch alone or with mates (who may catch hints). Trade journals break out rentals by type, but only after the money is spent, so that outlets must stock titles on the basis of the kinds of tapes patrons have been keen on before. "Couples" tapes may be up one year, down the next, as may be specific kinds of fetish tapes in straight, gay, and lesbian subgenres; confused signals go back up the chain to producers, who scratch their heads and try something else.

More than any other medium, the VCR has demonstrated the fragility of sexual taxonomies. Joshua Meyrowitz observed in *No Sense of Place* that television opened bedrooms, boardrooms, men's clubs, offices, police precincts, and political caucuses to everyone's gaze, a process that undermined not just ideas of childhood and privacy but also racial discrimination and gender inequity. Adult videotapes have removed the secrecy and mystery from sex and thus chipped away at concepts of the forbidden. Watching hard-core tapes, Americans learn that sticking various things in various orifices of various genders or, for that matter, eschewing penetration in favor of reaching climax some other way is a matter of personal choice. Watching a president's privacy being invaded (somewhat ironically, given Clinton's lackluster defenses of the rights of individuals against unwarranted government intrusion) probably reinforced that conviction.

As for the Internet and digital technologies that rampant connectivity will engender, it is still too early to say much. Computers are indifferent to tastes and mores, but commerce, as usual, has a way of accomplishing what the Communications Decency Act could not. As more and more sex Web sites charge for access, requiring passwords, proof of age, and credit card information, minors find themselves shut out.[4] In the meantime, it seems silly to keep debating whether or not pornography has a right to exist when it so manifestly flourishes in cyberspace or to keep complaining about the commercialization of sex when literally everything else has long since been commodified. A capitalist system means that all ideas—good, bad, indifferent, whether subject to Gresham's law or not—must be distributed by commercial media. There would appear to be no other option. But the marketplace is never praised for its discrimination. Does that mean that American culture is going to the dogs? Obviously.

NOTES

1. R. E. Ortega, "The New Morality," *Penthouse*, 30:8 (April 1999): 104.
2. The Barron Centers (New York and Beverly Hills), *New York Times*, 10 May 1999, p. A16.
3. Quoted by Richard Goldstein, "Through the Peephole," *Village Voice*, 18 May 1999, p. 65.
4. David Kushner, "Smuggler's Notch," *Village Voice*, 18 May 1999, p. 36.

9

The Landscape of the Body

NUDITY, FASHIONS, FETISHES, BODY MODIFICATIONS, AND SEXUAL TECHNOLOGIES

Cultural meanings of pornography are intimately bundled with irrational conceptions of the human body. A still influential mode of thought holds that pornography derives its impact from the shame with which Americans regard their bodies and fluids. Augmenting shame is fear, which can be deepened by the mystery of sexuality, about which scientists and the rest of us still understand very little. Of late, however, with the rise to prominence of gender issues, the matter has become more complicated. A significant segment of the feminist antiporn movement shares a traditional American revulsion toward the physical mechanics of sex, a mind-set that is ironic at a time when lesbians, for example, are rediscovering and redefining (reinventing?) their bodies in terms of both discourse and anatomy.

Academic criticism has recently begun to focus on the social and political construction of bodies, often as literary studies that purport to "read" bodies as texts; the more ethereal of these decline to consider actual corporeality, which in some cases is anathematized as mere "essentialism"—an assumption that says more about the authors' levels of comfort with their own bodies than anything else. Typical is Francis Barker's *The Tremulous Private Body: Essays on Subjection*, on the state's attempts to exercise control of the individual citizen's body; Barker, like the authors of a flood of similar books, thinks that conceptions of the body reflect stages of cultural victimization. That cultural factors do help shape our expectations of what bodies should look like seems obvious enough, but the degree to which individual physical appearance conforms to ideals may well involve factors such as class, or so argues Michael Hatt in " 'Making a

Man of Him': Masculinity and the Black Body in Mid-Nineteenth-Century American Sculpture," which theorizes on the social construction of the black male nude as an erotic icon. Feminist and deconstructionist theories assert that there is little "truth" to anatomy, that bodies, in a sense, are the products of ways of seeing that, in turn, are conditioned by ethnic, age, or gender assumptions that vary across regions, cultures, and periods.

In his *Symbolic Exchange and Death*, Jean Baudrillard asserts, "The entire contemporary history of the body is the history of its demarcation, the network of marks and signs that have since covered it, divided it up, annihilated its difference and its radical ambivalence in order to organise it into a structural material for sign-exchange, equal to the sphere of objects, to resolve its playful virtuality and its symbolic exchange (not to be confused with sexuality) into sexuality taken as a determining agency, a *phallic* agency entirely organised around the fetishization of the phallus as the general equivalent" (101). In this and other works, Baudrillard dilates on the concept of the simulacra, an artifice that functions erotically. The publisher's ad for *Tattoo, Torture, Mutilation, and Adornment: The Denaturalization of the Body in Culture and Text*, edited by Francis E. Mascia-Lees and Patricia Sharpe, asserts that "contemporary theory across a wide range of disciplines denaturalizes the body and reveals it to be a social construction. Cultural practices which deform, adorn, mutilate, and obliterate the body illustrate that it is an important site for the inscription of culture," that is, that the body bears cultural messages written upon it by special interest groups following agendas determined by economic and political influences— including, of course, those academic groups most vocal today. The sheer number of ephemeral bodies discovered in a kind of academic "culture space" has led to backlash; in *Thinking through the Body*, Jane Gallop suggests that scholars concentrate on finding a "style" for the body to replace endless theorizing about an "authorless" text. Still others point toward performance studies as a better source of insight.

An ambitious gathering of materials is the multivolume *Fragments for a History of the Human Body*, edited by Michael Feher, Ramona Naddaff, and Nadia Tazi, who have collected artistic, social, political, and medical comment on, and illustrations of, representations of bodies over time. The essays in *The Making of the Modern Body: Sexuality and Society in the Nineteenth Century*, edited by Catherine Gallagher and Thomas Lacquer, discuss Victorian concepts of gender and sexuality along with taxonomies of the body that still resonate in erotic imaginations. Especially interesting are discussions of moral judgments about reproduction, evolution, and spirituality that ranked males higher in cultural hierarchies. In *Making Sex: Body and Gender from the Greeks to Freud*, Lacquer theorizes that sharp distinctions between the two sexes began to emerge only in the eighteenth century, as anatomy itself began to assume political force and influence when women's sexuality was subordinated and made passive, a process completed by Freudian theories of penis envy. Lacquer observes that the popular values and mores of any given period determine the metaphors we use to discuss the body, sex, and gender. The essays in *Sex, Sensibility, and the Gendered Body*, edited by Janet Holland and Lisa Adkins, discuss the construction of female bodies by educational, sociological, legal, medical, and cultural representations through examinations of the body as text. Contributors to *The Sex of Things: Gender and Consumption in Historical Perspective*, edited by Victoria de Grazia with Ellen Furlough, range across nineteenth-century pinups and modern media depictions. Zillah R. Eisenstein's *The Female Body and the Law* maintains that generations of decisions have narrowed the legal standing of women by regulating their bodies.

Jennifer Terry and Jacqueline Urla contrast the conceptions of "normal, healthy" bodies constructed by medicine and science with equally constructed concepts of the homosexual body, the infertile body, the HIV-infected body, and other examples in *Deviant Bodies: Critical Perspectives on Difference in Science and Popular Culture*. The subject of the ideal or conventional female body has evoked a flood of publications by—say detractors—women who do not like theirs. Giving the lie to such detractors is Elizabeth Grosz, whose *Volatile Bodies: Toward a Corporeal Feminism* discusses the body's functions and attributes, especially as a conduit of erotic pleasure. Especially interesting are *Body Guards: The Cultural Politics of Gender Ambiguity*, edited by Julia Epstein and Kristina Straub, who collect essays dealing with social construction versus "essentialism," the latter a sometimes lame postmodern attempt to "explain" why two arms and ears are standard human issue rather than a number that fluctuates across cultures; and *The Female Body: Figures, Styles, Speculations* and *The Male Body: Features, Destinies, Exposures*, both edited by Laurence Goldstein, who brings together contributions by art historians, anthropologists, literary scholars, sociologists, and artists on the male and female body as both an anatomical and culturally constructed artifact. The essays indicate that the "body" as a form of discourse has become common to academic—chiefly feminist—criticism of literature, art, and culture. As just one example, the bodies described in *Sexy Bodies: The Strange Carnalities of Feminism*, an aptly titled anthology edited by Elizabeth Grosz and Elspeth Probyn, will be unfamiliar to the uninitiated, since they are (re)constructed by cultural theorists in discourse often untethered to popular experience.

In *Running Scared: Masculinity and the Representation of the Male Body*, a survey of masculine images veiled in various media, Peter Lehman attempts to demonstrate "how both avoiding the sexual representation of the male body and carefully controlling its limited explicit representations work to support patriarchy" (5). Kenneth R. Dutton traces idealized representations of the male form from Greek kouroi to pinups and strippers in *The Perfectible Body: The Western Ideal of Physical Development*. Alan M. Klein's *Little Big Men: Body Building Subculture and Gender Construction*, perhaps the best of similar texts, discusses the gender implications of powerful male physiques (see also **Gender Disputations: The Male Nude, the Male Pinup, and the Lesbian Photograph** in Chapter 12). Mere academic speculation on "the body" pales beside the more precise sensitivity of pornography producers and distributors, such as Vince Migliore, owner of Manhattan's Gay Pleases shop. Michael Musto says in "The Little Shop of Hornies" that Migliore "can tell you all about trends in gay iconography: 'the beefy, manicured leatherman' has replaced last year's 'buffed-up California boy' " (45).

Critics studying an open-crotch photo in *Penthouse, Blueboy*, or *On Our Backs* draw on postmodern vocabularies to describe the body as the "site" of desire. Even postmodernists are aware of paradoxes, as Pasi Falk notes in *The Consuming Body*. Contemporary pornographic videotapes represent sex by means of "real" bodies; that is, the representations are not "real," being images, but anyone can see that the performers *are* "real" in the sense that their "presence" is being asserted and recorded, says Falk. Such approaches reflect ancient tensions. For decades, pornographic images seemed to capture quotidian realities: flesh was mute, and bodies opaque, much as in the days before bosons and mesons, electrons and protons were thought to be bedrock reality. Even now, as William Irwin Thompson has remarked, "the body is the romantic landscape of the scientific age."[1] Unwilling to accept that characterization, postmodernists deconstruct the body's features; the body becomes a text, a locus that is shaped by cultural forces. The question is, How articulate are these images? Are penises and vaginas something more than their sheer physicality? Is an act of congress freighted with meaning, or is the act itself the meaning? The sex is "real" enough in that it can produce children or transmit HIV, but how important is the *representation* of the act? Such questions can be traced at least as far back as Michel Foucault's *The History of Sexuality*, which warned against the conflation of desire, language, and sexuality into absolutes. Elizabeth Wilson reviews the theories of Foucault and other critics as they apply to the study of bodies in "Fashion and the Postmodern Body."

Since the eroticism of pornographic scenarios usually has nothing to do with reproduction or other consequences of unfettered carnality (women do not become pregnant in porn videos, nor do men develop rashes), pornography has always been theoretically free to turn categories inside out, if only by passing out dildos to anyone who wanted one. Traditional pornographers have long foregrounded what seemed the socially subversive claim that women possess a sexuality so powerful that they will mate with anything: men, women, animals, machines, fruit, and so on. To be sure, the frustrated woman who seduced another woman in erotic genres was usually marking time until an available penis wandered along. Even within the closed erotic narrative, coupling with another woman did not "make" a female "lesbian"—quite the contrary, since she was simply succumbing to a masculinized drive oblivious to boundaries. Because of these assumptions, males besotted with female bodies sometimes cannot understand why their wives and girlfriends are not equally mesmerized by the sight of a lasciviously posed female.

Until recently, however, pornographic authors—always excepting de Sade— have usually balked at making the same assumptions about males; a male who masturbated or fellated another's penis or anally penetrated him was definitively homosexual, and such narratives were relegated to a clear-cut gay genre. Nowadays major male film and video stars such as Tom Byron and Joey Silvera accept inverted roles by permitting anal penetration by women wearing strapon dildos, and while these roles fall within even older pornographic traditions of dominance and submission, they may signal a shift of sorts, as evidenced by the appearance of Shar Rednour's *Bend Over Boyfriend* (1998), an instructional video made for heterosexual women who enjoy penetrating their male lovers with strap-on dildos (it is already so popular that a sequel is in the works). In general, however, the pornographer's typical response to incursion is to spin off specific behavior into different genres and to create new ones if necessary. Thus, while prohibitions against male–male contact in films aimed at heterosexuals have wavered, they erode only so far. The result has been a flood of relatively new bisexual and "she-male" (pre-op transsexual) scenarios. In the latter category, stereotypes of appearance, bizarre though they may be, still prevail. For theorists, however, the freedom associated with pornographic representation is an opportunity to reconstruct sexuality and toy with gender.

Some critics further finesse categories previously thought immutable by speculating on future landscapes of flesh, on "cyborgs," gender engineering, and highly artificial eroticism. Arthur and Marilouise Kroker's *Body Invaders: Panic Sex in America*, contains essays on the place of the body in American culture, with Baudrillardian reflections on fashion as a capitalistic phenomenon, and on gender dynamics of the future. Contributors to *Posthuman Bodies*, edited by Judith Halberstam and Ira Livingston, offer futuristic looks at "queers," transgenders, postgenders, and automated teller machines. Worth noting in this regard, though it speaks more subtly to questions of eroticism, is cyborg theorist Donna Haraway's work, in particular, her "The Biological Enterprise: Sex, Mind, and Profit from Human Engineering to Sociobiology." In *The Last Sex: Feminism and Outlaw Bodies*, "dedicated to resisters against the will to purity, the current manifestation of cultural fascism," Arthur and Marilouise Kroker endorse what they designate a "transgenic gender," a gender outside traditional or even physical categories, one that is constructed by technologies such as body modification, traditional pornographic media, and digitalized graphical interfaces.

CONCEPTS OF BEAUTY

Standards, forms, and ideals of attractiveness shape our conceptions of desirable bodies, say social constructionists. That makes aesthetics the real culprit, although thinking so seems a recrudescence of clichés about beauty's being no more than skin-deep, a suspicion long and insincerely held in Western tradition. Restrictive notions of beauty, say Puritans old and new, lead inevitably to sexual and gender inequities. Those seeking early evidence in America need only look at a quasi-pornographic artifact such as Alexander Walker's 1846 text, *Beauty:*

Analysis and Classification of Beauty in Woman. When even a recent conventional historian such as Edwin M. Schur decries the commercialization of sex in *The Americanization of Sex*, logic compels him to conclude that censoring pornography probably means regulating the cosmetics and fashion industry—the beauty business—as well. H. G. Beigel's "Sex and Human Beauty" is a dated, but still interesting, discussion of the relationship between physical symmetries, aesthetic, ethnic, and racial assumptions, and cultural eroticism. A very basic, extremely well researched, and far-reaching history of American ideals of female beauty is Lois W. Banner's aptly titled *American Beauty*, an excellent starting point for any scholar. "Beauty isn't a moral quality," says a character in Frederic Raphael's *After the War*, "it's a perishable commodity"[2]; and Vincent Canby noted some years ago that beautiful bodies such as Jane Fonda's had "become a multi-million dollar industry."[3] Feminist critics go further by insisting that fashion industries are a species of pornography because of their pernicious commodification of good looks.

The most strident argument is that advanced by Naomi Wolf in *The Beauty Myth: How Images of Beauty Are Used against Women*, which connects pornography with the exploitation of women by fashion, cosmetic, and diet industries that stereotype desirability and, in so doing, make women insecure and competitive. According to Wolf, beauty is mythical, without objective reality, merely the "currency" of a system of male dominance, part of a corporate manipulation of women. That women are oppressed by concepts of beauty is the thesis of Susan Brownmiller in *Femininity*, which discusses the power of aesthetic standards; of Kim Chernin in *The Obsession: Reflections on the Tyranny of Slenderness*, whose title is self-explanatory; of Susan Bordo in *Unbearable Weight: Feminism, Western Culture, and the Body*, which suggests that Westerners fear female fat as a symbol of power; of Arline Liggett and John Liggett in *The Tyranny of Beauty*, which condemns, among other things, silicone implants and cosmetic surgery, practices they compare to the ancient Chinese custom of binding women's feet; of Joseph Hansen and Evelyn Reed in *Cosmetics, Fashions, and the Exploitation of Women*, which is particularly good on the cosmetics industry. Kathy Peiss covers all these bases in her excellent cultural history, *Hope in a Jar: The History of America's Beauty Culture.* Just how important cosmetics are to the pornography industry should be apparent from a glance at the actresses on a porn video box cover. Some American women have learned to use nipple-rouges, labia highlighters, pubic trims, and other specialty adornments to entice their partners as a consequence of having watched such videos.

Although few scholars dispute the charges leveled against the beauty industry, one must be wary (as always with sexual polemics) of the figures sometimes bandied about. In her "Who Stole Feminism?" Christine Hoff Sommers points out that in her *Revolution from Within*, Gloria Steinem reproduced statistics advanced by Naomi Wolf in *The Beauty Myth.* Wolf claimed that 150,000 females die every year in the United States from anorexia—a disease Wolf sees as a form of oppression by a patriarchy that prizes female slimness. Sommers began checking this and other questionable statistics to find that Wolf (or her sources) had inflated the numbers more than a thousand times. The actual figures vary from year to year: in 1983, 101 women died from anorexia, in 1988, only 67, and in 1991, a still smaller 54. Sommers thinks that readers have to make careful distinctions between "gender feminists" and "equity feminists"; it is one thing to campaign for equality between males and females, Sommers says, but another to warp facts to fit ideologies. The point here is not that feminists are dishonest; it is a reminder that "facts" about ideologically heated topics are often suspect.

Wendy Chapkis also counsels common sense in *Beauty Secrets: Women and the Politics of Appearance.* Socially constructed or not, concepts of beauty and fashion are unlikely to lose their power, she says, and there are ways of sifting "erotica from insult" (142). Chapkis bases her thoughtful reflections on case histories. Similarly, Una Stannard speaks less ideologically of the psychic damage stemming from overblown emphasis on aesthetic appearance in "The Mask of Beauty." The bibliography is the most valuable component of Wolfgang Haug's *Critique of Commodity Aesthetics: Appearance, Sexuality, and Advertising in Capitalist Society,* a pretty standard attack on the commodification of beauty and sex focused on predominantly German examples. Jean Baudrillard's "Fashion, Or the Enchanting Spectacle of the Code," a chapter of his *Symbolic Exchange and Death,* investigates nudity and clothing as elements in a coded system of symbolic exchange in which desire is a commodity.

Robin T. Lakoff and Rachel L. Scherr include sections on beefcake and male beauty in *Face Value: The Politics of Beauty,* which is interesting precisely because it does extend political and ideological inquiry to images of masculinity as well as femininity. Stereotypes in advertising and pornography are covered by Edisol Dotson in *Behold the Man: The Hype and Selling of Male Beauty in Media and Culture,* which deals with ideals of fitness and attractiveness both heterosexual and homosexual. The discussion is lively, especially when it ventures into penis size, diet regimens, muscles, "cuteness," cosmetic surgery, and their correlations with self-esteem. The essayists in *Lesbians, Levis, and Lipstick: The Meaning of Beauty in Our Lives,* edited by Jeanine Cogan and Joanie Erickson, address dominant standards of attractiveness, concepts of weight and body shape, and templates of beauty in lesbians of color, among other topics. Dawn Atkins devotes most space to lesbians in *Looking Queer: Body Image and Identity in Lesbian, Bisexual, Gay, and Transgender Communities,* though her approach is compassionate and informative on all those groups ("square pegs" in round cultural categories) mentioned in the title.

General reviews of mores like *American Manners and Morals* by Mary Cable and her colleagues of necessity cover beauty, clothing, modesty, and related matters. Martha Banta's *Imaging American Women: Idea and Ideals in Cultural History* is superb on the shifting iconography of the American woman; her period chapters blend theory and research to provide exceptionally solid information; it is an extraordinary resource. Much more trendy is *Images of Women*, a videocassette produced by the National Film Board of Canada to survey images of women in pornography and in mass media; in this visual compilation, as in all such comment on the subject, the right-thinking condemn the ways in which visuality subordinates women to men, a charge that too often forestalls investigation of the reasons.

In contrast to cultural critics, sociobiologists look at beauty as an evolutionary strategy. A cluster of studies by D. Singh and his colleagues, "Female Judgment of Male Attractiveness and Desirability for Relationships: Role of Waist-to-Hip Ratio and Financial Status"; "Body Weight, Waist-to-Hip Ratio, Breasts and Hips: Role of Judgments of Female Attractiveness and Desirability for Relationships"; and "Ethnic and Gender Consensus for the Effect of Waist-to-Hip Ratio on Judgment of Women's Attractiveness" indicate that the depictions of specific body types to be found in sexually oriented magazines (e.g., *Playboy*) correspond to those physical attributes long associated with "reproductive success" and do so, moreover, across many different cultures. In other words, standards of beauty may, in fact, be correlated with perceived and actual reproductive capacity. Humans may choose partners using, at least, in part, a scale of attractiveness that, however socially constructed, may also function to signal evolutionary advantage. If that be true, then, as John Money points out in "Pornography in the Home: A Topic in Medical Education," nature is itself a pornographer, and lesser forms of pornography, such as those created by humans, may actually serve nature (see **Fetishized Loci of the Body** in this chapter).

Nancy Etcoff reviews many studies (on facial beauty, body symmetries, height, gait, and so on) in *Survival of the Prettiest: The Science of Beauty* (which sounds more Darwinian than it is) to conclude that personal attractiveness is leagued to biological drives as men and women try to assess the evolutionary advantages of producing children with prospective mates about whom they know little but exterior features. As Etcoff puts it, *beauty* is different from *fashion*—the quality that so many cultural critics mistake for "essentialism"—and taxing Madison Avenue with creating preferences is as silly as believing that "Coke or McDonald's created our cravings for sweet or fatty foods" (4). Sociobiologists do not believe that genetics explain fetishes. They acknowledge that elements such as personal tastes and preferences, psychological predispositions, class, fitness, health, and other factors may count but believe that science can also establish certain parameters in which aspects of beauty may correspond to sperm counts, social dominance, ease of impregnation, facility for childbirth, and other factors. As is the case with almost everything having to do with sexual representation, issues of nature versus nurture, or biology versus culture, constantly arise.

But, as Etcoff and others suggest, the insistence that beauty is an illusion masks a cluster of dirty little secrets: that beauty is irresistible, that it counts for far more than we are willing to acknowledge, that it can cause physical reactions in the beholder, that its power makes a shambles of political correctness. Beauty is essential to the pleasure that sexual representations provide. Pornography's power derives from this and other secret truths that we are compelled to deny in public. (See **Other Models** in chapter 19.)

BODIES NAKED

For Americans, clothing or its lack is an important signifier of eroticism. In the United States, the Supreme Court has ruled that nudity alone cannot be equated with obscenity or even with pornography, a distinction rejected by many Americans (and probably by the current chief justice), who still regard the unadorned body in any context as deliberate provocation. The more difficult distinction between *naked* and *nude* is as much a matter of taste as it is of semantics, but a body without clothes is still taboo for many Americans, who, unlike people in many other cultures, tend to equate nudity with sex. *The Body as a Medium of Expression* by Jonathan Benthall and Ted Polhemus, *Bodystyles* by Polhemus alone, and *Body Packaging: A Guide to Human Sexual Display* by Julian Robinson all study the human body as a sexual object and reflect on its presentation. The most provocative of the three is Robinson's discussion of teasing, posture, body language, and the display of erogenous zones, as in raised chest or out-thrust pelvis, flaccid or erect penis, shadowed or visible mons, and so on. Beth Anne Eck's "Body as Social Text: Meaning and Interpretation of the Nude" concludes that the meanings Americans impute to the nude body arise from their social backgrounds and that commodification more than any other factor has led to acceptance of nude images.

Historically fascinating are erudite studies of modesty and the cultural context of nudity by German sexologists of the 1920s, which were gathered into two impressive volumes replete with extraordinary photographs by Ernst Schertel; they are *Scham und Laster* and *Nachtheit als Kultur*; the contributors deal with taboos regarding the body across several cultures. Olivia Vlahos' *Body: The Ultimate Symbol* is another cross-cultural study of attitudes toward the body, its meaning, and the taboos it engenders. A different perspective is offered by Nancy M. Henley's *Body Politics: Power, Sex, and Nonverbal Communication*, which argues that power, status, and dominance govern body displays and profoundly affect sexual relationships. William N. Stephens' *A Cross-Cultural Study of Modesty and Obscenity*, as the title suggests, covers culturally mandated differences in dress as a means of disguising or emphasizing sexuality. More American in its orientation is Stephen Kern's *Anatomy and Destiny: A Cultural History of the Human Body*. The degree to which human shapes conform to a society's ideals of beauty and appropriateness, says Kern, fix the individual's racial and class status, determine success or failure in occupational and political pursuits, and, of course, influence her or his social and sexual relationships. Kern also discusses the role of repression in forming fetishes, though he may overstate the case for Victorian stringency.

Desmond Morris catalogs visual aspects of the body in terms of the responses they evoke in his socioanthropological text, *Body Watching*, a fascinating study illustrated with photographs that make his points. The Morris volume is an excellent companion to Erving Goffman's *Gender Advertisements*, an illustrated sociological study of how humans present themselves to others through visual posturing and performance. Goffman's many volumes explore human behavior as dramatization in situations defined by space or custom and offer many insights on modesty, display, and cultural coding. Paul Ableman's illustrated history of mores concerning the bare body in *Anatomy of Nakedness* deals with styles of display. Of value also is *The Future of Nakedness*, in which the philosopher John Langdon-Davies discusses socially sanctioned nudity, its purposes, its aesthetics, and its cultural context. Margaret Ruth Miles' *Carnal Knowing: Female Nakedness and Religious Meaning in the Christian West* reviews religious attitudes toward female nudity as part of the larger history of Christian doctrine that celebrates both shame and exaltation.

Social nudity, or nudism, which began as a movement extolling the hygienic aspects of going without clothes in Europe early in the century, has encountered a good deal of prejudice in this country, in part because nudist publications seemed to many Americans a species of pornography. An early attack on the alleged immorality of practitioners was Hugh Morris' *Facts about Nudism: The Real Truth about the Nudist Movement*, which charged nudists with conspiracy to destroy Western values; Morris' paranoid reflections on degeneracy resemble those of Max Nordau of the previous century and of Joseph McCarthy later on. Various defenses, like William Welby's *The Naked Truth about Nudism*, have tried to counter similar myths and have, perhaps, promoted others such as the equation of sunshine and health. *Sunshine and Health*, in fact, became the title of the official nudist magazine in the United States; it gave many Americans their first sight of pubic hair other than their own. In the puritanical 1950s, adolescents found its unretouched photos educational and erotic, as if to give credence to their elders' fears that such material was, in fact, pornographic. Official nudist publications are certainly not intended to arouse, but it would be ingenuous to assume, first, that the casual reader cannot be excited by either the photographs or the concept of people getting naked together or, second, that nudists themselves always behave puritanically. Even quasi-official nudists do sometimes engage in public sex on beaches (as opposed to chartered camps, where peer pressure prohibits unseemly contact), for example, or make hard-core films. In any case, several companies advertise nudist photographs and video productions, which might be said to constitute a subgenre of pornography, in men's magazines. (See **Sexuality in Public: Exhibitionism** in chapter 10.)

The ur-text of the domestic nudist movement is *The Joys of Nudism*, written by Ilsley Boone, the dean of American nudism and founder of the original American colony in Mays Landing, New Jersey. The major nudist organizations—most states now boast nudist clubs—have published their own texts as well. The photographs and narrative of *The All Revealing Nude: For Private*

Collection extol the virtues of nudism and proselytize for nudist lifestyles. Other standard works include *As Nature Intended: A Pictorial History of the Nudists*, by Adam Clapham and Robin Constable; *Therapy, Nudity, and Joy: The Therapeutic Use of Nudity through the Ages, from Ancient Ritual to Modern Psychology*, by Aileen Goodson, and *Nudism Comes to America*, by Frances Merrill and Mason Merrill (the last is old but excellent). Most of these volumes suggest that practitioners do not find nudity per se erotic. By contrast, Manfred F. DeMartino thinks the narcissistic aspects of nudism are related to sexual orientation, especially among women, or so he says in *The New Female Sexuality: The Sexual Practices and Experiences of Social Nudists, Potential Nudists and Lesbians*. A now somewhat dated but still excellent volume is *Social Nudism in America*, by Fred Ilfeld Jr. and Roger Laver; it has been superseded by *Nudist Society: An Authoritative, Complete Study of Nudism in America*, by William Hartman, Marilyn Fithian, and Donald Johnson, especially the edition updated by Iris Bancroft. Its pages deal frankly with the subject of nudist sexuality, a refreshing change from texts claiming that sex never crosses the practicing nudist's mind.

BODIES CLOTHED

The "ultimate purpose" of clothes, says J. C. Flugel in his pioneering study, *The Psychology of Clothes*, "is to add to the sexual attractiveness of their wearers, and to stimulate the sexual interest of admirers of the opposite sex and the envy of rivals of the same sex" (26). Kaja Silverman gives Flugel's ideas a feminist twist in "Fragments of a Fashionable Discourse" and there observes that "fashion constructs female subjectivity and female sexuality" (148). Edmund Bergler's *Fashion and the Unconscious* reduces fashion to variations on "seven themes: the breasts, waist, hips, buttocks, legs, arms and length (or circumference) of the body itself" (221). James Laver develops the sexual, social, and cultural symbolism of clothing in great detail in *Modesty in Dress*. Paul Tabori deals with provocative aspects of human clothing and ornamentation in *Dress and Undress: The Sexology of Fashion*, while Bernard Rudofsky foregrounds American fear of nudity in *The Unfashionable Human Body*; hatred of the body, he says, leads to artificial, ugly, and even absurd clothing styles. The indefatigable Adolph F. Niemoller, who commented on every aspect of erotica, published *Essays of an Erotologist*, devoted primarily to sex and clothing; it is still readable. Standard histories of costume rarely emphasize erotic dress, though they may well offer period background, so theoretical considerations of the cultural necessity for clothing are better starting points. Lawrence Langner's *The Importance of Wearing Clothes* is a study of attitudes and institutions, viewed historically and socially. Unlike most writers on mainstream fashion, Langner confronts issues of nudity and modesty and quotes G. B. Shaw to the effect that nobody really knows what makes clothing seductive. Anne Hollander says that a period's emphasis on one or another body parts (e.g., breast or leg or penis) determines not just fashion in clothing but also fashion in nudity and its portrayal; Hollander's *Seeing through Clothes* views clothing as a crucial sign of sexuality in Western art and society. In a compelling explanation of the perishability of pornography, Hollander says that "the nude of any age may seem erotically uninteresting to the eyes of another. We may even mistake an erotically intended image for an idealized one—if it lacks the shapes, proportions, and details we are accustomed to responding to in contemporary life" (88).

Although at first its breezy tone and lack of scholarship seem deficiencies, *Skin to Skin: Eroticism in Dress*, by Prudence Glynn, captivates with common sense and grasp of sensuality. Glynn observes, for instance, that a bared bosom can be of such "classic perfection that it transcend[s] accusations of indecency" (48–49). She pays almost as much attention to the "peacock" male in her determination to uncover the sexual impulses behind fashion. That sexual messages are conveyed by clothing is the thesis of Alison Lurie's *The Language of Clothes*, which is best when it focuses on contemporary fashions. Humans dress to exercise and display power, and all clothes are political, says Colin McDowell in *Dressed to Kill: Sex, Power, and Clothes*. We wear clothes, in the first place, not so much because we fear nudity as because we crave the aphrodisiac properties of fashion. As every couturier knows, says McDowell, clothes excite far more than bare skin. Where male clothes are concerned, the power of the penis is hidden, then represented in phallic shorthand: tight jeans, ridged briefs, or bulging shorts. Ruth P. Rubinstein's *Dress Codes: Meanings and Messages in American Culture* is unconcerned with pornography but does discuss the sexual meanings of clothing. Cultural, political, semiotic, and sexual meanings are taken up as well in the essays by various postmodernists collected by Sheri Benstock and Suzanne Ferriss for *On Fashion*. Similarly, Malcolm Barnard draws on Simmel, Derrida, Baudrillard, Jameson, and other theorists to analyze fashion as signifier for sexuality and gender (and class and ethnicity) in *Fashion as Communication*.

Valerie Steele's *Fashion and Eroticism: Ideals of Feminine Beauty from the Victorian Era to the Jazz Age* brims with information; she cites studies, events, and instances with great authority. For example, Steele notes that a study conducted in 1976 indicates that men and women disagree on what clothing makes women look sexy, a circumstance that will strike some as unremarkable, given the misunderstandings prevalent in gender communication. Steele's "Clothing and Sexuality" deals with contemporary erotic aspects of dress for men and women. Steele explains the differences between breasts exposed at a beach, flaunted in a topless bar, or provocatively revealed at a party. She also points out that male dress appeals most to women when it signifies wealth and power; upscale suits can thus be a turn-on for women looking for mates. Steele's wonderful *Fetish: Fashion, Sex and Power* advances these themes still further; the book explores "fashion as a symbolic system linked to the expression of sexuality—both sexual behavior (including erotic attraction) and gender identity" (4). Ted Polhemus' *Streetstyle* is a guide to bizarre and sometimes sexy fashions among subcultures, or "tribes," including those constructed around music and fringe lifestyles.

Fabrications: Costume and the Female Body, edited by Jane Gaines and Charlotte Herzog, also emphasizes contemporary fashion; the various contributors cover topics ranging from posing outfits for muscular women to garb for flash dancers. Brigette Nioche speculates on the motivations of people who wear revealing apparel in *The Sensual Dresser* and, of course, offers lots of appropriate examples. Dress is ambiguous, says Duncan Kennedy in "Sexual Abuse, Sexy Dressing, and the Eroticization of Domination": dressing provocatively both empowers and makes vulnerable its wearer, on one hand, asserting autonomy, and, on the other, inviting abuse. For a variation on such observations, one can read two books on the peculiar colonial American practice of engaging in intercourse while fully clothed, sometimes by cutting slits in each partner's clothing (which might be an early clue as to why sex and violence are so often linked in the American psyche) or bringing one another to orgasm by rolling about dexterously. These are A. Monroe Aurand Jr.'s *Bundling in the New World* and Henry Reed Stiles' *Bundling: Its Origin, Progress and Decline in America*.

The fashion industry itself seems increasingly to resemble a pornographic subculture, at least as some critics see it. Part of their ire stems from traditionally Puritan antimaterialism, a view that deplores fashion because it adorns bodies corrupt by definition or because it commercializes the basic human need to shield flesh from the elements. Some think that fashion objectifies the human form, principally the female's, and thus—according to cliché—reduces women to sex objects. Others object to the revealing nature of contemporary clothing, which tends to flaunt the genitals or secondary sex characteristics and thus offends taste or morality. The most cynical observe that the fashion industry would have collapsed years ago from sheer irrationality had not couturiers taken their inspiration from costumes once limited to brothels. In this vein is Suzy Menkes' "Regressing, from 'Lolita' to Robbing the Cradle" on "paedophiliac fashion" that seems "perverse and weird" because it transforms women into little girls. In short, Menkes thinks that the clothing industry lends itself too readily to fetishism. (See also **Celebrity and Fashion Nudity in Ads** in chapter 17.)

BODIES GENDERED BY FASHION AND STYLE

While feminists often attack "artificial" standards of beauty and the fashion and cosmetic industries they engender as the root of various evils, gays and lesbians wrestle with different issues. They understand the constructed aspects of clothing and appearance but must cope with their imposition by a culture ignorant of, and even hostile to, their gender identities. Gays and lesbians may flaunt "deviant" clothing as a means of asserting and celebrating difference, or they may wish to redefine style as a means of establishing community, but historically the problem has been invisibility within the greater culture. Theorists thus often speak of clothing as the most visible outward sign of gender.

Such questions can be traced to Foucault's insistence that practice takes precedence over theory. Social construction, once one gets beyond all the talk of power, is at base trendiness, packaging, and style, and wags sometimes ask whether "fashion follows fucking," or vice versa. If two homosexuals want to formally unite, must one of them wear drag to the wedding? What kind of body language do homosexuals use as "come-on" signals? Must gays employ the body language of women, "vogueing," for example, because their own subculture lacks indigenous seductive signals? The title of *What Color Is Your Handkerchief? A Lesbian S/M Sexuality Reader*, by Samois, the San Francisco S/M Support Group, refers to the lesbian practice of wearing differently colored handkerchiefs in the hip pocket to indicate whether one is a "top" or "bottom" partner. How does one distinguish merely by sight a gay penis or lesbian labia from heterosexual genitalia? Is being able to do so important? Is it impolite to notice that Alice B. Toklas had a moustache? For years, such questions were supposed to disturb only heterosexual males, who thought that gays and lesbians were recognizable only if they affected feminine gestures or wore butch clothing. That anatomy does not seem to be objective turns out to be an issue of importance to the homosexual community as well.

The title of Kath Weston's article, "Do Clothes Make the Woman? Gender, Performance Theory, and Lesbian Eroticism," puts the question succinctly. Her answer is that gender is not self-evident from the clothes people wear, nor— and here she appears to argue somewhat with Foucault—from the way they act or behave. (See also: **Gay and Lesbian Theater and Performance** in chapter 10.) Articles such as "Queer Fashion," Tim Goetz's photoessay for *Outweek* on clothing trends for gays and lesbians, are staples of gay and lesbian general interest magazines, while those such as "Deviant Dress," Elizabeth Wilson's musings on lesbians and fashion, appeal to feminist critics. Katrina Rolley's "Cutting a Dash: The Dress of Radclyffe Hall and Una Troubridge" analyzes the historical and cultural imperatives underlying the masculine dress of Hall and her lover. Rolley also looks at the dress of other famous lesbian couples such as Colette and Polaire and Vita Sackville-West and Violet Trefusis in "Love, Desire and the Pursuit of the Whole: Dress and the Lesbian Couple." Rolley has expanded these essays in her *The Lesbian Dandy: The Role of Dress and Appearance in the Formation of Lesbian Identities*. Working in a similar vein in "The Mythic Mannish Lesbian: Radclyffe Hall and the New Woman," Esther Newton speaks of the historic American equation of costume and sexual identity: "For bourgeois women, there was no developed female sexual discourse; there were only male discourses—pornographic, literary, and medical— *about* female sexuality. To become avowedly sexual, the New Woman had to enter the male world, either as a heterosexual in male terms (a flapper) or as—or with—a lesbian in male body drag (a butch)" (573). Inge Blackman and Kathryn Perry get down to cases in "Skirting the Issue: Lesbian Fashions for the 1990s." They deal with styles of clothing from "lipstick lesbian" outfits to masculine ensembles as aids to gender identification and orientation. In their view, fashion can assist the lesbian in "constructing one self after another, exposing her desires in a continual process of experimentation" (77).

Trying to understand gender semiotics leads Susan W. Rollins and Peter C. Rollins into forays among comic books, the merchandising of Madonna, cross-dressing, punk clothing styles, and the fiction of Anaïs Nin as material for *Gender in Popular Culture: Images of Men and Women in Literature, Visual Media, and Material Culture.* According to the Rollinses, current experimentation with clothing and body depictions attests to belief that power should stem from ability and other factors like personality, skill, competence, and merit—not from outdated norms of "masculinity." The academic fascination with gender representations in popular culture evident in *Queer Studies: A Lesbian, Gay, Bi-sexual, and Transgender Anthology,* edited by Brett Beenyn and Mickey Eliason, shades from serious reflections on the cultural implications of gender-bending to Clark Kent–style fantasies, the sort of daydreams that postmodernism encourages. Fred Davis devotes two chapters to the ambivalences of erotic fashions, especially where gender is concerned, in *Fashion, Culture, and Identity.* The essays in *Dress and Gender: Making and Meaning,* edited by Ruth Barnes and Joanne B. Eicher, consider dress as one means of shaping identity through ethnographic examinations of cultures in Asia, Europe, Africa, and the Americas. Mark Simpson focuses on bodybuilding, tattooing, pornography, advertising, sports, and other areas of American life in a broad examination of how gay men appropriate macho styles in *Male Impersonators: Gay Men Performing Masculinity.*

BODIES CROSS-DRESSED

Transvestism, or cross-dressing, should perhaps be discussed in chapter 10, **Performance**, but is included here because the focus is as much on clothing and masquerade as behavior. Effeminate and fey styles have during the last half century or so constituted a virtual subculture analyzed from different perspectives by Susan Sontag in her classic "Notes on Camp" (1964), by the three essays on camp in the second edition (1984) of Richard Dyer's *Gays and Film,* and more recently by the contributors to David Bergman's *Camp Grounds: Style and Homosexuality,* who cover tendencies toward camp from the time of Walt Whitman to more institutionalized forms since. John Degen's attempt to bring precision to a definition led to "Camp and Burlesque: A Study in Contrasts," while Andrew Ross sees camp as a hopelessly vague "operation of taste" (136) in "Uses of Camp," but the literature on the subject is vast. Moe Meyer offers a brief, but solid, historical overview of camp as a term for exaggerated gesture in "The Signifying Invert: Camp and the Performance of Nineteenth-Century Sexology." Meyer has also edited *The Politics and Poetics of Camp*, a grouping of essays on aspects of what is essentially a mode of performance.

Pamela Robertson's *Guilty Pleasures: Feminist Camp from Mae West to Madonna* examines iconographic figures who exaggerate and parody femininity. As gender barriers have deliquesced, cross-dressing, traditionally considered pathological behavior, has become not only accepted but celebrated. (See chapter 4, **Bibliographies and Reference Tools**, Bullough [*Cross-Dressing*].) Since merely listing current cultural manifestations would be tedious, one need only think of the delicious spectacle of white-bread star Julie Andrews appearing in the long-running Broadway show and film *Victor/Victoria*. The humorous appeal of cross-dressing in literature, drama, and film from *Charley's Aunt* to *Victor/Victoria* is the subject of Corinne Hart Sawyer's "Men in Skirts and Women in Trousers, from Achilles to Victoria Grant: An Explanation of a Comedic Paradox."

Transvestism is attractive to critics who find in the deliberate confusion of roles a vision of chaos and potentiality. To others, especially feminist critics, transvestism is a kind of poaching, because males who dress as women can pretend to enjoy the female domain without abandoning any of the perks of male power. In any case, academics have rushed to judgment, and the number of books on transvestism is surging. Sexual politics depend on orientation: for heterosexual males, dressing up in women's clothes is generally regarded as fetishistic, since the object of desire remains the female. For homosexual males, cross-dressing is not usually designated fetishistic, since the object of desire is another male. Or so the theories go; blurred boundaries seem inevitable. At any rate, cross-dressing has interested Americans for some time. Mark Twain's *Following the Equator* (1897) contains a chapter on the gender ambiguities of dress; those interested in his treatment should read Susan Gillman's *Dark Twins: Imposture and Identity in Mark Twain's America.*

Female impersonators have long been popular, much more so than male impersonators, who are only now appearing in significant numbers on lesbian stages; the parodic elements of "drag" shows, the comic spectacle of members of the dominant gender assuming the costume of the other, protected them from excessive censure. Transvestism, like many tastes, can generate both performance and discourse. Anthony Slide's *Great Pretenders: A History of Female and Male Impersonation in the Performing Arts* chronologically treats notable impersonators and costuming from the eighteenth century to the present, as does Catherine Chernayeff, Jonathan David, and Nan Richardson's *Drag Diaries*, a history of cross-dressing subcultures, especially good on the famous and the stylish. Still more comprehensive is *Drag: A History of Female Impersonation in the Performing Arts*, by Roger Baker, with Peter Burton and Richard Smith, which begins with transvestism in the court of Elizabeth I and concludes with reflections on the grunge dress of musicians in the United States; their history is both scholarly and amusing. Another history dealing with transvestism as performance is Peter Ackroyd's *Dressing Up—Transvestism and Drag: The History of an Obsession*, which has a fine bibliography on the subject and is excellent on transvestism in early America. *The Mysteries of Sex: Women Who Posed as Men and Men Who Impersonated Women*, the reprint of a book by C.J.S. Thompson published privately in the 1930s, when discussion skirted legality, is not sensational by modern standards. C. J. Bulliet's classic history of transvestism, *Venus Castina*, first published in 1928, is organized around capsule biographies of famous female impersonators. Esther Newton's *Mother Camp: Female Impersonators in America* is an authoritative anthropological study of drag queens who use cross-dressing as a way of overcoming their sense of powerlessness. *Minette: Recollections of a Part Time Lady*, the autobiography of Steve Watson, a drag queen popular in the 1950s and 1960s, provides information on the underground and quasi-public stage circuits for female impersonators in the United States. E. Carlton Winford's historical look at *Femme Mimics* is helpful on the traveling shows of drag queens in America during the 1950s. In a spirit of gender equity, Home Box Office's *Real Sex* has run "Girls Girls Girls," a segment on Suzanne Bartsch's traveling tour of male transvestites determined to "empower themselves through expression," and "Girls Will Be Boys," a visit to a lesbian theater starring women in male drag complete with artificial phalluses. *Male to Female: La Cage aux Follies*, by Vicki Goldberg, compiles portraits of famous transvestites, drag queens, and transsexuals, with some commentary. (See **Documentary Photographs** in chapter 12, Goldin).

Significant studies include Virginia Prince's *Understanding Cross-Dressing*, a psychological examination of the phenomenon by perhaps the most tireless American promoter of transgenderism, a term that applies to those who shape their lives by clothing rather than surgery; Deborah Heller Feinbloom's *Transvestites and Transsexuals: Mixed Views*, a scholarly study of homosexual transvestites and both male and female transsexuals; and David O. Caudwell's *Transvestism: Men in Female Dress*, a collection of comment by various authorities followed by autobiographies of practicing transvestites. Annie Woodhouse's *Fantastic Women: Sex, Gender, and Transvestism* is an excellent cultural and psychological study somewhat overshadowed by Marjorie Garber's *Vested Interests: Cross-Dressing and Cultural Anxiety*, which discusses transvestism as a definitive modern phenomenon by citing, among other examples, the astonishing appeal it holds for audiences of afternoon television talk shows like *Donahue*. Garber believes that the transvestite symbolizes the construction of identities as perhaps no other illustration can. He/she destabilizes boundaries between genders and sexes, and represents the fluidity of desire; his/her "style" is a signifier that undermines signification. As is evident from *Jacques Lacan and the Ecole Freudienne: Feminine Sexuality*, edited by Juliet Mitchell and Jacqueline Rose, the psychoanalyst Jacques Lacan invented a kind of spatial analogue of sexuality; the possession of a phallus puts one in the first space, while its absence puts one in the second. Lacan distinguished between penis and phallus, the first being real but trivial, the second being symbolic but potent, a separation that has endeared him to gender theorists, since it makes sexuality itself into a kind of discourse that can be embraced or rejected. Following Lacan, Garber puts transvestites in a sort of third space, defined as seeming, appearance, or representation: "Transvestism is a space of possibility structuring and confounding culture: the disruptive element that intervenes, not just a category crisis of male and female, but the crisis of category itself" (17).

The self-reflexivity of Garber's work manifested itself when author and book became hot topics in various media. The autobiography of a famous transvestite and star of Warhol films is the late Holly Woodlawn's *A Low Life in High Heels: The Holly Woodlawn Story*, written with Jeff Copeland; it is fairly explicit. Another, also associated with Warhol, is Candy Darling, whose *Candy Darling* reflects on the transvestite's career and motivations. Both books stress the anguish behind compulsion. Morgan Holliday's *The Morgan Mystique: Morgan Holliday's Essential Guide to Living, Loving, and Lip Gloss*, written with Peter Hawkins, offers advice on costumes, removing body hair, cosmetics, and etiquette to transvestite wanna-bes. *Hiding My Candy: The Autobiography of the Lady Chablis*, by The Lady Chablis, illustrates the porosity of mainstream and margin: the memorist, a Savannah drag queen, was featured in John Berendt's best-selling *Midnight in the Garden of Good and Evil* and capitalized on the first book's popularity. J. J. Allen's *The Man in the Red Velvet Dress: Inside the World of Cross-Dressing* explores the transvestite and transsexual underground of Los Angeles. Veronica Vera's *Miss Vera's Finishing School for Boys Who Want to Be Girls* contains narratives of successes drawn from the former porn star's training course for transvestites, an actual commercial enterprise.

Wide-ranging essays on cross-dressing in theater, cabaret, opera, dance, and modern performance from happenings to "vogueing" have been collected by Lesley Ferris in *Crossing the Stage: Controversies on Cross-Dressing*. The *New Yorker* ran Guy Trebay's "Letter from Downtown: Cross-Dresser Dreams," a respectful profile of RuPaul, a black drag queen now a fixture of the Manhattan night scene. RuPaul makes his own statements in *Lettin' It All Hang Out: An Autobiography*. Robert/"Stella," a British transvestite, discusses his reasons for dressing as a lady's maid in "Stella through the Looking Glass," while in the same volume Laura Kipnis explores "She-Male Fantasies and the Aesthetics of Pornography." Movie treatments of transvestism are covered by several works: Ralph Judd's *Drag Gags* and *Drag Gags Return*, the pages of which are mostly captioned film stills, and Rebecca Bell-Metereau's *Hollywood Androgyny*, a historically rich commentary on the appeal of gender reversals in scripts from Chaplin shorts to *The Rocky Horror Picture Show*. The popularity of the documentary film *Is Paris Burning?* attests to continuing interest. Of several critical essays on that film (1990), Jack Goldsby's "Queens of Language: *Paris Is Burning*" offers the most insight into Harlem drag queens and "vogueing."

BODIES MODIFIED

Armando R. Favezza's *Bodies under Siege: Self-Mutilation in Culture and Psychiatry*, an authoritative text, is the best place to begin research into body modification. Favezza deals with historical and contemporary examples of self-mutilation as responses to social and personal pathologies. V. Vale and Andrea Juno provide the most general map of the American contemporary scene in *Modern Primitives: An Investigation of Contemporary Adornment and Ritual*, which interviews devotees of piercing, tattooing, scarification, and other trends in body modification; the volume is a must. *Body Play/Modern Primitives Quarterly*, edited by Fakir Musafar, an exponent of body modification, features articles on extreme corseting to reshape the body, piercing, branding, tattooing, and other forms of deliberate mutation. Musafar is one subject of Charles Gatewood's *Bizarre Rituals: Dances Sacred and Profane*, a videotape exploration of bodies and modification in ritual settings as diverse as Mardi Gras, S/M clubs, and American Indian dances. *The Customized Body*, composed mostly of photographs chosen by Ted Polhemus and Housk Randall, depicts men and women fond of body shaping, painting, tattooing, piercing, scarifying, and dressing in exotic corsets, masks, shoes, and jewelry.

Body Building

Probably the most common form of modification is bodybuilding. David L. Chapman's *Sandow the Magnificent: Eugen Sandow and the Beginnings of Bodybuilding* tells the story of Sandow, who promoted bodybuilding (as display rather than prowess) by posing in a G-string. Though his overtly sexual photos were widely collected by both males and females, Sandow set in train the lightly masked erotic representations especially appealing to gays, a tradition examined in considerable detail in works on gay culture (see especially **Gender Disputations: The Male Nude, the Male Pinup, and the Lesbian Photograph** in chapter 12). While bodybuilding was once widely regarded as "a deviant activity," says Yvonne Wiegers in "Male Bodybuilding: The Social Construction of a Masculine Identity," it is now considered a "process of becoming," a step toward self-realization by a "somatic culture" (147). As Wiegers describes it, the dynamic that has cycled bodybuilding into respectability is similar to that by which pornography moves toward mainstreams. Samuel Fussell's *Muscle* discusses the symbolic significance of representations of masculinity conveyed by constructed bodies, and Kenneth Dutton's *The Perfectible Body* speaks of the ways that the male body can be shaped and exploited through such regimens.

Leslie Heywood traces the more recent appearance of the female bodybuilder as sex object in *Bodybuilders: A Cultural Anatomy of Women's Body Building*, as do Maria R. Lowe in *Women of Steel: Female Body Builders and the Struggle for Self-Definition* and the contributors to *Building Bodies*, edited by Pamela Moore. Robert Mapplethorpe's *Lady Lisa Lyon* (with text by world traveler

Bruce Chatwin), an almost perfectly realized pictorial sequence on the athlete Lisa Lyon, spurred the women's bodybuilding movement. Lyon's muscular nudity lent a heightened self-consciousness to a body blooming with healthy sexuality; she seems a Venus for the women's movement. (For Mapplethorpe, see **Period Histories of Erotic/Pornographic Photographs** in chapter 12.) Men's magazines frequently run pictorials on women athletes. Typical is "Hard Bodies," for which photographer Arny Freytag has shot buffed-up athletes from different sports to show the effects of barbells and Nautilus machines on breasts and buttocks. Although Paul B. Goode's *Physique: An Intimate Portrait of the Female Fitness Athlete* contains dozens of photographs of seminude women bodybuilders, the effect contrasts with those of Mapplethorpe and Freytag in that they are oddly nonerotic; in Goode's pictures, a breast seems to be just another muscle, and his interviews with his subjects indicate that the women's matter-of-fact approach to their bodies takes objectification in stride. Female bodybuilding as a pursuit nonetheless shades toward glamour, says Marion Roach in "Female Bodybuilders Discover Curves," an article on the displacement of female bodybuilding contests by fitness events that emphasize more feminine attributes, sexy costumes, and different styles of posing. Standouts among popular contemporary hard-core porn stars with athletic backgrounds are Tiffany Millions, a former wrestler, and Rocki Roads, a former gymnast. Producers of soft-core wrestling videos, such as those in which scantily clad "catfighters" claw at each others' breasts in the ring, or the more specialized scenarios in which muscular women use their crotches to pin men's shoulders to the mat, often recruit performers from gyms.

Tattooing

Almost as common as bodybuilding is tattooing, whose surge in popularity has put at least one parlor in every college town. A viewer of erotic videotapes would soon lose count of the number of tattoos sported by performers of all genders, but inked images erotic or otherwise clearly appeal to growing segments of the general population. Numerous texts attempt with varying degrees of success to explain the cachet, but the illustrations essential to all the books suggest that part of the attraction is voyeuristic. The most theoretical is *Tattoo, Torture, Mutilation, and Adornment: The Denaturalization of the Body in Culture and Text*, edited by Francis Mascia-Lees and Patricia Sharpe, a collection of essays designed to demonstrate that culture can almost literally write messages upon the body as it is shaped by social forces. A different perspective is that of Clinton R. Sanders, who agrees that body modification can be traced to social roots but describes tattooing as a genuine lower-class art form, much like graffiti as a form of quasi-sexual expression. His *Customizing the Body: The Art and Culture of Tattooing* is extremely lucid and has become a standard text. *The Painted Body*, by Michel Thévoz, the curator of the Collection de l'Art Brut in Lausanne, Switzerland, offers examples of early (Indian) and modern decoration, tattooing, and body art as part of the volume's historical sweep; Thévoz includes a good bibliography. *The Decorated Body*, by Robert Brain, and *Decorated Man*, by Charles Lenars and Josette Lenars and Andre Virel, adopt a cross-cultural approach to the history of scarification, tattooing, and piercing. Daniel Wojcik treats piercing and tattooing as a shock aesthetic in *Punk and Neo-Tribal Body Art*. Donna Gaines' "Tattoo's Back" surveys the proliferation of tattoos among professors, queer couples, rock stars, and, of course, sex workers.

Albert Morse's *The Tattooists*, based on interviews with notable tattooists, looks at tattooing as an art form with fetishistic implications. One of these, George Burchett with Peter Leighton, reflects on a career in *Memoirs of a Tattooist: From the Notes, Diaries and Letters of the Late "King of the Tattooists."* R.W.B. Scott and Christopher Gooch are equally straightforward in their linkage of tattooing with sexuality in *Art, Sex and Symbol: The Mystery of Tattooing*. An early, wide-ranging study of tattoos among circus performers, sailors, and prostitutes, with a very good bibliography, is Albert Parry's *Tattoo: Secrets of a Strange Art*. Samuel M. Steward also deals with tattoos as psychological and social emblems of specific subcultures in *Bad Boys and Tough Tattoos: A Social History of the Tattoo with Gangs, Sailors, and Street-Corner Punks, 1950–1965;* the text, part of a gay and lesbian studies series, sketches some of the artists as well. Significant in these and other texts is the association of tattoos with bikers, outlaws, convicts, and the lower classes generally, a connection that biker and other monthly tattoo magazines still claim. Such magazines trade in images but also the sexual folklore of tattooing, augmented by sometimes shrill attempts by aficionados to resist the co-option of a symbolic expression they consider their own.

The growing acceptance of tattoos by the middle class once again reveals patterns of cultural absorption of the outré, the forbidden, or the dangerous that is the central dynamic of pornography. Interesting reflections on that dynamic can be found in Marc Blanchard's "Post-Bourgeois Tattoo: Reflections on Skin Writing in Late Capitalist Societies" and Arnold Rubin's "Tattoo Renaissance"; a flood of other academic explications of the subject is on the way. Rubin's *Marks of Civilization* contains fascinating essays on cultural variations in tattooing among denizens of tattoo parlors. Taken together, several photographic works span an enormous range of explicitness. Recommended are Spider Webb's *Heavily Tattooed Men and Women*, Tim O'Sullivan's *Exposé: The Art of Tattoo*, Charles Gatewood's *Primitives: Tribal Body Art and the Left Hand Path*, and Chris Wroblewski's *The Art and Craft of Tattoo: Skin Show* and *Tattoo: Pigments of Imagination*. Wroblewski also took the photographs for Andy Cooper's *Tattoo Art: Tätowierte Frauen/Skin Fantasies on Tattooed Women*, a dual-language text on bodies as erotic landscapes; some of the illustrations are reproduced in Wroblewski's *Tattooed Women*. Easily the most useful text on tattooed women, however, is Margot Mifflin's *Bodies of Subversion: A Secret History of Women & Tattoo*, an engaging chronicle of women who have illustrated their bodies as expressions of womanhood and personal statement. *Tabu Tattoo: Erotic Body Art* is a new zine devoted to tattooing of genitals and depictions of erotic scenes on skin. Ron Athey incorporates piercing and tattooing in his performance art, which led to an uproar when blood suspected of being HIV-positive came in proximity to an audience. Jeff Spurrier reviews Athey's career and philosophy in "Blood of a Poet." Ron Athey is author and subject of a section in an issue of *Theatre Forum*, which synopsizes the script of Athey's *4 Scenes in a Harsh Life*, interviews Athey, and prints the text of a panel discussion on Athey's work, the censorship he has endured, and the body modification, piercing, and tattooing that are the themes of his stage work.

Piercing

The contemporary appeal of piercing, says Trish Hall in "Piercing Fad Is Turning Convention on Its Ear," indicates that shifts in cultural signification foster willingness to modify bodies. Where once gay males wore rings in their left ear to indicate their sexual orientation, now heterosexual males are piercing theirs. Hall traces the piercing of nipples in both men and women to the Victorian era, when women oppressed by shibboleths against ornamentation pierced nipples in order to wear jewels underneath their corsets. Hall also notes the growing popularity of piercing navels and genitals at emporiums like the Gauntlet, with stores in San Francisco and West Hollywood, whose staff does 5,000 such piercings a year. Fashion governs the sizes, shapes, and materials of the rings and jewels the wearer wishes inserted. Suzy Menkes remarks on the large number of supermodels on the fashion runways who are having their bodies pierced or tattooed in "Body Piercing Moves into the Mainstream." The *New Yorker* ran a "Talk of the Town" piece on Don Kopka, a professional body-piercer of labia, nipples, and scrotums for the Gauntlet in Manhattan called "The Holes in Some of the Parts." Kopka speaks of his techniques and discusses the preferences of his customers.

Newsweek also published "Think of It as Therapy," in which Patrick Rogers and Rebecca Crandall theorize that explosive growth of body piercing among middle-class Americans reaches some need to exercise control over their bodies, and that effects may be beneficial. That is the message of Vicki Glembocki's personal account of her piercing in "A Ring in Her Navel": "It may sound corny, but by piercing my navel I've taken back my body. I've learned to be proud of something I had always dreamed of changing. It feels great. And I've started thinking about having my nipples pierced too" (138). By contrast, Guy Trebay focuses on the appeal of the primitive as the force behind widespread piercing of nipples and genitals among punksters in "Primitive Culture: At Large with the Pierced and Tattooed Love Boys (and Girls)." *PFIQ Quarterly*, a journal for "Piercing Fans International," carries articles and photographs on piercing intimate body parts. Finally, those attracted to light body decoration as opposed to permanent modification should note among the triumphs of American merchandising two ersatz developments, both popular with porn stars. The first is the temporary tattoo, which can be applied as an ornament before an erotic encounter, then washed off. The second is clip-on jewelry (rather like ear clips for those without pierced lobes) that requires no piercing. Current catalogs offer tension nipple loops capable of suspending chains and novelties (e.g., "The Tittie Twinkler") and organ jewelry made of Austrian crystals that dangle from a shaft inserted in vagina or anus; these, for swingers who feel uncomfortable without some adornment at orgies, are often visible in amateur porn videotapes (see **Sexual Aids and Equipment** in chapter 4, Adam and Eve). In fact, all of these body modifications have become staples of porn films, which make visual capital out of tattoos, cock rings, genital jewelry, and resculpted body parts. Roughly a third of female performers now sport piercings, and the number of pierced male performers is rising rapidly. Actresses will ostentatiously insert studs in their tongues before performing fellatio, for example, or insist on intercourse in positions where the light can catch their labial jewels.

Cosmetic Surgery

So strong is the American fetish for big breasts that female porn stars whose expertise at intercourse is as polished as Joe Montana's at football nevertheless feel compelled to have their breasts enlarged, and reviewers routinely note that a movie was shot before or after the leading lady's surgery. Cultural equations falter here: does porn stimulate a desire for enormous breasts and impossible curves, or is porn merely emulating, even parodying, a liposuction-, silicone-crazed Hollywood ideal? Since porn films are often self-reflexive and fetish-oriented, some not only highlight large bosoms but discuss the desirability of enhancement. Typical is *Girls of Silicone Valley* (1991), directed by Loretta Sterling, who juxtaposes footage of actresses before and after breast enlargement, then shoots the actual operation as performed on Jamie Leigh. Leaving aside transsexual surgery, which still fuels the pornographic imagination, breast enlargement or implantation veers away from eroticism into the heart of American culture, where middle-class face-lifts, tummy tucks, cellulite removal, buttock tightening, and other cosmetic interventions are common party chatter. More cultural in their ruminations are Kathy Davis' *Reshaping the Female Body: The Dilemma of Cosmetic Surgery*, which reflects on the pressures women feel to enhance their bodies, and Elizabeth Haiken's *Venus Envy: A History of Cosmetic Surgery*, which explores the role of surgery in altering the attributes of race, ethnicity, aging, and gender. Steven Findlay looks at the costs behind the rising popularity of surgery in "Buying the Perfect Body," which notes that the average breast enlargement in 1989 ran $2,000—as opposed to the $50,000 plus that stars such as Demi Moore spend on virtually undetectable surgery. Sylvia Plachy and James Ridgeway interview doctors who enlarge the breasts of sex workers in *Red Light: Inside the Sex Industry* (183–187). Siliconing of breasts can be tax-deductible for performers; Martha Barnette cites the case of Chesty

Love, whose stripping career turns on achieving her goal of "the world's biggest boobs," and her success at persuading the Internal Revenue Service (IRS) to allow the cost as a business expense. "Stacked like Me," by former Yale professor and feminist Jan Breslauer, reveals why she had her breasts augmented along with another 50,000 Americans annually. The cosmetics industry itself plans a glossy magazine, *Form & Figure*, to capitalize on the huge market for aesthetic surgery for faces, breasts, fannies, and so on. Has pornography increased the desire for cosmetic surgery? No one has ever done a study, but it is worth remembering that breast implants used to be associated almost exclusively with strippers and porn starlets. Hundreds of thousands of ordinary American women now have them.

RADICAL ENGINEERING

Large adult emporiums reserve shelf space for magazines and videotapes on transsexuals—always to be distinguished from homosexuals and transvestites— engaged in intercourse with performers of assorted genders. Anne Balsamo, in "On the Cutting Edge: Cosmetic Surgery and the Technological Production of the Gendered Body," and Marjorie Garber, in "Spare Parts: The Surgical Construction of Gender," reflect on the motivations behind such drastic body modification, the cultural anathemas that surround operations, and the social and metaphysical implications for the construction of gender. Balsamo suggests that even ordinary technologies reinforce gender assumptions and patterns in *Technologies of the Gendered Body: Reading Cyborg Women*. One of the fastest growing pornographic subgenres is the "she-male" videotape. The stars of these tapes are sometimes called preop transsexuals, a label that may be disingenuous, since they seem comfortable in a transitional state defined by hormone-induced breasts and curves *and* fully functional penises. They typically engage in vaginal sex with women and anal sex with men in the same film. Several postop transsexuals have appeared in hard-core films as females, perhaps as a way of validating their new identities.

Videos centered on female transsexuals are rarer. Annie Sprinkle discusses *Linda/Les and Annie: The First Female to Male Transsexual Love Story*, in which Sprinkle and her real-life lover star, in *Post Porn Modernist* (96–99). Jessica Berens' "Becoming a Man" is a sympathetic portrait of Mark Rees, a British transsexual who has rejected phalloplasty ("Surely a man is more than a penis"), that is, surgery in which the subject's own tissue from a donor site is reconstructed. It is "a complicated series of procedures which bring risk of infection, leakage and blockage. . . . Progress in prosthetics offers permanent stiffness or an inflatable appendage that must be pumped by hand. In America, where micro-vascular surgery is being developed, penile reconstruction has a better reputation" (123). But in "The Body Lies," Amy Bloom's *New Yorker* report on female-to-male transsexuals, a female doctor comments on a male colleague's surgical construction of penises for the new males: "And of course

Dr. Laub was making them huge. I mean, really. . . . Well, Dr. Laub is a guy. I guess he figured that if you want one—Anyway, now they're a little closer to average" (44).

Freighted with psychological and physical complexity, transsexuality shades into realms beyond the purview of this guide. Transsexuals endure so much pain, psychic as well as physical, that one hesitates to call their longing pornographic, and yet pornography has served to establish the kind of sexual folklore that is a prerequisite for a sexual minority's assertion of identity and its recognition of community. The ur-text is *The Transsexual Phenomenon*, in which sexologist Harry Benjamin sympathetically identified the syndrome and which still serves as a kind of bible for the transsexual community, but it should be read along with Edward Sagarin's "Transsexualism: Legitimation, Amplification, and Exploitation of Deviance by Scientists and Mass Media," a history of the cultural construction of this form of "deviance." Sagarin's *Deviants and Deviance: An Introduction to the Study of Disvalued People and Behavior* is also extremely informative. Gordene Olga MacKenzie's *Transgender Nation* argues with the theories of Robert Stoller, John Money, and Richard Green and also provides a fine chapter on "Images of Transsexuals and Transgenderists in American Popular Culture." *Transgender Warriors*, by Leslie Feinberg, profiles notable transgressors of gender boundaries from Joan of Arc to RuPaul and Dennis Rodman, though Feinberg could have begun with Tiresias and run forward to J. Edgar Hoover.

Not surprisingly, transsexuals have gravitated toward extensive reconsiderations of gender. Holly Devor's *Gender Blending: Confronting the Limits of Duality* contains sober reflections, while Kate Bornstein's *Gender Outlaw: On Men, Women, and the Rest of Us* focuses on transgender as a foundation of a politics of gender and sexuality. In *Read My Lips: Sexual Subversion and the End of Gender*, Riki A. Wilchins argues forcefully that lesbians and transsexuals are pioneers in the struggle to end the dominance of gendered categories. Anne Bolin's *In Search of Eve: Transsexual Rites of Passage* describes stages in psychological awareness in a culture that is rigidly gendered. Caroline Cossey's *My Story* recounts the tribulations of a famous transsexual, a former male whose career apogee was a modeling stint for *Playboy*. Gretchen Edgren's text, "The Transformation of Tula: The Extraordinary Story of a Beautiful Woman Who Was Born a Boy," accompanied the photographs in *Playboy*. Sinister motives are attributed to transsexual engineering by *Changing Sex: Transsexualism. Technology, and the Idea of Gender*, in which Bernice L. Hausman suggests that advances in endocrinology and plastic surgery have permitted the medical establishment to make heterosexuals out of "intersexuals." *Transformation*, a journal devoted to cross-dressing and transsexuality, combines serious articles with practical advice for males who wish to pass as women. *Cross-Talk*, another zine, is written by and for transvestites and transsexuals. *Gender Euphoria* is a monthly newsletter devoted to issues of transsexuality. Marianne Macy visits a transsexual support group and spends time with transsexuals at home and in clubs in *Working Sex: An Odyssey into Our Cultural Underworld. Current Concepts in Transgender Identity*, edited by Dallas Denny, gathers essays on aspects of transgendered personalities and physicalities, some altered by surgical intervention.

FETISHES

Fetishes, loosely (and inaccurately) defined as categories of desire, often become synecdoches for pornography for both critics and aficionados. Catalogs of porn films, for instance, will frequently break out inventories in terms of "Anal," "Big Breasts," "Big Dicks," "Tattoos," and so on. The term *fetish* has different meanings for the anthropologist than it does for colleagues in other disciplines, says Thomas A. Sebeok in "The Word 'Fetish' and Its Uses in Anthropology." To anthropologists, a fetish is a venerated object; it does not necessarily have erotic connotations. To cultural critics, a fetish is variously a commodity in a capitalist economy, a form of discourse, a surrogate for some value, a fixation on some event or space, or a perversion involving sexual obsession, views advanced by the essayists in *Fetishism as Cultural Discourse*, edited by Emily Apter and William Pietz, who offer an excellent bibliography arranged around these perspectives. Pietz's historical observations are especially pertinent. He points out that the church recognized the power of fetishes in its denunciations of witchcraft and rowdy carnivals and explicitly associated fetishes with aberrant female behavior. According to Pietz, Western culture thus actually began debate on the subject hundreds of years before Freud linked fetishism to phallicism.

To sexologists, a fetish is *the* stimulus to an individual's desire, a syndrome of connotations whose whole point is that it doesn't make sense to those who cannot respond to the object, let alone to those who do. To pornographers, the formal and even institutional mechanics that fetishes reveal in operation make their tropes congenial to representation and equally attractive to cultural critics, who can thus enliven aesthetic, feminist, psychological, political, and Marxist theories. Somewhat sloppier definitions of fetishes animate a lively text, *Fetishes, Florentine Girdles, and Other Explorations into the Sexual Imagination*, edited by Harriet Gilbert, who includes almost anything that could possibly be designated a fixation, from lingerie to temple carvings; the book is a hodgepodge of popular conceptions of obsession. For the record, however, the "official" American definition is that found in the *Diagnostic and Statistical Manual of Mental Disorders* (the so-called DSM) of the American Psychiatric Association, which designates as fetishism "recurrent, intense sexually arousing fantasies, sexual urges or behaviors involving the use of nonliving objects (e.g., female undergarments)" (526).

Freud's short piece on "Fetishism" (in volume XXI of the *Standard Edition* or in the Strachey edition of *Sigmund Freud: Collected Papers*) claims that fetishes hold power over males who cannot acknowledge that women have no penises. According to the Freudian scenario, the child, nonplussed to see that his mother has no penis, redirects his fascination toward her corset or shoes or whatever catches his eye. Modern psychological interpretations suggest that a fetish hides a fear of castration. Feminist folklore sometimes holds that women are morally superior because, unlike men, they are not subject to fetishes, but in "Lesbian Fetishism?" Elizabeth Grosz, like William Pietz, challenges that view. Grosz says that "in psychoanalytic terms it makes no sense for women to be fetishists, and it is unimaginable that women would get sexual gratification from the use of inanimate objects or mere partial objects *alone*." But, Grosz notes, "this is analogous to the claim that pornography, like fetishism, is a male preserve; in itself it remains inadequate as a form of sexual satisfaction for it reduces women to the position of (voyeuristic/fetishistic) objects, not subjects" (101). In her view, Freud's denial of fetishism for women may actually discriminate against them. After all, fixations on objects have the advantage of redirecting desire in subversive directions, *away* from the penis, away from the whole phallocentric erotic realm, and thus may actually help liberate women. These and similar reflections are extended in Grosz's *Space, Time, and Perversion*. Laura Mulvey combines the Freudian concept of fetish, whose source is assumed to be the mother's body, and the Marxist concept, whose source is assumed to be the denigration of the worker's labor-value, in "Some Thoughts on Theories of Fetishism in the Context of Contemporary Culture." Jon Stratton also blends Freudian and Marxist theory in discussing artifacts of popular culture (from film stars and supermodels to robots) as fetishes in *The Desirable Body: Cultural Fetishism and the Erotics of Consumption*.

Topics of the essays in *Female Fetishism*, by Lorraine Gammon and Merja Makinen, range from traditional rubber and leather fashions to bulimia and food obsessions, which the authors suggest may be considered female fetishes; Gammon and Makinen insist on the rich ironies of fetishistic attractions and warn against trying to "read" their complexities too narrowly or pigeonhole them as forms of female commodification. Postmodernist theory generally suggests that one person's fetish, like another person's deviation, is the consequence of discourse shaped by power, whether the discourse is wielded by a medieval priest, a nineteenth-century burgher, a twentieth-century feminist, or a contemporary psychoanalyst. The amazing force, far stronger than tepid literary postulations of power, with which fetishes grip the psyche nevertheless give poststructuralists pause and has led theorists like Jacques Lacan and others to rewrite Freud. Worth consulting is "Fetishism: The Symbolic, the Imaginary, and the Real" by Lacan and Wladimir Granoff, who claim that fetishism as a perversion has no corresponding neurosis. Fetishism has also proved irresistible to French poststructural critics such as Baudrillard and Derrida, but tracing their approaches takes us some distance from American porn (though French poststructural theories may well function as fetishes for American academics who may or may not be neurotic).

In any case, fetish theory is suffused with politics. As Peter Lehman notes in *Running Scared: Masculinity and the Representation of the Male Body*, some feminists, following Lacan, assert that a belief in the vaginal orgasm turns the phallus itself into a fetish, since it enhances the value of a large penis that can penetrate the vagina fully, whereas faith in the clitoral orgasm restores the balance (146). In a larger sense, some theorists prefer to believe that fetishes are not fetishes at all but a matter of choice and taste; asserting that sex is the consequence of free will rather than a biological or psychological imperative implies that men choose to be brutes (as opposed to succumbing to forces beyond their control), an important tenet for radical feminists. According to extreme versions of "late capitalism" theories, humans in the future should be able to choose their sexual identities and fixations by shopping, just as consumers purchase products from supermarkets.

One pioneer was Wilhelm Stekel, whose *Sexual Aberrations: The Phenomena of Fetishism in Relation to Sex* still deserves a place on any shelf. His text covers a vast range of fetishes, from bust and buttock to rubber and orthopedic fixations. Always a renegade, if something of a monomaniac on the subject, Robert J. Stoller attributes fetishes to uncathected hostility in *Observing the Erotic Imagination* and his *Perversion: The Erotic Form of Hatred*. It would be difficult to improve upon the first volume's definition: "a fetish is a story masquerading as an object" (155). That is, the fetish encapsulates the psychological history of the person drawn to it, though the circuit between fantasy and behavior may remain idiosyncratic. In any case, sexologists generally use *fetish* to designate a surrogate for more logical or "normal" genital fixations. The surrogate can be another erogenous zone, like breasts or buttocks, or some artificial substitute, like clothing, that entices and excites. Whatever else one might say about fetishes, they add variety, spice, and depth to pornography. In a sense, fetishism in pornography is less about signification—since symbol is there made specific—than it is a matter of packaging. As John Matlock observes, "Cloth, clothing, and costume fetishes probably appear with such frequency because they are both the most socially acceptable of the potential obsessions (clothes, unlike dead bodies and women's hair, are household items—easy-to-obtain, portable, and hoardable) and also the most easily stolen (you can't bring home a foot; women's tresses are cut with difficulty; odors and voices can't be packaged)."[4]

Pornography often purveys images understood as fetishes. Some Americans erroneously assume that anybody can be turned into a sexual predator by exposure to generic pornography, that is, any grouping of explicit words or images, in the same way that they assume that generic religious symbology can set off a mass murderer who hears voices telling him to kill. It seems obvious that most people are drawn in a mildly fetishistic way to certain physical characteristics; some women prefer small buttocks on men, while others are keen on wedge-shaped chests, body hair, or small nipples. Ordinarily, however, we call a person a fetishist when he or she responds sexually *only* to the specific object or image: lactating women, say, or men in studded leather jockstraps. In other words, fetishes are themselves highly specific, and pornographic genres, because they can be tailored to desire, can represent fetishes precisely. Given this premise, whose validity should be apparent from even the most cursory glance at the thousands of fetishistic instances of pornography, it is silly to maintain that sexuality involves monolithic responses. Two of the most common myths, that *all* men are turned on by images of brutalized women or that *all* women are stimulated by rape fantasies, are hopelessly naive, not to say dangerous.

That point cannot be overemphasized, says the cultural anthropologist Jack Weatherford. He carried out a lengthy field study by working in an adult emporium (whose real name he disguised as "the Pink Pussy") in an American metropolis. His *Porn Row* has become a classic of ethnography. In a famous passage, Weatherford recalled that

I was surprised to learn that many of the men to whom I doled out all those quarters each night expressed a dislike for pornography in general although they sought one variety of it in particular. The men who could not have an orgasm without looking at big breasts ignored everything else in the store. Another, who fantasized about blond pubic hair, showed no interest in big breasts unless they happened to be on a woman who also had blond pubic hair. The man who liked pictures of transvestites thought that the customer who bought pictures of young men was sick, and the men who liked bondage had no common interest with the men who wanted the soft-core magazines. Often it seemed that the men who liked to read written stories had little interest in the picture magazines. Each man had a narrow range of fantasy and showed interest only in the precise kind of pornography that sustained this fantasy; as far as he was concerned, the rest was trash. There were no connoisseurs of pornography as a whole, no little old men in raincoats who got equal thrills from bondage, incest, and interracial rape. Even within the extreme monotony of pornography, there was a marked specialization of fetishes and fantasies that kept the users separate and isolated in their antisocial pleasures. (45)

A similar point is made by Robert Stoller, who says in *Observing the Erotic Imagination* that where fetishes are concerned, "*every detail counts*" (49). Although the common sense of such observations as Stoller's and Weatherford's is often ignored, anyone who has spent more than a few minutes in an adult bookstore or arcade can confirm it.

Straightforward discussions of fetishes are staples of every issue of *Adult Video News*, whose editors advise managers of adult bookstores and video rental outlets on what fetishes are popular at the moment and what kind of tapes to stock for fetish customers. Typical is Sam Masters' list of categories in "Alternative Sexuality and the Video Retailer": bondage, female domination, infantilism, male domination, transvestite and transsexual, foot worship, large breast, enemas. These are not exhaustive and vary in popularity from month to month and year to year. *Fetish Times*, a catholic journal intent on cataloging tastes, sooner or later gets around to most of them. Any adult bookstore carries magazines, few of scholarly intent, devoted to piercing (of nipples, labia, penises), light spanking, bondage, depilation, latex and rubber garments, lactation, scatology, urolagnia, anal intercourse, interracial sex, fellatio, cunnilingus, blond hair, shaved labia, large penises, fat women, pregnant women, erotic wrestling/ boxing, lingerie, masturbation with various objects, and so on.

Critical approaches to particular fetishes in pornography vary widely in merit, comprehensiveness, and accuracy. Since no list could cover them all, the student may begin with some of the classic studies of the most popular fetishes and work out to the margins. Most texts on fetishes concentrate on the authors' favorites, which may or may not imply that the writers engage in obsessional pursuits. Some deal with ornamentation of the body, some with body parts, some with specific physical activities. Berkeley Kaite's *Pornography and Difference* is a good place to start; Kaite ranges over various fetishes in modern porn films and photos and focuses on some more than others (e.g., shoes, jewelry, leather, lingerie) as means of transgressing boundaries of masculinity and femininity.

UNDERWEAR AND OTHER FETISH GARMENTS

Though published in the 1920s, *Sittengeschichte des Intimsten, Intime Toilette, Mode und Kosmetik im Diest der Erotik*, volume X of *Sittengeschichte der Kulturwelt und ihrer Entwicklung in Einzeldarstellungen*, edited by Leo Schidrowitz, is still an authoritative source on erotic clothing fetishes, cosmetics, and fashions, especially undergarments. Volume I, *Sittengeschichte des Intimen: Bett, Korsett, Hemd, Hose, Bad, Abtritt. Die Geschichte und Entwicklung der intimen Gebrauchsgegenstände*, contains some material as well, principally on corsets and costumes worn for lounge and bed. One of the early American histories of lingerie, fleshed out with an excellent annotated bibliography, is Richard Cortes Holliday's *Unmentionables: From Fig Leaves to Scanties*, published in 1933; it is thorough and well documented. So is a more recent work by Claire Paillochet, *Unmentionables: The Allure of Lingerie*, which, though French, refers constantly to American garments and styles. *Vogue* magazine has compiled several histories of clothing from text and pictures in its pages: Christina Probert's *Fashion in Vogue since 1910: Lingerie* offers a quick trip through the magazine's last several decades (other volumes in the series include *Shoes* [1981]). Elizabeth Ewing's *Dress and Undress: A History of Women's Underwear* is an extremely readable, reliable text, as are Alison Carter's *Underwear: The Fashion History*, Marianne Thesander's *The Feminine Ideal*, and Karoline Newman and her colleagues' *A Century of Lingerie: Icons of Style in the Twentieth Century*. Unfortunately, few works are devoted to male underwear, though Valerie Steele's *Fetish* contains a few useful pages (127–131). One account is Gary M. Griffin's *The History of Men's Underwear: From Union Suits to Bikini Briefs*, though one would hardly call it scholarly. Almost as ephemeral is Richard Dyer's brief essay, "Brief Affairs," on the sexual significance of display of men's shorts, jockstraps, and briefs. *Undergear*, a sales catalog devoted to men's undergarments, is aimed at both gays and heterosexuals and is a staple of newsstands everywhere, along with its counterpart, the quarterly *International Male*.

Edward Holzman's photographs illustrate *Dreams of Eros*, a catalog of lingerie for women *and* men. Just as catholic is *Unmentionables: A Brief History of Underwear*, for which Elaine Benson and John Esten pull together cartoons, ads, movie stills, and other artistic representations to illustrate the evolution of underwear of men and women. Despite its whimsicality, the book indicates the degree to which underwear has become fetishistic and how universal patterns of appeal are. Many Americans are familiar with the catalogs of Frederick's of Hollywood. The company itself, long since a cultural institution, has published a pictorial history of itself, *Frederick's of Hollywood, 1947–1973: 26 Years of Mail-Order Seduction*, using pages reproduced from years of lingerie and clothing catalogs. The volume makes clear that the special needs of erotic dancers have profoundly influenced lingerie used by housewives. (For lingerie photographs, see **Fetish Photographs** in chapter 12 but also note the prevalence of lingerie in erotic photos in early periods.) According to Dodie Kazanjian's article "Victoria's Secret Is Out," the lingerie chain grew from 5 stores and a mail catalog with grosses of $6 million in 1982 to 500 stores grossing $900 million in 1992.

The standard work on corsets, a favorite fetish, is David Kunzle's *Fashion and Fetishism: A Social History of the Corset, Tight-Lacing and Other Forms of Body-Sculpture in the West*. Less authoritative and less oriented toward fetishistic appeal but still comprehensive and relevant is Norah Waugh's *Corsets and Crinolines*, which depicts American examples. Beatrice Fontanel's more recent *Support and Seduction: A History of Corsets and Bras* is a compendium of facts, folklore, and illustrations; typical is the story of Caresse Crosby's invention of the modern soft bra that lightly separated the breasts (89). *Figure-Training Fundamentals: For Women of Distinction and Discernment*, a manual for women (and men) who wish to "train" their bodies, is also replete with historical lore on corsetry. One of the stranger homages to corsets, girdles, and lingerie is *Girls from Girdleville* (1992), a vaguely "Western" film by Eric Kroll, which features women cinched in corsets and girdles ankling ponderously around in a desert. Rowdy Yates' review, "Girls from Girdleville," compares Kroll's work to the lingerie movies of Irving Klaw and notes that Kroll himself owns a large collection of fetish photos. *Real Sex: 6* devotes considerable footage to the making of Kroll's film. Wallace Reyburn's *Bust-Up: The Uplifting Tale of Otto Titzling and the Development of the Bra*, is a silly history of the brassiere. Equally amusing but more contemporary is Dave Barry's Knight-Ridder–distributed column on the cleavage-inducing Wonderbra called "Men May Find 'Wonderbra' Simply 'Wunderbar.' " Introduced at the end of 1993, the Wonderbra drove "hard news" stories off the pages of daily newspapers everywhere and unleashed dozens of columns by pundits who found the new brassiere of enormous cultural importance; Barry's column is more readable than most. (See **Fetish Photographs** in Chapter 12, especially *Bizarre Classix, Bizarre Fotos, Bizarre Katalogs*, Klaw, Kloster, Kroll, and Rosen). Steele's *Fetish* also covers virtually all the identifiable clothing fetishes and is nicely illustrated.

Pictures of models in bathing suits are sometimes provocative enough to qualify as soft-core porn, yet as a fetish category the bathing suit is mild. Even so, who could measure the volume of ink devoted to the annual swimsuit issue published by *Sports Illustrated?* On a slow week journalists will tease out 500 words on the decline of Western morality as prefigured in the skimpy cut of bikinis featured in the magazine. (For more on the magazine's swimsuit pictures, see **Female Pinups, Centerfolds, and Magazine Pictorials** in Chapter 12.) The swimsuit event in the Miss America Pageant served the same purpose for previous generations of journalists. Banner's *American Beauty* follows the evolution of the pageant in terms of its influence on ideals of beauty and also its galvanizing effect on the sensibilities of feminists. A. R. Riverol's *Live from Atlantic City: The History of the Miss America Pageant before, after and in spite of Television* is a more straightforward history, rich in anecdotes and journalistic nuggets. Perhaps the most famous event associated with the pageant never happened at all, or so says an indignant Suzanne Braun Levine in "The Truth Was Burned." According to Levine, journalists invented the "bra-burning" episode of 7 September 1968, when feminists gathered on the Boardwalk to protest the pageant's pernicious effects on women. The women involved *did* throw into a "Freedom Trash Can" many symbols of female oppression—"steno pads, dishrags, diapers, copies of *Playboy* magazine, as well as girdles, false eyelashes, and, yes, bras"—but no one *burned* them. Media still refer to feminists as "bra-burners," however, a circumstance that says more about journalists than feminists, says Levine.

Scholars of swimsuits should dip into *Making Waves: Swimsuits and the Undressing of America* if only because Lena Lencek and Gideon Bosker document the shrinking coverage of swimsuits in the ongoing American affair with beaches and pools. Typical of superficial comment is *The Bikini*, edited by Pedro Silmon, a picture book with modest text on about thirty years of the abbreviated swimsuit. Slightly more informative is the entry on the "Topless Bathing Suit" (the one on the "Dallas Cowboys Cheerleaders" is pretty good, too) in Frank Hoffmann and William G. Bailey's *Sports and Recreation Fads*. Better still is Roberta Smith's "Demure to Demystified: Swimsuits' Hall of Fame," a report on an exhibition of bathing costumes at the Fashion Institute of Technology in New York City in August 1990. Among other themes, the exhibition traced the decline of taboos against the display of bodies. Richard Martin and Harold Koda based their text *Splash! A History of Swim Wear* on the exhibit; the volume includes pictures ranging from the turn-of-the-century cover-ups to the bikini, monokini, and thongs of the present by photographers as diverse as Louise Dahl-Wolf to Helmut Newton. A chapter in Jennifer Craik's *The Face of Fashion: Cultural Studies in Fashion*, entitled "States of Undress: Lingerie to Swimwear" addresses eroticism more directly. Lest the point be lost, swimwear—and all the other clothing items mentioned here—is common not only to the cultural mainstream but also to the pornographic genres that parody mainstream concerns. A computer could easily compile a huge list of soft- and hard-core heterosexual films revolving around swimsuits, for example, or a similar group of gay films in which plots turn on jockey shorts.

Surprisingly popular is the fetish for rubber and latex garments—underwear, body stockings, masks, and so on. Though hardly academic, the inevitable book to glance at here is Maurice North's *The Outer Fringe of Sex: A Study in Sexual Fetishism*, a text centered on the fascination with rubber clothing. By covering themselves from head to toe in rubber, North says, rubber fetishists transform themselves into penises, as if the garments were condoms. North points out that some aficionados are aroused by the actual sensation of the garments, either wearing the material themselves or caressing it on the bodies of their partners, while others are satisfied with pictures of models decked in shiny latex or neoprene. The latter representations form an important, if minor, subgenre of pornography. Theories advanced in explanation of the fetish's appeal range from arrested development at the rubber diaper stage to fantasies of restraint, suffocation, and genderlessness and are enumerated in Clavel Brand's *The Rubber Devotee and the Leather Lover*. Despite its generalized title, Brand's *Fetish: An Account of Unusual Erotic Desires* devotes most of its pages to interviews with those favoring leather, rubber, and bondage. More specialized is Mick Farren's discussion of the role of *The Black Leather Jacket* in various subcultures. Gillian Freeman singles out rubber garment periodicals as best-sellers in *The Undergrowth of Literature*. (For leather, see **Sadomasochism** in Chapter 10, especially Grumley and Galucci, Thompson, Townsend.) Those wishing to keep abreast might consult *Fantasy Fashion Digest*, best described as a compass for strange realms of clothing, with information on dozens of stores, catalogs, and mail-order houses. Finally, *Skin Two*, published in England but distributed in the United States, exhaustively treats fetish ware at the rubber and neoprene extreme in a series of issues that are more books than magazines. *The Best of Skin Two*, edited by Tim Woodward, contains fascinating accounts of obsessions.

Understanding the totemistic associations of fur fetishes has not progressed much beyond the classic novel on the subject, Leopold von Sacher-Masoch's *Venus in Furs*, although Gilles Deleuze, who rewrote *Venus in Furs* in *Masochism: An Interpretation of Coldness and Cruelty*, interprets the fetish as crucial to the distancing of the masochist from his social environment. Leather is quite a different material, with its own feel and smell. Edward Podolsky and Carlson Wade deal mostly with images of dominant women in corsets and leather boots. The text of their *Erotic Symbolism: A Study of Fetichism in Relation to Sex* shares space with extensive illustrations that have functioned as fetishes in Eastern and Western countries; Podolsky and Wade demonstrate that fetishes can be disguised as respectable clothing. Fixations on feet or footwear, leather or otherwise, are common to another representational subgenre. Americans with that fetish usually concentrate on depictions of patent leather pumps, stiletto heels, high-topped, leather lace-ups, rubber boots, or—rarely "and"—related paraphernalia—as opposed to foot-binding in the Oriental manner, or so says William A. Rossi in *The Sex Life of the Foot and Shoe*, a text whose utility is hard to assess except for its solid bibliography. Alan E. Murray's *Shoes and Feet to Boot* is a fetishistic text in itself, but scholars would do better to look at some of the photographs and drawings commissioned by Irving Klaw in the 1950s (for more on Klaw, see **Models and Techniques** in Chapter 12, and **Hearings, Panels, Commissions, and Other Forums for Dramatizing Sexual Expression** in chapter 5). These, or imitations, still circulate, although any number of mostly soft-core contemporary magazines feature women (and men) clomping around in ten-inch-high Capezios. Shared fascination can constitute community, or so says the writer styled Chicklet in "Das Boot Brigade: An International Contact Club Encourages Pride Among Men with a Passion for Boots." Worth looking at also is the performance artist Ann Magnuson's "Hell on Heels," an essay that combines history and personal experience with tottering about on high heels.

FETISHIZED LOCI OF THE BODY

Breasts

Although it hardly needs saying in a country where late-night talk show hosts routinely joke about Dolly Parton's silhouette, the female breast is the American fetish-object of choice, and it can never be omitted from examinations of American fashion, modesty, or pornography. The "celebrity" Dianne Brill forthrightly explains how a lucrative public persona can be invented around large breasts and cynical merchandising in *Boobs, Boys and High Heels;* her book resembles others on or by women whose bust size brought them fame. "You'd be surprised how tits figure in a girl's career," said studio head Louis B. Mayer in 1937,[5] an observation unrivaled in its directness. Patrick Dennis' mock biography of Belle Poitrine ("beautiful bosom"), the wonderfully illustrated *Little Me*, is a spoof of actresses whose success derives from extraordinary mammaries; the social comment is delicious. *Breasts*, a charming look at the enormous variety of mammaries by Meema Spadola and Thom Powers, holds the record as cable-provider Cinemax's most-watched documentary.

More serious is Pam Carter's extraordinarily astute *Feminism, Breasts, and Breastfeeding*, which explores the "sexualization of breasts" as illuminated in terms of their actual function; Carter discusses breast-feeding itself in different venues, especially the taboos that encode the practice in the West, and draws on women's own experience of their breasts as appendages that both nurture and attract. Susan Thames and Marin Gazzaniga have collected essays on breast hygiene, breast size, breast fantasies, topless bars, and representational issues in *The Breast*. Probably the single most informative text, however, is *A History of the Breast*, in which Marilyn Yalom succinctly traces styles of shaping, spreading, compressing, uplifting, and augmenting breasts so that their display conforms to standards of beauty and eroticism over the ages. Her survey ranges across religion, medicine, politics, literature, photography, pornography, and film and virtually invents a discourse for discussing a subject Americans often shy away from.

Quasi-medical texts by authors who lack the courage of their obsessions begin with Adolph F. Niemoller's *The Complete Guide to Bust Culture*, a fetishistic celebration disguised as advice on hygiene. Excerpts from the work of the great German sexologist Curt Moreck make up the text of *Breast Fetishism*, mostly as the publisher's excuse for photographs of stunning bosoms, although Moreck's reflections on the aesthethics involved are always worth reading. Else K. LaRoe's *The Breast Beautiful*, on the other hand, offers genuinely useful advice to those who want to sculpt breasts; it is informative on cosmetic surgery and general hygiene, though written too long ago to serve as an index to modern methods of bosom enhancement, let alone their dangers.

Profiles, by Baron Wolman, is a pretentious pictorial text on the breast, considerably more reserved in its tone than Dennis Bee's *Breasts! A Study of Fetishisms*, whose commentary is much racier. Those unacquainted with the depth of bosom fixation might consult Timothy Burr's "Burr Identification of Breast Analysis," in *BISBA*, an attempt to classify all women by mammary size and type; its looniness approaches sublimity. In a culture mesmerized by large breasts, preferences for modest sizes can seem political statements. *The Genuine Article*, a newsletter published by Frank Wallis, advocates an aesthetic that gives primacy to natural breasts and decries silicon and other enhancements. Another zine, *Small Tops*, worships small breasts, though most adult book or film services offer magazines and movies cataloged under headings such as "Tiny Titties." For engaging skepticism, one can hardly do better than Nora Ephron's "A Few Words about Breasts," probably the definitive essay on the subject. It is a splendid riff on the American predilection for large breasts, written by a woman endowed with intelligence instead of a *belle poitrine* ("beautiful bosom"). Told again and again by family and friends that breast size does not matter, Ephron closes with this reflection, famous now as a boffo conclusion: "I have thought about their remarks, tried to put myself in their place, considered their point of view. I think they are full of shit" (474).

Unlike European women, who routinely sunbathe topless, American beachgoers are traditionally modest except on Florida, New York, and California coasts. (For domestic behavioral protocols governing disrobing, applying lotion with panache, and reclining in revealing sunning postures, see Dave Patrick's *California's Nude Beaches*.) During the 1960s topless fashions for beach and evening wear nevertheless enjoyed a surprising vogue in the United States. As might be expected, *Playboy* chronicled the brief trend in several pictorial articles. Typical are "No Cover, No Minimum" (1966) and "The Nude Look" (1965), illustrated looks at the topless phenomenon that began in 1964, when socialites attended galas bare-breasted or in transparent clothing; the photo-essays provide information about designers and interview women who wear the clothing. More recently, in "See-Through Still Tries to Find Light of Day," the *New York Times* fashion columnist Suzy Menkes notes that designers are bringing back transparent chiffon, a trend that required advice on the proper display of nipples in the 1990s. With so many modern designers again baring breasts, nipple rouge may become a staple of ladies' handbags.

Legs, Navels, Feet, Buttocks

Few solid texts deal with the popular American fetish for legs. As Simon Landers observes in *Legs: A Study in Fetishism*, a fascination with "gams" may actually be rooted in a fixation on stockings or shoes or in a more "normal" interest in the vagina. If the latter is the case, legs as a surrogate for genitalia may have lost some of their appeal as open-crotch pictures have multiplied. Another factor behind flagging interest may be the decline of the silk stocking; nylon panty hose apparently lack the necessary cachet (and make a different sound when legs are crossed), though illustrated catalogs from Victoria's Secret and smaller companies offering vintage-style undies and hose may take up some of the slack. Madison S. Lacy and Don Morgan altered the title of their book, *Leg Art: Sixty Years of Hollywood Cheesecake*, to *Hollywood Cheesecake: Sixty Years of America's Favorite Pinups*, presumably because Americans no longer recognized a genre that evolved from the silent-film era to the present; Lacy and Morgan include reminiscences by "leg-art" photographers. But the fetish has hardly disappeared: in *Leg*, Diana Edkins and Betsy Jablow have collected fetishistic illustrations drawn from advertisements, cinema, art, and other media, with an insightful Foreword by fashion designer Donna Karan. Dian Hanson, editor of a raft of magazines including *Leg Show*, tries to explain to women that the fetish grips only a male minority in her "Just My Opinion." Less obvious as a fetish is the fascination with navels, though erotica collectors have long prized Jay Hahn-Lonne's *Navel Revue*, an "autobiographical" study of a man's obsession with belly buttons, allegedly "published by his heirs" in 1930. Like so many personal accounts, it is more descriptive than analytical. *Beautiful Bare Feet*, whose title describes the fixation (feet rather than legs) of its readership pretty well, runs photos and articles clotted with obsession. Such texts should be read with caution.

Although his research ended in the 1920s, Alfred Kind is still the authority on buttock worship. Kind's *Buttock Fetishism*, like Moreck's *Breast Fetishism*, cited earlier, is actually a reprint of the relevant pages from Kind and Moreck's *Gefilde der Lust*, a massive investigation of the human fascination with rear ends, brilliantly researched and modestly illustrated. Both reprints, assembled by Jack Brussel, are available in major libraries; Kind's original text is extremely rare but deals with buttocks as the primary sexual presentation site in primates. Unlike social constructionists, evolutionary biologists insist that well-developed human breasts are an evolutionary ploy, a redundant form of sexual coding in that they give the male more than one chance to be aroused. The physician and sexologist John Money speaks for many anthropologists and sociobiologists when he observes in "Pornography in the Home: A Topic in Medical Education" and other places that the fascination of breasts for humans stems from their similarities to buttocks; they serve as sexual markers by attracting attention from the front of the body as well. If such authorities are correct in their assumption that sexual attraction is programmed, then rear ends are the default drive. Such reflections animate Jean-Luc Hennig's *The Rear View: A Brief and Elegant History of Bottoms through the Ages*, a recent popular book on fannies.

Gesäss Erotik, another work from German sexologists working in the 1920s, has been reprinted also. Edited by Ernst Schertel, the essays are ostensibly on buttock fetishes but are really concerned with enemas. Modern adult bookstores carefully distinguish between enemas and feces, which are usually quite different obsessions, one anal, penetrative, and yet sanitized, the second scatalogical, more clearly fetishistic, and more taboo, and devote separate shelves to each. The modern authority on the first is David Barton-Jay, whose *The Enema as an Erotic Art and Its History* is thorough to a fault. The Schertel volume, however, quotes extensively from pornographic literature and contains exceptional illustrations. Long valued as a pornographic text in its own right is John Gregory Bourke's *Scatalogic Rites of All Nations* (1891), a quasi-anthropological study of practices involving urine and feces in cultures around the world. It has been widely circulated over the years in America; the 1934 edition boasts a Foreword by Sigmund Freud, and Louis P. Kaplan has recently edited it once again. Still more contemporary is Paul Spinrad's *The RE/Search Guide to Bodily Fluids*, a catalog of erotic responses to excreta from semen to feces that dilates on their significance as fetishes and symbols. Among William Ian Miller's reflections on sensual input that nauseates are several concerned with the feces, urine, mucus, semen, saliva, blood, pus, and other fluids to emanate from human orifices. Miller's *The Anatomy of Disgust* points out that for some people disgust is essential to eroticism: "Sex is perceived as dirty, bestial, smelly, messy, sticky, slimy, oozy, and that is precisely, for many, its attraction" (103).

Oral Sex

Fellatio and cunnilingus have acquired near-fetishistic status in American culture over the last three decades; both now lie well within the boundaries of "normal" foreplay. (See **The "Cum Shot"** in chapter 13, especially Faust.) Most narratives on oral sex appear in guides to better sex, where mouth-to-genital techniques are subordinated to those for genital-to-genital intercourse. Some Americans apparently believe that oral contact with penis or clitoris is not *real* sex, a distinction advanced as well by President Clinton and his supporters during the Lewinsky affair. Illustrated books such as Donald Gilmore's *Soixante-Neuf-69* appeared in the 1960s; their interest is dependent wholly on the photographs. Preferable to most is Robert Harkel's *The Picture Book of Oral Love*, which sometimes speculates on cultural meanings. The classic American text, replete with exotic publishing history, is *Oragenitalism: An Encyclopaedic Outline of Oral Technique in Genital Excitation*, written by Gershon Legman under the anagrammatic name Roger-Maxe de La Glannège, the kind of historical and cultural survey that only a scholar of his stature can write; it is still the only book worth reading on the subject. Cultural acceptance can be measured in signs ranging from jokes involving blow jobs, song titles that play on oral sex (e.g., Janis Joplin's "Down on Me"), references to "sucking dick" in mainstream movies, sales of over-the-counter vaginal fresheners, ads for syrups to sweeten penises and vulvas, and Marilyn Monroe's famous definition of stardom as having reached a stage where it is at last unnecessary to give blow jobs to producers. A website run by women, gettingit.com, suggests that because foods alter the taste of sperm, men who hope for blow jobs should eat fruits and avoid meat in order to make their ejaculate tastier to sex partners (see Tasty).

Anality

Anality recurs in pornography from the works of de Sade to contemporary videotapes such as the multicassette *Caught from Behind* and *Rump Humpers*, two of a dozen series devoted to heterosexual anal intercourse, not to mention innumerable gay films. Jack Morin's *Anal Pleasure and Health: A Guide for Men and Women* is a how-to guide, but references to anality in representation can be found in Linda Lovelace's *Inside Linda Lovelace*, in which the actress boasts of her proficiency at anal intercourse in her movies, and in Joseph W. Slade's "Recent Trends in Pornographic Films," which noted a surge in anal scenes in hard-core films of the 1970s. The authority on anality in Western culture, however, is Norman O. Brown, whose *Life against Death: The Psychoanalytic Meaning of History* and, to a lesser extent, his *Love's Body*, find in such obsessions stimuli for the development of Western civilization. One of the chapters of Susie Bright's *Suzie Sexpert's Lesbian Sex World* argues for increased attention to anal sex as a means of gender-bending; since everybody has an easily penetrated anus, she thinks that it can serve as a universal erotic zone. The skirmish lines of the gender wars advance and recede under various symbolic banners. One side might call for ending the tyranny of the phallus by condemning penetration altogether, while Bright and others advocate that men be fucked in the interests of equity; to one degree or another, the latter thesis has always been implicit in many pornographic genres. In "Is the Rectum a Grave?" probably the most notorious of recent essays on pornography, sexuality, and gender, Leo Bersani endorses the spiritual aspects of anality. Being fucked in the ass, he says, is a "self-shattering" experience.

Hair

Among traditional fetishes recurrent in representation are those revolving around hair and hairstyles. Bill Severn's *The Long and Short of It: Five Thousand Years of Fun and Fury over Hair*, ostensibly occasioned by parental ire over androgynous long hair on teenagers during the 1960s, addresses hair fetishism throughout history. Wendy Cooper subjects the significance of hair to deep cultural and sexual investigation in *Hair Sex Society Symbolism*, probably the most astute analysis outside the literature of psychoanalysis. According to Charles Berg, women's hair symbolizes the penis for certain men. Its display is an acceptable substitute for the phallus, and stroking it symbolizes stroking of a thicker shaft; the more unkempt the hair, the more suggestive the sexuality, or so he says in *The Unconscious Significance of Hair. Haircults: Fifty Years of Styles and Cuts* reviews twentieth-century barbering; author Dylan Jones gives some attention to sexual implications. In "Hair-Jewelry as Fetish," Pamela A. Miller deals with decorations, although her focus veers away from the sexual associations prized by the true hair fetishist. In her zine *Hair to Stay*, editor-publisher Pam Winter runs articles on hirsute women, includes photos of herself and others with thick axillary and pubic hair, and reviews porn videos and other materials in which bushy hair functions as a fetish.

Special Settings

Literature, photography, painting, and motion pictures sometimes achieve erotic effect by setting intercourse in unusual, lightly fetishized environments. Several dozen current pornographic videocassettes, for example, capitalize on nudity and intercourse recorded in public places (see **Sexuality in Public: Exhibitionism** in chapter 10). For the most part, Rob Moore's edition of *The Field Guide to Outdoor Erotica* is a how-to guide to sex in the outdoors; the essays are presented, in part, as aids to fantasy for those who have a taste for intercourse au naturel. Ian Keown's *Lover's Guide to America* identifies resorts, hideaways and honeymoon hotels equipped with mirrored ceilings and other equipment of the sort found in porn genres. Finally, though we are stretching the concept of fetish and erotic commentary, Jack Rudloe entitled his marine biology text *The Erotic Ocean: A Handbook for Beachcombers and Marine Naturalists* and laced it with sensual metaphors linking sea foam and sperm. Allen Guttmann addresses sexual aspects (clothing, contact, metaphors) of organized sports in the United States and makes specific reference to pornography in *The Erotic in Sports.*

Odors

Odors and smells as triggers to desire, because they are harder to represent in erotica, have attracted smaller numbers of investigators. Iwan Bloch's *Oderatus Sexualis: A Scientific and Literary Study of Sexual Scents and Erotic Perfumes* was one of the first. More discreet is Adolph F. Niemoeller's *Sex and Smell*, which ranges over fragrances and odors. More recent is Richard K. Champion's *The Sweet Smell of Sex: A Study of an Abnormal Obsession*, on the aphrodisiac qualities of smells and perfumes. Ruth Winter and Kathleen McAuliffe discuss pheromones as attractants in "Hooked on Love: Chemical Sex." As a minor historical footnote, the first porn film in Smell-o-Vision, called

Smells Like Sex (directed by Steve Perry), is distributed with a scratch 'n' sniff card. The title of Alan Hirsch's *Scentsational Sex: The Secret to Using Aroma for Arousal* is self-explanatory, as is Michelle Kodis' *Love Scents: How Your Natural Pheromones Influence Your Relationships, Your Moods, and Who You Love*, though the latter is more scholarly than the former, with excellent glossary and notes. The less pleasant side of the fetish is the subject of Harvey T. Leathem's *Scatology: The Erotic Response to Bodily Scent*. Franz-Marie Feldhaus' *Ka-Pi-Fu, und andre Verschämte Dinge* also covers scatology, smells, flatulence, urolagnia, and related fetishes; the book illustrates the truism that the "science" of the past can become the folklore of the present. Folkloristic describes the approach of *It's a Gas: A Study of Flatulence* by Eric S. Rabkin and Eugene M. Silverman, whose "history" of the subject is amusing as well as informative. Two other texts cover the lore that combines exotic scents with magic: *Magica Sexualis: Mystic Love Book of Black Arts and Secret Societies*, by Emile Laurent and Paul Nagour, and *Magical and Ritual Use of Perfumes*, by Richard A. Miller and Iona Miller. Legions of texts serve as guides to "spiritual" sex. Typical is J. William Lloyd's *The Karezza Method: Or, Magnetation, the Art of Connubial Love*, one of the earliest on a periodically popular form of coitus interruptus. (See **Representational/Aphrodisiac Food and Drink** in chapter 11.)

At this writing, the current favorite fetishes among cultural critics revolve around sadomasochism. Sadomasochists are similar to postmodern academics in that both examine relationships in enactments of power. Despite porno efforts to redefine sex in general as dominance and submission, however, sadomasochism remains a highly ritualized, extremely circumscribed mode of sexual expression and is considered in chapter 10, **Performance**, as are some of the fetishes connected with S/M.

GENITALS AND THEIR FOLKLORE

Motif-indexed or not, stories about genitalia form an important category of folklore, and one measure of gender inequity is that more ink has been devoted to penises than to vaginas. Slight but interesting is Alain Danielou's *The Phallus: Sacred Symbol of Male Power*, which deals with religious representations of the penis, mostly ancient. (See also **Sexuality, Religion, and Blasphemy** in chapter 15.) Edward Karsh's *The Membrum Virile* is an enormous compendium of penis lore but is hard to find. More accessible and just as amusing is Alexandra Parsons' *Facts and Phalluses: A Collection of Bizarre and Intriguing Truths, Legends, and Measurements*, whose title is self-descriptive. Similar in title and approach is Kit Schwartz's *The Male Member: Being a Compendium of Fact, Fiction, Foibles and Anecdotes about the Male Sexual Organ in Man and Beast*. Both Parsons and Schwartz are fond of statistics: how long? how short? how thick? how much and how often does the male ejaculate? how many penises are circumcised? So is Mark Strage, whose *The Durable Fig Leaf* purports to be a history of the penis, though its best moments have to do with artistic, literary, and medical representations both well known and obscure. Strage rejects the "illogic" of "polemical" arguments linking penis and rape advanced by writers like Susan Brownmiller and Susan Griffin but does observe that "the constellation of his conflicting emotions regarding the organ of his malehood has profoundly affected the manner in which man has organized his civilization, ordered his institutions, treated women and his fellow men, and even expressed the creations of his own imagination" (17). Strage is also a good source of information on American patents granted for devices for maintaining erections. Courtesan-columnist Xaviera Hollander draws on her experience for observations of the male anatomy in *Xaviera on the Best Part of a Man*. Brian Richards' *The Penis* is a novelty book on "man's best friend" for the coffee-table trade and not nearly so amusing as the classic from the 1930s called *The Demi-Wang*, by Peter Long/Long Peter, a ribald linguistic riff.

Typical of many similar articles is Jim Boyd's "The Last Taboo: The Hung and Unsung" on alleged preferences of women for men with large penises. Boyd furnishes a list of celebrities reputedly so endowed and sidebar information on a nationwide organization of men with large organs. Boyd's reflections continue a tradition begun by Mark Twain, whose comic "Mammoth Cod" celebrated the alleged virtues of large penises. In "What's It Worth to You?" Bruce Handy deflates the myth that John Dillinger's penis has been preserved by the FBI. The Smithsonian doesn't have it either, he says, but Walter Reed Hospital does archive a few unfamous penises. Leonore Tiefer treats the penis as a social construction in "In Pursuit of the Perfect Penis: The Medicalization of Male Sexuality." The word "impotence," for example, betrays "the social construction of male sexuality" when media, medicine, and technology combine to produce a medicalization of male sexual dysfunction, whose jargon Tiefer reviews. Tiefer thinks that if our culture could emphasize other, that is, nonpenis forms of sex, then men would feel less pressure to perform, and the concept of dysfunction would not weigh so heavily in sexual discourse. (That might mean that former presidential candidate Bob Dole would lose his day job as spokesperson for Viagra, of course.) Peter Lehman comments on the penis folklore prominent even in medical literature in his *Running Scared*.

Naomi Schor and Elizabeth Weed have edited "The Phallus Issue" of *differences*, mostly Lacanian and post-Lacanian denigrations of the phallus as the symbol and instrument of patriarchy, though the obsessiveness of the essays could just as easily be read as a celebration of its power. In any case, Lacanian psychology makes a cultural, if not sexual, fetish of the phallus. Lee Alexander Stone's *The Power of a Symbol*, retitled *The Story of Phallicism*, is a classic study of phallic imagery. Probably the most trenchant observation about the phallus—as opposed to the penis—is Sallie Tisdale's in *Talk Dirty to Me: An Intimate Philosophy of Sex*: "If every man thought his penis were good enough, there wouldn't be so many phallic symbols. . . . The assumption endures that women want—and *should* want—a penis, while men want bigger ones. But what women want is a phallus—that is, male power. . . . The phallus counts because *no* one has one. (At least, not one big enough. Phalluses can never be too big)" (237–238).

American obsession with the size of penises has been fed by pornographic genres, most recently by hard-core films and tapes, whose male stars can appear just as unbalanced by their sparlike erections as their counterparts with balloon-like breasts. In *Private Dicks*, an HBO documentary by Meema Spadola and Thom Powers, twenty-five men ranging from a paraplegic to actor Jonah Falcon, who boasts a thirteen-and-a-half-inch penis, display and sometimes measure their organs on-screen. Gary M. Griffin's *Penis Enlargement Methods: Fact and Phallusy*, while better than most such books on the subject, is notable chiefly because it attests to perennial fascination. Someday a scholar with a sense of humor will ferret through the mountains of ads, pamphlets, brochures, and folk-lore on the mythos of phallic tinkering, but until then this book will have to do. Doogie Wowser's "The Dick of Your Dreams" reviews Griffin's book as well as *Penis Power Quarterly*, a periodical devoted to penis enhancement, and films such as *Huge Dicks*, featuring John Holmes, Long Dong Silver, Long Dan Silver, and Mr. MX (perhaps the nation's only enduring memory of the once-favored medium-range missile). Or, those in a hurry can opt for surgery. As John Taylor explains in "The Long, Hard Days of Dr. Dick," Dr. Melvyn Rosenstein, the "Henry Ford" of cosmetic penis surgery, charges $5,900 to enlarge a member. Says Taylor in a Lacanian/Baudrillarian aside: "In [Rosenstein's] world, the phallus altogether replaces the penis, which ceases to exist as a tissued, vascular organ and instead becomes a technological replica of itself, a marvel of artifice that the ancient Egyptians might have worshipped" (130). The history of circumcision at times seems secondary to the illustrations of tissue in *Foreskin*, by Bud Berkeley and Joe Tiffenbach, but their remarks are keyed to a survey about foreskins that the authors conducted among male respondents.

Sex and Circumcision: A Study of Phallic Worship and Mutilation in Men and Women, by Felix Bryk, is a reprint of a classic German text from the 1930s, heavily illustrated and long regarded as quasi-pornographic. At this writing, various world organizations are lobbying against clitoridectomies, or female circumcision (see **Sexual Aids and Equipment** in chapter 4, Sanderson). The practice is not native to America, however, and appears in contemporary domestic sexual mythology only because of recent immigration. During the Victorian period, physicians sometimes recommended surgical intervention to curtail masturbation in women, as noted by John Duffy in "Masturbation and Clitoridectomy: A Nineteenth-Century View." In any case, it does not figure in pornographic representation: actresses in contemporary hard-core videos almost universally depilate their pubic hair so that clitorides are visible. Because women's desire is the implicit theme of most heterosexual videos, American pornographers would regard clitoridectomies as obscene. Before she became an antiporn crusader, the actress Holly Rider, celebrated by *Screw* magazine as the owner of the most beautiful genitals in America, used her generously endowed clitoris to simulate intercourse with other women. While Rider has rivals, films featuring large clitorides are not so numerous as to constitute a genuine sub-genre.

Genitology: Reading the Genitals, by Dr. Seymore Klitz and Dr. Ima Peeper, is a tongue-in-cheek (see authors' pseudonyms) treatise on the semiotics of genitalia. Kit Schwartz's *The Female Member: Being a Compendium of Facts, Figures, Foibles, and Anecdotes about the Loving Organ*, a companion volume to his text on penises, surveys the folklore of vaginas and clitorides. Freud's "Das Medusenhaupt," a note on the fear inspired in males by female genitalia, echoes in analytic literature. One of the best explications of the "vagina dentata" (vagina with teeth) syndrome is psychiatrist Karen Horney's "The Dread of Women," which can be read with Verrier Elwin's "The Vagina Dentata Legend," by an anthropologist who traces the motif across cultures. *The Female Eunuch* has become a classic text on women's sexuality partly because of Germaine Greer's marshaling of folklore on the vagina. Thomas P. Lowry's *The Classic Clitoris: Historic Contributions to Scientific Sexuality* offers a variety of perspectives, and *The Clitoris*, a text (with A-V packet) put together by Lowry and Thea Snyder Lowry, presents wide-ranging comment on hygiene, orgasms, clitoridectomies, and related matters. Mary Jane Sherfey's now famous revisionist view of female orgasm, *The Nature and Evolution of Female Sexuality*, is also highly informative on clitorides, vaginas, and other topics.

THE FOLKLORE OF MASTURBATION

Genital lore surfaces in the literature on masturbation, a human activity whose ubiquity is matched only by American reticence about its pleasures and satisfactions. Virtually all that we "know" about masturbation is folklore best studied by ethnographers. Depictions of masturbation are staples of pornography, one of whose classic aims is to foster it as a solitary experience or a shared one. Given the press of time and the difficulties some people have in achieving orgasm, that would seem a worthy goal, but it would be an understatement to say that the view is not widely held. Although millions of their fellow citizens masturbate every day, too many Americans worry that the experience is either harmful or at least fraudulent. Americans who endorse masturbation as a boon are outnumbered by those who either condemn it (Edward Taylor and Catharine MacKinnon come to mind) or ignore any mention of it in the hope that they might somehow be thought to be exempt from its blandishments. The educator A. S. Neill (author of *Summerhill*), who advocated that children be free to experiment, was once asked if he were not worried about their masturbating. His reply was memorable: "Well," he said, "it doesn't seem to have harmed you and me."[6] In 1994 political pressure forced President Clinton to dismiss his surgeon general, Joycelyn Elders, for suggesting that schools could do worse than teach students how to masturbate as an alternative to unsafe sex with partners. Myth and folklore, in short, are tenacious.

Probably the most authoritative survey is *Histoire d'une grande peur: la masturbation*, by Jean Stengers and Anne van Neck, who trace references to classical texts and include examples of famous masturbators such as Guy de Maupassant, said to indulge himself up to two dozen times a day to spur the inventiveness of his pen. The origins of pathological responses to masturbation can be laid at the door of S. A. Tissot (1718–1797), a Swiss physician who published *On Onanism, Or a Physical Dissertation on the Ills Produced by Masturbation* (1758)[7] to claim that the practice led not only to mental instability but also to physiological damage. According to Tissot, sex of any kind caused a rush of blood to the brain, leaving the neural system starved (the Freudian implications are titillating) and the mind at risk. Tissot's delusions figure in E. H. Hare's "Masturbatory Insanity: The History of an Idea," which enumerates variations on the notion that self-abuse leads to madness. Alex Comfort also covers Tissot's misguided notions (70–74) and even more splendidly erroneous convictions in Chapter 3 ("The Rise and Fall of Self-Abuse") of *The Anxiety Makers*, a history of attempts by medical establishments to combat masturbation, repudiate sexual experimentation, and endorse chastity. Ludmilla Jordanova categorizes Tissot's treatise as the fountainhead of medical misrepresentations of sexuality in "The Popularisation of Medicine: Tissot on Onanism." Equally readable is "The Frightful Consequences of Onanism: Notes on the History of a Delusion," for which Robert H. MacDonald gathers other absurdities (myths that masturbation causes pimples, hair loss, hair growth on palms, insomnia, feeblemindedness, weak genes, bed-wetting, diminished strength, spiritual anomie, etc.) that have afflicted the gullible. Most histories of Victorian sexuality touch on attitudes toward masturbation (see **Period Studies** in Chapter 5).

Vern L. Bullough and Martha Voght note that masturbation was often mistakenly conflated with both homosexuality and birth control in "Homosexuality and Its Confusion with the 'Secret Sin' in Pre-Freudian America." Bullough and Voght focus on advocates like the aptly named Dr. Alfred Hitchcock, who in 1842 chided his fellow physicians for not recognizing that virtually all illnesses in America were "caused" by masturbation. Bullough and Voght report that in the 1890s most physicians thought that girls were more likely to masturbate than boys, perhaps because they could do so more surreptitiously (e.g., on bicycles, whose seats seemed ideal for the purpose).

Peter Wagner's article, "The Veil of Medicine and Morality: Some Pornographic Aspects of the *Onania*," discusses a journal that was both imported and reprinted in the colonies in the early 1700s. Devoted to the evils of masturbation, it titillated audiences with the semisalaciousness of its content. "Authorities" continued to warn the young. "The Vice That Has No Name," William Styron's review of the Grove Press 1967 reissue of *Light on Dark Corners*, an 1894 sexual guide by B. G. Jefferis and J. L. Nichols, laughs at the period's folklore, especially regarding masturbation. Other Americans, of course, have found "self-abuse" both rewarding and amusing. In "Some Remarks on the Science of Onanism" (1879), an address delivered to the Stomach Club, Mark Twain reminded his audience that Benjamin Franklin insisted that "masturbation is the mother of invention" (23). Peter Gay's *The Bourgeois Experience: Victoria to Freud* (294–318) is also excellent on American medical and popular attitudes toward masturbation from the colonial period to the nineteenth century. Freud's "Concluding Remarks to a Discussion on Masturbation" is, of course, well known and is the subject of Annie Reich's "The Discussion of 1912 on Masturbation and Our Present-Day Views."

Pornography often figures in what might be called masturbation therapy in the treatment of sex offenders, who are first shown violent sexual images, then switched to "nondeviant" porn, and encouraged to masturbate; the intent is to refocus fantasies through "reconditioning," while the patient's hands provide cheap sources of energy. Lawrence Wright describes the practice in "A Rapist's Homecoming" (62). Wright also calls the plethysmograph, the device used to measure the erections of males exposed to erotic images, a "sexual lie detector" and compares it to *Screw's* "Peter Meter," then wonders if the magazine had the device in mind when it gave the movie review column the name. Urologists routinely provide men's magazines or more explicit material to assist patients who need sperm counts.

If both popular and poststructuralist accounts are to be believed, American men are either born knowing how to masturbate, are hegemonically tutored by the culture, or learn from male-inscripted pornography in the course of adolescence, while culturally victimized women require special instruction. That seems on the surface to be an egregiously sexist assumption (or, to use the fashionable term, a social construction), and the contention does not have the credibility of such clearly discriminatory practices as the Chinese binding of female feet, but its power is manifest in the many instruction manuals aimed at teaching women how to achieve orgasm on their own. It may well be, as some feminist writers assert, that ignorance of how to masturbate properly helped to subordinate women's sexuality to men's. One obvious means of redressing the balance would be to ensure that pornography be friendly and accessible to women.

Being able to bring one's self to orgasm, with or without mechanical assistance, is a form of empowerment. That is the message of Betty Dodson, labial artist and masturbation expert, who has held many workshops over the last several decades to proselytize for masturbation as one key to women's sexual health. Among her several volumes are *Liberating Masturbation: A Meditation on Self Love*, a rationale for masturbation, and *Self Love and Orgasm*, reflections on body images, effective masturbation techniques, and the role of fantasies. Joani Blank and Honey Lee Cottrell have published *I Am My Lover*, eight photoessays illustrating masturbation techniques of different women, and Jack Morin and Blank have written a pleasant, knowledgeable treatise on autoeroticism for all genders called *The Private Side of Sex*. Morin has also published *Men Loving Themselves: Images of Male Self-Sexuality*, a photographic essay on male masturbation that is both didactic and titillating. Joani Blank declared May National Masturbation Month in 1997, and her store, Good Vibrations, has been promoting the occasion ever since (see Good Vibrations, Spring 1997).

William Stekel's 1950 text *Auto-Eroticism* insisted that masturbation as a habit would grow along with the sophistication of culture and warned that *not* masturbating could lead to years of analysis. Stekel did not go as far as Wilhelm Reich, a Freudian Marxist who believed that the proletariat was retarded by sexual frustration and thus prevented from realizing its full revolutionary consciousness. Reich's efforts to safely discharge the sexual energy of the masses through engineered orgasm is the subject of "Orgonomy," a chapter in *Fads and Fallacies in the Name of Science* by Martin Gardner, a longtime columnist for *Scientific American*. The problem, of course, is that humans characterize masturbation so differently. In "Speaking about Sex: Sexual Pathology and Sexual Therapy as Rhetoric," Thomas S. Szasc contrasts the old view of masturbation as a pathological activity with the more modern view that it is therapeutic, only to conclude that sexual behavior in the main is just sexual behavior and that we had better try to call it that instead of coloring our language. Such logic, of course, would topple many religious and ideological edifices. Though united in their faith in the evils of pornography, conservatives and antiporn feminists diverge on their views of masturbation. As Richard Posner notes in *Sex and Reason*, the two groups "undermine each other": "The feminists fear that pornography causes rape; [conservatives such as Irving] Kristol that it causes the substitution of masturbation for intercourse. Since rape is a form of intercourse, Kristol must believe that pornography reduces the incidence of rape, while feminists must believe that it reduces the incidence of masturbation" (374).

A popular American text on the most universal of sexual practices is Suzanne and Irving Sarnoff's *Sexual Excitement and Sexual Peace*, a book-length study of the place of masturbation in an active sexual life, the fantasies that assist the practice, and methods that have proved favorites over time. It seems odd to speak of a balanced approach to a form of sex enjoyed by millions, but if there is such a thing, the Sarnoffs manage it, using a tone that is by turns solemn and reasonable, and they never once suggest that masturbation causes acne. One of Avodah K. Offit's essays in her *Night Thoughts: Reflections of a Sex Therapist* espouses a commonsense view of masturbation as both therapy and recreation. Hans Richter also treats both male and female pleasure in *Joys of Masturbation*, a how-to manual. The best-known texts by therapists William H. Masters and Virginia Johnson, *Human Sexual Response* and *Human Sexual Inadequacy*, are authoritative on the subject. Jodi Lawrence's *The Search for the Perfect Orgasm* traces the history of a virtual American fetish and documents not only the hope sometimes vested in masturbation as a source of personal pleasure but also its role in the evolution of the folklore of ideal mutual satisfaction (i.e., as a spur to crossing the finish line together).

A different perspective is that of Lynn Segal, whose "Sweet Sorrows, Painful Pleasures: Pornography and the Perils of Heterosexual Desire" notes that women like Lonnie Barbach and Betty Dodson put masturbatory pleasure at "the heart of heterosexual pleasure and desire" in order "to sidestep the difficulties of moving beyond or outside all the dominant representations of heterosexual desire as the desire of, or for, the phallus" (81). But Leonore Tiefer, the biologist, is more blunt. In *Sex Is Not a Natural Act and Other Essays*, Tiefer says that "the debate about pornography is in large part a debate about masturbation. I think the reason no one talks about *women's* use of pornography and *women's* interest in pornography has to do with discomfort with the idea of women masturbating" (133). Catherine Bennett comments on a detectable preference for masturbation in an age of AIDS in "View from a Broad: Why All Men Are Wankers." She reviews fiction that foregrounds masturbation and quotes various males on the benefits of the practice: "masturbation is clearly now the primary form of sex, with anything else second-best. Karl Kraus, another of those sexy Viennese sages, got there years ago. 'A woman occasionally is quite a serviceable substitute for masturbation,' he said generously, adding: 'It takes an abundance of imagination, to be sure.' " In one installment of his regular column for *Penthouse*, "The Penis Page," Bill Lawren wonders why—aside from the fun— men masturbate. Recreation and satisfaction are two reasons, obviously, but Lawren also reports on the work of Robin Baker and Mark Bellis of the University of Manchester, who believe that men masturbate to provide healthier, stronger sperm for sexual competition. Bernard Arcand discusses the relationship of pornography to masturbation at length in "The Sin of Onan." Finally, Paula Bennett and Vernon A. Rosario have collected materials under the title *Solitary Pleasures: The Historical, Literary, and Artistic Discourses of Autoeroticism*, whose postmodern contributors find cultural inscriptions in acts of masturbation; the volume lends credence to observers who equate cultural theory itself with masturbation.

SEXUAL AIDS, TOYS, CONTRIVANCES, AND IMPLEMENTS

Not all sexual devices are representational. Dildos are usually shaped like phalluses, and lifesize latex dolls are molded to resemble anatomically correct men and women, but the category of sexual aids also embraces creams and lotions, condoms plain, ornamental, and flavored, penis pumps, cock rings, restraints, whips, nipple whisks, labia spreaders, chains, rectal plugs, ben-wah balls, anal balls, nipple clips, hanging baskets designed for intercourse, and on— and on. Used as aids to masturbation or intercourse—or merely as objects of art or intrigue—they occupy prominent places in pornographic genres.

For the historical context for sexual technologies, the researcher might begin with Anthony Astrachan's "Patented Sex," a photo-essay on vintage sex devices—mostly loony—patented by Americans. More extensive is Hoag Levins' *American Sex Machines: The Hidden History of Sex at the U.S. Patent Office*, which unsuccessfully answers such questions as "who really invented the bra?" Among the examples in *Absolutely Mad Inventions: Compiled from the Records of the United States Patent Office,* by A. E. Brown and H. A. Jeffcott Jr., are the "Mobile Bust-Form," a sort of brassiere that vibrates when its wearer walks, so as to mimic the natural sway of unfettered breasts without any loss of support, and a "Lorelei Bait," a fishing lure in the shape of a nude woman, presumably attractive to horny male fish. Not all devices were intended to make sex pleasurable. Vern L. Bullough's "Technology for the Prevention of 'Les Maladies Produites par La Masturbation' " unearths some astonishing American patents for devices to forestall masturbation by either sex. Parents and physicians were to affix these to the genitals of suspect children, sometimes using wrenches. In the latter category were contraptions resembling chastity belts, which, while hardly an American invention and never widespread in this country, were staples of erotic literature. Esar Levine, publisher of Panurge Press, put together a volume of excerpts of erotica featuring chastity belts, adding his own commentary on the motives of people who used them, called *Chastity Belts: An Illustrated History of the Bridling of Women.* The fascination lasted long enough for John Dingwall, himself a notable dealer in erotica, to publish *The Girdle of Chastity: A Fascinating History of Chastity Belts,* which gives some space to the few American versions ever constructed.

Roger Blake's *Sex Gadgets* covers the paraphernalia of self-arousal. More comprehensive, better researched, and much funnier is *The Humor and Technology of Sex*; author Paul Tabori alludes to literary humor and popular jokes, especially those in which appliances appear. Manfred F. DeMartino's encyclopedic review of scientific and popular literature on self-stimulation, a spectrum that ranges from auto-fellation to self-induced suffocation, acknowledges the inventiveness of ancestors unblessed with the ability to order erotic contrivances by mail. DeMartino's comprehensive *Human Autoerotic Practices* contains essays by Albert Ellis, Morton Hunt, Patricia Brooks, David C. Gordon, Helen Kaplan, Masters and Johnson, Alex Comfort, Betty Dodson, Lonnie Barbach, and many others. Several medical and psychological authorities contribute essays to *Sexual Self-Stimulation,* edited by R.E.L. Masters, whose several sexology volumes, like this one, employ a tone midway between popular and academic. The nonscholarly *Auto-Erotic Acts and Devices,* by "Victor Dodson," gravitates toward the picturesquely bizarre, as does *Auto-Erotic Devices,* by Harvey T. Leathem with Hugh Jones, who discuss several dozen devices in "case histories." Americans have long been titillated by reading about, or looking at, pictures of gadgets that other humans inserted into themselves, wrapped their genitals in, or stimulated some part of the body with, and publishers have always obliged them. Typical of such texts is *Erotica Contrivances,* anonymously printed in 1922; it features sexual machines that seem a little dangerous now. In *Male Orgasm thru Auto-Erotic Devices,* Joel Lang refers to aids that will strike some readers as weird, other as wonderfully imaginative. The plots of stag films and modern videotapes have often turned on inventions ranging from vacuum pumps fitted on penises to piston-driven engines whose extensions probe vaginas. The current favorite, featured most recently in some of the Seymore Butts videotapes, is the "Sybian," an extremely powerful, saddle-shaped electrical appliance with a vibrator that can be introduced in a politically correct position. Elaborate controls permit women to adjust the speed of vibration, the depth of penetration, and the angle of rotation while straddling the device. Less expensive is a time-honored technology: in "On a Particular Form of Masturbation in Women: Masturbation with Water," E. Halpert notes that using bath faucet and shower jets for clitoral stimulation is more common than employing douche nozzles and that subjects report high degrees of satisfaction; such scenes recur in porn films. Rachel Maines also explores sexual applications of hydrotherapy in *The Technology of Orgasm.*

Any number of popular books on how to improve one's sex life advocate the use of sexual aids and toys; representative examples are Xaviera Hollander's *Xaviera's Fantastic Sex*, Alexandra Penny's *Great Sex*, and Jay Wiseman's *Sex Toy Tricks: More than 125 Ways to Accessorize Good Sex*, all of which talk about erogenous zones, genital techniques, video stimulants, and sex aids of all sorts. Toys in Babeland, a Manhattan emporium, is the subject of Lynn Yaeger's "Fun with Lipsticks and Dildos." Yaeger looks at how an upscale marketing that displays sex appliances in appealing packages on elegant shelves produces sales and comfort for customers. Even Andrea Dworkin's *Intercourse*, which deplores heterosexual intercourse, seems kindly disposed toward such technologies: according to Dworkin, women who insist on sexual experience can at least use dildos and vibrators as a way of avoiding contact with males. Susie Bright's brightly titled *Suzie Sexpert's Lesbian Sex World* evaluates accoutrements like latex and leather panties, dildos, nipple clamps, and softly lined body restraints for the well-equipped lesbian home. Sexual appliances are of special value to the physically challenged and receive ample attention in *Enabling Romance: A Guide to Love, Sex and Relationships for the Disabled (and the People Who Care About Them)* by Ken Kroll and Erica Levy Klein. If a picture is worth 1,000 words, then Bernard F. Stehle's *Incurably Romantic*, beautifully rendered photographs of love and sex between the "physically different," may be even more instructive.

In *The Durable Fig Leaf*, Mark Strage has a lot of fun discussing the toys used by researchers to measure arousal. He notes that Karl Freund developed the penile plethysmograph, a volumetric device for detecting erections, in order to keep homosexuals out of the Czech army. If the device sensed an erection when the inductee was shown homosexual porn, he was rejected (123). Freund outlines both the early applications and the proper fitting of the plethysmograph, a ring that fits snugly around the penis and emits electronic signals to researchers, in "A Laboratory Method for Diagnosing Predominance in Homo- or Hetero-Erotic Interest in the Male." The plethysmograph has become a favorite tool of porn researchers, who wire subjects to test arousal during the exhibition of movies. In the spirit of political correctness, the vaginal photoplethysmograph, a tamponlike device fitted with a photoelectric cell, measures arousal in women by recording the flow of secretions. As one might expect, both devices have given rise to a subcategory of folklore around social science laboratories, whose technicians have been rumored to place side bets on the erections and secretions of especially willing subjects.

CONDOMS

Casanova introduced condoms, made then from sheep intestines and known as "French Letters," to readers of his *Memoirs*, and the vulcanization of rubber in the mid-nineteenth century ensured their appearance in other pornographic genres. In an age of AIDS, more porn movie performers are sporting them now, and none too soon (at least two major stars are reportedly HIV-positive). Condoms enjoy ambivalent status: on one hand, they are sober instruments of birth control; on the other, they are sexual artifacts in their own right, suffused with a folklore that highlights their shape, construction, and decoration. The vastness of the literature is evident from a bibliography on "Condoms" available from the Kinsey Institute. The standard, if stuffy, history of contraceptive technologies, Norman E. Himes' *Medical History of Contraception*, begins with Roman sheaths and itemizes subsequent variations over the centuries. Of popular histories, the best is Jeannette Parisot's *Johnny Come Lately: A Short History of the Condom*. Another popular text, *The Curious History of Contraception* by Shirley Green, covers potions, pills, douches, sponges, vasectomies, sterilizations, and other methods along with condoms of many types. By far the most scholarly treatment is James S. Murphy's *The Condom Industry in the United States*, a dry, thorough investigation replete with dates, personalities, marketing statistics, and industry analysis. Here readers can learn about major brands, manufacturing plants, testing procedures, and industry arguments over sizes. Much lighter in tone are Gary M. Griffin's *Condom Encyclopedia: What Size Is Your Condom?* and M. K. Neilman's *Condom Mania! The Illustrated Condom Handbook*. Among other things, the former sketches cultural and racial assumptions about penis size and condom lore. The pictures in the latter indicate an astonishing—not to say goofy—array of colors, shapes, and materials. Funnier yet is *The Great Cover-Up: A Condom Compendium*, by Susan Zimet and Victor Goodman, who assemble cartoons, jokes, songs, and anecdotes to send a serious message about the necessity of using condoms. Though written from a British perspective, *Rubber Up! Every Gay Man's Guide to Condoms*, by Edward King and Chris Markham, offers lively discussion of "condom politics," condom selection, their use with toys and appliances, lubricants, and safe sex.

Karen Houppert discusses the shortcomings of the new "Reality"-brand condom for women, a disposable sheath for the vagina that Houppert describes as a polyurethane G-string with an inverted pouch in "Reality Check: Condom Con Job?" On that subject, Jim Shelley's "Tunnel of Glove" is more specific. Shelley's girlfriend field-tests the female condom, which sells at three for $7.50. Inserting it, she claims, is like "trying to compress a Slinky that has been dipped in mustard," but she thinks the protection it offers is wonderful since it is much less likely to break than a male condom. Shelley remarks that intercourse with a woman wearing it is uncomfortable for the male and that during oral sex the male will think of a "shower curtain banging in [his] face" (44). Porn movie producers generally avoid these and dental dams—polyurethane sheets fitted over the mouth for safe oral sex (they act as a barrier against the transmission of disease)—because they obscure the genitals for the camera. The absence of commentary on dental dams reflects cultural hierarchies. Although there is nothing gender-specific about dental dams, they are used mostly by lesbians going down on each other; the word of mouth on them has yet to make its way into the mainstream.

A sometimes unstated premise is that mechanical sex, jointly or as solitary masturbation, is preferable to sex in which the partners are at risk. Ted Mc-Ilvenna and his colleagues at the Institute for the Advanced Study of Sexuality are intent on explicating AIDS and other sex-specific medical problems, but they also include a chapter on eroticizing sexual aids, safety measures, and gadgets in *The Complete Guide to Safe Sex*. Erotic appliances, say advocates, can be the salvation of women in a risky sexual and social environment. *Safe Sex: The Ultimate Erotic Guide, with Photos by Fred Bissonen*, by John Preston and Glenn Swann, uses explicit illustration and focuses on reducing risk. Cindy Patton and Janis Kelly comment on prophylactic devices, especially dental dams, dildos, vibrators, and other tools in *Making It: A Woman's Guide to Sex in the Age of AIDS*, an English/Spanish guide to safe hetero-, bi-, and lesbian sex. Beverly Whipple and Gina Ogden adopt a similar strategy in *Safe Encounters: How Women Can Say Yes to Pleasure and No to Unsafe Sex*, which covers a substantial assortment of toys.

DILDOS

Chief and oldest of sexual instruments is the dildo, which has figured in literature since the third century B.C., when Herondas of Alexander wrote *A Private Chat*, a play whose comedy turned on a dildo as it passed from woman to woman.[8] Classic texts of more recent centuries include *Dildoides* (1706), which is usually ascribed to Samuel Butler, and *Le godimiché royal suivi du Mea Culpa* (1789), a French treatise on its use by aristocratic ladies, including Marie Antoinette, who, folklore has it, was skilled in its use on herself and others. Peter Wagner chronicles the public affection for narratives about dildos, as detailed in quasi-medical texts 200 years ago, in "The Discourse on Sex— Or Sex as Discourse: Eighteenth Century Medical and Paramedical Erotica." Gershon Legman notes in "Erotic Folksongs and Ballads" that Louis Perceau wrote a study of the literature of dildos under the name Alexandre de Vérineau called *Les Priapées* in 1921 (493).[9] Dildos occupy places of honor in hundreds of pornographic novels and stories, and millions of Americans buy models fabricated of space-age materials in hundreds of shapes and sizes.

Edward Kelly noted in the mid-1970s that cultural acceptance, though gradual, seemed lasting in "A New Image for the Naughty Dildo?" Dildos are now big business, a fact easily inferred from "The Feel of Real," a video report on reproductions of porn star genitals by Doc Johnson Enterprises, by far the largest U.S. maker of sexual appliances. (Doc Johnson was founded in the 1970s by Reuben Sturman, the most notorious of pornographers, now in federal prison for tax evasion.) The video footage features Mark Wallice and Nikki Tyler as their genitals are cast in molds. Women purchase the neoprene penises of their favorite stars to use as dildos, just as men buy the meticulously reproduced vaginas and anuses of their favorite actresses for leisure-time penetration. Doc Johnson has become virtually a generic term for sexual aids, largely because of its conflation with "Johnson" as a slang synonym for penis. "A Cock Goes to Court" describes Jeff Stryker's suit against Doc Johnson Enterprises; the successful suit by Stryker (aka Peyton), a leading gay porn star, asked for additional royalties on the company's sale of a dildo made from a mold of Stryker's celebrated organ. The case points up the historically interesting gender-inversion of dildos. The literature of dildos usually represents the appliances as beloved of females, when, in practice, they are also often purchased by homosexuals. Tales of dildos that allegedly become stuck in colons and have to be removed, still vibrating, by emergency room doctors constitute an enduring subcategory of urban myth; almost every hospital in America cherishes its own legend. As dildos have become ubiquitous, however, these folktales have been supplanted— though the suspension of disbelief required is greater—by the narrative of the emergency surgical removal of a live gerbil introduced into the rectum by (invariably) a major male celebrity.

Dildos have become politically charged as lesbians have tried to stake out territory of their own. Pornographers aiming at a heterosexual market have frequently employed dildos in narratives, photographs, and movies (1) to suggest a female desire so insatiable that women resort to phallic substitutes in the absence of an available male, (2) to assist in the opening up of vaginas so that audiences can get a better look, and (3) to identify performers as lesbians by masculinizing their intercourse in a way that fingers and tongues cannot. While statistically the last function may actually be less common than the others, it may well be the most iconographic. In the last several years, all-female porn videotapes in series such as *Strap-On Sally* have constituted a subgenre of ersatz lesbianism, but dildos worn in harnesses or wielded by hand also enliven series such as *San Francisco Lesbians*, made by avowed lesbians.

The ideological problem for some lesbians is penetration itself, with or without a dildo, because it implies participation in patriarchal power structures. For others, penetration is acceptable so long as it is accomplished without penises. Strongly informed by Lacanian psychology, the acute phallic symbolism shapes debate. As wags observe, for Freudians, a cigar is sometimes only a cigar, not necessarily a fetish; for Lacanians, a cigar is never just a cigar, because phallicism, the aura of the erect as opposed to the flaccid penis, is the literal locus of social, political, and economic power in Western culture. In "Taking On the

Phallus," Colleen Lamos endorses the dildo as "undermin[ing] the authority of the penis, discrediting phallic power while simultaneously, and paradoxically, assuming such power for itself" (102). Lamos cites surveys on lesbian use of dildos and figures on the number sold annually. Susie Bright also says in *Suzie Sexpert's Lesbian Sex World* that dildos are acceptable because they give pleasure and because they can be appropriated in good conscience given their historical association with lesbians. Besides, says Bright, dildos don't have to *look* like penises and don't have to be fully inserted. A dildo shaped like, say, a bunny, can do just as good a job on a clitoris.

The ur-texts on the subject, however, are Judith Butler's *Bodies That Matter: On the Discursive Limits of Sex* (especially the chapter entitled "The Lesbian Phallus and the Morphological Imaginary") and *Gender Trouble: Feminists and the Subversion of Identity.* Butler believes that dildos enable lesbians to carry out what she calls a "subversive repetition" of heterosexual sexuality and thereby to achieve an identity of their own. Using a dildo on one's self or a partner may thus be a political statement (and a source of ideologically sanctioned fun). Those interested in the growing corpus of dildo theory can consult several articles that outline the dimensions of the controversy and sketch the rich fantasies and folklore engendered by the topic: June Reich's "Genderfuck: The Law of the Dildo"; Heather Findlay's "Freud's 'Fetishism' and the Lesbian Dildo Debates"; and Julia Creet's "Daughter of the Movement: The Psychodynamics of Lesbian S/M Fantasy." Already dildo theory has branched out to consider the political correctness of lesbian "fisting," that is inserting one's clenched hand into the vagina or anus of one's partner. Because a fist resembles the symbol of male aggression, some lesbians reject it, while others—especially those in the S/M camps—extrapolating from an ideology that privileges fingers, think that knuckles merely add zest. Issues in the future will doubtless turn on whether cucumbers, carrots, and other vegetable dildo-substitutes are organically grown and whether they are domestic or foreign in origin, since the imperatives of multiculturalism might well mandate recognition of Third World agricultural quotas. In any case, the dildo debates are a fascinating example of folklore. During the 1960s and 1970s, liberal creeds held that lesbians *never* used dildos, and to suggest otherwise was to malign the gender. Nowadays, by contrast, it is hard to find a lesbian publication that does not carry ads for advanced instrumentation. Finally, scholars should consult Dorothy Allison's "The Theory and Practice of the Strap-On Dildo," a charming personal account.

VIBRATORS

The dildo of today occupies a particular niche in the history of technology because it so often marries older handworked and hand-carved artifacts with modern miniaturized electronics, as if deliberately to twit Walter Benjamin. Partly because they appeal to all genders, contemporary dildo-shaped vibrators seem quintessentially pornographic to many Americans; researchers for the

Meese Commission were mesmerized by them. Vibrators need not penetrate to be effective, of course, and some do not resemble dildos at all. According to Rachel Maines, the principal authority on the technology, the phallic shape is a twentieth-century development, though she stops short of saying that the shape was socially constructed (its similarity to a popular body part seems too logical). Maines' brilliant feat of scholarship, "Socially Camouflaged Technologies: The Case of the Electromechanical Vibrator," since expanded into a book, *The Technology of Orgasm: "Hysteria," the Vibrator, and Women's Sexual Satisfaction*, reminds us that women suffering from "hysteria" in the nineteenth century were routinely digitally masturbated by their doctors, who thought orgasm an effective treatment. Many patients thought so, too, so many that physicians quite literally had their hands full; the vibrator evolved as a laborsaving device. At first, then, electric vibrators (though Maines identifies an early steam-powered model) made it possible for doctors to treat, that is, masturbate, more women, but the technology eventually cost them their practices by permitting patients to stimulate themselves—and thus, to an extent, to regain control of their bodies. Making the vibrator compact, battery-operated, and phallic thoroughly domesticated it into one of the most ubiquitous appliances in the bedrooms of Americans of every gender (see **Pornography, Birth Control, and Racism** in chapter 3).

When vibrators began to surface openly in the United States in the early 1960s, they evoked detractors but also advocates such as Albert Ellis, whose *If This Be Sexual Heresy* embraced their benefits. Zooming sales in the next decade prompted articles such as Frederick Massey's "A New Look at Sex Toys." Howard Smith and Brian Van Der Horst visited the Manhattan Pleasure Chest emporium (one of several such stores in major cities) in 1976 to sample the products and the ambience of the place in "The Pleasure Chest." During the 1970s, moreover, saleswomen in the United States and Canada modeled sex aid parties on the famous Tupperware socials convened at neighborhood homes. John Masters reported on the dynamics of one such event in "Dingdong! Eros Calling." He observes that the women-only sex-aid party educates and titillates in a safe and secure setting. George Mazzei's *Good Vibrations: The Vibrator Owner's Manual of Relaxation, Therapy, and Sensual Pleasure* acquaints the newcomer with the features of many types of vibrators and gives tips to veterans as well. Joani Blank chose a similar title for her *Good Vibrations: The Complete Guide to Vibrators*, now in an updated edition. Blank's is a sophisticated guide to various styles and models, many of them field-tested by veterans, who share tips on the qualities of different materials, the sensations they evoke, what body positions and angles are most conducive to orgasm, how to fit harnesses, how to keep appliances clean, what lubricants are truly slippery, and lots of other advice. Blank has directed a videotape, *Carol Queen's Great Vibrations: An Explicit Consumer Guide to Vibrators*, in which performance artist Queen demonstrates standard and innovative applications of vibrators. In one segment of Home Box Office's *Real Sex: 3*, an interviewer visits Blank and her historically unique collection of dildos and vibrators. Finally, dildos are now so common in America that at least one mail-order house (Adam and Eve) offers a suction-cup base convenient for holding standard-sized vibrators on dashboards, computers, coffee tables, refrigerators, and other surfaces where one might need them close to hand (1995 catalog).

NOTES

1. William Irwin Thompson, *At the Edge of History: Speculations on the Transformation of Culture* (New York: Harper Colophon, 1972), p. 146.

2. Public Broadcasting System, Part V, aired 5 February 1990.

3. Vincent Canby, "Middle-Aged and Not Quite Middle Class [review of film *Stanley and Iris*]," *New York Times*, 9 February 1990, C1.

4. John Matlock, "Masquerading Women, Pathologized Men: Cross-Dressing, Fetishism, and the Theory of Perversion, 1882–1935," *Fetishism as Cultural Discourse*, ed. Emily Apter and William Pietz (Ithaca, NY: Cornell University Press, 1993), pp. 31–61.

5. Quoted by Tony Crawley, *Screen Dreams: The Hollywood Pinup: Photographs from the Kobal Collection* (New York: Delilah Communications, 1982), p. 5.

6. A. S. Neill, Lecture, New York University, 3 March 1967.

7. Tissot's first edition, published in Latin, went though various editions in various languages, some of them identified by Peter Wagner, *Eros Revived* (London: Secker and Warburg, 1988), pp. 19–20, 411.

8. Peter James and Nick Thorpe, *Ancient Inventions* (New York: Ballantine, 1994), p. 182.

9. I have not seen the Perceau text, but Legman is almost never mistaken.

REFERENCES

Ableman, Paul. *Anatomy of Nakedness*. London: Orbis, 1982.

Ackroyd, Peter. *Dressing Up—Transvestism and Drag: The History of an Obsession*. New York: Simon and Schuster, 1979.

Adult Video News. Upper Darby, PA, 1983–1996; Van Nuys, CA, 1996–: AVN, annual.

The All Revealing Nude: For Private Collection. N.p.: May Company, 1968.

Allen, J. J. *The Man in the Red Velvet Dress: Inside the World of Cross-Dressing*. New York: Carol Publishing Group/Birch Lane, 1996.

Allison, Dorothy. "The Theory and Practice of the Strap-On Dildo." *Skin: Talking about Sex, Class and Literature*. Ithaca, NY: Firebrand Books, 1994, pp. 127–134.

American Psychiatric Association. *Diagnostic and Statistical Manual of Mental Disorders*. 4th ed. rev. Washington, DC: APA, 1994.

Apter, Emily, and William Pietz, eds. *Fetishism as Cultural Discourse*. Ithaca, NY: Cornell University Press, 1993.

Arcand, Bernard. "The Sin of Onan." *The Jaguar and the Anteater: Pornography Degree Zero*, trans. Wayne Grady. New York: Verso, 1993, pp. 227–243.

Astrachan, Anthony. "Patented Sex." *Playboy*, 23:9 (September 1976): 113–115.

Athey, Ron. *4 Scenes in a Harsh Life*, with an interview and panel discussion. *Theatre Forum*, 6 (Winter–Spring 1995): 59–68.

Atkins, Dawn. *Looking Queer: Body Image and Identity in Lesbian, Bisexual, Gay, and Transgender Communities.* Binghamton, NY: Haworth Press, 1998.

Aurand, A. Monroe, Jr. *Bundling in the New World.* [Lancaster,] PA: Aurand Press, 1938.

Baker, Roger, with Peter Burton and Richard Smith. *Drag: A History of Female Impersonation in the Performing Arts.* New York: New York University Press, 1995.

Balsamo, Anne. "On the Cutting Edge: Cosmetic Surgery and the Technological Production of the Gendered Body." *Camera Obscura*, 28 (1992): 207–238.

———. *Technologies of the Gendered Body: Reading Cyborg Women.* Durham, NC: Duke University Press, 1995.

Banner, Lois W. *American Beauty.* Chicago: University of Chicago Press, 1983.

Banta, Martha. *Imaging American Women: Idea and Ideals in Cultural History.* New York: Columbia University Press, 1987.

Barker, Francis. *The Tremulous Private Body: Essays on Subjection.* New York: Methuen, 1984.

Barnard, Malcolm. *Fashion as Communication.* New York: Routledge, 1996.

Barnes, Ruth, and Joanne B. Eicher, eds. *Dress and Gender: Making and Meaning.* Oxford, England: Berg Publishers, 1993.

Barnette, Martha. "Beauty Loopholes." *Allure*, April 1997, pp. 192–195, 222.

Barry, Dave. "Men May Find 'Wonderbra' Simply 'Wunderbar.' " *Columbus (Ohio) Dispatch*, 27 February 1994, p. 31.

Barton-Jay, David. *The Enema as an Erotic Art and Its History.* New York: Barton-Jay Projects, 1984.

Baudrillard, Jean. *Symbolic Exchange and Death*, trans. Iain Hamilton Grant. Thousand Oaks, CA: Sage, 1993.

Beautiful Bare Feet. North Hollywood, CA, 1992–. Bimonthly.

Bee, Dennis. *Breasts! A Study of Fetishisms.* New York: Debon Distributors, [1965].

Beenyn, Brett, and Mickey Eliason, eds. *Queer Studies: A Lesbian, Gay, Bi-sexual, and Transgender Anthology.* New York: New York University Press, 1996.

Beigel, H. G. "Sex and Human Beauty." *Journal of Aesthetics and Art Criticism*, 12:1 (September 1953): 83–92.

Bell-Metereau, Rebecca. *Hollywood Androgyny.* 2d ed. New York: Columbia University Press, 1993.

Benjamin, Harry. *The Transsexual Phenomenon.* New York: Julian Press, 1966.

Bennett, Catherine. "View from a Broad: Why All Men Are Wankers." *Esquire*, 4:4 (May 1994): 168.

Bennett, Paula, and Vernon A. Rosario II, eds. *Solitary Pleasures: The Historical, Literary, and Artistic Discourses of Autoeroticism.* New York: Routledge, 1995.

Benson, Elaine, and John Esten. *Unmentionables: A Brief History of Underwear.* New York: Simon and Schuster, 1996.

Benstock, Sheri, and Suzanne Ferriss, eds. *On Fashion.* New Brunswick NJ: Rutgers University Press, 1994.

Benthall, Jonathan, and Ted Polhemus. *The Body as a Medium of Expression.* New York: Dutton, 1975.

Berendt, John. *Midnight in the Garden of Good and Evil: A Savannah Story.* New York: Random House, 1994.

Berens, Jessica. "Becoming a Man." *Gentleman's Quarterly*, May 1994, pp. 120–123.

Berg, Charles. *The Unconscious Significance of Hair.* New York: Citadel, 1959.

Bergler, Edmund. *Fashion and the Unconscious.* New York: Robert Brunner, 1953; rpt. Madison, CT: International Universities Press, 1987.

Bergman, David. *Camp Grounds: Style and Homosexuality.* Amherst: University of Massachusetts Press, 1993.

Berkeley, Bud, and Joe Tiffenbach. *Foreskin.* San Francisco: Berkeley and Tiffenbach, 1984.

Bersani, Leo. "Is the Rectum a Grave?" *October,* 43 (Winter 1987): 197–222.

Blackman, Inge, and Kathyrn Perry. "Skirting the Issue: Lesbian Fashions for the 1990s." *Feminist Review,* 34 (1990): 67–78.

Blake, Roger. *Sex Gadgets,* aka *The Stimulators.* Cleveland, OH: Century, 1968.

Blanchard, Marc. "Post-Bourgeois Tattoo: Reflections on Skin Writing in Late Capitalist Societies." *Visual Anthropology Review,* 7:2 (1991): 11–21.

Blank, Joani, producer and director. *Carol Queen's Great Vibrations: An Explicit Consumer Guide to Vibrators.* San Francisco: Good Vibrations/Down There, 1997.

———. *Good Vibrations: The Complete Guide to Vibrators,* rev. ed. Burlingame, CA: Down There Press, 1989.

Blank, Joani, and Honey Lee Cottrell. *I Am My Lover.* Burlingame, CA: Down There Press, 1978.

Bloch, Iwan (aka Eugen Dühren, aka Albert Hagen). *Die Sexuelle Osphresiologie.* Charlottenburg, Germany: H. Barsdorf, 1901; rpt. *Oderatus Sexualis: A Scientific and Literary Study of Sexual Scents and Erotic Perfumes.* New York: Panurge Press, 1934.

Bloom, Amy. "The Body Lies." *New Yorker,* 18 July 1994, pp. 38–44, 46–49.

Body Play/Modern Primitives Quarterly, ed. Fakir Musafar. San Francisco: Insight Books, 1992–.

Bolin, Anne. *In Search of Eve: Transsexual Rites of Passage.* South Hadley, MA: Bergin and Garvey, 1988.

Boone, Ilsley. *The Joys of Nudism.* New York: Greenberg Publishing, 1934.

Bordo, Susan. *Unbearable Weight: Feminism, Western Culture, and the Body.* Berkeley: University of California Press, 1993.

Bornstein, Kate. *Gender Outlaw: On Men, Women, and the Rest of Us.* New York: Verso/Routledge, 1994.

Bourke, John Gregory. *Scatalogic Rites of All Nations.* Washington, DC: Lowdermilk, 1891; rpt. *A Dissertation upon the Employment of Excrementious Remedial Agents in Therapeutics, Divination, Witchcraft, Love-Philtre, etc. in All Parts of the Globe.* New York: American Anthropological Society, 1934; rpt. *The Portable Scatalog,* ed. Louis P. Kaplan. New York: Morrow, 1994.

Boyd, Jim. "The Last Taboo: The Hung and Unsung." *Penthouse,* 23:8 (April 1992): 48–50, 52.

Brain, Robert. *The Decorated Body.* New York: Harper and Row, 1979.

Brand, Clavel. *Fetish: An Account of Unusual Erotic Desires.* London: Senate, 1997.

———. *The Rubber Devotee and the Leather Lover.* Vol. I of *The Kinky Crowd,* London: Luxor Press, 1970.

Breslauer, Jan. "Stacked like Me." *Playboy,* 44:7 (July 1997): 64–66, 68.

Bright, Susie. *Suzie Sexpert's Lesbian Sex World.* Pittsburgh: Cleis Press, 1990.

Brill, Dianne. *Boobs, Boys and High Heels.* New York: Penguin, 1992.

Brown, A. E., and H. A. Jeffcott, Jr. *Absolutely Mad Inventions: Compiled from the Records of the United States Patent Office.* New York: Dover, 1970; rpt. 1932.

Brown, Norman O. *Life against Death: The Psychoanalytic Meaning of History*. Middletown, CT: Wesleyan University Press, 1959.

————. *Love's Body*. New York: Random House, 1966.

Brownmiller, Susan. *Femininity*. New York: Simon and Schuster, 1984.

Bryk, Felix. *Sex and Circumcision: A Study of Phallic Worship and Mutilation in Men and Women*. North Hollywood, CA: Brandon House, 1967.

Bulliet, C. J. *Venus Castina: Famous Female Impersonators, Celestial and Human*. New York: Bonanza Books, 1956, 1970.

Bullough, Vern L. "Technology for the Prevention of 'Les Maladies Produites par La Masturbation.' " *Technology and Culture*, 28 (October 1987): 828–832.

Bullough, Vern L., and Martha Voght. "Homosexuality and Its Confusion with the 'Secret Sin' in Pre-Freudian America." *Journal of the History of Medicine*, 28:2 (1973): 143–155.

Burchett, George, and Peter Leighton. *Memoirs of a Tattooist: From the Notes, Diaries and Letters of the Late "King of the Tattooists."* New York: Crown, 1958.

Burr, Timothy. *BISBA*. Trenton, NJ: Hercules, 1965.

Butler, Judith. *Bodies That Matter: On the Discursive Limits of Sex*. New York: Routledge, 1993.

————. *Gender Trouble: Feminists and the Subversion of Identity*. New York: Routledge, 1990.

[Butler, Samuel?]. *Dildoides. A Burlesque Poem. By Samuel Butler, Gent. With a Key Explaining Several Names and Characters in Hudibras*. London: N.p., [1706?].

Cable, Mary, et al. *American Manners and Morals*. New York: American Heritage, 1969.

Carter, Alison. *Underwear: The Fashion History*. New York: Drama Books, 1992.

Carter, Pam. *Feminism, Breasts, and Breastfeeding*. New York: St. Martin's, 1995.

Caudwell, David O., ed *Transvestism: Men in Female Dress*. New York: Sexology Corporation, 1956.

Caught from Behind. (20 vols., 1982–1997). Hal Freeman, dir. Chatsworth, CA: Hollywood Video.

Champion, Richard K. *The Sweet Smell of Sex: A Study of an Abnormal Obsession*. London: Canova Press, 1969.

Chapkis, Wendy. *Beauty Secrets: Women and the Politics of Appearance*. Boston: South End Press, 1986.

Chapman, David L. *Sandow the Magnificent: Eugen Sandow and the Beginnings of Bodybuilding*. Champaign: University of Illinois Press, 1994.

Chernayeff, Catherine, Jonathan David, and Nan Richardson. *Drag Diaries*. New York: Chronicle Books, 1995.

Chernin, Kim. *The Obsession: Reflections on the Tyranny of Slenderness*. New York: Harper and Row, 1981.

Chicklet. "Das Boot Brigade: An International Contact Club Encourages Pride among Men with a Passion for Boots." *Advocate*, 10 March 1992, pp. 64–65.

Clapham, Adam, and Robin Constable. *As Nature Intended: A Pictorial History of the Nudists*. Los Angeles: Elysium, 1986.

"A Cock Goes to Court." *Adult Video News*, 8:12 (November 1993): 48.

Cogan, Jeanine, and Joanie Erickson, eds. *Lesbians, Levis, and Lipstick: The Meaning of Beauty in Our Lives*. Binghamton, NY: Haworth Press, 1998.

Comfort, Alex. *The Anxiety Makers*. London: Nelson, 1967.

Cooper, Andy, with photographs by Chris Wroblewski. *Tattoo Art: Tätowierte Frauen/ Skin Fantasies on Tattooed Women*. Vienna: Christian Brandstatter Verlag, 1985.

Cooper, Wendy. *Hair Sex Society Symbolism*. New York: Stein and Day, 1971.

Cossey, Caroline. *My Story*. London: Faber and Faber, 1991.

Craik, Jennifer. *The Face of Fashion: Cultural Studies in Fashion*. London: Routledge, 1994.

Creet, Julia. "Daughter of the Movement: The Psychodynamics of Lesbian S/M Fantasy." *differences*, 3:2 (Summer 1991): 135–159.

Cross-Talk. P.O. Box 944, Woodland Hills, CA 91365.

Danielou, Alain. *The Phallus: Sacred Symbol of Male Power*. Rochester, VT: Inner Traditions, 1995.

Darling, Candy. *Candy Darling*. New York: Haunman, 1992.

Davis, Fred. *Fashion, Culture, and Identity*. Chicago: University of Chicago Press, 1992.

Davis, Kathy. *Reshaping the Female Body: The Dilemma of Cosmetic Surgery*. New York: Routledge, 1995.

de Grazia, Victoria, with Ellen Furlough, eds. *The Sex of Things: Gender and Consumption in Historical Perspective*. Berkeley: University of California Press, 1996.

Degen, John A. "Camp and Burlesque: A Study in Contrasts." *Journal of Dramatic Theory and Criticism*, 1 (1987): 87–94.

Deleuze, Gilles [and Leopold von Sacher-Masoch]. *Masochism: An Interpretation of Coldness and Cruelty*, trans. Jean McNeil. New York: Braziller, 1971; *Sacher-Masoch: An Interpretation*. London: Faber and Faber, 1971; *Masochism*. New York: Zone Books, 1989.

DeMartino, Manfred F. *Human Autoerotic Practices*. New York: Human Sciences Press, 1979.

———. *The New Female Sexuality: The Sexual Practices and Experiences of Social Nudists, Potential Nudists and Lesbians*. New York: Julian Press, 1969.

Dennis, Patrick [E. E. Tanner]. *Little Me: The Intimate Memoirs of That Great Star of Stage, Screen, and Television, Belle Poitrine, As Told to Patrick Dennis, with Photos by Cris Alexander*. New York: Dutton, 1961.

Denny, Dallas, ed. *Current Concepts in Transgender Identity*. New York: Garland, 1998.

Devor, Holly. *Gender Blending: Confronting the Limits of Duality*. Bloomington: Indiana University Press, 1989.

Dingwall, John. *The Girdle of Chastity: A Fascinating History of Chastity Belts*. New York: Clarion Press, 1959.

Dodson, Betty. *Liberating Masturbation: A Meditation on Self Love*. New York: Bodysex Designs, 1974.

———. *Self Love and Orgasm*. New York: Betty Dodson, 1983.

Dodson, Victor [Newbern, John, and Peggy Roderbaugh.] *Auto-Erotic Acts and Devices*. Los Angeles: Medco, 1967.

Dotson, Edisol Wayne. *Behold the Man: The Hype and Selling of Male Beauty in Media and Culture*. Binghamton, NY: Haworth Press, 1998.

Duffy, John. "Masturbation and Clitoridectomy: A Nineteenth-Century View." *Journal of the American Medical Association*, 187 (1963): 246–248.

Dutton, Kenneth R. *The Perfectible Body: The Western Ideal of Physical Development*. New York: Continuum, 1995.

Dworkin, Andrea. *Intercourse*. New York: Free Press, 1987.

Dyer, Richard. "Brief Affairs." *The Matter of Images: Essays on Representation*. New York: Routledge, 1993, pp. 123–125.

————, ed. *Gays and Film*. Rev. ed. New York: New York Zoetrope, 1984.

Eck, Beth Anne. "Body as Social Text: Meaning and Interpretation of the Nude." Ph.D. dissertation, University of Virginia, 1996.

Edgren, Gretchen. "The Transformation of Tula: The Extraordinary Story of a Beautiful Woman Who Was Born a Boy." *Playboy*, 38:9 (September 1991): 103–105.

Edkins, Diana, and Betsy Jablow, eds. *Leg*. Los Angeles: General Publishing Group, 1997.

Eisenstein, Zillah R. *The Female Body and the Law*. Berkeley: University of California Press, 1989.

Ellis, Albert. *If This Be Sexual Heresy*. New York: Lyle Stuart, 1963.

Elwin, Verrier. "The Vagina Dentata Legend." *British Journal of Medical Psychology*, 19 (1941): 439–453.

Ephron, Nora. "A Few Words about Breasts." *The Best of Modern Humor*, ed. Mordecai Richler. New York: Knopf, 1983, pp. 467–474.

Epstein, Julia, and Kristina Straub. *Body Guards: The Cultural Politics of Gender Ambiguity*. New York: Routledge, 1991.

Erotica Contrivances. N.p., 1922.

Etcoff, Nancy. *Survival of the Prettiest: The Science of Beauty*. New York: Doubleday, 1999.

Ewing, Elizabeth. *Dress and Undress: A History of Women's Underwear*. London: Batsford, 1978.

Falk, Pasi. *The Consuming Body*. Thousand Oaks, CA: Sage, 1994.

Fantasy Fashion Digest. Strictly Speaking, P.O. Box 8006, Palm Springs, CA 92263.

Farren, Mick. *The Black Leather Jacket*, New York: Abbeville Press, 1985.

Favezza, Armando R. *Bodies under Siege: Self-Mutilation in Culture and Psychiatry*. Baltimore: Johns Hopkins University Press, 1987.

"The Feel of Real." *Real Sex: 21*. Produced and directed by Patti Kaplan. New York: HBO, 1998.

Feher, Michael, Ramona Naddaff, and Nadia Tazi, eds. *Fragments for a History of the Human Body*. 4 vols. New York: Zone Books, 1987–1994.

Feinberg, Leslie. *Transgender Warriors: Making History from Joan of Arc to Dennis Rodman*. Boston: Beacon Press, 1996.

Feinbloom, Deborah Heller. *Transvestites and Transsexuals: Mixed Views*. New York: Delacorte, 1976.

Feldhaus, Franz-Marie. *Ka-Pi-Fu, und andre Verschämte Dinge*. Berlin-Friedenau: Privatdruck, 1921.

Ferris, Lesley, ed. *Crossing the Stage: Controversies on Cross-Dressing*. London: Routledge, 1993.

Fetish Times. Van Nuys, CA, 1974–.

Figure-Training Fundamentals: For Women of Distinction and Discernment. Tustin, CA: Versatile, 1988.

Findlay, Heather. "Freud's 'Fetishism' and the Lesbian Dildo Debates." *Feminist Studies*, 18:3 (Fall 1992): 563–580.

Findlay, Steven. "Buying the Perfect Body." *U.S. News and World Report*, 1 May 1989, pp. 68–75.

Flugel, J. C. *The Psychology of Clothes*. London: Hogarth Press, 1930.

Fontanel, Beatrice. *Support and Seduction: A History of Corsets and Bras*, trans. Willard Wood. New York: Abrams, 1997.

Form & Figure. New York, 1999–.

Foucault, Michel. *The History of Sexuality*, trans. Robert Hurley. 3 vols. New York: Pantheon, 1978–1987.

Frederick's of Hollywood, 1947–1973: 26 Years of Mail-Order Seduction. New York: Castle, 1973.

Freeman, Gillian. *The Undergrowth of Literature*. London: Nelson and Sons, 1967; rpt. London: Panther, 1969.

Freud, Sigmund. "Concluding Remarks to a Discussion on Masturbation." *Standard Edition of the Complete Psychological Works of Sigmund Freud*, ed. James Strachey. 24 vols. London: Hogarth Press and the Institute of Psycho-Analysis, 1953–1975, 12, pp. 241–254.

———. "Das Medusenhaupt [The Medusa's Head]." *Standard Edition of the Complete Psychological Works of Sigmund Freud*, ed. James Strachey. 24 vols. London: Hogarth Press and the Institute of Psycho-Analysis, 1953–1975, 18, pp. 273–274.

———. "Fetishism." *Sigmund Freud: Collected Papers*, ed. James Strachey. New York: Basic Books, 1959, pp. 105–106.

———. *Standard Edition of the Complete Psychological Works of Sigmund Freud*, ed. James Strachey. 24 vols. London: Hogarth Press and the Institute of Psycho-Analysis, 1953–1975.

Freund, Karl. "A Laboratory Method for Diagnosing Predominance in Homo- or Hetero-Erotic Interest in the Male." *Behaviour Research and Therapy*, 1 [1963]: 85–94.

Freytag, Arny. "Hard Bodies." *Playboy*, 43:8 (August 1996): 60–69.

Fussell, Samuel. *Muscle*. New York: Poseidon Press, 1991.

Gaines, Donna. "Tattoo's Back." *Village Voice*, 26 May 1998, pp. 55–56.

Gaines, Jane, and Charlotte Herzog, eds. *Fabrications: Costume and the Female Body*. New York: Routledge, 1990.

Gallagher, Catherine, and Thomas Lacquer, eds. *The Making of the Modern Body: Sexuality and Society in the Nineteenth Century*. Berkeley: University of California Press, 1987.

Gallop, Jane. *Thinking through the Body*. New York: Columbia University Press, 1988.

Gammon, Lorraine, and Merja Makinen, eds. *Female Fetishism*. London: Lawrence and Wishart, 1994; *Female Fetishism: A Postmodern Condition?* New York: New York University Press, 1995.

Garber, Marjorie. "Spare Parts: The Surgical Construction of Gender." *The Lesbian and Gay Studies Reader*, ed. Henry Abelove, Michele Aina Barale, and David M. Halperin. New York: Routledge, 1993, pp. 321–338.

———. *Vested Interests: Cross-Dressing and Cultural Anxiety*. New York: Routledge, 1991.

Gardner, Martin. "Orgonomy." *Fads and Fallacies in the Name of Science*. New York: Dover, 1957, pp. 250–262.

Gatewood, Charles. *Bizarre Rituals: Dances Sacred and Profane*. Belmont, CA: Gauntlet, 1992.

———. *Primitives: Tribal Body Art and the Left Hand Path*. San Francisco: Flash Publications, 1992.

Gay, Peter. *The Bourgeois Experience: Victoria to Freud*. New York: Oxford University Press, 1984.

Gender Euphoria. San Antonio, 1991–.

Gilbert, Harriet, ed. *Fetishes, Florentine Girdles, and Other Explorations into the Sexual Imagination.* New York: HarperPerennial, 1994.

Gillman, Susan Kay. *Dark Twins: Imposture and Identity in Mark Twain's America.* Chicago: University of Chicago Press, 1989.

Gilmore, Donald. *Soixante-Neuf-69.* Torrance, CA: Monogram Books, 1968.

Glembocki, Vicki. "A Ring in Her Navel." *Playboy,* 41:2 (February 1994): 82–83, 118, 134, 136–138.

Glynn, Prudence. *Skin to Skin: Eroticism in Dress.* New York: Oxford University Press, 1982.

Le godimiché royal suivi du Mea Culpa. Paris: N.p., 1789.

Goetz, Tim. "Queer Fashion." *Outweek,* 23 May 1990, pp. 42–53.

Goffman, Erving. *Gender Advertisements.* New York: Harper and Row, 1976, 1979.

Goldberg, Vicki. *Male to Female: La Cage aux Follies.* Zurich: Édition Stemmle, 1995.

Goldsby, Jack. "Queens of Language: *Paris Is Burning.*" *Queer Looks: Perspectives on Lesbian and Gay Film and Video,* ed. Martha Gever, Pratibha Parmar, and John Greyson. New York: Routledge, 1993, pp. 108–115.

Goldstein, Laurence, ed. *The Female Body: Figures, Styles, Speculations.* Ann Arbor: University of Michigan Press, 1992.

———. *The Male Body: Features, Destinies, Exposures.* Ann Arbor: University of Michigan Press, 1995.

Good Vibrations. *Good Vibes Gazette.* 1210 Valencia St., San Francisco, CA 94110, quarterly; also mail order catalog.

Goode, Paul B. *Physique: An Intimate Portrait of the Female Fitness Athlete.* New York: Thunder's Mouth, 1997.

Goodson, Aileen. *Therapy, Nudity, and Joy: The Therapeutic Use of Nudity through the Ages, from Ancient Ritual to Modern Psychology.* Los Angeles: Elysium Growth Press, 1991.

Green, Shirley. *The Curious History of Contraception.* New York: St. Martin's, 1971.

Greer, Germaine. *The Female Eunuch.* New York: McGraw-Hill, 1971.

Griffin, Gary M. *Condom Encyclopedia: What Size Is Your Condom?* Los Angeles: Added Dimensions, 1991.

———. *The History of Men's Underwear: From Union Suits to Bikini Briefs.* Los Angeles: Added Dimensions, 1991.

———. *Penis Enlargement Methods: Fact and Phallusy.* Rev. ed. Los Angeles: Added Dimensions, 1991.

Grosz, Elizabeth. "Lesbian Fetishism?" *Fetishism as Cultural Discourse,* ed. Emily Apter and William Pietz. Ithaca, NY: Cornell University Press, 1993, pp. 101–115.

———. *Space, Time, and Perversion.* New York: Routledge, 1995.

———. *Volatile Bodies: Toward a Corporeal Feminism.* Bloomington: Indiana University Press, 1994.

Grosz, Elizabeth, and Elspeth Probyn, eds. *Sexy Bodies: The Strange Carnalities of Feminism.* New York: Routledge, 1995.

Guttmann, Allen. *The Erotic in Sports.* New York: Columbia University Press, 1996.

Hahn-Lonne, Jay. *Navel Revue.* N.p.: Privately published by his heirs, 1930.

Haiken, Elizabeth. *Venus Envy: A History of Cosmetic Surgery.* Baltimore: Johns Hopkins University Press, 1997.

Hair to Stay. Pam Winter, Box 80667, South Dartmouth, MA 02748.

Halberstam, Judith, and Ira Livingston, eds. *Posthuman Bodies*. Bloomington: Indiana University Press, 1995.

Hall, Trish. "Piercing Fad Is Turning Convention on Its Ear." *New York Times*, national ed., 19 May 1991, p. 17.

Halpert, E. "On a Particular Form of Masturbation in Women: Masturbation with Water." *Journal of the American Psychoanalytic Association*, 21 (1973): 525–530.

Handy, Bruce. "What's It Worth to You?" *New York Times Magazine*, 13 February 1994, p. 82.

Hansen, Joseph, and Evelyn Reed. *Cosmetics, Fashions, and the Exploitation of Women*. New York: Pathfinder Press, 1986.

Hanson, Dian. "Just My Opinion: Perfect Strangers." *Leg Show*, September 1994, pp. 4–5.

Haraway, Donna. "The Biological Enterprise: Sex, Mind, and Profit from Human Engineering to Sociobiology." *Radical History Review*, 20 (Spring/Summer 1979): 206–237.

Hare, E. H. "Masturbatory Insanity: The History of an Idea." *Journal of Mental Science*, 108 (1962): 1–25.

Harkel, Robert. *The Picture Book of Oral Love*. New York: Cybertype, 1969.

Hartman, William, Marilyn Fithian, and Donald Johnson. *Nudist Society: An Authoritative, Complete Study of Nudism in America*. New York: Crown Publishers, 1970; rev. and enlarged by Iris Bancroft as *Nudist Society: The Controversial Study of the Clothes-Free Naturist Movement in America*. Los Angeles: Elysium Growth Press, 1991.

Hatt, Michael. " 'Making a Man of Him': Masculinity and the Black Body in Mid-Nineteenth-Century American Sculpture." *Oxford Art Journal*, 15:1 (1992): 21–35.

Haug, Wolfgang. *Critique of Commodity Aesthetics: Appearance, Sexuality, and Advertising in Capitalist Society*, trans. R. Bock. Minneapolis: University of Minnesota Press, 1986.

Hausman, Bernice L. *Changing Sex: Transsexualism, Technology, and the Idea of Gender*. Durham, NC: Duke University Press, 1995.

Henley, Nancy M. *Body Politics: Power, Sex, and Nonverbal Communication*. Englewood Cliffs, NJ: Prentice-Hall, 1977.

Hennig, Jean-Luc. *The Rear View: A Brief and Elegant History of Bottoms through the Ages*, trans. Margaret Crosland and Elfreda Powell. New York: Crown, 1995.

Heywood, Leslie. *Bodybuilders: A Cultural Anatomy of Women's Body Building*. Piscataway, NJ: Rutgers University Press, 1998.

Himes, Norman E. *Medical History of Contraception*. Boston: Allen and Unwin, 1936; reissued with a new preface by Christopher Tietze. New York: Schocken, 1970.

Hirsch, Alan. *Scentsational Sex: The Secret to Using Aroma for Arousal*. Boston: Element, 1998.

Hoffmann, Frank, and William G. Bailey. *Sports and Recreation Fads*. Binghamton, NY: Haworth Press, 1991.

"The Holes in Some of the Parts." *New Yorker*, 4 October 1993, pp. 70–71.

Holland, Janet, and Lisa Adkins, eds. *Sex, Sensibility, and the Gendered Body*. New York: St. Martin's, 1996.

Hollander, Anne. *Seeing through Clothes*. New York: Avon, 1975.

Hollander, Xaviera. *Xaviera's Fantastic Sex*. New York: Signet, 1978.

————. *Xaviera on the Best Part of a Man*. New York: Signet, 1975.

Holliday, Morgan, with Peter Hawkins. *The Morgan Mystique: Morgan Holliday's Essential Guide to Living, Loving, and Lip Gloss*. Toronto, Ontario: Holliday Productions, 1990.

Holliday, Robert Cortes. *Unmentionables: From Fig Leaves to Scanties*. New York: Long and Smith, 1933.

[Holzman, Edward]. *Dreams of Eros*. Los Angeles: Artisan Marketing, 1988.

Home Box Office. "Dildos and Vibrators." *Real Sex: 3*. Produced and directed by Patti Kaplan. New York: HBO, 1992.

————. "Girls Girls Girls." *Real Sex: 5*. Produced and directed by Patti Kaplan. New York: HBO, 1993.

————. "Girls Will Be Boys." *Real Sex: 9*. Produced and directed by Patti Kaplan. New York: HBO, 1994.

————. "The Making of *Girls from Girdleville*." *Real Sex: 6*. Produced and directed by Patti Kaplan. New York: HBO, 1993.

Horney, Karen. "The Dread of Women: Observation on a Specific Difference in the Dread Felt by Men and by Women Respectively for the Opposite Sex." *International Journal of Psychoanalysis*, 13 (1932): 348–360.

Houppert, Karen. "Reality Check: Condom Con Job?" *Village Voice*, 3 March 1992, p. 26.

Huge Dicks. Montreal: VMC Canada, 1992.

Ilfeld, Fred, Jr., and Roger Laver. *Social Nudism in America*. New Haven, CT: College and University Press, 1964.

International Male. San Diego: Brawn of California, 1975–.

Jones, Dylan. *Haircults: Fifty Years of Styles and Cuts*. London: Thames and Hudson, 1990.

Jordanova, Ludmilla. "The Popularisation of Medicine: Tissot on Onanism." *Textual Practice*, 1 (1987): 68–79.

Judd, Ralph. *Drag Gags* and *Drag Gags Return*. San Francisco: Ralph Judd Communications, 1991, 1992.

Kaite, Berkeley. *Pornography and Difference*. Bloomington: University of Indiana Press, 1995.

Karsh, Edward. *The Membrum Virile*. San Francisco: Penury Publishing, 1969.

Kazanjian, Dodie. "Victoria's Secret Is Out." *Vogue*, April 1992, pp. 218–226.

Kelly, Edward. "A New Image for the Naughty Dildo?" *Journal of Popular Culture*, 7:4 (Spring 1974): 804–809.

Kennedy, Duncan. "Sexual Abuse, Sexy Dressing, and the Eroticization of Domination." *Sexy Dressing Etc: Essays on the Power and Politics of Cultural Identity*. Cambridge: Harvard University Press, 1993, pp. 126–214.

Keown, Ian. *Lover's Guide to America*. New York: Collier Macmillan, 1974.

Kern, Stephen. *Anatomy and Destiny: A Cultural History of the Human Body*. Indianapolis: Bobbs-Merrill, 1975.

Kind, Alfred. *Buttock Fetishism*. New York: International Press of Sexology, 1965.

Kind, Alfred, and Curt Moreck. *Gefilde der Lust*. Vienna: Verlag für Kulturforschung, 1930.

King, Edward, and Chris Markham. *Rubber Up! Every Gay Man's Guide to Condoms*. London: Cassell, 1996.

Kipnis, Laura. "She-Male Fantasies and the Aesthetics of Pornography." *Dirty Looks:*

Women, Pornography, Power, ed. Pamela Church Gibson and Roma Gibson. London: British Film Institute, 1993, pp. 124–143.

Klein, Alan M. *Little Big Men: Body Building Subculture and Gender Construction*. New York: State University of New York Press, 1993.

Klitz, Dr. Seymore, and Dr. Ima Peeper. *Genitology: Reading the Genitals*. Hollywood, CA: Gen Publications, 1983.

Kodis, Michelle, with David Moran and Deborah Houy. *Love Scents: How Your Natural Pheromones Influence Your Relationships, Your Moods, and Who You Love*. New York: Dutton, 1998.

Kroker, Arthur, and Marilouise Kroker, eds. *Body Invaders: Panic Sex in America*. Montreal: New World Perspectives, 1987.

———. *The Last Sex: Feminism and Outlaw Bodies*. New York: St. Martin's, 1993.

Kroll, Eric, director. *Girls from Girdleville*. San Francisco: Eric Kroll Photography, 1992.

Kroll, Ken, and Erica Levy Klein. *Enabling Romance: A Guide to Love, Sex and Relationships for the Disabled (and the People Who Care about Them)*. New York: Harmony Books, 1992.

Kunzle, David. *Fashion and Fetishism: A Social History of the Corset, Tight-Lacing and Other Forms of Body-Sculpture in the West*. Totowa, NJ: Rowman and Littlefield, 1982.

Lacan, Jacques, and Wladimir Granoff. "Fetishism: The Symbolic, the Imaginary, and the Real." *Perversions, Psychodynamics, and Therapy*, ed. Sandor Loran. London: Tavistock, 1956, pp. 265–275.

Lacquer, Thomas. *Making Sex: Body and Gender from the Greeks to Freud*. Cambridge: Harvard University Press, 1990.

Lacy, Madison S., and Don Morgan, eds. *Leg Art: Sixty Years of Hollywood Cheesecake*. New York: Citadel, 1981; rpt. *Hollywood Cheesecake: Sixty Years of America's Favorite Pinups*. New York: Citadel, 1983.

The Lady Chablis. *Hiding My Candy: The Autobiography of the Lady Chablis*. New York: Pocket Books, 1996.

La Glannège, Roger-Maxe de [Gershon Legman]. *Oragenitalism: An Encyclopaedic Outline of Oral Technique in Genital Excitation Part 1: Cunnilinctus*. New York: Privately printed, 1940; rep. and exp. (with *Part II: Fellation and the Sixty-Nine*) by Legman under his own name, as *Oragenitalism*. New York: Julian Press, 1969; rpt. London: Duckworth, 1972; rpt. as *The Intimate Kiss*. New York: Paperback Library, 1971.

Lakoff, Robin Tolmach, and Rachel L. Scherr. *Face Value: The Politics of Beauty*. London: Routledge and Kegan Paul, 1984.

Lamos, Colleen. "Taking On the Phallus." *Lesbian Erotics*, ed. Karla Jay. New York: New York University Press, 1995, pp. 101–124.

Landers, Simon. *Legs: A Study in Fetishism*. New York: Debon, 1965.

Lang, Joel. *Male Orgasm thru Auto-Erotic Devices*. Chatsworth, CA: Prairie, 1972.

Langdon-Davies, John. *The Future of Nakedness*. New York: Harper and Brothers, 1968.

Langner, Lawrence. *The Importance of Wearing Clothes*. New York: Hastings House, 1959.

LaRoe, Else K. *The Breast Beautiful*. New York: House of Field, 1960.

Laurent, Emile, and Paul Nagour. *Magica Sexualis: Mystic Love Book of Black Arts and Secret Societies*, trans. Raymond Sabatier. New York: Falstaff Press, 1934.

Laver, James. *Modesty in Dress: An Inquiry into the Fundamentals of Dress*. Boston: Houghton Mifflin, 1969.

Lawren, Bill. "The Penis Page." *Penthouse*, 25:10 (June 1994): 70, 128, 130, 162.

Lawrence, Jodi. *The Search for the Perfect Orgasm*. Los Angeles: North, 1973.

Leathem, Harvey T. *Scatology: The Erotic Response to Bodily Scent*. North Hollywood, CA: Barclay House, [1967].

Leathem, Harvey T., with Hugh Jones. *Auto-Erotic Devices*. Cleveland, OH: Century Books, 1968.

Legman, Gershon. "Erotic Folksongs and Ballads: An International Bibliography." *Journal of American Folklore*, 103 (October/December 1990): 417–501.

Lehman, Peter. *Running Scared: Masculinity and the Representation of the Male Body*. Philadelphia: Temple University Press, 1993.

Lenars, Charles, Josette Lenars, and Andre Virel. *Decorated Man*. New York: Abrams, 1980.

Lencek, Lena, and Gideon Bosker. *Making Waves: Swimsuits and the Undressing of America*. San Francisco: Chronicle, 1989.

Levine, Esar, ed. *Chastity Belts: An Illustrated History of the Bridling of Women. Containing Numerous Explanatory Excerpts from Curious and Facetious Books*. New York: Panurge Press, 1931.

Levine, Suzanne Braun. "The Truth Was Burned." *Media Studies Journal*, 12:3 (Fall 1998): 110–111.

Levins, Hoag. *American Sex Machines: The Hidden History of Sex at the U.S. Patent Office*. Holbrook, MA: Adams Media, 1996.

Liggett, Arline, and John Liggett. *The Tyranny of Beauty*. London: Gollancz, 1989.

Lloyd, J. William. *The Karezza Method: Or, Magnetation, the Art of Connubial Love*. [New York?]: Privately printed, 1931.

Long, Peter/Long Peter. *The Demi-Wang*. New York: Privately printed, 1931.

Lovelace, Linda. *Inside Linda Lovelace*. Los Angeles: Pinnacle, 1973.

Lowe, Maria R. *Women of Steel: Female Body Builders and the Struggle for Self-Definition*. New York: New York University Press, 1998.

Lowry, Thomas P., ed. *The Classic Clitoris: Historic Contributions to Scientific Sexuality*. Chicago: Nelson-Hall, 1978.

Lowry, Thomas P., and Thea Snyder Lowry, with Thomas G. Morricone et al. *The Clitoris*. St. Louis: W. H. Green, 1976.

Lurie, Alison. *The Language of Clothes*. New York: Random House, 1982.

MacDonald, Robert H. "The Frightful Consequences of Onanism: Notes on the History of a Delusion." *Journal of the History of Ideas*, 28 (1967): 423–431.

MacKenzie, Gordene Olga. *Transgender Nation*. Bowling Green, OH: Bowling Green State University Popular Press, 1994.

Macy, Marianne. *Working Sex: An Odyssey into Our Cultural Underworld*. New York: Carroll and Graf, 1996.

Magnuson, Ann. "Hell on Heels." *Allure*, September 1994, pp. 128–131.

Maines, Rachel. "Socially Camouflaged Technologies: The Case of the Electromechanical Vibrator." *IEEE Technology and Society Magazine*, 8:2 (June 1989): 3–23.

———. *The Technology of Orgasm: "Hysteria," the Vibrator, and Women's Sexual Satisfaction*. Baltimore: Johns Hopkins University Press, 1998.

Mapplethorpe, Robert, and Bruce Chatwin. *Lady Lisa Lyon*. New York: Viking, 1963.

Martin, Richard, and Harold Koda. *Splash! A History of Swim Wear*. New York: Rizzoli, 1990.

Mascia-Lees, Francis, and Patricia Sharpe, eds. *Tattoo, Torture, Mutilation, and Adornment: The Denaturalization of the Body in Culture and Text*. Albany: State University of New York Press, 1992.

Massey, Frederick. "A New Look at Sex Toys." *Sexology*, 40:4 (November 1973): 6–10.

Masters, John. "Dingdong! Eros Calling." *MacLeans*, 94 (2 February 1981): 29–31.

Masters, R.E.L., ed. *Sexual Self-Stimulation*. Los Angeles: Sherbourne Press, 1967.

Masters, Sam. "Alternative Sexuality and the Video Retailer." *Adult Video News*, 8:12 (November 1993): 60, 62.

Masters, William H., and Virginia Johnson. *Human Sexual Response* and *Human Sexual Inadequacy*. Boston: Little, Brown, 1970.

Mazzei, George. *Good Vibrations: The Vibrator Owner's Manual of Relaxation, Therapy, and Sensual Pleasure*. New York: Hawthorne, 1977.

McDowell, Colin. *Dressed to Kill: Sex, Power, and Clothes*. London: Hutchinson, 1992.

McIlvenna, Ted, et al. *The Complete Guide to Safe Sex*. San Francisco: Specific Press, 1987.

Menkes, Suzy. "Body Piercing Moves into the Mainstream." *New York Times*, 23 November 1993, p. B4.

———. "Regressing, from 'Lolita' to Robbing the Cradle." *New York Times*, 29 March 1994, p. B4.

———. "See-Through Still Tries to Find Light of Day." *New York Times*, 18 May 1993, pp. B1, B4.

Merrill, Frances, and Mason Merrill. *Nudism Comes to America*. New York: Knopf, 1932.

Meyer, Moe. "The Signifying Invert: Camp and the Performance of Nineteenth-Century Sexology." *Text and Performance Quarterly*, 15 (1995): 265–281.

———, ed. *The Politics and Poetics of Camp*. New York: Routledge, 1994.

Meyers, Kathy. "Fashion 'n' Passion." *Screen*, 223:3/4 (September/October 1982): 89–97.

Mifflin, Margot. *Bodies of Subversion: A Secret History of Women & Tattoo*. New York: Juno Books, 1998.

Miles, Margaret Ruth. *Carnal Knowing: Female Nakedness and Religious Meaning in the Christian West*. Boston: Beacon, 1989.

Miller, Pamela A. "Hair-Jewelry as Fetish." *Objects of Special Devotion: Fetishes and Fetishism in Popular Culture*. Bowling Green, OH: Bowling Green State University Press, 1982, pp. 89–106.

Miller, Richard A., and Iona Miller. *Magical and Ritual Use of Perfumes*. Rochester, VT: Inner Traditions, 1990.

Miller, William Ian. *The Anatomy of Disgust*. Cambridge: Harvard University Press, 1997.

Mitchell, Juliet, and Jacqueline Rose, eds. *Jacques Lacan and the Ecole Freudienne: Feminine Sexuality*. London: Macmillan, 1982.

Money, John. "Pornography in the Home: A Topic in Medical Education." *Contemporary Sexual Behavior: Critical Issues in the 1970s*, ed. Joseph Zubin and John Money. Baltimore: Johns Hopkins University Press, 1973, pp. 409–440.

Moore, Pamela, ed. *Building Bodies*. Piscataway, NJ: Rutgers University Press, 1998.

Moore, Rob, ed. *The Field Guide to Outdoor Erotica.* Moscow, ID: Solstice Press, 1988.

Moreck, Curt [Konrad Hammerling]. *Breast Fetishism.* New York: International Press of Sexology, 1965.

Morin, Jack. *Anal Pleasure and Health: A Guide for Men and Women.* Burlingame, CA: Down There Press, 1981.

———. *Men Loving Themselves: Images of Male Self-Sexuality.* San Francisco: Down There Press, 1988.

Morin, Jack, and Joani Blank. *The Private Side of Sex.* Burlingame, CA: Down There Press, 1982.

Morris, Desmond. *Body Watching.* New York: Crown, 1985.

Morris, Hugh. *Facts about Nudism: The Real Truth about the Nudist Movement.* New York: Padell, 1935.

Morse, Albert. *The Tattooists.* San Francisco: Albert L. Morse, 1977.

Mulvey, Laura. "Some Thoughts on Theories of Fetishism in the Context of Contemporary Culture." *October,* 65 (Summer 1993): 3–20.

Murphy, James S. *The Condom Industry in the United States.* Jefferson, NC: McFarland and Co., 1990.

Murray, Alan E. *Shoes and Feet to Boot.* Chapel Hill, NC: Orange Printshop, 1950.

Musto, Michael. "The Little Shop of Hornies." *Village Voice,* 31 December 1996, pp. 44–46.

National Film Board of Canada. *Images of Women.* Videocassette. Montreal: National Film Board of Canada, 1991.

Neilman, M. K. *Condom Mania! The Illustrated Condom Handbook.* New York: Metro Press, 1988.

Newman, Karoline, et al. *A Century of Lingerie: Icons of Style in the Twentieth Century.* London: Chartwell, 1998.

Newton, Esther. *Mother Camp: Female Impersonators in America.* Englewood Cliffs, NJ: Prentice-Hall, 1972; rpt. Chicago: University of Chicago Press, 1979.

———. "The Mythic Mannish Lesbian: Radclyffe Hall and the New Woman." *Signs,* 9 (1984): 557–575; rpt. *The Lesbian Issue: Essays from Signs.* Berkeley: University of California Press, 1985, pp. 7–25.

Niemoeller, Adolph F. *The Complete Guide to Bust Culture.* New York: Harvest House, 1939.

———. *Essays of an Erotologist.* Little Blue Book B-516. Girard, KS: Haldeman-Julius, 1946.

———. *Sex and Smell.* Girard, KS: Haldeman-Julius, 1947.

Nioche, Brigette. *The Sensual Dresser.* New York: Oxford University Press, 1981.

"No Cover, No Minimum." *Playboy,* 13:11 (November 1966): 144–153.

North, Maurice. *The Outer Fringe of Sex: A Study in Sexual Fetishism.* London: Odyssey Press, 1981.

"The Nude Look." *Playboy,* 12:11 (November 1965): 88–99.

Offit, Avodah K. *Night Thoughts: Reflections of a Sex Therapist.* New York: Congdon and Lattes, 1981.

O'Sullivan, Tim. *Exposé: The Art of Tattoo.* New York: Citadel Press, 1993.

Paillochet, Claire. *Unmentionables: The Allure of Lingerie,* trans. Anne Collier and Christel Petermann. New York: Delilah Books, 1984.

Parisot, Jeannette. *Johnny Come Lately: A Short History of the Condom.* London: 1987.

Parry, Albert. *Tattoo: Secrets of a Strange Art.* New York: Simon and Schuster, 1933.

Parsons, Alexandra. *Facts and Phalluses: A Collection of Bizarre and Intriguing Truths, Legends, and Measurements*. New York: St. Martin's, 1990.

Patrick, Dave. *California's Nude Beaches*. Los Angeles: Bold Type, 1988.

Patton, Cindy, and Janis Kelly. *Making It: A Woman's Guide to Sex in the Age of AIDS*. Ithaca, NY: Firebrand Books, 1990.

Peiss, Kathy. *Hope in a Jar: The History of America's Beauty Culture*. New York: Holt, 1998.

Penis Power Quarterly. Los Angeles: Added Dimensions (4216 Beverly Blvd., CA 90004), 1993–.

Penny, Alexandra. *Great Sex*. New York: Putnam's, 1985.

Perry, Steve, dir. *Smells like Sex*. Chatsworth, CA: VCA, 1996.

PFIQ Quarterly. San Francisco, 1989–.

Plachy, Sylvia, and James Ridgeway. *Red Light: Inside the Sex Industry*. New York: Powerhouse Books, 1996.

Podolsky, Edward, and Carlson Wade. *Erotic Symbolism: A Study of Fetichism in Relation to Sex*. New York: Epic, 1960.

Polhemus, Ted. *Bodystyles*. Harpenden, Herfortshire, England: Lennard Press, 1988.

———. *Streetstyle: From Sidewalk to Catwalk*. New York: Thames and Hudson, 1994.

Polhemus, Ted, and Housk Randall. *The Customized Body*. New York: Serpent's Tail, 1996.

Posner, Richard. *Sex and Reason*. Cambridge: Harvard University Press, 1992.

Preston, John, and Glenn Swann. *Safe Sex: The Ultimate Erotic Guide, with Photos by Fred Bissonen*. New York: NAL, 1986.

Prince, Virginia. *Understanding Cross-Dressing*. Los Angeles: Chevalier Publishing, 1976.

Probert, Christina. *Fashion in Vogue since 1910: Lingerie*. New York: Abbeville, 1982.

Rabkin, Eric S., and Eugene M. Silverman. *It's a Gas: A Study of Flatulence*. Ann Arbor, MI: Xenos, 1991.

Rednour, Shar, director. *Bend Over Boyfriend*. San Francisco: Fatale Films, 1998.

Reich, Annie. "The Discussion of 1912 on Masturbation and Our Present-Day Views." *Psychoanalytic Study of the Child*, 6 (1951): 80–94.

Reich, June. "Genderfuck: The Law of the Dildo." *Discourse*, 15:1 (Fall 1992): 112–127.

Reyburn, Wallace. *Bust-Up: The Uplifting Tale of Otto Titzling and the Development of the Bra*. Englewood Cliffs, NJ: Prentice-Hall, 1972.

Richards, Brian. *The Penis*. New York: Valentine Products, 1977.

Richter, Hans. *Joys of Masturbation*. Palm Springs, CA: MFM, 1982.

Riverol, A. R. *Live from Atlantic City: The History of the Miss America Pageant before, after and in spite of Television*. Bowling Green, OH: Bowling Green State University Popular Press, 1992.

Roach, Marion. "Female Bodybuilders Discover Curves." *New York Times*, 10 November 1998, p. D9.

Robert/"Stella." "Stella Through the Looking Glass." *Dirty Looks: Women, Pornography, Power*, ed. Pamela Church Gibson and Roma Gibson. London: British Film Institute, 1993, pp. 73–85.

Robertson, Pamela. *Guilty Pleasures: Feminist Camp from Mae West to Madonna*. Durham, NC: Duke University Press, 1996.

Robinson, Julian. *Body Packaging: A Guide to Human Sexual Display*. Topanga, CA: Elysium, 1988.

Rogers, Patrick, with Rebecca Crandall. "Think of It as Therapy." *Newsweek*, 31 May 1993, p. 65.

Rolley, Katrina. "Cutting a Dash: The Dress of Radclyffe Hall and Una Troubridge." *Feminist Review*, 35 (1990): 54–66.

———. *The Lesbian Dandy: The Role of Dress and Appearance in the Formation of Lesbian Identities*. London: Cassell, 1996.

———. "Love, Desire and the Pursuit of the Whole: Dress and the Lesbian Couple." *Chic Thrills*, ed. Juliet Ash and Elizabeth Wilson. Berkeley: University of California Press, 1993, pp. 30–39.

Rollins, Susan W., and Peter C. Rollins. *Gender in Popular Culture: Images of Men and Women in Literature, Visual Media, and Material Culture*. Cleveland, OK: Ridgemont Press, 1994.

Ross, Andrew. "Uses of Camp." *No Respect: Intellectuals and Popular Culture*. New York: Routledge, 1989, pp. 135–170.

Rossi, William A. *The Sex Life of the Foot and Shoe*. New York: Dutton, 1976.

Rubin, Arnold. "Tattoo Renaissance." *Marks of Civilization: Artistic Transformations of the Human Body*, ed. Arnold Rubin. Los Angeles: Museum of Cultural History, 1988, pp. 233–262.

Rubinstein, Ruth P. *Dress Codes: Meanings and Messages in American Culture*. Boulder, CO: Westview Press, 1995.

Rudloe, Jack. *The Erotic Ocean: A Handbook for Beachcombers and Marine Naturalists*. New York: Dutton, 1984.

Rudofsky, Bernard. *The Unfashionable Human Body*. Garden City, NY: Anchor/Doubleday, 1971.

Rump Humpers. (18 vols., 1991–1994). No director credited. Woodland Hills, CA: Glitz Video.

RuPaul. *Lettin' It All Hang Out: An Autobiography*. New York: Warner, 1995.

Sacher-Masoch, Leopold von. *Venus in Furs and Selected Letters of Leopold von Sacher-Masoch*, trans. Uwe Moeller and Laura Lindgren. New York: Blast Books.

Sagarin, Edward. *Deviants and Deviance: An Introduction to the Study of Disvalued People and Behavior*. New York: Praeger, 1975.

———. "Transsexualism: Legitimation, Amplification, and Exploitation of Deviance by Scientists and Mass Media." *Deviance and Mass Media*, ed. Charles Winick. Beverly Hills, CA: Sage, 1978, pp. 243–262.

Samois. *What Color Is Your Handkerchief? A Lesbian S/M Sexuality Reader*. San Francisco: Samois, 1979.

San Francisco Lesbians. (6 vols., 1990–1994). No director credited. Tennent, NJ: Pleasure Productions.

Sanders, Clinton R. *Customizing the Body: The Art and Culture of Tattooing*. Philadelphia: Temple University Press, 1989.

Sarnoff, Suzanne, and Irving Sarnoff. *Sexual Excitement and Sexual Peace*. New York: Evans, 1979.

Sawyer, Corinne Holt. "Men in Skirts and Women in Trousers, from Achilles to Victoria Grant: An Explanation of a Comedic Paradox." *Journal of Popular Culture*, 21: 2 (Fall 1987): 1–18.

Schertel, Ernst, ed. *Gesäss Erotik*. Berlin: Pergamon Verlag, 1931; rpt. 1970.

————. *Nachtheit als Kultur.* Leipzig: Panthenon Verlag, 1929.

————. *Scham und Laster.* Leipzig: Panthenon Verlag, 1927.

Schidrowitz, Leo, ed. *Sittengeschichte der Kulturwelt und ihrer Entwicklung in Einzeldarstellungen.* 10 vols. and supplement to vol. 2. Vienna/Leipzig: Verlag für Kulturforschung, 1926–30. I: *Sittengeschichte des Intimen: Bett, Korsett, Hemd, Hose, Bad, Abtritt, Die Geschichte und Entwicklung der intimen Gebrauchsgegenstände* (1926); II: *Sittengeschichte des Lasters: die Kulturepochen und ihre Leidenschaften* (1927), and *Ergänzungsband* (1927); III: *Sittengeschichte von Paris: die Grosstadt, ihe Sitten und ihre Unsittlichkeit* (1926); IV: *Sittengeschichte des Proletariats: des Weg vom Leibes-zum Maschinensklaven, die sittliche Stellung und Haltung des Proletariats* (1926); V: *Sittengeschichte des Theaters, Ein Darstellung des Theaters, seiner Entwicklung und Stellung in zwei Jahrhunderten* (1926); VI: *Sittengeschichte der Liebkosung und Strafe, Die Zärtlichkeitsworte, Gesten und Handlungen der Kulturmenschheit und ihr Gegenpol der Strenge* (1928); VII: *Sittengeschichte des Geheimen und Verbotenen. Eine Darstellung der geheimen und verborgen gehaltenen Leidenschaften der Menschheit, die Einstellung der Staatsgewalt zum Geschlechtsleben der Gesellschaft* (1930); VIII: *Sittengeschichte des Hafens und der Reise, Eine Beleuchtung des erotischen Lebens in der Hafenstadt, im Hotel, im Reisevehikel, Die Sexualität des Kulturmenschen während des Reisens in fremden Milieu* (1927): IX: *Sittengeschichte der Revolution, Sittenlockerung und Sittenverfall, Moralgesetze und sexualethische Neuorientierung in Zeiten staatlicher Zersetzung und revolutionären Umsturzes* (1930); X: *Sittengeschichte des Intimsten, Intime Toilette, Mode und Kosmetik im Dienst und Erotik* (1929).

Schor, Naomi, and Elizabeth Weed. "The Phallus Issue." Special issue of *differences*, 4: 1 (1992).

Schur, Edwin M. *The Americanization of Sex.* Philadelphia: Temple University Press, 1988.

Schwartz, Kit. *The Female Member: Being a Compendium of Facts, Figures, Foibles, and Anecdotes about the Loving Organ.* New York: St. Martin's, 1988.

————. *The Male Member: Being a Compendium of Fact, Fiction, Foibles and Anecdotes about the Male Sexual Organ in Man and Beast.* New York: St. Martin's, 1985.

Scott, R.W.B., and Christopher Gooch. *Art, Sex and Symbol: The Mystery of Tattooing.* South Brunswick, NJ: A. S. Barnes, 1974.

Screw. New York: Milky Way Productions, 1969–.

Sebeok, Thomas A. "The Word 'Fetish' and Its Uses in Anthropology." *American Journal of Semiotics*, 6:4 (1989): 51–65.

Segal, Lynn. "Sweet Sorrows, Painful Pleasures: Pornography and the Perils of Heterosexual Desire." *Sex Exposed: Sexuality and the Pornography Debate*, ed. Lynn Segal and Mary McIntosh. New Brunswick, NJ: Rutgers University Press, 1993, pp. 65–91.

Severn, Bill. *The Long and Short of It: Five Thousand Years of Fun and Fury over Hair.* New York: David McKay, 1971.

Shelley, Jim. "Tunnel of Glove." *Details*, January 1994, p. 44.

Sherfey, Mary Jane. *The Nature and Evolution of Female Sexuality.* New York: Random House, 1972.

Silmon, Pedro, ed. *The Bikini.* New York: Diadem Books, 1986.

Silverman, Kaja. "Fragments of a Fashionable Discourse." *Studies in Entertainment*, ed. Tania Modleski. Bloomington: Indiana University Press, 1986, pp. 138–152.

Simpson, Mark. *Male Impersonators: Gay Men Performing Masculinity*. New York: Routledge, 1994.

Singh, D. "Female Judgment of Male Attractiveness and Desirability for Relationships: Role of Waist-to-Hip Ratio and Financial Status." *Journal of Personality and Social Psychology*, 69 (1995): 1089–1101.

Singh, D., and R. Young. "Body Weight, Waist-to-Hip Ratio, Breasts and Hips: Role of Judgments of Female Attractiveness and Desirability for Relationships." *Ethology and Sociobiology*, 16 (1995): 483–507.

Singh, D., and S. Luis. "Ethnic and Gender Consensus for the Effect of Waist-to-Hip Ratio on Judgment of Women's Attractiveness." *Human Nature*, 6 (1995): 51–65.

Skin Two. London: Woodward, 1985–.

Slade, Joseph W. "Recent Trends in Pornographic Films." *Society*, 12 (September/October 1975): 77–84; rpt. *Film in Society*, ed. Arthur Asa Berger. New Brunswick, NJ: Transaction/Dutton, 1980, pp. 121–135.

Slide, Anthony. *Great Pretenders: A History of Female and Male Impersonation in the Performing Arts*. Radnor, PA: Wallace-Homestead, 1986.

Small Tops. P.O. Box 801434, Santa Clarita, CA, 91380.

Smith, Howard, and Brian Van Der Horst. "The Pleasure Chest." *Village Voice*, 31 May 1976, p. 28.

Smith, Roberta. "Demure to Demystified: Swimsuits' Hall of Fame." *New York Times*, 10 August 1990, p. C22.

Sommers, Christine Hoff. "Who Stole Feminism?" *Allure*, May 1979, pp. 174–177.

Sontag, Susan. "Notes on Camp [1964]." *A Susan Sontag Reader*. New York: Vintage, 1983, pp. 105–119.

Spadola, Meema, and Thom Powers, producers and directors. *Breasts*. New York: Cinemax, 1996.

———. *Private Dicks*. New York: HBO, 1998.

Spinrad, Paul. *The RE/Search Guide to Bodily Fluids*. San Francisco: RE/Search, 1995.

Sprinkle, Annie [Ellen F. Steinberg]. *Post Porn Modernist*. Amsterdam: Art Unlimited, 1991.

Spurrier, Jeff. "Blood of a Poet." *Details*, February 1995, pp. 106–111, 140.

Stannard, Una. "The Mask of Beauty." *Women in Sexist Society*, ed. Vivian Gornick and Barbara K. Moran. New York: Basic Books, 1971.

Steele, Valerie. "Clothing and Sexuality." *Men and Women: Dressing the Part*, ed. Claudia Brush Kidwell and Valerie Steele. Washington, DC: Smithsonian Institution Press, 1989, 42–63.

———. *Fashion and Eroticism: Ideals of Feminine Beauty from the Victorian Era to the Jazz Age*. New York: Oxford University Press, 1985.

———. *Fetish: Fashion, Sex and Power*. New York: Oxford University Press, 1995.

Stehle, Bernard F. *Incurably Romantic*. Philadelphia: Temple University Press, 1985.

Stekel, Wilhelm. *Auto-Eroticism: A Psychiatric Study of Onanism and Neurosis*, trans. James S. Van Teslaar. New York: Liveright, [1950].

———. *Sexual Aberrations: The Phenomena of Fetishism in Relation to Sex*, trans. Samuel Parker. 2 vols. New York: Liveright, 1930; rpt. [c.1958], 1971.

Stengers, Jean, and Anne van Neck. *Histoire d'une grande peur: la masturbation.* Brussels: Editions de l'Université de Bruxelles, 1984.

Stephens, William N. *A Cross-Cultural Study of Modesty and Obscenity.* Halifax, Nova Scotia, Canada: Dalhousie University Press, 1969.

Sterling, Loretta [Ed de Roos]. *Girls of Silicone Valley.* Sun Valley, CA: Filmco, 1991.

Steward, Samuel M. *Bad Boys and Tough Tattoos: A Social History of the Tattoo with Gangs, Sailors, and Street-Corner Punks, 1950–1965.* New York: Haworth Press, 1990.

Stiles, Henry Reed. *Bundling: Its Origin, Progress and Decline in America.* N.p.: Privately printed, n.d.

Stoller, Robert J. *Observing the Erotic Imagination.* New Haven, CT: Yale University Press, 1985.

———. *Perversion: The Erotic Form of Hatred.* New York: Pantheon, 1975.

Stone, Lee Alexander. *The Power of a Symbol.* Chicago: Pascal Covici, 1925; rpt. and rev. *The Story of Phallicism,* 1927.

Strage, Mark. *The Durable Fig Leaf: A Historical, Cultural, Medical, Social, Literary, and Iconographic Account of Man's Relations with His Penis.* New York: Morrow, 1980.

Strap-On Sally. (8 vols., 1993–1996). Jim Gunn, director. Tennent, NJ: Pleasure Productions.

Stratton, Jon. *The Desirable Body: Cultural Fetishism and the Erotics of Consumption.* New York: St. Martin's/Manchester University Press, 1996.

Styron, William. "The Vice That Has No Name." *Harpers Magazine,* February 1968, 97–100.

Szasc, Thomas S. "Speaking about Sex: Sexual Pathology and Sexual Therapy as Rhetoric." *Challenges in Sexual Science,* ed. Clive Davis. Lake Mills, IA: Society for the Scientific Study of Sex, 1983, pp. 1–7.

Tabori, Paul. *Dress and Undress: The Sexology of Fashion.* London: New English Library, 1969.

———. *The Humor and Technology of Sex.* New York: Julian Press, 1969.

Tabu Tattoo: Erotic Body Art. Hoboken, NJ, 1997–.

Tasty. http://www.gettingit.com.

Taylor, John. "The Long, Hard Days of Dr. Dick." *Esquire,* September 1995, pp. 120–128, 130.

Terry, Jennifer, and Jacqueline Urla. *Deviant Bodies: Critical Perspectives on Difference in Science and Popular Culture.* Bloomington: Indiana University Press, 1995.

Thames, Susan, and Marin Gazzaniga, eds. *The Breast.* New York: Global City Press, 1994.

Thesander, Marianne. *The Feminine Ideal.* New York: Reaktion Books/Consortium, 1997.

Thévoz, Michel. *The Painted Body.* New York: Skira/Rizzoli, 1984.

Thompson, C.J.S. *The Mysteries of Sex: Women Who Posed as Men and Men Who Impersonated Women.* New York: Causeway Books, 1974.

Tiefer, Leonore. "In Pursuit of the Perfect Penis: The Medicalization of Male Sexuality." *American Behavioral Scientist,* 29:5 (May–June 1986): 579–599.

———. *Sex Is Not a Natural Act and Other Essays.* Boulder, CO: Westview Press, 1995.

Tisdale, Sally. *Talk Dirty to Me: An Intimate Philosophy of Sex.* New York: Doubleday, 1994.

Tissot, Samuel Auguste. *L'onanisme: ou dissertation physique sur les maladies produites par la masturbation*. Paris: Chez Bossange, Masson et Besson, 1800, a rpt. of the 1760 ed. published in Lausanne.

Transformation. Orange, CA, 1989–.

Trebay, Guy. "Letter from Downtown: Cross-Dresser Dreams." *New Yorker*, March 22, 1993, pp. 49–54.

———. "Primitive Culture: At Large with the Pierced and Tattooed Love Boys (and Girls)." *Village Voice*, 12 November 1991, pp. 37–39.

Twain, Mark [Samuel Clemens]. *Following the Equator: A Journey Around the World*. Hartford, CT: American Publishing Company, 1897.

———. "Some Remarks on the Science of Onanism." *The Mammoth Cod, an Address to the Stomach Club*. Waukegan, WI: Maledicta Press, 1976.

Undergear. San Diego: Brawn of California, quarterly.

Vale, V., and Andrea Juno. *Modern Primitives: An Investigation of Contemporary Adornment and Ritual*. San Francisco: RE/Search, 1989.

Vera, Veronica. *Miss Vera's Finishing School for Boys Who Want to Be Girls*. New York: Main Street, 1997.

Vlahos, Olivia. *Body: The Ultimate Symbol*. New York: Lippincott, 1979.

Wagner, Peter. "The Discourse on Sex—Or Sex as Discourse: Eighteenth Century Medical and Paramedical Erotica." *Sexual Underworlds of the Enlightenment*, ed. George Rousseau and Roy Porter. Chapel Hill: University of North Carolina Press, 1988, pp. 9–38.

———. "The Veil of Medicine and Morality: Some Pornographic Aspects of the *Onania*." *British Journal for Eighteenth-Century Studies*, 6 (1983): 179–184.

Walker, Alexander. *Beauty: Analysis and Classification of Beauty in Woman*. New York: William H. Colyer, 1846.

Wallis, Frank. *The Genuine Article*. P.O. Box 641741, San Francisco 94109.

Watson, Steven [Minette], and Ray Dobbins. *Minette: Recollections of a Part Time Lady*. New York: n.p., 1979.

Waugh, Norah. *Corsets and Crinolines*. Boston: Boston Book and Art Shop, 1954.

Weatherford, Jack. *Porn Row*. New York: Arbor House, 1986.

Webb, Spider, comp. and ed. *Heavily Tattooed Men and Women*. New York: McGraw-Hill, 1976.

Weeks, Jeffrey. *Against Nature: Essays on History, Sexuality and Identity*. London: Rivers Oram Press, 1991.

Welby, William. *The Naked Truth about Nudism*. London: Thorsons, 1950.

Weston, Kath. "Do Clothes Make the Woman? Gender, Performance Theory, and Lesbian Eroticism." *Genders*, 17 (Fall 1993): 1–21.

Whipple, Beverly, and Gina Ogden. *Safe Encounters: How Women Can Say Yes to Pleasure and No to Unsafe Sex*. New York: McGraw–Hill, 1988.

Wiegers, Yvonne. "Male Bodybuilding: The Social Construction of a Masculine Identity." *Journal of Popular Culture*, 32:2 (Fall 1998): 147–161.

Wilchins, Riki A. *Read My Lips: Sexual Subversion and the End of Gender*. Ithaca, NY: Firebrand, 1997.

Wilson, Elizabeth. "Deviant Dress." *Feminist Review*, 35 (1990): 67–74.

———. "Fashion and the Postmodern Body." *Chic Thrills*, ed. Juliet Ash and Elizabeth Wilson. Berkeley: University of California Press, 1993, pp. 3–15.

Winford, E. Carlton. *Femme Mimics*. Dallas, TX: Winford, 1954.

Winter, Ruth, and Kathleen McAuliffe. "Hooked on Love: Chemical Sex." *Omni* (May 1984): 78–79, 81.

Wiseman, Jay. *Sex Toy Tricks: More than 125 Ways to Accessorize Good Sex.* San Francisco: Greenery Press, 1996.

Wojcik, Daniel. *Punk and Neo-Tribal Body Art.* Jackson: University Press of Mississippi, 1995.

Wolf, Naomi. *The Beauty Myth: How Images of Beauty Are Used against Women.* New York: William Morrow, 1991.

Wolman, Baron. *Profiles.* Mill Valley, NY: Square Books, 1974.

Woodhouse, Annie. *Fantastic Women: Sex, Gender, and Transvestism.* New Brunswick, NJ: Rutgers University Press, 1989.

Woodlawn, Holly, with Jeff Copeland. *A Low Life in High Heels: The Holly Woodlawn Story.* New York: HarperCollins, 1992.

Woodward, Tim, ed. *The Best of Skin Two.* London: Kasak Books, 1993.

Wowser, Doogie. "The Dick of Your Dreams." *Adam Film World*, 15:2 (August 1993): 44–45.

Wright, Lawrence. "A Rapist's Homecoming." *New Yorker*, 4 September 1995, pp. 56–62, 64–69.

Wroblewski, Chris. *The Art and Craft of Tattoo: Skin Show.* London: Dragon's Dream, 1981.

———. *Tattoo: Pigments of Imagination.* New York: Alfred van der Marck, 1987.

———. *Tattooed Women.* New York: Virgin Publications, 1991.

Yalom, Marilyn. *A History of the Breast.* New York: Knopf, 1997.

Yaeger, Lynn. "Fun with Lipsticks and Dildos." *Village Voice*, 11 August 1998, p. 16.

Yates, Rowdy. "Girls from Girdleville." *Film Threat Video Guide*, no. 5 (1992): 35.

Zimet, Susan, and Victor Goodman. *The Great Cover-Up: A Condom Compendium.* New Paltz, NY: Civan, 1989.

10

Performance

OBSCENE AND/OR PORNOGRAPHIC ACTS

For purposes of this section, indecent, erotic, or pornographic *performance* refers to activity that is public or quasi-public and deliberate in its exhibitionism, as in theatrical settings. (Prosecutors habitually describe lewd performances as *obscene*, which can obscure the sexuality of the activity.) Although sex in a house of prostitution or a massage parlor may include elements of voyeurism, it is ambiguous in its theatricality, since the settings are not quite "public" and for that reason may best be understood as terrain for ethnographers or anthropologists. Performances mix at least some elements of display and drama, such as exhibitionism, role-playing, voyeurism, and deliberate shock. Sometimes events are staged, as in theaters, and sometimes they spring from a setting—such as a gay steambath or heterosexual sex club—that encourages spontaneity. Tourists and college students flock to oil, mud, or jello wrestling; competitions to determine "best buns" (all genders), largest penis, biggest breasts, prettiest navel, most elaborate tattoos or body piercings; wet T-shirt, "mooning," farting, lascivious banana-eating and condom-decorating contests; nude aerobic demonstrations, Jane Fondaesque workouts, and so on. The commentary on such events is generally too slight to be included here, in part because the activities fall more easily into the category of the dopey or the ribald rather than the obscene or the pornographic. One important exception is the work of Jean Baudrillard, who finds such material fascinating. Baudrillard's "What Are You Doing after the Orgy?" attempts to discriminate among audiences for mud-wrestling, male strippers, peep shows, and traditional erotic iconography. Some of Baudrillard's reflections in *Simulations* on figuration, power, substance, and simulacra apply to sexual theatricality; Baudrillard himself has made a career out of dramatizing the obvious.

In recent years the term *performance* has come to stand for events and spaces in which issues of sexuality and gender are "negotiated" and dramatized; *performance theory* refers to the growing body of criticism on these subjects. Postmodern cultural critics refer to readings of even traditional texts as "performances." Suzanne Lacy and Leslie Labowitz published an account of the first "Take Back the Night" march, predecessor of a now-popular annual feminist event on campuses around the country, as "November 18, 1978: Take Back the Night: San Francisco, CA" in *High Performance*, the national journal of performance art. Jerri Allyn and her colleagues similarly wrote up the founding of the lesbian archives in New York for the magazine as a performance event under the title "Oral Herstory of Lesbianism" for the same issue. Explicit protest qualified as performance as early as the 1970s. *TDR* carried Lee Baxandall's "Spectacles and Scenarios: A Dramaturgy of Radical Activity," an article centered on a Grinnell College demonstration against the visit of a *Playboy* photographer, when ten male and female students stripped naked to protest. While not quite a manifesto, Baxandall's essay is one of the best rationales for radical performance art. Carole Tornellan's "Keep Your Fly Buttoned: Putting Desire, Danger and Pleasure Back in the Streets" covers a performance by various women artists occasioned by a "sexist" advertisement for "Levi's 500" blue jeans. Sometimes the confrontation surmounts staging entirely. *Good Girls/Bad Girls: Feminists and Sex Trade Workers Face to Face*, edited by Laurie Bell, is not simply a splendid source of information; it is also the account of the 1985 International Woman's Day Congress (Toronto) that brought feminists together with members of the Canadian Organization for the Rights of Prostitutes. Lively discussion pitted the two groups against each other. To the degree that the encounter was a contest, such comparisons being unfair, the working women generally made the professional feminists look foolish, in large part because their experience dramatized what theory simply cannot.

Mandatory reading includes any of Erving Goffman's books on performance; *Behavior in Public Places* is highly recommended. Goffman's many volumes explore human behavior as performance in situations (hence, the school called "situationism") defined by space or custom and offer many insights on modesty, display, and shock—in short, appropriate and inappropriate ways of presenting ourselves to others. Goffman makes distinctions between foreground, background, and "middle space," areas that shape our behavior and dictate degrees of intimacy. Humans are more "onstage" in foregrounded space, while they behave quite differently in the background, the most intimate realm, and adopt hybrid behavior in the less formal, but also less casual, middle arenas. What makes blatantly sexual activity so shocking is that we expect it to remain out of public view or, at the very least, to take place in settings at some distance from common scrutiny. A less academic variation of this thesis animates *Life-Show: How to See Theater in Life and Life in Theater*, by John Lahr and Jonathan Price. "Etiquette ritualizes suppression," they point out (53), and explicit performance can achieve effects by violating it.

THE AMERICAN EROTIC STAGE

Arthur Maria Rabenalt's five-volume *Mimus Eroticus*, the great history of international erotic theater, devotes only a few pages to American examples. Because the public or quasi-public nature of performance made erotic manifestations vulnerable to prosecution, few domestic histories record what were often marginal, ephemeral, rarely repeated stagings. Generally speaking, American historians have not yet undertaken the formidable task of tracking down the many isolated newspaper notices of arrests and prosecutions from various periods. That means that students must rely on the fugitive references in biographies of playwrights and performers or in chronicles of popular culture or prostitution. A distinguished example of the latter category is Timothy J. Gilfoyle's *City of Eros: New York City, Prostitution, and the Commercialization of Sex, 1790–1920*, which covers sex industries in America's major city, in particular, the bawdy houses and bars where lewd exhibitions took place considerably removed from respectable gaze. Gilfoyle's meticulous scholarship on the "sporting world" draws on documents ranging from district attorney's papers to pornographic magazines, and he has appended a remarkable bibliography of interest to any scholar of sexuality. One of his sources is Edward Van Every's *Sins of America as Exposed by the Police Gazette*. In its early incarnation, the *Gazette* drew its material from the music halls and bordellos that sometimes featured exhibitions; references to prizefights, circuses, dancing, and other elements of the "sporting world" of cities in the last half of the nineteenth century are mixed in with indecent performance. Peter Fryer's survey of sexual reticence, with numerous examples of attempts to censor productions on the English and American stages, is *Mrs. Grundy: Studies in Sexual Prudery*. To many pre-twentieth-century people, the make-believe world of the theater encouraged lascivious fantasy, and women, when they were at last permitted to appear onstage (prior to the modern era, female roles were usually played by males), seemed little better than prostitutes. The unsavory reputation of actresses, says Tracy C. Davis in "The Actress in Victorian Pornography," meant that the character of the actress became a stereotypic staple of many genres of pornography.

Abe Laufe's *The Wicked Stage: A History of Theater Censorship and Harassment in the United States*, whose scope extends from colonial performance to *Oh! Calcutta!*, is the best single work on theater that transgressed taboos in America and is most enlightening about the outspoken drama of the 1920s. Less comprehensive, but still excellent, general surveys are Abel Green and Joe Laurie Jr.'s two-volume *Show Biz: From Vaude to Video*, which offers considerable information on nude tableaux, burlesque, and raunchy drama, and Lewis Erenberg's splendid *Steppin' Out: New York Nightlife and the Transformation of American Culture, 1890–1930*, an indispensable lens for the study of cabaret, jazz and dance clubs, and other forms of popular amusement. Eroticism is hardly the subject of T. Allston Brown's three-volume *A History of the New York Stage from 1732 to 1901*, but it is extremely useful for its comprehensive treatment of early dramatic presentations, some of which got in trouble with the law. Jack W. McCullough traces the modest, yet startling, "nudity" of the tableau vivant (for which performers "froze" in scenes imitating famous paintings or statues) from its first appearance in America in 1832 to its demise in the 1890s in *Living Pictures on the New York Stage*. John Elsom's *Erotic Theatre* is good on early British performance but deals significantly with American examples only since the 1960s.

Sodom by the Sea: An Affectionate History of Coney Island, by Oliver Pilat and Jo Ranson, covers the vulgar shows of America's most notorious amusement park, as does, to a more reticent extent, John Kasson's *Amusing the Million: Coney Island at the Turn of the Century*. Kathy Peiss' *Cheap Amusements: Working Women and Leisure in Turn-of-the-Century New York* looks at titillating entertainment aimed at women. David Nasaw's *Going Out: The Rise and Fall of Public Amusements* provides excellent background, with chapters on "The Indecent Other" and "The Pernicious Motion Pictures" and a running commentary on cabarets, gaming halls, and low entertainment of all sorts. Robert Bogdan's *Freak Show: Presenting Human Oddities for Amusement and Profit*, which examines a popular form of entertainment during a century stretching from 1840 to 1940, and Leslie Fiedler's somewhat more theoretical *Freaks: Myths and Images of the Secret Self* both touch on the erotic exploitation of freaks. Daniel P. Mannix's *Freaks: We Who Are Not as Others* also deals with the sexuality implicit in the process by which society marginalizes the different. Rosemarie Garland Thomson's *Freakery: Cultural Spectacles of the Extraordinary Body* is a more straightforward history of freaks and bizarre exhibits in America to the present. An illustrated section on "Girlie Shows" (235–264) in Charles Fish's *Blue Ribbons and Burlesque: A Book of County Fairs* recalls fairground shows featuring mostly tired women performing for rubes. Arthur L. Lewis' *Carnival* also discusses freak shows, sexual performance, "cootch shows," and con games on the midway. For *Girl Show: Into the Canvas World of Bump and Grind*, beyond question the best volume on carnival "peelers," A. W. Stencell draws on reminiscences of circus barkers, fair folk and marvellous archives of photos. Stencell describes fairway shows constructed around flesh, from Hawaiian hula dancers to hoochie-coochie girls and jaded burlesque queens, a robust form of entertainment that faded when fairgrounds lost their allure to "titty bars" and clubs. In "Black Bodies, White Bodies: Toward an Iconography of Female Sexuality in Late Nineteenth-Century Art, Medicine, and Literature," Sander L. Gilman points out that the practice of displaying blacks nude on slave blocks helped to construct erotic public iconographies. Patricia Hill Collins notes in *Black Feminist Thought* that such wholesale objectification of black women rendered them spectacles of erotic entertainment.

Walker Gilmer's *Horace Liveright, Publisher of the Twenties* contains chapters on John Sumner and the New York Society for the Suppression of Vice, whose minions harassed Liveright. In 1927 police, acting on the usual complaints from the New York Society for the Suppression of Vice, raided three plays in Manhattan[1]: *The Virgin Man, Sex* (produced by and starring Mae West), and *The Captive*, a drama with a lesbian theme by Edouard Boudet. Horace Liveright bought the rights to the Boudet show and remounted it, then had to fight clamors for censorship. Information on Mae West's battles with authority over her work onstage can be found in *Mae West*, by George Eells and Stanley Musgrove, in West's autobiography, *Goodness Had Nothing to Do with It*, and in her *Playboy* "Interview" of 1971. More scholarly are "Mae West Live: *Sex, The Drag*, and 1920s Broadway," Marybeth Hamilton's article on West's prosecuted plays of the 1920s, "raw and unvarnishedly staged plays by a working-class actress fresh out of burlesque" (99); *"When I'm Bad I'm Better": Mae West, Sex, and American Entertainment*, Hamilton's full-length cultural study of the actress; *Too Much of a Good Thing: Mae West as Cultural Icon*, Ramona Curry's characterization of West as an officer in the gender wars; and *Mae West: Empress of Sex*, Maurice Leonard's no-holds-barred account of West's sensationalization of sexual templates. Angela Carter writes persuasively about Mae West's impersonations of an impersonation of female sexuality in *Nothing Sacred*, though W. C. Fields may have captured her talent for self-parody more succinctly. Fields, an occasional costar, called West "a plumber's idea of Cleopatra."[2] At any rate, she is often cited as an example of feminine "masquerade." Studying West can tell the scholar a great deal about pornography, whose effect is often achieved by a hyperbole that calls attention to its own exaggeration. If pornography is at base the performance of sexuality and gender, then Mae West was the first American porn diva.

Partly as a consequence of official vigilance, American theater during the 1940s and 1950s, save for the occasional homosexual theme, the odd scandal, and the equally sporadic avant-garde performance (see **Performance Art** in this chapter), was pretty bland and remained so until the 1960s. Two books offer some information on the transitional period: Elsom's *Erotic Theatre* compares undercurrents in the theater of the 1950s with the raucous themes that erupted in the 1960s and early 1970s, while Gillian Hanson's *Original Skin: Nudity and Sex in Cinema and Theatre*, a surprisingly solid text, contrasts the artistic, social, and political shock associated with states of undress in the 1960s with practices earlier in the century.

The rise of explicit theater in the 1960s and 1970s accompanied the flowering of the youthful counterculture, whose influence on the popular stage peaked with *Hair*, a spectacle that included nude performers belting out "The Age of Aquarius." Pocket Books published the script of *Hair*, by Jerome Ragni and James Rado, in an edition laced with photos. Howard Junker's "Theater of the Nude" is excellent on the use of nudity by more commercial playwrights like Tom O'Horgan in the 1960s. The book version of *Oh! Calcutta!* by Kenneth Tynan and his colleagues reproduces the scripts by Jules Feiffer, Sam Shepard,

Samuel Beckett, and the other authors of the skits but does not include the skits (e.g., "I Dance to Make My Titties Bounce") omitted from the final staging. *Oh! Calcutta!*, of course, ran for years on Broadway, where its bare performers and simulated sex titillated tens of thousands of Americans. Kenneth Tynan, the force behind the show, includes an unpublished interview originally scheduled for *Playboy* in his *The Sound of Two Hands Clapping*. Questioned by the interviewer as to what he wanted critics to say about the show, Tynan replied: "What we are asking for is a response to private acts performed in public. And I don't think there's a vocabulary for that yet, certainly not a critical one" (143–144). The interview allows Tynan to speak of play, eroticism, the force of taboo, and the necessity for masturbation. Raina Barrett's *First Your Money, Then Your Clothes: My Life and Oh! Calcutta!*, by one of the performers, recounts experiences on- and offstage. Among her anecdotes are the cast's methods of dealing with sudden male erections (the actresses hid them with *their* bodies). C. Robert Jennings speaks with other cast members like Margo Sappington (now a choreographer for the Joffrey Ballet) on the pleasures and pitfalls of performing nude and their reactions to audience attitudes toward the show's scenes of simulated intercourse in "Shaping Up for 'Oh! Calcutta!' "

Scholars interested in erotic plays from this period should investigate playwrights such as Kenneth Bernard, Michael McClure, Rochelle Owens, and others with similarly raucous voices. John Lahr's "The Theater's Voluptuary Itch," focuses on flesh and sexuality in Bruce Jay Friedman's *Scuba Duba*, Michael McClure's *The Beard*, Paul Foster's *Tom Paine*, and other plays. *Access: The Supplementary Index to Periodicals* is an excellent guide to other reviews of local and regional experimental theater with sexual content. Harold Clurman's "New Playwrights: Boys and Girls on the Burning Deck" chronicles efforts at shock by the LaMama Theatre and by various playwrights and performers, such as those in *The Dirtiest Show in Town*, one of the nudest of musicals. *Playboy* ran photos and text on the nude musical mounted by Earl Wilson Jr. at the Village Gate, "Let My People Come: The Last Dirty Word in Musicals"; as the show closed each evening, a still-nude cast mingled with the departing audience.

The new freedom naturally stimulated a great deal of comment. Previous taboos against nudity onstage, says Martin Esslin, resulted from the audience's fear that the performers would be embarrassed, and when that did not happen, dramatic nudity became accepted. Indeed, Esslin insists, nudity is now so commonplace in our culture that the theater cannot ignore it. In his "Nudity: Barely the Beginning?" Esslin notes that in a play like McClure's *The Beard*, "it is not the sexual act, but the *unorthodox* sexual act—cunnilingus—which matters. The public display of a practice that many members of the audience indulge in themselves, but that they regard as deviant or especially sinful, must have a reassuring effect. If it can be shown publicly, it may not be so horrifically sinful as they had, in their tortured minds, believed it to be" (181–182).

Action of the sort Esslin finds so revolutionary is usually simulated. "Triple Treat" is an interview with Samara, a mostly simulated-sex performer, by the

Reverend Kellie Everts, herself a self-styled "Stripper for Christ," whose perspective is inimitable. Samara says, "When I go out there, I'm putting on an act. I'm not getting no rocks off, believe me. In all my years of working, I've never come on stage, with a girl, with a guy, or with myself. When I go out there, it's just like putting on a business suit and going downtown to work" (38). Even simulated sex can be disruptive, according to some critics. In "Sex Acts on Stage: Where Does Art Get Off?" Ross Wetzsteon considers performances as diverse as Charles Ludlam's and Marilyn Chambers's and the difficulties inherent in staging sexual acts for public viewing, not the least of which is their power to arouse and thus jeopardize the artistic experience. Using Susan Sontag's always pertinent observation—"There are some elements in life—above all, sexual pleasure—about which it isn't necessary to have a position" (77)—Wetzsteon observes that his objection is not a matter of politics or ideology, just a recognition that the sight of a sexual act seems to undermine themes and ideas. Others think that erotic and even obscene theater functions as a necessary alternative to conventional drama, that it stakes out an intellectual position by presenting that which society would suppress. The most succinct statement is enunciated by Jean Genet, quoted by Tony Duvert in "Other People's Eroticism": "In fact, the existence of specifically 'pornographic' works calls to mind Jean Genet's remark when he was asked why his theatre was obscene: because, he said, 'the other theatre is not' " (120).

Richard Schechner discusses his intent as a theorist of shock in mounting erotic performance at the Performance Garage in New York in "Pornography and the New Expression." Probably the most famous of these events was Schechner's *Dionysus in '69*, a modern version of Euripedes' *The Bacchae*, in which the actors, frequently nude, interacted with the audience in the performance space; the script holds up well. Schechner's "News, Sex, and Performance Theory," a reconsideration of eroticism in the theater, contrasts the carefully crafted and staged sex simulated in performance with the immediacy of the reporting of sexual matters in print and electronic media. Margaret Croyden's *Lunatics, Lovers and Poets: The Contemporary Experimental Theatre* critiques various troupes of the 1970s, from the Living Theatre to the Performance Group, in a narrative that recalls the ferment swirling about dramaturges from Grotowski to Brook. Such theorists exalt a romantic frenzy that pushes performers and audience to the boundaries of excess and sometimes beyond, says Jon Fabre in *The Power of Theatrical Madness*. "A Little Treatise on Eroticism," by Jan Kott, a Polish theorist of great influence on New York theater in the 1960s, suggests, "Eroticism is the verification of the partner who has been created by oneself." Erotic theater became an international phenomenon in the late 1960s and has remained so to a degree ever since. "Eroplay," a personal account of erotic performances in various cities around the world by Frank Moore, stresses the revolutionary aspects of a theater of sexual frankness and the ease with which it leaps borders.

Aldo Rostagno, Julian Beck, and Judith Malina provide accounts of the company's origins, selections from performances, and excerpts from reviews of one of the most important erotic troupes in *We, the Living Theatre*. Stefan Brecht's "Family of the f.p.: Notes on the Theatre of the Ridiculous" is an excellent early article on this equally significant group. "Playhouse of the Ridiculous," a photo-essay, captures the raunchy, gender-bending spirit of the troupe. The collaboration between the explicit avant-garde playwright Kenneth Bernard and John Vaccaro, the director of the Playhouse of the Ridiculous, extended from the strangely fetishistic *The Moke-Eater* (1968) to the gender-bending *The Sixty Minute Queer Show* (1977); Gerald Rabkin delves into the relationship in "The Kenneth Bernard–John Vaccaro Ten-Year Queer Show."[3] Dan Isaac critiques "Ronald Tavel: Ridiculous Playwright," one of the founders of the Theatre of the Ridiculous. "The AIDS Crisis Is Ridiculous," Gregg Bordowitz's memorial to Charles Ludlam, the other founder of the Ridiculous Theatre Company, concludes that Ludlam profoundly influenced modern theater, a judgment that seems reasonable. Concurring is Charles McNulty, whose "The Ridiculous Theatrical Company: Still Mocking after All These Years," updates what is by now a semirespectable image. The scripts of Ludlam's works have been published as *The Complete Plays*, and Rick Roemer discusses all of them in *Charles Ludlam and the Ridiculous Theatrical Company: Critical Analyses of 29 Plays*. Valuable comment, much of it recorded on the spot, forms the reminiscences of many experimental plays from the 1960s on by Richard Kostelanetz in *On Innovative Performance(s): Three Decades of Recollections on Alternative Theatre*. Since performances by groups such as the Performance Garage and the Living Theatre varied from night to night, Kostelanetz's annotations of different visits to the same play help capture ephemeral and fleeting elements.

In 1990 the politically charged attacks on the National Endowment for the Arts made the NEA-funded New York City Opera hesitate before opening its production of Arnold Schoenberg's *Moses und Aron*, since naked "virgins" appeared in several scenes. The opera went ahead, as reported in "Nude Characters to Remain in City Opera Production," by A. Kozinn. Senator Helms and the NEA aside, critics in the 1990s not only took nudity on the Broadway stage for granted but also felt comfortable commenting on the size of penises in plays with gay themes. Allan Havis calls Mac Wellman "the dean of anti-naturalists" in his "Mac Wellman on '7 Blowjobs'" interview for *Theatre Forum*, which also reproduces the script of the play, a dramatic attack on Jesse Helms as influenced by Donald Wildmon. Such works are flash points in the cultural wars. Perhaps because of the enhanced candor, the challenge to playwrights is more likely to be framing a conflict in unconventional terms rather than seeking deliberately to shock.

PERFORMANCE ART

Some critics distinguish avant-garde and/or experimental drama, both of which usually rely on some form of narrative, however unconventional, to tell stories, from performance art, in which the body and/or persona of the performer is used to convey aesthetic, moral, or political messages. The distinctions, loose at best, often collapse. Though performance art really began in the early part of this century on the Continent, it has grown steadily in the United States, where it is now a form pretty much dominated by women artists.

RoseLee Goldberg's *Performance Art: From Futurism to the Present* provides the best historical overview of performance art in America because she begins with movements in 1909 and progresses through significant groups like Fluxus later on. "Happenings," a performance form popular in the 1960s, though with earlier roots in Dada and other schools, emphasized the spontaneity of groups brought together to interact. Happenings frequently fostered mild sexual contact, nudity, and obscene language. The rationale is explained by Al Hansen in *A Primer of Happenings and Time/Space Art*, which refers to these events, some of them quite complex, mostly in large, urban environments. Another text, similar in intent, is Michael Kirby's *Happenings*; Kirby briefly explores the roles and relationship of voyeurism and exhibitionism. Henry M. Sayre's *The Object of Performance: The American Avant-Garde since 1970*, though not exclusively concerned with erotic manifestations in the 1970s, gives them their due in the course of thoughtful essays ranging over photography and other media. The essays in *Happenings and Other Acts*, edited by Mariellen Sandford, recall famous events, as do those in *Collective Consciousness: Art Performances of the Seventies*, edited by Jean Dupuy. Nina Felshin has edited *But Is It Art? The Spirit of Art as Activism*; essays cover modern performance artists (e.g., Suzanne Lacy) and an aesthetic consciousness that deliberately affronts.

Susan Rubin Suleiman's "Pornography and the Avant-Garde" explores the connections between pornographic impulses and cutting-edge drama. The periodical *High Performance* reports monthly on avant-garde performance artists, and virtually any issue will furnish the researcher with a wealth of information. Typical articles are "Paul McCarthy: A Penis Painting Appreciated: American Hotel, October 1, 1980," on recent work by McCarthy, with a retrospective look at his 1973 event, during which he publicly painted the windshield of a Volkswagen with his penis; Linda Burnham's follow-up article, "Paul McCarthy: The Evolution of a Performance Artist," published five years later; and Lewis Macadams' ". . . It Started Out with Death . . . ," on Boston performance artist Alex Grey, whose nude performances can be distinguished, the author believes, from the public disrobings of less serious artists.

One notable facet of explicit performance art is the degree to which women have claimed it as an endeavor. Amelia Jones' *Body Art: Performing the Subject*, which is especially trenchant on the work of Hannah Wilke, makes clear this trend. Explicit body art/performance adopts the classic posture of pornography, which historically has been to subvert established conventions, values, and tastes. Although not particularly concerned with erotic manifestations of the female body, Elizabeth Bell's "Performance Studies as Women's Work: Historical Sights/Sites/Citations from the Margin" maintains that performance has become central for women's studies, a thesis that appears plausible in view of the swelling literature on the subject. Both heterosexual and lesbian women, moreover, seem more prolific, explicit, and public than male performance artists.

Even so, women are feeling their way along, rejecting or reappropriating male images and creating their own, so that female performance art is still very much in transition, says Catherine Elwes in "Floating Femininity: A Look at Performance Art by Women." Ann Daly is typical of many feminist critics who question whether women performance artists may be falling victim to the sexist syndromes they attempt to deconstruct by appearing nude or in explicit postures in "Are Women Reclaiming or Reinforcing Sexist Imagery?" The other side of this argument is that the violation of taboo undermines dominant ideologies, a function as old as pornography itself, or so argues Jon Erickson in "Appropriation and Transgression in Contemporary American Performance: The Wooster Group, Holly Hughes, and Karen Finley." The drama critic C. Carr agrees. "Watch a taboo break, and it speaks to the taboo events of your own life" (25), she says in *On Edge: Performance at the End of the Twentieth Century*. Carr is very knowledgeable about the East Village (New York City) scene of the 1980s, but also about the influence of AIDS on performance art, the controversy over federal funding by the NEA, the Cincinnati trial of the museum director who mounted the Mapplethorpe show, and the artistry of Linda Montano and David Wojnarowicz, and astute as well on sex roles, racism, and violence in art.

Lucy R. Lippard analyzes the ways in which artists ranging from Carolee Schneemann to Hannah Wilke seize a vulgar form, deconstruct it, and reconstruct it as a new form of discourse in "The Pains and Pleasures of Rebirth: European and American Women's Body Art." Lippard thinks that performance media cleave along gender and sexual fault lines, noting that men treat women's bodies as objects, where women see them as "process." If largely semantic, the distinction seems an honest attempt to discriminate. The heavily illustrated *More than Meat Joy: Complete Performance Works and Selected Writings*, by Carolee Schneemann, records her reprise of a notorious work, *Meat Joy*, as well as *Interior Scroll* (1975), in which the nude artist reads from a long tape slowly tugged from her vagina. Grace Glueck offers a very astute assessment of a Schneemann retrospective at the New Museum of Contemporary Art (New York City) in 1996 in "Of a Woman's Body as Both Subject and Object." Moira Roth's *The Amazing Decade: Women and Performance Art in America, 1970–1980* is an especially important collection of essays on women's experiments with sexual shock and includes excerpts from many scripts, including Carolee Schneemann's "Interior Scroll," (1975), Womanhouse of Los Angeles Collective's performance of Judy Chicago's "Cock and Cunt" (1972), Suzanne Lacy's "Three Weeks in May" (1977), and Hannah Wilkes's "Starification Object Series (S.O.S.)" (1975). Just as useful are the interviews and personal accounts of sixteen performance artists (Acker, Bright, Coleman, Export, Finley, Galás, hooks, Hughes, Lunch, Kerr and Malley, Montano, Ronell, Sapphire, Schneemann, Sprinkle) collected by V. Vale and Andrea Juno as *Angry Women*. The artists discuss their art, which may devolve upon masturbation, S/M, menstruation, violence, and a host of other topics; it is the best single source on explicit performance by contemporary women artists, with extensive bibliographies for each woman.

The body language of contemporary performance is a vibrant alternative to the bloodless discourse of textual scholarship, though both aim at the aesthetic and cultural deconstruction of gender and sexuality. For example, *High Performance* said of Annie Sprinkle's *Bosom Ballet*, a performance piece in which the actress bounces her breasts rhythmically, "Showing her tits spills over the limits of sexiness and exaggerates by analogy our exaggerated interest in seeing or having large breasts, until humor overtakes self-consciousness" (quoted in Sprinkle's *Post Porn Modernist*, 67). That performance can expose the limitations of traditional textuality is the conclusion of Cindy Lutenbacher's "Theater X's *A History of Sexuality*," which reports on a Minneapolis theater group trying to dramatize Foucault's work and thereby to establish a new sexual discourse; the effect, she says, is leaden. In "Graphing Porn," Michael Feingold reviews *The History of Pornography* (Ohio Theater, New York City) and another ambitious attempt to stage *Excerpts from the Attorney General's Report on Pornography* (Hard Place Theater, New York City); he decides that didacticism causes both efforts to fail. In a similar review, "Porn Again: Bringing the Attorney General's Report to the Stage," Norine Dworkin suggests that the results of the attempt to deconstruct the text of the report onstage are mixed. Boredom is the real enemy, since the cast reads the entire list of 2,325 pornographic magazines compiled by the commission as its only original research. Besides, she says, the tongue does not exactly glide across titles like *A Cock between Friends*, and cast members have trouble keeping straight faces. Writing about a government-staged event in "Being There: Performance as Mise-en-Scène, Abscene, Obscene, and Other Scene," Kimberly W. Benston compares and contrasts the Clarence Thomas–Anita Hill hearings with Amiri Baraka's *Slave Ship*, both of which she sees as powerful performances of identity.

Lenora Champagne, Ellie Covan, Diane Torr, Robbie McCauley, Arlene Raven, Rachel Rosenthal, Martha Wilson, Carolee Schneemann, Laurie Anderson, Holly Hughes, Diamanda Galás, and many others voice their intentions in Maria Beatty's videotape, *Sphinxes without Secrets: Women Performance Artists Speak Out*. Extended clips of performances by Rosenthal, Hughes, Galás, and McCauley make clear that feminist performance art attempts to undermine cultural phobias about women's bodies; to combat racism, sexism, and homophobia; to break the male gaze by returning control of women's bodies to themselves; and to subvert convention generally. According to the artists, women have dominated the form because it is flexible, unprofitable, and unconstrained by males, whose erotic fantasies do not have to be satisfied by performers. As Hughes puts it, such performances permit women to "excavate themselves." Splendid photos of occasionally explicit performances by Karen Finley, Diamanda Galás, Holly Hughes, Penny Arcade, and others make up Dona Ann

McAdams' *Caught in the Act: A Look at Contemporary Multimedia Performance*, which features a fine Introduction by C. Carr.

Elinor Fuchs discusses female performers ranging from Carolee Schneemann to Elisabeth LeCompte, Kathy Acker, Karen Finley, and Annie Sprinkle, all of whom confront audiences with explicit nudity and/or sexuality by way of exploring the nature of sex, gender, eroticism, and obscenity in "On Staging the Obscene Body." Fuchs thinks that the transgression inherent in such performance has consequences for personal and social consciousness and may in the future bridge ruptures between women with very different views of sexuality. "Interrogating the Boundaries of Women's Art: New Work in Video by Four Women," by Liz Kotz, covers work by Leslie Singer, Azian Nurudin, Cecilia Doughtery, and Valerie Soe, some of whom use nudity and sexual imagery in performance. Critics of feminist performance art often single out Karen Finley for the fertility of her imagination and the explicitness of her images. Finley has startled audiences with a succession of works such as the wonderfully comic *I Like the Dwarf on the Table When I Give Him Head* (1983). Lynda Hart's "Karen Finley's Dirty Work: Censorship, Homophobia, and the NEA" finds that the shocking nature of Finley's stuffing yams between her buttocks or exposing her genitals evokes anxieties in audiences and an urge to suppress in politicians.

In "Belly Laughs and Naked Rage: Resisting Humor in Karen Finley's Performance Art," Maria Pramaggiore interprets Finley's ambivalent humor and unprovocative nudity in *The Constant State of Desire*. Lenora Champagne folds in her own interpretive commentary with texts of performances by Holly Hunter, Karen Finley, Laurie Anderson, and others in *Out from Under: Texts by Women Performance Artists*. *TDR* has printed the text of Finley's "The Constant State of Desire," which offers the scholar the chance to study the performance as written discourse. In a retrospective on Finley's career, Michael Brenson reviews the artist's installation at Franklin Furnace in "Effects of Men's Desires on the Lives of Women." Responding to comment that a performance offended critics of the National Endowment for the Arts, which provided some support, Finley tells Brenson: " 'My work is against violence, against rape and degradation of women, incest and homophobia.' 'When I smear chocolate on my body it is a symbol of women being treated like dirt.' " Finley opposes obscenity and pornography by utilizing what other people consider obscenity and pornography, a comprehensible paradox given the host of ambivalences that roil culture. It is also the central paradox of pornography itself: outrageous expression can simultaneously offend and educate, arouse and disgust, degrade and exalt.

Home Box Office's cable production, *Real Sex: Wild Cards*, interviews numerous stripper/performance artists such as Annie Sprinkle and Lily Burana and includes footage of their acts. In one of the sequences, Burana observes that "the sex industry is the real source of funding for the [performing] arts, not the NEA." Like strippers and formally trained dramatists, actresses in pornographic films have graduated into performance art as a way of validating their experiences and of expressing a female sexuality free of the conventions of male-oriented cinema. Later, Burana changes her mind. In "The Old Bump and Grind: Can Stripping Support the Arts?" Burana says that government cuts in support for the arts have been so deep that stripping cannot furnish enough to offset them. Worse, given the moral climate of the nation, stripping burns out performers too quickly and provides only the most clichéd reflections on the body. Even so, says Angela Tribelly in "Burlesque Is Back, a Step Ahead of the Law," the art of erotic dancing is endlessly adaptable. To defy Mayor Giuliani's crackdown on strip clubs, she says, club owners have reduced nudity in order to represent dancing as performance art, a ploy that recalls strategies of promoters during LaGuardia's similar efforts at censorship in the 1930s and a reminder that ingenuity can still triumph.

Since most porn stars consider themselves performers, not prostitutes, moving across genre boundaries seems both natural and fulfilling. Arlene Raven's "Looking beneath the Surface: Deep inside Porn Stars," while a largely disapproving review of the *Deep inside Porn Stars* performance at New York's Franklin Furnace in 1984, includes interviews with principal performers Annie Sprinkle and Veronica Vera and represents a genuine desire to understand what Sprinkle and the others are trying to do. The porn director Candida Royalle staged *Deep inside Porn Stars* (1984) as a theatrical version of a policy meeting she organized for women porn performers, who spoke at length of their emotional and intellectual responses to their profession, their roles in the industry, and the benefits and penalties of sexual representation. Linda Montano's "Summer Saint Camp 1987, with Annie Sprinkle and Veronica Vera," an account of a sort of feminist-porn workshop conducted in Kingston, New York, includes a story by Vera and a "scrapbook" by Sprinkle; the two refer to themselves as "Sex National Treasures" and as "feminist/activist porn stars." Sprinkle's "Performance Hits: Bosom Ballet Folklorica, How to Be a Sex Object, and a Public Cervix Announcement" were staged at Dominique's Harmony Burlesk Theater in New York (June 1989) and in other venues. Sprinkle's autobiography, *Post Porn Modernist*, recaps her experiences as porn star, editor of the zine *Piss Art*, Rip Off Press comix character, and Neikrug Gallery photographer.

The protean Sprinkle, whose experience—which seemingly includes intercourse with the widest possible sampling of humans and objects—invests her with enormous authority, asserts that "almost *all* the top women performance artists today have at one time worked in commercial sex" (47) and believes that pornographic genres beyond question profoundly influence culture today. Numerous critics have observed that because Sprinkle uses her body as an instrument (she invites members of the audience to inspect her vagina), she is a performance artist of great credibility and that in a sense she illustrates the pertinence of Lawrence Durrell's remark that "nymphomania is a form of virginity"; she is cheerful, ebullient, and warm, as if she had remained entirely untouched by sexual experiences that many Americans think of as degrading. Sprinkle recalls her participation in the 1984 Prometheus Project staged in the Performance Garage by Richard Schechner, as a dominatrix in New York's Hell-

Fire Club, and her acts in various other locations. Steven Chapple and David Talbot interview Sprinkle for *Burning Desires: Sex in America—A Report from the Field* and find her fascinating, irrepressible, articulate, and witty. In yet another "Interview with Annie Sprinkle," she tells David Aaron Clark: "Actually I see Woman [*sic*] against Pornography as kind of sex workers in themselves. They're as much a part of the porn world as porn themselves, because they're always busy with it. Their whole lives are based around porn. So is mine. I don't see that it's that different" (124–125). She says that she might even enjoy sex with Andrea Dworkin.

In "A Provoking Agent: The Pornography and Performance Art of Annie Sprinkle," Linda Williams says: "Defenders of performance art have . . . often found it necessary to distinguish this art from pornography. While I agree that this art is not pornography, I am suspicious of attempts to draw the line too vigorously between performance art on the one hand and pornography on the other" (176). Henry M. Sayre makes a similar point in his comment on Annie Sprinkle's "A Hundred Blow Jobs" in "Scars: Painting, Photography, Performance, Pornography, and the Disfigurement of Art." In performance, he says, what "*looks* like pornography" often isn't (72). Chris Straayer details the ways in which Sprinkle deconstructs pornography in "The Seduction of Boundaries: Feminist Fluidity in Annie Sprinkle's Art/Education/Sex" as part of her cultural comment on American eroticism, though the article is really an argument as to whether women can actually ejaculate. Sprinkle speaks at length of her performance art in *Angry Women*, edited by V. Vale and Andrea Juno, as do a number of others represented in that volume. Don Vaughan's "From Reel to Real: A Conversation with Annie Sprinkle" recounts her many-faceted career as porn star and performance artist and her latest ventures into publishing books, postcards, and games.

In "Ejaculatory Television: The Talk Show and the Postmodern Subject," Shannon Bell, who studies stripping, discusses her participation on *The Shirley Show*, a Canadian talk show modeled on American versions, in a session devoted to "Women Making Pornography for Women." Bell admires women performers who "since the mid-'80s have been critiquing the pornography, prostitution, and stripping industries and have also been producing works that examine sexualities (Gwendolyn in Toronto, Annie Sprinkle in New York, Scarlot Harlot in San Francisco)" (9). The performance artist Scarlot Harlot (Carol Leigh) has scattered autobiographical musings throughout *Sex Work: Writings by Women in the Sex Industry*, edited by Frédérique Delacoste and Priscilla Alexander. Some of the performers find that their avant-garde positions are lonely. In "Stop the Sexual Revolution: I Want to Get Off," Lily Burana claims that she wants the rest of the world to catch up with her, because she can't find partners as sophisticated as herself. Lisa Palac's interview with another major performer, "Viva La Pussy: Love, Sex, and Being Female with Ann Magnuson," allows for self-irony on the part of the recording artist (*Power of Pussy*), movie star (*The Hunger*), and multimedia performer. In her history of feminist foregroundings of the body, *The Explicit Body in Performance*, a revision of a dissertation entitled "The Explicit Body in Feminist Performance, 1963–1993," Rebecca Schneider examines the collision of symbolic and literal meanings of the body in the work of such notables as Schneemann, Sprinkle, Finley, and Magnuson.

GAY AND LESBIAN THEATER AND PERFORMANCE

Performance theory has profoundly reshaped the presentation of gender on the stage. Plays with homosexual themes or characters almost always encountered official repression in America, since the subject matter was by definition obscene or pornographic. The most comprehensive history is Carl Miller's *Stages of Desire: Gay Theatre's Hidden History*; it deals chiefly with the English stage from the fourteenth century to the nineteenth century. More focused on the numerous arrests and prosecutions of the 1920s and 1930s in the United States is Kaier Curtin's *"We Can Always Call Them Bulgarians": The Emergence of Lesbians and Gay Men on the American Stage;* the notes are rich in contemporary source citations. Donald Lee Loeffler's *An Analysis of the Treatment of the Homosexual Character in Dramas Produced in the New York Theatre from 1950 to 1968* complements Curtin's study. The "Sex and Performance" issue of *TDR* contains Terry Helbing's "Gay Plays, Gay Theatre, Gay Performance" and Emily L. Sisley's "Notes on Lesbian Theatre," both of which highlight gender issues and trace cultural consequences. John M. Clum's *Acting Gay: Male Homosexuality in Modern Drama* offers close readings of major works of English and American gay male drama. A solid Introduction by William Hoffman to his edition of *Gay Plays: The First Collection* provides a brief history and cultural critique. Otis Stuart's "No Tongues, Please—We're Queer: The Same-Sex Kiss on the New York Stage" is a history of the same-sex kiss on the stage, always disturbing to audiences but particularly so, Stuart argues, in an age of AIDS. Don Paulson's fascinating *An Evening at the Garden of Allah: A Gay Cabaret in Seattle*, written with Roger Simpson, focuses on gender enactments at a nightclub in the Northwest.

Wayne Kostenbaum analyzes the fascination opera holds for gays, who apparently respond erotically to its power and glamour in *The Queen's Throat: Opera, Homosexuality, and the Mystery of Desire*, a text whose insights can be applied to mainstream and marginal drama as well. Corinne Blackmer and Patricia J. Smith carry Kostenbaum's ideas in different directions. Their *En Travesti: Women, Gender, Subversion, Opera* argues that opera empowers women and undermines heterosexual hierarchies. Pornographic representations—or representations called pornographic—have moved to centrality in the politics of identity. Here issues of biological sex, gender, sexual orientation, and what is sometimes called the presentation of self find fertile ground. To conventional rosters of identities can be added transsexuals, bisexuals, butches and femmes, and devotees of sadomasochism. The overriding question, the rationale for experimentation, is this, Are identities to be defined by biological and social categories, or are they to be defined by what people *do* and the relationships they form? Susan Rubin Suleiman traces the impact of avant-garde sensibilities on literature, art, and performance in *Subversive Intent: Gender, Politics, and the Avant-Garde*. Peggy Phelan also deconstructs performance as political statement as theater grapples with gender and sexual issues in *Unmarked: The Politics of Performance*. Like Suleiman, Phelan ranges across media and is especially good on the representations of Mapplethorpe, Schor, and Sherman. Close readings of pornographic images and performances uncover the fluidity of categories ordinarily used to marginalize people.

Teresa de Lauretis' "Sexual Indifference and Lesbian Representation" advances proposals for building lesbian theater. De Lauretis insists that lesbian performance must attempt to differentiate itself from male models of dramatic presentation. Representation of the lesbian is "still unwittingly caught in the paradox of socio-sexual (in)difference . . . (homo)sexuality being in the last instance what can not be seen" (177). She amplifies this theme in *The Practice of Love: Lesbian Sexuality and Perverse Desire*. "Lesbian theatre, like the lesbian experience, is very much a case of hide-and-seek," says Nina Rapi in "Hide and Seek: The Search for a Lesbian Theatre Aesthetic." "What you hide is that which still 'dare not speak its name' and what you seek is that which affirms your existence" (147). Performance, in short, assists lesbians in inventing niches and identities. It does so, says Sue-Ellen Case, through masquerade. In a now-famous essay, "Towards a Butch-Femme Aesthetic," Case singles out elements of parody in lesbian experience and speaks of butch-femme roles as one type of masquerade among many. Among other works to study lesbianism as performance, two are notable. Elaine Creith's *Undressing Lesbian Sex: Popular Images, Private Acts and Public Consequences* has uncommon breadth, discriminating carefully between private and public sensibilities. Rosa Ainley interviews scores of lesbians on topics ranging from fashion to behavior, noting a tendency of lesbians to merge into nontransgressive roles, for *What Is She Like? Lesbian Identities from 1950s to 1990s*.

While Jill Dolan agrees that much pornography is hostile to women in "The Dynamics of Desire: Sexuality and Gender in Pornography and Performance," she says that even performance genres that might be considered male-oriented can be liberating when appropriated by lesbian performers. In "Desire Cloaked in a Trenchcoat," Dolan dissects explicit gender representation onstage, explores the different reactions by men and women, but centers on what she calls "lesbian spectatorship" as evoked by *Dress Suits to Hire*, by Holly Hughes, Peggy Shaw, and Lois Weaver. Dolan elaborates on these and other observations in her *Presence and Desire: Essays on Gender, Sexuality, Performance*. Kate Davy's "Reading Past the Heterosexual Imperative: *Dress Suits to Hire*" justifies the pornographic scenes in that lesbian performance work. Rebecca Schneider's interview with the artist in "Holly Hughes: Polymorphous Perversity and the Lesbian Scientist" casts light on Hughes' intent. Useful also are several anthologies. *Making a Spectacle: Feminist Essays on Contemporary Women's Theatre*, edited by Lynda Hart, and *Acting Out: Feminist Performances*, edited by Hart and Peggy Phelan, contain essays on lesbian theater, Finley, Hughes, and other performers. The essays in *Performing Feminisms*, edited by Sue-Ellen Case, and *Cruising the Performative: Interventions into the Representation of Ethnicity, Nationality, and Sexuality*, edited by Case, Philip Brett, and Susan Leigh Foster, are also generally helpful. Those in the latter volume deal with subjects such as transvestism, Michael Jackson's penis, John Rechy's explorations of gay undergrounds, and other sprightly topics. Rosemary K. Curb has gathered plays by Jane Chambers, Janis Astor Del Valle, Gloria Dickler, Maria Irene Fornes, Carolyn Gage and Sue Carney, Shirlene Holmes, Joan Lipkin, Susan Miller, Patricia Montley, Canyon Sam, Joan Schenkar, Megan Terry, and Paula Vogel for *Amazon All Stars: Thirteen Lesbian Plays*. Very up-to-date is *Acts of Passion: Sexuality, Gender, and Performance*, edited by Nina Rapi and Maya Chowdry, who have included performance texts, performance experiences, and remarks by directors, performers, theorists, playwrights, and authors of lesbian works.

EROTIC DANCE

Nude dancing as entertainment in the United States was long associated with burlesque, whose raucous comedy nurtured what eventually came to be known as striptease. The most analytical study of burlesque is Robert Allen's *Horrible Prettiness: Burlesque and American Culture*, whose title indicates a degree of academic disdain for the subject, not to mention over-the-top academic theory. In addition to providing an excellent historical survey of burlesque until the 1930s, Allen covers posters, magazines, and stereographs on burlesque, includes a fine discussion of "cooch" dancing, and appends a splendid bibliography of sources and collections. In some respects, burlesque would seem the classic example of sexual expression as it spirals toward the center of a culture's regard, having produced a generation of Bert Lahrs, Red Buttonses, Ann Corios, and Fanny Brices who transformed theaters, nightclubs, and film. Irving Zeidman's *The American Burlesque Show*, excellent on this sort of cultural context, is also important for its caution. Zeidman observes that "burlesque, unfortunately, has never been any of the fancy or sentimental things ascribed to it—neither now nor then. It has never been a lusty form of folk expression or a national forum for satire or a showcase for knockabout hilarious slapstick. If burlesque ever became too talented, it ceased to be burlesque. It became vaudeville or musical comedy and even, as in the case of E. E. Rice extravaganzas of the [eighteen] eighties, light opera" (43).

The quarterly *Cavalcade of Burlesque*, published between 1951 and 1955, furnishes an incomparable historical record; Introductions by comedians like Jack E. Leonard and Joey Bishop and photos of notable ecdysiasts supplement often solid essays and scripts of famous routines. Valuable also, though rare, are programs like *The Streets of Paris*, a souvenir booklet from the "girlie show" at the International Exposition of 1933 in Chicago. Bernard Sobel's *Burleycue: An Underground History of Burlesque Days* suggests that the genre reached its heyday in the early 1930s, though H. M. Alexander's *Strip Tease: The Vanished Art of Burlesque*, published near the end of that decade, maintained that authentic dancing had already disappeared. Sobel's later *A Pictorial History of Burlesque* offers a more recent perspective on the evolution and demise of burlesque, with particular reference to striptease queens. The coverage in Richard Wortley's *A Pictorial History of Striptease: 100 Years of Undressing to Music* is more international than American.

Three European histories with pretentious titles are nonetheless valuable because the traditions they cover contrast sharply with the evolution of American striptease, which serves as a running parallel in each text. François des Aulnoyes' *Histoire et philosophie du strip-tease: Essai sur L'erotisme au music hall* argues that striptease developed from the imagery of classical art; Denys Chevalier's *Metaphysique du striptease* concentrates on the aesthetic basis of voyeurism; Jean Charvill's *Histoire et sociologie du strip-tease* offers fairly standard sociological analysis. All are illustrated, but the pictures are supported by learned pages on subjects such as the inspiration that led to the adaptation of a retrotechnology like the bicycle clip—an open-ended band of coiled metal fitted around a trouser leg to prevent cloth from snagging in the bike's sprocket chain—to the need to mask the striptease dancer's pubic hair. French designers sewed the coil into a *cache-sexe* that, clamped between the thighs, thrilled audiences, since the cloth triangle appeared to float on the *mons* itself. French interest in this form of eroticism reaches a kind of apotheosis in Roland Barthes' "Striptease," in which the French critic says that "striptease—at least Parisian striptease—is based on a contradiction: Woman is desexualized at the very moment when she is stripped naked. We may therefore say that we are dealing in a sense with a spectacle based on fear, or rather on the pretense of fear as if eroticism here went no further than a sort of delicious terror, whose ritual signs have only to be announced to evoke at once the idea of sex and its conjuration" (84). Redolent of the long-standing French equation of orgasm and death (*le petit morte*), such statements doubtless appeal to contemporary American critical sensibilities even as they affront the enthusiast who simply likes to see an occasional beautiful bare breast. As if to prove that the French have no monopoly on portentous comment, *Revelations: Essays on Striptease and Sexuality*, by Margaret Dragu and A.S.A. Harrison, characterizes striptease in North America as a mature art with strong overtones of social satire and cosmic spirituality; this hard-to-find work deserves more attention.

Richard A. Posner observes in *Sex and Reason*, "The key to understanding the striptease is the ambiguity . . . of nudity as a signal of intentions. For nudity to be an erotic signal, it must be associated with sex, so the norm of privacy in sexual relations entails the rejection of public nudity, and public nudity in turn implies a transgression of sexual norms. There are of course degrees of nudity. The stronger the nudity taboo, in the sense of the more fully clad the body is expected to be, the smaller is the amount of nudity required to imply a sexual context and therefore to convey an erotic signal" (363). So far as trenchant observations on public nudity go, however, it would be difficult to improve on Marshall McLuhan's remark. Taken by friends to a bar where women were dancing nude, the media pundit insisted: "They're *not* naked. They're wearing *us.*"[4] The public gaze envelops and clothes.

Joel Harvey contextualizes striptease as one of the elements of burlesque, discusses the social mores of the 1920s and 1930s, and suggests that striptease helped create a market for other kinds of pornography in *"American Burlesque as Reflected through the Career of Kitty Madison, 1916–1931."* Ann Corio's *This Was Burlesque*, written with Joe DiMona, is the book version of the show that Corio toured until the 1970s; it contains many items of historical interest. Ralph G. Allen also gathered famous blackouts and bawdy routines for his traveling road show *Sugar Babies*, a homage to classic burlesque, and published them as *The Best Burlesque Sketches as Adapted for Sugar Babies and Other Entertainments.* Jill Dolan uncovers an unsurprising sexism in some of these routines in her " 'What, No Beans?': Images of Women and Sexuality in Burlesque Comedy."

Randolph Carter focuses on the pioneer producer/innovator of burlesque revues in *The World of Flo Ziegfeld*, while Marjorie Farnsworth's *The Ziegfeld Follies* concentrates more on staging and performers in the shows. One of the narrative devices in Charles Castle's *The Folies Bergère* is a running comparison between the Parisian *Folies* and Ziegfeld's *Follies*. Castle quotes Ziegfeld as observing of his American imitators: "These orgies of nakedness are disgusting, worse than one can find in the lowest dives of Europe and they make one ashamed of ever having anything to do with revues" (105). Linda Mizejewski's *Ziegfeld Girl: Image and Icon in Culture and Cinema* is a cultural study of the type of performer who appeared in the *Follies*, and as such complements the several memoirs of former showgirls; an example of the latter is Marcelle Earle's *Midnight Frolic: A Ziegfeld Girl's True Story*, written with Arthur Homme, Jr. Jerry Stagg's *The Brothers Shubert* and Morton Minsky and Milt Machlin's *Minsky's Burlesque: A Fast and Funny Look at America's Bawdiest Era* provide readable, accurate accounts of Ziegfeld's principal competitors; the latter appends some famed burlesque skits and routines. Rowland Barber tells the apocryphal story of the "accidental" invention of striptease, when a showgirl's bra strap snapped, and the police descended (all this as late as 1925!) in *The Night They Raided Minsky's.*

Ken Murray's *The Body Merchant: The Story of Earl Carroll* reviews the career of the impresario whose fleshy shows caused sensations in the 1930s and 1940s and includes biographies and photos of celebrated showgirls. Stephen N. Vallillo finds much to praise in the extravaganzas of Earl Carroll and Florenz Ziegfeld in "Broadway Reviews in the Teens and Twenties: Smut and Slime?" The title essay of *Hot Strip Tease and Other Notes on American Culture*, written by Geoffrey Gorer with an English sniff, calls striptease in the United States of the 1930s a dismal business. No discussion of erotic dancing during the early part of the century can omit Josephine Baker, the American who danced across Europe, revitalized nude performance in France, and went on to become a war hero and Parisian legend. Of the many commentaries, three biographies best detail her life and career: Lynn Haney's *Naked at the Feast: A Biography of Josephine Baker* and Phyllis Rose's *Jazz Cleopatra: Josephine Baker In Her Time* put her dancing in context, while Jean-Claude Baker and Chris Chase's *Josephine: The Hungry Heart* draws on the recollections of one of her many adopted children to sketch a warm and courageous personality. Len Rothe's *The Bare Truth: Stars of Burlesque of the 1940s and 1950s*, a slight, but perky, history of performers who redefined burlesque dancing during the period Rothe thinks most important, is replete with anecdotes and reminiscences about the careers of Scarlett O'Hara, Zorita, Lily St. Cyr, Wendee Gayle, Tempest Storm, Pepper Powell, Blaze Fury, and Betty Howard, among others. *The Queens of Burlesque: Vintage Photographs of the 1940s and 1950s*, Rothe's companion volume, furnishes a pictorial record of lavish costumes and charming routines by the performers highlighted in the history. A. W. Stencell devotes a chapter of *Girl Show: Into the Canvas World of Bump and Grind* to Blaze Fury, perhaps the wildest stripper ever to appear on an American stage.

Those interested in autobiographies of stars should begin with Georgia Southern's *Georgia: My Life in Burlesque*, an unapologetic and poignant book by the greatest of all American strippers that should dispel any doubt that she was a brilliant artist; Southern also provides portraits of colleagues such as Hinda Wassau, Georgia's only serious rival to artistic eminence. Autobiographies of other performers include Blaze Starr's *My Life*, a book made into a mainstream film that emphasized her relationship with Louisiana governor Earl Long; Tempest Storm's *The Lady Is a Vamp*, a sanitized narrative loaded with the dropped names of celebrities who posed or slept with her; and Gypsy Rose Lee's *Gypsy*, whose career also spawned a musical and movie. The talents of all three were formidable, and it is not hyperbolic to call them (and Southern) *beloved* by American audiences. Additional information on Lee is available in Erik Lee Preminger's memoir of his mother, *Gypsy and Me: At Home and on the Road with Gypsy Rose Lee*, and in the autobiography of Lee's sister, June Havoc, in *More Havoc*. The *Betty Pages Annual*, devoted to the famous pinup model Bettie (the correct spelling) Page, documents Page's brief foray into striptease in the 1950s and includes an extensive, illustrated filmography of Irving Klaw films featuring striptease artists such as Page, Lili St. Cyr, Tempest Storm, Rosita and Her Pigeons, and many lesser-known ecdysiasts.

In "Candy Barr," an interview in *Oui*, the most notorious of American strippers recalls her dancing in Dallas and her friendship with Jack Ruby (owner of the Theater Lounge and killer of Lee Harvey Oswald), as does Gary Cartwright's "Candy: Taking the Wrapper Off a Texas Legend." Cartwright maintains that Barr was set up for the marijuana charge that sent her to prison as a sop to the public morality of a corrupt state. In one of those peculiarly American ironies that attend the infusion of eroticism into the larger culture, Barr's sentence was delayed because Twentieth Century Fox had hired her to teach Joan Collins how to strip for the latter's role in *Seven Thieves* (1959). In her autobiography, *Past Imperfect*, Collins recalls that this "down to earth girl with an incredibly gorgeous body and an angelic face . . . taught me more about sensuality than I had learned in all my years under contract." Collins echoed her bosses' judgment that Barr was "the best stripper in America" (160–161). Annie Ample's *The Bare Facts: My Life as a Stripper* and Yvette Paris' *Queen of Burlesque: The Autobiography of Yvette Paris* recount the experiences of more recent *artistes* working in classic traditions. Liz Renay's *My First 2,000 Men*, a memoir by the former actress and model, also covers her years as a stripper.

Lauri Lewin's *Naked Is the Best Disguise: My Life as a Stripper* is reflective and rewarding in its personal, social, and cultural analysis of the profession; her book covers her five years, not all of them pleasant, in clubs in Boston's Combat Zone. Roswell Angier's *". . . A Kind of Life": Conversations in the Combat Zone*, a series of interviews with sex workers in Boston's adult district, presents an unflattering and realistic view of the striptease profession. Mary Wagner's "Donna from 'Live Show,' " an unromanticized interview with a stripper, is also a grim portrait. Marilyn Salutin's "Stripper Morality" examines the economic and social motivations of professionals, as does Chi Chi Valenti's "Steamed Clams." In "The Choice of Stripping for a Living: An Empirical and Theoretical Explanation," Jacqueline M. Boles and Albeno O. Gabrin find that multiple motivations, not all of them economic, lead women to this occupation; the conclusion (that exhibitionism, the need for approval, and confidence in one's skill play a role, for instance) will strike many as obvious, but statistical confirmation helps. Interviews conducted by Tim Keefe for *Some of My Best Friends Are Naked: Interviews with Seven Exotic Dancers* provide additional insights into those strippers who reveal their histories, which defy pigeonholing. The stage names of the seven are Minx Manx, Ann More, Lilith, Phoenix, Lusty Lipps, Attila the Honey, and Jackie; they discuss childhoods in broken homes, sexual beliefs, relationships with audiences and club owners, compensation, working conditions, backstage tedium, unpleasant encounters, job satisfaction, the wearing effects of travel, drugs in the industry, talent, beauty, and so on. They talk freely with Keefe, who worked backstage for six years in a San Francisco peep show.

In "Teasing, Flashing and Visual Sex: Stripping for a Living," James K. Skipper Jr. and Charles H. McCaghy examine the interactions of performers and audiences, some of whom, like those males who masturbate in the front row, are as interesting as the women onstage. Skipper and McCaghy have written a series of sociological articles on stripping. "Stripteasers: The Anatomy and Career Contingencies of a Deviant Occupation" covers the class origins and economic background of strippers. "Stripteasing: A Sex-Oriented Occupation" looks at idiosyncrasies of different performers in a culture that rewards exhibitionism. McCaghy and Skipper (note order of authors) theorize that the relatively high incidence of lesbianism among strippers stems from a narcissism that encourages bodily display and that may actually lead certain types of personalities into the stripping subculture in "Lesbian Behavior as an Adaptation to the Occupation of Stripping."

Sociologists frequently patronize strippers by assuming that the profession is deviant, that all strippers were abused as children, and that all are animated by the need for male approval, but some probe more deeply. Better than most is Jacqueline Boles' dissertation, "The Nightclub Stripper: A Sociological Study of a Deviant Occupation," which provided data for the Boles and Gabrin article cited earlier. Other dissertations of merit are Rona Hildy Halpern's "Female Occupational Exhibitionism: An Exploratory Study of Topless and Bottomless Dancers," which examines the psychology of performers; Michael D. Angioli's "Body Image Perception and Locus of Control in Semi-Nude and Nude Female Dancers," which suggests that dancers employ physical grace to control audiences; and Dean J. M. Mooney's "Shame, Body Image and Locus of Control in Male and Female Exotic Dancers," which is notable because it deals with psychological syndromes of sexual authority in both male and female performers. The common view of stripping is that the stripper is exploited, at the mercy of club owners, the male gaze, and patriarchal society at large. Implicit in some of these essays is what may be the most startling truth of all: that striptease venues demonstrate, above all, that the males in the audience *lack* any kind of significant power (or they would not be there in the first place). Strip clubs may actually function in a Marcusian sense: making sexuality public renders it affectless, nonphysical, and sanitized to the point of capitalist spirituality. Academics are drawn to striptease because performances enact gender: performers perform *for each other* as much as for patrons, for instance, while males in the audience perform their gender roles of macho protectors, fatherly patriarchs, and romantic swains *for each other* as well as for the dancers. Katherine H. Liepe-Levinson's "*A Striptease Poetics*" investigates the ways in which female and male striptease upholds and transgresses gender roles and the status quo. Liepe-Levinson bases her study on visits to sixty clubs in seven major cities and finds that sexual pleasure, body shapes and styles, and gender stratification are not nearly so inflexible as folklore would lead us to believe.

The stripper/porn actress Seph Weene acknowledges that she exploits the power over men that performing naked gives her in "Venus." Amber Cooke, an articulate dancer, is impatient with ideologies and says she refuses to be stereotyped by feminists or anyone else in Laurie Bell's "Sex Trade Workers and Feminists: Myths and Illusions, an Interview with Amber Cooke." The volume in which that interview appears, *Good Girls/Bad Girls: Feminists and Sex Trade Workers Face to Face*, edited by Bell, offers many insights into explicit dancers, as does *Sex Work: Writings by Women in the Sex Industry*, edited by Frédérique Delacoste and Priscilla Alexander. Notable chapters in the latter volume are "Good Girls Go to Heaven, Bad Girls Go Everywhere" (131–134), by "Aline," a former topless dancer who had fun at the time and has no bad memories, and

"Stripper" (175–180), by Debi Sundahl, a dancer (and publisher and filmmaker) who says that performing at the Lusty Lady Theater in Seattle and the O'Farrell in San Francisco enriched her life. Erika Langley's *The Lusty Lady: Photographs and Texts* documents daily routines at the Lusty Lady, a Seattle peep show run entirely by women. HBO's "Through the Looking Glass" also covers the Lusty Lady arcade by interviewing its female managers and performers.

Two other surveys of women in sex industries are informative, though both concentrate on subjects in Great Britain: Nickie Roberts, herself a former stripper, collects stories of strippers, porn stars, and prostitutes in *The Front Line: Women in the Sex Industry Speak*, as does Rachel Silver in *The Girl in Scarlet Heels: Women in the Sex Business Speak Out*. The Silver volume is remarkable because most of the subjects she interviewed suggest that their careers provide a high degree of autonomy, allow them to feel liberated, and give them self-respect along with pleasure. Silver is nonetheless careful to include those who feel victimized and exploited, objectified and degraded, even abused. The San Francisco O'Farrell Theater, notorious for graphic acts (dancers penetrated themselves with dildos or engaged in intercourse onstage) in the 1970s and 1980s, figures prominently in David McCumber's study of its owners in *X-Rated: The Mitchell Brothers, a True Story of Sex, Money, and Death* and in John Hubner's more analytic *Bottom Feeders: From Free Love to Hard Core—The Rise and Fall of Counterculture Heroes Jim and Artie Mitchell*. Both biographers talk to some of the performers. Even more gritty are the investigations by Sylvia Plachy and James Ridgeway published as *Red Light: Inside the Sex Industry*. They interview performers in different sectors and classes of the industry, mostly in New York and New Jersey.

Stripped Bare: A Look at Erotic Dancers (1989), a video profile by Caitlin Manning and Glen Foster, bases discussion of eroticism, sexuality, and exploitation on footage of San Francisco nude dancers. Another feminist documentary about strippers at the Market Street Cinema in San Francisco is Petra Mueller and Elizabeth Dewey's *Live Girls Nude* (1989). Liz Kotz refers to both films in her "Striptease East and West: Sexual Representation in Documentary Film," a comparison of Eastern (India) striptease with American. The popularity of lesbian burlesque, or rather, lesbians stripping for lesbian audiences, is manifest in *BurLEZk Live* (1989) and *BurLEZk II* (1990), two videotapes shot on location in lesbian bars from Fatale Video/Blush Entertainment. Videotapes of vintage stripteasers, ranging from burlesque headliners to the uncelebrated, are available from many video companies as nostalgia items. Chief among collections is the three-reel *Grindhouse Follies*, compiled by Mike Varney, who juxtaposes old-style burlesque routines with footage of headliners.

"Topless," a *Playboy* survey of the topless phenomenon that began in 1964, covers bars and restaurants staffed by bare-breasted waitresses as they interact with patrons. Eric Kroll's *Sex Objects* finds varied perspectives on clients and customers in interviews with strippers, massage parlor employees, and other sex workers. It is much superior to Bob Hoddeson's also-dated *The Porn People:*

A First-Person Documentary Report, which seems overly fascinated with "open-crotch" strippers, those who invite close inspection of the genitals; their responses are framed in the clichés of the mid-1970s. More recent and more substantial is Terry J. Prewitt's "Like a Virgin: The Semiotics of Illusion in Erotic Performance"; in addition to annotating a (not entirely persuasive) "grammar" of strip performances (topless, table dancing, lap dancing), he finds that the relationship between stripper and customers essentially asserts family values, and he draws parallels between strippers and music videos by Cyndi Lauper and Madonna. Dan Barry talks with Milton Anthony, owner of Billy's Topless, the most venerable strip bar in New York City, forced by new draconian zoning laws in Manhattan to costume its nude dancers, in "Under Siege, a Topless Bar Will Cover Up." The memory banks of Anthony, the last remaining Manhattan impresario, are archives begging for an oral historian. Very much worth reading are the several essays on stripping in "Striptease," a special issue of *TDR* devoted to erotic performance theory.

Lap dancing is a recent "up close and personal" version of striptease in which for a fee the nude dancer sits on the lap of the clothed consumer. The performance is a kind of game, because the patron is generally not permitted to fondle while the dancer writhes lasciviously in an effort to bring him to orgasm in the midst of the crowded room. According to Tuppy Owens, whose *The (Safer) Sex Maniac's Bible: A World Review of Sexuality, Listings of Erotic Clubs in all Major Cities, and Fun and Games for Your Delectation* lists major strip palaces, lap dancing originated at the O'Farrell Theatre in San Francisco (sec. 13, n.p.). Not so, says Al Goldstein in "Lap Dancing": the practice originated when "burlesque collided with dime-a-dance—when a g-string was run over by a taxi" (64); he interviews several New York lap dancers. In "Couch Dancing," another term for the practice, Keith McWalter confesses to guilt at paying a gorgeous woman to gyrate naked in his lap. In assessing the popularity of such encounters, McWalter fears that American males cannot respond to "real" women, that is, the warts-and-all type, because they are overwhelmed by plastic images of beauty as manifest in airbrushed centerfolds and silicon-enhanced dancers. Vinita Srivastava visits lap dancing night for women at New York's Silverado in "Women Lap It Up." Here female dancers perform for other women, who *are* allowed to touch the performers.

A good antidote to the many heavy-handed ethnographic studies and sociological analyses of strippers and audiences is "The American Male: The Naked Truth," a charming essay on topless bars by James Truman, who maintains that one reason men enjoy them is that there they can be ravished by the beauty of breasts, a response admittedly complex but primarily aesthetic. Also in this category is "Reporter Tries Burlesque: I'll Cry Tomorrow but I'll Strip Tonight," in which the journalist Victoria Hodgetts herself tries stripping at the Ivar Theatre in Los Angeles and learns to see beyond her moralizing, concluding that psychological, aesthetic, and cultural needs drive both performers and audiences toward erotic dramaturgy. One of the more interesting phenomena of recent years is the transformation of strippers into genuine performance artists. Catherine Saalfield, in her review of Divianna Ingravallo's *Gone Bad*, an explicit show, notes that the lesbian performance artist is also a burlesque stripper; the review is entitled "Performance Gone Good." Melanie Bush's "Gyneconomy" reports on Manhattan's the Blue Angel, a cabaret owned by Ute Hanna, herself an ex-stripper, who provides a comfortable environment for the women who dance there. (Manhattan's recent zoning crackdown has closed many clubs.)

(For photojournalistic studies of nude performers, see **Documentary Photographs** in chapter 12, especially Angier, Baronio, Futterman, Gelpke, Goldin, Goude, Kroll [1977], Meiselas, Morey.)

Articles on males stripping for females usually concentrate on audience response, as in a *Time* essay on Chippendale's, "And Now Bring On the Boys"; Rebecca Clark's "Male Strippers: Ladies' Night at the Meat Market," which details stripper rituals and audience participation; and Judith Brackley's "Male Strip Shows," which observes that women enjoy watching such performances because of the illusion of control that the audience pretends to exert over the performers. Best in this category is Judith Liepe-Levinson's "Striptease: Desire, Mimetic Jeopardy, and Performing Spectators," which gives the same weight to male stripping as to female, with intelligent comment on spectatorship and performance. Guy Trebay's "Only Looking: Scenes from a Go-Go Planet" reports on male go-go dancers at the Gaiety and other theaters in Manhattan. In Chapter 4 of *Re-Making Love: The Feminization of Sex*, Barbara Ehrenreich, Elizabeth Hess, and Gloria Jacobs include several pages on Chippendale's, which operates numerous male-stripper franchises for women audiences. Sheila Sobell Moramarco reports appreciatively on her visit to one of those establishments in "Male Strippers." The "Bare and Bold" segment of Home Box Office's *Real Sex: 9* records the views of dancers of the Mr. Nude Universe strip show for women, and "Ladies Night" in *Real Sex: 20* does the same for African American male strippers. Probably the most interesting account, however, can be found in Marianne Macy's *Working Sex: An Odyssey into Our Cultural Underworld*. Macy notes that males dance for women (sometimes on special nights) at some 2,000 American clubs. Macy follows Dianah and Kirk, a stripper couple; she dances for males, he for females. Sylvia Plachy and James Ridgeway visit males who dance for gay and straight audiences and talk as well to women who perform in lesbian clubs in *Red Light: Inside the Sex Industry*, which devotes more pages to strippers than to any other category of workers. (For incomes of strippers, see **Performance** in Chapter 21.)

Heidi Mattson, a Brown University student, has written that her job moonlighting as a stripper at Boston's Foxy Lady is safe, comfortable, profitable, and fun. Mattson's book, *Ivy League Stripper*, has not endeared her to campus feminists. An article by Kathy Healy, "The New Strippers," expresses amazement at the sudden recent popularity of the dance form, which she attributes to the need for voyeurism as a form of "safe sex" in an age of AIDS. "Edge of Night Life," which ran in the *New Yorker*, is a respectful notice of the male burlesque review at the Gaiety Theater in Manhattan's Times Square, as well as of the more conventional female strippers at Goldfinger's farther south. In "The Barest in the Land," HBO reports on the Miss Nude World International dance contest; the winner becomes the highest-paid stripper in the world. Several major Hollywood studios have released films on lap dancing and/or striptease; notable are *Exotica* [Miramax, 1994], *Showgirls* [United Artists, 1995], and *Striptease* [Castle Rock/Columbia Tri-Star, 1996]). A better indicator of the cultural importance of the subject is the sheer number of mainstream American movies set in bars and showrooms, a genre that critic Joe Bob Briggs calls the "titty-bar film."

In a different category is "serious" dance, and here the best overview is Judith Lynne Hanna's *Dance, Sex and Gender: Signs of Identity, Dominance, Defiance, and Desire*, intended as a guide for further study, with rich bibliographic suggestions for the investigation of dance, gender, and eroticism. Perhaps the most authoritative of all texts on the subject, Hanna's investigation of the erotic wellsprings of dance, rhythm, and music will repay any reader. The essays in Helen Thomas' *Dance, Gender and Culture* sometimes trip over their own theory and are not so clearly focused on the sexuality involved. *Democracy's Body: Judson Dance Theater, 1962–1964*, by Sally Banes, chronicles two crucial years when avant-garde performers at New York City's Judson Church experimented with nudity and sexual themes in dance. Banes' even more narrowly focused *Greenwich Village 1963: Avant Garde Performance and the Effervescent Body* documents the vibrant expression of that year, as recalled by one of the most incisive critics of the dance scene in the 1960s. "Dance and Sexual Politics," a special issue of *Dance Theatre Journal*, gathers several important essays on the sexual semiotics of dance, most of which parse body and gender issues. Serious dancers take off their clothes in order to highlight naturalness, beauty, vulnerability, affirmation, and rationality, says Deborah Jowitt in "Getting It Off: Why Dancers Bare All for Art." *Labyrinths: Robert Morris, Minimalism, and the 1960s*, by Maurice Berger, studies an artist who during the 1960s mounted sexually explicit performances often incorporating dance at Judson Church and other sites. Michael Moon's "Flaming Closets" draws parallels between Nijinsky's erotic dances and those depicted in Jack Smith's avant-garde film *Flaming Creatures*. The representation of masculinity in the twentieth century, as constructed by choreographers from Martha Graham to Pina Bausch, is the subject of Ramsey Burt's *The Male Dancer: Bodies, Spectacle and Sexuality;* Burt contrasts an institutionalized dance that privileges heterosexuality and an avant-garde choreography that disrupts gender and hegemony. Finally, *Contact Quarterly* has published a special issue on "Gender and Sexual Identity" in dance. Of the several articles, the most interesting is Paul Langland's interview with gender-bending dancer Diane Tott, who uses grotesqueries to illuminate the intent of her performances.

SEXUALITY IN PUBLIC: EXHIBITIONISM

Scholars have recently focused on the public nudity and lewd behavior sanctioned by seasonal celebrations in major American cities. Samuel Kinser's *Carnival American Style: Mardi Gras at New Orleans and Mobile* brings semiotic, anthropological, and folkloristic perspectives to comparisons of modern, medieval, and Renaissance festivals. Jack Kugelmass' "Wishes Come True: Designing the Greenwich Village Halloween Parade" examines the folkloristic elements of the (largely gay) Halloween celebration in New York, which features nudity, body adornment, tranvestism, sexual exaggeration (e.g., in the form of huge papier-mâché penises), and other forms of exuberant hyperbole. Says Kugelmass, "the expansion of the threshold of the sexual self is intricately connected to expansion of the self in other domains as well, and this manifests itself in all kinds of expressive culture, including religious beliefs and practices" (462). Kugelmass has also published *Masked Culture: The Greenwich Village Hollywood Parade*, a picture book of the parades. Ken Werner's *Halloween* is a photo-study of the San Francisco Halloween celebration in the Castro district, also a mostly gay affair featuring sexually grotesque costumes and behavior. Denise L. Lawrence has written two ethnographic essays on the artists' parade in Pasadena, California, "Parades, Politics, and Competing Urban Images: Doo Dah and Roses" and "Rules of Misrule: Notes on the Doo Dah Parade in Pasadena."

Of the several works in which the influential theorist Mikhail Bakhtin dilates on the "carnivalesque" as a linguistic and performance subversion of social order, his *Rabelais and His World* is perhaps the most pertinent here. Feminist variations on Bakhtin, some related to the body as spectacle (see **Nudity, Fashions, Fetishes, Body Modifications, and Sexual Technologies** in chapter 9), some to freakishness, some to performance, have multiplied. The most interesting is Mary Russo's *The Female Grotesque: Risk, Excess and Modernity*, which links Freud and Bakhtin and ventures into the image of the grotesque in several media, including performance. According to Russo, grotesque female figures can help reconfigure both performance and spectatorship because they counter conventional images of women. In "Frame, Flow and Reflection: Ritual and Drama as Public Liminality," Victor Turner says that "the subversive potential of the carnivalized feminine principle becomes evident in times of social change when its manifestations move out of the liminal world of Mardi Gras into the political world itself" (42). Helpful in this regard are the theoretical essays in *Rite, Drama, Festival, Spectacle: Rehearsals toward a Theory of Cultural Performance*, edited by John J. MacAloon; the contributors consider large-scale public celebrations, some of which involve nudity and explicitness.

These activities may be distinguished from *streaking*, a fad popular in the 1970s, as appreciated by George Pleasant in *The Joy of Streaking: A Guide to America's Favorite Pastime*. The fad generated *The Sensuous Streaker*, a short-lived magazine devoted to running naked in public venues such as football stadiums, awards banquets, and graduations. Carol Queen's *Exhibitionism for the Shy*, an exhortation to take control of one's sexual life, has some amusing pages on semipublic exposure; she suggests that Americans take cues from cultures where women (and men) regard exhibitionism as their birthright. D. Cox and D. Daitzman have edited an authoritative *Exhibitionism*, which covers the many psychological and social aspects of sexual behavior in public; especially helpful is the book's chapter on "Exhibitionism: An Overview." Females who take off their clothes in public may be said to be *performing*, but males who reveal themselves are called *deviant*, presumably because doing so seems a willful undercutting of masculine authority. The medical syndromes are detailed by John M. MacDonald in *Indecent Exposure*, a text on men who expose themselves to unsuspecting women or children as an aberration. Popular specialty items in many video catalogs are cassettes shot in public places. These feature "flashing" by women exposing their breasts, raising their skirts, or removing their panties in crowds; exhibitionistic sex by men and women coupling on beaches, in bars, on park benches, or on the street at Mardi Gras; and staged events such as Wet T-Shirt, Perfect Ass, Tiny Bikini, Nude Skiing, Nude Marathons, and Blowjob contests at spring breaks in coastal resorts, as well as other sexual high jinks in full view of passersby. Voyeur Video is perhaps the best known of such companies. In a separate category are events for which a woman has semipublic intercourse with dozens of men, usually in order to sell novelty videotapes. Until recently, the world champion was porn star Jasmine, whose couplings with 300 men were observed by Anthony Haden-Guest in "World's Biggest Gang Bang II." The current (1999) record-holder for marathons is the performer Houston. Greg Alves directed *The World's Biggest Gang Bang III: The Houston 500* (with the 500 x-ed out and replaced with 620), a videocassette that records Houston's intercourse with 620 men.

ORGIASTIC PERFORMANCE

The most authoritative and accessible book on orgies as performance is Karl Toepfer's *Theatre, Aristocracy, and Pornocracy: The Orgy Calculus*, a fascinating history of orgiastic sex as performance on the clandestine stage. The section called "A Postmodern Example of Orgy" recounts Toepfer's participation in a contemporary performance. Toepfer's text is invaluable for its discussion of sexual performance as a substrate of class values and for its resurrection of Pierre-Joseph Proudhon's obscure manuscript, *La Pornocratie ou les femmes dans les temps modernes* (1858/1859? published 1875), which attributes erotic power to women, speaks of an ideal state he calls "pornocracy," and speculates on the economic relationship between labor and pleasure.

In contrast to the Bakhtinian ideology of carnival, the ideology of orgy, which strives to realize its objectives through secrecy, is consistently the production of an aristocratic impulse, in the sense that desires satisfied through an orgy mark those who feel them as members of a *highly privileged class* of persons. An orgy enhances the difference between one *class* of persons (its participants) and "the rest," those excluded from the performance. Orgy culture is subculture or counter-culture, but not a revolutionary culture which posits orgy as a model for the transformation of social reality. Orgy is possible because orgiasts believe either that social reality needs no major changes or that a utopian intersection of desire and necessity embracing an entire society will not happen soon enough, if ever. But this observation does not mean that orgy lacks a utopian dimension. (13)

Toepfer develops paradoxes of privacy versus public display and the overwhelming of individual bodies through a communal experience of sexuality by a class whose "collective ecstasy is greater than the happiness of any individual or of an entire society" (13).

Bruno Partridge's *A History of Orgies*, a chronicle of texts rather than performances, is readable but too dated to marshal material on American examples and too off the mark to be relevant here. Far more informative are the essays in *Sittengeschichte des Theaters*, volume V of the massive *Sittengeschichte der Kulturwelt und ihrer Entwicklung in Einzeldarstellungen*, edited by Leo Schidrowitz. The volume covers "secret" theatricals only until the turn of the century, and the range is from classic to late European examples, but it is, as always, accurate in its identification of traditions. Sometimes political, more often merely prurient, such performances featured sexual congress between straights and gays, usually of the upper class, for whom the quasi-public theatrical exaggeration was a stimulant. For *Voluptas Ludens: Erotische Geheimtheater, 17. 18. und 19. Jahrhundert*, a history of secret erotic theater in Europe over three centuries, Arthur Maria Rabenalt drew heavily on a rare text, *Les Théâtres clandestins* (Paris: Plessis, 1905), by Gustav Capon and Robert Yve-Plessis, who speak knowledgeably of stage presentations of intercourse during the same period. One section of Richard Wunderer's *Treibhaus der Erotik: Pansexualismus und Orgiasmus in erotischen Wunschträumen und sexueller Wirklichkeit* traces secret European theater. Two works by Peter Gorsen, *Sexualästhetik: zur bürgerlichen Rezeption von Obzönität und Pornographie* and *Sexualästhetik: Grenzformen der Sinnlichkeit im 20. Jahrhundert*, discuss the ways in which the consciousness of sexuality has redefined the artistic sensibilities of the twentieth century. The two books cover sexually explicit performance, including staged intercourse, with some long looks at American performers. Gorsen highlights the "Orgien-Mysterien" Theater of Hermann Nitsch, a German ensemble group devoted to the serious exploration of obscenity and sexuality through drama; no American theatrical troupe comes close to rivaling the "O-M" in explicitness.

SEX SHOWS

The liberalized climate for exhibitionism in the 1960s and 1970s fostered commercial spectacles in large American cities. Edward J. Mishan condemns sexual displays in public in *Pornography, Psychedelics and Technology: Essays on the Limits to Freedom*. Performers in sex shows are among the people interviewed by Eberhard Kronhausen and Phyllis Kronhausen for *The Sex People: Erotic Performers and Their Brave New Worlds*. From the 1970s until the 1980s, bars in tenderloin districts in New York and San Francisco presented nude male and female dancers who permitted sexual contact in the form of oral sex or (usually) incomplete intercourse. Blair Sabol shakes her head over the performances at the Anvil and other working-class bars in the meatpacking district of lower Manhattan. Her title, "This Box Lunch Will Kill Your Appetite," refers to the practice of local workers taking their lunch to the bars, ordering drinks, then for a dollar or two engaging in public cunnilingus with the women dancing on the bar in front of them. Bruce David's "Honeysuckle Divine" speculates on the performer's muscular control, as demonstrated in her act at various storefronts in New York. She puffs cigarettes with her labia and shoots Ping-Pong balls from her vagina, all the while keeping up a patter about alleged affairs with LBJ and Illinois Senator Everett Dirksen. The climax of the show is signaled by an explosion of talcum powder that Divine loads into her vagina, then expels with great force. In *Learned Pigs and Fireproof Women*, a marvelous book on spectacle, Ricky Jay compares Divine to Le Pétomane, the legendary French music hall performer, whose act consisted of virtuoso farting (307).

The sex show scene—in New York, at least—during this period was self-reflexive, as if it were deliberately creating legends. If Honeysuckle Divine could shoot a Ping-Pong ball twenty feet, then another performer would break her record. A storefront on 7th Avenue would spread the word that its female performers would simultaneously service three partners, while a gay bar in the West Village would promote the length of its performers' penises. Major porn stars such as Tish Ambrose appeared in the minitheaters of the various Show World emporiums in the Times Square area. There they would have intercourse in front of audiences with local males recruited for their ability to maintain erections for four shows a day. Usually, however, performers were drawn from the floating population of the city and remained anonymous, except for stage-names, as they writhed on platforms in arcades and peep-show booths. Their traces, more ephemeral than the needle-tracks on their arms, can be found only in the pages of *Screw* and other tabloids; these wrote up shows from week to week and sometimes noted performers. Otherwise, as is so often the case, sexual performance became the stuff of anonymous low porn.

Indefatigable in their curiosity about the Manhattan sex scene, Howard Smith and Brian Van Der Horst devoted one *Village Voice* column to Rod Swenson, a low-rent impresario of mid-1970s storefront sex, in "It's Hard to Stay Hot." With a master's degree in drama from Yale, Swenson seemed a cut above his rivals in Times Square. His "Sex Fantasy Theatre" played in twin theaters in the Show World Complex at Eighth Avenue and 42d Street, grossing $20,000 a week. The shows foregrounded actual sex between people of various genders; one of the production numbers concluded with a chorus line of performers with objects dangling from different orifices. Says Swenson: "My aim is to create a truly honest and living theatre. I'm fascinated by what happens when people have sex in front of other people. My performers are former dancers, computer programmers, schoolteachers—some are college students. I don't hire hookers. We're all people who are exploring our own sexuality." Swenson and one of his performers, Wendy O. Williams, eventually founded the Plasmatics, a musical group. Bernard Arcand points out in *The Jaguar and the Anteater* that live performances have given way to advanced technology and are rare today, "partly because the craze for them has died out, but also because live shows are very expensive to mount and bring in very little in return. If only for physiological reasons, no live show could ever be repeated as often as a video can be replayed" (262, n. 21).

For a time, however, sincere or not, the refrain of "exploring our own sexuality" reverberated in several semipublic arenas. From at least the 1950s on, one of those arenas had been the gay bathhouse, where sex gradually assumed institutionalized proportions. John Rechy's *The Sexual Outlaw: A Documentary* is a raw tour of the gay underground sex scene, of interest not least because of the author's reputation as a writer of innovative fiction. The behavior Rechy depicts is alien, driven, desperate. Dotson Rader's "Notes from the Underground: St. James Baths," on public sex in a West Coast gay bathhouse, is graphic and straightforward in its treatment of the exhibitionistic sex in such venues. Among the recollections of David Wojnarowicz in *Memories That Smell like Gasoline: Art and Memoirs* are experiences of public sex in gay bathhouses and movie theaters; included are drawings by the artist. *Policing Public Sex: Queer Politics and the Future of AIDS Activism*, by writers collectively known as Dangerous Bedfellows, deals with sex clubs, bathhouses, cinemas, and Times Square retreats open to gays.

Dan Rosen's "Sex Goes Public: The Straights Follow" notes that the voyeurism that accelerated actual sex and, in turn, mirrored it soon leaped beyond gay bathhouses like the Ansonia in Manhattan and led directly to heterosexual spectacle, sometimes just down the hall, as with the many chambers of Plato's Retreat in the Ansonia building. This arena was heterosexual, though the appeal was similar: men and women, strangers to one another, met to have sex in couples or clusters. For information on bathhouses in the process of sexual metamorphosis from a gay to a heterosexual clientele, John Vater's article on a San Francisco venue, "The Sutro Baths," is helpful. Howard Smith and Leslie Harlib describe the oral sex in the pool and the intercourse in mattress-filled rooms in the most famous heterosexual emporium of the 1970s in their article "Plato's Retreat." Probably the best critique is offered by Buck Henry in "My Night at Plato's Retreat," an amusing, but incisive, look at the couplings that took place there. Perhaps the most rationalized of theatrical events were those set at Sandstone, a name that became synonymous with group sex. Tom Hatfield's *The Sandstone Experience*, on the Sandstone Sex Commune, is an account of the resort/therapeutic institute that for more than a decade encouraged public sex. Participants might meet in the pool to work out sexual anxieties and frustrations or explore fantasies by "pleasuring" one another. *Thy Neighbor's Wife*, Gay Talese's lightly fictionalized account of the American sexual revolution, offers information on the institutionalized promiscuity in venues such as Sandstone and Plato's Retreat.

SWINGING

The ethos and dramatic purpose of sex staged in what were essentially nightclubs like Plato's Retreat differed, at least at first, from the middle-class phenomenon known as swinging. Swingers often justify their behavior in terms of healthy experimentation. As they see it, swinging saves marriages in danger of succumbing to boredom; by retaining their sexual freedom, wives and husbands cleave to one another out of choice. Swinging thus preserves and even extends family values. Swinging takes place in loosely organized events designed as therapy for the oversexed and/or entertainment for the jaded. Swinging, or "wife-swapping," as journalists labeled the behavior, began to attract attention in America in the 1950s, and the ordinariness of the participants seems to mock Toepfer's insistence on the aristocratic impulse behind the orgiastic impulse. Where the Sandstone experience was fairly exclusive, sited as it was in an expensive retreat, swinging occurred in neighborhoods, sometimes in private homes, sometimes in local motels. On the other hand, swing meets were closed off to the wider public, restricted to people who knew one another or who had been invited to participate. Open theater performances such as those at Plato's Retreat required only payment of an admission fee, and one was then free to have intercourse (provided that desired participants were willing) or merely observe. By contrast, swingers usually arrived with lasagna or curry for potluck dinners, inquired after each other's children, and discussed neighborhood events or exchanged recipes before pairing off.

The Groupsex Tapes, a study of swinging couples in the United States by H. E. Margolis and Paul Rubenstein, evolved from interviews with over 100 participants in group-sex events. Margolis and Rubenstein discuss swingers' magazines and other channels of communication. Carolyn Symonds' ethnographic investigation, "Sexual Mate-Swapping: Violation of Norms and Reconciliation of Guilt," concludes that mate-swappers are middle-class citizens. Their ability to shield their children from their activities and to reconcile the pull of fidelity and adventure puts a positive spin on swinging. Lawrence Lipton generally praises sexual performance, swinging, open marriages, and so on in *The Erotic Revolution: An Affirmative View of the New Morality*. Additional information on the phenomenon in the 1960s can be found in *The Records of the San Francisco Sexual Freedom League*, by Jefferson Poland and Valerie Alison, *Group Sex: An Eyewitness Report on the American Way of Swinging*, by Gilbert Bartell, and *The Wonderful World of Penthouse Sex: Radical Sex in the Establishment*, edited by Marco Vassi. As such texts pointed out, swinging provided the plots for many early hard-core features (wife or husband would agonize over whether to participate, then, once initiated, would couple with everyone in sight, thus realizing happiness).

Trends vectored together as some swingers found it easier to attend gatherings scheduled by entrepreneurs rather than organize orgies in their own homes, though some complained that *gesellschaft* replaced *gemeinschaft* (i.e., commercial relationships replaced personal ones). When sex clubs began to appear in major cities in the mid-1970s, numerous local and national magazines sent reporters to cover the "fuck-scene." For "Is There Life after Swinging?" a *Time* reporter took his girlfriend in 1978 to a club "scene" described as hopelessly middle-class, unimaginative, and sweaty. The bolder reporters participated, coupling with partners they thought attractive, or joining daisy chains, while others declined, commenting on the action with various degrees of aloofness. The articles they filed can be traced in *Access: The Supplementary Index to Periodicals* for those years under "Sex Shows." Over time, the threat of AIDS significantly reduced the phenomenon. Now, says Ellis Henican in "Swinging Swings Back," there are only about twenty couples-only sex clubs in the United States, scattered "in cities, suburbs, and small towns. About half of them provide facilities for on-premise sex," the other half just meeting places for people who then go to motels or homes (59). Le Trapeze, the midtown Manhattan sex club, is the center. All of the participants are average Americans, claims Henican, who interviews Robert McGinley, president of the North American Swing Club Association and author of a guidebook called *Etiquette in Swinging*. Henican does observe that many medical authorities are appalled at the increased risk of AIDS that attends sex on this scale.

Steven Chapple and David Talbot cover orgies staged by contemporary entrepreneurs in their more recent *Burning Desires: Sex in America—A Report from the Field*. Chapple and Talbot devote several pages to "jack-offs" and "jill-offs," groups of usually naked or provocatively clad men and women who publicly masturbated themselves and each other in what passed for large-scale safe sex in the 1990s. Michael Kelly visits Le Trapeze in "Sex Is Back" to find that clubgoers are cautious but can still get into public sex. New sex clubs, like San Francisco's Club Ecstacy, which caters to women only, are reviewed from time to time; see "Real Girl World." Guy Trebay's "Culture Club: A Lesbian Landmark's Preservation" centers on the Clit Club, a dyke bar, but also chronicles the history of other Manhattan lesbian night spots such as the Sahara, the Duchess, Bonnie and Clyde, Peaches, She-Scape, Crazy Nanny, and Cubbyhole, some of which have fostered sex on the premises. Brief as it is, Trebay's is an important historical reference guide to the formation of an erotic consciousness. Swinging has inspired representation (books, photos, films, etc.) for at least two decades. Magazines with titles such as *Odyssey Express, ConneXion*, and *Unreal People* are numerous, as are videotapes of swinging groups. Ads in some of the magazines recruit swingers for such tapes, sometimes by offering the chance to have intercourse with professional performers, a genre called "pro-am" (professional-amateur; see **Amateur Films and Videos** in Chapter 13).

SADOMASOCHISM

Of all the forms of erotic performance, the ones that often bring debate to a halt are sadism and masochism, terms coined by Richard von Krafft-Ebing in *Psychopathia Sexualis* in 1885. Reactions to sadomasochism (aka S and M, S&M, and S/M) shape the current controversy on pornography, not least, perhaps, because of Michel Foucault's personal fondness for it, a factor that doubtless colored his discourse on sex as power. Thanks largely to Foucault, the reflex equation of sex and power is as much a cliché in critiques of pornography as the "cum shot" has become in pornographic movies: sadomasochistic representations are the favorite targets of antiporn crusaders. The reasons are obvious: such scenarios illustrate far more clearly but also far more narrowly than other pornographic genres the power relationships that antiporn advocates hope to uncover in all sexual acts and representations. Less doctrinaire critics find it hard to discount the self-parodic aspects of S/M genres and sometimes argue that for precisely that reason they cannot function as representative of other genres. Even so, when even the Parent–Teacher Association (PTA) endorses fellatio, sadomasochistic performances still seem bizarre enough to disturb liberal apologists for porn. Sadomasochism thus fills an almost necessary niche in the hierarchy of fast-eroding sexual taboos. The furor that greeted exhibitions of Robert Mapplethorpe's S/M photographs in the early 1990s is but one example.

Gayle Rubin says in "Thinking Sex: Notes for a Radical Theory of the Politics of Sexuality" "The use of S/M imagery in anti-porn is inflammatory. It implies that the way to make the world safe for women is to get rid of sadomasochism. The use of S/M images in the movie *Not a Love Story* was on a moral par with the use of depictions of black men raping white women, or of drooling old Jews pawing young Aryan girls, to incite racist or anti-Semitic frenzy" (298). Despite the best efforts of antiporn feminists, trying to define pornography as a subset of sadomasochism is like trying to define Protestantism as a species of Pentecostal snake-handling. In this regard, the parallels between S/M performance and religious ritual are fairly obvious, as Ann McClintock points out in "Maid to Order: Commercial S/M and Gender Power," one of the best essays on the subject. McClintock makes clear that she is not speaking of men who beat up their wives: "S/M is the most liturgical of forms, sharing with Christianity a theatrical iconography of punishment and expiation: washing rituals, bondage, flagellation, body-piercing, and symbolic torture. Like S/M, the economy of Christianity is the economy of conversion: the meek exalted, the high made low. Mortifying the flesh exalts one in the eyes of the Master" (106). More important to McClintock, perhaps, is that S/M means "a subculture of organized fetishism" (113), with lots of ritualized patterns ranging from piercing to bondage. McClintock is conventional only when she condemns the commodification of sexuality by trying to distinguish between "*reciprocal* S/M for mutual pleasure, and *consensual* S/M organized as a commercial exchange" (227); the former she thinks more acceptable than the latter. For McClintock and many other critics, commerce is the real source of evil in sexual matters. Lynda Hart's *Between the Body and the Flesh: Performing Sadomasochism* argues that sadomasochism, especially in its lesbian and queer guises, is a means of making sense of life, finding meaning in experience, and "bearing witness" to the power of sexuality. In her reading, S/M challenges and transgresses an "erotics of power" (202) by exploring a "place" where the self can be recovered. Hart's book includes an excellent bibliography.

Most devotees of S/M prize its ritualistic character and celebrate its dramaturgical aspects; it is an extreme version of one of pornography's central reasons for being—the role-playing that eroticism makes possible. In S/M scenarios, humans exchange roles, playing out a script of master and slave that is as much parody and inversion of traditional roles as it is an assertion of power and submission. The vast preponderance of such scenarios involves submissive males and dominant females in what is clearly theater. Carol Siegel's interesting thesis is that modern male masochism descends from traditions of courtly love, in which knight submitted to lady; Siegel's *Male Masochism: Modern Revisions of the Story of Love* extrapolates from literature and film. Jessica Benjamin's "Master and Slave: The Fantasy of Erotic Domination" is a thoughtful piece on the differences between actual aggression and consensual sadomasochistic fantasies. Benjamin rejects the idea that sadism is a defining characteristic of male-oriented porn, arguing in particular with the group of essays in Laura Lederer's book *Take Back the Night*, "labeled, with characteristic simplemindedness, 'Who Benefits'—as if violent or derogatory attitudes toward women made men happy, healthy, and wise" (297). One thing seems certain: S/M scenarios bear little relationship, causal or otherwise, to actual aggression. As Mistress Lilith Lash, a veteran writer, director, and star of S/M films, points out in "Pain, Pleasure and Poetry," "a man who's just been fucked up the ass while wearing false eyelashes and crotchless pink panties is very unlikely to rape or kill" (52).

Perhaps the most telling cultural comment on S/M in the 1990s is the new zoning practice in New York City that has relegated adult bookstores, topless bars, and peep shows to the fringes of the city. Because no one complained about the S/M "dungeons," and because even the police think that they are harmless, establishments like the Vault and Paddles have been permitted to remain open. Denise Kiernan quotes one emporium as saying, "We don't offer sex. We're a house of domination," in "Spank You Very Much," which also points out that only affluent males patronize dungeons where being paddled or led about on a leash can cost $180 a session. Chapter 6 of Gertzman's *Bookleggers and Smuthounds: The Trade in Erotica, 1920–1940* points out that American police did not recognize flagellation as an erotic category until the mid-1930s, a phenomenon that attests both to the social construction of sexual practice and to the naïveté of authorities.

For background, scholars can consult Arthur Maria Rabenalt's *Theatrum Sadicum*, which, though centered on de Sade's theater as a historical phenomenon, follows its themes and elements in modern examples of sadistic theater. The essays in Annie LeBruin's *Petits et grand theatres du Marquis de Sade* argue that de Sade himself conceived of his extreme behavior as a form of theater in keeping with eighteenth-century philosophies of moral freedom. *Sittengeschichte des Theaters*, by Leo Schidrowitz, also attributes a strong moral dimension to sadomasochistic dramaturgy; Schidrowitz early on characterized S/M as performance. The ur-text is the seventeenth-century *A Treatise on the Use of Flogging in Medicine and Venery*, by "Meibomius," the pen name of Heinrich Meibaum (1590–1633), a German physician who recommended flagellation as a form of therapy, especially for impotence (the only English translation is in the British Museum). *An Illustrated History of the Rod*, an often-reprinted nineteenth-century volume (original c.1877) by a minister named William M. Cooper, dwells lasciviously on flagellation as a didactic ritual of liberation; its theme of spiritual exaltation is typical of dozens of other examples of what has become a pornographic genre. Whips and rods are common to S/M scenarios because they can be iconographic, say the essayists gathered by Ernest Schertel for his classic *Die Komplex der Flagellomanie*. Another classic study is Wilhelm Stekel's *Sadism and Masochism: The Psychology of Hatred and Cruelty*, still a good reference tool. The most illuminating historical survey, however, is Jonathan Dollimore's *Sexual Dissidence: Augustine to Wilde, Freud to Foucault*, which covers and interprets many documents on "perversions."

Several studies of the performance aspects of sadomasochism make use of American examples. The first is Gini Graham Scott's *Dominant Women, Submissive Men: An Exploration in Erotic Dominance and Submission*, a wide-ranging investigation of the S/M scene, with particular emphasis on live performances at New York City's Chateau; chapters include S/M couples and communities, the role of fantasy, "toys and techniques" such as bonds, bracelets, racks, and whips, fantasy tapes and letters from professional mistresses to their "slaves," and an important index of magazines and books dealing with the subject. Scott argues that because the female dominant/male submissive model is widespread in America, the practice can almost be considered definitive, at least in terms of formal dramaturgy. (The well-documented popularity of lesbian S/M has challenged such assertions.) Thomas Weinberg and G. W. Levi Kamel have edited *Studies in Sadomasochism*, which excerpts classic studies by Richard von Krafft-Ebing, Sigmund Freud, Havelock Ellis, and Paul Gebhard, to which are added interviews and autobiographical essays by contemporary practitioners. The volume contains an essential essay, Gerhard Falk and Thomas Weinberg's "Sadomasochism and Popular Western Culture," which sets the behavior in a rich context. Another chapter discusses S/M theater in New York City, such as that conducted by the Till Eulenspiegel Society, the Chateau, and the Project, all of which performed S/M fantasies onstage with frequent audience participation in the late 1970s and early 1980s (151–159). The revised edition, edited by Weinberg alone, contains additional material.

Works about celebrated dominatrices (who abuse mostly male clients), with reflections on the performance aspects of sadomasochism, include *Whips and Kisses: Parting the Leather Curtain*, the memoirs of "Mistress Jacqueline," a West Coast dominatrix, as told to Catherine Tavel and Robert H. Rimmer; *The House of Pain: The Strange World of Monique Von Cleef, the Queen of Humiliation*, by Monique Von Cleef with William Waterman, a New Jersey woman whose customer files were exposed by police raids in the 1970s; *Tied up with Love: The Making of Mistress Antoinette*, by Jeanette Luther, a dominatrix of extensive experience; and *The Correct Sadist: The Memoirs of Angel Stern*, by Terence Sellers, the story of a New York dominatrix, with extensive forays into various associated fetishes like coprolagnia and urolagnia, rubber garments, and transvestism; the volume gives special emphasis to popular scenarios. Nick Broomfield's documentary, *Fetishes: Mysteries and Domination at Pandora's Box*, interviews professional mistresses and their male customers in the course of exploring various facilities designed for fantasy. Paul Theroux's essay on a Manhattan dominatrix, "Nurse Wolf," appeared in the *New Yorker*. Martha Stein directly observed prostitutes working with more than 1,200 clients, a study published as *Lovers, Friends, Slaves . . .* ; one section deals with dominatrices and their masochistic customers, who exhibit patterns that reflect both classic and personal masochistic need. Marianne Macy speaks to many dominatrices, though she devotes the most space to Ava Taurel, a thoughtful professional, in *Working Sex: An Odyssey into Our Cultural Underworld*. Thaïs E. Morgan's "A Whip of One's Own: Dominatrix Pornography and the Construction of a Post-Modern (Female) Subjectivity" deals with S/M as a parodic reinscription of gender roles, mostly in fiction and photos, but she also points out that the codes of pornography are extremely complex and that viruall all definitions reflect self-serving agendas.

Any serious student of S/M must at some point read Susan Shellogg's *Unnatural Acts*, the witty, literate, reflective, and insightful autobiography of a career "Mistress," who identifies the two "nodes" of the Scene as New York and San Francisco and divides "old-style S/M," recognizable by its iconographic costume, from what she calls newer, more commercialized styles promoted on afternoon television shows such as *Donahue* and *Sally Jessy Raphael*. Shellogg says that humans need an Other, and that S/M practitioners neatly fit the role for Americans who dote on S/M's "alien mystery, its separation from themselves. To admit that the sexual dynamic of S-M influences their lives would be just too terrifying. Not only would it challenge the safe and secure foundation of their safe and secure world, it would deprive them of that Otherness, that ability to point a finger, which serves to keep their own world stable" (50). She describes sadomasochists as fetishists short-circuited by childhood experience, "locked into an endless loop of repetitive erotic drudgery, as if they were mules tied to a mill wheel. The fetishist's partner may be changed, and in this aspect only he craves novelty. The actual fantasy itself is repeated endlessly, like some nightmarish Greek myth" (146). After so long studying hunger, she concludes that "any woman who has ever looked full into the face of male sexual need comes away changed" (79), but she notes that lesbians, homosexuals, and heterosexual females are also prone to fetish. Of interest also is Shellogg's account of her affair with the artist Andrés Serrano and of her first career as a fashion model.

Lynn S. Chancer explores the psychological wellsprings of ritual in *Sadomasochism in Everyday Life: The Dynamics of Power and Powerlessness. A Sexual Profile of Men in Power*, by Sam Janus, Barbara Bess, and Carol Saltus, investigates the phenomenon of powerful men who seek out professional dominatrices to allay their own guilt through ritual expiation. The subjects, chief executive officers (CEOs) and wielders of influence, engage in transvestism, bondage and discipline, sadism and submission in an effort to come to terms with the ambiguities of power. Robert Stoller argues in *Pain and Passion: A Psychoanalyst Explores the World of S-M* and *Perversion: The Erotic Form of Hatred* that the psychological "scripts" that sadomasochists follow have been formed from erotic conflicts shaped in childhood. Walter Braun studies flagellation, S/M, and related practices drawn from many literary and cultural sources in *The Cruel and the Meek*. Equally dated now and more concerned with literary examples is Gerald Greene and Caroline Greene's *S-M: The Last Taboo*, which argues for recognizing sadomasochism as a powerful sexual force assaulting a kind of final frontier. More recent is *Thy Rod and Thy Staff: New Light on the Flagellatory Impulse*, by Edward Anthony, who outlines the essential elements and implements of S/M scenarios, dissociates the true enthusiast from the pedophilia with which S/M was once linked, and wades through the rivers of ink expended on the subject. Ian Gibson's *The English Vice: Beating, Sex, Shame in Victorian England and After* traces the fetish through British newspapers, where it undergoes interesting transformations in the public mind; scholars of American culture should nonetheless find the work useful. "The Many Faces of S/M," a special issue of *Gauntlet*, contains articles by Pearl Chavez, Charlie LaTour, S. B. Forrest, David Aaron Clark, David Steinberg, and Ariel Hart on the S/M scene, on well-known dominants, and on various protocols and practices.

A compilation of arguments that consensual S/M is healthy and appealing forms the text of *Different Loving: An Exploration of the World of Sexual Dominance and Submission*. Here Gloria G. Brame, William D. Brame, and Jon Jacobs interview practitioners, theorists, and other commentators such as Pat Califia, Gayle Rubin, and Fakir Musafar on activities ranging from bondage to water sports. Although most of the text veers away from the heavier forms of S/M, the sections on theatrical contours are valuable. Sadomasochism has been misrepresented by both psychiatrists and journalists, says Bill Thompson in *Sadomasochism: Painful Perversion or Pleasurable Play?* Thompson believes that the practice is a "natural" part of many healthy sex lives, especially in its promotion of fantasy. In "Erotic Power and Trust," Carol Queen suggests separating dominance and submission from sadism and masochism, preferring to "conceptualize each sort of play on a continuum, rather like Kinsey saw heterosexuality and homosexuality blur into each other via bisexuality," but notes elements

common to dominance/submission and S/M. Both are usually ritualized in a *scene*, which can be delimited by costume, by the assumption of fantasy personae and, most important, by the agreement of the participants. They will usually assume roles, commonly called *top* and *bottom*, which correspond to master and servant, dominant and submissive, sadist and masochist, respectively. Most S/M scenes will have at least one of each. The bottom allows the top to take control of the scene, but power is rarely conceded unconditionally. Usually the participants have agreed upon a scenario and established basic limits. (229)

The effect, she says, is to "break down" fear of sexuality.

Wagner Heller and Pauly Heller were among the first observers to notice an upsurge of theatrical S/M, a phenomenon they reported on in 1959 in *Der Fla-gellantismus und Verwandte Formen Exzentrischer Sexualität im Amerika*. Two interesting articles review more recent staged fantasies: Catherine Burgheart and Sam Blazer visit the Project, Belle de Jour Theatre, and Plato's Retreat, sites for the dramatic and explicit acting out of sexual scenes, as reported in "Sex Theatre"; Arlene de Strulle comments on themes, performers, scenery, and dramaturgy at the Project in "Sexual Fantasy Theatre." Various filmmakers have produced both documentaries and pornographic scenarios, far too many, in fact, even to list. S/M performances took place sporadically at theaters in San Francisco and reached a kind of apogee at the O'Farrell, when the Mitchell Brothers filmed Marilyn Chambers' act in 1985; the result can serve as an example. Framed by interviews with the star, the action in *Never a Tender Moment* moves from Chambers' body contact with members of the audience to a garishly staged set piece. Here two leather-clad dominatrices attach chains to rings in Chambers' pierced labia, torment her with various appliances, then anally fist her. During all these encounters, Chambers plays directly to the audience encircling the stage and in the interview framing the scenarios speaks about her intentions. As readers of Michael Musto's column in the *Village Voice* know, the Vault, located in New York's West Village, is the leading venue for S/M theater now. Elissa Wald's *Meeting the Master*, about the "darker side of desire," is an apology for S/M first self-published (then taken up by a major press) by a stripper and performance artist.

Pat Califia and Robin Sweeney have drawn on narratives of lesbian "leather sex" for *Second Coming: A Leatherdyke Reader*. G. W. Levi Kamel's "Leathersex: Meaningful Aspects of Gay Sadomasochism," also reprinted in the Weinberg and Kamel volume, studies individual psychopathology as a form of social bonding and differentiation in theatrical settings. Two dozen essays gathered by Mark Thompson also deal with the structures of community engendered by S/M mostly among gays in *Leatherfolk: Radical Sex, People, Politics, and Practice*; the contributors cover costume, symbols, and iconography in their focus on the heightened consciousness that grows out of dominance and submission. Since its first appearance in the 1970s Larry Townsend's *The Leatherman's Handbook* has become a definitive guide to the gay use of leather, especially in S/M scenarios, for which it provides a map of preferences and protocols. Townsend's legendary status in the S/M world is evident in the collection of his views published by Victor Terry as *Master of Masters*. Townsend's *To Take a Slave and Other Stories of Male/Male S/M* combine fiction and memoir. Joseph W. Bean's *Leathersex O & A: Questions about Leathersex and the Leathersex Lifestyles Answered* speaks to novices and the curious in eleven thematic chapters. In the same league is Geoffrey Mains' *Urban Aboriginals: A Celebration of Leather Sexuality*, which branches into physiology in an effort to explain the gratifications of practices such as anal-fisting. (See also **Fetish Photographs** in Chapter 12, especially Gatewood, Grumley, and Gallucci.) A. X. Naerssen, Mart van Dijk, Geert Hoogeveen, Dick Visser, and Gertjan van Zessen argue in "Gay SM in Pornography and Reality" that participants make clear distinctions between reality and performance, merely using fantasies as cues. Guy Baldwin outlines the rules of engagement for gay scenes in *Ties That Bind: The S/M/ Leather/Fetish Erotic Style: Issues, Commentary and Advice*.

Masochism is quite different from sadism in both its goals and its expression, especially where pornography is concerned, says Giles Deleuze in *Masochism: An Interpretation of Coldness and Cruelty*, which centers around Sacher-Masoch's famous text, *Venus in Furs*, as revised by Deleuze; Deleuze's postmodern reading finds the "volatile presence of a terrible coldness" at the heart of masochism. Margaret Ann Hanly's *Essential Papers on Masochism* also ranges over rituals as paths to understanding psychological need through pain. Vintage texts include *Masochism in Modern Man*, in which Theodor Reik tries to advance beyond Freudian explanations for masochism, and *Sexual Masochism*, in which Edward Podolsky and Carlson Wade offer medical perspectives on the syndrome. Another classic work is Joachim Pauly's *Die Anglolagnie*, so titled because of the popular conception that flagellation is a British taste; a later, mostly pictorial supplement is *Der Sexuelle Fetischism*. Pauly's narrative deals with bondage and discipline as well as flagellation and is heavily illustrated, with some references to American examples. Maria Marcus' *A Taste for Pain* explores the roots and outlines the manifestations of female masochism. Christina Abernathy's *Miss Abernathy's Concise Slave Training Manual* is as much a guide for submissives as their masters. *Learning the Ropes: A Basic Guide to Safe & Fun S-M Lovemaking*, by Race Bannon, *Screw the Roses, Send Me the Thorns: The Romance and Sexual Sorcery of Sadomasochism*, by Molly Devon and Phillip Miller, *S/M 101: A Realistic Introduction*, by Jay Wiseman, and *The Loving Dominant*, by John Warren, are manuals of protocol and etiquette. Two complementary texts by Dottie Easton and Catherine A. Liszt, *The Bottoming Book: Or How to Get Terrible Things Done to You by Wonderful People* and *The Topping Book: Or, Getting Good at Being Bad*, provide instructions on how to enjoy submissiveness and dominance, respectively. Being an effective top in a sadomasochistic relationship means knowing how to monitor the pain of the submissive, how to use instruments, and so on; taking pleasure in submission means knowing what one wants, one's limits, and so on. Both volumes include lists of publications, organizations, and clubs.

Perhaps the single most interesting essay on the subject is "Unlikely Obsession: Confronting a Taboo," in which the *New Yorker* columnist and film critic Daphne Merkin grapples with her need to be spanked by sexual partners. In *The Joy of Suffering*, Shirley Panken offers case histories and therapies. The pages on female masochism in Linda Williams' *Hard Core* are excellent. Rachel Rosenthal's "Performance Notes: Taboo Subjects: Performance and the Masochist Tradition" explains her participation in masochistic performances in which she was suspended from hooks embedded in her flesh. For *Bob Flanagan: Super Masochist*, V. Vale and Andrea Juno collect material on a late victim of cystic fibrosis who takes up masochism as a means of recapturing control of his body. Kirby Dick, as if to illustrate once again the cultural appropriation of marginal materials, shot *Sick: The Life and Death of Bob Flanagan, Supermasochist*, a movie about Flanagan's life. Deborah Ryder, a disabled woman who is also a masochist, argues for access to pornography for the disabled in "Lady O." David Aaron Clark's "Happiness in Slavery: The Making of a Masochist" is a personal account of the appeal of masochism, developed over visits to the Vault and to a professional mistress. "Stella through the Looking Glass," by Robert/"Stella," who dresses in female clothes for his mistress, attempts to explain his motivations. In *Le Musée des Supplices*, Roland Villeneuve gathers images of sadomasochism from films, photographs, and advertisements to assert their pervasiveness in popular media.

LESBIAN S/M

For the extreme antiporn feminist, sex is power, and pornography is an expression of male sadism; women who collaborate in any sex act are themselves masochistic. For such feminists, lesbian sex merely reproduces masculine norms and nowhere more clearly than when lesbians practice sadomasochism. Lesbian sadomasochism is perhaps the ultimate litmus test of feminist sexual politics. As put by B. Ruby Rich in "Feminism and Sexuality in the 1980s": "Nowhere has this Manichean struggle between updated bourgeois respectability and its opposite become more attenuated than in the debate over lesbian sadomasochism" (529). In "The Feminist Ethics of Lesbian S/M," Mandy Merck similarly observes, "The Sex Wars have taught us the error of attempting to fuse our political and sexual imaginaries, but they have also demonstrated the futility of trying to keep them apart" (266). Also useful are the psychological reflections in Parveen Adams' "Of Female Bondage."

As the title suggests, most of the perspectives in *Against Sadomasochism: A Radical Feminist Analysis*, edited by Robin Ruth Linden, Darlene R. Pagano, Diana E. H. Russell, and Susan Leigh Starr, oppose lesbian sadomasochists, a sizable group, who, their detractors say, simply mirror male power obsessions. Arguments range from the claim that women who practice S/M are traitors to feminism, secret men-male sympathizers, sick, reactionary, or just too plain sensual to be ideologically correct. The two dozen essays map the rift between feminists who wish to practice marginal sexual behavior and/or write and enjoy pornography and those who reject sex as a source of pleasure (either physical or spiritual) or who feel that the realization of female sexuality must be postponed until after the political triumph of radical feminism. Perhaps the best of the collection is Judith Butler's "Lesbian S & M: The Politics of Disillusion," which observes that "S & M also believes in the wrongness of conscience, and seeks the radical inversion of the Judeo-Christian ethic which is renowned for its contempt for desire. [Advocates of S/M] accuse moral feminists of continuing this anti-sex tradition. In turn, moral feminists charge that SM has merely appropriated patriarchal power relations and brought them into lesbianism in faintly disguised form" (171).

The most powerful counterstatements to those who condemn lesbian S/M can be found in *Coming to Power: Writings and Graphics on Lesbian S/M* and *What Color Is Your Handkerchief? A Lesbian S/M Sexuality Reader*, both collectively written volumes from Samois, the San Francisco S/M Support Group (named after Anne-Marie's estate in *The Story of O*, by Pauline Réage, the pen name of Dominique Aury). Chief spokesperson in this group is the articulate and talented Pat Califia, whose Preface to her *Macho Sluts* stresses the consensual and theatrical basis of sadomasochism. She has edited a how-to guide called *The Lesbian S/M Safety Manual*. Califia's more recent *Public Sex: The Culture of Radical Sex* defends sadomasochists, leatherfolk, and public, theatrical sex in general. Julia Creet adopts a postmodern position based on language as an enveloping environment and psychology as a Lacanian construct (in which females accept the authority of the father) to suggest that S/M fantasies allow lesbians to recover an "outlaw status" in "Daughter of the Movement: The Psychodynamics of the Lesbian S/M Fantasy." Not so, says Tania Modleski, who insists in *Feminism without Women* that although lesbian S/M inverts conventional gender schemes, the new pattern is one of "initiating the woman into the symbolic order, but transferring and transforming a patriarchal system of gender inequities into a realm of difference presided over by women" (156–157). Finally, Katrien Jacobs' " 'The Lady of Little Death': Illuminated Encounters and Erotic Duties in the Life and Art of Maria Beatty" examines the ways in which the artist constructs a film version of herself through the iconography of sadomasochism.

NOTES

1. See the *New York Times*, 10 February 1927, sec. 1, p. 8.
2. Quoted by Louise Brooks, *Lulu in Hollywood* (New York: Knopf, 1982), p. 80.

3. As a side note, when Ken Bernard and I were both teaching in New York, I introduced him to Vaccaro.

4. Quoted in Tom Wolfe (writer/narrator), *The Video McLuhan: Cassette 2, 1965– 1970* (Toronto: McLuhan Productions, 1996), at 56 minutes.

REFERENCES

Abernathy, Christina. *Miss Abernathy's Concise Slave Training Manual.* San Francisco: Greenery Press, 1996.

Access: The Supplementary Index to Periodicals, 1975–. Syracuse, NY: Gaylord Professional Publishers, 1975–1977; Evanston, IL: J. G. Burke Publishers, 1978–.

Adams, Parveen. "Of Female Bondage." *Between Feminism and Psychoanalysis,* ed. Teresa Brennan. New York: Routledge, 1989, pp. 247–265.

Ainley, Rosa. *What Is She Like? Lesbian Identities from 1950s to 1990s.* New York: Cassell, 1996.

Alexander, H. M. *Strip Tease: The Vanished Art of Burlesque.* New York: Knight Publishers, 1938.

Aline. "Good Girls Go to Heaven, Bad Girls Go Everywhere." *Sex Work: Writings by Women in the Sex Industry,* ed. Frédérique Delacoste and Priscilla Alexander. Pittsburgh: Cleis Press, 1987, pp. 131–134.

Allen, Ralph G. *The Best Burlesque Sketches as Adapted for Sugar Babies and Other Entertainments.* New York: Applause Theatre Books, 1995.

Allen, Robert C. *Horrible Prettiness: Burlesque and American Culture.* Chapel Hill: University of North Carolina Press, 1991.

Allyn, Jerri, et al. "Oral Herstory of Lesbianism." *High Performance,* 2:4 (Winter 1979/ 1980): 16–25.

Alves, Greg. *The World's Biggest Gang Bang III: The Houston 500.* Van Nuys, CA: Metro Video, 1999.

Ample, Annie. *The Bare Facts: My Life as a Stripper.* Toronto: Key Porter, 1988.

"And Now Bring On the Boys." *Time,* 6 August 1979, p. 69.

Angier, Roswell. *". . . A Kind of Life": Conversations in the Combat Zone.* Danbury, NH: Addison House, 1976.

Angioli, Michael D. "Body Image Perception and Locus of Control in Semi-Nude and Nude Female Dancers." Ph.D. dissertation, United States International University, 1982; Ann Arbor, MI: UMI Dissertation Service, 1982.

Anthony, Edward. *Thy Rod and Thy Staff: New Light on the Flagellatory Impulse.* Boston: Little, Brown, 1996.

Arcand, Bernard. *The Jaguar and the Anteater: Pornography Degree Zero,* trans. Wayne Grady. New York: Verso, 1993.

Aulnoyes, François des. *Histoire et philosophie du striptease: Essai sur L'erotisme au music hall.* Paris: Pensée Moderne, 1958.

Baker, Jean-Claude, and Chris Chase. *Josephine: The Hungry Heart.* New York: Random House, 1993.

Bakhtin, Mikhail. *Rabelais and His World,* trans. Helene Iswolsky. Bloomington: Indiana University Press, 1984.

Baldwin, Guy. *Ties That Bind: The S/M/Leather/Fetish Erotic Style: Issues, Commentary and Advice,* ed. Joseph Bean. Los Angeles: Daedalus, 1993.

Banes, Sally. *Democracy's Body: Judson Dance Theater, 1962–1964.* Ann Arbor, MI: UMI Research Press, 1980.

———. *Greenwich Village 1963: Avant Garde Performance and the Effervescent Body.* Durham, NC: Duke University Press, 1993.

Bannon, Race. *Learning the Ropes: A Basic Guide to Safe & Fun S-M Lovemaking.* San Francisco: Daedalus Publishing, 1993.

Barber, Rowland. *The Night They Raided Minsky's.* New York: Simon and Schuster, 1960.

"The Barest in the Land." *Real Sex: 20.* Produced and directed by Patti Kaplan. New York: HBO, 1998.

Barrett, Raina. *First Your Money, Then Your Clothes: My Life and Oh! Calcutta!* New York: Morrow, 1973.

Barry, Dan. "Under Siege, a Topless Bar Will Cover Up." *New York Times*, 29 April 1998, p. A24.

Bartell, Gilbert D. *Group Sex: An Eyewitness Report on the American Way of Swinging.* New York: Signet, 1971.

Barthes, Roland. "Striptease." *Mythologies*, trans. Annette Lavers. New York: Hill and Wang, 1975, pp. 84–87.

Baudrillard, Jean. *Simulations.* New York: Semiotext(e), 1983.

———. "What Are You Doing after the Orgy?" trans. Lisa Liebmann. *Art forum*, 22 (October 1983): 42–46.

Baxandall, Lee. "Spectacles and Scenarios: A Dramaturgy of Radical Activity." *TDR*, 13:4 (Spring 1969): 5–71.

Bean, Joseph W. *Leathersex Q & A: Questions about Leathersex and the Leathersex Lifestyles Answered.* San Francisco: Daedalus, 1996.

Beatty, Maria. *Sphinxes without Secrets: Women Performance Artists Speak Out.* New York: Beatty, 1991; dist. San Francisco: Art Commission.

Bell, Elizabeth. "Performance Studies as Women's Work: Historical Sights/Sites/Citations from the Margin." *Text and Performance Quarterly*, 13:4 (October 1993): 350–374.

Bell, Laurie. "Sex Trade Workers and Feminists: Myths and Illusions, an Interview with Amber Cooke." *Good Girls/Bad Girls: Feminists and Sex Trade Workers Face to Face*, ed. Laurie Bell. Seattle: Seal Press, 1987, pp. 190–203.

Bell, Shannon. "Ejaculatory Television: The Talk Show and the Postmodern Subject." *Fuse*, 14: 5/6 (1991): 7–11.

Benjamin, Jessica. "Master and Slave: The Fantasy of Erotic Domination." *Powers of Desire: The Politics of Sexuality*, ed. Ann Snitow, Christine Stansell, and Sharon Thompson. New York: Monthly Review Press, 1983, pp. 280–299.

Benston, Kimberly W. "Being There: Performance as Mise-en-Scène, Abscene, Obscene, and Other Scene." *PMLA*, 107:3 (May 1992): 434–449.

Berger, Maurice. *Labyrinths: Robert Morris, Minimalism, and the 1960s.* New York: HarperCollins, 1990.

Bergman, David, ed. *Camp Grounds: Style and Homosexuality.* Amherst: University of Massachusetts Press, 1993.

Betty Pages Annual. New York: Black Cat Books, 1991.

Blackmer, Corinne, and Patricia J. Smith. *En Travesti: Women, Gender, Subversion, Opera.* New York: Columbia University Press, 1995.

Bogdan, Robert. *Freak Show: Presenting Human Oddities for Amusement and Profit.* Chicago: University of Chicago Press, 1988.

Boles, Jacqueline M. "The Nightclub Stripper: A Sociological Study of a Deviant Occupation." Ph.D. dissertation, University of Georgia, 1973; Ann Arbor MI: UMI Dissertation Service, 1993.

Boles, Jacqueline M., and Albeno O. Gabrin. "The Choice of Stripping for a Living: An Empirical and Theoretical Explanation." *Sociology of Work and Occupations,* 1: 1 (February 1974): 4–17.

Bordowitz, Gregg. "The AIDS Crisis Is Ridiculous." *Queer Looks: Perspectives on Lesbian and Gay Film and Video,* ed. Martha Gever, Pratibha Parmar, and John Greyson. New York: Routledge, 1993, pp. 208–224.

Brackley, Judith. "Male Strip Shows." *Ms,* 9:5 (November 1980): 68–70, 84.

Brame, Gloria G., William D. Brame, and Jon Jacobs. *Different Loving: An Exploration of the World of Sexual Dominance and Submission.* New York: Random House, 1993.

Braun, Walter. *The Cruel and the Meek.* New York: Lyle Stuart, 1967.

Brecht, Stefan. "Family of the f.p.: Notes on the Theatre of the Ridiculous." *TDR,* 13:1 (Fall 1968): 117–142.

Brenson, Michael. "Effects of Men's Desires on the Lives of Women." *New York Times,* 21 May 1990, p. C13.

Broomfield, Nick, dir. *Fetishes: Mysteries and Domination at Pandora's Box.* New York: HBO/A-Pix, 1996.

Brown, T. Allston. *A History of the New York Stage from 1732 to 1901.* 3 vols. New York: Dodd, Mead, 1903.

Burana, Lily. "The Old Bump and Grind: Can Stripping Support the Arts?" *Village Voice,* 5 May 1998, pp. 138–140.

———. "Stop the Sexual Revolution: I Want to Get Off." *Future Sex,* 6 (March–May 1994): 14–15.

Burgheart, Catherine, with Sam Blazer. "Sex Theatre." *TDR,* 25:1 (March 1981): 69–78.

BurLEZk Live and *BurLEZk II.* San Francisco: Fatale Video/Blush Entertainment, 1989, 1990.

Burnham, Linda. "Paul McCarthy: The Evolution of a Performance Artist." *High Performance,* 8:1 (issue 29; 1985): 37–43.

Burt, Ramsey. *The Male Dancer: Bodies, Spectacle and Sexuality.* New York: Routledge, 1995.

Bush, Melanie. "Gyneconomy." *Village Voice,* 21 May 1996, pp. 27–30.

Butler, Judith. "Lesbian S & M: The Politics of Disillusion." *Against Sadomasochism: A Radical Feminist Analysis,* ed. Robin Ruth Linden, Darlene R. Pagano, Diana E. H. Russell, and Susan Leigh Starr. East Palo Alto, CA: Frog in the Well, 1982.

Califia, Pat. *Public Sex: The Culture of Radical Sex.* Pittsburgh: Cleis Press, 1994.

———, ed. *The Lesbian S/M Safety Manual.* Denver, CO: Lace, 1988.

Califia, Pat, and Robin Sweeney, eds. *Second Coming: A Leatherdyke Reader.* Boston: Alyson, 1995.

"Candy Barr [interview]." *Oui,* 5:6 (June 1976): 81–84, 110–113.

Capon, Gustav, and Robert Yve-Plessis. *Les Théâtres clandestins.* Paris: Plessis, 1905.

Carr, C. *On Edge: Performance at the End of the Twentieth Century.* Hanover, NH: Wesleyan University Press, 1994.

Carter, Angela. *Nothing Sacred.* London: Virago, 1982.

Carter, Randolph. *The World of Flo Ziegfeld.* New York: Praeger, 1974.

Cartwright, Gary. "Candy: Taking the Wrapper Off a Texas Legend." *Texas Monthly,* 4 (December 1976): 99–103, 188–192.

Case, Sue-Ellen, ed. *Performing Feminisms.* Baltimore: Johns Hopkins University Press, 1990.

———. "Towards a Butch-Femme Aesthetic." *Discourse,* 11:1 (Fall-Winter 1988–1989): 55–73. Rpt. *Making a Spectacle: Feminist Essays on Contemporary Women's Theatre,* ed. Lynda Hart. Ann Arbor: University of Michigan Press, 1989, pp. 282–300.

Case, Sue-Ellen, Philip Brett, and Susan Leigh Foster, eds. *Cruising the Performative: Interventions into the Representation of Ethnicity, Nationality, and Sexuality.* Bloomington: Indiana University Press, 1995.

Castle, Charles. *The Folies Bergère.* New York: Franklin Watts, 1985.

Cavalcade of Burlesque. Philadelphia: Burlesque Historical Co., 1951–1955.

Champagne, Lenora. *Out from Under: Texts by Women Performance Artists.* New York: Theatre Communications Group, 1992.

Chancer, Lynn S. *Sadomasochism in Everyday Life: The Dynamics of Power and Powerlessness.* New Brunswick, NJ: Rutgers University Press, 1992.

Chapple, Steven, and David Talbot. *Burning Desires: Sex in America—A Report from the Field.* New York: Signet, 1990.

Charvill, Jean. *Histoire et sociologie du strip-tease.* Paris: Editions Planète, 1969.

Chevalier, Denys. *Metaphysique du striptease.* Paris: Pauvert, 1960.

Clark, David Aaron. "Happiness in Slavery: The Making of a Masochist." *Future Sex,* 6 (March–May 1994): 10–11.

———. "Interview with Annie Sprinkle." *Gauntlet,* 1:5 (1993): 123–130.

Clark, Rebecca. "Male Strippers: Ladies' Night at the Meat Market." *Journal of Popular Culture,* 19:1 (1985): 51–55.

Clum, John M. *Acting Gay: Male Homosexuality in Modern Drama.* New York: Columbia University Press, 1992.

Clurman, Harold. "New Playwrights: Boys and Girls on the Burning Deck." *Theatre 4: The American Theatre 1970–1971.* New York: Scribner's, 1972, pp. 166–177.

Collins, Joan. *Past Imperfect: An Autobiography.* New York: Simon and Schuster, 1984.

Collins, Patricia Hill. *Black Feminist Thought.* New York: Routledge, 1990.

Cooper, William M. [James Glass Bertram]. *An Illustrated History of the Rod.* Ware, England: Wordsworth, 1988.

Corio, Ann, with Joe DiMona. *This Was Burlesque.* New York: Grosset and Dunlap, 1968.

Cox, D., and D. Daitzman, eds. *Exhibitionism.* New York: Garland, 1980.

Creet, Julia. "Daughter of the Movement: The Psychodynamics of the Lesbian S/M Fantasy." *differences,* 3:2 (Summer 1991): 135–146.

Creith, Elaine. *Undressing Lesbian Sex: Popular Images, Private Acts and Public Consequences.* New York: Cassell, 1996.

Croyden, Margaret. *Lunatics, Lovers and Poets: The Contemporary Experimental Theatre.* New York: Delta, 1974.

Csicsery, George Paul. *The Sex Industry.* New York: NAL, 1973.

Curb, Rosemary Keefe, ed. *Amazon All Stars: Thirteen Lesbian Plays.* New York: Applause Theatre Books, 1998.

Curry, Ramona. *Too Much of a Good Thing: Mae West as Cultural Icon.* Minneapolis: University of Minnesota Press, 1996.

Curtin, Kaier. *"We Can Always Call Them Bulgarians": The Emergence of Lesbians and Gay Men on the American Stage.* Boston: Alyson Publications, 1987.

Daly, Ann. "Are Women Reclaiming or Reinforcing Sexist Imagery?" *High Performance,* 12:22 (Summer 1989): 18–19.

"Dance and Sexual Politics." Special issue of *Dance Theatre Journal,* 7:2 (Autumn 1989).

Dangerous Bedfellows [Ephen G. Colter, Wayne Hoffman, Eva Pendleton, Alison Redick, David Senlin]. *Policing Public Sex: Queer Politics and the Future of AIDS Activism.* Boston: South End Press, 1996.

David, Bruce. "Honeysuckle Divine." *Gallery* (February 1975): 22–25.

Davis, Tracy C. "The Actress in Victorian Pornography." *Theatre Journal,* 41 (October 1989): 294–315.

Davy, Kate. "Reading Past the Heterosexual Imperative: *Dress Suits to Hire.*" *TDR,* 33:1 (Spring 1989): 153–170.

de Lauretis, Teresa. *The Practice of Love: Lesbian Sexuality and Perverse Desire.* Bloomington: Indiana University Press, 1994.

———. "Sexual Indifference and Lesbian Representation." *Theatre Journal,* 40:2 (May 1988): 155–177; rpt. *The Lesbian and Gay Studies Reader,* ed. Henry Abelove, Michele Aina Barale, and David M. Halperin. New York: Routledge, 1993, pp. 141–158.

de Strulle, Arlene. "Sexual Fantasy Theatre." *TDR,* 20: 1 (March 1976): 64–74.

Delacoste, Frédérique, and Priscilla Alexander, eds. *Sex Work: Writings by Women in the Sex Industry.* Pittsburgh: Cleis Press, 1987.

Deleuze, Gilles [and Leopold von Sacher-Masoch]. *Masochism: An Interpretation of Coldness and Cruelty,* trans. Jean McNeil. New York: Braziller, 1971; *Sacher-Masoch: An Interpretation.* London: Faber and Faber, 1971; *Masochism.* New York: Zone Books, 1989.

Devon, Molly, and Phillip Miller. *Screw the Roses, Send Me the Thorns: The Romance and Sexual Sorcery of Sadomasochism.* Fairfield, CT: Mystic Rose, 1995.

Dick, Kirby, dir. *Sick: The Life and Death of Bob Flanagan, Supermasochist.* New York: Avalanche Films/Lexicon Home Entertainment, 1998.

Dolan, Jill. "Desire Cloaked in a Trenchcoat," *TDR,* 33:1 (Spring 1989): 59–67.

———. "The Dynamics of Desire: Sexuality and Gender in Pornography and Performance." *Theatre Journal,* 39:2 (May 1987): 156–174; rpt. *The Feminist Spectator as Critic.* Ann Arbor: University of Michigan Press, 1988, pp. 59–81.

———. *Presence and Desire: Essays on Gender, Sexuality, Performance.* Ann Arbor: University of Michigan Press, 1993.

———. " 'What, No Beans?': Images of Women and Sexuality in Burlesque Comedy." *Journal of Popular Culture,* 18 (Winter 1984): 37–48.

Dollimore, Jonathan. *Sexual Dissidence: Augustine to Wilde, Freud to Foucault.* Oxford: Clarendon Press, 1991.

Dragu, Margaret, and A.S.A. Harrison. *Revelations: Essays on Striptease and Sexuality.* London, Ontario: Nightwood Editions, 1988.

Dupuy, Jean, ed. *Collective Consciousness: Art Performances of the Seventies.* New York: New York Performing Arts Journal Publications, 1980.

Duvert, Tony. "Other People's Eroticism," trans. Joan Templeton. *Antaeus*, 4 (Winter 1976): 117–125.

Dworkin, Norine. "Porn Again: Bringing the Attorney General's Report to the Stage." *Village Voice*, 30 October 1990, p. 100.

Earle, Marcelle, with Arthur Homme, Jr. *Midnight Frolic: A Ziegfeld Girl's True Story.* Basking Ridge, NJ: Twin Oaks, 1999.

Easton, Dottie, and Catherine A. Liszt. *The Bottoming Book: Or How to Get Terrible Things Done to You by Wonderful People.* San Francisco: Greenery Press, 1995.

———. *The Topping Book: Or. Getting Good at Being Bad.* San Francisco: Greenery Press, 1995.

"Edge of Night Life." *New Yorker*, 11 January 1993, p. 9.

Eells, George, and Stanley Musgrove. *Mae West.* New York: Morrow, 1982.

Ehrenreich, Barbara, Elizabeth Hess, and Gloria Jacobs. *Re-Making Love: The Feminization of Sex.* Garden City, NY: Anchor/Doubleday, 1986.

Elsom, John. *Erotic Theatre.* New York: Taplinger, 1974.

Elwes, Catherine. "Floating Femininity: A Look at Performance Art by Women." *Women's Images of Men*, ed. Sarah Kent and Jacquiline Morreau. London: Pandora, 1990, pp. 164–193.

Erenberg, Lewis. *Steppin' Out: New York Nightlife and the Transformation of American Culture, 1890–1930.* Westport, CT: Greenwood, 1981.

Erickson, Jon. "Appropriation and Transgression in Contemporary American Performance: The Wooster Group, Holly Hughes, and Karen Finley." *Theatre Journal*, 42 (May 1990): 225–236.

Esslin, Martin. "Nudity: Barely the Beginning?" *Reflections: Essays on Modern Theatre.* Garden City, NY: Doubleday, 1969, pp. 179–182.

Everts, Kellie. "Triple Treat." *Sex Work: Writings by Women in the Sex Industry*, ed. Frédérique Delacoste and Priscilla Alexander. Pittsburgh: Cleis Press, 1987, pp. 37–38.

Fabre, Jon, with photos by Robert Mapplethorpe. *The Power of Theatrical Madness.* London: Institute of Contemporary Arts, 1986.

Farnsworth, Marjorie. *The Ziegfeld Follies.* New York: Bonanza Books, 1956.

Feingold, Michael. "Graphing Porn." *Village Voice*, 22 January 1991, p. 87.

Felshin, Nina, ed. *But Is It Art? The Spirit of Art as Activism.* Seattle: Bay Press, 1995.

Fiedler, Leslie. *Freaks: Myths and Images of the Secret Self.* New York: Simon and Schuster, 1978.

Finley, Karen. "The Constant State of Desire." *TDR*, 32:1 (T117, 1988): 139–151.

Fish, Charles. *Blue Ribbons and Burlesque: A Book of County Fairs.* Woodstock, VT: Countryman Press, 1998.

Fryer, Peter. *Mrs. Grundy: Studies in Sexual Prudery.* London: Dobson, 1965.

Fuchs, Elinor. "On Staging the Obscene Body." *TDR*, 33:1 (Spring 1989): 33–58.

"Gender and Sexual Identity." Special Issue. *Contact Quarterly*, 21:2 (Summer/Fall 1995): 16–25.

Gertzman, Jay A. *Bookleggers and Smuthounds: The Trade in Erotica, 1920–1940.* Philadelphia: University of Pennsylvania Press, 1999.

Gibson, Ian. *The English Vice: Beating, Sex, Shame in Victorian England and After.* Newburyport, MA: Duckworth UK, 1995.

Gilfoyle, Timothy J. *City of Eros: New York City, Prostitution, and the Commercialization of Sex, 1790–1920.* New York: Norton, 1992.

Gilman, Sander L. "Black Bodies, White Bodies: Toward an Iconography of Female Sexuality in Late Nineteenth-Century Art, Medicine, and Literature." *Critical Inquiry*, 12:1 (1985): 205–243.

Gilman, Susan. *Dark Twins: Imposture and Identity in Mark Twain's America*. Chicago: University of Chicago Press, 1989.

Gilmer, Walker. *Horace Liveright, Publisher of the Twenties*. New York: David Lewis, 1970.

Glueck, Grace. "Of a Woman's Body as Both Subject and Object." *New York Times*, 6 December 1996, p. C29.

Goffman, Erving. *Behavior in Public Places*. Glencoe, IL: Free Press, 1963.

Goldberg, RoseLee. *Performance Art: From Futurism to the Present*. New York: Harry Abrams, 1988; rev. of *Performance: Live Art 1909 to the Present*. New York: Abrams, 1979.

Goldstein, Al. "Lap Dancing." *Penthouse*, 26:7 (March 1995): 60–62, 64, 111.

Gorer, Geoffrey. *Hot Strip Tease and Other Notes on American Culture*. London: Cresset, 1937.

Gorsen, Peter. *Sexualästhetik: zur bürgerlichen Rezeption von Obzönität und Pornographie*. Hamburg: Rowohlt, 1972.

———. *Sexualästhetik: Grenzformen der Sinnlichkeit im 20. Jahrhundert*. Hamburg: Rowohlt, 1987.

Gosselin, Chris, and Glen Wilson. *Sexual Variations: Fetischism, Sadomasochism, Transvestism*. New York: Simon and Schuster, 1980.

Green, Abel, and Joe Laurie Jr. *Show Biz: From Vaude to Video*. 2 vols. New York: Holt, 1951.

Greene, Gerald, and Caroline Greene. *S-M: The Last Taboo*. New York: Grove Press, 1973.

Haden-Guest, Anthony. "World's Biggest Gang Bang II." *Penthouse*, 28:10 (June 1997): 134–136, 150, 166, 202.

Halpern, Rona Hildy. "Female Occupational Exhibitionism: An Exploratory Study of Topless and Bottomless Dancers." Ph.D. dissertation, United States International University, 1981; Ann Arbor, MI: UMI Dissertation Service, 1981.

Hamilton, Marybeth. "Mae West Live: *Sex, The Drag*, and 1920s Broadway." *TDR*, 36:4 (Winter 1992): 82–100.

———. *"When I'm Bad I'm Better": Mae West, Sex, and American Entertainment*. New York: Harper, 1994.

Haney, Lynn. *Naked at the Feast: A Biography of Josephine Baker*. London: Robson, 1981.

Hanley, Margaret Ann, ed. *Essential Papers on Masochism*. New York: New York University Press, 1995.

Hanna, Judith Lynne. *Dance, Sex and Gender: Signs of Identity, Dominance, Defiance, and Desire*. Chicago: University of Chicago Press, 1988.

Hansen, Al. *A Primer of Happenings and Time/Space Art*. New York: Something Else, 1965.

Hanson, Gillian. *Original Skin: Nudity and Sex in Cinema and Theatre*. London: Tom Stacy, 1970.

Hart, Lynda. *Between the Body and the Flesh: Performing Sadomasochism*. New York: Columbia University Press, 1998.

————. "Karen Finley's Dirty Work: Censorship, Homophobia, and the NEA." *Genders*, 14 (Fall 1992): 1–15.

————, ed. *Making a Spectacle: Feminist Essays on Contemporary Women's Theatre.* Ann Arbor: University of Michigan Press, 1989.

Hart, Lynda, and Peggy Phelan, eds. *Acting Out: Feminist Performances.* Ann Arbor: University of Michigan Press, 1993.

Harvey, Joel. "American Burlesque as Reflected through the Career of Kitty Madison, 1916–1931." Ph.D. dissertation, Florida State University, 1980.

Hatfield, Tom. *The Sandstone Experience.* New York: Crown, 1975.

Havis, Allan. "Mac Wellman on '7 Blowjobs.' " *Theatre Forum*, 1 (Spring 1992): 20–23.

Havoc, June. *More Havoc.* New York: Harper and Row, 1980.

Healy, Kathy. "The New Strippers." *Allure*, June 1992, pp. 96–99, 115.

Helbing, Terry. "Gay Plays, Gay Theatre, Gay Performance." *TDR*, 25:1 (March 1981): 35–46.

Heller, Wagner, and Pauly Heller. *Der Flagellantismus und Verwandte Formen Exzentrischer Sexualität im Amerika.* Hamburg: Hans W. Lassen, 1959.

Henican, Ellis. "Swinging Swings Back." *Penthouse*, 25:3 (November 1993): 54–56, 58–59, 63, 72, 113–114.

Henry, Buck. "My Night at Plato's Retreat." *Playboy*, 25:5 (May 1978): 160–163, 183–186.

Hoddeson, Bob. *The Porn People: A First-Person Documentary Report.* Watertown, MA: American Publishing Co., 1974.

Hodgetts, Victoria. "Reporter Tries Burlesque: I'll Cry Tomorrow but I'll Strip Tonight." *Village Voice*, 8 March 1976, 108–109.

Hoffman, William, ed. *Gay Plays: The First Collection.* New York: Avon Books, 1979.

Home Box Office. "Bare and Bold." *Real Sex: 9.* Produced and directed by Patti Kaplan. New York: HBO, 1994.

————. *Real Sex: Wild Cards.* Produced and directed by Patti Kaplan. New York: HBO, 1995.

Hubner, John. *Bottom Feeders: From Free Love to Hard Core—The Rise and Fall of Counterculture Heroes Jim and Artie Mitchell.* New York: Doubleday, 1993.

"Is There Life after Swinging?" *Time*, 16 January 1978, p. 53.

Isaac, Dan. "Ronald Tavel: Ridiculous Playwright." *TDR*, 13:1 (Fall 1968): 106–116.

Jacobs, Katrien. " 'The Lady of Little Death': Illuminated Encounters and Erotic Duties in the Life and Art of Maria Beatty." *Wide Angle*, 19:3 (1997): 13–40.

Janus, Sam, Barbara Bess, and Carol Saltus. *A Sexual Profile of Men in Power.* New York: Warner, 1978.

Jay, Ricky. *Learned Pigs and Fireproof Women.* New York: Villard Books, 1987.

Jennings, C. Robert. "Shaping Up for 'Oh! Calcutta!' " *Playboy*, 17:7 (July 1970): 7–76, 78, 196–197.

Jones, Amelia. *Body Art: Performing the Subject.* Minneapolis: University of Minnesota Press, 1998.

Jowitt, Deborah. "Getting It Off: Why Dancers Bare All for Art." *Village Voice*, 5 May 1998, p. 143.

Junker, Howard. "Theater of the Nude." *Playboy*, 15:11 (November 1968): 99–104, 197.

Kamel, G. W. Levi. "Leathersex: Meaningful Aspects of Gay Sadomasochism." *Deviant Behavior: An Interdisciplinary Journal*, 1:2 (January–March 1980): 171–191.

Kasson, John. *Amusing the Million: Coney Island at the Turn of the Century.* New York: Hill and Wang, 1978.

Keefe, Tim. *Some of My Best Friends Are Naked: Interviews with Seven Exotic Dancers.* San Francisco: Barbary Coast Press, 1992.

Kelly, Michael. "Sex Is Back." *Playboy,* 37:5 (May 1990): 122–124, 162–163, 165–166, 168.

Kiernan, Denise. "Spank You Very Much." *Village Voice,* 21 November 1995, p. 8.

Kinser, Samuel. *Carnival American Style: Mardi Gras at New Orleans and Mobile.* Chicago: University of Chicago Press, 1990.

Kirby, Michael. *Happenings.* New York: Dutton, 1965.

Kostelanetz, Richard. *On Innovative Performance(s): Three Decades of Recollections on Alternative Theatre.* Jefferson, NC: McFarland, 1994.

Kostenbaum, Wayne. *The Queen's Throat: Opera, Homosexuality, and the Mystery of Desire.* New York: Poseidon Press, 1993.

Kott, Jan. "A Little Treatise on Eroticism." *Evergreen Review,* 43 (October 1966): 54–55.

Kotz, Liz. "Interrogating the Boundaries of Women's Art: New Work in Video by Four Women." *High Performance,* 12:4 (Winter 1989): 36–41.

———. "Striptease East and West: Sexual Representation in Documentary Film." *Framework,* 38/39 (1992): 47–63.

Kozinn, A. "Nude Characters to Remain in City Opera Production." *New York Times,* 2 July 1990, p. A14.

Krafft-Ebing, Richard von. *Psychopathia Sexualis,* trans. Franklin S. Klaf. 1886; New York: Stein and Day, 1965.

Kroll, Eric. *Sex Objects: An American Photodocumentary.* Danbury NH: Addison House, 1977.

Kronhausen, Eberhard, and Phyllis Kronhausen. *The Sex People: Erotic Performers and Their Brave New Worlds.* Chicago: Playboy Press, 1975.

Kugelmass, Jack. *Masked Culture: The Greenwich Village Hollywood Parade.* New York: Columbia University Press, 1995.

———. "Wishes Come True: Designing the Greenwich Village Halloween Parade." *Journal of American Folklore,* 104 (Fall 1991): 443–465.

Lacy, Suzanne, and Leslie Labowitz. "November 18, 1978: Take Back the Night: San Francisco, CA." *High Performance,* 2:4 (Winter 1979/1980): 32–34.

"Ladies Night." *Real Sex: 20.* Produced and directed by Patti Kaplan. New York: HBO, 1998.

Lahr, John. "The Theater's Voluptuary Itch." *Evergreen Review,* 56 (July 1968): 32–41, 88–92.

Lahr, John, and Jonathan Price. *Life-Show: How to See Theater in Life and Life in Theater.* New York: Viking, 1973.

Langland, Paul. "Between the Cracks; An Interview with Diane Tott on Gender and Sexual Identity in the New Dance/Performance Scene." *Contact Quarterly,* 21:2 (Summer/Fall 1995): 16–25.

Langley, Erika. *The Lusty Lady: Photographs and Texts.* New York: Scalo, 1997.

Lash, Mistress Lilith. "Pain, Pleasure and Poetry." *Sex Work: Writings by Women in the Sex Industry,* ed. Frédérique Delacoste and Priscilla Alexander. Pittsburgh: Cleis Press, 1987, pp. 50–52.

Laufe, Abe. *The Wicked Stage: A History of Theater Censorship and Harassment in the United States.* New York: Frederick Ungar, 1978.

Lawrence, Denise L. "Parades, Politics, and Competing Urban Images: Doo Dah and Roses." *Urban Anthropology*, 11 (1982): 155–176.

———. "Rules of Misrule: Notes on the Doo Dah Parade in Pasadena." *Time Out of Time: Essays on the Festival*, ed. Alessandro Falassi. Albuquerque: University of New Mexico Press, 1987, pp. 123–136.

LeBruin, Annie, ed. *Petits et grand theatres du Marquis de Sade.* Paris: n.p., [1989].

Lederer, Laura, ed. *Take Back the Night: Women on Pornography.* New York: William Morrow, 1980.

Lee, Gypsy Rose. *Gypsy.* New York: Harper, 1957.

Leonard, Maurice. *Mae West: Empress of Sex.* New York: Carol/Birch Lane, 1991.

"Let My People Come: The Last Dirty Word in Musicals." *Playboy*, 1:7 (July 1974): 145–147.

Lewin, Lauri. *Naked Is the Best Disguise: My Life as a Stripper.* New York: Morrow, 1984.

Lewis, Arthur L. *Carnival.* New York: Trident Press, 1970.

Liepe-Levinson, Katherine H. "Striptease: Desire, Mimetic Jeopardy, and Performing Spectators." *TDR*, 42:2 (Summer 1998): 9–37.

———. "A Striptease Poetics." Ph.D. dissertation, City University of New York, 1993.

Linden, Robin Ruth, Darlene R. Pagano, Diana E. H. Russell, and Susan Leigh Star, eds. *Against Sadomasochism: A Radical Feminist Analysis.* East Palo Alto, CA: Frog in the Well, 1982.

Lippard, Lucy R. "The Pains and Pleasures of Rebirth: European and American Women's Body Art." *Art in America*, 64 (May–June 1976): 73–81.

Lipton, Lawrence. *The Erotic Revolution: An Affirmative View of the New Morality.* Los Angeles: Sherbourne, 1965; New York: Pocket Books, 1966.

Loeffler, Donald Lee. *An Analysis of the Treatment of the Homosexual Character in Dramas Produced in the New York Theatre from 1950 to 1968.* New York: Arno Press, 1975.

Ludlam, Charles. *The Complete Plays.* New York: Harper and Row, 1989.

Lutenbacher, Cindy. "Theater X's *A History of Sexuality*." *Theater*, 20 (Spring–Summer 1989): 85–90.

Luther, Jeanette (aka "Mistress Antoinette"). *Tied up with Love: The Making of Mistress Antoinette.* Tustin, CA: Versatile, 1987.

Macadams, Lewis. ". . . It Started Out with Death . . ." *High Performance*, 5 (Spring–Summer 1982): 43–49.

MacAloon, John J., ed. *Rite, Drama, Festival, Spectacle: Rehearsals toward a Theory of Cultural Performance.* Philadelphia: Institute for the Study of Human Issues, 1984.

MacDonald, John M. *Indecent Exposure.* Chicago: Charles C. Thomas, 1973.

Macy, Marianne. *Working Sex: An Odyssey into Our Cultural Underworld.* New York: Carroll and Graf, 1996.

Mains, Geoffrey. *Urban Aboriginals: A Celebration of Leather Sexuality.* San Francisco: Gay Sunshine, 1991.

Malina, Judith, and Julian Beck. *Paradise Now.* New York: Vintage, 1971.

Manning, Caitlin, and Glen Foster. *Stripped Bare: A Look at Erotic Dancers.* Derry, NH: Chip Taylor Communications, 1989.

Mannix, Daniel P. *Freaks: We Who Are Not as Others*. San Francisco: RE/Search, 1976, 1990.

"The Many Faces of S/M." Special issue of *Gauntlet*, 15 (1998).

Marcus, Maria. *A Taste for Pain*, trans. Joan Tate. New York: St. Martin's, 1981.

Margolis, H. E., and Paul Rubenstein. *The Groupsex Tapes*. New York: McKay, 1971.

Mattson, Heidi. *Ivy League Stripper*. New York: Arcade, 1995.

McAdams, Dona Ann. *Caught in the Act: A Look at Contemporary Multimedia Performance*. New York: Aperture, 1998.

McCaghy, Charles H., and James K. Skipper Jr. "Lesbian Behavior as an Adaptation to the Occupation of Stripping." *Social Problems*, 17 (Fall 1969): 262–270.

McClintock, Ann. "Maid to Order: Commercial S/M and Gender Power." *Dirty Looks: Women, Pornography, Power*, ed. Pamela Church Gibson and Roma Gibson. London: British Film Institute, 1993, pp. 207–231; excerpted in *Skin Two*, 14 (1994): 70–71.

McCullough, Jack W. *Living Pictures on the New York Stage*. Ann Arbor, MI: UMI Research Press, 1983.

McCumber, David. *X-Rated: The Mitchell Brothers, a True Story of Sex, Money, and Death*. New York: Simon and Schuster, 1992.

McNulty, Charles. "The Ridiculous Theatrical Company: Still Mocking after All These Years." *Theater*, 23:3 (Summer/Fall 1992): 67–69.

McWalter, Keith. "Couch Dancing." *New York Times Magazine*, 6 December 1987, p. 38.

Meibomius, John Henry [Heinrich Meibaum or Meibom]. *A Treatise on the Use of Flogging in Medicine and Venery*. Paris [New York]: Isidore Liseux, 1898 [1920s?]; originally published as *De Usu Flagrorum* (1630?), but translated as *A Treatise of the Use of Flogging in Venereal Affairs*. Leiden, 1639?

Merck, Mandy. "The Feminist Ethics of Lesbian S/M." *Perversions: Deviant Readings*. New York: Routledge, 1993, esp. pp. 236–266.

Merkin, Daphne. "Unlikely Obsession: Confronting a Taboo." *New Yorker*, 26 February and 4 March 1996, pp. 98–100, 102, 104, 111–115.

Miller, Carl. *Stages of Desire: Gay Theatre's Hidden History*. New York: Cassell, 1996.

Minsky, Morton, and Milt Machlin. *Minsky's Burlesque: A Fast and Funny Look at America's Bawdiest Era*. New York: Arbor House, 1986.

Mishan, Edward J. *Pornography, Psychedelics and Technology: Essays on the Limits to Freedom*. London: Allen and Unwin, 1980.

Mistress Jacqueline, as told to Catherine Tavel and Robert H. Rimmer. *Whips and Kisses: Parting the Leather Curtain*. Buffalo, NY: Prometheus, 1991.

Mitchell Brothers. *Never a Tender Moment*. San Francisco: Mitchell Brothers Releasing Group, 1985.

Mizejewski, Linda. *Ziegfeld Girl: Image and Icon in Culture and Cinema*. Durham, NC: Duke University Press, 1999.

Modleski, Tania. *Feminism without Women: Culture and Criticism in a "Postfeminist" Age*. New York: Routledge, 1991.

Montano, Linda. "Summer Saint Camp 1987, with Annie Sprinkle and Veronica Vera." *TDR*, 33:1 (Spring 1989): 94–119.

Moon, Michael. "Flaming Closets." *Bodies of the Text: Dance as Theory, Literature as Dance*, ed. Ellen W. Goellner and Jacqueline Shea Murphy. New Brunswick, NJ: Rutgers University Press, 1995, pp. 57–78.

Mooney, Dean J. M. "Shame, Body Image and Locus of Control in Male and Female Exotic Dancers." Ph.D. dissertation, University of Detroit, 1991; Ann Arbor, MI: UMI Dissertation Service, 1991.

Moore, Frank. "Eroplay." *TDR*, 33:1 (Spring 1989): 120–131.

Moramarco, Sheila Sobell. "Male Strippers." *Playboy*, 25:6 (June 1978): 50.

Morgan, Thaïs E. "A Whip of One's Own: Dominatrix Pornography and the Construction of a Post-Modern (Female) Subjectivity." *American Journal of Semiotics*, 6:4 (1989): 109–136.

Mueller, Petra, and Elizabeth Dewey. *Live Girls Nude*. San Francisco: 1989.

Murray, Ken. *The Body Merchant: The Story of Earl Carroll*. Pasadena, CA: Ward Ritchie Press, 1976.

Musto, Michael. "La Dolce Musto." *Village Voice*. Weekly column, 1993–.

Naerssen, A. X., Mart van Dijk, Geert Hoogeveen, Dick Visser, and Gertjan van Zessen. "Gay SM in Pornography and Reality." *Journal of Homosexuality*, 13 (Winter 1986/Spring 1987): 111–119.

Nasaw, David. *Going Out: The Rise and Fall of Public Amusements*. New York: Basic Books, 1993.

Owens, Tuppy. *The (Safer) Sex Maniac's Bible: A World Review of Sexuality, Listings of Erotic Clubs in All Major Cities, and Fun and Games for Your Delectation*. London: Tuppy Owens, 1990.

Palac, Lisa. "Viva La Pussy: Love, Sex, and Being Female with Ann Magnuson." *Future Sex*, 6 (March–May 1994): 24–28.

Panken, Shirley. *The Joy of Suffering*. New York: Jacob Aronson, 1973.

Paris, Yvette. *Queen of Burlesque: The Autobiography of Yvette Paris*. Buffalo, NY: Prometheus, 1989.

Partridge, Bruno. *A History of Orgies*. New York: Bonanza Books, 1960.

"Paul McCarthy: A Penis Painting Appreciated: American Hotel, October 1, 1980." *High Performance*, 3 (Fall–Winter 1980): 80–81.

Paulson, Don, with Roger Simpson. *An Evening at the Garden of Allah: A Gay Cabaret in Seattle*. New York: Columbia University Press, 1996.

Pauly, Joachim. *Die Anglolagnie*. Hamburg: Hans Lassen, 1956.

———. *Der Sexuelle Fetischism*. Hamburg: Hans Lassen, 1967.

Peiss, Kathy. *Cheap Amusements: Working Women and Leisure in Turn-of-the-Century New York*. Philadelphia: Temple University Press, 1986.

Phelan, Peggy. *Unmarked: The Politics of Performance*. New York: Routledge, 1993.

Pilat, Oliver, and Jo Ranson. *Sodom by the Sea: An Affectionate History of Coney Island*. Garden City, NY: Doubleday, Doran, 1941.

Plachy, Sylvia, and James Ridgeway. *Red Light: Inside the Sex Industry*. New York: Powerhouse Books, 1996.

"Playhouse of the Ridiculous." *Avant-Garde*, September 1968, pp. 12–24.

Pleasant, George. *The Joy of Streaking: A Guide to America's Favorite Pastime*. New York: Ballantine, 1974.

Podolsky, Edward, and Carlson Wade. *Sexual Masochism*. New York: Epic Publishing, 1961.

Poland, Jefferson F., and Valerie Alison. *The Records of the San Francisco Sexual Freedom League*. New York: Olympia, 1971.

Posner, Richard A. *Sex and Reason*. Cambridge: Harvard University Press, 1992.

Pramaggiore, Maria. "Belly Laughs and Naked Rage: Resisting Humor in Karen Finley's

Performance Art." *New Perspectives on Women and Comedy*, ed. Regina Barreca. Philadelphia: Gordon and Breach, 1992, pp. 47–63.

Preminger, Erik Lee. *Gypsy and Me: At Home and on the Road with Gypsy Rose Lee*. New York: Ballantine, 1986.

Prewitt, Terry J. "Like a Virgin: The Semiotics of Illusion in Erotic Performance." *American Journal of Semiotics*, 6:4 (1989): 137–152.

Queen, Carol. "Erotic Power and Trust." *The Erotic Impulse: Honoring the Sensual Self*, ed. David Steinberg. New York: Jeremy P. Tarcher/Perigee, 1992, pp. 225–234.

———. *Exhibitionism for the Shy*. San Francisco: Down There Press, 1995.

Rabenalt, Arthur Maria. *Mimus Eroticus*. 5 vols. Hamburg: Verlag für Kulturforschung, 1965–1967.

———. *Theatrum Sadicum*. Emsdetten: Lechte, 1963.

———. *Voluptas Ludens: Erotische Geheimtheater, 17. 18. und 19. Jahrhundert*. Munich: Verlag der Schaumbuhne, 1962.

Rabkin, Gerald. "The Kenneth Bernard–John Vaccaro Ten-Year Queer Show." *Soho Weekly News*, 16 June 1977, pp. 17–20.

Rader, Dotson. "Notes from the Underground: St. James Baths." *Evergreen Review*, 58 (September 1968): 17, 85–92.

Ragni, Jerome, and James Rado. *Hair*. New York: Pocket Books, 1970.

Raphael, Lennox. "Notes from the Underground: Censorship." *Evergreen Review*, 67 (June 1969): 20–21, 92.

Rapi, Nina. "Hide and Seek: The Search for a Lesbian Theatre Aesthetic." *New Theatre Quarterly*, 9 (May 1993): 147–158.

Rapi, Nina, and Maya Chowdry, eds. *Acts of Passion: Sexuality, Gender, and Performance*. Binghamton, NY: Haworth Press, 1998.

Raven, Arlene. "Looking Beneath the Surface: Deep inside Porn Stars." *High Performance*, 7:4 (Issue 28, 1984), 24–27, 90–91.

"Real Girl World." *Future Sex* (March–May 1994): 13.

Rechy, John. *The Sexual Outlaw: A Documentary*. New York: Grove, 1977.

Reik, Theodor. *Masochism in Modern Man*, trans. Margaret H. Beigel and Gertrud M. Kurth. New York: Farrar, Straus, 1941.

Renay, Liz. *My First 2,000 Men*. Fort Lee, NJ: Barricade Books, 1992.

Rich, B. Ruby. "Feminism and Sexuality in the 1980s." *Feminist Studies*, 12:3 (1986): 529–532.

Robert/"Stella." "Stella through the Looking Glass." *Dirty Looks: Women, Pornography, Power*, ed. Pamela Church Gibson and Roma Gibson. London: British Film Institute, 1993, pp. 73–85.

Roberts, Nickie. *The Front Line: Women in the Sex Industry Speak*. London: Grafton Books, 1986.

Roemer, Rick. *Charles Ludlam and the Ridiculous Theatrical Company: Critical Analyses of 29 Plays*. Jefferson, NC: MacFarland, 1997.

Rose, Phyllis. *Jazz Cleopatra: Josephine Baker In Her Time*. New York: Vintage, 1991.

Rosen, Dan. "Sex Goes Public: The Straights Follow." *Playboy*, 24:7 (July 1977): 99–101, 126–129.

Rosenthal, Rachel. "Performance Notes: Taboo Subjects: Performance and the Masochist Tradition." *High Performance*, 4 (Winter 1981–1982): 22–25.

Rostagno, Aldo, with Julian Beck and Judith Malina. *We, the Living Theatre*. New York: Ballantine, 1970.

Roth, Moira, ed. *The Amazing Decade: Women and Performance Art in America, 1970–1980*. Los Angeles: Astro Artz, 1983.

Rothe, Len. *The Bare Truth: Stars of Burlesque of the 1940s and 1950s*. Atglen, PA: Schiffer Publications, 1998.

———. *The Queens of Burlesque: Vintage Photographs of the 1940s and 1950s*. Atglen, PA: Schiffer Publications, 1998.

Rowland, Willard D. *The Politics of TV Violence: Policy Uses of Communication Research*. Beverly Hills, CA: Sage, 1983.

Royalle, Candida, dir. *Deep inside Porn Stars*. Club 90, New York City, 26 January 1984.

Rubin, Gayle. "Thinking Sex: Notes for a Radical Theory of the Politics of Sexuality." *Pleasure and Danger: Exploring Female Sexuality*, ed. Carole S. Vance. Boston: Routledge and Kegan Paul, 1984, pp. 267–319.

Russo, Mary. *The Female Grotesque: Risk, Excess and Modernity*. New York: Routledge, 1995.

Ryder, Deborah. "Lady O." *Tales from the Clit: A Female Experience of Pornography*, ed. Cherie Matrix. San Francisco: AK Press, 1996, pp. 17–20.

Saalfield, Catherine. "Performance Gone Good." *Outweek* (23 May 1990): 66, 72.

Sabol, Blair. "This Box Lunch Will Kill Your Appetite." *Village Voice*, 20 September 1976, pp. 16, 23.

Salutin, Marilyn. "Stripper Morality," *Transaction*, 8:8 (June 1974): 12–22; also in *The Sexual Scene*, ed. John H. Gagnon and William Simon. 2d ed. New Brunswick, NJ: Transaction/Dutton, 1973, pp. 167–192.

Samois. *Coming to Power: Writings and Graphics on Lesbian S/M*. 2d ed. Boston: Alyson Publishers, 1982.

———. *What Color Is Your Handkerchief? A Lesbian S/M Sexuality Reader*. San Francisco: Samois, 1979.

Sandford, Mariellen, ed. *Happenings and Other Acts*. New York: Routledge, 1995.

Sayre, Henry M. *The Object of Performance: The American Avant-Garde since 1970*. Chicago: University of Chicago Press, 1990.

———. "Scars: Painting, Photography, Performance, Pornography, and the Disfigurement of Art." *Performing Arts Journal*, 46 (1994): 64–74.

Schechner, Richard. *Dionysus in '69*. New York: Farrar, Straus, and Giroux, 1970.

———. "News, Sex, and Performance Theory." *Between Theater and Anthropology*. Philadelphia: University of Pennsylvania Press, 1985, pp. 295–324.

———. "Pornography and the New Expression." *The Perverse Imagination*, ed. Irving Buchen. New York: New York University Press, 1970, pp. 103–114.

Schertel, Ernst, ed. *Die Komplex der Flagellomanie*. Berlin: Pergamon Verlag, 1932.

Schidrowitz, Leo, ed. *Sittengeschichte des Theaters. Ein Darstellung des Theaters, seiner Entwicklung und Stellung in zwei Jahrhunderten*. Vol. V of *Sittengeschichte der Kulturwelt und ihrer Entwicklung in Einzeldarstellungen*. 10 vols. plus suppl. (1926–1930). Vienna/Leipzig: Verlag für Kulturforschung, 1927.

Schneemann, Carolee. *More than Meat Joy: Complete Performance Works and Selected Writings*, ed. Bruce McPherson. New Paltz, NY: Documentext, 1979.

Schneider, Rebecca. *The Explicit Body in Performance*. New York: Routledge, 1997.

———. "Holly Hughes: Polymorphous Perversity and the Lesbian Scientist." *TDR*, 33:1 (Spring 1989): 171–183.

Scott, Gini Graham. *Dominant Women, Submissive Men: An Exploration in Erotic Dominance and Submission.* New York: Praeger, 1983; aka *Erotic Power: An Exploration of Dominance and Submission.* Secaucus, NJ: Citadel Press, 1983.

Screw. New York, 1968–.

Sellers, Terence. *The Correct Sadist: The Memoirs of Angel Stern.* New York: Vitriol Publishing, 1983.

The Sensuous Streaker, 1:1. New York: Magazine Management, 1974.

"Sex and Performance Issue." *The Drama Review,* 25:1 (March 1981).

Shellogg, Susan. *Unnatural Acts.* New York: Barricade Books, 1994.

Siegel, Carol. *Male Masochism: Modern Revisions of the Story of Love.* Bloomington: Indiana University Press, 1995.

Silver, Rachel. *The Girl in Scarlet Heels: Women in the Sex Business Speak Out.* N. Pomfret, VT: Trafalgar Square, 1994.

Sisley, Emily L. "Notes on Lesbian Theatre." *TDR,* 25:1 (March 1981): 47–56.

Skipper, James K., Jr., and Charles H. McCaghy. "Stripteasers: The Anatomy and Career Contingencies of a Deviant Occupation." *Social Problems,* 17 (Winter 1970): 391–405.

———. "Stripteasing: A Sex-Oriented Occupation." *Studies in the Sociology of Sex,* ed. James M. Henslin. New York: Appleton-Century-Crofts, 1971, pp. 275–296.

———. "Teasing, Flashing and Visual Sex: Stripping for a Living." *The Sociology of Sex: An Introductory Reader,* ed. James M. Henslin and Edward Sagarin. Rev. ed. 1978, pp. 169–184.

Smith, Howard, and Brian Van Der Horst. "It's Hard to Stay Hot." *Village Voice,* 25 October 1976, p. 26.

Smith, Howard, and Leslie Harlib. "Plato's Retreat." *Village Voice,* 3 October 1977, p. 20.

Sobel, Bernard. *Burleycue: An Underground History of Burlesque Days.* New York: Farrar, Reinhart, 1931.

———. *A Pictorial History of Burlesque.* New York: Putnam, 1956.

Sontag, Susan. "Notes on Camp." *Against Interpretation.* New York: Farrar, Straus, and Giroux, 1966, pp. 275–292.

Southern, Georgia. *Georgia: My Life in Burlesque.* New York: Signet, 1972.

Sprinkle, Annie [Ellen F. Steinberg]. "Performance Hits: Bosom Ballet Folklorica, How to Be a Sex Object, and a Public Cervix Announcement." Dominique's Harmony Burlesk Theater, New York City, 15, 16, 17 June 1989; Performance flyer.

———. *Post Porn Modernist.* Amsterdam: Art Unlimited, 1991.

Srivastava, Vinita. "Women Lap It Up." *Village Voice,* 5 December 1995, pp. 9–10.

Stagg, Jerry. *The Brothers Shubert.* New York: Random House, 1968.

Starr, Blaze, as told to Huey Perry. *My Life.* New York: Praeger, 1974.

Stein, Martha. *Lovers, Friends, Slaves . . .* New York: Berkeley Medallion, 1974.

Stekel, Wilhelm. *Sadism and Masochism: The Psychology of Hatred and Cruelty,* trans. Louise Brink. 2 vols. New York: Liveright, 1929, 1953.

Stencell, A. W. *Girl Show: Into the Canvas World of Bump and Grind.* Toronto: ECW Press, 1999.

Stoller, Robert. *Pain and Passion: A Psychoanalyst Explores the World of S-M.* New York: Plenum Press, 1991.

———. *Perversion: The Erotic Form of Hatred.* New York: Dell, 1975.

Storm, Tempest, with Bill Boyd. *The Lady Is a Vamp*. Atlanta: Peachtree Publishers, 1987.

Straayer, Chris. "The Seduction of Boundaries: Feminist Fluidity in Annie Sprinkle's Art/Education/Sex." *Dirty Looks: Women, Pornography, Power*, ed. Pamela Church Gibson and Roma Gibson. London: British Film Institute, 1993, pp. 156–175.

The Streets of Paris. Chicago: Paris Art Company, 1933.

"Striptease." Special issue of *TDR*, 42:2 (Summer 1998).

Stuart, Otis. "No Tongues, Please—We're Queer: The Same-Sex Kiss on the New York Stage." *Village Voice*, 2 February 1993, p. 90.

Suleiman, Susan Rubin. "Pornography and the Avant-Garde." *The Poetics of Gender*, ed. Nancy Miller. New York: Columbia University Press, 1986, pp. 117–136.

———. *Subversive Intent: Gender, Politics, and the Avant-Garde*. Cambridge: Harvard University Press, 1990.

Sundahl, Debi Sundahl. "Stripper." *Sex Work: Writings by Women in the Sex Industry*, edited by Frédérique Delacoste and Priscilla Alexander. Pittsburgh: Cleis Press, 1987, pp. 175–180.

Symonds, Carolyn. "Sexual Mate-Swapping: Violation of Norms and Reconciliation of Guilt." *Studies in the Sociology of Sex*, ed. James M. Henslin. New York: Appleton-Century-Crofts, 1971, pp. 81–109.

Talese, Gay. *Thy Neighbor's Wife*. New York: Dell, 1981.

Theroux, Paul. "Nurse Wolf." *New Yorker*, 15 June 1998, pp. 50–60, 62–63.

Thomas, Helen, ed. *Dance, Gender and Culture*. New York: St. Martin's, 1995.

Thompson, Bill. *Sadomasochism: Painful Perversion or Pleasurable Play?* New York: Cassell, 1993.

Thompson, Mark, ed. *Leatherfolk: Radical Sex, People, Politics, and Practice*. Boston: Alyson Press, 1991.

Thomson, Rosemarie Garland. *Freakery: Cultural Spectacles of the Extraordinary Body*. New York: New York University Press, 1996.

"Through the Looking Glass." *Real Sex: 18*. Produced and directed by Patti Kaplan. New York: HBO, 1997.

Toepfer, Karl. *Theatre, Aristocracy, and Pornocracy: The Orgy Calculus*. New York: PAJ Publications, 1991.

"Topless." *Playboy*, 13:9 (September 1966): 160–167, 187–188, 190–191.

Tornellan, Carole. "Keep Your Fly Buttoned: Putting Desire, Danger and Pleasure Back in the Streets." *High Performance*, 13:3 (Fall 1990): 38–41.

Townsend, Larry. *The Leatherman's Handbook*. New York: Olympia Press, 1972; rpt. Beverly Hills, CA: Larry Townsend, 1983; rpt. *The Leatherman's Handbook II*. New York: Carlyle Communications, 1989; *The Original Leatherman's Handbook*. Beverly Hills, CA: LT Publications, 1993.

———. *Master of Masters*, ed. Victor Terry. Beverly Hills, CA: LT Publications, 1997.

———. *To Take a Slave and Other Stories of Male/Male S/M*. Los Angeles: L. Townsend, 1995.

Trebay, Guy. "Culture Club: A Lesbian Landmark's Preservation." *Village Voice*, 27 June 1995, p. 20.

———. "Only Looking: Scenes from a Go-Go Planet." *Village Voice*, 16 February 1993, pp. 27–29.

Tribelly, Angela. "Burlesque Is Back, a Step Ahead of the Law." *New York Times*, 5 October 1998, p. B3.

Truman, James. "The American Male: The Naked Truth." *Vogue*, 179 (June 1989): 241.

Turner, Victor. "Frame, Flow and Reflection: Ritual and Drama as Public Liminality." *Performance in Postmodern Culture*, ed. Michel Benamou and Charles Caramello. Madison: Coda Press, 1977, pp. 35–55.

Tynan, Kenneth. *The Sound of Two Hands Clapping*. New York: Holt, Rinehart, and Winston, 1975.

Tynan, Kenneth, et al. *Oh! Calcutta!* New York: Grove Press, 1969.

Vale, V., and Andrea Juno, eds. *Angry Women*. San Francisco: RE/Search, 1992.

———. *Bob Flanagan: Super Masochist*. San Francisco: RE/Search, 1994.

Valenti, Chi Chi. "Steamed Clams." *Village Voice*, 3 September 1991, p. 30.

Vallillo, Stephen N. "Broadway Reviews in the Teens and Twenties: Smut and Slime?" *TDR*, 25:1 (March 1981): 25–34.

Van Every, Edward. *Sins of America as Exposed by the Police Gazette*. New York: Stokes, 1931.

Varney, Mike, comp. *Grindhouse Follies*. 3 reels. P.O. Box 33664, Seattle: Something Weird Video, 1991.

Vassi, Marco, ed. *The Wonderful World of Penthouse Sex: Radical Sex in the Establishment*. New York: Penthouse/General Media, 1975.

Vater, John. "The Sutro Baths." *Oui*, 5 (April 1976): 70–74.

Vaughan, Don. "From Reel to Real: A Conversation with Annie Sprinkle." *Gauntlet*, 14 (1997): 13–19.

Village Voice. New York, 1959–.

Villeneuve, Roland. *Le Musée des Supplices*. Paris: Éditions Azur-Co, 1968.

Von Cleef, Monique, with William Waterman. *The House of Pain: The Strange World of Monique Von Cleef, the Queen of Humiliation*. Secaucus, NJ: Lyle Stuart, 1973.

Voyeur Video. Catalog of Travel/Adventure, Nudist, and Public Sex Videocassettes. DDI, P.O. Box 77902, San Francisco 94107.

Wagner, Mary. "Donna from 'Live Show.'" *Heresies*, 5:1 (issue 17; 1984): 31–33.

Wald, Elissa. *Meeting the Master: Stories about Mastery, Slavery, and the Dark Side of Desire*. Los Angeles: Wald, 1994; New York: Grove, 1996; London: Abacus, 1998.

Warren, John. *The Loving Dominant*. New York: Masquerade, 1994.

Webb, Peter. *The Erotic Arts*. Boston, New York: Graphic Society, 1975.

Weene, Seph. "Venus." *Heresies* [Sex issue], 12 (1981): 36–38.

Weinberg, Thomas, and G. W. Levi Kamel, eds. *Studies in Sadomasochism*. Buffalo, NY: Prometheus Books, 1983; rev. ed. T. S. Weinberg, *S & M: Studies in Dominance and Submission*. Buffalo, NY: Prometheus, 1995.

Wellman, Mac. "7 Blowjobs." *Theatre Forum*, 1 (Spring 1992): 24–33.

Werner, Ken. *Halloween*. San Francisco: RE/Search, 1990.

West, Mae. *Goodness Had Nothing to Do with It*. Englewood Cliffs, NJ: Prentice-Hall, 1959.

———. "Interview." *Playboy*, 18:1 (January 1971): 71–78.

Wetzsteon, Ross. "Sex Acts on Stage: Where Does Art Get Off?" *Village Voice*, 22 March 1976, 76–77.

Williams, Linda. Hard Core: Power, Pleasure, and the Frenzy of the Visible. Berkeley: University of California Press, 1989.

————. "A Provoking Agent: The Pornography and Performance Art of Annie Sprinkle." *Dirty Looks: Women, Pornography, Power*, ed. Pamela Church Gibson and Roma Gibson. London: British Film Institute, 1993, pp. 176–191.

Wiseman, Jay. *S/M 101: A Realistic Introduction*. San Francisco: Greenery Press, 1996.

Wojnarowicz, David. *Memories That Smell like Gasoline: Art and Memoirs*. San Francisco: Artspace Books, 1992.

Wortley, Richard. *A Pictorial History of Striptease: 100 Years of Undressing to Music*. Secaucus, NJ: Chartwell, 1976.

Wunderer, Richard. *Treibhaus der Erotik: Pansexualismus und Orgiasmus in erotischen Wunschträumen und sexueller Wirklichkeit*. Schmiden bei Stuttgart: Freya, 1967.

Zeidman, Irving. *The American Burlesque Show*. New York: Hawthorne, 1967.

11

Erotic and Pornographic Art

EROTIC FIGURATION

Because entries on erotic-verging-on-pornographic art could easily swamp this *Guide*, the list in this section is highly selective; it is intended to be representative of American artists rather than exhaustive. Scholars trying to find material on relative unknowns will find *Art in America* useful; each month the editors print notices of gallery openings, museum exhibitions, displays in alternative spaces, dealers, and catalogs, and each year they print an annual index keyed to artists. Helpful also are magazines as diverse as the glossy *New Art Examiner* and the tabloid *Flash Art*, which dutifully report on erotic works and exhibitions. Although no serious art journal can ignore the constant experimentation with sexual representation on the contemporary scene, few cover such subjects as well. Publishers in recent years have issued photographic compilations of erotic art (painting, sculpture, crafts, artifacts) from around the world, most of it ancient, European, or Oriental rather than American and therefore outside our scope. As in other sections of this book, the emphasis is on American examples, though the international circulation of art makes that qualification difficult to enforce. The distinction has more to do with working environment than place of birth: for example, despite his numerous exhibitions in America, the contemporary erotic surrealist Hans Bellmer is excluded here because he is a German who has worked most of his life in France, in favor of a lesser artist like Tomi Ungerer, who is French but has spent much of his career in the United States.

As we have indicated elsewhere, the term *pornographic* is rarely applied to one-of-a-kind objects of art whose relative scarcity and singularity give them economic value and confer upon them the label "erotic" even when the intent

and the execution make them indistinguishable from mass-produced artifacts
currently out of cultural favor.

HISTORIES OF EROTIC ART

(For generalized texts on erotic art, see chapter 4, **Bibliographies and Reference Tools**, especially Burt, Clapp, Corinne, Erotic Art.)

Historians of art have attributed many once-anonymous images to notable
painters and thus have come to recognize erotica as a tributary of mainstream
Western creativity. Many works still occupy a shadow realm, however, sometimes because the talent of the artist was not sufficient to make vulgarity interesting, sometimes because the artist simply declined to sign the canvas. We are
more apt to characterize even a well-executed but unsigned drawing as "low"
pornography simply because we have nothing to link it to. Yet, because the
impulse to render explicit scenes is so strong as to be primal, Carlo Ferrero, in
a chapter on anonymous art in *Les Cinq Sens D'Eros*, speculates that skilled
illustrators may have on occasion not signed works in order to endow them with
mystery. Crude or not, a clandestine representation may actually gain power
from being unattributable; without the baggage of provenance and biography,
we are forced to confront the work itself. The images that Ferrero reproduces
for his text are fascinating.

Among general historical surveys are Edward Lucie-Smith's *Sexuality in
Western Art*, who goes even further than Ferrero in his conviction that the drive
to represent sexuality has been an irresistible force in Western art from at least
Botticelli through Mapplethorpe and Cindy Sherman. Lucie-Smith's *Ars Erotica: An Arousing History of Erotic Art* covers works from all periods and nationalities, arranged thematically. Though no longer current, Peter Webb's *The
Erotic Arts* is superior to Lucie-Smith's many volumes. Webb labors sometimes
successfully on sexual nuances, while Lucie-Smith thinks he has a handle on
definition. As Lucie-Smith puts it in *Eroticism in Western Art*: "A distinction is
sometimes attempted between those representations of erotic activity which are
merely erotic, and those which qualify for the loaded adjective 'pornographic.'
The distinction is based, for example, on the question of whether or not the
penis can actually be seen entering the vulva, or if some 'deviant' sexual practice
such as fellatio is represented" (183–184). Poul Gerhard is similarly blunt in
Pornography in Fine Art from Ancient Times to the Present; for him, sexuality
energizes art, and he thinks calling some types erotic and others pornographic
unnecessarily clouds appreciation. Gerhard has published two other volumes,
The Pillow Book, or a History of Naughty Pictures, and *Pornography or Art*,
both comprising mostly pictures of lesser-known artists. Other standard works
are Volker Kahmen's *Erotic Arts Today*, a comprehensive look at twentieth-century art until the 1970s, with a good index to artists working in erotic veins,
and Jean Rodolphe's *Mit den Fünf Sinnen: Gesicht, Gefühl, Gehör, Geschmack*

Geruch: Ein Erotisches Bilderbuch, which explores representations aimed at the five senses.

The five volumes of Arthur Maria Rabenalt's *Mimus Eroticus* constitute one of the most thorough and authoritative histories of every kind of erotic theater, but volumes four and five, entitled *Beitrage zur Sittengeschichte der erotischen Szenik im Zwanzigsten Jahrhundert*, also break out works of art, giving precedence to those of modern provenance. Similarly ambitious in scope but much more popular in tone is *Love's Picture Book: Love, Lust and Pleasure*, a broad survey of erotic expression in various cultures by Ove Brusendorff and Paul Henningsen. *L'Art et l'Amour* is a mild history of sex, love, and romance in illustration, mostly painting, from many cultures; author Florent Fels includes excellent reproductions. Paul Tabori's *A Pictorial History of Love*, a narrative told in text and illustrations, has a pleasantly gritty perspective. Heavier by contrast, *Studies in Erotic Art*, edited by Theodore Bowie and Cornelia V. Christenson, features very learned chapters by Theodore Bowie, Otto J. Brendel, Paul H. Gebhard, Robert Rosenblum, and Leo Steinberg on materials in the art collections of the Kinsey Institute. These range from treatises on Greco-Roman artifacts to Picasso's drawings, with occasional comparison to American works. Freudian doctrine governs Guiseppe Lo Duca's *Die Erotik in der Kunst: die Welt des Eros* as it moves from early cave paintings into the twentieth century; it is a highly discursive, but fine, survey, though somewhat hampered by the reduced size of hundreds of illustrations. Robert Melville's *Erotic Art of the West* divides discussion of works clustered by subject: the kiss, fellatio, penetration, masturbation, lesbianism, homosexuality, transvestism, incest, specific fetishes such as hair, breast, vulva, penis, sperm, and larger categories such as violence and symbolism. Wayland Young's *Eros Denied*, while primarily concerned with tracing sexual expression in the West, devotes considerable attention to sculpture and painting that have been suppressed over the centuries.

Cary von Karwath's *Die Erotik in der Kunst* is an important work on pictorial erotica before 1900. Extremely rare, it is notable for photographs of the erotic murals for Versailles painted by François Boucher; the originals were destroyed by American Customs when they were sent to the United States (see Legman, *The Horn Book*, 127). The volume's plates are explicit. In a class by itself is Paul Englisch's *Irrgarten der Erotik: Eine Sittengeschichte uber das gesamte Gebiet der Weltpornographie*, an important reference tool because of its extensive bibliographic and biographic information on publishers, editors, authors, and artists working in what was primarily European erotica from the early eighteenth to the early twentieth centuries, though American examples crop up. John Grand-Carteret covers sexual images in French drawing over two centuries in *Die Erotik in der französischen Karikatur*. Still more important is Eduard Fuchs' three-volume *Geschichte de Erotischen Kunst*. This 1912 edition is an amplification of Fuchs' 1904 *Das Erotischen Element in der Karikatur*. Between 1912 and 1926 he expanded the 1912 edition into the three-volume *Geschichte de*

Erotischen Kunst, often called the most comprehensive of all histories of erotic art. A separate volume, Fuchs' *Die grossen Meister der Erotik*, deals with erotic paintings by the greatest artists. Fuchs' *Illustrierte Sittengeschichte von Mittelalter biz zur Gegenwart* also traces shifting moral and aesthetic standards in art from the Middle Ages to the twentieth century; the six volumes of this history are close in intent and perspective but not in scope to the six volumes of *Bilderlexicon der Erotik*. The *Bilderlexicon* has never been surpassed. Its pages and illustrations cover representation in art, literature, science, and cultural discourse of all sorts; essays focus on the psychology and aesthetic principles of expression, the politics and economics of the marketplace, and the historical context of different periods and nations. The last two volumes contain essays on recent art, with Peter Gorsen's on contemporary painting being perhaps the best. Rounding off German expertise is the nine-volume *Bibliotheca Germanorum Erotica and Curiosa*, the first eight compiled by Hugo Hayn and Alfred N. Gotendorf and the ninth, and most modern, by Paul Englisch. (The set supersedes Hayn's other internationally oriented bibliographies.) What makes the period's German art criticism of erotica so significant is that it emphasizes the role of folklore and lower-class imagery in the evolution of artistic sensibilities. Almost as magisterial is the three-volume *Ars Erotica* of Bodo Harenberg, whose German text carefully examines mostly European erotic woodblock prints from the eighteenth century to the present; the illustrations are beautifully reproduced.

Bernhardt J. Hurwood's *The Golden Age of Erotica* examines a period of flourishing sexual representation. Despite its orientation toward literature of the eighteenth and nineteenth centuries and despite the reputation of the book's first publisher, the text contains astute remarks about illustration and plastic art of the same period. An encyclopedia of sexual behavior written by Ludwig Knoll and Gerhard Jaekel is illustrated by artists minor and major. In effect, *Lexicon der Erotik* functions as an art history because the authors are careful to identify the artist and the provenance of each work. Most of the reproductions are of nineteenth- and twentieth-century drawings and paintings that graphically interpret sexual behavior. Peter Weiermair has edited text by Isabelle Azoulay, Georges Bataille, Hans-Jürgen Döpp, Claudia Gehrke, Volmar Sigusch, and Weiermair himself and added illustrations drawn from the collection of the Frankfurter Kunstverein for *Erotic Art from the 17th to the 20th Century*, an exceptionally intelligent volume, though the focus is primarily German and French painting. Bradley Smith's *Erotic Art of the Masters: The 18th, 19th, 20th Centuries* reproduces and comments on works by famous artists, as does his *Twentieth Century Masters of Erotic Art*, which expands on the material in the former. Roberta Haynes and Rick Hauser based their video, *Secret World of Erotic Art*, on Smith's two volumes. The narrative tends to be sappy at times, but it contextualizes works by Boucher, Calder, Courbet, Daumier, Hokusai, Ingres, Karhu, Louedin, Manet, Masson, Medvedev, Millet, Picasso, Rowlandson, Ting, Toulouse-Lautrec, Utamaro, and others. Guiseppe Lo Duca's *Die*

Erotik im 20. Jahrhundert, while similar to the larger work by Lo Duca cited earlier, focuses on modern trends and ventures into advertising and popular arts.

In most examples previously cited, illustrations are subordinated to text. The reverse is the case with many histories of erotic art. Francis Carr's *European Erotic Art*, for example, is a brief and somewhat superficial survey of art from cave drawings to the present, with good plates. In this category also are two volumes compiled by Gilles Néret. In his *Erotica Universalis*, 700 illustrations trace erotic paintings from prehistoric times to the present. Americans represented are few, though several highlighted artists, such as Grosz, Stanton, Wille, and Eneg, worked in the United States. Moreover, many of the reproductions, from book illustrations to lithographs, have circulated widely in America. Néret's *Erotic Art* is composed of nineteenth- and twentieth-century paintings by artists from Matisse to Bellmer, without much comment. Néret's *Twentieth Century Erotic Art*, however, is a much more intelligent volume, with reproductions not often found together. Its fine selection of often explicit images includes those by many Americans: Georgia O'Keeffe, Claes Oldenburg, Jackson Pollock, Edward Hopper, Eric Fischl, William N. Copley, Andy Warhol, Jeff Koons, Roy Lichtenstein, Philip Pearlstein, Mel Ramos, Larry Rivers, David Salle, and Cindy Sherman. Néret's critical observations are insightful and direct, and his bibliography lists major exhibitions and catalogs. The redoubtable and perhaps pseudonymous Donald H. Gilmore, commentator on many forms of erotica, has loaded his *Sex and Censorship in the Visual Arts* with illustrations of comics, photos, and painting, much of it American; the comment is pedestrian. The pictures in Jack Bacon's *Eros in Art* are more interesting than the text, which is conventional and shaded toward international, rather than American, examples. Better is Richard Bentley's *Erotic Art*, though its scope is a pretty standard list of erotic works of art; it, too, is chiefly a picture book. Abe Richards and Robert Irvine spread 150 pictures of paintings and sculpture drawn from collections such as those owned by Somerset Maugham and King Farouk throughout *An Illustrated History of Pornography*.

CRITICAL APPROACHES

(For aesthetic theories of erotica and pornography, see **Aesthetics: Pornography as Art** in Chapter 6.)

Though hardly an authority on art, the popular sex therapist Ruth Westheimer cuts through pretense in *The Art of Arousal*. Her commonsense, if politically incorrect, view is that arousal is a legitimate goal of art, that arousal is not as easy to achieve as one might think, and that successful images can function didactically and therapeutically—like any other form of art. She discusses erotic themes and images in mainstream painting, sculpture, prints, and drawings and recommends some for their ability to stimulate. Peter Gorsen, whose expertise led to his being invited to update the *Bilderlexicon*, believes that pornographic impulses are inextricably linked to aesthetic sensibilities and that pornographic artifacts serve as models for artists in need of fresh templates. Gorsen's *Sexualästhetik: Grenzformen der Sinnlichkeit im 20. Jahrhundert* traces the ways in which the consciousness of sexuality has redefined the artistic landscape of the twentieth century. While he has recourse mostly to European examples, his sections on Carolee Schneemann and performance, bondage illustration, dildos and other artifacts, cartoons, fetishes, and Richard Lindner are consistently provocative. The collective theme of the essays in *On the Margins of Art Worlds*, edited by Larry Gross, is similar: that marginal art forms from graffiti to animation actually define the art considered mainstream.

Mark Dery reaffirms the subversive nature of Americans working with graffiti, electronic media, zines, cyberpublishing, and various art forms, characterizing them as cultural terrorists/artists in *Culture Jamming, Hacking, Slashing and Sniping in the Empire of Signs*. So does Linda S. Kauffman, whose *Bad Girls and Sick Boys: Fantasies in Contemporary Art and Culture* is an impassioned defense of trangression in art; she specifically includes pornography and ventures into areas that other critics shy away from, such as the atrocity art of J. G. Ballard. Russell Ferguson, Martha Gever, Trinh T. Minh-ha, and Cornel West have edited a group of essays on minority representations in art, with particular reference to issues of colonialism and gender, into a volume called *Out There: Marginalization and Contemporary Cultures. Féminimasculin: Le sexe de l'art*, a comprehensive and beautifully illustrated volume on mostly contemporary work, including American artifacts and artists, contains more than a dozen essays on gender as an accelerant of artistic endeavor. The catalog of a 1984 exhibit organized by Marcia Landsman and published as *Difference: On Representation and Sexuality* uses illustrations to explore variations on gender and sexuality in twentieth-century art. Linda Weintraub, Arthur Danto, and Thomas McEvilley range widely over experimental art, some of it explicit, during the last two decades, in *Art on the Edge and Over*. Edward Lucie-Smith has covered similar territory with *Race, Sex and Gender: Issues in Contemporary Art*, which explores art in categories such as "transgressive," "feminist," and "minority sexuality." Some of these categories include explicit works. James Gardner challenges such assumptions in *Culture or Trash? A Provocative View of Contemporary Painting, Sculpture, and Other Costly Commodities*, an attack on the cultural (and financial) values assigned to graffiti, "outsider art," and erotica.

Christopher Macy's *The Arts in a Permissive Society* sidles up to eroticism in art, the novel, cinema, television, and theater in language so prudish, with allusions so reticent, that its conclusions seem fearful. *Sex in the Arts: A Symposium*, edited by John F. Mcdermott and Kendall B. Taft, contains even more dated, still more diffident essays on a variety of artistic subjects, from nude sculpture to painting and theater; modern readers may find themselves rechecking the title to ascertain that the participants are, in fact, talking about sex. Both works are cited here only because they are so often found in bibliographies on eroticism in the arts. As a reminder that laughter is probably the best critique of issues raised by sexual representation in public venues, scholars should glance at Dan Greenberg's *Porno-graphics: The Shame of Our Art Museums*, a tongue-in-cheek lampoon of the conservative outrage occasioned by "obscene" paintings and artifacts in museums. Greenberg's reconstructive/deconstructive collages take classic paintings and make them less "obscene" (or more, depending on one's perspective) by altering the originals in hilarious ways. Similarly, Eugene C. Burt's brief essay, "Humor in Erotic Art," is important because of its reminder that one justification of explicit art is its often comic dimension. "On Eros and Erotic Art," a cluster of "Statements by Erotic Writers, Photographers, Poets, and Artists," contains remarks by Tee Corinne, Anne Rice, Duane Michaels, and Ron Raffaelli, among others, on why they create in erotic genres. One of these, Mark Chester, says: "The pain of living is so beastly and so great that it is unbearable. But then the joy of sex, sexuality and eroticism is so beautiful and so powerful that it almost makes life bearable. I can't help it: I believe in hard dicks" (101).

(See also **Censorship of Art** in chapter 20, especially Clapp, Carmilly-Weinberger, Dubin, and Heins.)

ARTISTIC REPRESENTATIONS OF THE BODY

Feminist and fundamentalist critiques of the body have reawakened a puritanical shame toward the physicality of sex, a syndrome that has generated an outpouring of texts on anatomy. Probably the best-known study of the artistic rendering of the body is Kenneth Clark's *The Nude: A Study in Ideal Form*, whose genuine insights are almost overwhelmed by a classically dull discussion of painting and sculpture. On the other hand, Clark almost single-handedly invented an elevated, if bland, discourse suited to talking about the naked human form without embarrassment. When Sister Wendy Beckett speaks about the "lovely floss of pubic hair" on a model in a painting on the BBC art shorts carried on PBS, she can do so because Clark made the topic safe. Clark believes that art sublimates and/or transcends the eroticism of nudity; consequently, he ignores those nude figures with warts in search of his ideal. Gill Saunders' *The Nude: A New Perspective* takes a similarly broad approach to the visual arts, as does Edward Lucie-Smith's *The Body: Images of the Nude*, both of whom offer reflections on the effect that depictions of the unclothed body have on conceptions of gender and sexuality. Both recognize that erotic and pornographic are seamless, as does Margaret R. Miles. Miles' *Carnal Knowing: Female Nakedness and Religious Meaning in the Christian West* suggests that artistic status has traditionally masked the erotic appeal that has always been central to representations of the female nude and that the deception was abetted by Christian doctrine. The contributors to *The Body Imaged: The Human Form in Visual Culture since the Renaissance*, edited by Kathleen Adler and Marcia Pointon, cover the human figure in art, mostly painting but with some reference to photography. Museum-oriented treatments of the nude are legion, of course, and are recognizable by their assumption that the artist under discussion was motivated by cool detachment. In this category, for instance, is Friedrich Bayl's *Der Nackete Mensch in der Kunst*, a chronicle of the male nude with little reference to gender or sexuality. Mya Cinotti's *The Nude in Painting* is remarkable only because it treats graphic nudes rather than the idealized variety as a matter of course. For *The Artist and the Nude: An Anthology of Drawings*, Mervyn Levy compiled several dozen, chiefly from the eighteenth and nineteenth centuries, and discusses them in terms of intent and effect. Ronald Pearsall's *Tell Me, Pretty Maiden: The Victorian and Edwardian Nude* explores the iconography of the nude in paintings by British artists such as Alma-Tadema, Leighton, and Burne-Jones and traces their reception in the United States and their influence on illustrators.

The best single survey of American representations of the nude in just about every style, their numerous examples carefully considered, compared, and contrasted, is William H. Gerdts' *The Great American Nude: A History in Art*. Gerdts draws on biographies of painters and sculptors to recount the details of professional response and public reception. Noting that American artists like West, Stuart, and Copley had to flee America to learn to draw the nude in Europe, Gerdts credits realist Thomas Eakins with insisting on life drawing for his students in this country in the face of public outcry and graphs the gradually warming temperatures of a more tolerant climate that ensued to encourage Luks, Bellows, Glackens, and Henri. He also ventures into pictures of bathing beauties and barroom cuties. Gerdts appends a valuable bibliography of important exhibitions, including the Brooklyn Museum's landmark 1961 exhibition, *The Nude in American Painting*, whose catalog is still matchless. Scholars can find ample comment on specific artists who pushed against convention in histories, critical texts, and catalogs of their works that are simply too numerous to be listed here. Lois W. Banner's *American Beauty* and Martha Banta's *Imaging American Women: Idea and Ideals in Cultural History* discuss the representation of women in high and low art; both histories chart shifting aesthetic climates with great precision. Suzanne L. Kinser places John Sloan's paintings, etchings, and illustrations of prostitutes at the intersection of genteel tradition and modern commerce during the Progressive Era in "Prostitutes in the Art of John Sloan." John Baker studies Sloan's penchant for depicting sex workers as human critiques of city life in "Erotic Spectacle in the Art of John Sloan: A Study of the Iconography, Sources and Influences of a Subject Matter Pattern." Sloan, the great urban realist of the period, continued to depict the denizens of New York's Tenderloin District when he became editor of the radical journal *The Masses* and prodded artists such as George Bellows, Boardman Robinson, Stuart Davis, Glenn Coleman, Art Young, and Robert Minor to take on subjects such as "women's rights, sex relations, birth control, and prostitution" (237). For the scholar interested in the burlesque queens and other naked figures of Reginald Marsh (1898–1954), Marilyn Cohen's catalog of the Whitney Museum retrospective, *Reginald Marsh's New York: Paintings, Drawings, Prints and Photographs*, reproduces the faintly scandalous paintings of the 1930s, and it and

Norman Sasowsky's collection of the Paris bordello etchings and performance drawings, *The Prints of Reginald Marsh*, would be logical starting points. One of the most interesting analyses of Marsh's eroticized images, so popular in the 1930s that they collectively became known as the "Marsh girl," is "Sex for Sale: Reginald Marsh's Voluptuous Shopper," by Ellen W. Todd, who believes that Marsh's "sirens" were less threatening than career women and thus more easily accepted.

In *Image of the Body*, a text concerned with the "metamorphoses" that representations of the human body have undergone throughout history, Michael Gill recounts the story of Thomas Eakins' dismissal from the University of Pennsylvania in the 1870s for removing a loincloth from a male model in order to exhibit musculature for a painting class; the case demonstrated American society's profound fear of the male body. Ironically, says Gill, the year before, the same university had allowed faculty, their spouses, and students to be photographed in the nude as part of a scientific experiment that would become famous as Muybridge's *The Human Figure in Motion*. Gill's pages are especially helpful on the nude women painted by Alice Neel, the penis constructions of Louise Bourgeois, and the voluptuous sculptures of Mary Frank. Gill, who seems to have inherited the mantle of Kenneth Clark, believes that the artistic nude brought "a new concept to humanity's contemplation of itself" only when in the nineteenth-century Manet painted *Olympia*, the alert, cynical nude staring out of the frame that some viewers still find pornographic (x–xi). According to Gill, Manet's "ironic questioning of the whole genre" of the female nude forced audiences to look at actual bodies rather than idealized forms of it—to see rawness and sexuality. In "Manet, 'Olympia,' and Pornographic Photography," Gerald Needham also refers to an editorial the same year in the English *Saturday Review* complaining that porn photos, especially stereoscopic ones, were for sale on every London street corner. As have other historians, Needham insists that pornographic photos heavily influenced painters such as Manet. Although it does not concentrate on erotic material, Ian Dunlop's *The Shock of the New* is a classic study of the disruptive force of novelty on artistic establishments; Dunlop, too, thinks of Manet's revisions as pivotal.

In "The Female Nude: Pornography, Art, and Sexuality," Lynda Nead reviews various theories of the nude from Clark and Berger, to Nochlin and Webb; her conclusion is that "pictures of the female nude are not *about* female sexuality in any simplistic way; they also testify to a particular cultural definition of male sexuality and are part of a wider debate around representation and cultural value" (293). Nead quite reasonably characterizes that debate as a struggle over imperfect statistics and cultural and political ambiguities; artists and critics assert the value of beautiful images, while antiporn feminists assert the deleterious effects of male dominance. As Nead observes, "The meanings of eroticism and obscenity, sensuality and sexuality, art and pornography, change over time, their boundaries shaped by the forms and institutions of culture and society" (294). Nead also notes that paintings of nude women, as examples of higher culture, have been separated from photographs, which do not enjoy the same status (286–287). Nead has expanded these insights in *The Female Nude*, which further contrasts the traditions of the art nude with recent feminist criticism and current arguments concerning gender and sexuality.

The question of authorship, the way the body is created on canvas, says Marcia Pointon in *Naked Authority: The Body in Western Painting, 1830–1908*, is crucial in art, since intent, conscious or otherwise, genders and sexualizes the representation. Contributors to *The Female Body in Western Culture: Contemporary Perspectives*, edited by Susan Rubin Suleiman, adopt a reader/text approach to terrain ranging from the pastels of Degas to "Medical Discourse in the 'Women's Film' of the 1940s"; the bodies as a consequence seem occasionally ethereal, but some of the essays find the incorporeality itself quite erotic, and most dutifully insist that representations of the female body express ideologies of patriarchy and misogyny. Though more trenchant on photographic images, both *The Male Nude*, by Margaret Walters, and *The Male Nude: A Modern View*, by François de Louville, analyze many drawings and paintings as well. Edward Lucie-Smith, not surprisingly, has compiled *Adam: The Male Figure in Art* to add to the shelf of erotic art books he has already published. Abigail Solomon-Godeau studies various images of the male nude in terms of period fashions of masculinity in *Male Trouble: A Crisis in Representation*. "Nudes Now" is an excellent period piece on ten American artists of the nude, including Richard Diebenkorn and Alfred Leslie. Rosemary Betterton studies the ways women artists from Kollwitz forward deal with the female body in *Intimate Distance: Women, Artists and the Body*.

Few critiques are as succinct as "Hers," a flawless essay by an artist who refuses to use moral, aesthetic, and political compasses to chart the myriad of universes embodied in flesh. Here the painter Maureen Mullarkey observes that the struggles of female artists to capture the female nude have been made more difficult not just by the opposition of male critics and curators but also by feminist ideology: "It takes a puritanical bent as severe as Increase Mather's to reduce the nude to its nudity. Since classical times, the nude, male or female, has been an art form designed to testify to the physical world's capacity for beauty, grace, occasional nobility.... While sexuality is implicit in the nude, that is not its first concern. Even if it were, sexuality is as amenable to artistic interpretation as anything else. The innocence or degradation of the nude owes little to gender but everything to the sensibility of the artist."

EROTIC PAINTING AND DRAWING

Several scholars have explored the erotic aspects of early cultures of North America and compiled cartographies of the artifacts of the inhabitants. One of the broadest is *Exotic Art*, compiled by W. Forman and B. Forman, who traverse Africa, Oceana, Southeast Asia, and the early Americas. A superficial text mars Jules Griffon's *Pictorial History of Erotography*, which is redeemed by illustrations of art and artifacts from around the globe, including some primitive North American examples. Hughes de Jouvancourt's *Eros Eskimo* covers erotica as diverse as paintings and drawings on walrus hide to scrimshawed dildos. By far the best look at the subject, however, is Philip Rawson's *Primitive Erotic Art*, whose chapters study native Central and North American art, chiefly artifacts, in terms of their sexual imagery and their probable roles in older cultures. Between these early periods and the present the critical cabinet seems largely barren, and period comment can be found only in the larger surveys of erotic art in the United States.

Charlotte Hill and William Wallace reproduce many drawings and paintings in the three volumes of *Erotica: An Illustrated Anthology of Sexual Art and Literature*, although these are chiefly European in origin, and the attributions are erratic; Hill and Wallace seem to use the illustrations to space out the literary excerpts. Despite its title, Simon Wilson's "Short History of Western Erotic Art" deals chiefly with American pop art, photo-realism, and their successors, with good treatment of Warhol, Oldenburg, Wesselman, Kitaj, and so on. More comprehensive on the subject, though not focused exclusively on erotic aspects, is Tilman Osterwald's *Pop Art*, which traces the sources, styles, and themes of pop art as manifest in works by Johns, Rauschenberg, Lichtenstein, Oldenburg, Rosequist, Warhol, Wesselman, and lesser-known artists. Among other techniques, pop artists borrowed girlie pictures from men's magazines, snipped or copied erotic synecdoches from advertisements, and wove these into collages and prints of deliberate artifice that seemed at times as much the product of testosterone as artistic impulse. Bradley Smith's *Erotic Art of the Masters: The 18th, 19th, and 20th Centuries* devotes extensive coverage to works by Larry Rivers, Tom Wesselman, Henriette Francis, Morton Kaish, Mel Ramos, Robert Andrew Parker, Willem de Kooning, Robert Broderson, Martha Edelhart, Andy Warhol, and George Segal; among its excellent illustrations is Wesselman's "Great American Nude #87," "which made erotic art history" because of its explicit fellatio. In Tom Gardner's interview, "Tom Wesselman: 'I Like to Think That My Work Is about All Kinds of Pleasure,'" perhaps the boldest of pop artists explains his intent with particular reference to the highly sexualized *Great American Nude* series of the 1960s. Under the pseudonym Slim Stealingworth, Wesselman discusses his career and his predilection for the nude form and the sinuous curve in *Tom Wesselman*. Asked about his depictions of breasts, Wesselman speculates on the symbolism of anatomical parts in "Wesselman's Fancy Footwork": "A tit by itself loses its titness. If she's on her back, the tit looks like a mountain" (47).

During the 1960s, erotic art began appearing in semirespectable galleries in the United States and abroad. H. Wurdemann visited a cluster of Los Angeles galleries specializing in erotic fare in "Stroll on La Cienega" for the journal *Art in America*. These included the David Stuart, Ferus, Dalzell Hatfield, Felix Landau, Comara, Zora, and Dwan Galleries, a grouping of exhibits ranging from the erotic to the scabrous. A companion piece in the same magazine, John

Russell's "London Pornocrats," found that British audiences took the erotic art exhibited there in stride, perhaps because it tended to be less explicit than the shows in America. Brian O'Doherty's "Urogenital Plumbing," a review of the *Erotic Art '66* show at the Janis Gallery in New York, concentrated on works by Allen Jones, Jim Dine, Richard Lindner, George Segal, Marisol, Andy Warhol, R. B. Kitaj, Larry Rivers, Tom Wesselman, and Mimmo Rotella. *Newsweek's* startled review of the same show was entitled "Eros in Polyester." From then on, most major art journals covered shows that previously would have been too scandalous for their pages. Typical was "Seized," a special issue of *Art and Artists*, which reported on the Janis show and other upwellings of erotic impulse.

"Erotic Art," a special issue of *Art and Artists*, covers the contemporary art scene from Richard Lindner to Louise Bourgeois and captures the excitement of erotic experimentation in the late 1960s and early 1970s. Lindner, a German pop artist working in America, was turning out female nudes. Rolf-Gunter Dienst critiques the robotic implications of those figures in "Richard Lindner," while Hilton Kramer looks at the pinup aspects in "Lindner's Ladies"; *Richard Lindner*, D. Ashton's full-length study, though dated now, gives due thought to the man's erotic force. Richard Morphet wrote the Introduction to the catalog for Claes Oldenburg's *Claes Oldenburg: An Exhibition of Recent Erotic Fantasy Drawings*, a collection that experiments with congeries of flesh. The show ran from November to December 1975 at London's Mayer Gallery. Following up the exhibit, Elizabeth Claridge contrasts Oldenburg with an artist she thinks different in style, sexual orientation, and focus, though she thinks the fantasies they embody are both compelling, in "Aspects of the Erotic—1: Warhol, Oldenburg." Roy Lichtenstein's *The Prints of Roy Lichtenstein: A Catalogue Raisonne, 1948–1993*, compiled by Mary Lee Corlett with an Introduction by Ruth E. Fine, reproduces all his prints and posters, some of which are erotic. Diane Waldman delves into Lichtenstein's painting and sculpture as exemplars of the conflict between high and popular art in *Roy Lichtenstein*. Jim Dine's *Prints 1970–1977* contains modest comment on prints by Dine such as *Oo La La* (1970), which features an erect penis, and *Four Kinds of Pubic Hair* (1971), which are humorously self-reflexive etchings. For prints of the penis and vulva drawings seized by London police, scholars will have to find the Robert Fraser Gallery catalog (with Introduction by Cyril Barrett), *Dine*, for the show that ran in London from September to October 1966. Sam Hunter's updated and expanded edition of *Larry Rivers* is probably the most comprehensive text on Rivers, but another solid study is Helen A. Harrison's *Larry Rivers*; both put his outrageous creations in proper cultural and artistic context. Rivers himself, writing with Arnold Weinstein, revels in the image of bad boy of American art, as somewhat embellished in *What Did I Do? The Unauthorized Autobiography of Larry Rivers*; the narrative is centered, of course, on the life and career of the self-described painter, musician, designer, actor, addict, and "erotomane." Rivers' most notorious work, "Lampman Loves It" (1966), is an assemblage in

which a bending male figure is sodomized by another figure with a light bulb
for a penis. Photographs of that work recur in texts on erotic art.

The nudes of Philip Pearlstein, usually considered the dean of living realists,
possess a graphic quality some find offensive. Janet Hobhouse's *The Bride
Stripped Bare: The Artist and the Female Nude in the Twentieth Century* (a title
that is itself a play on the title of one of Marcel Duchamps' works), deals with
mostly British or European painters but devotes a chapter each to Willem de
Kooning and Philip Pearlstein. Hobhouse agrees with many critics that the models in Pearlstein's paintings are rendered so dispassionately that they are de-
tached from their environment by the absence of any sign of social status. In
this regard, she says, Pearlstein's work "has its greatest affinity with pornography in its use of persons for its own ends, though those ends seem so utterly
different from simple sexual arousal" (275). In "Filthy Pictures: Some Chapters
in the History of Taste," a marvelous essay on the subject of figurative representations of erotica, Barbara Rose finds that modern paintings and photographs
grapple with the culture's confused perspectives on sexuality. An objectified
body does not lose its eroticism, she says; eroticism persists precisely in unappealing physical distortions and awkward poses. Rose has in mind the paintings
of Pearlstein, which reward close looking with magnified insight into the human
condition and into sexuality itself.

Eleanor Heartney outlines the controversy surrounding David Salle's explicit
pop representations of women in "David Salle: Impersonal Effects," while Joyce
Fernandes attacks their sexist, misogynistic, and pornographic aspects in "Exposing a Phallocentric Discourse: Images of Women in the Art of David Salle."
Janet Malcolm comes to the defense of America's premier postmodernist painter
in "Forty-One False Starts." As Malcolm points out, Salle once did paste-ups
and layouts for a men's magazine and, as a consequence, uses in his paintings
a collection of pinups that he took with him from *Stag*, but "the idea of Salle
as pornographer is laughable" (54). Malcolm observes that Salle's art "refuses
to be any one thing or to find any one thing more interesting, beautiful, or
significant than another" (68). The images in David Salle's *David Salle* demonstrate that "vulgarity" is essential to Salle's attempt to probe reality. Lisa
Phillips' essay in that volume, "His Equivocal Touch in the Vicinity of History"
(22–31), is valuable because it reviews the images of other artists in an attempt
to historicize the vulgarity that she thinks becomes classical abstraction, and
contrasts Salles figures with those in porn itself: "Salle's women elude our normal frame of reference. The chilling banality of pornography is preserved
through Salle's repertoire of gesture and pose, but he has abandoned pornography's descriptive detail of genitalia, its displacement to secondary sex characteristics (skin, hair, etc.)" (29). A generous sampling of plates allows readers
to see for themselves. Lisa Liebmann's comment on Salle's controversial dip-
tych canvases of the female nude makes up the text of Salle's *David Salle,
1979–1994*. *David Salle*, the catalog of a 1983 Dutch exhibit, contains essays

by W.A.L. Beeren and Carter Ratcliff, the latter on Salle and eroticism of the New York school.

Forays into eroticism by Eric Fischl, an artist often compared to Salle, have evoked similar responses. In an interview with Bruce Ferguson published as "Eric Fischl: chez lui, avec les tableaux," the painter offers a rationale for his splendid, exuberant nudes. Fischl's frank, seductive, and provocative treatment of taboos in more than 100 works of 1986 are the subject of essays by Richard S. Field, Elizabeth Armstrong, E. L. Doctorow, and other critics in *Scenes and Sequences: Recent Monotypes by Eric Fischl*. Fischel's *Scenes before the Eye* features plates of nudes, including the one intended as homage to George Platt Lynes, the homoerotic photographer. "Sex and Success," Mark Stevens' review of a Whitney Museum show, argues that Fischl's sexual sensibility colors even his paintings of domesticity. Eric Fischl's *Eric Fischl* is an excellent, illustrated catalog of Fischl's work, including the untitled sequence of 1984 paintings depicting couples in intercourse, the "Dog Days" sequence of 1985, depicting, among other things, a woman stroking her lover's erect penis on a balcony, and "First Sex," a pensive oil of 1985, in which a reclining woman, clutched by one youth, opens her legs to the erection of a second. In the volume's principal essay, Peter Schjeldahl calls Fischl "the first great painter of the United States in decline" (11). A similar thesis informs *The Postmodern Scene: Excremental Culture and Hyper-Aesthetics*, by Arthur Kroker and David Cook, who think of Fischl as central to an understanding of an exhausted artistic sensibility and a blasted political landscape whose surfaces they tour in a chapter entitled "Post Modern America in Ruins: Are We Having Fun Yet?"

Robert Creeley introduces Ronald B. Kitaj's *R. B. Kitaj: Pictures/Bilder*, an exhibition catalog from the late 1970s, by praising his mastery of human figures and the eroticism that lends them piquancy. Frederic Tuten interviews the artist in "Art Profile: R. B. Kitaj" on the occasion of his 1994 show (London, Los Angeles, New York). Asked why he thinks life drawing is so important, the American expatriate responds: "It's *not* important if you want to do art by standing on your head and jerking off in a Macy's window. Or if you want to paint monochrome canvases. Or if you like to plant umbrellas around the Grand Canyon. All that is great stuff. But if you want to draw the human form to the standard of, say, Adolph von Menzel—which I suspect nobody in America, save for maybe David Hockney can do—then you'll have to teach it to yourself over the course of many intensive years" (36). Probably the best single monograph on the artist is Marco Livingstone's *R. B. Kitaj*.

David Littlejohn reports on an artist who says that his work "recontextualizes" erotica and renders it nonpornographic in "Who Is Jeff Koons and Why Are People Saying Such Terrible Things about Him?" Koons' *The Jeff Koons Handbook*, with an Introduction by Robert Rosenblum, contains dry-transfer photos of the artist and his former wife, the Honorable Ilona Staller, aka Cicciolina, the Italian porn star and member of Parliament, engaged in various explicit sexual acts. Though they are largely indistinguishable from the sort of images routinely found in hard-core porn magazines, especially since Staller is wearing her trademark costume of open-cup merry widow corset, white silk stockings, and chapelet of daisies (all she wears in her many hard-core films), Koons presents these as artistic creations. "The Honorable Cicciolina," a video segment, profiles the star and Koons as he poses her. Carter Ratcliff, Rhonda Lieberman, and JoAnna Isaak critique those works in "Jeff Koons: Not for Repro." Among hostile critics is Michael Kimmelman, whose "Onward into the Realm of Porno and Promo" condemns the paintings and adorned photographs of Koons and Cicciolina as cheap and pornographic. Adam Gopnik's "Lust for Life," written about the New York Gallery show of Koons' sex sequences called "Made in Heaven," is probably the most balanced review. In *Race, Sex, and Gender: Issues in Contemporary Art*, Edward Lucie-Smith notes that some of the more explicit images, such as those in which Koons anally penetrates Staller, are deliberately designed to affront antiporn feminists and thus may serve as political statement of the sort well within the province of art (102–103). Those who wish to make up their own minds should consult the layout on "Koons" in *Art Press*, which comments on Koons' deliberate exploitation of pornography and reproduces the most graphic examples. *Koons* is a catalog of the 1992 exhibition at the San Francisco Museum of Modern Art.

Novelties from the brush of an American primitive are collected in G. L. Pauly's *The Weird Sexual Fantasies of G. L. Pauly: Reproductions from Original Watercolor Paintings; weird* is an accurate description. Drawings and caricatures of futuristic sex, by an artist very popular in the United States during the 1960s and early 1970s, are reproduced in Tomi Ungerer's *Fornicon* and *Totempole: Erotische Zeichnungen 1968–1975*. Tomi Ungerer's *The Underground Sketchbook of Tomi Ungerer* contains Jonathan Miller's comments on the fantastic eroticism of the artist. The erotic drawings of Gerald Gooch are the subject of David Zack's "West Coast: Kama Sutra to the Life." Andrew Tilly discusses techniques of line and representation in *Erotic Drawings*, using mostly familiar examples by Rowlandson, Boucher, and Picasso but also venturing into lesser-known experiments by Willem de Kooning and Tom Wesselman; most interesting are the explicit male nudes of Sandra Fisher and the fetishistic images of Nancy Grossman. Norman Lindsay's *Selected Pen Drawings* are amusing conceits. Brad Benedict has gathered 176 illustrations from 108 artists and illustrators such as Warhol, Allen Jones, Robert Blue, and Mel Odom, leaving only modest space for comment in *The Blue Book*. L. L. Eisenhauer's "Bob Delford Brown" critiques the artist's pop assemblies and sometimes explicit collages. Richard Merkin, a New York erotic artist who works in several media, is best known for a seriograph portfolio of photomontage, *Paris de Nuit*. The send-ups of pornography drawn by Brian Nissen have been published as *Voluptuario* by Nissen and Carlos Fuentes, who wrote the narrative.

Gerrit Henry comments on paintings by William Copley that satirize American views of patriotism and sex in "William Copley," the review of a show at the Brooks Jackson Iolas Gallery in New York. Though struck by Copley's painting of a half-nude Barbara Fritchie, the reviewer observes that "one is never 100 percent sure whether the American obsession with sex is being satirized or acclaimed." In "Larry Blizard," Ellen Lubell remarks on the imaginative erotic uses of bananas as rendered in paintings by Larry Blizard, who depicts them peeled, phallic, and intertwined. Nicholas A. Moufarrege's "The Erotic Impulse" finds enormous erotic diversity in an important show featuring the work of Kathleen Thomas, Andy Warhol, Hannah Wilke, Lucas Samaras, Louise Bourgeois, Jedd Garet, Al Calderaro, John Altoon, Vernon Fisher, Jim Nutt, Robert Mapplethorpe, Claes Oldenburg, Janet Cooling, and many others. *Nude, Naked, Stripped*, the catalog of a show held at the Hayden Gallery of MIT 13 December 1985–2 February 1986, contains useful commentary on work by Alice Neel, Lucas Samaras, Robert Mapplethorpe, Cheri Eisenberg, Greer Lankton, Chuck Close, John Coplans, Peter Hujar and others.

Constance Franklin weaves comment by artists around illustrations of their work in the two volumes entitled *Erotic Art by Living Artists*; of the twenty-six artists represented in volume I, Jan ten Broeke is perhaps the most articulate in explaining the motivation behind erotic painting. Some of the images collected by Franklin, including those by Ron Barsano, David Fraley, Philip Sherrod, Steve Larson, Paul Kolosvary, and Sherry Lane, are reproduced in "Erotic Art," an article in *Penthouse*. *Helter Skelter: L.A. Art in the 1990s*, an exhibition catalog edited by Catherine Gudis, contains essays centered on a show mounted from January to April 1992; the explicitness of some entries attracted little attention, presumably because they were hung in a museum. "Sensual and Erotic Art Exhibition," Susan Reifer's illustrated review of the Fifth Annual Sensual and Erotic Art Exhibition at the Desmond Gallery in Los Angeles (1995), reproduces works by Robert Blue, John Paul Thornton, Dandra Chang, Gillian Burrows, Marc Greenblum and Ken Marcus, John Russo, Daniel Miller, Carlos Saenz, Moline of Tucson, Luis Monsalve, Dawn Mears, Rick Penn-Kraus, Mickey Kaplan, Bernadette McNulty, Lee Thomas, Fritz Ptasnyski, and Karin Swildens. This show, comprising works in various media, was quickly closed by embarrassed managers of the mall in which the gallery is located. Susan Tallman covers Barbara Bloom's *Pictures from the Floating World* show, which features explicit iconography, in "Private and Public." For "Art in Heat," a review of a show at the Halstead Gallery in 1986, Kathryn Hixson reflects on the significance of group gropes, body parts, and messy sex in works by Jim Matusek, Liz Wolf, Dan Galemb, Anne Scott, and J. E. Horwich. Peter Schjeldahl's "Shock of the Good," an essay on Sue Williams, a "visual polemicist of feminist rage," finds that her fantastic sexual orgies reflect a "ravaged sensibility" of beauty and power. "Peep Galleries" points out that while the city's antisex drive has threatened New York's 144 sex shops, the Manhattan art world is taking up the slack, offering, among other exhibits, Andres Serrano's photo-exhibit "A History of Sex" (Paula Cooper Gallery); two performance artists in a presentation of intercourse called "Self-Portrait Porno Show" (Jack Tilton Gallery); Matthew Sandager's video-sex installation "Eros Electronica"; and an exhibit of nude photos of the ten-year-old Brooke Shields (American Fine Arts Gallery).

FEMINIST CRITIQUES AND CONTEMPORARY WOMEN ARTISTS

Sophisticated feminist critiques of erotic art can be wonderfully exciting, erudite, and witty. Like their counterparts in other schools of thought, less informed and more ideological feminist approaches sometimes shade into mindless philistinism, especially when they reject serious attempts to come to terms with the body as a landscape and end by trashing huge sections of European and American art. Even the latter can be valuable, however, in the same way that goofier Marxist treatises force us to reexamine the nature of eroticism. The better feminist critiques look more closely at what is going on in painting and drawing, often setting the aesthetic dynamics against cultural institutions. Easily the most authoritative feminist critic is Linda Nochlin. Her "Eroticism and Female Imagery in Nineteenth-Century Art" insists that a patriarchal culture creates the female nude for consumption and that the individual artist's personal vision is subsumed by this larger cultural construction. That means, among other things, that we need a new language and imagery for women's erotic needs. The other eleven essays by art historians that make up the volume in which this essay appears treat Courbet, Renoir, Viennese erotica, corsets, and other subjects. The volume *Woman as Sex Object: Studies in Erotic Art, 1730–1970*, edited by Thomas B. Hess and Nochlin, traces the objectification of the female figure by Western painters, sculptors, photographers, and designers, traversing erotic territories mostly European. Because the contributors exhibit a knowledge of art not often shared by modern theorists, the volume is indispensable (it was roundly condemned as a "dirty book" when it first appeared). Perhaps the funkiest of theoretical approaches is "Representing Pornography: Feminism, Criticism, and Depictions of Female Violation," by Susan Gubar, an essay centered on the work of Magritte, with extended references to other artists who affront political sensibilities by depicting women as sexual creatures. The stance is interesting chiefly because it suggests the caprice with which the term *pornography* is applied, since most critics would balk at so designating Magritte's art. Feminists are not alone in confusing the issue, of course; art critics and historians have long elided distinctions. In a larger sense, Gubar's approach indicates that theories that dismiss authorship in favor of reader-response have influenced visual studies. In a culture of free-floating signifiers, it would seem, authorship and intent are beside the point.

Two essays by Carol Duncan argue that males have used art to dominate women. The first, "The Esthetics of Power in Modern Erotic Art," plays with the metaphor of masculine artist painting with a phallic brush and thereby controlling what he depicts. The second, "Virility and Domination in Early Twentieth Century Vanguard Painting," is more doctrinaire than witty; it claims that modern artists often choose the female nude as a subject in order to objectify or savage women. A refreshing dissent is Wendy Lesser's *His Other Half: Men Looking at Women through Art*. Lesser attacks the thesis that male artists inevitably misrepresent and distort women, an argument she says itself discounts aesthetic impulses and libels many artists, and she draws on evidence from painting to film. According to Lesser, complex motives lie behind artistic achievements, and making them pass litmus tests of political correctness ignores their contributions to a cultural consciousness that is moving toward gender equity. Lesser surveys Degas' bathers, Marilyn Monroe, film stars, concepts of narcissism, D. H. Lawrence, and a host of subjects. An almost old-fashioned emphasis on women as aesthetic inspiration that varies from age to age animates *Power and Beauty: Images of Women in Art*, by Georges Duby and Michelle Perrot, who also argue that the iconography used to represent women is complex. Eunice Golden thinks in "The Male Nude in Women's Art: Dialectics of a Feminist Iconography" that the motivations of female painters are similar to those of males; that is, they generally aim at unmasking male phallic power, just as males try to uncover the power they perceive in female bodies. Sarah Kent and Jacqueline Morreau bring depth to this thesis in *Women's Images of Men*, which explores the many ways that women artists represent males. Lorraine Gammon and Margaret Marshment have edited uneven essays on images from Madonna to male nudes in *The Female Gaze: Women as Viewers of Popular Culture*; most suggest that these images are embodiments of manipulated desire.

Most of the essays in *Art and Sexual Politics: Women's Liberation, Women Artists, and Art History*, edited by Thomas B. Hess and Elizabeth C. Baker, attempt to finesse the question posed by Linda Nochlin as "Why Have There Been No Great Women Artists?" Probably no one will be satisfied with the answers. Some of the book's illustrations are erotic, like Kiki Kogelnik's "Liquid Injection Thrust" (1967), and the bottom-line conclusion is that women artists, erotic or otherwise, are *now* poised to take advantage of a climate more receptive to foregrounding their sexuality. Various critics have chronicled the surge of eroticism in works by women artists since the late 1960s, a decade whose vaunted "sexual revolution" triggered experimentation. Essays in *The Power of Feminist Art: The American Movement of the 1970s. History and Impact*, edited by Norma Bronde and Mary D. Garrard, provide background for growing explicitness in feminist art of the 1970s and examine the work of specific artists, as does Lucy R. Lippard's excellent *From the Center: Feminist Essays on Women's Art*, still one of the most important critical texts on the subject. Lippard's *The Pink Glass Swan: Selected Feminist Essays on Art* brings together some of her other provocative essays. In a play on Nochlin's title, Naomi Salman asks, "Why Have There Been No Great Women Pornographers?" Her answer is that various anxieties have barred women artists from looking at the male body with the degree of visible lust that is required.

Lawrence Alloway's "Women's Art in the Seventies" reflects on tentative forays by some artists into sexual imagery. Cindy Nemser interviewed a dozen women working in different media in *Art Talk: Conversations with Twelve Women Artists*; some of the talk explores the place of the explicit. Nemser's "Four Artists of Sensuality" critiques works by Eleanor Antin (*The King*, a 1974 videotape), Lynda Benglis (*Fredrica*, a 1974 collage, and *Female Sensibility*, a 1974 videotape), Judith Bernstein (*Big Horizontal*, a 1973 painting of a phallus), and Hannah Wilke (*Super Tart*, a 1974 performance piece, and *Untitled*, a 1974 terra cotta and liquitex vagina). Nemser concludes that all four provide "new insights into female sexuality" (75). Lisa Tickner charts erotic terrain traversed by members of the Women's Art Movement in "The Body Politic: Female Sexuality and Women Artists since 1970," one of the most comprehensive mappings of the decade. "The Male Nude: The Gaze Returned. Women Painters in the 1970s and Early 1980s," a survey in *Heresies*, covers many of the artists noted by critical studies already listed here: Nancy Grossman, Judith Bernstein, Hannah Wilke, and Joan Semmel are notable.

The best indicators of the growing power of women erotic artists are official efforts to suppress their work. Carol Jacobsen surveys women artists subjected to censorship over the past decade: Kathe Kowalski, Jacqueline Livingstone, Carolee Schneemann, Clarisse Sligh, Anita Steckel, Joan Semmel, and Hannah Wilke in "Redefining Censorship: A Feminist View." Robert G. Edelman's "Hannah Wilke," a review of the late great artist's March 1994 show at the Ronald Feldman Gallery in New York, recalls her struggle to be exhibited and understood. Chapter 3, "Witchcraft/Witch Art," of Heide Göttner-Abendroth's *The Dancing Goddess: Principles of a Matriarchal Aesthetic*, is devoted to the body art of Judy Chicago, (the American) Colette, Carolee Schneemann, and Mary Beth Edelson, along with European artists who work in explicit images. In *Visibly Female: Feminism and Art Today*, an anthology edited by Hilary Robinson, American and (mostly) British artists speak of their work. The best segment is "Behind the Fragments," a conversation conducted by Rosalind Coward, Yve Lomax, and Kathy Myers (297–306) on creating feminist erotica. *Feminist Art Criticism: An Anthology*, edited by Arlene Raven, Cassandra Langer, and Joanna Frueh, is an excellent collection of essays, some of which focus on erotic art. Especially notable in that volume is Maryse Holder's "Another Cuntree: At Last, a Mainstream Female Art Movement," which covers the erotic work of Nikki de Saint Phalle, Silvianna Goldsmith, Kiki Kogelnik, Sara d'Allesandro, Shelly Lowell, Marge Helenchild, Anne Sharp, Judith Bernstein, Anita Steckel, Arlene Love, Juanita McNeely, Martha Edelheit, and Joan Semmel, among others better known. Joanna Frueh's *Erotic Faculties*, a free-ranging work by a noted performance artist, contains performance pieces inspired by Louise Bourgeois and Hannah Wilke. Frueh's *Hannah Wilke: A Retrospective* analyzes the execution and merits of themes and motifs in the work of one of America's supreme erotic artists.

American audiences seem to expect female artists to be more circumspect than their male counterparts. In "The Female View of Erotica," Dorothy Sieberling suggests that women achieve erotic effects through softness and muted symbolism, though such remarks may strike some as recapitulating ancient gender stereotypes (sugar and spice versus snails and puppy dog tails). A year later, Sieberling and other critics were startled by the now-notorious ad/photo of artist Lynda Benglis, nude, in a macho pose, her hand gripping a giant, two-headed dildo, one end of which she has inserted into herself, the other of which she thrusts outward in aggressive statement. Sieberling's essay on the image, "The New Sexual Frankness: Good-Bye to Hearts and Flowers," asserted that women artists were taking advantage of a period propitious for bold sexuality. Benglis ran her famous ad/art photo on page 4 of the November 1974 issue of *Artforum* as a shockingly resonant riff on art, artists, sexuality, reticence, and gender. Writing about the scandal in the same issue of the journal, Robert Pincus-Witten in "Lynda Benglis: The Frozen Gesture" worried that the stunt might detract from less graphic paintings in which the artist's talent is undeniable. Thanks in part to Benglis, female artists who press against the envelope of respectability are growing in number and articulateness. Joyce Kozloff describes her work as "pornament" in *Patterns of Desire*, a narrative featuring watercolors of textured sensuality and collages of classic erotic images borrowed from Japanese woodcuts to European and art deco erotica. In her Introduction to the book, Linda Nochlin uses words like "appropriation," "demystification," "transgressive," and "playful" to describe Kozloff's often amusing variations on pornographic images, which Nochlin maintains can nonetheless function as "decorative art." *Bad Girls*, the catalog of the New York and Los Angeles shows edited by Marcia Tucker, while short on illustrations of "transgressive" work by Yoko Ono, Levine, Kruger, Holzer, Wilke, Sherman, and others, contains several solid essays on "bad" art as a tool for raising political consciousness. Arlene Raven's report/ review of several "bad girl" art shows in New York and Newark, New Jersey, "Is Bad Good or Bad?" says that the pornographic images and installations heighten women's consciousness and serve to reformulate principles and expectations. The artist Emma Amos reflects on her attempts to infuse her work with eroticism in "Changing the Subject."

EROTIC AND PORNOGRAPHIC BOOK AND MAGAZINE ILLUSTRATION

Because public display of candid sexual images was for so long out of the question, especially in large formats, one of the major genres of pornographic drawing and painting was the book illustration. Publishers of volumes of erotic literature could include prints of clandestine works by well-known artists but might also commission original drawings or paintings to illustrate scenes in a salacious narrative. Since they take their themes from fiction, such works often differ from those produced by artists in other media. By now, Americans are familiar with Aubrey Beardsley's bizarre illustrations for the books of Oscar Wilde; these were often sold as prints and posters during the 1960s. Less known are Crepax's illustrations for *Story of O*, though the French illustrator's cartoon version of that novel circulates widely in the United States. American collectors of erotica from the colonial period to the present have prized such illustrations, although eighteenth-century readers were doubtless not quite so familiar with Antoine Borel's engravings of Fanny Hill's ministrations to her lovers' genitals as contemporary teenagers are with R. Crumb's drawings of similarly comic scenes.

In recent years major galleries have mounted exhibits of mostly classic erotic book illustrations. The most comprehensive was the show at the Peter Biddulph Gallery in London, 10 June to 18 June 1986. The catalog, 589 entries with an Introduction by Peter Webb, was published as *The Forbidden Library: An Exhibition of Erotic Illustrations from the 18th Century to the Present Day*. More specialized are the two volumes of *Erotische Illustrationen französischer Klassiker*; the plates are principally eighteenth-century illustrations of French erotic fiction sprinkled with a few contemporary images, and the text is in German, French, Italian, and English. A similar three-volume compilation is *Ars Erotica: Die erotische Buchillustration im Frankreich des 18. Jahrhunderts*. Here Golo Jacobsen chronicles the history of French erotic illustration in the eighteenth century, while Ludwig von Brunn's impressive annotations lead the reader through hundreds of plates from editions of works considered scandalous (e.g., Cleland, Rousseau, de Sade, and Voltaire); some educated Americans and collectors would have seen them.

Just after the turn of the century the collector and bibliographer Bernhard Stern printed a volume composed of book jackets and plates of classic literary works from around the world entitled *Illustrierte Geschichte der Erotischen Literatur aller Zeiten und Völker*. His volume can be compared with Gordon Grimley's compilation, *Erotic Illustrations*, a study of images commissioned for classic erotica; again, most are European. The late William B. Ober, a New Jersey pathologist, dealt at length with erotic book illustration in two volumes, *Boswell's Clap and Other Essays* and *Bottoms Up! A Pathologist's Essays on Medicine and the Humanities*. Ober was particularly interested in images of flagellation, asphyxiation, and other bizarre acts and writes about them with wit, sympathy, and intelligence. (Shortly before he died, Ober told me that "if people had seen as many dead bodies as I have, they would learn to prize erectile tissue while they still can.") Though Philip Stewart is not concerned with specifically American examples, his "Indecency and Literary Illustration" explores the erotic motivation and collaboration of artists and writers. Like Ober, Stewart is drawn to illustrations in the many editions of Cleland's *Fanny Hill*, a volume long a staple of American collections.

Few American artists have specialized in erotic illustration of classic texts, and of those who did, few hold the stature of a Felicien Rops or Martin Van Maele. Gershon Legman's *The Horn Book: Studies in Erotic Folklore and Bibliography* mentions several who accepted commissions from American publishers; these include Keene Wallis, David Plotkin, Alexander King, Eric Stanton, and John Willie, though the latter are perhaps better known as fetish cartoonists. Easily the greatest of American artists to work in this genre was Mahlon Blaine. For the publisher Jack Brussel, for instance, Blaine copiously illustrated a collection of Ben Franklin's short esoterica called *Facetiae Frankliana* in the 1940s. Brussel brought out two folio editions of Blaine's work under the imprint of Walden Publications, the second of which, *Nova Venus*, is the better realized. Blaine's erotic illustrations for American editions of Verlaine, Voltaire, Flaubert, and others are the subjects of Gershon Legman's bibliographic Introduction to Blaine's *The Art of Mahlon Blaine*, which reproduces his finest work. One of the more fascinating experiments in this genre is Tee Corinne's homage to talented female illustrators in *Sapphistry: The Book of Lesbian Sexuality*, by Pat Califia. The volume contains drawings by Corinne in the style of these pioneers, who are introduced in capsule biographies. Corinne correctly gives precedence to the American Clara Tice (1888–1973), who during the 1920s and 1930s drew voluptuous scenes for various special editions of erotica. Tice is associated with American editions of the work of Pierre Louÿs; she illustrated *Woman and Puppet* and *The Adventures of King Pausole*, both by the French literary roué. In *Erotic Art of the Masters: The 18th, 19th, and 20th Centuries*, Bradley Smith says that Tice was the "greatest of all the women erotic illustrators" (176), a judgment widely accepted by collectors. A more obscure female contender is "Rhangild" or "Rahnghild" (Susan Aguerra?), who drew Tijuana Bibles and illustrations for erotic novels, such as the 1932 American edition of Leopold von Sacher-Masoch's *Venus in Furs*.

Alexander King's several works of autobiography speak from time to time of his experiments with book illustrations that he compared to George Grosz's, of his translation of Ovid, and of his relationships with magazine editors and book publishers; notable among the volumes is King's *Mine Enemy Grows Older*. Among modern masters of this meticulous form is John Boyce, whose illustrations originally drawn for the erotic fiction of Anais Nin have been reprinted in *Aphrodisiac*; Nin wrote the Introduction to the volume. Maureen Duffy's *The Erotic World of Faery* ventures briefly into illustrations of fairy tales, and Luis Royo's "Royo" might serve as an exemplar of sword and sorcery fantasy illustrations. Gwendolyn Layne draws on a great many examples in "Subliminal Seduction in Fantasy Illustration."

American magazine and paperback publishers frequently enlisted pinup artists to produce provocative covers and jackets for texts that were both sensational and sexy; the covers are often more memorable than the content. Francis Smilby's *Stolen Sweets: The Cover Girls of Yesteryear: Their Elegance, Charm, and Sex Appeal* is a slight and rather dull volume of little significant comment on classic images of women on magazine covers from the late nineteenth century to the 1930s. Better is Robert Lesser's *Pulp Art: Original Cover Paintings for the Great American Pulp Magazines*, a critical history and commentary on garish cover illustrations of the 1930s and 1940s. *The Spicy of Life: A Sampler of 50 Covers from the "Spicy" Pulps* brings together risqué covers with a brief discussion of the provenance of each. *Spicy: Naughty '30s Pulp Covers* is a set of thirty-nine trading cards; each card provides useful publication data, information on editorial staff, and circulation statistics for pulp magazines like *Stolen Sweets, Breezy, Pep*, and *Bedtime Stories*. A similar card set published by Kitchen Sink Press inspired Neil Wexler's "A Pocket Full of Pin-Ups," a nostalgic piece on pocket (4" by 6") pinup books of the 1950s such as *Carnival, Focus, She, Bold*, and *Show*. Harry Harrison identifies the sexy illustrations and magazine covers that helped to build an American audience for science fiction in *Great Balls of Fire! A History of Sex in Science Fiction*. Donald Palumbo discusses erotic imagery and themes in fantasy magazines in *Eros in the Mind's Eye: Sexuality and the Fantastic in Art and Film*, and, to a lesser degree, so do the contributors to Palumbo's *Erotic Universe: Sexuality and Fantastic Literature*.

Erotic anthologies that blend literary excerpts and reproductions of art have become popular in recent years. While generally chosen for their beauty or because they have been sanitized by institutional approval, the illustrations often carry captions that scholars might find useful. Typical of the genre are *Erotic by Nature: A Celebration of Life, of Love, and of Our Wonderful Bodies*, edited by David Steinberg; *Plaisirs d'Amour: An Erotic Guide to the Senses*, by Elizabeth Nash; and *Passionate Journey: Poems and Drawings in the Erotic Mood*, by Steve Kowit and Arthur Okamura.

PINUP PAINTINGS

Pinup artists, though distinguishable from pinup photographers, like them have helped to define the erotic sensibilities of Americans, and antiporn feminists routinely characterize both as pornographers. The information on pinup artists varies in substance and quality. The most authoritative volume, by the collector Charles G. Martignette and L. K. Meisel, is *The Great American Pin-Up*. Its 900 illustrations cover calendars, magazine covers, centerfolds, playing cards, and other formats, but only from World War II until the mid-1970s. Unlike other compilers of such images, Martignette and Meisel identify the artists and offer modest information on masters such as Rolf Armstrong, Zöe Mozert, Harry Aikman, and Alberto Vargas. Wider in their coverage, with more extensive comment, *The Illustrated History of Girlie Magazines* and *The Pin-Up: A Modest History*, both by Mark Gabor, offer general surveys with a heavy emphasis on American examples of the genre, as does Jacques Sternberg's *Pin Up*, which covers the period from the mid-nineteenth century to the eve of World War II. The European focus of Pierre Duvillars's *Pin-up: Femmes Fatales et Ingénues Libertines* allows only a brief look at American illustrations. Americans are, of course, familiar with many of the French pinups that Duvillars considers, as is obvious from *The Girls from La Vie Parisienne*, in which Paul Dinnage points out that the drawings of women from the French weekly reached audiences in the United States as soon as the magazine began publishing in

1863 and that the tabloid sold well in major U.S. cities in the 1920s. Bryon Stinson's "Pin-Ups of the Civil War" studies the embryonic domestic type. His article is a good companion piece to Edward Van Every's *Sins of America as Exposed by the Police Gazette*, which considers the influence of scandal magazines like the venerable *Police Gazette* in shaping the pinup in this country. Reid Austin's illustrated article, "The Petty Girl," covers the evolution of the figure that George Petty began drawing in 1933; the essay is a precursor of Austin's *Petty: The Classic Pin-Up Art of George Petty*, a fine biographical and critical study of Petty's life and art, with a Foreword by Hugh Hefner.

The work of Petty's principal rival is covered by Astrid Rossana-Conte in *Vargas: The Creator of the Pin-Up Girl, 20s–50s*. Rossana-Conte details the six-decade-long career of Alberto Vargas (1896–1982), who began working for impresario Florenz Ziegfeld to create an idealized woman known as "the Ziegfeld Girl." Vargas moved on to painting pictures of Hollywood film stars that adorned troop lockers in World War II, then hit his stride with illustrations for *Esquire* and *Playboy*. A California proprietorship still owns all rights to Vargas' work. Tom Robotham's *Varga* covers the peak years in the 1940s with *Esquire*, as detailed in eighty of Vargas' more famous paintings, together with photos of some of his better-known models. Collections include *Vargas: 20s–50s*, a poster book featuring the trademark sheen of flesh and the carefully highlighted voluptuous curves; *Vargas: The Esquire Years, A Catalogue Raisonne*, which features an appreciative Introduction by Kurt Vonnegut; and *Playboy's Vargas Girls*, which are drawn from the later work. Vargas himself coauthored with Reid Austin the volume called *Vargas*, probably the most comprehensive source of information on the most successful pinup artist in American history.

Another of Petty's rivals, Earl MacPherson, has published *The Earl from Oklahoma* and (with Merylene Schneider) *Memoirs of Earl MacPherson: The King of "Pin-Up Art."* Both books deal with the career of one of the most prolific of pinup painters, especially for ads and calendars. MacPherson flourished until the market collapsed after World War II with the rise of men's magazines specializing in photographs. (*Modern Man*, a popular pinup magazine in the 1950s, ran a pictorial on MacPherson himself in its June 1954 issue, or so says the man himself.) Irving Wexler's article, "King Pin-Up," contains recollections of Gil Elvgren, Peter Driben, Fritz Willis, and Bill Randall, other notable painters of pinups. In *Elvgren: His Life and Art*, Max Allan Collins and Drake Elvgren collect and comment on the pinup, calendar, and advertising art by the "Norman Rockwell of Cheesecake," Gil Elvgren, whose heyday was World War II. *Vignettes*, a four-volume set, reproduces the best-known work of Vargas, Elvgren, Rolf Armstrong, and Billy DeVorss, set in historical context.

The art critic Elizabeth Claridge has characterized the pop pinups of Mel Ramos as descendants from a tradition of artistic exaggeration in *The Girls of Mel Ramos*. Honey Truewoman has also criticized Ramos' works such as "Ode to Ang" (1972) and "Manet's Olympia" (1973), in which the artist places pinup figures in the settings of classic paintings, in "Realism in Drag." Ramos' works, says Truewoman, are not really satires, but "metaphors, parodies, travesties" (44). Robert Rosenblum has compiled many of the nudes in *Mel Ramos: Pop Art Images*. *Leg Art: Sixty Years of Hollywood Cheesecake*, edited by Madison S. Lacy and Don Morgan (and reissued under the title *Hollywood Cheesecake: Sixty Years of America's Favorite Pinups*), chronicles the evolution of the movie pinup, a form that spans both painting and photography. Fetishistic images of women—in bondage, sadomasochistic scenes, horror movies, comic books, and so on, some photographed, some drawn or painted—fill the twelve volumes of *Diva Obsexion*, a history of a male fascination with women caught in erotic frames, by Riccardo Morrocchi and other pop culture enthusiasts.

Most of the artists working in this vein have been male, but there are several notable exceptions. In their interview with the actress, "Mae West 1976," Anjelica Huston and Peter Lester include West's recollections of Florence Kosell, the artist who painted the provocative advertisement for *Sex*, the play with which West scandalized New York in the 1920s. Until quite recently, the only female pinup painter to rival Vargas or Petty was Zöe Mozert, famous for her pinup ad for *The Outlaw*, starring Jane Russell. Often called a pinup herself because of her habit of painting in the nude using her own voluptuous body as model, Mozert painted most of the major Hollywood starlets as pinups. The best article on her is "Zöe Mozert: Pin-Up's Leading Lady," by Marianne Ohl Phillips. The current leading female pinup artist is Olivia De Berardinis, known for the graphic symbolism and explicitly realized genitalia of her subjects. Her work in different media is collected, with comment by herself, editor Joel Beren, and Hugh Hefner, as *Let Them Eat Cheesecake: The Art of Olivia*. *Second Slice: The Art of Olivia* includes work from 1994 to 1997. *Penthouse* profiles a Japanese artist now working in California in "Sorayama," a portfolio and biography; the magazine carries one of Sorayama's fetishistic paintings in every issue.

Betty Pages Annual covers not just the photographs but also the painted pinups that Bettie Page inspired during her career as America's most famous model. The *Betty Page Portfolio* contains paintings of Page rendered by eight artists, including Dave Stevens. No fewer than three historians have studied pinups on aircraft. The broadest is *Airplane Nose Art: Over 350 Paintings on Aircraft*, edited by B. Munro, who selects a great many featuring skimpily clad women. Gary M. Valant's *Vintage Aircraft Nose Art* concentrates on World War II aircraft, especially bombers, while Ian Logan and Henry Nield's *Classy Chassy* surveys aircraft fuselage pinups (bombers and fighters) from World War II to the Korean War. "Provocative Art of the Pinup," a special issue of *Airbrush Action Magazine*, covers aircraft and other types of pinups, including contemporary ones. The magazine is a good source of information on the airbrush, which lends a voluptuous sheen and fullness to body parts in pinup paintings. The work of Boris Vallejo, an artist typical of specialists in smooth fantasy illustrations for magazines as diverse as *Penthouse* and *Heavy Metal*, has been collected as *Mirage*.

Several other critical approaches are relevant here. Karen Machover's text,

Personality Projection in the Drawing of the Human Figure, demonstrates a method of creating psychological and sexual profiles from the study of artists' renditions of anatomy. Carol A. Pollis' fascinating "Sensitive Drawings of Sexual Activity in Human Sexuality Textbooks: An Analysis of Communication and Bias" investigates the genre of medical illustration. Pollis observes that signs denoting age, ethnic status, class, and sexual identity are coded in such drawings and reflect the bias of illustrator, author, publisher, and intended audience. These signs mirror the difficulties of dealing with gender, social class, and sexuality, specifically with reference to masturbation, oral sex, and anal sex. In short, says Pollis, visual images replicate other forms of discourse, even in books like *The Joy of Gay Sex*, which contains no "sensitive drawings" (67) of homosexual anal sex; that there are none, she says, is a message in itself.

EROTIC/PORNOGRAPHIC OBJETS D'ART

Humans have always represented sex and sexuality by fashioning objects in the shape of naked figures or genitals, created toys that simulate intercourse, or merely transformed familiar things into suggestive artifacts. The most straightforward treatment is Harriet Bridgeman's Introduction to Cottie Burland's wonderfully illustrated *Erotic Antiques: Or Love Is an Antic Thing*, which discusses meerschaum pipes, lamps, statuary, snuffboxes, porcelains, bottles, scrimshaw, watches, cameos, seals, netsukes, woodcuts, furniture, dildos, ashtrays, fans, boxes, sauce-boats, medical figures (for diagnosis of shy patients), inkwells, lightbulbs, dishes, vases, bronzes, postcards, crystals, dolls, and a great many other objects. Most of the items are not American, though many are in American collections. Charlotte Hill and William Wallace scatter a few pictures of artifacts such as explicit snuffboxes and inkwells, most drawn from the collections of the Klinger auction house, throughout the three-volume *Erotica: An Illustrated Anthology of Sexual Art and Literature*. More specialized is R. Carrera's *Hours of Love*, a Swiss catalog and commentary on erotic timepieces, ornamental watches, and beautifully wrought clocks featuring carved or painted scenes of nudity or congress and mechanical escapements that mimic intercourse.

Bradley Smith's *The American Way of Sex: An Informal Illustrated History* covers artifacts such as erotically embellished clocks and streamlined dildos made in America. *Secret World of Erotic Art*, a videotaped version of two of Smith's histories of erotica by Roberta Haynes and Rick Hauser, provides a good look at artifacts lent by the Gichner Foundation: postcards, pipes, watches, prehistoric and American Indian crafts, necklaces, lingams, charms, statuary, porcelains, carvings, and toys. The various books and catalogs derived from the Kronhausen collection depict erotic artifacts from all over the world (see **Erotic Art** in chapter 4, Phyllis Kronhausen and Eberhard Kronhausen). The Kronhausens have also assembled a volume on *Erotic Bookplates*. Although not a well-established American genre, the bookplates are collectors' items in the United

States; these are mostly European examples. (For additional comment on book-plates from other countries, see Chapter 36 in Eugene Burt's *Erotic Art*.)

Holding somewhat different status than these vintage pieces are contemporary erotic folk crafts. The authorities here are two. Nancy Bruning Levine's *Hardcore Crafts* contains photos and commentary on explicitly sexual American works in wood, glass, clay, cloth, metal, enamel, and so on, together with capsule biographies of the artists. Broader still is Milton Simpson's more recent *Folk Erotica*, which covers around three centuries of erotic folk art, with particular reference to American examples such as Navajo kachina dolls, nineteenth-century carved canes and walking sticks, and other demotic artifacts, some comic, some beautiful, some crude in the extreme. Simpson's highly knowledgeable survey is mandatory reading for those interested in popular erotic Americana and, for that matter, popular culture generally; the illustrations are superb. Mac E. Barrick's "Folk Toys" deals with the mechanical and/or carved wooden figures such as wind vanes that simulate sexual intercourse, a popular item among mountain whittlers and craftsmen. The section on "Figurative" art (10–48) in *American Primitive: Discoveries in Folk Sculpture*, by Roger Ricco, Frank Maresca, and Julia Weissman, contains many examples of erotic figurines; the text is excellent on carnival figures, found objects, and "outsider" artifacts. Nina Hellman and Norman Brouwer have collected a few examples of mildly erotic objects in *A Mariner's Fancy: The Whaleman's Art of Scrimshaw*. An excellent essay on vaginal imagery as a motif of self- and sexual awareness in quilting and other "women's" folk art is "Cunts/Quilts/Consciousness" by Miriam Schapiro and Faith Wilding. Schapiro and Wilding set feminist art in the larger context of raised consciousness that occurred in the 1970s, when " 'Cunt art' " emerged as "a defiant challenge to depictions of submissive female sexuality." "For the first time many women produced work with their own naked bodies as subject, exploring them from their personal points of view. The body became the book: it was written upon, painted, photographed, ritually arranged, bathed in eggs, mud, blood . . . and draped in flowers, seaweed and other detritus of the natural and *man* made world" (7). It was, in short, a feminist attempt to appropriate the defiant purposes often thought to animate male-oriented pornography, to reclaim the vulgarity that seems somehow more truthful than official versions of reality.

The premier example of vaginal embroidery and ceramics, of course, is Judy Chicago's "Dinner Party" gallery/museum show, which consists of thirty-nine hand-painted china plates and their place mats and table settings, each representing a great woman and all symbolic of a history in which women's contributions to culture have been subsumed by their domestic roles. Chicago explains her intent in mounting the show, which has traveled widely in the United States, in *The Dinner Party: A Symbol of Our Heritage*. *Embroidering Our Heritage: The Dinner Party Needlework*, by Chicago and Susan Hill, provides the rationale for the needleworked vulva images and patterns produced for the exhibit. *Through the Flower*, Chicago's autobiography, asserts the female need for erotic expression and the artist's right to explore and express eroticism in the search for gender identity and autonomy. Not all feminists agree with her position, of course, but the contributors to *Sexual Politics: Judy Chicago's Dinner Party in Feminist Art History*, edited by Amelia Jones, zero in on the famous exhibit as a fault line in feminist art and the politics of identity. Occasioned by the Hammer Museum's exhibit of feminist art, some of it highly explicit, which has been influenced in some way by Chicago's precedents, the volume includes comment on what is virtually a who's who of American women artists of the last two decades. Another ceramicist who delves into sexuality is Howard Kottler; he is the subject of Patricia Failing's "Howard Kottler: Conceptualist and Purveyor of Psychosexual Allusions," a fairly heavy-handed analysis of images and shapes in his clay objects.

Cynthia Plaster Caster, a former groupie, is the possessor of what she thinks is the world's largest collection of casts of the penises of famous rock stars. Doug Simmons interviews her in "Harder They Come." The artist describes her techniques for erecting the subject's member, for mixing a suitable plaster, and for ensuring that the finished cast properly records veins, urethra, and idiosyncrasies of the shaft. Her formula for plaster is reproduced in Pamela Des Barres' *I'm with the Band: Confessions of a Groupie*. Jack Boulware's "Backstage Pass" identifies other casters, while Ellen Sanders' "The Case of the Cock-Sure Groupies" is a 1968 account of the art form. Heather Busch and Burton Silver have written a unique how-to book in *Kokigami: The Intimate Art of the Little Paper Costume*, which provides detailed instructions on constructing paper garments and hats to decorate penises, which then, properly attired, can participate in intimate puppet shows and other forms of entertainment. Finally, Douglas Wissing's "Erotica Whose Purpose Was Scholarly" reports on a well-attended exhibit of art from the Kinsey Archives displayed at the Fine Arts Gallery of Indiana University; the show included many esoteric objects.

REPRESENTATIONAL/APHRODISIAC FOOD AND DRINK

Collectors of erotica have traditionally prized treatises on aphrodisiacs and their alleged ability to stimulate desire or enhance sexual performance. The category is enormous, comprising potions, recipes, prescriptions, treatments, and secret rites. Modern examples include tracts on vitamin E, bee-balm, ginger root, massage, virility diets, kegel exercises, yoga, tantra, and any number of schemes shading toward quackery. The brief listing here includes texts in which linkages with sexual discourse or erotic imagery illuminate pornographic genres. For example, foods whose natural shapes or prepared forms counterfeit the images of phalluses, breasts, vulvas, or humans engaged in intercourse conform to a definition of pornography as sexual *representation*. Works on drugs, perfumes, chemicals, and other stimulants that are described in sexual imagery are also listed as a way of indicating scope. It hardly seems necessary to say so, but readers should approach these works with skepticism.

One of the cornerstones of American libraries of erotica has always been John Davenport's *Aphrodisiacs and Anti-Aphrodisiacs: Three Essays on the Power of Reproduction*, a famous English text published in 1869. It is filled with lore and myth that must have titillated readers at the time. The erotologist Alfred F. Niemoeller borrowed the title and many of the legends for his little Haldeman-Julius "blue book," called *Aphrodisiacs and Anti-Aphrodisiacs*. One of the first comprehensive American surveys of the subject, Harry E. Wedeck's *Dictionary of Aphrodisiacs*, aka *Love Potions through the Ages*, draws most of its entries from literature classical to modern. Two more recent broad looks are Gary Selden's *Aphrodisia: A Guide to Sexual Food, Herbs, and Drugs* and Raymond Stark's *The Book of Aphrodisiacs*; Stark appends a useful bibliography. *Aphrodisiacs: From Legend to Prescription*, by Alan Hull Walton, is more historical and most interesting on attempts to transplant monkey and goat glands to humans to increase sexual potency.

Pamela Allardice's *Aphrodisiacs and Love Magic: The Mystic Lure of Love Charms* recounts the lore of plants, herbs, fruits, games, and potions, while Richard A. Miller's *Magical and Ritual Use of Aphrodisiacs* emphasizes their religious and cabalistic associations. *Phantastica: Narcotic and Stimulating Drugs*, by Lewis Lewin, first published in 1931, became an underground classic for beats and hippies. The folklorist Eleanor Long examines some of the more persistent beliefs held by Americans, including those concerning the alleged properties of Spanish fly, in "Aphrodisiacs, Charms, and Philtres." Another enduring myth, that schools, prisons, and military barracks lace food with saltpeter, alleged to reduce sexual desire, has led to anxieties among male populations in such institutions, say George W. Rice and David F. Jacobs in "Saltpeter: A Folkloric Adjustment to Acculturation Stress." The most erudite and intelligent approach, however, is Peter V. Taberner's *Aphrodisiacs: The Science and the Myth*, which casts doubt on a lot of assumptions and also marshals a lot of information, including an excellent bibliography.

Eugene Schoenfield wrote a column for the *Berkeley Barb* on drugs and sex and other matters during the 1960s and has collected his advice in *Dear Dr. Hip*. Given the potential for drug abuse, pharmacists such as M. Laurence Lieberman have tried to provide accurate information. Lieberman's *The Sexual Pharmacy: The Complete Guide to Drugs with Sexual Side Effects* details the sexual potential—or lack thereof—of some 200 drugs. Less knowledgeable is the discussion of stimulating foods and vitamins, alcohol, drugs, and so on by Gary Null and Elayne Kahn; their *The Whole Body Health and Sex Book* is typical of large numbers of popular health volumes. In *Sex and Drugs: A Journey beyond Limits*, Robert Anton Wilson is cautious also in his assessment of sexual responses to hashish, LSD, and other substances frequently ingested in the 1960s and 1970s.

Recipes for seduction are standard elements in many pornographic genres and themselves constitute a minor subgenre. Writing under the cute pseudonym Pilaff Bey, Norman Douglas published *Venus in the Kitchen: Recipes for Seduction*, a book (originally published in 1952) which set formulas for cookbooks to follow. The appeal of *Fanny Hill's Cook Book* lies in the title and in the whimsically named recipes ("Crafty Ebbing Undressing") for food and drink offered by Lionel H. Braun and William Adams. Norma Ewalt's racy commentary on dishes and recipes chosen for titillation of the palate animates *Decadent Dinners and Lascivious Lunches*. Cookbooks are, of course, staples in the lists of many publishers, and eroticism adds zest, as in Greg Frazier and Beverly Frazier's *Aphrodisiac Cookery Ancient and Modern*. Another gastronomic treatise on eroticism, Robert Hendrickson's *Foods for Love*, was originally titled *Lewd Food: The Complete Guide to Aphrodisiac Edibles*. Martha Hopkins and Randall Lockridge tutor chefs in stimulating ingredients in *Intercourses: An Aphrodisiac Cookbook*. *The X-Rated Cookbook*, by Susan Sky and Louise Wolfe, is replete with "recipes for the bedroom," like Penis Colada and Nipple Nectar. "Phallic Foods," that is, those shaped like penises or reputed to foster erections, are the topics of Duncan Macdongald's essay of that title. Jo Foxworth promises 138 recipes favored by renowned madams from eras in which full-service whorehouses offered food as well as other attractions in *The Bordello Cookbook*.

Ron Stieglitz and Sandy Lesberg compile more than 100 recipes for sauces, some reputed to have aphrodisiac properties and, as if to invoke sympathetic magic, intersperse them with reproductions of vintage erotic French postcards in *Saucy Ladies*. Spurning such pretense, David Thorpe and Pierre le Poste call their explorations of the connections between edibles and sex *Rude Food* and use as their illustrations mostly pictures of the food itself. K. Rhein Merchant's "Come and Get It" offers recipes for cooking with semen (lower in fat and higher in protein than milk or eggs), which can be frozen for later use. Among the felicities of *Ladies' Own Erotica*, a volume assembled by the Kensington Ladies' Erotica Society, are some recipes that have turned on the ladies themselves. Karen Dwyer and Patrika Brown, operators of the Erotic Bakery at 582 Amsterdam in New York, specialize in baked goods in the shape of penises, vulvas, breasts, and figures crafted to order and promise that no cupcake request will be denied; they share their expertise in *The Erotik Baker Cookbook*, as they have already shared their wares with thousands of Manhattanites. Howard Smith and Leslie Harlib visit their store and sample their sweets in "Ladies Buntiful." So do Lucy Winer and Paula Koenigsberg, who report on the bakery as a place where fantasies take edible form in their documentary *Rate It X*.

Two unusual approaches to food and sexuality are Carol J. Adams' *The Sexual Politics of Meat: A Feminist-Vegetarian Critical Theory*, which has little to do with eroticism but speculates on gender differences associated with eating food, vegetables being women's food, steak men's, and Soledad de Montalvo's four-volume *Women, Food and Sex*; volume IV is on America. Some of the linkages

Montalvo makes are not always clear, but they indicate that Americans find the subject important. Sexual potency, a matter of concern for men, has made men receptive to pre-Viagra substances reputed to increase virility. Gary M. Griffin's *Aphrodisiacs for Men; Effective Virilizing Foods and Herbs* identifies those the author likes. Gary Brandner's *Vitamin E: Key to Sexual Satisfaction* is representative of the dozen or so volumes to sing the praises of various vitamins, supplements, salves, and ointments. In "The Entrée That Dare Not Speak Its Name," restaurant critic Jeff Weinstein asks if there is such a thing as gay food and, after sorting through various dishes, concludes that there is not. Donna Clark thinks otherwise; her *Queer Street Cookbook* is a reflection on culinary arousal, complete with gastronomically gendered recipes. The influence of gastronomic eroticism on mainstream culture manifests itself in a stream of holiday catalogs advertising edible novelties and in such literature as Isabel Allende's *Aphrodite: A Memoir of the Senses*, which recalls recipes such as Novice's Nipples and Harem Turkey.

Since roués have long thought that alcohol weakened a woman's inhibitions, specially concocted drinks are a staple of aphrodisiac folklore. The *Encyclopedia of Shooters* lists the ingredients for aptly named drinks such as Slippery Dick, Blow Job, Slippery Nipple, Pink Twat, Sit on My Face Sally, Red Panties, and Busted Cherry. Ted Saucier's *Bottoms Up* merely illustrates its pages with pictures of nude women, indulges in adolescent wit, and offers advice on the order of serving drinks in suggestive containers to make them more stimulating to female guests; the mixes, however, would probably get a home bartender through a party. In "Just Slip This into Her Drink . . . ," Frederic C. Appel dismisses most such stimulants as ineffectual or dangerous (e.g., Spanish fly) but also identifies a few that do heighten sexual experience.

Such subjects have, of course, invoked academic and scientific comment. Volume I of Claude Lévi-Strauss' wonderful anthropological text, *The Raw and the Cooked: Introduction to a Science of Mythology*, deals among many other things with the erotic aspects of food and eating and is a fine introduction for scholars. His metaphorical conceit, the notion that a culture always "cooks" nature, can be applied to the transformation of raw sex into a palatable commodity. Pages 92–106 of Rosalind Coward's *Female Desires*, which investigates the ways in which women are manipulated in a consumer culture, discuss the erotic aspects of food. Coward's essay, "Naughty but Nice: Food Pornography," asserts that "food pornography" is a "regime of pleasurable images" that contributes to the servitude of women and their cultural subordination because it emphasizes slenderness as a social ideal, a syndrome that promotes guilt at the same time that it stimulates eating. Although Octavio Paz's "Eroticism and Gastrosophy" is not about specific foods, it is a splendid riff on North American appetites and worth reading for its cultural reflections. William W. Weaver discusses mildly erotic edibles, with discussion behind the impulse to fabricate them, in *America Eats: Forms of Edible Folk Art*. Jan Avgikos' catalog, "Riproaring Rhopography," is an exhibit guide to Marilyn Minter's *100 Food Porn*, a series of paintings of food with sexual characteristics; Avgikos says that Minter also collaborated on a video commercial for the show with Ted Haimes. Finally, a notorious work that combines food and outrage is Les Krims' *Making Chicken Soup*, a book of photographs in which the photographer depicts his elderly mother, nude save for panties, making chicken soup; he includes the recipe.

KITSCH

These last examples might just as well be described as kitsch. No one has ever come up with a satisfactory explanation of just why making a swizzle stick or a hat in the shape of a nipple or a penis should be so compelling, but whether one considers them fetishes, totems, amusing toys, or mere vulgarities, they have proliferated everywhere. Novelty shops and mail-order businesses sell suggestive toothbrushes, key chains, cigarette lighters, ballpoint pens, mechanical contraptions, coffee cups, pillows, and so on. Four books that investigate kitsch, with occasional reference to its erotic aspects, are Jane Stern and Michael Stern's *The Encyclopedia of Bad Taste*; Curtis F. Brown's *Star-Spangled Kitsch: An Astounding and Tastelessly Illustrated Exploration of the Bawdy, Gaudy, Shoddy Mass-Art Culture in This Grand Land of Ours*; Gillo Dorfles' *Kitsch: The World of Bad Taste*; and Peter Ward's *Kitsch in Sync: A Consumer's Guide to Bad Taste*. All consider "naughty" artifacts, for example, pitchers in the shape of infants with penises for spouts, items shaped like breasts, buttocks, vulvas, and rectums, double-entendre toys, and risqué twists on every conceivable medium. In a familiar pattern that assigns vulgarity to the deliberately uncharted realm of "low" pornography, most cultural critics associate kitsch with lower-class, mass-market consumption as a way of distinguishing it from expensive, that is, acceptable, erotica.

Among the many dealers who market sexual kitsch, perhaps the most interesting is Bud Plant, who publishes *Bud Plant's Incredible Catalog*, page after page of posters, pinups (e.g., Betty Page), buttons, figurines, T-shirts, trading cards, and so on. A visit to any well-stocked seaside resort shop would locate some of these novelties. Eric Schmitt writes about public reaction on Long Island against pornographic or obscene messages on products like T-shirts, coffee mugs, bumper stickers, and greeting cards and against novelties like fortune cookies containing condoms and windup toys in the shape of breasts that jiggle in "Angry Shoppers Protest Cupidity in Valentine Vice," though the title of his article undermines the neighborhood's discontent. Alternative newspapers in urban centers routinely carry ads for kitsch. During 1994 the *Nuovo Newsweekly* of Indianapolis, for example, featured ads by Stoner's Funstores, merchants of "Funny, Goofy Crap since 1949": "Penis Straws, Blowup Dolls, Hand Buzzers, Bugs, Flash Paper, Boobie Mugs, Fart Plugs, Squirming Rat in a Trap, Whips, Crap, Puke, Vibrators, Cool Magic Tricks, Stink Bombs, Penis Squirtguns, Masturbation Kit, Snot Nose, Condom Lollipops, Cigarette Loads, Small Penis

Condoms, Shocking Lighters, Edible Panties and Body Paints, Farting Turds, Outrageous T-Shirts, Cards, Mugs, and Other Goofy Crap!"

Fascinating to Richard Carleton Hacker are the pinup labels of sexy women that decorated vintage cigar boxes, now collectors' items. His "Sex and the Cigar Box" discusses the development of chromolithography in the late nineteenth century. Another specialized article, on the labels featuring scantily clad women ("Squeeze Me") for fruit and vegetable boxes, is "Now, That's a Tomato: A Salute to Those Pinup Artists Who Elevated the Vegetable Crate to an Art Form." Howard Smith and Leslie Harlib discover wallpaper with erotic images and themes in "X-Rated Hang-Up." Terry Sullivan admires an S/M wallpaper designed by British pop artist Allen Jones in "Pop Tart: Wallpaper with Edge, in a Severely Limited Edition." The price is $250 per double roll, cheap for a material already on display in the Cooper-Hewitt Museum. Part of Bruce M. Newman's *Fantasy Furniture* is devoted to sensual and exotic furnishings like chairs, sofas, and lamps. An interesting recent phenomenon is the reappropriation of Barbie dolls by gay and lesbian artists, who work variations on the body as art as idiograph, says Erica Rand in *Barbie's Queer Accessories*.

ARCHITECTURE AND SCULPTURE

The erotic potential of architecture is the subject of Sivon C. Reznikoff's *Sensuous Spaces: Designing Your Erotic Interiors*, which is full of suggestions for rendering environments more stimulating. Reznikoff has a lot to say about the psychology of erotic design, and his bibliography is extensive. Traditional sexual assumptions govern the allocation of living areas, says Daphne Spain in *Gendered Spaces*, an ethnographic study of rooms and design: kitchens built for women, for example, or studies intended for men, or bedrooms and bathrooms refitted for intimacy. Diana I. Agrest's "Body, Logic, and Sex" also explores gender, sexuality, and sensuality in architectural terms, as do the essays in *Sexuality and Space*, edited by Beatriz Colomina; these speculate on voluptuous architecture, the gendering of structures and interiors, and the sexuality of space itself. Agrest, Patricia Conway, and Leslie Kanes Weisman have edited the wide-ranging *The Sex of Architecture*, whose chapter titles (e.g., "Gendered Spaces in Colonial Algiers" and "Female Fetish Urban Form") indicate perspectives. Gendered spaces as loci of eroticism are the topics of essays in *Desiring Practices: Architecture, Gender and the Interdisciplinary*, edited by Katerina Rüedi, Sarah Wigglesworth, and Duncan McCorquodale. What makes Christian Thomsen's *Sensuous Architecture: The Art of Erotic Building* interesting is its tour of locations from the Marquis de Sade's torture chambers to English country gardens and cyberspace.

Also comprehensive is Aaron Betsky's *Building Sex: Men, Women, Architecture, and the Construction of Sexuality*, which argues that architecture can literally construct sexuality by gendering and sensualizing living and working spaces. Betsky's *Queer Space: Architecture and Same-Sex Desire* provides radical reflections on gendered space, as do the essays in *Queers in Space: Communities, Public Places, Sites of Resistance*, edited by Gordon Brent Ingram, Anne-Marie Bouthillette, and Yolanda Retter, whose contributors link gay identity to private and public venues. Many of Edmund B. Feldman's chapters in *Varieties of Visual Experience* deal with representations of sex and gender in architectural forms, the role of fantasy in design, and the erotic elements of visualized art. Marco Frascari warns against the excesses that overemphasis on human sensuality can generate in *Monsters of Architecture: Anthropomorphism in Architectural Theory*. Suzanne Foley's *Space/Time/Sound: Conceptual Art in the San Francisco Bay Area: The 70s* is an exhibition catalog of a show mounted from December 1979 to February 1980 featuring large-scale installations, some with sexual themes, and is valuable because of an exceptional chronology of spatial works. "Dirty Furniture" is a "Talk of the Town" interview with Joe Hurley, designer and manufacturer of such specialized furniture as the Bend-Over Chair, the Multi-Position Stair Sofa, and the Kinky Headboard (the latter has built-in restraints), mostly for S/M enthusiasts but also for the average citizen who needs to unwind with a light beating.

Dozens of articles have been written on the eroticism implicit in car design. L. E. Sissman makes the motifs explicit in "Autoerotics: The Pleasure Principle in Car Design." Ron Boise and Alan Watts examine erotic sculpture fashioned from automobile parts in "Sculpture: The Kama Sutra Theme." Most commentary on erotic sculpture is reticent. Typical is "Modern Sculpture," by Edan Wright, who speaks of the sensuality of themes and surfaces in works by sculptors such as Saint-Gaudens. Most erotic art histories are concerned with painting and drawing, but a few give more than superficial attention to sculpture. Among the best are some of the essays in *Studies in Erotic Art*, edited by Theodore Bowie and Cornelia V. Christenson. Since they focus on materials in the Kinsey Institute, they are good at tracing influences and sketching cultural contexts. Jean Rodolphe's section on "touch" in *Mit den Funf Sinnen: Gesicht, Gefühl, Gehör, Geschmack, Geruch: Ein Erotisches Bilderbuch* deals with sculptured forms. While hardly about pornography, *The Nude: A Study in Ideal Form*, by Kenneth Clark, offers insights into sculpture that carry over into examinations of more vulgar forms, and Patrick Waldberg's *Eros in the Belle Epoque* devotes a few pages to erotic sculpture, mostly European. Bradley Smith's *Erotic Art of the Masters: The 18th, 19th, and 20th Centuries* is better on contemporary examples. The title of Brandt Aymar's *The Young Male Figure in Paintings, Sculptures, and Drawings, from Ancient Egypt to the Present* describes its approach to semierotic sculptures of young men, but Aymar is not really interested in explicit representations.

Easily the most readable history is William H. Gerdts' *The Great American Nude: A History in Art*, which covers the sculpted human figure in the United States from the frank nudity carved into seventeenth-century tombstones to the polyester women of John de Andrea and the plaster lovers of George Segal of the 1970s. Gerdts seems not to have missed any of the controversies that greeted the display of any statue of an unclothed human; it is a lively, informative, and entertaining work, the more so because of the author's expertise. His treatment of nude sculpture in the nineteenth century is first-rate, and his bibliography will lead the scholar to firsthand accounts of sculptors whose works caused scandal. Gerdts also covers Allen Jones, a British artist who fashioned fetishized plasticine female figures clad in leather into coffee tables, chairs, and hat stands that occasioned feminist protests in this country. Marina Warner's *Monuments and Maidens: The Allegory of the Female Form* discusses the preference for nude females as symbols of light, progress, and reform, all of which were personified as female in public; though Warner glosses over all but the most conventional erotic aspects of sculpture, the book is fascinating.

Carl Bode's "Marble Men and Brazen Ladies" is an amusing account of puritanical American attitudes toward nude sculpture and painting; he identifies some statues that scandalized. Ilene Susan Fort covers genres, exotic variations, and the role and place of nude figures across a wide spectrum, including Afro-American sculpture, in *The Figure in American Sculpture: A Question of Modernity*. In " 'Making a Man of Him': Masculinity and the Black Body in Mid-Nineteenth-Century American Sculpture," Michael Hatt studies the social forces that constructed images of black male nudes as erotic icons of physical power beneath a facade of cultural subservience. Seymour Howard's "Fig Leaf, Pudica, Nudity, and Other Revealing Concealments," which deals with the American practice of hiding the genitals in sculpted and painted works, asserts that doing so draws attention to the pubic area and heightens the erotic response by making the nudity seem mysterious and shameful, especially when the fig leaves are themselves of exuberant rococo design.

Paul Gardner's *Louise Bourgeois* and Deborah Wye's *Louise Bourgeois* review the career and output of the French American artist who created witty sculptures of penises, breasts, and other erotic assemblages in the 1960s and 1970s. Lucy R. Lippard also touches on erotic images and themes implicit or explicit in the artist's assemblages in "Louise Bourgeois from the Inside Out." In "New Thoughts for Jasper Johns' Sculpture," Roni Feinstein discusses some of Johns' sexier sculptures. The work of Mike Kelley, a West Coast artist who specializes in doll and paper constructions, some of them vulgar, is covered by Mark Kreemer in "Mike Kelley: A Fucked-Up Mirror of Dominant Image Making." Charles Hagen reviews Cindy Sherman's 1992 show of sexual and fetishistic assemblages at the Metro Pictures gallery in Soho in "Adventures in Anatomy." The show features sadomasochistic masks and contorted figures to suggest "sex as monstrous and mechanical." According to Jan Avgikos, in "Cindy Sherman: Burning Down the House," Sherman's "grimly humorous vignettes deep-throat the politics of pornographic representation" by asking, "Is the social economy of pornography different from that of art?" (75). "Nancy Grossman at Exit Art" reviews a gallery show by Grossman, who dresses her carved heads with S/M garb such as bondage masks. Sam Hunter and Don

Hawthorne tactfully discuss the "public" sexuality of some famous plaster sculptures in *George Segal*. Anne Doran's "The Dialectical Porn Rock" discusses artist Aura Rosenberg, who employs a "reverse fetishism" by pasting pornographic pictures on rocks, then recontextualizes the stones by placing them in various social settings, where the ensembles become objects of fun.

André Chabot speculates on the linkages between love and death manifest in the "thanatopsian eroticism" of funerary sculpture in *Érotique du Cimetière*, which includes a few American examples among the European. It is worth comparing Chabot's volume with David Robinson's *Saving Graces: Images of Women in European Cemeteries*, though the latter has no American sepulchral monuments similar in their eroticism. Diana Hume George and Malcolm A. Nelson range further, covering the erotic appeal of cemeteries as a form of cultural conditioning, in "Man's Infinite Concern: Graveyards as Fetishes." Tuppy Owens lists various modern "monuments" to porn, though American examples are not as spectacular as Italy's Pompeii or Norway's Vigeland, in *The (Safer) Sex Maniac's Bible* (sec. 31). Among American variations, Owens lists the footprints of porn stars set in the cement floor of New York City's Pussycat Theatre.

IMAGES AND THEMES

In recent years, critics have concentrated on themes and motifs to explain the lure of erotic art in specific periods. Some of these works are remarkable in their critical perspectives, their cultural breadth, and their exceptional scholarship. For example, *Cleopatra: Histories, Dreams and Distortions*, by Lucy Hughes-Hallett, is an exhaustive study of Cleopatra as a literary and artistic image that varied—child, queen, woman, lover, suicide, alien, priestess, killer, camp figure—according to the agendas of successive eras. Hughes-Hallett looks at the work of painters and artists, scholars, historians, moviemakers, playwrights, and folklorists to uncover a politics of sex, race, morality, and desire. Her approach has little to do with pornography per se but a great deal to say about eroticism and art. Similarly, Eunice Lipton's *Alias Olympia: A Woman's Search for Manet's Notorious Model and Her Own Desire* exhibits the same kind of research, a nonpolemic investigation of nudity, sexuality, and sensuality in a historical context rendered with great skill. Bram Dijkstra finds images of perverse women everywhere in the art of a culture approaching the end of an aesthetic tradition in *Idols of Perversity: Fantasies of Feminine Evil in Fin-de Siècle Culture*. Eva Kuryluk explores similar terrain in *Salome and Judas in the Cave of Sex: The Grotesque: Origins, Iconography, Techniques*. Roland Villeneuve explores strange forests of fantasy creatures in *La Musée du la Bestialité*, a study of the sexual associations to be found in artistic representations of animals and humans, mostly women and dogs, snakes, or horses. Two other texts by Villeneuve, *Fétichisme et amour* and *Le Diable: Erotologie de Satan*, are mostly compilations of reproductions, all of them interesting. The first deals with sexual fetishes (symbolic and explicit) in art; the second, with erotic images of Satan, who has often been depicted in lascivious Christian art and kitsch as a depraved demon with erect penis. Robert Benayoun's *Erotique du Surréalisme* deals with the role of the erotic in surrealistic art, literature, and cinema.

Many studies, of course, focus on fetishes or specific images that recur in art. David Kunzle's brilliant "The Corset as Erotic Alchemy: From Rococo Galanterie to Montaut's Physiologies," a wonderfully illustrated analysis of the role of the corset in both mainstream painting and popular illustration (as in *La Vie Parisienne*) during a significant period of modern art, is as valuable for its notes as for its insights. John Grand-Carteret's *Le décolleté et le retroussé, trois siècles de gauloiseries 1600–1900* devotes a lot of attention to the corset as well but also to many other items of women's clothing as erotic fetishes in paintings and illustrations that have been familiar to Americans over the last two centuries. Robert Anton Wilson's *The Book of the Breast* treats the female bosom as a symbol in art and popular culture, as does Romi's more ambitious *Mythologie du Sein*, which finds that breast images recur ubiquitously in literature, fashion, and advertising as well. Far better histories of the treatment of the breast in art are *Be Still My Beating Heart: Art of Many Ages Illustrating a Resonant Female Gesture*, a collection of reproductions of pictures of women holding or caressing their breasts, compiled by Benjamin Darling partly to heighten awareness of breast cancer, and *The Moons of Paradise: Reflections on the Breast in Art*, by Mervyn Levy, whose examples provide evidence for the aesthetic and spiritual significance he thinks drives all idealized erotic art. *Gefilde de Lust*, despite its age, is still one of the best texts on the fascination with human breasts and buttocks; the authors, Alfred Kind and Curt Moreck, include hundreds of pictures of artistic treatments of these body parts and index them by artist.

Genital images in art have received somewhat less attention. Although Georges Devereux does consider contemporary open-crotch depictions of the vagina in *Baubo, la Vulve Mythique*, his psychoanalytic approach draws most of its illustrations from ancient and classic art in order to investigate the mythic power associated with vulva. Gérard Zwang's *Le Sexe de la Femme* explores the eroticization of women through studies of vaginal imagery in art throughout history. The "vaginal artist" Betty Dodson advocates that women begin the process of controlling their own sexuality by familiarizing themselves with their organs in *Liberating Masturbation: A Meditation on Self-Love*, a book illustrated by Dodson's own paintings of vaginas. Similarly illustrated, with an excellent commentary, is Barbara Rose's "Vaginal Iconography," a look at erotic paintings by contemporary women artists. Meridee Merzer provides a brief look at figurations of genitalia as exhibited in art by Hannah Wilke, Judy Chicago, and Doug Johns in "Genital Art." In the hands of talented artists, these traditionally pornographic images shock and mesmerize. The late Hannah Wilke used "transgressive" images of vaginas—sculptured in chewing gum and applied to her body—as a way of forcing reconsideration of the female body and woman's sexuality, says Constance M. Shortlidge in "The Disruptive 'Cunts' of Hannah

Wilke." Wilke's vaginal sculptures and images are the focus of M. Savitt's review, "Hannah Wilke: The Pleasure Principle [at the] Ronald Feldman Fine Arts Gallery, New York." Leslie Camhi reviews an exhibit of the paintings of vulva by an artist inspired by pornographic magazines in "Lip Service: Ghada Amer." One should note that these images differ considerably in explicitness from, say, the gynecological flowers painted by Georgia O'Keeffe, who said, although "somewhat disingenuously," according to Sue Hubbard in "A Womb with a View," that she was weary of "the obsessive sexual analysis of her work" (32). Male critics have been reluctant to grant O'Keeffe her rightful artistic status, says Anna C. Chave in "O'Keeffe and the Male Gaze," precisely because they have not understood the feminine eroticism that infuses her painting; the essay is a good companion piece, both conceptually and historically, to those on Wilke.

"The Penis as Art" is an illustrated article on a show called "True Phallacy: The Myth of Male Power," mounted by Clark and Company, a Washington, D.C., gallery, and curated by Alison Maddex "to celebrate the beauty and power of the penis" in December 1993. Show and article feature phallic art by various artists, including Marilyn Minter, Rick Castro, and Joe Kaminski. Jeanne Siegel chronicles the depiction of male figures from the 1970s, when male artists "manipulated their own body parts," to the present, when the bodies seem more objectified, in "Unveiling the Male Body." Siegel begins with Bruce Nauman's wax figures, Robert Mapplethorpe's photographs of penises, Ariane Lopez-Huici's studies of masturbating men, then discusses the urinals and other constructions (*Male and Female Genital Wallpaper*, 1989) of Robert Gober, the nude studies of Matthew Weinstein, and the video footage of gymnasts by Matthew Barney.

The three volumes (plus two later supplements by other hands) of *Die Weiberherrschaft in der Geschichte der Menschheit*, a study of women in all their aspects (shameless, dominant, sadistic, masochistic, and so on) throughout history by Eduard Fuchs and Alfred Kind, contain extraordinary illustrations (more than 1,000 plates drawn from sculpture, paintings, and photography) of females from Athenian fishwives to leather-clad, twentieth-century dominatrices, as depicted in literature and art, with extended discussion of artists and techniques. Another massive work on the "perversity" of women is *Allmacht Weib; erotische Typologie der Frau*, six volumes authored or edited by various hands, each with 200 or more illustrations and photos depicting women as slaves, dominants, prostitutes, in corpulent, lustful, and evil forms, down through time, in all countries including America. Indexes and artist-registers guide the reader to themes and paintings. As just one more example of this curious genre, though we could easily add others, is a volume edited by Agnes, Countess Esterházy, who also edited the sixth volume of *Allmacht Weib*. Esterházy's *Die Perverse Frau* gathers modestly scholarly articles on female masturbation, promiscuity, bestiality, lesbianism, transvestism, prostitution, incest, exhibitionism, and so on into a universe of deviations that has been illustrated by tipping in plates by artists known and unknown.

The standard text on flagellation as an image in erotic literature and art is Ernst Schertel's *Der Flagellantismus in Literatur und Bildnerei* (1929–1932), revised and expanded into a twelve-volume edition in 1957. The most cursory glance at the more than 1,000 reproductions of sculpture, paintings, photographs, and drawings will detect the symbolic, iconographic, and dramaturgical elements of flagellation as an artistic theme. The work is invaluable as a source of information on pornography. It is massive, comprehensive, and rich in analysis by various authorities. The Klinger auction catalog, *Flagellanten: Darstellungen aus Drei Jahrhunderten*, provides some commentary on individual drawings, principally original illustrations from classic erotic fiction. The three volumes of Ernest Haverly's *Selected Studies of Sadism in Art* analyze images and themes of sadism and the iconography of cruelty in paintings, drawings, and photographs of various periods. A very idiosyncratic assortment of illustrations with some comment on flagellation as a theme in art and literature appears in Horace Bellows' *Art Album of Flagellation: Photos and Drawings from the Collection of Horace Bellow*. The two volumes are especially valuable because many of the pictures first appeared as illustrations for the wide body of fictional narratives, cartoons, and clandestine magazines around the turn of the century. In *Das skatologische Element in der Literatur, Kunst, und Volksleben*, Paul Englisch covers scatological images in art, though mostly in European examples. "Perversions" as motifs in literature and painting are the subject of *Das Sexual Problem in der Modernen Literatur und Kunst*, by Herbert Lewandowski, who includes homosexuality as a category along with flagellation, sadomasochism, and other forms of behavior that have given rise to artistic images. Homosexuality, of course, while no longer classed as "perverse," has informed art from its inception. While most of the general histories cited earlier usually touch upon gay or lesbian themes or motifs, critical attention has recently begun to factor homosexual genres out of the larger corpus of erotic art.

One final observation about this chapter. Because it attempts to limit the critical works to those that pay at least some attention to American artists, it ignores vast numbers of texts on every conceivable fetish addressed by artists of every nationality in virtually every medium. Those interested in ranging outside the United States should consult **Erotic Art** in Chapter 4, especially Burt and Scheiner.

GAY AND LESBIAN ART

One hesitates to perpetuate categories by separating gay and lesbian varieties from mainstream erotica; the classifications are those of historians and critics. Edward Lucie-Smith points out in *Race, Sex, and Gender: Issues in Contemporary Art* that homosexuality is generally recognized as a powerful force in

European art at least since the time of Leonardo and Michelangelo: "one persistent influence was the practice of working from the model. Artists were trained by drawing the nude and, until comparatively recent times, the male model was more often used than the female one." To show the difference between past and present practice, Lucie-Smith contrasts the academic drawings of male nudes in the past with those by the gay California artist Don Bachardy, whose intent is openly homoerotic (104). Ostensibly a coffee-table book, Cecile Beurdeley's *L'amour bleu* is a fine explication of homosexuality as expressed in attitudes and images in art and literature since antiquity, with some reference to American examples of varying explicitness. Selections from literary texts range from Plato to Tennessee Williams, with art from private collections around the world. Another once-notorious volume, Raymond de Becker's *L'Erotisme d'en Face*, still holds up well, though its treatment of homosexuality in the visual arts is dated now. Felix Lance Falkon's *A Historic Collection of Gay Art*, though short on analysis, is long on illustrations of homosexual painting, sculpture, and photos.

In *The Sexual Perspective: Homosexuality and Art in the Last 100 Years in the West*, Emmanuel Cooper also avers that homosexuality has enriched Western art. Cooper's excellent survey does not shy from the pornographic, and he includes photos by Robert Mapplethorpe and Duane Michaels to help make his points; the book concludes with the essay "Lesbians Who Make Art." The expanded and better-illustrated second edition gives even more attention to lesbian works and includes reflections on artistic responses to AIDS. John S. Barrington has reproduced drawings, paintings, and photographs from various homosexual magazines to chronicle gay visual expression during the late 1960s and early 1970s in *Contemporary Homo-Erotic Art*. Peter Horne and Reina Lewis assess the state of visual representation of gays and lesbians in the present in *Outlooks: Lesbian and Gay Sexualities and Visual Cultures*, which contains extensive commentary on artists such as Teresa Boffin and Sadie Lee. Cherry Smyth surveys contemporary artists in many countries who work in sculpture, mixed media, furniture, and other materials in *Damn Fine Art by New Lesbian Artists*. *Part Fantasy: The Sexual Imagination of Seven Lesbian Artists Explored through the Medium of Drawing*, the catalog of a New York show held 12 June–11 July 1992, features works by Ellen Cantor, Elise Dodeles, Nicole Eisenman, Daphne Fitzpatrick, Eliza Jackson, G. B. Jones, and Nicola Tyson. Interestingly, Jones' drawings reveal the influence of Tom of Finland. James C. Parkes' *A Queer Conceit: Towards an Aesthetic of Gay Art* reaches back to 1500 for sensibilities he thinks still animate the work of artists of the present. Whitney Davis has collected pieces by various critics for *Gay and Lesbian Studies in Art History*; they do not so much address gay art as a gay perspective on art. More whimsical are those in *Out in Culture: Gay, Lesbian, and Queer Essays on Popular Culture*, edited by Corey K. Creekmur and Alexander Doty; they span imaginative dildos and the drawings of Tom of Finland.

Sanford Schwartz reports on the Pennsylvania artist Charles Demuth's pornographic drawings, chiefly of males, that appeared on the market in the mid-1970s in "Auctions: Glimpsing the Hidden Demuth." "Charlie Was like That," by Kermit Champa, compares Demuth to Marcel Duchamp and Francis Picabia, all of whom aimed at a "pure" decadence. A decade later, the Whitney held a Demuth (1883–1935) retrospective, including the notorious watercolors of urinating sailors. Barbara Haskell's *Charles Demuth* is the catalog of the 1987 show; her critical biography/appreciation notes that Demuth separated his homoerotic drawings from his posters, portraits, cityscapes, and still lifes. Impressed by the explicit paintings, Arthur Danto in "Charles Demuth" speaks of the artist's eroticism, homosexuality, and the artistic undercurrents he set in motion. Arguing against that position is Jonathan Weinberg, who thinks Demuth differed from homosexual contemporaries like Marsden Hartley (1877–1943) precisely because the former wove gay themes into all his paintings, not just his "Turkish Bath" paintings (1916 and 1918) but even into his illustrations for books by Zola, Balzac, and Henry James. The last chapter of Weinberg's *Speaking for Vice: Homosexuality in the Art of Charles Demuth, Marsden Hartley, and the First American Avant-Garde*, entitled "Coming Home: Homosexuality and the American Avant-Garde" (195–219), looks at the role of homosexuality in innovative art in the early part of the twentieth century. Bruce Robertson's biography, *Marsden Hartley*, explores the artist's intentions, his homosexuality, and his forays into eroticism. In " 'Boy Crazy': Carl Van Vechten's Queer Collection," Jonathan Weinberg examines the twenty "scrapbooks"—collages or "homemade sex books" composed of pastiches of explicitly homosexual photos, stories, captions, and comic strips—that Van Vechten left to Yale University; the scrapbooks apparently inspired the artist.

Many Americans have illustrated gay themes. One of the most talented was George Quaintance (1915–1957), whose idealized, but strongly homoerotic, drawings and paintings appeared on magazine covers and were sometimes sold as single prints. The best of these have been reproduced in George Quaintance's *The Art of George Quaintance*, a catalog edited by Volker Janssen. Beyond question the most influential creator of gay pornographic illustration was Tom of Finland, the pseudonym of Touko Laaksonen (1920–1991). Finland began his career in Helsinki, but his reputation grew after he began illustrating magazines published in the United States in the 1950s, especially covers and inside art for *Physique Pictorial*. Instantly recognizable, his hulking butch figures are square-jawed, idealized types with enormous penises; these they wield in scenes of oral and anal group sex, with excursions into urolagnia and rape. An early edition of his work, *The Best of Tom of Finland*, published by AMG, has been superseded by several others. Many of the images in the two-volume *Tom of Finland Retrospective*, arranged chronologically in order to mark his evolving style, are reproduced as *Tom of Finland: The Art of Pleasure*, which highlights his "Queen" and "Rough Trade" periods of the 1940s and his "Fetish" period of the 1980s. The Tom of Finland Company has produced a videotape biography, *Daddy and the Muscle Academy: The Art, Life and Times of Tom of Fin-*

land, which traces through interviews the artist's influence on other artists and on gays in general. More carefully documented is F. Valentine Hooven's *Tom of Finland: His Life and Times*, a full-scale biography and assessment of the artist's influence on the gay community in the United States and abroad. Barney Michalchuk's *Queer Space: The Tom of Finland Museum and Archive* speculates on the possibilities of using twenty-four of Finland's images as a spatial form for constructing an architectural "queerness." Finland's pornographic images have come full capitalist circle in the Tom of Finland store on Eighth Avenue and 19th Street in Manhattan, where the stylish can purchase T-shirts and jeans emblazoned with his images. Bloomingdale's also sells them.

As Cooper, Lucie-Smith, and other critics have observed, Paul Cadmus' candid, voluptuous lines can be traced to Tom of Finland's style. Lincoln Kirstein's *Paul Cadmus* covers these and other influences on Cadmus. David Hockney also used Tom of Finland images from *Physique Pictorial* as models for early paintings of deliberately gay sexual interest, and the works of Gallucci and Warhol sometimes reveal Finland's pictorial influence. *Pop Out: Queer Warhol*, edited by Jennifer Doyle, Jonathan Flatley, and José Esteban Muñoz, contains essays by the editors and by Simon Watney, David James, Thomas Waugh, Michael Moon, Eve Sedgwick, Brian Selsky, Marcie Frank, Mandy Merck, and Sasha Torres on the queer erotic aspects of Warhol's pop art. Warhol's most explicit nudes, chiefly of males, are reproduced as *Andy Warhol Nudes*, with an essay by Linda Nochlin. (For extended discussion of Warhol, see **Avant-Garde Films: High Porn** in Chapter 13.) The most interesting essays in *Keith Haring*, edited by Germano Celant, are on the artist's graffiti and homoerotic images. Patrick Angus' scenes of gay lowlife in bars and male strip joints, such as the 1987 painting of a dancer waggling his penis in front of a spectator, are the subject of Douglas B. Turnbaugh's *Street Show: Paintings by Patrick Angus (1953–1992)*. The two memoirs by David Wojnarowicz, *Close to the Knives: A Memoir of Disintegration*, and *Memories That Smell like Gasoline*, constitute an extraordinary account of the man's career as homosexual and artist.

Heresies devoted a special issue to "Lesbian Art and Artists." One of the great resources on feminist executions of erotica, it directly engages lesbian art and artists and is mandatory reading for scholars. Lesbians face a special challenge, often enunciated by artists working in various media, but never better expressed than by Joyce Fernandes. In her "Sex into Sexuality," she explains the "invisibility" of lesbian women in art in political terms: "it is nearly impossible to represent lesbianism in a way that cannot be co-opted by the dominant (and inimical) heterosexual culture" (36). In one sense, pornography has always been one of the chief offenders in this regard, since heterosexual pornographic genres instantly seize on female same-sex relationships for erotic purposes; in another sense, however, pornography helps to create a lesbian identity. In any case, gay and lesbian artists have become more aggressive in using art to redefine erotic boundaries, as Robert Atkins' "Scene and Heard" column of 8 March 1994 indicates. Atkins reviews a show presented by the National Museum and Archives of Lesbian and Gay History at the Lesbian and Gay Community Service Center in the West Village (New York City): the art collective Fierce Pussy mounted the women's art installation, while Big Dicks Make Me Sweat Productions handled the men's exhibit in the rest rooms. Some vandalism was reported.

REFERENCES

Adams, Carol J. *The Sexual Politics of Meat: A Feminist-Vegetarian Critical Theory.* New York: Continuum, 1990.

Adler, Kathleen, and Marcia Pointon, eds. *The Body Imaged: The Human Form in Visual Culture since the Renaissance.* Cambridge: Cambridge University Press, 1993.

Agrest, Diana I. "Body, Logic, and Sex." *Architecture from Without: Theoretical Framings for a Critical Practice.* Cambridge: MIT Press, 1991.

Agrest, Diana I., Patricia Conway, and Leslie Kanes Weisman, eds. *The Sex of Architecture.* New York: Abrams, 1996.

Allardice, Pamela. *Aphrodisiacs and Love Magic: The Mystic Lure of Love Charms.* Garden City, NY: Avery Press, 1989.

Allende, Isabel. *Aphrodite: A Memoir of the Senses.* New York: Harper/Flamingo, 1998.

Allmacht Weib: erotische Typologie der Frau. Vienna and Leipzig: Verlag für Kulturforschung, 1928–1930. I: O. F. Scheuer and F. L. Wangen, *Das üppige Weib: Sexualleben und erotische Wirkung, künstlerische und karikaturistische Darstellung der dicken Frau vom Beginn bis heute* (1928); II: J. R. Birlinger, *Das grausame Weib: Sexualpsychologische und pathologische Dokumente von der Grausamkeit and Dämonie der Frau* (1929); III: Joachim Welzl, *Das Weib also Sklavin: Die Frau in gewollter und erzwungener Hörigkeit* (1929); IV: Erik Hoyer, *Das lüsterne Weib: Sexualpsychologie der begehrenden, unbefriedigten und schamlosen Frau* (1929); V: Rudolf Brettschneider, *Das feile Weib: Triebleben und Umwelt der Dirne* (1929); VI: Gräfin Agnes Esterházy, ed., *Das lasterhafte Weib: Bekenntnisse und Bilddokumente zu den Steigerungen und Aberrationen im weiblichen Triebleben* (1930).

Alloway, Lawrence. "Women's Art in the Seventies." *Art in America,* 64:3 (May/June 1976): 64–72.

Amos, Emma. "Changing the Subject." *"Bad Girls"/"Good Girls": Women, Sex, and Power in the Nineties,* ed. Nan Bauer Maglin and Donna Perry. New Brunswick, NJ: Rutgers University Press, 1998.

Appel, Frederic C. "Just Slip This into Her Drink . . ." *Sex American Style,* ed. Frank Robinson and Nat Lehrman. Chicago: Playboy Press, 1971, pp. 166–180.

Ars Erotica: Die erotische Buchillustration im Frankreich des 18. Jahrhunderts, with bibliographical entries by Ludwig von Brunn and an essay by Golo Jacobsen. 3 vols. Frankfurt: Schwerte, 1983–1989.

Art in America. New York, 1913–.

Art Press. "Koons." Issue no. 151 (1990).

Ashton, Dore. *Richard Lindner.* New York: Abrams, [1968].

Atkins, Robert. "Scene and Heard." *Village Voice,* 8 March 1994, p. 34.

Austin, Reid S. "The Petty Girl." *Playboy,* (February 1995): 79–85, 147.

———. *Petty: The Classic Pin-up Art of George Petty.* New York: Grammercy, 1997.

Avgikos, Jan. "Cindy Sherman: Burning Down the House." *Artforum*, 31:5 (January 1993): 74–79.

———. "Riproaring Rhopography." New York: Simon Watney Gallery, 1990.

Aymar, Brandt. *The Young Male Figure in Paintings, Sculptures, and Drawings, from Ancient Egypt to the Present*. New York: Crown, 1970.

Bacon, Jack. *Eros in Art*. Los Angeles: Elysium, 1969.

Baker, John. "*Erotic Spectacle in the Art of John Sloan: A Study of the Iconography. Sources and Influences of a Subject Matter Pattern*." M.A. thesis, University of Indiana; copy in the Kinsey Institute, Bloomington.

Banner, Lois W. *American Beauty*. Chicago: University of Chicago Press, 1983.

Banta, Martha. *Imaging American Women: Idea and Ideals in Cultural History*. New York: Columbia University Press, 1987.

Barrick, Mac E. "Folk Toys." *Pennsylvania Folklore*, 29:1 (1979): 27–34.

Barrington, John S. *Contemporary Homo-Erotic Art*. London: S & H, 1974.

Bayl, Friedrich. *Der Nackete Mensch in der Kunst*. Cologne: Verlag M. Dumont, 1964.

Bellow, Horace. *Art Album of Flagellation: Photos and Drawings from the Collection of Horace Bellow*. 2 vols. New York: Franco Publishing, 1937.

Benayoun, Robert. *Erotique du Surréalisme*. Paris: Pauvert, 1965.

Benedict, Brad. *The Blue Book*. New York: Indigo Books, 1983.

Bentley, Richard. *Erotic Art*. New York: Gallery Books, 1984.

Betsky, Aaron. *Building Sex: Men, Women, Architecture, and the Construction of Sexuality*. New York: William Morrow, 1995.

———. *Queer Space: Architecture and Same-Sex Desire*. New York: William Morrow, 1997.

Betterton, Rosemary. *Intimate Distance: Women, Artists and the Body*. New York: Routledge, 1996.

Betty Page Portfolio. Oregon City, OR: PortKar Industries, 1992.

Betty Pages Annual. New York: Black Cat Books, 1991.

Beurdeley, Cecile. *L'amour bleu*, trans. Michael Taylor. New York: Rizzoli, 1978.

Bey, Pilaff [Norman Douglas]. *Venus in the Kitchen: Recipes for Seduction*. San Francisco: Halo Books, 1992.

Bilderlexicon der Erotik, Ein bibliographisches und biographisches Nachschlagewerk, eine Kunst-und Literaturgeschichte für die Gebiete der erotischen Belletristik ... von der Antike zur Gegenwart. 6 vols. Vienna and Hamburg: Verlag für Kulturforschung, 1928–31, 1963. Edited by Leo Schidrowitz: I: *Kulturgeschichte*; II: *Literatur und Kunst*; III: *Sexualwissenschaft*; IV: *Ergänzungsband*. Edited by Armand Mergen: V and VI: *Sexualforschung: Stichwort und Bild*.

Blaine, Mahlon. *The Art of Mahlon Blaine*. East Lansing, MI: Peregrine, 1982.

———. *Nova Venus*. New York: Walden Publishers, 1939.

Bode, Carl. "Marble Men and Brazen Ladies." *The Anatomy of American Popular Culture*, ed. Carl Bode. Berkeley: University of California Press, 1959, pp. 92–105.

Boise, Ron, and Alan Watts. "Sculpture: The Kama Sutra Theme." *Evergreen Review*, 9 (June 1965): 64–67.

Bolen, Carl van. *Geschichte der Erotik*. 4th ed. Munich: Verlag Willy Verkauf, 1967.

Boulware, Jack. "Backstage Pass." *Sex American Style: An Illustrated Romp through the Golden Age of Heterosexuality*. Venice, CA: Feral House, 1997, pp. 118–127.

Bourgeron, Jean-Pierre. *Les Masques d'Eros: Les Objects Erotiques de Collection a Systeme*. Paris: Éditions de l'Amateur, 1985.

Bowie, Theodore, Otto J. Brendel, Paul H. Gebhard, Robert Rosenblum, and Leo Steinberg. *Studies in Erotic Art*, ed. Theodore Bowie and Cornelia V. Christenson. New York: Basic Books, 1970.

Boyce, John. *Aphrodisiac*. New York: Crown Publishing, 1976.

Brandner, Gary. *Vitamin E: Key to Sexual Satisfaction*. New York: Bell, 1971.

Braun, Lionel H., and William Adams. *Fanny Hill's Cook Book*. London: Odyssey Press, 1970.

Bronde, Norma, and Mary D. Garrard, eds. *The Power of Feminist Art: The American Movement of the 1970s. History and Impact*. New York: Abrams, 1994.

The Brooklyn Museum. *The Nude in American Painting*. Brooklyn, NY: Brooklyn Museum, 1961.

Brown, Curtis F. *Star-Spangled Kitsch: An Astounding and Tastelessly Illustrated Exploration of the Bawdy, Gaudy, Shoddy Mass-Art Culture in This Grand Land of Ours*. New York: Universe Books, 1975.

Brusendorff, Ove, and Paul Henningsen. *Love's Picture Book: Love, Lust and Pleasure*. London: Polybooks, 1973.

Burland, Cottie, with an essay by Harriet Bridgeman. *Erotic Antiques: Or Love Is an Antic Thing*. Galashiels, Selkirkshire, Scotland: Lyle Publications, 1974.

Burt, Eugene C. *Erotic Art: An Annotated Bibliography with Essays*. Boston: G. K. Hall, 1989.

———. "Humor in Erotic Art." *Libido: The Journal of Sex and Sensibility*, 3:1 (Winter 1990/1991): 12–17.

Busch, Heather, and Burton Silver. *Kokigami: The Intimate Art of the Little Paper Costume*. Berkeley CA: Ten Speed Press, 1990.

Camhi, Leslie. "Lip Service: Ghada Amer." *Village Voice*, 5 May 1998, p. 149.

Carr, Francis. *European Erotic Art*. London: Luxor Press, 1972.

Carrera, R. *Hours of Love*. Lausanne, Switzerland: Scriptar, n.d.

Celant, Germano, ed. *Keith Haring*. New York: Prestel, 1992.

Chabot, André. *Érotique du Cimetière*. Paris: Henri Veyrier, 1989.

Champa, Kermit. "Charlie Was like That." *Artforum*, 12:6 (March 1974): 54–59.

Chave, Anna C. "O'Keeffe and the Male Gaze." *Art in America*, 78:1 (January 1990): 114–125, 177, 179.

Chicago, Judy. *The Dinner Party: A Symbol of Our Heritage*. New York: Doubleday, 1979.

———. *Through the Flower*. New York: Doubleday, 1975.

Chicago, Judy, with Susan Hill. *Embroidering Our Heritage: The Dinner Party Needlework*. Garden City: Anchor/Doubleday, 1980.

Cinotti, Mya. *The Nude in Painting*, trans. M. D. Clement, Milan: Uffici Press, n.d.

Claridge, Elizabeth. "Aspects of the Erotic—1: Warhol, Oldenburg." *London Magazine*, 19 (February–March 1976): 94–101.

———. *The Girls of Mel Ramos*. Chicago: Playboy Press, 1975.

Clark, Donna. *Queer Street Cookbook*. London: Cassell, 1996.

Clark, Kenneth. *The Nude: A Study in Ideal Form*. Princeton: Princeton University Press, 1956.

Cohen, Marilyn. *Reginald Marsh's New York: Paintings, Drawings, Prints and Photographs*. New York: Whitney Museum of American Art/Dover Publications, 1983.

Collins, Max Allan, and Drake Elvgren. *Elvgren: His Life and Art*. Portland, OR: Collectors Press, 1998.

Colomina, Beatriz, ed. *Sexuality and Space*. New York: Princeton Architecture Press, 1992.

Cooper, Emmanuel. *The Sexual Perspective: Homosexuality and Art in the Last 100 Years in the West*. London: Routledge and Kegan Paul, 1986; 2nd ed. 1994.

Corinne, Tee, illustrator. *Sapphistry: The Book of Lesbian Sexuality*, by Pat Califia. Tallahassee, FL: Naiad Press, 1980.

Coward, Rosalind. *Female Desires*. New York: Grove Press, 1985; see also Coward's "Naughty but Nice: Food Pornography." *Ethics: A Feminist Reader*, ed. Elizabeth Frazer, Jennifer Hornsby, and Sabina Lovibond. Cambridge: Blackwell, 1992, pp. 132–138.

Creekmur, Corey K., and Alexander Doty, eds. *Out in Culture: Gay, Lesbian, and Queer Essays on Popular Culture*. Durham, NC: Duke University Press, 1995.

Danto, Arthur. "Charles Demuth." *The Nation*, 246 (23 January 1988): 101–104.

Darling, Benjamin, ed. *Be Still My Beating Heart: Art of Many Ages Illustrating a Resonant Female Gesture*. West Hollywood, CA: Tale Weaver, 1990.

Davenport, John. *Aphrodisiacs and Anti-Aphrodisiacs: Three Essays on the Power of Reproduction*. London: Privately printed, 1869.

Davis, Whitney, ed. *Gay and Lesbian Studies in Art History*. Binghamton, NY: Haworth Press, 1994.

de Becker, Raymond. *L'Erotisme d'en Face*. Paris: Pauvert, 1964; rpt. *The Other Face of Love*, trans. Margaret Crossland and Adam Daventry. New York: Bell, 1969; rpt. London: Neville Spearman, 1976.

de Berardinis, Olivia. *Let Them Eat Cheesecake: The Art of Olivia*, ed. Joel Beren. Malibu, CA: Ozone Productions, 1993.

———. *Second Slice: The Art of Olivia*. Malibu, CA: Ozone Productions, 1997.

de Louville, François. *The Male Nude: A Modern View*, ed. Edward Lucie-Smith. New York: Rizzoli, 1985; Oxford: Phaidon, 1985.

Dery, Mark. *Culture Jamming, Hacking, Slashing and Sniping in the Empire of Signs*. Westfield, NJ: Open Magazine Pamphlet Series, 1993.

Des Barres, Pamela. *I'm with the Band: Confessions of a Groupie*. New York: Beech Tree Books, 1987.

Devereux, Georges. *Baubo, la Vulve Mythique*. Paris: Jean-Cyrille Godefroy, 1983.

Dienst, Rolf-Gunter. "Richard Lindner," trans. Michael Werner. *Art and Artists*, 5:5 (August 1970): 54–57.

Dijkstra, Bram. *Idols of Perversity: Fantasies of Feminine Evil in Fin-de Siècle Culture*. New York: Oxford University Press, 1987.

Dine, Jim. *Prints 1970–1977*. New York: Williams College/Harper and Row, 1977.

Dinnage, Paul. *The Girls from La Vie Parisienne*. New York: Citadel Press, 1961.

"Dirty Furniture." *New Yorker*, 16 October 1995, p. 52.

Dodson, Betty. *Liberating Masturbation: A Meditation on Self-Love*. New York: Dodson, 1976.

Doran, Anne. "The Dialectical Porn Rock." *Grand Street*, 14:1 (Summer 1995): 135–145.

Dorfles, Gillo. *Kitsch: The World of Bad Taste*. New York: Universe Books, 1969.

Doyle, Jennifer, Jonathan Flatley, and José Esteban Muñoz, eds. *Pop Out: Queer Warhol*. Durham, NC: Duke University Press, 1996.

Duby, Georges, and Michelle Perrot. *Power and Beauty: Images of Women in Art*. New York: St. Martin's/I. B. Tauris, 1995.

Duffy, Maureen. *The Erotic World of Faery*. London: Hodder and Stoughton, 1972.

Duncan, Carol. "The Esthetics of Power in Modern Erotic Art." *Heresies*, 1 (1977): 46–50; rpt. *Feminist Art Criticism: An Anthology*, ed. Arlene Raven, Cassandra Langer, and Joanna Frueh. New York: HarperCollins, 1991, pp. 59–69.

———. "Virility and Domination in Early Twentieth Century Vanguard Painting." *Artforum*, 12 (December 1973): 30–39.

Dunlop, Ian. *The Shock of the New*. London: Weidenfeld and Nicolson, 1972.

Duvillars, Pierre. *Pin-up: Femmes Fatales et Ingénues Libertines*. Paris: Editions du XXe Siècle, 1951.

Dwyer, Karen, and Patrika Brown. *The Erotik Baker Cookbook*. New York: New American Library, 1983.

Edelman, Robert G. "Hannah Wilke." *ArtPress*, 191 (May 1994): iv.

Eisenhauer, L. L. "Bob Delford Brown." *Art and Artists*, 8:4 (July 1973): 34–37.

Encyclopedia of Shooters. Miami, FL: Contemporary Bar Publications, 1992.

Englisch, Paul. *Irrgarten der Erotik: Eine Sittengeschichte uber das gesamte Gebiet der Weltpornographie*. Leipzig: Lykeion, 1931.

———. *Das skatologische Element in der Literatur, Kunst, und Volksleben*. Stuttgart: Puttman Verlag, 1928.

"Eros in Polyester." *Newsweek*, 10 October 1966, pp. 102–103.

"Erotic Art." *Penthouse*, 25:7 (March 1994): 109–119.

"Erotic Art." Special issue of *Art and Artists*, 5:5 (August 1970).

Erotische Illustrationen französischer Klassiker. 2 vols. Hamburg: Verlag für Kulturforschung, 1964.

Esterházy, Gräfin Agnes. *Die Perverse Frau*. Leipzig: Hagenberg-Verlag, 1932?

Ewalt, Norma. *Decadent Dinners and Lascivious Lunches*. 2d ed. Frederick, CO: Renaissance House, 1985.

Failing, Patricia. "Howard Kottler: Conceptualist and Purveyor of Psychosexual Allusions." *American Craft*, 47:6 (December 1986/January 1987): 22–29.

Falkon, Felix Lance. *A Historic Collection of Gay Art*. San Diego: Greenleaf, 1972.

Feinstein, Roni. "New Thoughts for Jasper Johns' Sculpture." *Arts Magazine*, 54:8 (April 1980): 139–145.

Feldman, Edmund Burke. *Varieties of Visual Experience*. 4th ed. New York: Abrams, 1992.

Fels, Florent. *L'Art et l'Amour*. Paris: Editions Arc-en-ciel, 1952 or 1953.

Féminimasculin: Le sexe de l'art. Paris: Gallimard/Electa, 1995.

Ferguson, Bruce. "Eric Fischl: chez lui, avec les tableaux." *ArtPress*, 191 (May 1994): 24–30.

Ferguson, Russell, Martha Gever, Trinh T. Minh-ha, and Cornel West, eds. *Out There: Marginalization and Contemporary Cultures*. Cambridge: MIT Press and the New Museum of Contemporary Art, 1990.

Fernandes, Joyce. "Exposing a Phallocentric Discourse: Images of Women in the Art of David Salle." *New Art Examiner*, 14 (November 1986): 32–34.

———. "Sex into Sexuality." *Art and Artists*, 50:2 (Summer 1991): 35–39.

Ferrero, Carlo. *Les Cinq Sens D'Eros*. Paris: Solar, 1988.

Field, Richard S., Elizabeth Armstrong, E. L. Doctorow, et al. *Scenes and Sequences: Recent Monotypes by Eric Fischl*. Hanover, NH: Hood Museum of Art, Dartmouth College/Harry N. Abrams, 1990.

Fischl, Eric. *Eric Fischel*, Introduction by Peter Schjeldahl, ed. David Whitney. New York: Stewart, Tabori, and Chang, 1988.

———. *Scenes before the Eye*. Long Beach: California State University (Long Beach) Art Museum, 1986.

Flagellanten: Darstellungen aus Drei Jahrhunderten. Nuremburg: Klinger, n.d. [1982?].

Flash Art. Milan, 1992–.

Foley, Suzanne. *Space/Time/Sound: Conceptual Art in the San Francisco Bay Area: The 70s*. San Francisco: San Francisco Museum of Modern Art, 1981.

The Forbidden Library: An Exhibition of Erotic Illustrations from the 18th Century to the Present Day. London: Hobart and Maclean, 1986.

Forman, W., and B. Forman. *Exotic Art*. London: Spring Books, n.d.

Fort, Ilene Susan. *The Figure in American Sculpture: A Question of Modernity*. Los Angeles: Los Angeles County Museum of Art, 1994.

Foxworth, Jo. *The Bordello Cookbook*. Wakefield, RI: Moyer-Bell, 1998.

Franklin, Constance, ed. *Erotic Art by Living Artists*. Vol. I: Renaissance, CA: Directors Guild, 1988; Vol. II: Los Angeles: ArtNetwork, 1994.

Frascari, Marco. *Monsters of Architecture: Anthropomorphism in Architectural Theory*. Savage, MD: Rowman and Litchfield, 1991.

Frazier, Greg, and Beverly Frazier. *Aphrodisiac Cookery Ancient and Modern*. San Francisco: Troubador Press, 1970.

Frueh, Joanna. *Erotic Faculties*. Berkeley: University of California Press, 1996.

———. *Hannah Wilke: A Retrospective*, ed. Thomas H. Kochheiser. Columbia, MO: University of Missouri Press, 1989.

Fuchs, Eduard. *Das Erotische Element in der Karikatur*. Munich: Albert Langen, 1904; rev. and enl. *Geschichte der Erotischen Kunst. Erw. und Neubearb. des Werkes, das Erotische Element in der Karikatur, mit Einschluss der Ernsten Kunst*. Munich: Albert Langen, [1912]; rev. and enl. *Geschichte der Erotischen Kunst*. 3 vols. Munich: Albert Langen, 1912–1926; rpt. New York: AMS Press, 1972.

———. *Die grossen Meister der Erotik*. Munich: Albert Langen, 1930.

———. *Illustrierte Sittengeschichte vom Mittelalter bis zur Gegenwart*. 6 vols. (3 vols. each with a supplementary volume of plates, the latter later reprinted separately). Munich: Albert Langen, 1909–1928. I: *Die Renaissance* (1909) and *Ergänzungsband* (1909 and 1928); II: *Die galant Zeit* (1910) and *Ergänzungsband* (1911 and 1928); III: *Das bürgerliche Zeitalter* (1912) and *Ergänzungsband* (1912 and 1928).

Fuchs, Eduard and Alfred Kind. *Die Weiberherrschaft in der Geschichte der Menscheit*. 3 vols. Munich: Albert Langen, 1913–1914; first supplement: *Die Weibherrschaft. Ergänzungsband I*. Vienna-Leipzig: Verlag für Kulturforschung, 1930; second supplement, sometimes called vol. 4, by J. R. Birlinger: *Die Weibherrschaft von Heute. Ergänzungsband II*. Vienna-Leipzig: Verlag für Kulturforschung, 1931.

Gabor, Mark. *The Illustrated History of Girlie Magazines*. New York: Harmony, 1984.

———. *The Pin-Up: A Modest History*. New York: Universe Books, 1972.

Gammon, Lorraine, and Margaret Marshment, eds. *The Female Gaze: Women as Viewers of Popular Culture*. Seattle, WA: Real Comet Press, 1989.

Gardner, James. *Culture or Trash? A Provocative View of Contemporary Painting, Sculpture, and Other Costly Commodities*. New York: Carol Publishing Group/Birch Lane, 1995.

Gardner, Paul. *Louise Bourgeois*. New York: Universe Books, 1994.

Gardner, Tom. "Tom Wesselman: 'I Like to Think That My Work Is about All Kinds of Pleasure.' " *Art News*, 81 (January 1982): 67–72.

George, Diana Hume, and Malcolm A. Nelson. "Man's Infinite Concern: Graveyards as Fetishes." *Objects of Special Devotion: Fetishes and Fetishism in Popular Culture*. Bowling Green, OH: Bowling Green State University Press, 1982, pp. 136–150.

Gerdts, William H. *The Great American Nude: A History in Art*. New York: Praeger, 1974.

Gerhard, Poul. *The Pillow Book, or a History of Naughty Pictures*. London: Words and Pictures, 1972.

———. *Pornography in Fine Art from Ancient Times to the Present*. Los Angeles: Elysium, 1969.

———. *Pornography or Art*. London: Words and Pictures, 1971.

Gill, Michael. *Image of the Body*. New York: Doubleday, 1989.

Gilmore, Donald H. *Sex and Censorship in the Visual Arts*. San Diego: Greenleaf Classics, 1970.

Golden, Eunice. "The Male Nude in Women's Art: Dialectics of a Feminist Iconography." *Heresies* (issue 12: Sex Issue, 1981): 40–42.

Gopnik, Adam. "Lust for Life." *New Yorker*, 18 May 1992, pp. 76–78.

Gorsen, Peter. *Sexualästhetik: Grenzformen der Sinnlichkeit im 20. Jahrhundert*. Hamburg: Rowohlt, 1987.

Göttner-Abendroth, Heide. *The Dancing Goddess: Principles of a Matriarchal Aesthetic*, trans. Maureen T. Krause. Boston: Beacon Press, 1991.

Grand-Carteret, John. *Die Erotik in der französischen Karikatur*. Vienna: C. W. Stern, 1909.

———. *Le décolleté et le retroussé, trois siècles de gauloiseries 1600–1900*. Paris: Bernard, 1905.

Greenberg, Dan. *Porno-graphics: The Shame of Our Art Museums*. New York: Random House, 1969.

Griffin, Gary M. *Aphrodisiacs for Men: Effective Virilizing Foods and Herbs*. Los Angeles: Added Dimensions, 1991.

Griffon, Jules. *Pictorial History of Erotography*. City of Industry, CA: Collectors Publications, 1969.

Grimley, Gordon, comp. *Erotic Illustrations*. New York: Bell, 1974.

Gross, Larry, ed. *On the Margins of Art Worlds*. Boulder, CO: Westview Press, 1997.

Gubar, Susan. "Representing Pornography: Feminism, Criticism, and Depictions of Female Violation." *Critical Inquiry*, 13:4 (1987): 712–741.

Gudis, Catherine, ed. *Helter Skelter: L.A. Art in the 1990s*. Los Angeles: Los Angeles Museum of Contemporary Art, 1992.

Hacker, Richard Carleton. "Sex and the Cigar Box." *Playboy*, 41:7 (July 1994): 85–87.

Hagen, Charles. "Adventures in Anatomy." *New York Times*, 24 April 1992, p. B9.

Harenberg, Bodo. *Ars Erotica*. 3 vols. Madrid: Hahnes Jahn, 1995.

Harrison, Harry. *Great Balls of Fire! A History of Sex in Science Fiction*. London: Pierrot, 1977; aka *Great Balls of Fire: An Illustrated History of Sex in Science Fiction*. New York: Grosset and Dunlap, 1977.

Harrison, Helen A. *Larry Rivers*. New York: Harper and Row, 1984.

Haskell, Barbara. *Charles Demuth*. New York: Whitney Museum of Art, 1987.

Hatt, Michael. " 'Making a Man of Him': Masculinity and the Black Body in Mid-

Nineteenth-Century American Sculpture." *Oxford Art Journal*, 15:1 (1992): 21–35.

Haverly, Ernest. *Selected Studies of Sadism in Art*. 3 vols. New York: Dodson, 1937–1938.

Hayn, Hugo, Alfred N. Gotendorf, and Paul Englisch. *Bibliotheca Germanorum Erotica and Curiosa. Verzeichnis der gesamten deutschen erotischen Literatur mit Einschluss der Übersetzungen, nebst Beifügung Originale*. 3d ed. 9 vols. 1912–1914; Vol. IX, 1929; rpt. Hanau/München: Verlag Müller and Kiepeneuer, 1968.

Haynes, Roberta, and Rick Hauser. *Secret World of Erotic Art*. Vestron Video, 1985.

Heartney, Eleanor. "David Salle: Impersonal Effects." *Art in America*, 76:6 (June 1988): 120–129, 142.

Hellman, Nina, and Norman Brouwer. *A Mariner's Fancy: The Whaleman's Art of Scrimshaw*. St. Louis, MO: University of Washington Press, 1992.

Hendrickson, Robert. *Foods for Love*. New York: Stein and Day, 1980. Originally published as *Lewd Food: The Complete Guide to Aphrodisiac Edibles* (1974).

Henry, Gerrit. "William Copley." *Art News*, 80 (November 1981): 189.

Hess, Thomas B., and Elizabeth C. Baker, eds. *Art and Sexual Politics: Women's Liberation, Women Artists, and Art History*. New York: Macmillan, 1973.

Hess, Thomas B., and Linda Nochlin, eds. *Woman as Sex Object: Studies in Erotic Art, 1730–1970*. New York: Newsweek, 1972 (rep. vol. 38 of *Art News Annual*); London: Allen Lowe, 1973.

Hill, Charlotte, and William Wallace. *Erotica: An Illustrated Anthology of Sexual Art and Literature*. 3 vols. New York: Carroll and Graf, 1992, 1993, 1995.

Hixson, Kathryn. "Art in Heat." *New Art Examiner*, 14 (November 1986): 52–53.

Hobhouse, Janet. *The Bride Stripped Bare: The Artist and the Female Nude in the Twentieth Century*. New York: Weidenfeld and Nicolson, 1988.

Holder, Maryse. "Another Cuntree: At Last, a Mainstream Female Art Movement." *Off Our Backs*, 3:10 (September 1973): 11–17; rpt. *Feminist Art Criticism: An Anthology*, ed. Arlene Raven, Cassandra Langer, and Joanna Frueh. New York: HarperCollins, 1991, pp. 1–20.

"The Honorable Cicciolina." *Real Sex: 4*. Produced and directed by Patti Kaplan. New York: Home Box Office, 1992.

Hooven, F. Valentine, III. *Tom of Finland: His Life and Times*. New York: St. Martin's, 1995.

Hopkins, Martha, and Randall Lockridge. *Intercourses: An Aphrodisiac Cookbook*. Memphis, TN: Terrace Publishers, 1997.

Horne, Peter, and Reina Lewis. *Outlooks: Lesbian and Gay Sexualities and Visual Cultures*. New York: Routledge, 1996.

Howard, Seymour. "Fig Leaf, Pudica, Nudity, and Other Revealing Concealments." *American Imago*, 43:4 (Winter 1986): 289–293.

Hubbard, Sue. "A Womb with a View." *New Statesman & Society*, 6:248 (16 April 1993): 32–33.

Hughes-Hallett, Lucy. *Cleopatra: Histories, Dreams and Distortions*. London: Bloomsbury, 1990.

Hunter, Sam. *Larry Rivers*. New York: Harry M. Abrams, 1967; updated and exp. ed. New York: Rizzoli, 1989.

Hunter, Sam, and Don Hawthorne. *George Segal*. New York: Rizzoli, 1989.

Hurwood, Bernhardt J. *The Golden Age of Erotica*. Los Angeles: Sherbourne, 1965; rpt. *Erotica*. New York: Paperback Library, 1968.

Huston, Anjelica, and Peter Lester. "Mae West 1976." *Interview*, July 1994, pp. 92–93.

Ingram, Gordon Brent, Anne-Marie Bouthillette, and Yolanda Retter, eds. *Queers in Space: Communities, Public Places, Sites of Resistance*. Seattle: Bay Press, 1997.

Jacobsen, Carol. "Redefining Censorship: A Feminist View." *Art Journal*, 50 (Winter 1991): 42–55.

Jones, Amelia, ed. *Sexual Politics: Judy Chicago's Dinner Party in Feminist Art History*. Berkeley: University of California Press/Hammer, 1996.

Jouvancourt, Hughes de. *Eros Eskimo*. Montreal: Fugate, 1969.

Kahmen, Volker. *Erotic Arts Today*, trans. Peter Newmark. Greenwich, CT: New York Graphic Society, 1972; aka *Eroticism in Contemporary Art*. London: Studio Vista, 1972.

Karwath, Cary von. *Die Erotik in der Kunst*. Vienna: C. W. Stern, 1908.

Kauffman, Linda S. *Bad Girls and Sick Boys: Fantasies in Contemporary Art and Culture*. Berkeley: University of California Press, 1998.

Kensington Ladies' Erotica Society. *Ladies' Own Erotica: Tales, Recipes, and Other Mischiefs by Older Women*. Berkeley, CA: Ten Speed Press, 1984.

Kent, Sarah, and Jacqueline Morreau. *Women's Images of Men*. London: Writers and Readers, 1985.

Kimmelman, Michael. "Onward Into the Realm of Porno and Promo." *New York Times*, national ed., 29 November 1991, p. B6.

Kind, Alfred, and Curt Moreck. *Gefilde de Lust*. Vienna/Leipzig: Verlag für Kulturforschung, 1930.

King, Alexander. *Mine Enemy Grows Older*. New York: Simon and Schuster, 1958.

Kinser, Suzanne L. "Prostitutes in the Art of John Sloan." *Prospects*, 9 (1984): 231–254.

Kirstein, Lincoln. *Paul Cadmus*. New York: Imago, 1984.

Kitaj, Ronald B. *R. B. Kitaj: Pictures/Bilder*. London: Marlborough Fine Arts, 1977.

Knoll, Ludwig, and Gerhard Jaekel. *Lexicon der Erotik*. Zurich: Ferenczy Verlag, 1970.

Koons, Jeff. *The Jeff Koons Handbook*. New York: Rizzoli, 1992.

———. *Koons*. Museum Catalog. San Francisco: San Francisco Museum of Modern Art, 1992.

Kowit, Steve, and Arthur Okamura. *Passionate Journey: Poems and Drawings in the Erotic Mood*. Berkeley, CA: City Miner Books, 1984.

Kozloff, Joyce. *Patterns of Desire*. New York: Hudson Hills, 1990.

Kramer, Hilton. "Lindner's Ladies." *Playboy*, 20:3 (March 1973): 96–101.

Kreemer, Mark. "Mike Kelley: A Fucked-Up Mirror of Dominant Image Making." *Art-Press*, 183 (September 1993): E5–E8.

Krims, Les. *Making Chicken Soup*. N.p.: Humpy Press, 1972.

Kroker, Arthur, and David Cook. *The Postmodern Scene: Excremental Culture and Hyper-Aesthetics*. New York: St. Martin's, 1986.

Kronhausen, Phyllis, and Eberhard Kronhausen. *Erotic Bookplates*. New York: Bell, 1970.

Kunzle, David. "The Corset as Erotic Alchemy: From Rococo Galanterie to Montaut's Physiologies." *Woman as Sex Object: Studies in Erotic Art, 1730–1970*, ed. Thomas B. Hess and Linda Nochlin. New York: Newsweek, 1972, pp. 91–165.

Kuryluk, Eva. *Salome and Judas in the Cave of Sex: The Grotesque: Origins, Iconography, Techniques*. Evanston, IL: Northwestern University Press, 1987.

Lacy, Madison S., and Don Morgan, eds. *Leg Art: Sixty Years of Hollywood Cheesecake*. New York: Citadel, 1981; rpt. *Hollywood Cheesecake: Sixty Years of America's Favorite Pinups*. New York: Citadel, 1983.

Landsman, Marcia. *Difference: On Representation and Sexuality*. New York: New Museum of Contemporary Art, 1984.

Layne, Gwendolyn. "Subliminal Seduction in Fantasy Illustration." *Eros in the Mind's Eye: Sexuality and the Fantastic in Art and Film*, ed. Donald Palumbo. Westport, CT: Greenwood, 1986, pp. 95–110.

Legman, Gershon. *The Horn Book: Studies in Erotic Folklore and Bibliography*. New York: University Books, 1964.

"Lesbian Art and Artists." Special Issue of *Heresies*, 3 (1977).

Lesser, Robert. *Pulp Art: Original Cover Paintings for the Great American Pulp Magazines*. New York: Grammercy, 1997.

Lesser, Wendy. *His Other Half: Men Looking at Women through Art*. Cambridge: Harvard University Press, 1991.

Levine, Nancy Bruning, ed. *Hardcore Crafts*. New York: Ballantine, 1976.

Lévi-Strauss, Claude. *The Raw and the Cooked: Introduction to a Science of Mythology: Volume I*, trans. John and Doreen Weightman. Chicago: University of Chicago Press, 1969.

Levy. Mervyn. *The Artist and the Nude: An Anthology of Drawings*. New York: Potter, 1965.

———. *The Moons of Paradise: Reflections on the Breast in Art*. London: Arthur Barker, 1962.

Lewandowski, Herbert. *Das Sexual Problem in der Modernen Literatur und Kunst*. Dresden: Paul Aretz, 1927.

Lewin, Lewis. *Phantastica: Narcotic and Stimulating Drugs*. New York: Dutton, 1931, 1964.

Lichtenstein, Roy. *The Prints of Roy Lichtenstein: A Catalogue Raisonne, 1948–1993*, comp. Mary Lee Corlett, with Introduction by Ruth E. Fine. New York: Hudson Hills Press/National Gallery of Art, 1994.

Lieberman, M. Laurence. *The Sexual Pharmacy: The Complete Guide to Drugs with Sexual Side Effects*. New York: New American Library, 1988.

Lindsay, Norman. *Selected Pen Drawings*. New York: Bonanza Books, 1968.

Lippard, Lucy R. *From the Center: Feminist Essays on Women's Art*. New York: Dutton, 1976.

———. "Louise Bourgeois from the Inside Out." *Artforum*, 13:7 (March 1975): 26–33.

———. *The Pink Glass Swan: Selected Feminist Essays on Art*. New York: New Press, 1995.

Lipton, Eunice. *Alias Olympia: A Woman's Search for Manet's Notorious Model and Her Own Desire*. New York: Scribner's, 1992.

Littlejohn, David. "Who Is Jeff Koons and Why Are People Saying Such Terrible Things about Him?" *ARTnews*, 92:4 (April 1993): 90–94.

Livingstone, Marco. *R. B. Kitaj*. New York: Thames and Hudson, 1992.

Lo Duca, Guiseppe. *Die Erotik im 20. Jahrhundert*. Basel: Kurt Desch, 1967.

———. *Die Erotik in der Kunst: die Welt des Eros*. Munich: Verlag Kurt Desch, 1965; rpt. *Erotique de l'Art*. Paris: Le Jeune Parque, 1966.

Logan, Ian, and Henry Nield. *Classy Chassy*. New York: A and W Visual Library, 1977.

Long, Eleanor. "Aphrodisiacs, Charms, and Philtres." *Western Folklore*, 32:3 (1973): 153–163.

Louÿs, Pierre. *The Adventures of King Pausole*, illustrated by Clara Tice. N.p.: Pierre Louÿs Society, 1926.

———. *Woman and Puppet*, illustrated by Clara Tice. New York: Rarity Press, 1932.

Lubell, Ellen. "Larry Blizard." *Arts*, 51:7 (March 1977): 41.

Lucie-Smith, Edward. *Adam: The Male Figure in Art.* New York: Rizzoli, 1998.

———. *Ars Erotica: An Arousing History of Erotic Art.* New York: Rizzoli, 1997.

———. *The Body: Images of the Nude.* London: Thames and Hudson. 1981.

———. *Sexuality in Western Art.* London: Thames and Hudson, 1991; rev. of *Eroticism in Western Art.* New York: Praeger, 1972.

———. *Race, Sex and Gender: Issues in Contemporary Art.* New York: Abrams, 1994.

Macdongald, Duncan. "Phallic Foods." *International Journal of Sexology*, 5:4 (May 1952): 206–208.

Machover, Karen. *Personality Projection in the Drawing of the Human Figure.* Chicago: Charles C. Thomas, 1949.

MacPherson, Earl. *The Earl from Oklahoma.* Dewey, AZ: MacPherson, 1993.

MacPherson, Earl, and Merylene Schneider. *Memoirs of Earl MacPherson: The King of "Pin-Up Art."* Detroit: Stabur Press, 1991.

Macy, Christopher, ed. *The Arts in a Permissive Society.* London: Pemberton, 1971.

Malcolm, Janet. "Forty-One False Starts." *New Yorker*, 11 July 1994, pp. 50–62, 64–68.

"The Male Nude: The Gaze Returned. Women Painters in the 1970s and Early 1980s." *Heresies*, 6:4 (1989): 46–49.

Martignette, C. G., and L. K. Meisel. *The Great American Pin-Up.* Berlin: Benedikt Taschen, 1995.

Mcdermott, John F., and Kendall B. Taft, eds. *Sex in the Arts: A Symposium.* New York; Harper, 1932.

Melville, Robert. *Erotic Art of the West.* New York: Putnam, 1973; London: Weidenfeld and Nicolson, 1974.

Merchant, K. Rhein. "Come and Get It." *Gallery*, 22:3 (March 1994): 141–142, 144, 154.

Merkin, Richard. *Paris de Nuit.* Providence, RI: Merkin, 1980.

Merzer, Meridee. "Genital Art." *Penthouse*, 7:2 (1975): 44–46.

Michalchuk, Barney R. *"Queer Space: The Tom of Finland Museum and Archive."* M.E.Des. thesis, University of Calgary, 1995.

Miles, Margaret Ruth. *Carnal Knowing: Female Nakedness and Religious Meaning in the Christian West.* Boston: Beacon Press, 1989.

Miller, Richard A. *Magical and Ritual Use of Aphrodisiacs.* Rochester, VT: Inner Traditions, 1985.

Montalvo, Soledad de. *Women, Food and Sex.* 4 vols. Austin, TX: American Atheist Press, 1988.

[Morrocchi, Riccardo, et al]. *Diva Obsexion.* 12 vols. Firenze, Italy: Glittering Images, 1992.

Moufarrege, Nicholas A. "The Erotic Impulse." *Arts*, 57 (November 1982): 5.

Mullarkey, Maureen. "Hers." *New York Times*, 29 August 1985, p. C2.

Munro, B., ed. *Airplane Nose Art: Over 350 Paintings on Aircraft.* New York: Crescent, 1984.

"Nancy Grossman at Exit Art." *New Yorker*, 23 September 1991, p. 10.

Nash, Elizabeth. *Plaisirs d'Amour: An Erotic Guide to the Senses*. San Francisco: Harper-Collins, 1995.

Nead, Lynda. *The Female Nude*. London: Routledge, 1992.

———. "The Female Nude: Pornography, Art, and Sexuality." *Signs*, 15 (Winter 1990): 323–335; rpt. in *Sex Exposed: Sexuality and the Pornography Debate*, ed. Lynne Segal and Mary McIntosh. New Brunswick, NJ: Rutgers University Press, 1993, pp. 280–294.

Needham, Gerald. "Manet, 'Olympia,' and Pornographic Photography." *Woman as a Sex Object: Studies in Erotic Art, 1730–1970*, ed. Thomas B. Hess and Linda Nochlin. New York: Newsweek, 1972, pp. 81–89.

Nemser, Cindy. *Art Talk: Conversations with Twelve Women Artists*. New York: Scribner's, 1975.

———. "Four Artists of Sensuality." *Arts*, 49 (March 1975): 73–79.

Néret, Gilles. *Erotic Art*. Berlin: Benedikt Taschen, 1994.

———. *Erotica Universalis*. Berlin: Benedikt Taschen, 1994.

———. *Twentieth Century Erotic Art*, ed. Angelika Muthesias and Burkhard Riemschneider. Berlin: Benedikt Taschen, 1994.

New Art Examiner. Chicago, 1973–.

Newman, Bruce M. *Fantasy Furniture*. New York: Rizzoli, 1989.

Niemoeller, Alfred F. *Aphrodisiacs and Anti-Aphrodisiacs*. Girard, KS: Haldeman-Julius, 1937.

Nissen, Brian, and Carlos Fuentes. *Voluptuario*. New York: St. Martin's, 1996.

Nochlin, Linda. "Eroticism and Female Imagery in Nineteenth-Century Art." *Woman as Sex Object: Studies in Erotic Art, 1730–1970*, ed. Thomas B. Hess and Linda Nochlin. New York: Newsweek, 1972, pp. 8–15.

———. *Women, Art, and Power, and Other Essays*. New York: Harper and Row, 1989.

"Now, That's a Tomato: A Salute to Those Pinup Artists Who Elevated the Vegetable Crate to an Art Form." *Playboy*, 40:12 (December 1993): 103–107.

Nude, Naked, Stripped. Cambridge: MIT Committee on the Visual Arts/Hayden Gallery, 1986.

"Nudes Now." *Art Voices*, 5:3 (Summer 1966): 35–45.

Null, Gary, and Elayne Kahn. *The Whole Body Health and Sex Book*. New York: Pinnacle, 1976.

Ober, William B. *Boswell's Clap and Other Essays*. Carbondale: Southern Illinois University Press, 1979.

———. *Bottoms Up! A Pathologist's Essays on Medicine and the Humanities*. Carbondale: Southern Illinois University Press, 1987.

O'Doherty, Brian, "Urogenital Plumbing." *Art and Artists*, 1:8 (November 1966): 14–19.

Oldenburg, Claes. *Claes Oldenburg: An Exhibition of Recent Erotic Fantasy Drawings*, with Introduction by Richard Morphet. London: Mayer Gallery, 1975.

"On Eros and Erotic Art: Statements by Erotic Writers, Photographers, Poets, and Artists." *The Erotic Impulse: Honoring the Sensual Self*, ed. David Steinberg. New York: Tarcher/Perigee, 1992, pp. 101–106.

Osterwald, Tilman. *Pop Art*, trans. Iain Galbraith. Cologne: Benedikt Taschen Verlag, 1990.

Owens, Tuppy. *The (Safer) Sex Maniac's Bible: A World Review of Sexuality Listings of Erotic Clubs in All Major Cities, and Fun and Games for Your Delectation.* London: Tuppy Owens, 1990.

Palumbo, Donald. *Eros in the Mind's Eye: Sexuality and the Fantastic in Art and Film.* Westport, CT: Greenwood, 1986.

———, ed. *Erotic Universe: Sexuality and Fantastic Literature.* Westport, CT: Greenwood, 1986.

Parkes, James Cary. *A Queer Conceit: Towards an Aesthetic of Gay Art.* London: Cassell, 1996.

Part Fantasy: The Sexual Imagination of Seven Lesbian Artists Explored through the Medium of Drawing. New York: Trial Balloon, 1992.

Pauly, G. L. *The Weird Sexual Fantasies of G. L. Pauly: Reproductions from Original Watercolor Paintings.* Los Angeles: Diverse Industries, 1978.

Paz, Octavio. "Eroticism and Gastrosophy." *Daedalus*, 117 (Summer 1988): 227–249.

Pearsall, Ronald. *Tell Me, Pretty Maiden: The Victorian and Edwardian Nude.* London: Grange Books, 1981.

"Peep Galleries." *New York Times Magazine*, 6 September 1998, p. 19.

"The Penis as Art." *Penthouse*, 25:8 (April 1994): 43–51.

Phillips, Lisa. "His Equivocal Touch in the Vicinity of History." *David Salle*, ed. Janet Kardon. Philadelphia: Institute of Contemporary Art, University of Pennsylvania, 1986, pp. 22–31.

Phillips, Marianne Ohl. "Zöe Mozert: Pin-Up's Leading Lady." *The Betty Pages Annual.* New York: Black Cat Books, 1991, pp. 151–163.

Pincus-Witten, Robert. "Lynda Benglis: The Frozen Gesture." *Artforum*, 13:3 (November 1974), p. 54.

Plant, Bud. *Bud Plant's Incredible Catalog.* P.O. Box 1689, Grass Valley, CA 95945.

Pointon, Marcia. *Naked Authority: The Body in Western Painting, 1830–1908.* New York: Cambridge University Press, 1991.

Pollis, Carol A. "Sensitive Drawings of Sexual Activity in Human Sexuality Textbooks: An Analysis of Communication and Bias." *Journal of Homosexuality*, 13 (Fall 1986): 59–74.

"Provocative Art of the Pinup." Special issue of *Airbrush Action Magazine*, 13 (October 1997).

Quaintance, George. *The Art of George Quaintance*, ed. Volker Janssen. Berlin: Janssen-Verlag, 1989.

Rabenalt, Arthur Maria. *Mimus Eroticus.* 5 vols. Hamburg: Verlag für Kulturforschung, 1965–1967. I: *Die erotische Schauszenik in der antiken Welt* (1965); II: *Das Venusische Schauspiel im Mittelalter und in der Renaissance* Part I (1965): III: *Das Venusische Schauspiel im Mittelalter und in der Renaissance* Part II (1965); IV: *Beitrage zur Sittengeschichte der erotischen Szenik im Zwanzigsten Jahrhundert* Part I (1965); V: *Beitrage zur Sittengeschichte der erotischen Szenik im Zwanzigsten Jahrhundert* Part II (1967).

Rand, Erica. *Barbie's Queer Accessories.* Durham, NC: Duke University Press, 1995.

Ratcliff, Carter, Rhonda Lieberman, and JoAnna Isaak. "Jeff Koons: Not for Repro." *Artforum*, 30 (February 1992): 82–87.

Raven, Arlene. "Is Bad Good or Bad?" *Village Voice*, 19 April 1994, p. 88.

Raven, Arlene, Cassandra Langer, and Joanna Frueh, eds. *Feminist Art Criticism: An Anthology.* New York: HarperCollins, 1991.

Rawson, Philip. *Primitive Erotic Art.* New York: Putnam, 1973.

Reifer, Susan. "Sensual and Erotic Art Exhibition." *Penthouse*, 27:5 (January 1996): 55–65.

Reznikoff, Sivon C. *Sensuous Spaces: Designing Your Erotic Interiors.* New York: Whitney Library of Design, 1983.

Rice, George W., and David F. Jacobs. "Saltpeter: A Folkloric Adjustment to Acculturation Stress." *Western Folklore*, 32:3 (1973): 164–179.

Ricco, Roger, Frank Maresca, and Julia Weissman. *American Primitive: Discoveries in Folk Sculpture.* New York: Knopf, 1988.

Richards, Abe, and Robert Irvine. *An Illustrated History of Pornography.* Los Angeles: Athena Books, 1968.

Rivers, Larry, with Arnold Weinstein. *What Did I Do? The Unauthorized Autobiography of Larry Rivers.* New York: Aaron Asher Books, 1992.

Robert Fraser Gallery. *Dine.* London: Fraser, 1966.

Robertson, Bruce. *Marsden Hartley.* New York: Abrams/Smithsonian Institution, 1995.

Robinson, David. *Saving Graces: Images of Women in European Cemeteries.* New York: Norton, 1995.

Robinson, Hilary, ed. *Visibly Female: Feminism and Art Today: An Anthology.* New York: Universe Books, 1988.

Robotham, Tom. *Varga.* Ft. Wayne, IN: Arlington Press, 1991.

Rodolphe, Jean. *Mit den Fünf Sinnen: Gesicht, Gefühl, Gehör, Geschmack, Geruch: Ein Erotisches Bilderbuch.* Munich: Karl Schustek, 1968.

Romi. *Mythologie du Sein.* Paris: Pauvert, 1965.

Rose, Barbara. "Filthy Pictures: Some Chapters in the History of Taste." *Artforum*, 3:8 (May 1965): 21–25.

———. "Vaginal Iconography." *New York Magazine*, 7 (11 February 1974): 59.

Rosenblum, Robert, ed. *Mel Ramos: Pop Art Images.* Cologne: Benedikt Taschen, 1997.

Rossana-Conte, Astrid. *Vargas: The Creator of the Pin-Up Girl, 20s–50s.* Berlin: Benedikt Taschen, 1990.

Royo, Luis. "Royo." *Penthouse*, 27:4 (December 1995): 75–85.

Rüedi, Katerina, Sarah Wigglesworth, and Duncan McCorquodale, eds. *Desiring Practices: Architecture, Gender and the Interdisciplinary.* London: Black Dog Publishing, 1996.

Russell, John. "London Pornocrats." *Art in America*, 53:5 (October–November 1965): 125–127.

Sacher-Masoch, Leopold von, with illustrations by Rahnghild. *Venus in Furs*, no translator credited. New York: William Faro [Samuel Roth], [1932].

Salle, David. *David Salle.* Amsterdam: Museum Boymans-Van Beuningen Rotterdam, 26 February–17 April 1983.

———. *David Salle*, essay by Lisa Phillips, ed. Janet Kardon. Philadelphia: Institute of Contemporary Art, University of Pennsylvania, 1986.

———. *David Salle, 1979–1994*, designed and directed by Richard Pandiscio, text by Lisa Libemann, ed. David Whitney. New York: Rizzoli, 1994.

Salman, Naomi. "Why Have There Been No Great Women Pornographers?" *New Feminist Art Criticism*, ed. Katy Deepwell. Manchester: Manchester University Press/St. Martin's, 1995, pp. 119–125.

Sanders, Ellen. "The Case of the Cock-Sure Groupies." *The Realist*, 84 (November 1968): 1, 3.

Sasowsky, Norman. *The Prints of Reginald Marsh: An Essay and Definitive Catalog of*

His Linoleum Cuts, Etchings, Engravings, and Lithographs. New York: Potter/ Crown, 1976.

Saucier, Ted. *Bottoms Up*. New York: Greystone Press, 1954.

Saunders, Gill. *The Nude: A New Perspective*. New York: HarperCollins, 1989.

Savitt, M. "Hannah Wilke: The Pleasure Principle [at the] Ronald Feldman Fine Arts Gallery, New York." *Arts Magazine*, 50:1 (September 1975): 56–57.

Schapiro, Miriam, and Faith Wilding. "Cunts/Quilts/Consciousness." *Heresies*, 6:4 (1989): 6–17.

Schertel, Ernst, ed. *Der Flagellantismus als Literarisches Motiv*. 4 vols. Leipzig: Parthenon-Verlag, 1929–32; rev. and exp. ed. *Der Flagellantismus in Literatur und Bildnerei*. 12 vols. Schniden bei Stuttgart: F. Decker, 1957.

Schjeldahl, Peter. "Shock of the Good." *Village Voice*, 31 December 1996, p. 81.

Schmitt, Eric. "Angry Shoppers Protest Cupidity in Valentine Vice." *New York Times*, national ed., 13 February 1990, B1.

Schoenfield, Eugene. *Dear Dr. Hip*. New York: Grove Press, 1968.

Schwartz, Sanford. "Auctions: Glimpsing the Hidden Demuth." *Art in America*, 64 (September–October 1976): 102–103.

"Seized." Special issue of *Art and Artists*, 1:8 (November 1966).

Selden, Gary. *Aphrodisia: A Guide to Sexual Food, Herbs, and Drugs*. New York: Dutton, 1979.

"Sex Issue." *Heresies*, 12 (1981).

Shortlidge, Constance M. "The Disruptive 'Cunts' of Hannah Wilke." Paper delivered at the Popular Culture/American Culture Conference, Chicago, April 1994.

Sieberling, Dorothy. "The Female View of Erotica." *New York Magazine*, 7 (February 11, 1974): 54–58.

———. "The New Sexual Frankness: Good-Bye to Hearts and Flowers." *New York*, 8 (17 February 1975): 37–39, 42, 44.

Siegel, Jeanne. "Unveiling the Male Body." *ArtPress*, 183 (September 1993): E12–E15.

Simmons, Doug. "Harder They Come." *Village Voice Rock & Roll Quarterly* (17 December 1991): 6–9.

Simpson, Milton. *Folk Erotica*. New York: HarperCollins, 1994.

Sissman, L. E. "Autoerotics: The Pleasure Principle in Car Design." *Audience*, 1:3 (May–June 1971): 14–21.

Sky, Susan, and Louise Wolfe. *The X-Rated Cookbook*. New York: Brown, 1977.

Smilby, Francis. *Stolen Sweets: The Cover Girls of Yesteryear: Their Elegance, Charm, and Sex Appeal*. Chicago: Playboy Press, 1981.

Smith, Bradley. *The American Way of Sex: An Informal Illustrated History*. New York: Gemini Smith, 1978.

———. *Erotic Art of the Masters: The 18th, 19th, and 20th Centuries*. New York: Erotic Arts Society, n.d.; rev. ed. La Jolla, CA: Gemini Smith, 1981.

———. *Twentieth Century Masters of Erotic Art*. La Jolla, CA: Gemini Smith, 1985.

Smith, Howard, and Leslie Harlib. "Ladies Buntiful." *Village Voice*, 7 November 1977, p. 30.

———. "X-Rated Hang-Up." *Village Voice*, 5 December 1977, p. 16.

Smyth, Cherry. *Damn Fine Art by New Lesbian Artists*. London: Cassell, 1996.

Solomon-Godeau, Abigail. *Male Trouble: A Crisis in Representation*. London: Thames and Hudson, 1997.

"Sorayama." *Penthouse*, 26:1 (September 1994): 226–233.

Spain, Daphne. *Gendered Spaces*. Chapel Hill: University of North Carolina Press, 1992.

Spicy: Naughty '30s Pulp Covers. Princeton, WI: Kitchen Sink Press, 1992.

The Spicy of Life: A Sampler of 50 Covers from the "Spicy" Pulps. Framingham, MA: Winds World Press, 1987.

Stark, Raymond. *The Book of Aphrodisiacs*. New York: Stein and Day, 1982.

Stealingworth, Slim [Tom Wesselman]. *Tom Wesselman*. New York: Abbeville, 1980.

Steinberg, David, ed. *Erotic by Nature: A Celebration of Life, of Love, and of Our Wonderful Bodies*. San Juan, CA: Shakti Press, 1988.

Stern, Bernhard. *Illustrierte Geschichte der Erotischen Literatur aller Zeiten und Völker*. Vienna/Leipzig: C. W. Stern, 1908.

Stern, Jane, and Michael Stern. *The Encyclopedia of Bad Taste*. New York: Harper-Perennial, 1991.

Sternberg, Jacques. *Pin Up*. New York: St. Martin's, 1974.

Stevens, Mark. "Sex and Success." *New Republic*, 21 April 1986, pp. 25–27.

Stewart, Philip. "Indecency and Literary Illustration." *South Atlantic Quarterly*, 90:1 (Winter 1991): 111–152.

Stieglitz, Ron, and Sandy Lesberg. *Saucy Ladies*. New York: Peebles Press, 1977.

Stinson, Bryon. "Pin-Ups of the Civil War." *Civil War Times Illustrated*, 8 (August 1969): 38–41.

Suleiman, Susan Rubin, ed. *The Female Body in Western Culture: Contemporary Perspectives*. Cambridge: Harvard University Press, 1986.

Sullivan, Terry. "Pop Tart: Wallpaper with Edge, in a Severely Limited Edition." *Gentleman's Quarterly*, November 1993, p. 33.

Taberner, Peter V. *Aphrodisiacs: The Science and the Myth*. Philadelphia: University of Pennsylvania Press, 1985.

Tabori, Paul. *A Pictorial History of Love*. London: Spring Books, 1966.

Tallman, Susan. "Private and Public." *Art in America*, 83:9 (September 1995): 88–95.

Thomsen, Christian W. *Sensuous Architecture: The Art of Erotic Building*. New York: Prestel, 1998.

Thorpe, David, and Pierre le Poste. *Rude Food*. New York: Ballantine, 1978.

Tickner, Lisa. "The Body Politic: Female Sexuality and Women Artists since 1970." *Art History*, 1:2 (1978): 236–251.

Tilly, Andrew. *Erotic Drawings*. New York: Rizzoli, 1986.

Todd, Ellen W. "Sex for Sale: Reginald Marsh's Voluptuous Shopper." *The "New Woman" Revised: Painting and Gender Politics on Fourteenth Street*. Berkeley: University of California Press, 1993, pp. 178–223.

Tom of Finland [Touko Laaksonen]. *The Best of Tom of Finland*. Los Angeles: AMG Studios, 1970?

———. *Tom of Finland: The Art of Pleasure*. Cologne: Benedikt Taschen Verlag, 1992.

———. *Tom of Finland Retrospective*. 2 vols. Los Angeles: Tom of Finland Co., 1988, 1991.

Tom of Finland Company. *Daddy and the Muscle Academy: The Art, Life and Times of Tom of Finland*. Los Angeles: Tom of Finland Co., 1992.

Truewoman, Honey. "Realism in Drag." *Arts*, 48:5 (February 1974): 44–45.

Tucker, Marcia, ed. *Bad Girls*. Cambridge: MIT Press and New Museum of Contemporary Art, 1994.

Turnbaugh, Douglas B. *Street Show: Paintings by Patrick Angus (1953–1992)*. London: Editions Aubrey Walter, 1992.

Tuten, Frederic. "Art Profile: R. B. Kitaj." *Interview*, July 1994, pp. 36–37.

Ungerer, Tomi. *Fornicon*. New York: Grove Press, 1969.

———. *Totempole: Erotische Zeichnungen. 1968–1975*. Zurich: Diogenes, 1976.

———. *The Underground Sketchbook of Tomi Ungerer*. New York: Viking, 1964.

Valant, Gary M. *Vintage Aircraft Nose Art*. Osceola, WI: Motorbooks International, 1987.

Vallejo, Boris, and Doris Vallejo. *Mirage*. New York: Thunder's Mouth, 1997.

Van Every, Edward. *Sins of America as Exposed by the Police Gazette*. New York: Stokes, 1931.

Vargas, Alberto. *Playboy's Vargas Girls*. Chicago: Playboy Press, 1972.

———. *Vargas: The Esquire Years, A Catalogue Raisonne*. New York: Van der Marck, 1987.

———. *Vargas: 20s–50s*. Berlin: Taschen Verlag, 1990.

Vargas, Alberto, and Reid Austin. *Vargas*. New York: Harmony House, 1978.

Vignettes. 4 vols. Los Angeles: Collectors Press, 1997. I: *Alberto Vargas: The Esquire Years*; II: *Rolf Armstrong: The Dream Girls*; III: *Billy DeVorss: The Classic Pin-Ups*; IV: *Gil Elvgren: The Wartime Pin-Ups*.

Villeneuve, Roland. *Fétichisme et amour*. Paris: Editions Azur-Co, 1968.

———. *Le Diable: Erotologie de Satan*. Paris: Editions Azur-Co, 1963.

———. *La Musée du la Bestialité*. Paris: Editions Azur-Co, 1969.

Waldberg, Patrick. *Eros Modern Style*. Paris: J. J. Pauvert, 1964; rpt. *Eros in La Belle Epoque*. New York: Grove Press, 1969.

Waldman, Diane. *Roy Lichtenstein*. New York: Guggenheim Museum, 1993.

Walters, Margaret. *The Male Nude*. New York: Paddington Press, 1978.

Walton, Alan Hull. *Aphrodisiacs: From Legend to Prescription*. Westport, CT: Associated Booksellers, 1958.

Ward, Peter. *Kitsch in Sync: A Consumer's Guide to Bad Taste*. London: Plexus, 1991.

Warhol, Andy. *Andy Warhol Nudes*, with an essay by Linda Nochlin. Woodstock, NY: Overlook Press, 1995.

Warner, Marina. *Monuments and Maidens: The Allegory of the Female Form*. London: Weidenfeld and Nicholson, 1985.

Weaver, William W. *America Eats: Forms of Edible Folk Art*. New York: Museum of American Folk Art, 1989.

Webb, Peter. *The Erotic Arts*. Boston: New York Graphic Society, 1975; rev. ed. New York: Farrar, Straus, and Giroux, 1983.

Wedeck, Harry E. *Dictionary of Aphrodisiacs*. New York: Philosophical Library, 1956; rpt. as *Love Potions through the Ages*. New York: Philosophical Library, 1963.

Weiermair, Peter, ed. *Erotic Art from the 17th to the 20th Century*. Zurich: Edition Stemmle, 1995.

Weinberg, Jonathan. " 'Boy Crazy': Carl Van Vechten's Queer Collection." *Yale Journal of Criticism*, 7:2 (1994): 25–49.

———. *Speaking for Vice: Homosexuality in the Art of Charles Demuth, Marsden Hartley, and the First American Avant-Garde*. New Haven, CT: Yale University Press, 1993.

Weinstein, Jeff. "The Entrée That Dare Not Speak Its Name." *Village Voice*, 27 June 1995, p. 43.

Weintraub, Linda, Arthur Danto, and Thomas McEvilley. *Art on the Edge and Over:*

Searching for Art's Meaning in Contemporary Society, 1970s–1990s. Litchfield, CT: Art Insights, 1996.

"Wesselman's Fancy Footwork." *Art Voices*, 5:3 (Summer 1966): 47.

Westheimer, Ruth. *The Art of Arousal.* New York: Abbeville, 1993.

Wexler, Irving. "King Pin-Up." *High Society*, 3:7 (December 1978): 52–54, 79–81.

Wexler, Neil. "A Pocket Full of Pin-Ups." *Gallery*, February 1994, pp. 112–114, 116.

Wilson, Robert Anton. *The Book of the Breast.* Chicago: Playboy Press, 1974.

———. *Sex and Drugs: A Journey beyond Limits.* Chicago: Playboy Press, 1973.

Wilson, Simon. "Short History of Western Erotic Art." *Erotic Art of the West*, by Robert Melville. New York: Putnam, 1973; London: Weidenfeld and Nicolson, 1974, pp. 11–31.

Winer, Lucy, and Paula Koenigsberg. *Rate It X.* New York: International Video, 1985.

Wissing, Douglas. "Erotica Whose Purpose Was Scholarly." *New York Times*, 23 November 1997, p. 47.

Wojnarowicz, David. *Close to the Knives: A Memoir of Disintegration.* New York: Vintage Books, 1991.

———. *Memories That Smell like Gasoline.* San Francisco: Artspace Books, 1992.

Wright, Edan. "Modern Sculpture." *Sex in the Arts: A Symposium*, ed. John F. Mcdermott and Kendall B. Taft. New York; Harper, 1932, pp. 253–277.

Wurdemann, Helen. "Stroll on La Cienega." *Art in America*, 53:5 (October–November 1965): 115–118.

Wye, Deborah. *Louise Bourgeois.* New York: Museum of Modern Art, 1982.

Young, Wayland. *Eros Denied.* New York: Grove Press, 1964.

Zack, David. "West Coast: Kama Sutra to the Life." *Art and Artists*, 5:5 (August 1970): 26–27.

Zwang, Gérard. *Le Sexe de la Femme.* Paris: Le Jeune Parque, 1967.

12

Erotic and Pornographic Photography

THE CAMERA AS EROTIC EYE

The history of erotic and pornographic photography begins with the invention of the camera itself, a circumstance that reinforces the thesis that the urge to represent sexuality helps drive the evolution of communication technologies. Early on, photographic representations of sexuality took high *and* low forms. Approve of elegant eroticism though we might, the appeal of the truly lubricious is strong. Executors of estates who have just come to terms with the revelation that the deceased deacon secretly stuffed a locked cabinet with classic erotic texts richly bound with pages still uncut can be shocked anew to discover hidden in the back a packet of dirty photos, provenance unknown, greasy from constant touch.

The more explicit the representation, the more anonymous it was. Photographers leave signatures, of course, and some who shot vintage pornography were known to historians and bibliographers. Thanks to the furor attending his posthumous exhibitions, many Americans know who Robert Mapplethorpe was, and others can recognize an erotic high-fashion lensman such as Helmut Newton or major photographers for *Playboy* or *Penthouse* such as Suze Randall and Richard Fegley. Most freelance journeymen who shoot the thousands of explicit frames for the hundreds of pornographic magazines published each year are familiar only to the agents who sell their slides and prints, and their individual styles are submerged in the flood. The works listed here provide comment mostly on high porn, that is, on photographs that scandalized one generation, then became eroticized for the next by shifts in moral and aesthetic perspectives. If a photograph were seized by American police as obscene, then it and/or its maker qualifies for the list, though no such list can be exhaustive. The Kinsey

Institute's massive photo archive, built from just such contraband, includes photos by Muybridge, Weston, Allen, Bellocq, Genthe, Outerbridge, and so on—artifacts, in short, now revered by museum curators and prized by collectors. The archive also holds close to 100,000 prints by photographers who left no other trace, just flotsam on a shore of limitless desire.

In order to keep the list within manageable limits, I have omitted standard scholarly texts on nude photography, most how-to manuals for taking nude photos, and virtually all of the pictorial guides to happier sex lives but—idiosyncratically—included some volumes simply because they have struck viewers as provocative. Included also are several anthologies on the grounds that images today travel widely and speak for themselves. Given the number of anthologies, however, I have been selective here as well, choosing those that make some effort to comment.

THEORETICAL AND GENERAL HISTORICAL APPROACHES

A short, but incisive, essay by a notable photographer is Grace Lau's "Confessions of a Complete Scopophiliac." Lau, who deliberately explores pornographic subjects to uncover the power of taboo and fetish, wants to create "erotic photography for women." Asked to define erotica and pornography, she replies that the question "always exasperates me because, of course, there are no definitive answers. Personally, I prefer images that conceal, rather than those that reveal all. Most men, however, need to be re-educated to appreciate images that stir the imagination, rather than those which assault the senses. Susan Sontag encapsulates the issue in "The Pornographic Imagination" (1967): " 'The issue is not, whether pornography, but the *quality* of pornography' " (195). Many art critics still think of photography as a usurper technology, hardly in the same league as painting.

Scholars may wish to consult general surveys of erotic arts for comment on photographs. An excellent starting point is Peter Webb's *The Erotic Arts*; appendixes deal with magazines and photographs. (For others, see **Histories of Erotic Art** in Chapter 11.) Perhaps the best single volume to confront the nature of erotic photographs is *Eros and Photography: An Exploration of Sexual Imagery and Photographic Practice*, a beautiful book of examples the editors, Donna-Lee Phillips and Lew Thomas, find erotic. Contributors discuss works by Robert Heinecken, Chris Enos, Joel-Peter Witkin, Arthur Ollman, and others historically important by way of analyzing what makes frames erotic. Two other books are mandatory reading: *Image Ethics: The Moral Rights of Subjects in Photographs, Film, and Television*, a series of essays, some bearing on sexual representation, edited by Larry Gross, John Stuart Katz, and Jay Ruby, and *The Body and the Lens: Photography 1839 to the Present*, a collection of pieces on politics, race, and gender in photographs of the human body, set in historical context and edited by John Pultz.

Variations on the "male gaze" arguments (see **The "Male Gaze": Visuality**

and Pornography in Chapter 6), not all of them doctrinaire, abound among feminist critics. One of the most balanced approaches to the subject is Abigail Solomon-Godeau's "The Legs of the Countess," a splendidly researched, brilliantly argued essay whose contention is that erotic photography reveals "the very reification it enacts" and "potentially subverts the very authority it apes" (306). Noting the fetishistic character of representations of the nude, with their limited repertoire of poses and their frequent concealing of the genitals, Solomon-Godeau observes that "the photographic nude inevitably disrupts these structures of containment and idealization, disrupts, in short, the propriety of the nude. What the painter elided, the photographer showed: not just pubic hair but dirty feet and, perhaps most disturbing, the face of the real woman, often including her direct and charmless gaze. The look of these women is rarely the inviting compliant expression that signals complicity between the desiring subject and the object of desire" (299).

George Eisler's *Naked to Nude*, a modest history of the human figure in the visual arts, tries to distinguish between the two terms; it also grapples with the differences in response evoked by paintings and photographs. Jorge Lewinski's *The Naked and the Nude: A History of the Nude in Photographs 1839 to the Present* may be more successful at establishing the difference, though it will, of course, satisfy nobody. Perhaps the best broad text on the subject of nude photography is *Nude Photographs, 1850–1980*, edited by Constance Sullivan, a volume of brief, but incisive, theoretical remarks. Of these, Ben Maddow and Robert Sobieszek are perhaps the most interesting; the latter argues that while an erotic image subordinates the humanity of the female figure and reifies it into an object of male desire, the process is the same whenever sexual roles are reversed. Just as beautifully illustrated, with a text whose intelligence lifts it above the plane of the coffee table, is William A. Ewing's *The Body: Photographs of the Human Form*, an excellent general history of images of specific body parts, though its chapter on erotica, which is restricted to photos of the 1920s and earlier, is disappointing. For *Nude: Theory*, editor Jain Kelly draws on text and pictures by Michaels, Kertesz, Clergue, Newton, and others; the result is a fine, modern sampling of theoretical perspectives. *The History of the Nude in Photography* by Peter Lacey and *The Nude in Photography* by Arthur Goldsmith are both well illustrated, well-researched histories of the evolution of genres and their major innovators; Americans figure more prominently in the second volume. Rod Ashford has compiled *Erotique: Masterpieces of Erotic Photography* from a very eclectic selection of female nudes, mostly from recent masters, though its text is weak in its sketchiness.

PERIOD HISTORIES OF EROTIC/PORNOGRAPHIC PHOTOGRAPHS

By most reckonings, the nude photo stands halfway between artistic transcendence and social taboo, a domain constantly in flux. Aesthetic considerations, often in conjunction with social and political reflections, form the basis for most critical texts on the nude. As a group, general histories focus on mainstream, "artistic" figure studies, with occasional digressions toward margins. Though vintage nudes may once have been regarded as pornographic, today's sophisticated viewers find most about as titillating as pictures of furniture. Assessment may well turn on whether the model is looking directly at the camera, displays pubic hair, or holds a penis or fingers a nipple. Depending in part on *when* it is shot and in part on the choice of subject, a photograph of explicit degree may seem at first an example of low pornography, then, as it accumulates critical approval, rise to the plateau of high pornography in which aesthetic intent is acknowledged, then reach a level called "erotic" that denotes our inability to see much sexuality at all in it.

In a highly readable essay, Bill Jay characterizes explicitness in early photography as a moral and aesthetic response to painting that had become too polite in "The Erotic Dawn of Photography," one of the best articles ever written on the subject. Partly to distinguish their art from older forms, says Jay, many early photographers of the nude deliberately shot "warts and all" frames that were not "painterly," and these offended audiences whose expectations had been shaped by familiarity with the brush. Nevertheless, Jay notes, some nineteenth-century painters welcomed photography as a visual aid; Renoir, for example, often worked from nude photographs of his models. (To Renoir, incidentally, Jay attributes the remark: "Never trust a man who is not excited by a pretty breast.") Jay's remarks are echoed by Abigail Solomon-Godeau, cited earlier. An essay by Gundolf Freyermuth, "Die Geschichte der erotischen Photographie," also suggests that the new technology of reproduction immediately opened up erotic possibilities simply not available before cameras.

The early decades of the erotic photograph have attracted magisterial scholarship, much of it German, on craftspeople and techniques. Some can be found in the *Bilderlexicon der Erotik*, greatest of all general histories of eroticism, especially the chapters on "Aktphotographie" and "Photographien." Primacy, however, goes to the indispensable, three-volume *Die Erotik in der Photographie*, edited by Erich Wulffen et al. Its content and commentary range from period catalogs and advertisements for hard-core prints and photo series, to nude photos of early MGM movie actresses; it comments on traffic, technologies, cultural reaction, official sanctions, photographers, subjects, and erotic themes. The third volume, essentially a photo album (*Ergänzungsband: Bilderatlas*), is extremely rare; it contains additional suppressed vintage photos, many from private collections, on fetishes and "perversities"; no historian of clandestine photography can fail to acknowledge it.

The most authoritative information on explicit daguerreotypes can be found in Hans Christian Adam's "Die Erotische Daguerreotypie." Rainer Wick's catalog of the Weingarter Museum's 1989 exhibition of the Uwe Scheid Collection of Erotic Daguerreotypes, *Die Erotische Daguerreotypie: Sammlung Uwe Scheid*, features historical comment by Wick and Grant Romer of the George Eastman House. Scheid's is the largest collection of sexually oriented daguerreotypes in the world; plates are replete with novelties such as hand-tinted nipples, labia, and penises. Romer says that erotic examples reproduced here were aesthetically and technically superior to most other forms of daguerreotypy, once more a reminder of the force with which eroticism drives technology. The standard volume on erotic stereographs is Serge Nazarieff's *The Stereoscopic Nude, 1850–1930*, a trilingual edition accompanied by 3-D glasses for viewing the images, most of which are nudes and some of which exhibit masturbation or intercourse, all produced for the stereoscopic viewer; most examples are European rather than American, but the historical commentary and technical citations are scholarly. "Questionable Subjects for Photography," an 1858 editorial in one of the earliest of photo magazines, deplores erotic stereographs, which had proliferated at a rapid rate in less than a decade. Two fascinating articles on erotic daguerreotypes are Elisabeth Lyon's "Unspeakable Images, Unspeakable Bodies," which contrasts nineteenth-century pictures of the Countess de Castiglione with modern images by artists such as Cindy Sherman; and Abigail Solomon-Godeau's "The Legs of the Countess" (cited earlier), also on the erotic stereographic daguerreotype.

The most important modern reference work on the early erotic photograph, the most comprehensive since Wulffen et al., is *Das Aktfoto: Ansichten vom Körper im fotografischen Zeitalter: Ästhetik—Geschichte—Ideologie*, edited by Michael Köhler and Gisela Barche; its wonderful selection of images is matched by learned essays on various aspects of erotic photographs. *Nus d'autrefois, 1850–1900*, by Marcel Bovis and François Saint-Julien, though hard to find, details successive photographic processes before the turn of the century and illustrates them with material from famous collections (Duchesne, Saint-Julian, Bovis, and Sirot). Serge Nazarieff surveys images by Auguste Belloc, Phillipe Derussy, Alexis Gouin, Bruno Braquehais, and anonymous practitioners in *Early Erotic Photography*. Gunther Bartosch's *Der Akt von Damals: Der Erotik in der frühen Photographie aus der privaten Sammlung Ernst und Gunter Bartosch* catalogs images from the 1850s to about 1900, mostly European, from the Ernst and Gunther Bartosch archives. Alfred de Montel's *Journal Intime Illustre d'Alfred de Montel* reproduces explicit nineteenth- and early twentieth-century photos from the French Bourgeron and Gantier archives, with a good Introduction. *Bilderlust: Erotische Photographien aus der Sammlung Uwe Scheid*, edited by Ulrich Domröse, Christian von Faber-Castell, Claudia Gabriele Philipp, Rainer Wick, and Reinhold Misselbeck, critiques a wide selection from the Scheid collection, including American examples of the present, but is most pertinent on pre-1900 plates of couples engaged in intercourse. Michael Köhler's *Ansichten vom Körper: Das Aktphoto 1840–1987* lacks the theoretical buttresses of the Köhler-Barche study but contains a few pages on the specifically pornographic photo; the English edition, *The Body Exposed: 150 Years of the Nude in Photography*, slightly updates the first volume, though again the commentary is slight. For *One Thousand Nudes from the Uwe Scheid Collection*, Michael Koetzle has selected examples ranging from daguerreotypes to modern Polaroids and collages, with excursions into pornography and ethnography.

Uwe Scheid himself has published three volumes, *Das Erotische Imago: der*

Akt in frühen Photographien, Das Erotische Imago II: das Aktphoto von 1900 bis heute, and *Freudinnen: Bilder der Zärtlichkeit: Der Doppelakt in frühen Photographien,* all of which give the provenance of specific photos from the first appearance of photographic plates up to sophisticated film stocks of today. The third volume, on couples in heated embraces, is the most explicit. Thomas P. Lowry's *The Story the Soldiers Wouldn't Tell: Sex in the Civil War* and Michael Musick's "Spirited and Spicy Scenes" examine catalogs of raunchy photographs sold to soldiers on both sides of the Civil War. Graham Ovenden and Peter Mendes draw chiefly on European and British examples such as nudes of children shot by Lewis Carroll in *Victorian Erotic Photography.* Mendes published some of the pictures as an article called "Victorian Erotic Photography." *Nudes of Yesteryear,* a collection of old photos and postcards gathered by Ralph Ginzburg as a subscription premium for his magazines, has no text; some appeared originally in *Eros* 1:3 (Autumn 1962). Carol Mavor's *Pleasures Taken: Performances of Sexuality and Loss in Victorian Photographs* discusses the era's photographs as elements in the schooling of sexual perceptions; Mavor thinks Lewis Carroll's photographs help explain Victorian attitudes toward women and children. The photo collection at the Kinsey Institute furnishes Linda Williams with subjects for "Corporealized Observers: Visual Pornographies and the 'Carnal Density of Vision,' " a survey of nineteenth-century erotic images. Philippe Jullian's *Le Nu 1900,* an academic treatment of nineteenth-century nude photographers, touches on American pioneers. The original eleven volumes of Eadweard Muybridge's photographic studies of men, women, and animals, so important to the development of motion pictures, are now available in a low-cost Dover edition, *Muybridge's Complete Animal and Human Locomotion,* with a helpful Introduction by Anita V. Mozley.

Eduard Fuchs' *Illustrierte Sittengeschichte von Mittelalter biz zur Gegenwart* deals with traffic in illicit photographs before and after the turn of the century and reproduces pages of catalogs from dealers of several decades. *Sittengeschichte des Hafens und der Reise,* edited by Leo Schidrowitz, traces the distribution of photographs by travelers through busy harbors around the world. The great erotica collector Gustav Gugitz contributed an essay on photos to Schidrowitz's *Sittengeschichte des Geheimen und Verboten.* Chapter 16 of Iwan Bloch's *Anthropological Studies in the Strange Sexual Practices of All Races in All Ages* examines the worldwide traffic in pornographic photographs and albums at the end of the nineteenth century. Curt Moreck's *Das Gesicht* is also authoritative on the international circulation of early erotic photographs and stereographs.

Outside of dealer catalogs, the artifacts of "low" pornography evoke a comment whose slipshod vulgarity seems mandatory. Captioning pornographic photos, like writing titles for old stag films, apparently requires deliberate crudity, presumably to establish authenticity by undercutting any pretension the genre might aspire to. Paul Aratow's *One Hundred Years of Erotica* reproduces mostly nude and fetish photos from 1845 to 1945, most of them French but with a sampling of American frames, some of them dated, none of them discussed in any depth. Similar shortcomings afflict "Petronius' " *Tool Box Scandals*, though it is interesting because of its collages of nineteenth- and twentieth-century hard-core prints. No more reliable are the two volumes of *Smut from the Past*, the first edited by Michael Perkins, the second by John Milton, each of whom encloses an excellent collection of vintage photographs in sniggering, anecdotal narrative; neither volume significantly identifies any of the pictures. The only virtue of G. G. Stoctay's two books, *America's Erotic Past: 1868–1940* and *The Illustrated Collector's Price Guide to Erotica*, is that they reproduce some classic hard-core images; the chronologies are eccentric, not to say useless, and the pictures are mostly Cuban or Continental. The texts of Judd Graham's *The Porno 20s* and Reinhart Seufert's *Porno-Photographics* are dopey excuses for displaying explicit images. Somewhat better is Edward J. Nelson's two-volume *Yesterday's Porno: A Pictorial History of Early Stag Photographs*, which has a brief Introduction that makes an attempt at cultural context. Much preferable to any of the foregoing are the photographs from the Vasta, Merkin, and Bélier Press collections included in *Caught Looking: Feminism, Pornography, and Censorship*, an anthology of excellent essays assembled by the Feminist Anti-Censorship Task Force (FACT).

E. J. Bellocq's portraits of naked prostitutes, the prints pulled by Lee Fried-lander from the defaced original glass plates, are reproduced in *Storyville Portraits: Photographs from the New Orleans Red Light District, circa 1912*. Al Rose's *Storyville, New Orleans: Being an Authentic, Illustrated Account of the Notorious Red-Light District* is an excellent companion volume because it details the environment and explains the provenance of many of Bellocq's pictures. *Alo Nudes*, probably the first collection of photos from the California studio of Al-bert Arthur Allen, features female nudes whose flaunted pubic hair, whimsical posing, and gamboling movements—often out of doors—undermined the studio genre. *Highlights and Shadows*, Arnold Genthe's collection of sensual images from the first two decades of the century, with plates by himself and others, includes the famous gauzy studies of nude avant-garde dancers such as Ruth St. Denis. The text of Thomas Walters' *Nudes of the 20s and 30s*, basically a picture book, is weak, and the reproductions are not exceptional.

The late 1920s and early 1930s were the "schonheit" (beauty) period of the Weimar Republic, which, in turn, was followed by "naturkeit" (nudism); both movements generated lots of Continental photos of nude men and women. There was nothing comparable in the United States, where nudity had to have an excuse, and marginal American publishers and importers of photo books had to retouch flesh unless the bodies themselves had been marginalized by race or ethnicity. Falstaff Press, for instance, printed the German Felix Bryk's *Voodoo-Eros: Ethnological Studies in the Sex-Life of African Aborigines*, which presented pictures of naked blacks embedded in an anthropological narrative, and also Robert Meadows' *A Private Anthropological Cabinet of 500 Authentic Racial-Esoteric Photographs and Illustrations*, a compilation of photos illustrating "racial types of beauty," mostly female. Similarly, the anonymous author of *The Secret Museum of Anthropology* illustrated the text with photographs of women from various cultures pirated from Ferdinand von Reitzenstein's *Das Weib bei den Naturvolkern.* These photo volumes were but the latest in a tradition that dates back to works such as C. H. Stratz's *Die Schönheit des weiblichen Körpers* (1898), which purported to furnish a "scale of beauty" based on photographs of women from many cultures. Pasi Falk uses Stratz's text as the starting point for speculation on pornography's role as "the excluded other" in "Pornography and the Representation of Presence." A version of the male gaze theory, Falk's argument is that the graphic image eliminates "interpretative and even representational distance" (213) because the photographed activity is "really happening." Stratz's work went through many editions before being expanded into *Die Rassenschönheit des Weibes.* The tradition extended to magazines, too. As Catherine Lutz and Jane Collins note in *Reading National Geographic,* the photographs in this glossy journal introduced many Americans, men and women, to nakedness and served for a time as a quasi-pornographic delight. In this regard, some of the contributors to *Anthropology and Photography, 1860–1920,* edited by Elizabeth Edwards, comment on the double standard by which "primitive" peoples could be photographed without clothing—as in the pages of the *National Geographic*—but American whites could not.

The great nude studies by the pioneering Edward Weston, scandalous for the direct detail of bodies waxed by the desert sun during the 1920s and 1930s, have been collected in *Edward Weston Nudes.* In addition to fine prints, the volume reprints daybooks, diaries, and letters of the photographer, as well as a memoir by Charis Wilson, his model and later wife, whose recollections as to Weston's intent and his perfectionism are trenchant. Alfred Stieglitz's photographs of his lover (and then wife), the artist Georgia O'Keeffe, affronted some Americans. O'Keeffe's pubic hair was visible in Stieglitz's "Thighs" (1918) and "Torso" (1919) sequences of photographs. Of several books exploring their personal and artistic relationship, Benita Eisler's *O'Keeffe and Stieglitz: An American Romance* is one of the more readable. In 1995, reported Peter Halpert in "Fantasy Buys," one of Stieglitz's shots of O'Keeffe in a lingerie pose sold for $400,000.

Tony Sansone's nudes of his own body, self-published in the 1930s as *Rhythm,* startled those few Americans who saw them. Worth noting also is the five-volume *The Body Beautiful,* edited by Heyworth Campbell, the most comprehensive compilation of pre–World War II American female nudes; the collection makes visible many styles and perspectives. Graham Howe's "Outerbridge: From Cubism to Fetishism" traces Paul Outerbridge's gravitation from cubist images to gender-bending erotic ones: "Outerbridge was mainly concerned with making images, shocking in their suggestiveness, about subjects which were naughty or taboo. Naked ladies wearing top hats that one might assume belonged to their male companions, satin sheets indicative of luxurious decadence, exotic hosiery and gloves, various kinds of masks and rubber bathing caps were his favorite props for the ritualized performance of sexual masquerade" (54). Outerbridge tried to get around the censorship of pubic hair by shaving the mons of his models and manipulating labia to obscure the cleft.

Once again, the most explicit photographs were anonymous. Consider two groups of photographs in the archives of the Kinsey Institute. Of the thousands of subjects pictured in that collection, only a few dozen have been identified. Several individual prints that were originally parts of three different sets feature a woman named Madeline Cobb. Kinsey archivist Eugene Slabaugh identified her from a group of stag films (e.g., *Piccolo Pete*) from the 1930s, presumably shot by the same producer, and called the "Chicago Series" for lack of a better designation; Cobb performed in several of these. Slabaugh managed to trace a portion of her life through arrests that generated tiny notices on back pages of the *Chicago Tribune*. An attractive blond with marcelled hair, Cobb was addicted to heroin. Arrested for prostitution in February 1936, she was sentenced to thirty days in the Chicago workhouse. On her release, she dropped from sight, then, several weeks later, was discovered floating in Lake Michigan, an apparent suicide; no one claimed the body. One of the photos, a profile of Cobb's torso and face with a man's penis in her mouth, has been made into a postcard; stage white on her neck and breasts glosses her sallow skin. Others show her seated, nude, legs spread, or in congress with different males and females. The photographs bear docket numbers indicating when they were seized by police departments in the Midwest. Some dates are in the 1950s, indicating that the photos had been in circulation for twenty years, though they were not widely dispersed. Eugene Slabaugh, who never doubted that the subjects of the artifacts he studied were human, is the only historian to mark Cobb's brief and unfortunate life.

The second group is larger, partly because the subject was visible to mainstream culture. She was Juanita Slusher, later known as the exotic dancer Candy Barr. This group spans two decades and includes a dozen pictures shot at the Dallas motel that was the setting for *Smart Alec* (1950–1951), the best known of all American stag films, as well as some stills from a striptease film made some years later (1959?) and another dozen studio shots, some of Barr nude, some in G-string and pasties. In the earlier scenes, the usually blond Barr is dark-haired but easily recognized by the lush curves and the puffy nipples of the famous *belle poitrine* ("beautiful bosom"). Half a dozen more photographs from the same set have since come to light; collectors who shared information with Joseph Slade for *Shades of Blue* report purchasing copies of some of the prints as late as 1975 in New York, Chicago, Oklahoma City, and Des Moines. Slade himself met an arcade owner with a stack of prints at the State Fair of Texas in Dallas in 1959. The prints are finely grained, shot with superior lenses and film stock, of better definition than those of Cobb. The photographer was also much more skilled. In the photo Slade added to the Kinsey archive, the nude Barr sits facing forward astride a reclining male once erroneously identified as Gary Crosby, son of Bing. If one drew diagonals from opposing corners, they would meet at exactly the point where his penis enters her. Each photo seems to have burned a place in the memory of men who saw it, and the number of individual prints gave rise to the legend that Barr had appeared in many films. Barr, too, spent time in prison for drugs, railroaded on a marijuana charge, it is said, by scandalized Texans. Yet her reputation, her film, and these photos combined to make her the favorite bad girl of a generation—graceful and aggressive, demure and wild. The pictures of Cobb and Barr are examples of a "low" pornography remote from the mainstream; every pose is far more explicit than anything printed by photographers who strove for "eroticism." (For Barr as a stripper, see **Erotic Dance** in Chapter 10.)

The revolutionary, progressively more graphic nudes shot by Bill Brandt over more than half a century have been gathered in *Bill Brandt: Behind the Camera: Photographs 1928–1983*. Similarly influential is the work of Robert Farber; some of the prints from a long career appear in his *Images of Woman*, a book of several dozen photos complemented by a technical text. In 1991 Lee Friedlander's stark images appeared in a New York gallery retrospective and were published as *Nudes*. In "Photography View: Seeing 'Olympia' Afresh," Charles Hagen compares the shock value of Friedlander's explicitly rendered female genitalia to a touchstone of Western eroticism, Manet's notorious painting. Lucas Samaras presents images in *Samaras Album: Autointerview, Autobiography, Autopolaroid* as a foray into the erotic, using his own body as subject. His *Sittings 8 × 10: 1979–1980* depict erotic tableaux with the artist himself seated in the margins as an observer. Probably the best single source for those unacquainted with his work, however, is *Samaras: The Photographs of Lucas Samaras*, whose pages contain merged, manipulated, multiple-exposure Polaroid images, many of intense erotic power. Pat Booth's *Self Portrait*, a volume of photographs by a model turned photographer of herself in the nude, documents the artist's attempts to reveal inner states beneath flesh captured in mostly black-and-white shots. Booth's candor and intent recall Sansone's. Will McBride's *I, Will McBride* collects the work of a remarkable photographer, painter, and sculptor of occasional erotic subjects, briefly notorious for *Show Me* (1974), a volume of photographs intended to make children feel more comfortable with sex, now virtually unobtainable (see Chapter 8, **Child Pornography**).

Rosalind Kraus and Norman Bryson survey Cindy Sherman's career from the black-and-white film stills for which Sherman posed as various B-movie celebrities to the photographed guises/simulations of old masters and finally to the close-ups of sexual masks and gadgets with which she is associated today in *Cindy Sherman: 1975–1993*. Arthur Danto has collected several dozen photos of the photo/performance artist in erotic and conventional poses inspired by movies and fashion styles in *Cindy Sherman: Untitled Film Stills*. Laura Kipnis' critique of Sherman in "She-Male Fantasies and the Aesthetics of Pornography" is at odds with Danto's. Danto thinks that Sherman's photos speak to all women affected by the tropes of movie narratives and that they mirror cultural themes and preoccupations; Kipnis thinks instead that Sherman's pictures are about the instabilities of gender and sexual difference. Mira Schor's "From Liberation to

Lack" attacks Sherman's photos as "phallic." The Museum of Modern Art recently bought an extensive collection of Sherman's prints for a huge sum.

Charles R. Callum began a trend in photographing "ordinary" Americans in the nude, then publishing the pictures in collections like *Dallas Nude: A Photographic Essay* and *New York Nude: A Photographic Essay*. The scholar may wish to compare national differences in volumes from other countries presumably inspired by Callum's. Recommended are the nude studies of French architects, teachers, lawyers, and other professionals in Arnaud Baumann's *Carnet D'Adresses*. Diane Schmidt's *Chicago Exhibition* typifies a popular American genre, shots of nude women posed against familiar urban landmarks. The eroticism derives from the "exhibitionistic" aspects of the frames, though it is usually clear that most passersby are unaware of what is happening. Nan Goldin provides the images, and Marvin Heifernan, Mark Holborn, and Suzanne Fletcher provide the text in *The Ballad of Sexual Dependency*, a series of powerfully rendered, highly evocative photographs of ordinary and odd selves, friends, and relatives, all of whom seem fixated on tugging at the roots of desire. It is one of the most successfully realized of all photographic studies of "real" sexuality, as will be apparent when contrasted to the many coffee-table books of high erotica popular in the 1970s, of which the glossy *L'Amour: The Ways of Love*, with text by Colin Wilson and photos by Piero Rimaldi, is representative.

Women photographers in the 1970s produced impressive erotic statements. Ruth Bernard's *The Eternal Body: A Collection of Fifty Nudes*, with a fine text by Margaretta K. Mitchell, evokes the majesty of the human body, which is often endowed with cool sensuality by Bernard's lens. *Women and Other Visions*, by Judy Dater and Jack Welpott, showcases the fresh and piquant eroticism of Dater's images. Some of Dater's more famous photos, the best of which depict females who seem only that second to have discovered their bodies, are included in *Women on Women*, edited by Deborah Turbeville et al.; the collection views women from many perspectives, not just the erotic. *The Blatant Image: A Magazine of Feminist Photography*, an annual edited by Tee Corinne, served for a few years as an outlet for feminist photographers who wished to explore sexuality and gender. A comprehensive survey of contemporary women photographers, some of them working in erotic modes, is *Reframings: New American Feminist Photographies*, edited by Diane Neumaier, a volume more valuable than most because of its scope and its comment by various critics. Rundu L. Staggers, the virtual creator of black photographic erotica in the United States, has shaped images into a narrative called *Body and Soul: Black Erotica by Rundu*.

Comparatively few talented contemporary photographers have moved into hard-core photographic genres, whose appeal rests, in part, on the shock of visible genital contact. Of those who have, the most notable are Ron Raffaelli and Suze Randall. Raffaelli has published three volumes of joyous couples engaged in intercourse; they vary in graphic detail on an ascending scale: *Raffaelli's Passion: An Erotic Portfolio; Desire*; and *Rapture: Thirteen Erotic Fantasies*. All three sequences constitute discrete visual narratives, and all are buttressed with technical data on film stock and lenses. Randall is the reigning female pinup photographer and one of the principal targets of the antiporn feminist film *Not a Love Story*, by Bonnie Klein, who taxes her with the exploitation of women. Randall's work appears almost monthly in one men's magazine or another. *Suze*, a hardcover collection, includes photos of herself as well as many famous layouts, rendered in a style that is best described as centered on moist labia. Both Randall and Raffaelli have made hard-core films as well. Explicit photos by Richard Kern, a filmmaker who specializes in erotic visuals, have been collected as *New York Girls*.

In "Arrested Development: Larry Clark Pins Adolescence to the Wall," a review of a retrospective exhibit, Vince Aletti calls Clark "the most idiosyncratic and influential photographer of his generation." Clark's most powerful collections, *Teenage Lust* and *Larry Clark, 1992*, contain images of oral-genital sex and intercourse and of nudity tinged with drugs and violence; both chronicle Clark's fascination with youth and transgression. Clark's first film, *Kids* (Shining Excaliber Films/Miramax, 1995), a harrowing movie about aimless adolescents, owes a good deal to the grittiness he sought out as a still photographer. Joel-Peter Witkin has in recent years published volumes that might be called postmodern assemblages of the grotesque; they force viewers to consider the freakish, the bizarre, and the macabre. Witkin's *Forty Photographs*, the catalog of a 1985 show, is a good introduction to his work, which bears some similarity to that of Diane Arbus. The images of fetishes, abnormalities, and naked skin in *Gods of Heaven and Earth* are more disturbing than erotic. Witkin's recent *Harm's Way: Lust and Madness, Murder and Mayhem* has more in common with the tabloid photojournalism of, say, Weegee. For this volume, Witkin selects images from nineteenth-century medical studies, turn-of-the-century crime scenes, nineteenth-century asylum photos, and the pornographic photo archive of the Kinsey Institute. Only the vintage prints from the latter group might be said to be erotic, and they are less representative than the others of what Witkin calls "a time resplendent in the atrocity we once called life." *Francesca Woodman* collects photographs by the late Woodman, who used her own body as a canvas for moods that are erotic, despairing, and wounded.

The American photographer who has achieved the most notoriety through explorations of sexual fringes, of course, is Robert Mapplethorpe. Paul Morrison's "Coffee Table Sex: Robert Mapplethorpe and the Sadomasochism of Everyday Life" argues that far from being subversive, Mapplethorpe's S/M images conform to Marcusian political practice. The theatricalization implicit in the fetishes documented by Mapplethorpe makes them "acceptable" expressions of domestic freedom in a state that controls sexuality by establishing limits to what can be said and revealed through surveillance. Stuart Morgan's catalog of the traveling Mapplethorpe show, *Robert Mapplethorpe, 1970–1983*, comments on the raw power behind startling, but contrived, images. Mapplethorpe's *Black Book* was preceded by *Black Males*, published earlier in Amsterdam. A more recent collection is Mapplethorpe's *Altars*, a series of iconographic studies ranging from religious artifacts to S/M scenarios. Richard Marshall's *Robert Mapplethorpe*, written before Senator Helms made the photographer into a symbol of depravity, is a fine overview of Mapplethorpe's work. Probably the most comprehensive volume to date is Robert Mapplethorpe's *Mapplethorpe*, which gathers more than 300 photos, including those of the sexual undergrounds Mapplethorpe was drawn to, with a sympathetic Introduction by Arthur Danto, who thinks that the man's commercialism sapped his talent. Danto's *Playing with the Edge: The Photographic Achievement of Robert Mapplethorpe* nonetheless praises the impulses that drove the photographer toward extremes. Recommended are Jack Fritscher's *Mapplethorpe: Assault with a Deadly Camera: A Pop Culture Memoir, an Outlaw Reminiscence* and Patricia Morrisroe's *Mapplethorpe: A Biography*; the first finds Mapplethorpe subversive, while the second notes that the risks he took were always calculated. For a cultural barometer more accurate than political rhetoric, one might note the recent Quality Paperback Book Club catalog that offered a CD-ROM of 450 Mapplethorpe photos, including documentary footage by the BBC and commentary on Mapplethorpe's aesthetic of "perfect form" (15).

Studio nudes have always provoked pornographers. If professional studies emphasized body profiles, pornographers shot their models frontally. If studio technicians daubed bodies with stage white or slathered them with oil, pornographers parodied the makeup or highlighted pimples and moles. If glamour photographers airbrushed the pubic hair of their subjects, pornographers shot their models with hirsute open crotches. Pubic hair is almost acceptable now, so pornographers shave genitals of both sexes.

But pornographers also provoke mainstream artists. The increasing candor with which artists insist on rendering bodies creates problems for gallery owners, publishers, and arts organizations. A. D. Coleman suggests that the tenor of work by reputable artists in the 1970s has changed pitch in "Erotica: The Arrival of the Explicit." The quasi legality of hard-core images, Coleman thinks, has pushed artists over boundaries previously recognized by custom and statute. Now galleries display pictures of penises erect and vaginas ajar. The catalog of the Demarais Studio, *Erotic Photography, an Exhibition*, reproduces unusual photographs by eighty-five American photographers, such as Robin Schwartz and Annie Sprinkle, who submitted prints to a national competition. *Be/ing without Clothes*, Minor White's catalog of a show held at the Massachusetts Institute of Technology in November 1970, includes work by Kroll, Cunningham, and others. "Sexual Devolution: Naughty Pictures Never Die, They Just Fade Away," Anne M. Russell's review of "Rated-X," the annual show (since 1982) of erotic photos held at Neikrug Photographica gallery in New York City, remarks on the loss of force that occurs when tabooed subjects are exposed; the pictures she mentions are by Annie Sprinkle, Marie-Claire Montanari, and thirty others. Merry Alpert's *Dirty Windows* reproduces the images from Alpert's exhibit of photos clandestinely shot through the window of a Manhattan sex club at the Bonni Benrubi Gallery; Alpert's prints say more about surveillance than voyeurism, though she makes nice juxtapositions between images of hands holding penises and fingers clutching currency.

Notable anthologies are *Nude Photography: The Art and Technique of Nine Modern Masters*, by Peter Lacey; *The Naked Eye: Great Photographs of the Nude*, edited by David Bailey, with a text by Martin Harrison persuasive as to why they are great; and *New American Nudes: Recent Trends and Attitudes*, edited by Arno Minkkinen. The last is an evenhanded celebration of male and female nudes by photographers such as Marsha Burns, Duane Michaels, Robert Mapplethorpe, Kelly Wise, Minnette Lehmann, Peter Hujar, Arthur Tress, Reed Estabrook, Ralph Gibson, Linda Swartz, Jeffrey Silverthorne, and others; the chosen images were winnowed from more than 4,000. *Contemporary American Erotic Photography* anthologizes works by Dunas, Kane, Mapplethorpe, Marcus, and others, while *Masterpieces of Erotic Photography* includes photos by Art Kane and Duane Michaels among foreign entries (e.g., Haskins, Bailey, Skrebinski, Vogt, Sieff). The photographs in *Exquisite Creatures*, edited by Jim Cline, are chiefly nude studies of women by Jim Dine, Robert Mapplethorpe, Roy Volkmann, Deborah Turbeville, and others, but the Introduction by Donald Barthelme lifts the volume above the ordinary. *Sensual Images*, edited by the PIE Books staff, presents erotic nudes by photographers of several nations, noting that growing explicitness is an international phenomenon.

Although Jeff Dunas achieved fame largely as a photographer of pinups, his melding of background and flesh often transcends the genre. *Voyeur*, images shot between 1979 and 1983, is representative of his several books. Dunas also edits a bimonthly called *Collectors Photography*, which in its first few years was devoted entirely to photography of the female nude, with historical and critical essays, interviews, and comment by a diverse group of photographers; later issues cover different subjects as well. Still tightly focused is *Erotica*, a British journal edited by Julia Thompson. Historical essays and illustrations are less frequent than photos by contemporary artists like Chris Wroblewski, Jeanloup Sieff, Katarina Jebb, Grace Lau, Jeanette Jones, Craig Morey, China Hamilton, Gerard Malanga, Karen Rosenthal, and many others.

FEMALE PINUPS, CENTERFOLDS, AND MAGAZINE PICTORIALS

The pinup is difficult to define precisely, since it may be a painting, a photograph, or some other graphic design. That said, *pinup* today usually designates a revealing photograph of a woman or man in a format large enough to draw the eye. While hardly restricted to the United States, pinups have evolved in recognizable American styles. Those who want to contrast European and American compositions should glance at *Heavenly Bodies: The Complete Pirelli Cal-*

endar Book, a compendium of Continental pinups published over decades by the Pirelli Tire Company. Complementing that volume is *The Pirelli Calendar, 1964–1997*, a collection of profusely illustrated essays on aspects of an artifact found in garages around the world. (See also **Pinup Paintings** in Chapter 11.)

Mark Gabor's *The Art of the Calendar* is only partially devoted to the pinup calendar, but his *The Illustrated History of Girlie Magazines* covers magazine photos and drawings that often doubled as pinups; his *The Pin-Up: A Modest History* focuses more precisely on the genre, despite the book's disjointed organization, and includes examples of the male pinup. *The Pin-Up from 1852 to Today*, by Ralph Stein, is superficial, despite a chronological outline that is better structured than Gabor's. Stein's perspective shapes "History of Pin-Ups," one segment of a *Playboy* videocassette. Provocative calendars and posters are arranged historically by Michael Colmer in *Calendar Girls: A Lavishly Illustrated, Colourful History Spanning Six Decades*; it stops well short of the *Sports Illustrated* swimsuit pinups. In recent years, the latter have generated miles of newspaper copy, not all of it from feminist journalists. For HBO, Susan Froemke and Albert Maysles shot *Sports Illustrated Swim Suits USA: America the Beautiful*, a documentary that follows assignment editors, photographers, and models. Michael MacCambridge devotes a few pages to the swimsuit editions that have become a staple in *The Franchise: A History of Sports Illustrated Magazine*.

Richard Wortley's *Pin-ups Progress: An Illustrated History of the Immodest Art* is international in scope, with commentary on more British and Continental examples than American, as is Jacques Sternberg's *Pin Up*, though the latter has a more limited range—from the mid-nineteenth century to the eve of World War II—and more astute comment. By contrast, Allen Chellas' survey, *Cheesecake: An American Phenomenon*, makes a strong case for American distinctiveness. The number of pinups produced in this country has been phenomenal, or so says Arthur Amsie, a former pinup photographer interviewed by Irving Wexler in "King Pin-Up." Amsie owns the Girl Whirl, a gallery of 200,000 classic pinup paintings and photos. Amsie also reminisces about pinups of the 1950s in *The Betty Pages Annual*. None of these works, however, are as interesting as the several pages called "Entomology of the Pin-Up Girl" that Andre Bazin devotes to the genre in *What Is Cinema?* or the brief remarks Thomas B. Hess offers in "Pinup and Icon," which reviews the influence of the pinup on painters as diverse as Manet, De Kooning, Rauschenberg, Wesselman, and Rivers.

Period studies are erratic. The most authoritative discussion of nineteenth-century pinups is Patrice Boussel's *Erotisme Galanterie au 19e Siècle*, whose text explores thematic categories. Robert Lebeck's *Playgirls of Yesteryear* concentrates on French postcards and pinups, some of which made their way to collectors in America; the German edition, *Playgirls von Damals*, contains an informative Afterword by Manfred Sack. *Nudes of Yesteryear* reproduces without comment turn-of-the-century postcards and photo sets. John Costello compares pinups of World War I with those of World War II (187–194) in his *Love, Sex and War: Changing Values 1939–1945*. One chapter of *Parade of Pleasure:*

A Study of Popular Iconography in the U.S.A., a generally unflattering portrait of American media by Geoffrey Wagner, lifts an eyebrow at Yankee fondness for pinups, especially those of women whose skirts have been blown above the waist.

"G.I. Pin-ups" identifies popular Hollywood pinups, with particular reference to the shot of maillot-clad Betty Grable as long-stemmed flower. Beginning in the 1920s, American film studios shot photos of barely clad actors and actresses, especially the latter. Heinrich Ludwig reproduces nude shots of some American ingenues in "Die Erotik im Film." The Kobal collection (now in London), probably the largest archive of Hollywood glamour photographs from the 1920s through the 1940s (most by Kobal himself), has provided illustrations for many volumes. Kobal's *Hollywood Glamour Portraits: 145 Photos of Stars 1926–1949* and *Gods and Goddesses of the Movies* offer an index to the eroticism of earlier decades. Additional insights can be found in Kobal's biography, *People Will Talk. Screen Dreams: The Hollywood Pinup: Photographs from the Kobal Collection*, with reproductions by Ed Caraeff and an excellent text by Tony Crawley, contains many images of scantily clad stars and starlets from Louise Brooks and Erroll Flynn, to Morgan Fairchild and Mel Gibson. The work of three major Hollywood stylists has also been collected: George Hurrell's *Hurrell's Hollywood Portraits: The Chapman Collection* features seductive, brilliantly lit portraits; Bernard of Hollywood's *Pin-Ups: A Step Beyond, a Portfolio of Breathtaking Beauties* depicts actresses in postures of desire; Bruno of Hollywood's *Figure Photography* adds cinematic sheen to male and female nudes. Bernard's classic photos of fifty-three cheesecake stars (e.g., Mara Corday, Ava Norring, Lily St. Cyr) of the 1940s, 1950s, and 1960s, classified as redheads, blonds, and brunets, have been recently issued on a CD-ROM entitled *Bernard of Hollywood's Pin-Ups.*

Mary Beth Haralovich notes the willingness of moviemakers to please fans in "Film Advertising, the Film Industry and the Pin-Up: The Industry's Accommodations to Social Forces in the 1940s," whose thesis is that producers used the pinup to add spice to ads as a way of circumventing the restrictions of the Motion Picture Producers and Distributors of America (MPPDA) and the Production Code Administration. *Hollywood Cheesecake: Sixty Years of America's Favorite Pinups*, edited by Madison S. Lacy and Don Morgan, indicates the enduring appeal of movie star pinups. "The Cult of the Love Goddess in America" by Winthrop Sargeant centers on the endlessly reproduced over-the-shoulder look of Betty Grable, who peered out of troop lockers during World War II. Similarly, Jane Gaines comments on the ironies of the army's using feminine beauty to promote aggression in "In the Service of Ideology: How Betty Grable's Legs Won the War." After the war, pinups reminded a reticent middle class of the robustness of sensuality. Joanne Meyerowitz surveys reactions by women to pinups in men's magazines in "Women, Cheesecake, and Borderline Material: Responses to Girlie Pictures in the Mid-Twentieth Century United States"; she analyzes letters to magazines as diverse as *Esquire, Playboy,*

Life, and *Ebony*. Meyerowitz found that some women endorsed the magazines and their pictorials because they empowered women by asserting their sexuality against decades of repression, while others condemned them as dehumanizing and demeaning; the split over the inscription and interpretation of sexual codes, says Meyerowitz, continues today. Russ Meyer's *The Glamour Camera of Russ Meyer* also documents the irreverence of an allegedly staid period. Before Meyer became celebrated as a cinematographer, he photographed bare-breasted celebrities such as Dianne Webber, Jayne Mansfield, Joy Lansing, and Mamie Van Doren. David K. Frasier's *Russ Meyer—the Life and Films: A Biography and a Comprehensive, Illustrated, and Annotated Filmography and Bibliography*, though primarily concerned with Meyer's movies, is useful on Meyer's photographic work and favorite models, some of whom are very articulate. (For other critical work on Meyer, see **Exploitation Films** in Chapter 13.)

Some of Meyer's photos appeared in *Playboy*, a venue that gave the pinup new respectability as monthly centerfold. The centerfold, in turn, sanitized conventional sexiness. Exposure sometimes propelled models to careers on-screen. Often, however, the magazine operates in reverse to validate the sexiness of women who want to jump-start a new career or juice a dessicated one; unlike centerfold models, they pose for lavish pictorials after extensive negotiation by agents who time layouts to promote a movie, a television series, or a book; the spread on presidential–daughter, Patti (Reagan) Davis, is a notable example. Of the large number of movies and television programs making use of centerfolds as a plot device, only one need serve as example: *Posing: Inspired by Three Stories* describes how posing for *Playboy* affected the lives of three women. *Playboy*'s response to the program was to invite American housewives to pose; hundreds of wives and mothers applied, and the article/pictorial that resulted, "Domestic Bliss," exemplifies the safe, domesticated eroticism that is the magazine's current stock-in-trade.

As Eugene Burt points out in *Erotic Art: An Annotated Bibliography with Essays* (282), any discussion of pinups published before the 1970s must take into account the airbrushing of pubic hair: Burt cites Elyce Wakerman's *Air-Powered: The Art of the Air Brush* as the standard text. Not until the late 1960s, when *Penthouse* began to reveal pubic hair, would matters change. Close-ups of pubic hair gave way to shaved labia, to depiliated recta, and, in the case of *Penthouse*, to actual genital contact. *Playboy*'s Thirtieth Year Aniversary Issue includes a retrospective on its Playmates: "Thirty Memorable Years: Three Decades of the Best, the Brightest, the Most Beautiful Women to Grace These Pages" that graphs evolution. Every issue now includes a reshooting of Playmates turned mothers and grandmothers but still proud of their bodies. An interesting indicator of the Playmate's current cultural status, as noted by Mark Schone in "Centerfolds Emeritus," is the Playboy Playmate Alumni Association, comprising former models who share a newsletter and a health plan.

Playboy Press recycles the magazine's gauzy, feel-good photos in dozens of softcover books and videos that can be found anywhere. The most comprehensive collection is Gretchen Edgren's *The Playmate Book: Five Decades of Centerfolds*, which contains more than 500 photos ranging from 1953 to 1996, with interpolations from Hugh Hefner's personal collection all embedded in reminiscences by photographers, models, and readers. Despite its age, Thomas Meehan's "We Like to Find a Late-Maturing Girl" is probably the best article on the process of creating a *Playboy* centerfold. Similarly dated but still useful is Herbert Richardson's "Playboy Playmates," on interpreting the elements of pictorials.

Most critical articles reach the far from fresh conclusion that Playmates just do not seem like real women or that the sexual appeal of burnished buttocks and nipples seems tainted by commerce; as such, they belong to what is virtually an antiporn genre of hackneyed prudish response. One such analysis is "Playmate of the Month: Naked but Nice," in which Richard A. Kallan and Robert D. Brooks examine the practice of encapsulating the Playmate in a contextual environment made iconographic by photos and allusions to family, friends, and traditional politics. Mary Riege Laner looks at the layouts of eleven magazines to find that where the occupations of the models were indicated (46 percent), the majority were entertainers or employed in lower-class occupations the author considers nonthreatening to males, presumably to emphasize that the women were dumb, in "Make-Believe Mistresses: Photo-Essay Models in the Candy-Sex Magazines." Cultural agendas can cue pinup practice in other ways: in "Anatomy Lessons: The Destiny of a Textbook, 1971–72," Rosalind A. Coleman and James Rolleston study an anatomy textbook that included female pinups as illustrations; the authors note that such practice would be unacceptable now because of social change. That change has come about, in part, because women now occupy workplaces once exclusively male. Pinning pictures of scantily clad women on office walls can offend coworkers. Richard Goldstein considers walls themselves rather than the precise content of messages in "Wall of Change," an article on fashion in displaying pin-ups in offices and workplaces; Goldstein observes that like graffiti such works sometimes suggest "not sexism, but sexual transgression."

MODELS AND TECHNIQUES

Sometimes models regret having posed. A case in point is Tim Conaway's "The Hite Report Exposed," a review of *The Hite Report* accompanied by open-crotch nude photos of the author, Sherry Hite, taken in her early days as a would-be model. Bettie Page, easily the most famous pinup model of the 1950s, now in her seventies, has no misgivings. Page typifies the period to a rare degree. (Page's spelling is *Bettie*; a dissertation could be written on the reasons she has come to be known as *Betty*.) A native of Tennessee, Page has become a cult figure, though she lived until quite recently in obscurity. Page was a fresh-faced brunet of graceful proportions; her slim body set a standard displaced only by Marilyn Monroe's lush curves in the next decade. Page's history confirms the thesis that the pornography of one generation can enrich the culture of succeeding periods. Willie Morris, former editor of *Harper's* magazine, has dissected her appeal in "The Wild One: Betty Page, the First Naked Woman in America." For Morris, she was "the even darker side of Marilyn": "Her body was of the Fifties, *my* Fifties, full and opulent as the replenishing epoch itself, not the taut, slender, athletic silhouette of the Nineties models nor of today's high-ballasted strippers with the silicone aspect" (68). Morris noted that photographers shot more than 500,000 photos of Page before she found religion at age thirty-four. He knows she has stories to tell but, for the sake of keeping fantasy alive and mysterious, begs her not to "tell anybody, not even Oprah" (69). Reams of text speculate on Page's mystery, which stemmed, in part, from her mastery of the art of pivoting her body on her trademark high heels to emphasize both buttocks and breasts.

Irving Klaw's favorite model, Page appeared in his *Movie Star News* and *Model Parade* in dozens of photo sequences and in one-reel, soft-core films, often in bondage scenes or other "bizarre" situations. Part of her appeal was relentless good cheer: in a typical bondage photo the bra-and-panty-clad Page is trussed with rope knots that appear to have been tied by inept Boy Scouts, but she always seems to be having fun. She remains perhaps the only American model to attain the status of Kiki de Montparnasse (Alice Irene), the inspiration of so many Parisian photographers and painters of the 1920s. An industry has grown up around the artifacts of her career, and original prints, especially those in which Page's pubic hair has not been airbrushed, sell for high prices. Unlike many figure models of her period (and unlike Kiki, whose fame rested, in part, on her lack of pubic hair), Page did not depilate her labia, and that "naturalness"—revealed in the rarest, most surreptitiously distributed shots—enhanced her mystery in an era when pubic hair seemed more frightening to Americans than communism. The dimensions of the craze are detailed in Buck Henry's "The Betty Boom." Soon after Henry's article appeared, the television show *Lifestyles of the Rich and Famous* aired a segment on Page in November 1992. In a follow-up to that show, Bob Schapiro's "Betty Page Update" traces her life from 1957, when she dropped out of modeling after the Kefauver Senate hearings targeted Irving Klaw. Schapiro interviewed Page, almost seventy and living in southern California, for the television program. As media revved up the cycle of cultural appropriation, photos of Page would soon appear even in the *New York Times Magazine*.

The publicity drew her out. Page herself has contributed a memoir to the second volume of the *Betty Pages Annual*, published by Greg Theakston, whose biographical treatment of Page in the initial volume is complemented by Harlan Ellison's fevered Introduction: "She was an icon, Venus on the spikeheel, the goddess Astarte come again . . ." (8). Extensive biographical material also appears in James Silke's *Betty Page: Queen of Hearts*, a commentary that draws on Silke's massive collection of pinups. Karen Essex and James L. Swanson's *Bettie Page: Life of a Pin-Up Legend*, a biography based on interviews, is generally admiring, while Richard Foster's *The Real Bettie Page: The Truth about the Queen of the Pinups*, an unromanticized chronicle of her failed marriages, trial for attempted murder, and commitment to an asylum debunks her legendary status. Foster's bibliography of Page's memorabilia and magazine appearances is amazing. Page's own response to these charges and the story of her religious conversion are recorded in Kevin Cook's "Bettie Page Interview: My Story—The Missing Years."

A biennial periodical, *The Betty Pages: The Magazine Dedicated to Tease*, is devoted to Page photos and memorabilia; collectors can order Page posters, pinups, buttons, figurines, T-shirts, and trading cards from *Bud Plant's Incredible Catalog*. Plant sells three videos: *The Betty Page Story* (parts 1 and 2) and *Betty Page: Raw and Exposed*. Part of William Grimes' article entitled "Lurid! Licentious! Collectible! The Flip Side of the 1940's and 50's" deals with the collectibility of Page memorabilia. *Betty Page Outdoors* reproduces shots taken on outings on Long Island by members of photo clubs for whom Page served as a model. Bélier Press has published several volumes in which Page figures prominently, with comment by J. B. Rund. The four-volume *Betty Page: Private Peeks* generously samples studio poses; volume III has an Introduction by artist Richard Merkin. The five numbers of *Betty Page in Bondage*, originally published by Klaw, feature her in various restraints, ropes, cages, and costumes; the first number includes biographical information. *Betty Page Confidential*, a collection of Page photos shot by Bunny Yeager in the 1950s, contains a reasonably complete filmography of Page's bondage movies for Klaw and an even more valuable list of the magazine pictorials featuring the model. *Betty Page: Volume I: The Glamourous Betty Page*, and *Volume II: Dedicated to Betty Page*, edited by Stefano Piselli, Riccardo Morrocchi, and Marco Giovannini, comment on photo sequences; volume II includes movie stills and a filmography. Two 3-D picture books of Page photos assembled by Ray Zone are *Betty Page, Captured Jungle Girl* and *The Betty Page 3-D Picture Book*. The Introduction to the latter volume is by Dave Stevens, who speculates on her cultural significance; Stevens himself modeled the female character in his *The Rocketeer* (now a mainstream film) on the pinup queen. Two bound poster collections are also available: eight artists have done renditions of Page for *The Betty Page Portfolio*, and Stevens' *Just Teasing: The Dave Stevens Poster Book* reproduces some of his own work. *Betty Page: Queen of Pin-Up* is an excellent recent compilation of photos; additional information is available from her largest fan club, the Betty Scouts of America. Those skeptical about Page's cult status need only enter her name in any Internet search engine; the websites devoted to her number in the hundreds. The search will also turn up the latest incarnation of Movie Star News, Irving Klaw's original enterprise.

In 1949 Tom Kelley shot the most famous pinup of the twentieth century; its aura swelled with the career of its subject. First published as the *"Golden Dreams"* Calendar by the John Baumgarth Company of Melrose Park, California, in 1953, the nude photograph of Marilyn Monroe ignited fantasies across the nation when *Playboy* reproduced it as the centerfold for its first edition in 1953. That photo and nude photographs of Monroe by other artists are now part of the legends detailed in biographies and texts too numerous to list; the reader need only look under "M" in the biography section of a local library. Norman Mailer's *Marilyn* is perhaps the most overblown hagiography, and for balance one might look at Gloria Steinem's *Marilyn/Norma Jean*, a volume laced with photographs by George Barris. Susan Griffin's hyperbolic *Pornography and Silence* contains an extended riff (201–217) on Monroe as an icon of the pornographic imagination; it can serve as exemplar of feminist antiporn screeds on the actress. The subtext of other studies of Monroe is that the culture has by now raised the goddess' body, suffused with glamour and mystique, to a transcendent, panerotic or supererotic plane. That line of thought has reached an apogee—or nadir—in *American Monroe: The Making of a Body Politic*, in which the late S. Paige Baty claims that our fetishized image of Monroe is now inscribed with the whole of American culture, and vice versa. At such junctures, one may wonder whether commerce or criticism is the more ghoulish.

Worth noting, however, is Kathyrn N. Benzel's "The Body as Art: Still Photographs of Marilyn Monroe," a close study of some of these images, especially the Kelley calendar. Of articles tracing Monroe's impact on American culture, the most unique is "L.A.'s Museum of Contemporary Art and the Body of Marilyn Monroe," in which Jo-Anne Berelowitz demonstrates how an architect visualized a building as Marilyn Monroe's body to add sensuality to the design; the circumstance suggests sexism inherent in architecture, says Berelowitz, but also attests to the metaphorical power of Monroe's image. Another indicator of Monroe's importance is *Marilyn*, the 1993 opera by Ezra Laderman and Norman Rosten; it was reviewed by Edward Rothstein in "New Milieu for Monroe: Some Like It Operatic." Legend has Monroe as the naked woman masturbating in the short film *Apples, Knockers, and the Coke Bottle* (1955?), but Neil Wexler persuasively identifies the lady in question as model Arlene Hunter (116) in "A Pocket Full of Pin-Ups." Clark Kidder and Madison Daniels have identified all the known early Monroe magazine appearances in *Marilyn Monroe unCovers*, and Denis C. Jackson provides the going rates for artifacts in *The Price and Identification Guide to Marilyn Monroe*. For those seeking a quick study, however, John Updike's "The Nude Marilyn," illustrated with some of the original Kelley outtakes and with a sampling of other figure studies by photographers celebrated and obscure, offers clues to understanding the significance of her body.

The story of Diane Webber, "Queen of Nudists" and model for many of America's great glamour photographers, frames Gay Talese's book *Thy Neighbor's Wife*. *Calendar Model*, by Gloria Gale, the autobiography of a ubiquitous nude figure during the 1950s, is a cut above such memoirs in that it is truly interesting. Information on Donna Brown and Joann Rydell, who like Page also modeled for Irving Klaw, can be found in *Irving Klaw, "The Pin-up King" Catalogs*, which also featured strippers such as Blaze Starr, Tempest Storm, and

Lili St. Cyr. Klaw's catalogs capsuled biographies of his models for customers eager for contextualization; the strategy resembled *Playboy*'s biographical notes on its centerfolds. The more than 100 Klaw catalogs are collectors' items now. Another famous model helped define the field by turning photographer herself. Most pinup photographers were male, but Bunny Yeager practiced with her own body to learn how to heighten the sexuality of other women. Her *How I Photograph Myself* and her *100 Girls: New Concepts in Glamour Photography*, both of which emphasized lighting and posture, were influential in the 1960s. Yeager's *Bunny's Honeys* is a recent collection of her vintage photos. Photos of Yeager herself can be found in *Va Va Voom! Bombshells, Pinups, Sexpots, and Glamour Girls*, for which Steve Sullivan has assembled pictures and biographies of famous pinups such as Page, Eve Meyer, Dianne Webber, Candy Barr, Joi Lansing, Mamie Van Doren, and many others.

In *The Girl in the Centerfold: The Uninhibited Memoirs of Miss January*, Surrey Marshe regards her experience as a Playmate in ambivalent terms; she remains disturbed by the fantasy images that models foster. Remarkably few *Playboy* models have publicly voiced second thoughts, and remarkably few have moved into hard-core genres (although one who did, Teri Weigel, instantly achieved star status in the video industry). Perhaps the best-known Playmate of recent years, Dorothy Stratton, was killed by her estranged husband and was eulogized in film biographies, one by her lover, director Peter Bogdanovich, called *The Killing of the Unicorn*. A former photographer's model (not for *Playboy*) who does feel degraded and exploited by her experiences is the subject of Laura Lederer's "Then and Now: An Interview with a Former Pornography Model." Two collections provide authentic background, though in both the recollections of strippers, prostitutes, and porn stars outnumber those of models. These are *The Front Line: Women in the Sex Industry Speak*, edited by Nickie Roberts, and *Sex Work: Writings by Women in the Sex Industry*, edited by Frédérique Delacoste and Priscilla Alexander. Among the various sex workers Bob Hoddeson interviews for *The Porn People: A First-Person Documentary Report* are nude models for walk-in photographers during the 1970s; their descriptions of working conditions are gritty. Less disillusioned are the models represented in *The Sex People: Erotic Performers and Their Brave New Worlds*, by Eberhard Kronhausen and Phyllis Kronhausen, also written at a time when nudity was touted as revolutionary. To judge by her breathless prose, Liz Renay had a splendid time modeling, or so she says in *My First 2,000 Men*, the memoir of a career highlighted by stripping and acting (in John Waters' films).

Martin Schreiber's early black-and-white photographs of Madonna Ciccone, as she was known before her fame, have been published as *Madonna Nudes 1979*. Madonna's *Sex*, with photographs by Steven Meisel and art by Fabien Baron, was a publishing sensation in 1992. The volume contains photographs of the barely clothed celebrity visiting the Vault, New York's S/M palace, and posing with partners of various genders. Calvin Tomkins' review of *Sex*, entitled "Madonna's Anticlimax," concludes: "sadly, her book is going to give pornography a bad name" (39), though Tomkins admires the volume itself, which seems "more about layout than getting laid" (39). David Aaron Clark's "Madonna Exposed" suggests that the sexuality revealed in Meisel's photographs for *Sex* is pretty ersatz. Mimi Udovich, Kate Tentler, Vince Aletti, and Simon Frith attempt not so much to counter such arguments as to appreciate Madonna's images of her stylized body parts as cultural statements in brief, linked essays called "In Defense of *Sex*." Of these, Udovich's remarks are the most interesting. She observes: "While the dismissal of *Sex* is not 100% uniform, it does achieve a consensus on several points. The strangest of these is that it is at least unusual and perhaps impossible to say anything intelligent about pornography" (22). Essays in *Madonnarama: Essays on Sex and Popular Culture*, edited by Lisa Frank and Phil Smith, consider the celebrity's propensity for self-exposure and how such images feed and draw on popular culture.

Peter Basch, highly regarded as a glamour photographer during the 1950s and 1960s, moved easily between pinup and studio genres, and offers advice on both types in *The Nude as Form and Figure*. Peter Gowland's *Peter Gowland's Glamour Camera* and *The Secrets of Photographing Women* distill what another photographer learned over many years in the trade. Perhaps the best of similar insights by a professional on just what makes pictures erotic is Peter Barry's *The Art of Erotic Photography*. Another standard text is Roger Hicks' *Techniques of Pin-Up Photography*, a practical guide to choosing lenses and instructing models to lower shoulders, flex legs, lift breasts, wet lips, and so on. Of all the technical guides that professional photographers might keep handy, however, *John Hedgecoe's Workbook of Nudes and Glamour* is the one most often found in studios.

It should not need saying, but usually does, that taking erotic photographs is much harder than people think, a point stressed by Annie Sprinkle, who includes photographs from her various publications (e.g., *The Sprinkle Report: A Newsletter of Piss Art*) in *Post Porn Modernist*. Especially notable are those from her "Sluts and Goddesses" project, for which she photographed ordinary women in seductive costumes and poses. *Real Sex*, the Home Box Office video series, carried a segment called "Sluts and Goddesses" to document the experiment. Professional André Rival handed the shutter release to his models, who triggered the camera when they were satisfied with their poses. Published as *Self-Images: 100 Women*, the results are fascinating. Except for a few instances in which the subjects clown, the images are those of women trying to look beautiful rather than provocative, and the effect is charming—not sensual.

That the pinup is a powerful cultural force is obvious from the enormous number of amateurs who attempt to capture poses of themselves in the style of centerfolds. In major cities, for instance, boudoir/glamour photography studios offer citizens a comfortable and safe environment for having themselves photographed nude. Typical are two establishments in Columbus, Ohio: Linda's Boudoir Photography Studio and Oliver's Loft: A Studio for Gentlemen; all the television networks have run stories on them. J. A. Dickerson reports on the phenomenon, discusses the rationale of the boudoir print as souvenir of sensual youth, and includes expert tips in "Boudoir Portraiture." Mario Venticinque's *Boudoir Photography: The Fantasy Exposed* is a technical guide to setting up a studio devoted to walk-in clients. Sometimes such photographs represent rebellion. George Myers Jr. notes in "Writers Express Love in All Ways" that the novelist Katharine Anne Porter insisted that her lovers take nude photographs of her, which she then sent to disapproving family members. Sometimes exhibitionism is the driving force. *Gallery* has for twenty-five years featured "The Girl Next Door"; readers send in photos of wives or girlfriends to compete for model fees and prizes. From these editors choose one to be photographed by a professional as a layout in the next issue. James N. Goode's *How to Create and Sell Amateur Erotic Videos and Photos: Cashing In on the Amateur Craze* probably overstates the market for amateur photos, but it would appear, nonetheless, to be substantial. Moreover, the appeal of the amateur subject is a reminder that the photographic genres of pornography have not changed much from their inception. Internet Web sites exhibit amateur photos; the oldest is AAAAA Amateurs Web, on which are posted soft- and hard-core images by and of men and women.

Anonymous Americans have taken tens of millions of explicit shots of equally anonymous friends, lovers, and models; millions more are now surging across the Net. It is here, at the edge of a wilderness of images, leagues beyond the cultural mainstream at a boundary drawn by the imperatives of *low* pornography, that we should be reminded of how little we know about sex and its representation. Flesh remains mute, but these human landscapes hold meaning for scholars bold enough to interpret them. After all, the average Americans who take the shots do so in the hope of capturing *something*.

EROTIC POSTCARDS

Picture postcards began to appear shortly before the turn of the century, materially assisted by a craze for collecting them, especially among women. In his *Pictures in the Post*, a good general history of collecting mania, Richard Carline suggests that eroticizing the postcard was a marketing strategy designed to encourage men to collect. *Picture Postcards of the Golden Age: A Collector's Guide*, by Tonie Holt and Valmai Holt, is a tool for the hobbyist with only modest reference to erotic subcategories and is a good companion to Carline's history, as is Martin Willoughby's *A History of Postcards*, which is excellent on sepia-toning and captioning, chromolithographs and hand-painted genres. Americans have collected cards since well before the turn of the century, a trend accelerated by soldiers bringing back large numbers from Paris in World War I. More recently, U.S. souvenir shops have sold nude photo postcards, usually of women on a beach, and various manufacturers now offer classic and offbeat nudes. (American versions of off-color "seaside" British kitsch—both are more "dirty" than erotic—are common, but there seems to be no essay on American bad taste comparable to George Orwell's study, "The Art of Donald McGill," who set the standard for the British genre. Samples of McGill's postcard drawings are on view in Alan Wykes' *Saucy Seaside Postcards: An Illustrated Disquisition.*)

Perhaps because these card-stock rectangles are more easily preserved than other photographic artifacts, erotic postcards have attracted excellent scholars, most of them European. *Erotic Postcards*, by William Ouellette and Barbara Jones Ouellette, whose superb volume is complete with technical details of printing processes, publishers, and provenances, is the best reference work. They respond to the question often asked by noncollectors, Did anyone ever mail these postcards, say, one picturing a smiling woman caressing a large penis? Answer: Every now and then, and every now and then one reached its destination; but mostly, no, and the Ouellettes do not advise franking one now. Also scholarly is Erik Nørgaard's *With Love: The Erotic Postcard*, a history of the period 1890–1930, which breaks down the genre into categories of nudity and sexual behavior; the German edition, *In Liebe Dein: Sexpostkarten aus Grossvaters Pornokiste*, contains comment by Michael Schiff. The now-classic study, *L'Age d'or de la carte postale*, by the erotica historian Ado Kyrou, is comprehensive and excellent, especially in its discussion of styles of nudity, piquancies of props, and degrees of lasciviousness. Jules Griffon's *The Golden Years: Masterpieces of the Erotic Postcard* is notable because its focus includes the 1940s and 1950s. Just as popular in tone but with an ambitious intent and an excellent bibliography is *Post Card Album, and Also a Cultural History*, by Anatole Jakovsky and Carl Lauterbach, who discuss mostly French cards. In *French Undressing: Naughty Postcards from 1900 to 1920*, Paul Hammond's brief, solid text contrasts the development of the erotic postcard with that of "dirty" comic strips and movies and covers hand-tinted cards, collages, and other novelties. Collecting cards, he suggests, helped to bolster the concept of pornography as a realm of the forbidden.

Patrick Waldberg's *Eros Modern Style* marshals examples to support the thesis that turn-of-the-century card manufacturers defused outrage by suppressing pubic hair and by dressing up erotic representations with settings of antiquity or allegory. The massive archive of Robert Lebeck has generated several volumes by the collector, each devoted to particular fetishes. Lebeck's *Busen, Strapzen, Spitzhoschen* covers French postcards featuring models in lingerie. His *Die Erotische Postkarte* offers a more general account, while *Kehr Seiten* concentrates on postcards emphasizing female buttocks. The latter two volumes are combined in an American edition called *Playgirls of Yesteryear* and a similar German edition, *Playgirls von Damals*; the second has an interesting Afterword by Manfred Sack. More romantic, less explicit photos make up Lebeck's *The Kiss*. Very explicit cards from the late nineteenth century are reprinted with an Introduction by Alfred de Montel in *Cartes Postales Pornographiques de la Belle Epoque*; these range from mild (women inserting dildos) to strong (couplings by multiple partners). Robert Merodack's *Mignones, Mignonettes* covers

French postcards from the 1920s and 1930s. Two volumes of pictures, poorly dated and with little text, are *Nude 1900: A Look at French Postcards* and *Nude 1925: A Look at French Postcards*. Of slight merit also is Ferruccio Farina's *Venus Unveiled*, though the photos are well reproduced. Finally, the German publisher Taschen has been issuing historically interesting sexual images in postcard form (thus rejuvenating the format, and perhaps reinventing the genre) under the title *Thirty Postcards*, each by a celebrated photographer; examples of the series are photos by Elmer Batters, Doris Kloster, and Bunny Yeager. The *Vasta Collection*, a CD-ROM, contains 300 vintage erotic postcards. In *Lost, Lonely and Vicious: Postcards from the Great Trash Films*, Michael Barson has pulled together stills from B-movies that are provocative, though hardly pornographic by most definitions. Finally, even Jacques Derrida has published *The Post Card: From Socrates to Freud and Beyond* in order to speak of voyeurism and the erotic aspects of communication; from it readers will unfortunately discover little about postcards, eroticism, or voyeurism that they do not already know.

VENDING MACHINE CARDS, CIGARETTE CARDS, AND TRADING CARDS

Mrs. John King Van Rensselaer's *The Devil's Picture Books: A History of Playing Cards* (1893) mentions images of sexual suggestiveness within a larger moral critique of cards employed for gambling. W. Gurney Benham is more concerned with political images in *Playing Cards: The History and Secrets of the Pack* but provides some information on sexualized images. Over the decades, various erotic photo-card novelties, usually incorporating pictures of scantily clad or nude women, have included playing cards, cigarette cards, matchboxes and matchbooks, photos embedded in plastic to form cups, keychains, letter openers, and so on. Collectors specialize in each of these artifacts, but only those items with large markets generate guides and handbooks, and there do not seem to be many. A well-known dealer is Bud Plant, whose *Bud Plant's Incredible Catalog* lists his inventory of novelties.

Robert C. Allen comments on cigarette cards, stereoscopic cards, and mutoscope flip cards in *Horrible Prettiness: Burlesque and American Culture*. Two classic handbooks, I. O. Evans' *Cigarette Cards and How to Collect Them* and Alfred J. Cruse's *All about Cigarette Cards* both note the appeal of the erotic type collected by smokers in the late nineteenth and early twentieth centuries. Werner Bokelberg is the authority on saucy cards sold by machines in train stations and public amusement areas beginning in the 1930s. His *Vending Machine Cards: Pin-Up Girls von Gestern* is profusely illustrated. More recently, trading cards modeled on baseball cards have become a collecting craze. In an interview with Plant's staff entitled "Bud Plant's Incredible Catalog," Stacey Taylor notes that the company's best-selling trading cards include *Painted Ladies, Bizarre Detectives, Spicy Naughty '30s* (most of them artwork rather than photos) and of course, three different Betty Page photo sets. Neil Wexler's "A Pocket Full of Pin-Ups" covers some of the more famous classic pinups reproduced in smaller card-stock formats for traders and hobbyists. More recently, publishers of porn film magazines have created trading cards of stars. Deidre Holland's card, for example, features a frontal nude on one side, and her measurements, some personal history—her Dutch nationality and her marriage to fellow star Jon Dough—and her screen credits on the other. *Adam Film World* includes a couple of dozen in selected issues for its subscribers and sells complete sets by mail order, while *Adult Video News* reports regularly on which sets are selling well.

Mark Kernes reports on the brisk exchange of cards in "Adult Industry Ogles T & A at Glamourcon II." Dealers and collectors come together in conventions like Glamourcon, there to buy, sell, and swap adult comic books, vintage photos, and classic pinups. "It may seem strange that wall calendars from the '40s and three-for-a-nickel erotic 'trading cards' could now sell for hundreds of dollars apiece," but, says Kernes, nostalgia adds zest to commerce. Collectors' motivations doubtless vary. At one end of the scale are those who collect for reasons similar to people who collect stamps or matchbooks. At the other are aficionados who admire the skill of sexual performers. Anyone doubting that Ginger Lynn, Debi Diamond, and Ashlyn Gere are not virtuoso sexual performers on a par with, say, athletes such as Joe Montana or Steffi Graf should watch their films: at their best, they bring sublimity to sexual acts, and the cards, in some dim sense, are an indication of respected prowess. *Penthouse* recently launched its own line of cards featuring monthly Pets (*Playboy* has long offered them), advertising them as collectibles in the tradition of the cigarette and baseball cards made possible by the invention of lithography; the article is Jane Girrand's "Scenes." Finally, Annie Sprinkle is marketing cards of "drag kings," porn stars, and "pleasure activists" under the title *Annie Sprinkle's Post Modern Pin-Ups Playing Cards: Pleasure Activist Playing Cards*. The deck comes with a booklet of biographies of each performer to assist in choosing roles and is now offered by the Quality Paperback Book of the Month Club. Sprinkle has also printed up some "postporn postcards" as *XXXOOO: Love and Kisses from Annie Sprinkle*. The idea has taken hold: Laura Corn's *101 Grreat Quickies*, a paperback bound with coupons depicting sexual acts (e.g., cunnilingus) that partners can exchange with each other as requests, are typical of other sex-oriented games played with cards.

GENDER DISPUTATIONS: THE MALE NUDE, THE MALE PINUP, AND THE LESBIAN PHOTOGRAPH

The male nude and the early male pinup occupy disputed territory between high and low pornography. Westerners have usually characterized the female form as more aesthetically and sexually appealing than the male, a preference doubtless fed by homophobia. Two essays by Michael Kimmelman address some of these distinctions. "The Body as Provocateur and Victim," a review of the 1990 *Figuring the Body* exhibition at the Boston Museum of Fine Arts, observes that Elsa Dorfman's photograph of a naked Allen Ginsburg reinforces the propensity to think of photographs of nude women as artistic and photographs of nude men as obscene. On the other hand, Kimmelman's "Peering into Peepholes and Finding Politics: Pornography or Feminist Bullying?," a report on the attempt by the head of the National Museum of American Art to censor "Muybridge I" by Sol LeWitt on the grounds that its "connotation" (not its intent) was "degrading" to women, discusses this inequity from the standpoint of antiporn feminist ideology. (After more than half the other artists in the show demanded that their works also be removed, the director backed down and hung the work, as reported by Barbara Gamarekian in "Closing of Art Show Is Demanded.") When Jacqueline Livingston tried to exhibit her photographs of a radical sexual consciousness at Cornell University, the controversy over the exposed penises reverberated for months. Howard Smith interviews Livingston in "Ruckus Aroused: The Male Nude Taboo."

In any case, critical attention to photographs of male nudes has become intense only recently. Margaret Walters' *The Male Nude*, spanning various visual arts, is the best general historical analysis of the subject and the most scholarly; among her observations is that male nudes usually stress hard edges, muscularity, and phallic power. She also points out that while male artists may distort or take liberties in depicting the genitalia of women, they are more scrupulous in their rendering of the phallus. *Life Class: The Academic Male Nude, 1820–1920*, edited by Stephen Boyd, surveys male nudes over a century that overlaps the invention of photography and compares the subdued eroticism of formal salon photographs with raunchier descendants; Boyd charts the erosion of reticence as evolving aesthetics loosened restraint. François de Louville's *The Male Nude: A Modern View* is a broad, competent survey of contemporary pictures drawn from a traveling exhibit. The catalog of a recent important exhibition, with a fine historical essay by Alasdair Foster, is *Behold the Man: The Male Nude in Photography*. Similarly, *The Male Nude in Photography*, the catalog for a show at the Pfeiffer Gallery in New York, features comment by the editor, Lawrence Barnes. Using the work of six photographers who deliberately challenge societal prohibitions, Robert Mapplethorpe, Lucas Samaras, John Coplans, George Dureau, Joel-Peter Witkin, and Dusan Makavejev, Melody D. Davis considers what happens when the male becomes "spectacle rather than spectator" in her excellent *The Male Nude in Contemporary Photography*, which deals, in large part, with the spatial construction of gender. A balanced feminist perspective animates "The Erotic Male Nude," by Sarah Kent, who finds that photographs can speak more directly to contemporary male and female desire than paintings and speculates at length on the positioning of the penis in various frames, because, she claims, if there is no female to dominate, the phallus is the only thing that will impress an audience. Companion volumes edited by Peter Weiermair, *Male Nudes by Women* and *The Male Nude: A Male View*, attest to the differences that women and men bring to the subject. *Women See Men*, edited by Yvonne Kalmus, Rikki Ripp, and Cheryl Wiesenfeld, is a collection of images and criticism inspired by women photographers shooting male subjects, some of whom are erotically posed.

As Peter Weiermair points out in *The Hidden Image*, a study of nineteenth- and twentieth-century photographs of nude males, gender uncertainty has traditionally made the male nude problematic. Heterosexual viewers found a degree of perversity in the "masking" of both object and origin of desire. Homosexual viewers, on the other hand, searched for cues that the images were pitched at them; the uncertainty may or may not have contributed to eroticism; desire sometimes seemed spurious. One of the more interesting attempts to grapple with signifiers of gender is Hal Fischer's approach, articulated in "Toward a Gay Semiotic," part of the splendid *Eros and Photography*, edited by Donna-Lee Phillips and Lew Thomas. Fischer has expanded his insights into *Gay Semiotics: A Photographic Study of Visual Coding among Homosexual Men*, on signs and cues expressed in dress, posture, and visual styles; numerous photos complement the text. Though it contains mostly nonexplicit examples, James Gardiner's *Who's a Pretty Boy Then? One Hundred and Fifty Years of Gay Life in Photographs* offers candid photographs of gay life with remarkable straightforwardness and sympathy.

Ostensibly directed at females, male pinups may actually be aimed at homosexuals. Although *Playgirl* might run fiction and articles geared to a female readership, for instance, the editors knew that the centerfolds of naked men held strong appeal for homosexual males and tried to adjust the advertisements carried in the magazine's pages accordingly. Angela Carter's "A Well Hung Hang-Up" suggests that women enjoy male pinups as substrates for fantasy, just as males prize pictures of women, but doubts that explicitness is essential, let alone large penises, which do not universally turn on women. She is echoed by Germaine Greer, whose "What Do We Want from Male Pin-Ups?" argues that editors need to learn what those stimuli are instead of favoring semierect members. By contrast, Christie Jenkins knows the parts she likes and soliloquizes on the objects of female voyeurism in the illustrated *A Woman Looks at Men's Buns*. Heterosexual comment on male pinups is sketchy; typical are brief and diffident passages in Mark Gabor's *The Pin-Up*. Richard Dyer's "Don't Look Now: Richard Dyer Examines the Instabilities of the Male Pin-Up" examines images of men aimed at female audiences and the reticence with which they respond. The intent of the pinup, he says, is to establish an anticipation of phallicism that can rarely be matched by any individual penis, hence, the instabilities. Since the male pinup can also appeal to gays, erotic possibilities are fixed by the gender of the viewer; Dyer draws on Margaret Walters' *The Male Nude* in its assumptions about class and power.

Early gay photographers maintained low profiles, and critics are still cautious. Estelle Jussim's *Slave to Beauty: The Eccentric Life and Controversial Career of F. Holland Day, Photographer, Publisher, Aesthete* is a tepid, timid biography of an important turn-of-the-century American photographer of homoerotic images but does discuss Day's friendship with—and photographs of—Aubrey Beardsley and Oscar Wilde. The 1975 exhibition catalog of a show mounted in the Wellesley College Museum, *The Photographic Work of F. Holland Day*, by Ellen F. Clattenberg, subordinates the male nudes to more acceptable experiments, but religious, "decadent," and homoerotic images have been collected in Day's *F. Holland Day: Suffering the Ideal*. Day's *Selected Texts and Bibliography* have been collected and edited by Verna Posever Curtis and Jane Van Nimmen. Included is Day's "Photography Applied to the Undraped Figure" (43–46), in which Day insists that there must be a reason for shooting a nude, a rationale that explains his preference for poses and settings that are pensive, pastoral, or quasi-religious.

Just before and after the turn of the century, the most common poses were "classic," a label that could justify revealing the penis to a viewer. Because prosecution was nevertheless a threat, most prints were shot anonymously. Of those who did create a recognizable body of work, the photographer most often identified with homoerotic images was without doubt the German Wilhelm von Gloeden, who took an astonishing number of male nudes in more than a dozen countries, though his most popular were those of Sicilian boys. They are often elegantly posed (with models embracing Greek columns, for instance). Widely reproduced, his prints are staples of collections of vintage gay photos. Charles Leslie's Introduction to *Wilhelm Von Gloeden, Photographer* is informative about the man and the market for such photos at the turn of the century and is devoted chiefly to Sicilian sequences. A modest, but excellent, collection is Wilhelm Von Gloeden's *Photographs of the Classic Male Nude*. Tom Waugh, the leading authority on early gay images, writes about Von Gloeden's shaping of erotic sensibilities in "The Third Body: Patterns in the Construction of the Subject in Gay Male Narrative Film." Looking at one of Von Gloeden's photographs, Waugh says that "these two bodies together predicated in turn a third body, an implied gay subject, the invisible desiring body of the producer-spectator behind the camera in front of the photograph, but rarely visualized within the frame" (141–142).

Another prolific master was George Platt Lynes, a German-turned-American fashion photographer of the 1930s and 1940s, who shot highly theatrical erotic frames. James Crump identifies many of these and some of females as well in *George Platt Lynes: Photographs from the Kinsey Institute*. One of the essays in the book, Crump's "George Platt Lynes and the Avant-Garde" (137–147) traces Platt Lynes' influence on experimental photography. The homoerotic illustrations in Platt Lynes' *Photographs 1931–1955* overlap Crump's volume somewhat, but the texts of both are valuable. Large numbers of Platt Lynes' homoerotic photographs appear in the fourth volume of *Der Mann in der Photographie* under the pseudonym "Roberto Rolf." Jack Woody has also edited some of the homoerotic photos shot by the painter Paul Cadmus, working with his fellow painter Jared French and his wife, Margaret French, in a volume entitled *Collaboration: The Photographs of Paul Cadmus, Margaret French, and Jared French*. Photographers and artists often moved in the same circles, with the former taking pictures of the latter. David Leddick's *Naked Men: Pioneering Male Nudes, 1935–1955* traces some of the permutations in pictures of Tennessee Williams, Christopher Isherwood, Yul Brynner, and others shot by Platt Lynes, Paul Cadmus, and Lincoln Kirstein (the arts patron).

The mostly formal male nudes of Minor White (1908–1976), who began shooting in the 1940s, are featured in *Minor White: Rites and Passages*. The work of one of the most talented American gay photographers appears in George Dureau's *George Dureau: New Orleans*, edited by Edward Lucie-Smith, who notes that unlike those of Robert Mapplethorpe, Dureau's images reveal the personalities of his subjects, who are physically challenged—dwarfs, cripples, or misshapen. Jeff Perrone discusses some of Duane Michaels' forays into gay eroticism in "Duane Michaels: The Self as Apparition," although Max Kozloff's Introduction to *Now Becoming Then: Photographs by Duane Michaels* is probably the most comprehensive approach to a complex sensuality. Michaels himself speaks of his intent in his volume *The Nature of Desire*, though that intent may be better illustrated in Michaels' *Homage to Cavafy: Ten Poems by Constantine Cavafy: Ten Photographs by Duane Michaels*. Artists working with male models today include Arthur Tress (*Facing Up*), Warren Truitt (*Textures*), Don Whitman (*Mountain Men*), Jim French (*Man*), Michael Huhn (*Photos*), George Machado (*Masculine*), Bruce Weber (*Bear Pond*), and Tom Bianchi (*Out of the Studio*), though the list could be extended considerably. It is worth noting that both Bianchi and Herb Ritts have published books featuring the same gay couple (who are themselves lecture-circuit advocates of same-sex marriage)—Bianchi's *Bob and Rod* and Ritts' *Duo: Photographs of Bob Paris and Rod Jackson*—in embraces. One of the functions of erotica is to domesticate passion over time, so that these reflections on gay couples and gay marriage may well advance the acceptance of gay relationships just by appearing on coffee tables. *Fun? Game: Male Models Revealed*, by Joe Lalli, with an Afterword by Paul Cadmus, fits easily on such tables.

James Smalls analyzes what he calls "fetish and fantasy" images of interracial homosexuality taken by Carl Van Vechten in the 1930s and 1940s in "Public Face, Private Thoughts: Fetish, Interracialism, and the Homoerotic in Some Photographs by Carl Van Vechten." Kobena Mercer considers the aesthetic, cultural, and racial implications of explicit images of the black male nude, with particular reference to the depiction of the phallus in a series of essays: "Skin Head Sex Thing: Racial Difference and the Homoerotic Imaginary," "Imaging the Black Man's Sex," and "True Confessions: A Discourse on Images of Black Male Sexuality" (the latter was coauthored with Isaac Julien). In examining the notion that "anatomy is truth," Mercer's criticism centers on Robert Mapplethorpe's photographs of black men. "Just Looking for Trouble: Robert Mapplethorpe and Fantasies of Race" asks whether Mapplethorpe's photos of large black penises "reinforce or undermine racist myths about black sexuality" (103). Mercer first thinks that the photographs do reproduce racial stereotypes, then decides that Mapplethorpe was exploding clichés: from that perspective the bodies seem starkly different in their nonwhiteness and intense sexuality. In "Reading Racial Fetishism: The Photographs of Robert Mapplethorpe" (partly a revision of the earlier "Imaging the Black Man's Sex"), Mercer recognizes Mapplethorpe's photos of "beautiful black men" as maps of "the political unconscious we all inhabit as embodied subjects of identity, desire, and history" (329).

Toward the end of the last century, pinups masquerading as bodybuilding images began to appear in gay subcultures. These featured muscular males clad only in what was called a "posing strap" to cover genitals; they circulated as single pinups or as portfolios, less often as magazines or bound volumes. The best introduction to this genre is David Chapman's *Adonis: The Male Physique Pin-Up, 1879–1940*. Many such photos employed sailor themes and images, a fact noted in Tom Waugh's "Photography, Passion, and Power" but examined in detail in Thomas Sokolowski's *The Sailor 1930–45: The Image of an American Demigod*. In "Lurid! Licentious! Collectible! The Flip Side of the 1940's and 50's," William Grimes talks with William O'Connor of New York's Wessel O'Connor Gallery, which has held several exhibits of physique photos. O'Connor says that during the 1940s and 1950s, some twelve to eighteen studios in California printed circumspect male nudes until the Supreme Court ruled in 1966 that a full frontal male figure was not in itself obscene. Glen Mannisto's "1950s Male Nude Photography," a review of the major decade survey show at Bookbeat Gallery in Oak Park, Michigan, featuring work by the Western Photography Guild and Bruce of Los Angeles (Bruce Bellas), argues that the latter exercised a strong influence on Robert Mapplethorpe. *Bruce of Los Angeles*, edited by Jim Dolinksy, reproduces examples of Bruce of Los Angeles' work; Dolinksy traces the history of Bellas' studio. Bruno of Hollywood published discreet male nudes mixed in with female studies in *Figure Photography*, one of several volumes to display a prolific talent. Another popular Californian was Bill Hillgardner, whose *Physique* collects his bodybuilder photos. Increased tolerance in the 1960s led to the disappearance of the posing strap; thereafter, the male model could sport an erect or semierect penis. "Hard-On Art: A History of Physique Art from the Forbidden 40s to the Explicit 80s" by Jerry Mills and Dwight Russ charts this shift. Useful information on the Athletic Model Guild can also be found in John W. Rowberry's *Gay Video: A Guide to Erotica* and in Paul Alcuin Siebenand's *The Beginnings of Gay Cinema in Los Angeles: The Industry and the Audience*. Even better for general readers is Richard Dyer's *Now You See It: Studies on Lesbian and Gay Film*, which explores the photographic industry that nurtured gay cinema. (For female bodybuilders, see **Body Building** in Chapter 9.)

Most surveys of male nudes attempt to deal with homoerotic appeal, but Allen Ellenzweig's *The Homoerotic Photograph* is the most straightforward; it is a critical history of artists from Eakins to Mapplethorpe. Emmanuel Cooper has recently updated *Fully Exposed: The Male Nude in Photography*, a sumptuously illustrated volume whose text speaks frankly of homoerotic modern and postmodern images by artists such as Lea Andrews, Diane Arbus, Imogen Cunningham, Frank Eugene, Yvonne Gregory, Annie Leibovitz, Robert Mapplethorpe, George Platt Lynes, Arthur Tress, Bruce Weber, and many other Americans and Europeans. The need to preserve what remains of hundreds of gay photos that have been lost is the topic of "The Old Erotica," by G. Duay. Two essays by Tom Waugh analyze vintage gay photos and films. The broader of the two is "A Heritage of Pornography," while "Photography, Passion, and Power" covers artifacts of the 1940s; both stress the weight that images have acquired as historical markers of identity. Waugh's book, *Hard to Imagine: Gay Male Eroticism in Photography and Film from Their Beginnings to Stonewall*, in a sense supersedes these essays; it is a splendid resource, far more gritty, explicit, and honest than more circumspect histories and absolutely indispensable to the scholar.

These and other historical documents indicate that unlike gay porn, photographs of lesbian encounters frequently slipped through legal screens because they were assumed to target heterosexual male desire and because they seemed far less threatening to the male order of society. If one accepts the view that hard-core pornography constitutes the "real," that is, the truly authentic, discourse of sexuality in our culture, then images and terms function to fix categories such as race, ethnicity, gender, class, and desire. But the matter is far from simple. What makes those categories authentic? In considering photographs depicting lesbian sexuality, it is instructive to look at a series of coffee-table books that became popular in America during the 1970s. These were elegant, glossy volumes of women in erotic embraces, popular because they were ersatz couplings satisfying to a wide range of viewers comfortable with erotica, or what we have called high pornography. Here, close-ups of genitalia are subordinated to generic caresses. Since the subjects were female, arranged by male photographers, their homoeroticism was not threatening, as might have been the case if the models were male or the photographers women. A far from exhaustive list might include M. Richard Kirstel's *Pas De Deux*; J. Frederick Smith's *Sappho: The Art of Loving Women* and *Sappho by the Sea*; Wingate Paine's *Mirror of Venus*, with essays by Francoise Sagan and Federico Fellini; Peter Barry's *The Love of Two Women*; Ron Adams and Julia Adams' *Woman Times Two: A Photo Essay*; and Roy Volkmann's *Two Women in Love*.

Recent criticism of such images deals with the semiotics of gender difference, a larger issue than simply putting female bodies into frames made familiar by heterosexual preferences. In short, say lesbian critics, lesbian pornography, in order to be authentic, must escape the imprisoning effects of the "male gaze" and the tropes of culturally sanctioned erotica. Is it possible for a photograph of a woman's body to be so coded that the viewer can tell whether the figure is intended as the object of desire for other women rather than for men? That question leads to considerations of "spectatorship," or how different gender audiences respond to images. Readers of *On Our Backs, Bad Attitude: A Lesbian*

Sex Magazine, and other lesbian sex zines can search for hints in the open-crotch displays, which at first glance look identical to centerfolds aimed at males but which on closer inspection may reveal different visual cues. Jan Zita Grover's "Dykes in Context: Some Problems in Minority Representation" outlines these and other issues for the lesbian photographer. Perhaps the most admirable and ambitious photographic attempt to undermine gender conventions is *Eye to Eye: Portraits of Lesbians*, by "JEB," the professional signature of Joan E. Biren. An artist who clearly sees "fashion" as an opportunity, Biren offers nude and erotic studies of lesbians in situations that startle, such as a telephone linewoman working topless. Given the subject and the intent, it is difficult to characterize (perhaps the real point) the book, save to say that it represents genuine experimentation with the presentation of the lesbian body, which is depicted in a variety of poses and settings, some traditional, some not, that are designed to evoke "difference." It is a conscious attempt to escape from the body types and styles prized by a dominant heterosexual culture and to assert sensuality that can be understood "outside" that context. Ultimately, however, viewers must register the meaning of the images themselves.

The Passionate Camera: Photography and Bodies of Desire, edited by Deborah Bright, reproduces and comments on photographs featuring sex radicals and queer eroticism. Richard Dyer draws on Joan Biren's work in *The Matter of Images: Essays on Representations*. In Chapter 4, "Seen to be Believed: Some Problems in the Representation of Gay People as Typical," Dyer tries to identify cues or signs of gayness, since sexual orientation is otherwise not visible, in an attempt to establish typologies. Dyer observes that gay types are connected "to other enormously complex sign systems, for example, competing conceptions of nature and mythologies such as Christianity or the vampire tale" (50). *Stolen Glances: Lesbians Take Photographs*, a historical grouping by Tessa Boffin and Jean Fraser, depicts lesbian lifestyles from Alice B. Toklas and Gertrude Stein to the age of AIDS. Sexual tension animates Cathy Cade's *A Lesbian Photo Album: The Lives of Seven Lesbian Feminists*, which also ranges widely across subjects and contexts both domestic and public. The lesbian collective called Kiss and Tell has produced *Drawing the Line: Lesbian Sexual Politics on the Wall (Kiss and Tell)*, which reproduces forty explicit photos from a traveling show, with comment. Persimmon Blackbridge, Lizard Jones, and Susan Stewart, three members of Kiss and Tell, have assembled the wonderfully titled *Her Tongue on My Theory: Images, Essays and Fantasies*, which contains essays and images challenging stereotypes of lesbians, especially those advanced by antiporn feminists. The most helpful volume for scholars looking for information on specific artists is *Nothing but the Girl: The Blatant Lesbian Image, a Portfolio and Exploration of Lesbian Erotic Photography*, edited by Susie Bright and Jill Posener, who append biographies to print captions. Represented are Honey Lee Cottrell, Tee Corinne, Morgan Gwenwald, Della Grace, Jill Posener, and many others. Perhaps the most remarkable thing about *The Wild Good:*

Lesbian Photographs and Writings on Love, edited by Beatrix Gates, is that its eroticism has made it a staple of the Quality Paperback Book of the Month Club.

The doyenne of American lesbian photographers, Tee Corinne, has been interviewed by Alice Henry in "Images of Lesbian Sexuality [an Interview with Tee Corinne]." Here Corinne speaks of the experience she strives to capture and the need for women to understand their sexuality. To the charge that feminist genital imagery encourages female objectification, Corinne replies, "That's hiding from ourselves." She says that women cannot avoid their own sexuality or its beauty, pleasure, and responsibilities. She wants "squishy and beautiful" images that she contrasts with the "soft romantic" (and ersatz) sapphic photos of British photographer David Hamilton; she wants her work "to have that kind of texture and presence of wrapping around you and becoming an intense present experience, rather than a voyeuristic experience, where you are over here looking at something over there" (10). Corinne earned her credentials by publishing *Lesbian Images in the Fine Arts*, a survey of considerable depth. Her own photographs of women, remarkable for their close-ups of vulvas, can be found as illustrations sandwiched between the poems of Jacqueline Lapidus in *Yantras of Womanhood*. Those unfamiliar with Corinne's work might look first at the sequence of two women sitting on a park bench with their hands under each other's skirts, photographs characterized by a sensibility both aesthetic and authoritative, in *Erotic by Nature: A Celebration of Life, of Love, and of Our Wonderful Bodies*, edited by David Steinberg. As factors in creating eroticism, says Corinne in the Henry interview, elegance and attention to relationships have merit, "but I think it is important to focus on sexuality" because there is such a "hunger for information."

Gillian Rodgerson's "Lesbian Erotic Explorations" examines an assortment of lesbian erotica but focuses on the photos of Della Grace, whose *Love Bites* (1991) is aimed at a female audience of lesbians who feel excluded by the women's movement and condemned for their sexuality. Grace says, "I think pornography is a very subjective term that's very charged politically and I don't set out to take erotica and I don't set out to do pornography. I'm happy if someone gets an erotic buzz" (277). U.S. Customs seized *Love Bites* when the domestic publisher imported a copy from England, presumably because it ventures into the world of lesbian sadomasochism. In any case, the demand for explicit images is soaring, as attested by M. G. Soares' *Butch/Femme*, an anthology of work by five lesbian photographers.

FETISH PHOTOGRAPHS

(For works with significant fetish illustrations, see **Fetishes** in Chapter 9, especially Edkins and Jablow, Fontanel, Gilmore, Harkel, Kroll, Lacey and Morgan, Moreck, and Woodward. Most sources devoted to a single fetish, such as the vast number of books and magazines featuring breasts, are merely compilations of photographs with no significant commentary or context; those are ignored here.)

In "Photography and Fetish," an influential essay, Christian Metz argues that the still photograph, unlike the motion picture, has itself become a fetish because of the former's greater capacity for objectification (Metz suggests that film cannot be fetish—as a surrogate for the thing itself—because it is a narrative form and in that sense nonartifactual). Taking a cue from anthropological studies of remote tribes convinced that cameras steal souls, Metz suggests that photographs freeze the living into postures of death, so that subjects are "dead for having been seen" (85). Thus, though hardly an airtight taxonomy, since virtually any photograph can be fetishistic, fetishistic genres include frames in which sexuality arises from singularities of body, costume, or pose. In "The Pleasures of Looking: The Attorney General's Commission on Pornography versus Visual Images," Carole S. Vance points out that the commission focused on the most fetishistic and sadomasochistic photos as an excuse to condemn all sexual images.

The vintage prints in *Wheels and Curves: Erotic Photographs of the Twenties*, a compilation of photos of buffed bare women and highly polished automobiles, attest to an early understanding that the car, in its guise as mobile bedroom, would alter Western sexual mores forever. Here, according to compilers W. Honscheidt and Uwe Scheid, the automobile serves as sexual fetish. Michael Koetzle and Uwe Scheid have collected turn-of-the-century erotic photos of underdressed women smoking in *Feu d'Amour: Seductive Smoke* in order to discuss the cigarette as prop and fetish. *L'Amour fou: Photography and Surrealism*, by Rosalind Kraus and Jane Livingston, with an essay by Dawn Ades, chronicles eroticism in surrealistic photography. Robert Benayoun's *Erotique du Surréalisme*, noting that surrealism toyed with fetishes as keys to experience, provides examples from motion pictures and still photographs. J. K. Potter, a modern surrealist, manipulates genitalia to render them explicitly symbolic; the photo-essay "Potter" offers a sampling, more of which can be found in his *Horripilations: The Art of J. K. Potter*. Joani Blank has collected thirty-two color photos by various photographers (including Tee Corinne) in an effort to show the amazing varieties of women's genitalia, all of them rendered in close-ups of great beauty in *Femalia*. Though not quite a semiotic text, the volume indicates the enormous variation in vulvic contours. Scholars might wish to contrast the nooks and crannies of these genital landscapes with the clefts and folds found in centerfolds of men's magazines.

Lingerie has always figured prominently in photography, and the number of books and magazines given over to pictures of women modeling lingerie is beyond number. Gilles Néret has constructed a photographic history of women so clad in *1000 Dessous: A History of Lingerie*; although it has no commentary, the photos illustrate an amazing variety of costumes over many decades. Historically significant also is *Petit Catalogue des Fetichismes*, a collection that includes pre-twentieth-century women in drawers, pantaloons, and chemises from the great Bourgeron archive; most are European. Where lingerie informs desire, much depends on the cachet of the models. Some are stiff, runway mannequins, but others fall easily into the dreamy poses that most *couturiers* want. Traditionally, lingerie models have been paid more than other clotheshorses, and the folklore surrounding them is extensive: photographers prefer to shoot lingerie frames just as the model is beginning to menstruate, so that the breasts will be fuller; studios stock flesh-colored Band-Aids handy to cover nipples so they will not protrude through fabric, a reversal of the ancient practice at strip-show theaters, where stagehands filled trays with ice that the performers could use to erect their nipples before going onstage; lingerie models carry tissues to wear inside sheer panties, so as to mask pubic hair and reduce the necessity of retouching the photographs; models cross their ankles so as to part the buttocks and thus make derrieres look rounder or arch their backs in order to lift the breasts outward, and so on. Dozens of lingerie photographers have published books of such "secrets." Perhaps the best is *Erotic Lingerie*, by the accomplished glamour lensman Peter Barry, who served as mentor to a generation of glamour and fashion photographers in the 1950s and 1960s. The social history of women's underwear, as women progress from subordinate to more equal status, is the subject of Mitchell Gray and Mary Kennedy's *The Lingerie Book*, which is illustrated sensuously.

If styles in lingerie evolve, so do the ways in which they are displayed, says Michael Gross in "Lingerie Catalogues: Changing Images," a look at a genre of soft-core porn that has riveted adolescents since Sears and Roebuck first sent catalogs through the mail. The revolutionary realism—as opposed to the usual frozen artificiality—of the women photographed by Guy Bourdin for Bloomingdale's *Sighs and Whispers* catalog of 1976 has made it a collector's item,[1] but similar shifts have occurred even in Montgomery Ward catalogs, which experimented briefly in the 1970s with revealing undie ads. Rosetta Brooks maps the "spaces of erotic encounter" in Bourdin's photos in "Sighs and Whispers in Bloomingdale's: A Review of a Bloomingdale Mail-Order Catalogue for Their Lingerie Department." "Stephanie's Secret" is a photo-essay on the reigning queen of lingerie models, Stephanie Seymour, known to millions as the woman in the Victoria's Secret catalogs; her "look," her poise, her posture, and her fondness for rock stars etched templates for dozens of other models. The best single source of information is the "Lingerie" issue of *American Photo*; historical essays range across craftspeople as diverse as Bruno of Hollywood and Sante D'Orazco, the latter the photographer of Victoria's Secret catalogs.

Bondage, discipline, flagellation, and sadomasochism have generated vast numbers of photographs. Serge Nazarieff's *Jeus de Dames Cruelles: Photographies 1850–1960* draws on the collections of Alexander Dupouy and Gerald de Reinich-Cessac to sample a century's fetish images; considerable numbers from the American studio of Irving Klaw indicate a brisk international traffic. The majority depict women engaged in bondage and spanking. (See also **Images**

and Themes in Chapter 11, especially Bellow, Fuchs and Kind, Haverly, and Schertel, for books that contain photographs along with paintings.) The anonymously edited *Painful Memories* reproduces vintage S/M and fetish (bondage, enemas, flagellation, etc.) photos, some from Kinsey Institute archives. Edward Reynolds pulls many anonymous European prints together to punctuate his reflections on *Der Flagellantismus in der Photographie*. Friedrich Thelen has collected photographs of whipping from the 1950s in *Das Verhalten der Flagellanten in Realitat und Phantasie*. Interspersed with narratives and reminiscences of the subjects, the frames feature male and female "victims," some of them American.

More than a hundred of Irving Klaw's photo-illustrated circulars, called *Irving Klaw, "The Pin-up King" Catalogs*, are prized by collectors. Issue number 2 of *The Betty Pages: The Magazine Dedicated to Tease* contains a feature entitled "Irving Klaw, Emperor of Tease." Volume I of *The Betty Pages Annual* contains several chapters on Klaw, notably "Tease on Trial," which recounts testimony before the Kefauver Committee. Bélier Press has reproduced most of the pictures and photographs of Irving Klaw: these include enormous numbers of prints of women in bondage and discipline roles, in boxing scenarios, in skimpy fetish garb, in striptease sequences, and in photo-narratives from conventional to bizarre. Bélier Press has published the two-volume *Amateur Bondage*; the five-volume *Bizarre Classix*; the four-volume *Bizarre Fotos: From the Archives of Irving Klaw* (more than 1,000 images); and the four-volume *Bizarre Katalogs* issued by Klaw and other publishers. All have been compiled and often annotated by J. B. Rund, an authority on erotic imagery in the first half of the twentieth century. A web browser programmed for "Irving Klaw" or "Movie Star News" (Klaw's 14th Street shop in Manhattan during the 1940s and 1950s) will pull up quite a lot of websites, some of which sell copies of Klaw photos and films. A more specialized collection, drawn, in large part, from the Bélier Press archive, is *Photographies de John Willie*, which records the artist's obsessions with bizarre outfits, poses, and scenarios.

The encyclopedic, twelve-volume *Diva Obsexion*, edited by Riccardo Morrocchi and his colleagues, reproduces fetishistic images of women from all media. Essays by Morrocchi and Stefano Piselli treat fetish models of various nationalities in their *The Golden Age of Exotic Gals: Sultry Strippers and Fetish Models*, which is concerned mostly with photography of the 1940s and 1950s. Popular media provide the images for *Glamour Girls of 1943*, a CD-ROM heavy on images of women in bra and panties, mild bondage, wrestling, and other fetishized activities. Eric Kroll has shot women in leather, corsets, spandex, net, stiletto heels, stockings, and rubber for his recent *Fetish Girls*, a companion volume to his *Fetish Tapes*; many other fetish images by Kroll have been gathered in Kroll's *Beauty Parade*, a compilation of his photographs (see **Fetish Films** in Chapter 13). Although Kroll insists that he does not know much about sex, he thinks the photographs help give sexuality meaning. Kelly Klein has gathered fetish photos of well-known models shot by well-known photographers in *Under World*; Anne Rice comments on the iconography of the shocking, beautiful, and erotic images. One collection of the late Elmer Batters' photographs of women in stockings has been edited by Eric Kroll as *From the Tip of the Toes to the Top of the Hose*, and another, similar in its focus on lingerie and legs, has been edited by Dian Hanson as *Elmer Batters: Legs That Dance to Elmer's Tune*; both Kroll and Hanson provide brief, but astute, comment on one of the most prolific of fetish photographers, although it is not always clear whether it was stockings, knees, legs, or undepiliated labia that intrigued Batters. Steve Diet Goedde comments on posed and theatrical models sporting leather, latex, spandex, and other accessories prized by bondage and discipline enthusiasts in *The Beauty of Fetish*.

Bizarre tastes inform Charles Gatewood's *Forbidden Photographs*, whose subjects are people engaged in ritualistic fetishes. Gatewood also collaborated with William Burroughs on a volume of erotic freaks entitled *Sidetripping*. Three volumes by Michael A. Rosen, *A Sexual Magic: The S-M Photographs, Sexual Portraits: Photographs of Radical Sexuality*, and the aptly titled *Sexual Art: Photographs That Test the Limits*, are straight-on treatments of transvestites, sadomasochists, leather-wearers, and other fetishists, presented without apology or justification, though with more than a little exhibitionism on the part of the subjects. As is so often the case with erotic visual genres, the photos invite the viewer's complicity; the subjects occupy environments in which public display is assumed and accepted. Doris Kloster, editor of the zine *FAD*, has shot bizarre subjects for her semidocumentary *Doris Kloster: Photographs*, which captures the rituals of sadomasochism and cross-dressing at balls, dances, and other exhibitionist spaces. Her second volume, *Forms of Desire*, explores similar terrain. The poor design of Grace Lau's *Grace Lau: A Retrospective: Adults in Wonderland*, a volume of her photos of male strippers, cross-dressers, and S/M enthusiasts, mutes the force of this talented artist; however, the often bizarre images are always striking. Michael Grumley and Ed Gallucci explore similar subcultures in *Hard Corps: Studies in Leather and Sadomasochism*. The ambiguity of intent and execution, as in the photographs of Robert Mapplethorpe, sometimes makes it difficult to decide whether the images should be classified as erotic or emetic.

Finally, any collector will have run across books of photographs of the sort usually published in magazines but gathered into volumes by marginal publishers during the 1960s and 1970s. They have become collectors' items. An example is James Bellah's two-volume *Anal and Oral Love*, but there are many others.

DOCUMENTARY PHOTOGRAPHS

Some excursions into the bizarre, especially those that involve clothing or body modification, shade into ethnography. The photographer most sensitive to gender-bending is Nan Goldin. Her *The Other Side* collects her photographs of transvestites and transsexuals exhibited at the Pace-McGill Gallery (New York City) in 1993, a show praised because it avoided the trivialization of cross-dressing rampant in other media. *The Other Side* looks unflinchingly at transvestites and transsexuals in erotic fantasies that reveal their attempts to transcend gender. Goldin calls the illustrations from a Whitney Museum of Art exhibit (held from 30 October 1996 to 5 January 1997) a "diary," as if this great voyeur/recorder of cultural and sexual transformations were shooting pages in a journal. *I'll Be Your Mirror*, the book version of the exhibit, plumbs the mysteries of relationships that Goldin thinks appear in photographs of bodies. Some of Goldin's pictures also appear in *The American Trip*, edited by Philip Monk, the catalog of a show featuring the work of Larry Clark, Goldin, Cady Noland, and Richard Prince (the other three venture into different erotic forms). Jeanette Jones' photographs of pre- and postoperative transsexuals, some of them posed explicitly, have been published as *Walk on the Wild Side*.

Performers who appear nude have always attracted photojournalists because of the erotic tension that nakedness in public heightens. Probably the most insightful is Marilyn Futterman's *Dancing Naked in the Material World*, which catches dancers in motion and repose in Atlanta; Futterman was herself a waitress in a "titty bar," working sporadically from 1979 until 1992 to get close to the performers, who range from veteran ecdysiasts to working mothers and all of whom speak of their working conditions as well as their aspirations, defeats, and triumphs. Susan Meiselas' gritty and incisive *Carnival Strippers* focuses on performers in "girl shows" in New England state fairs between 1973 and 1975. Futterman emphasizes the humanity of her subjects; Meiselas captures the interaction between dancers and blue-collar audiences. Anyone who does not appreciate the class distinctions inherent in all forms of pornography, in particular, this kind of performance, will find Meiselas' photos instructive. Craig Morey's *Studio Nudes*, which poses strippers against the angles of studio backdrops instead of within the ecology of the stage, is notable for the illustrations' stark texture, a surface gray rather than provocative. Morey's lens freezes bodies that ordinarily would be exciting in motion. Michael Read sifts through the recently discovered archive of a Los Angeles photographer who took pictures of burlesque queens and go-go dancers of the 1960s in "The Life and Times of Raoul Gradvohl." Gradvohl documented styles of naked dance as they were fading from a decade that equated freedom with the motion of breasts in space; his photos constitute an archive of the ephemeral.

More idiosyncratic are the paintings, drawings, and photographs by Jean-Paul Goude in *Jungle Fever*, a traverse through storefront theaters and adult arcades of Manhattan. Goude's camera is relentless in its exposure, though most of his subjects manage to co-opt it in some way. Among the most stunning photographs are those of Kellie Everts, the "Christian Stripper," of Honeysuckle Divine, who could "smoke" cigarettes with her vagina, and of the androgynous Grace Jones. Goude's sequences of "beaver shots" (female pubic hair) are less interesting. The photographs in Joyce Baronio's marvelous *42nd Street Studio*, for which she invited male and female sex performers to sit for her camera, capture them in moments of vulnerable beauty; the expressiveness demonstrates that Baronio is easily the most compassionate of the photographers working with such subjects, a point made by critic Linda Nochlin, who contributes a fine Introduction to the volume. In "Tripping the Light Fantastic: Joyce Baronio on 42nd Street," Edmund White observes that "though almost all of [Baronio's] recent pictures portray sex performers and strippers, none of them is pornographic. Though each model seems to be releasing a fantasy as if it were a pheromone, the work is in no sense surrealistic. And though the models might be considered exotic, the pictures resolutely avoid sensationalism. They are noble, often tender, and always admiring studies of healthy bodies and entranced faces" (35). Any one of Baronio's images would grace a wall in any museum.

By contrast, Allan Porter's pictures in Andre Gelpke's *Sex-Theatre: Eine fotographische Documentation mit einer Einleitung von Allan Porter*, which offers studies of variously gendered performers from various countries, including the United States, have a sensational cast; their explicitness undermines Gelpke's textual reflections. Worth noting also are the photographs in Roswell Angier's *". . . A Kind of Life": Conversations in the Combat Zone*, whose text offers empathic portraits of sex workers in Boston's "Combat Zone." The result of a study funded by the New York State Council on the Arts, Eric Kroll's *Sex Objects* combines photographs, text, and extensive interviews with women who service customers in massage parlors. Jerry Yulsman's *Oh, Copenhagen!* records an American journalist's exploration of the Danish sex scene at the end of the 1960s. Yulsman's camera documents the schizophrenic lifestyle of Scandinavian hippies: they perform in sex shows to support communes where they raise children and strive for satisfying lifestyles. Justice Howard's "PornARTraphy," by a photographer of porn performers, speaks of his attempts to turn their bodies into art. Ian Gittler's photographs of well-known video porn performers, published as *Pornstar*, present his subjects working on sets, but also in repose, exhilaration, comic moments, and anguished reflections; the second thoughts of the burned-out photographer, who once shot stills for producers, depict the industry as exploitive and callous. Gittler's text, however, is neither naive nor cynical; he chronicles drug-use, tedium, tawdriness, and the human cost of what is often an unpleasant business, but he clearly likes the performers, and befriended many of them. In "The Taboo Artist: Andres Serrano Goes for the XXX," Richard Goldstein reviews Serrano's explicit photographs for his show at the Paula Cooper Gallery in New York. The images include males ejaculating, transsexuals displaying their fabricated breasts, grandmothers enjoying intercourse, a female banker stroking the erect penis of her horse, and various genders (sometimes improbably) copulating.

NOTE

1. Marvin Traub, former chairman of Bloomingdale's, says that these were the "kind of photos that, today, could get your National Endowment grant dropped. The taste level was so high, however, that [the project] convinced me." Marvin Traub, with Tom Tei-

cholz, *Like No Other Store . . . The Bloomingdale's Legend and the Revolution in American Marketing* (New York: Times Books, 1993), pp. 148–151.

REFERENCES

Adam, Hans Christian. "Die Erotische Daguerrotypie." *Das Aktfoto: Ansichten vom Körper im fotografischen Zeitalter: Ästhetik, Geschichte, Ideologie*, ed. Michael Köhler and Gisela Barche. Munich: Stadtmuseum, 1985, pp. 56–61.

Adams, Ron, and Julia Adams. *Woman Times Two: A Photo Essay*. Sausalito, CA: Astarte Enterprises, 1975.

Adam Film World and Adult Video Guide. Los Angeles: Knight Publishing, 1968–.

Adult Video News. Upper Darby, PA: AVN, 1983–1996; Van Nuys, CA, 1996–.

Aletti, Vince. "Arrested Development: Larry Clark Pins Adolescence to the Wall." *Village Voice*, 13 October 1997, pp. 99–100.

Allen, Albert Arthur. *Alo Nudes*. Oakland, CA: Allen Art Studios, [*Amateur* 1918?].

Allen, Robert C. *Horrible Prettiness: Burlesque and American Culture*. Chapel Hill: University of North Carolina Press, 1991.

Alpert, Merry. *Dirty Windows*. New York: Scalo, 1995.

Amateur Bondage, comp. J. B. Rund. 2 vols. New York: Bélier Press, 1978.

Angier, Roswell. *". . . A Kind of Life": Conversations in the Combat Zone*. Danbury, NH: Addison House, 1976.

Aratow, Paul. *One Hundred Years of Erotica: A Photographic Portfolio of Mainstream American Subculture, 1845–1945*. San Francisco: Straight Arrow Books, 1971.

Ashford, Rod, ed. *Erotique: Masterpieces of Erotic Photography*. London: Carlton Books, 1998.

Bailey, David, ed. *The Naked Eye: Great Photographs of the Nude*, with text by Martin Harrison. London: Barrie and Jenkins, 1987.

Barnes, Lawrence, ed. *The Male Nude in Photography*. Waitsfield, VT: Vermont Crossroads Press, 1980.

Baronio, Joyce. *42nd Street Studio*. New York: Pyxidium Press, 1980.

Barr, Candy [Juanita Slusher]. Photo sets. Photographic Archives, Kinsey Institute for Sex, Gender, and Reproduction. University of Indiana, Bloomington.

Barry, Peter. *The Art of Erotic Photography*. New York: Crescent, 1983.

———. *Erotic Lingerie*. Guildford, Surrey, England: Arlington House/Crown, 1984.

———. *The Love of Two Women*. N.p.: Eurasia Distributors, 1979.

Barson, Michael, ed. *Lost, Lonely and Vicious: Postcards from the Great Trash Films*. New York: Pantheon, 1988.

Bartosch, Gunter. *Der Akt von Damals: Der Erotik in der frühen Photographie aus der privaten Sammlung Ernst und Gunter Bartosch*. Munich: Herbig, 1976.

Basch, Peter. *The Nude as Form and Figure*. New York: Amphoto, 1966.

Batters, Elmer. *Elmer Batters: Legs That Dance to Elmer's Tune*, ed. Dian Hanson. Cologne: Benedikt Taschen, 1997.

———. *From the Tip of the Toes to the Top of the Hose*, ed. Eric Kroll. Berlin: Benedikt Taschen Verlag, 1995.

———. *Thirty Postcards*. Berlin: Benedikt Taschen Verlag, 1995.

Baty, S. Paige. *American Monroe: The Making of a Body Politic*. Berkeley: University of California Press, 1995.

Baumann, Arnaud. *Carnet D'Adresses*. Paris: Le Dernier Terrain Vague, 1984.

Bazin, Andre. "Entomology of the Pin-Up Girl." *What Is Cinema?* Berkeley: University of California Press, 1967, pp. 158–162.

Bellah, James. *Anal and Oral Love*. 2 vols. Los Angeles: Ultima Books, 1970.

Bellocq, E. J. *Storyville Portraits: Photographs from the New Orleans Red Light District, circa 1912*. New York: Museum of Modern Art, 1970.

Benayoun, Robert. *Erotique du Surréalisme*. Paris: J. J. Pauvert, 1965.

Benham, W. Gurney. *Playing Cards: The History and Secrets of the Pack*. London: Ward Lock, 1931.

Benzel, Kathryn N. "The Body as Art: Still Photographs of Marilyn Monroe," *Journal of Popular Culture*, 25:2 (Fall 1991): 1–29.

Berelowitz, Jo-Anne. "L.A.'s Museum of Contemporary Art and the Body of Marilyn Monroe." *Genders*, 17 (Fall 1993): 22–40.

Bernard, Ruth. *The Eternal Body: A Collection of Fifty Nudes*. Carmel, CA: Photography West Graphics, 1986; rpt. San Francisco: Chronicle, 1994.

Bernard of Hollywood. *Bernard of Hollywood's Pin-Ups*. Los Angeles: Corel, 1995.

———. *Pin-Ups: A Step Beyond, a Portfolio of Breathtaking Beauties*. Hollywood: Bernard of California, 1950.

Betty Page: Private Peeks. 4 vols. New York: Bélier Press, 1980.

Betty Page: Queen of Pin-Up. Berlin: Benedikt Taschen Verlag, 1995.

Betty Page in Bondage. New York: Mutrix [Irving Klaw], 1960–1961.

Betty Page Outdoors. New York: Modern Age, n.d. [1950s].

The Betty Page Portfolio. Oregon City, OR: Port Kar Industries, 1992.

Betty Pages Annual. 2 vols. New York: Black Cat Books, 1991, 1994.

The Betty Pages: The Magazine Dedicated to Tease. New York: Pure Imagination/Black Cat, 1988–.

Betty Scouts of America. Fan Club run by Steve Brewster, 2641 South 53d St., Kansas City, KS 66106.

Bianchi, Tom. *Bob and Rod*. New York: St. Martin's, 1994.

———. *Out of the Studio*. New York: St. Martin's, 1991.

Bilderlexicon der Erotik, Ein bibliographisches und biographisches Nachschlagewerk, eine Kunst- und Literaturgeschichte für die Gebiete der erotischen Belletristik . . . von der Antike zur Gegenwart. 6 vols. Vienna and Hamburg: Verlag für Kulturforschung, 1928–31, 1963. Edited by Leo Schidrowitz: I: *Kulturgeschichte*; II: *Literatur und Kunst*; III: *Sexualwissenschaft*; IV: *Ergänzungsband*. Edited by Armand Mergen: V and VI: *Sexualforschung: Stichwort und Bild*.

Bizarre Classix, comp. J. B. Rund. 5 vols. New York: Bélier Press, 1977–1980.

Bizarre Fotos: From the Archives of Irving Klaw, comp. J. B. Rund. 4 vols. New York: Bélier Press, 1978.

Bizarre Katalogs, comp. J. B. Rund. 4 vols. New York: Bélier Press, 1979.

Blank, Joani, ed. *Femalia*. San Francisco: Down There Press, 1993.

The Blatant Image: A Magazine of Feminist Photography, ed. Tee Corinne. Sunny Valley OR: 1981–1985.

Bloch, Iwan (aka Eugen Dühren, aka Albert Hagen). *Anthropological Studies in the Strange Sexual Practices of All Races in All Ages*, trans. Keene Wallis. Berlin: 1902; rpt. New York: Anthropological Press, 1933.

Bloomingdale's. *Sighs and Whispers*. New York: New York Times, 1976.

Boffin, Tessa, and Jean Fraser, eds. *Stolen Glances: Lesbians Take Photographs.* San Francisco: Harper, 1991.

Bogdanovich, Peter. *The Killing of the Unicorn: Dorothy Stratten, 1960–1980.* New York: Morrow, 1984.

Bokelberg, Werner. *Vending Machine Cards: Pin-Up Girls von Gestern.* Dortmund: Harenberg, 1980.

Booth, Pat. *Self Portrait.* London: Quartet Books, 1983.

Boussel, Patrice. *Erotisme Galanterie au 19e Siècle.* Paris: Berger-Levrault, 1979.

Bovis, Marcel, and François Saint-Julien. *Nus d'autrefois, 1850–1900.* Paris: Arts et Metiers Graphiques, 1953.

Boyd, Stephen, ed. *Life Class: The Academic Male Nude, 1820–1920.* London: Éditions Aubrey Walter/GMP, 1989.

Brandt, Bill. *Bill Brandt: Behind the Camera: Photographs 1928–1983.* New York: Aperture, 1985.

Bright, Deborah, ed. *The Passionate Camera: Photography and Bodies of Desire.* New York: Routledge, 1998.

Bright, Susie, and Jill Posener, eds. *Nothing but the Girl: The Blatant Lesbian Image, a Portfolio and Exploration of Lesbian Erotic Photography.* London: Wellington House, 1995.

Brooks, Rosetta. "Sighs and Whispers in Bloomingdale's: A Review of a Bloomingdale Mail-Order Catalogue for Their Lingerie Department." *Zoot Suits and Second-Hand Dresses: An Anthology of Fashion and Music,* ed. Angela McRobbie. Boston: Unwin Hyman, 1988, pp. 183–188.

Bruce of Los Angeles [Bruce Bellas]. *Bruce of Los Angeles,* ed. Jim Dolinsky. Berlin: Bruno Gmünder Verlag, 1990.

Bruno of Hollywood. *Figure Photography.* New York: Photo Guild, 1945?

Bryk, Felix. *Voodoo-Eros: Ethnological Studies in the Sex-Life of African Aborigines,* trans. Mayne Sexton. New York: Falstaff, 1933.

Burt, Eugene C. *Erotic Art: An Annotated Bibliography with Essays.* Boston: G. K. Hall, 1989.

Cade, Cathy. *A Lesbian Photo Album: The Lives of Seven Lesbian Feminists.* Oakland, CA: Waterwomen Books, 1987.

Callum, Charles R. *Dallas Nude: A Photographic Essay.* New York: Amphoto, 1977.
———. *New York Nude: A Photographic Essay.* New York: Amphoto, 1981.

Campbell, Heyworth, ed. *The Body Beautiful.* 5 vols. New York: Dodge, 1935–1939.

Carline, Richard. *Pictures in the Post.* Rev. ed. London: Gordon Fraser, 1971.

Carter, Angela. "A Well Hung Hang-Up." *Arts in Society,* ed. Paul Barker. Glasgow: Fontana/Collins, 1977, pp. 73–78.

Chapman, David. *Adonis: The Male Physique Pin-Up, 1879–1940.* London: Éditions Aubrey Walter/GMP, 1990.

Chellas, Allen, ed. *Cheesecake: An American Phenomenon.* Dunellen, NJ: Hillman Periodicals, 1953.

Clark, David Aaron. "Madonna Exposed." *Gauntlet,* 5 (1993): 18–23.

Clark, Larry. *Larry Clark, 1992.* New York: Thea Westreich; Cologne: Gisela Captain, 1992.
———. *Teenage Lust.* New York: Clark, 1983.

Clattenberg, Ellen F. *The Photographic Work of F. Holland Day.* Wellesley, MA: Wellesley College Museum, 1975.

Cline, Jim, ed. *Exquisite Creatures*. New York: Morrow, 1985.

Cobb, Madeleine. Cluster of photographs, 1930s. Photography Archives, Kinsey Institute for Sex, Gender, and Reproduction, Indiana University, Bloomington.

Coleman, A. D. "Erotica: The Arrival of the Explicit." *Camera 35*, 24:9 (September 1979): 20–35.

Coleman, Rosalind A., and James Rolleston. "Anatomy Lessons: The Destiny of a Textbook, 1971–72." *South Atlantic Quarterly*, 90:1 (Winter 1991): 153–173.

Collectors Photography. 9021 Melrose Avenue, Los Angeles, CA 90069. 1986–.

Colmer, Michael. *Calendar Girls: A Lavishly Illustrated, Colourful History Spanning Six Decades*. London: Sphere, 1976.

Conaway, Tim. "The Hite Report Exposed." *Hustler*, 3:10 (April 1977): 71–75.

Contemporary American Erotic Photography. New York: Grove/Weidenfield, 1984.

Cook, Kevin. "Bettie Page Interview: My Story—The Missing Years." *Playboy*, 45:1 (January 1998): 134–136, 184–189.

Cooper, Emmanuel. *Fully Exposed: The Male Nude in Photography*. 2d ed. New York: Routledge, 1995.

Corinne, Tee. *Lesbian Images in the Fine Arts*. San Francisco: Privately issued, 1978.

Corinne, Tee, with Jacqueline Lapidus. *Yantras of Womanhood*. Tallahassee, FL: Naiad Press, 1982.

Corn, Laura. *101 Grreat Quickies*. Oklahoma City, OK: Park Avenue, 1997.

Costello, John. *Love, Sex and War: Changing Values 1939–1945*. London: Collins, 1985.

Crawley, Tony, and Ed Caraeff. *Screen Dreams: The Hollywood Pinup: Photographs from the Kobal Collection*. New York: Delilah Communications, 1982.

Crump, James, with an Introduction by Bruce Weber. *George Platt Lynes: Photographs from the Kinsey Institute*. Boston: Bulfinch, 1993.

Cruse, Alfred J. *All about Cigarette Cards*. London: Perry Colour, [1943?].

Danto, Arthur C. *Cindy Sherman: Untitled Film Stills*. New York: Rizzoli, 1990.

———. *Playing with the Edge: The Photographic Achievement of Robert Mapplethorpe*. Berkeley: University of California Press, 1995.

Dater, Judy, and Jack Welpott. *Women and Other Visions*. New York: Morgan and Morgan, 1975.

Davis, Melody D. *The Male Nude in Contemporary Photography*. Philadelphia: Temple University Press, 1991.

Day, F. Holland. *F. Holland Day: Suffering the Ideal*, with an essay by James Crump. Santa Fe, NM: Twin Palms, 1995.

———. *Selected Texts and Bibliography*, ed. Verna Posever Curtis and Jane Van Nimmen. New York: G. K. Hall, 1995.

Delacoste, Frédérique, and Priscilla Alexander, eds. *Sex Work: Writings by Women in the Sex Industry*. Pittsburgh: Cleis Press, 1987.

Demarais Studio. *Erotic Photography, an Exhibition*. Trenton, NJ: Demarais Studio Press, 1981.

Derrida, Jacques. *The Post Card: From Socrates to Freud and Beyond*, trans. Alan Bass. Chicago: University of Chicago Press, 1987.

Dickerson, J. A. "Boudoir Portraiture." *Petersens Photography Magazine*, 14 (March 1986): 18–21.

"Domestic Bliss." *Playboy*, 39:8 (August 1992): 116–125.

Domröse, Ulrich, Christian von Faber-Castell, Claudia Gabriele Philipp, Rainer Wick, and Reinhold Misselbeck, eds. *Bilderlust: Erotische Photographien aus der Samm-lung Uwe Scheid.* Heidelberg: Edition Braus, 1991.

Duay, G. "The Old Erotica." *Gay,* 2:65 (6 December 1971): 65.

Dunas, Jeff. *Voyeur.* New York: Melrose, 1983.

Dureau, George. *George Dureau: New Orleans,* ed. Edward Lucie-Smith. London: GMP, 1985; rpt. *New Orleans.* East Haven, CT: InBook/GMP Publishers U.K., 1991.

Dyer, Richard. "Don't Look Now: Richard Dyer Examines the Instabilities of the Male Pin-Up." *Screen,* 23:3/4 (September–October 1982): 61–73; rpt. in Dyer's *Only Entertainment.* New York: Routledge, 1992, 103–120; rpt. *The Sexual Subject: A Screen Reader in Sexuality,* by the editors of *Screen.* New York: Routledge, 1992, pp. 265–276.

———. *The Matter of Images: Essays on Representations.* New York: Routledge, 1993.

———. *Now You See It: Studies on Gay and Lesbian Film.* New York: Routledge, 1990.

Edgren, Gretchen, ed. *The Playmate Book: Five Decades of Centerfolds.* Los Angeles: General Publishing Group, 1996.

Edwards, Elizabeth, ed. *Anthropology and Photography, 1860–1920.* New Haven, CT: Yale University Press, 1992.

Eisler, Benita. *O'Keeffe and Stieglitz: An American Romance.* New York: Doubleday, 1991.

Eisler, George. *Naked to Nude.* London: Thames and Hudson, 1977.

Ellenzweig, Allen. *The Homoerotic Photograph: Male Images from Durieu/Delacroix to Mapplethorpe.* New York: Columbia University Press, 1992.

Erotica, ed. Julia Thompson. London, 1993–.

Essex, Karen, and James L. Swanson. *Bettie Page: Life of a Pin-Up Legend.* Los Angeles: General Publishing Group, 1995.

Evans, I. O. *Cigarette Cards and How to Collect Them.* London: Jenkins, 1937.

Ewing, William A. *The Body: Photographs of the Human Form.* San Francisco: Chronicle Books, 1994.

Falk, Pasi. "Pornography and the Representation of Presence." *The Consuming Body.* Thousand Oaks, CA: Sage, 1994, pp. 186–217.

Farber, Robert. *Images of Woman.* New York: Amphoto, 1980.

Farina, Ferruccio. *Venus Unveiled.* Madison, WI: Magna, 1989.

Feminist Anti-Censorship Task Force (FACT). *Caught Looking: Feminism, Pornography, and Censorship.* New York: Caught Looking, 1986.

Fischer, Hal. *Gay Semiotics: A Photographic Study of Visual Coding among Homosexual Men.* Berkeley: NFS Press, 1978; rpt. and expanded from Fischer's "Toward a Gay Semiotic." *Eros and Photography,* ed. Donna-Lee Phillips and Lew Thomas. San Francisco: Camerawork/NFS Press, 1977.

Foster, Alasdair. *Behold the Man: The Male Nude in Photography.* Edinburgh: Stills Gallery, 1988.

Foster, Richard. *The Real Bettie Page: The Truth about the Queen of the Pinups.* New York: Carol Publishing Group/Birch Lane, 1997.

Frank, Lisa, and Phil Smith, eds. *Madonnarama: Essays on Sex and Popular Culture.* Pittsburgh: Cleis Press, 1993.

Frasier, David K. *Russ Meyer—the Life and Films: A Biography and a Comprehensive, Illustrated, and Annotated Filmography and Bibliography.* Jefferson, NC: McFarland, 1990.

French, Jim. *Man.* New York: French, 1972.

Freyermuth, Gundolf S. "Die Geschichte der erotischen Photographie." *Der Erotische Augenblick*, ed. Gundolf S. Freyermuth and Ranier Fabian. Hamburg: stem-Buch in Verlag Gruner, 1984, pp. 323–335.

Friedlander, Lee. *Nudes.* New York: Pantheon, 1991.

Fritscher, Jack. *Mapplethorpe: Assault with a Deadly Camera: A Pop Culture Memoir, an Outlaw Reminiscence.* Mamaroneck, NY: Hastings House, 1994.

Froemke, Susan, and Albert Maysles. *Sports Illustrated Swim Suits USA: America the Beautiful.* New York: HBO, 1993.

Fuchs, Eduard. *Illustrierte Sittengeschichte von Mittelalter biz zur Gegenwart.* 6 vols. (3 vols. each with a supplementary volume of plates, the latter later reprinted separately). Munich: Albert Langen, 1909–1928. I: *Die Renaissance* (1909) and *Ergänzungsband* (1909 and 1928); II: *Die galant Zeit* (1910) and *Ergänzungsband* (1911 and 1928); III: *Das bürgerliche Zeitalter* (1912) and *Ergänzungsband* (1912 and 1928).

Futterman, Marilyn. *Dancing Naked in the Material World.* Buffalo, NY: Prometheus, 1992.

Gabor, Mark. *The Art of the Calendar.* New York: Harmony, 1976.

———. *The Illustrated History of Girlie Magazines.* New York: Harmony, 1984.

———. *The Pin-Up: A Modest History.* New York: Universe Books, 1972.

Gaines, Jane. "In the Service of Ideology: How Betty Grable's Legs Won the War." *Film Reader,* 5 (1982): 47–59.

Gale, Gloria. *Calendar Model.* New York: Frederick Fell, 1957.

Gamarekian, Barbara. "Closing of Art Show Is Demanded." *New York Times,* national ed., 13 July 1991, p. 13.

Gardiner, James. *Who's a Pretty Boy Then? One Hundred and Fifty Years of Gay Life in Photographs.* New York: Serpent's Tail, 1992.

Gates, Beatrix, ed. *The Wild Good: Lesbian Photographs and Writings on Love.* New York: Anchor Books, 1996.

Gatewood, Charles. *Forbidden Photographs.* New York: Flash Productions, 1981.

Gatewood, Charles, and William Burroughs. *Sidetripping.* New York: Strawberry Hill, 1975.

Gelpke, Andre. *Sex-Theatre: Eine fotographische Documentation mit einer Einleitung von Allan Porter.* Munich: Mahriert-Lueg, 1981.

Genthe, Arnold, ed. *Highlights and Shadows.* New York: Greenburg, [1930s].

"G.I. Pin-ups." *Motion Picture Herald,* 153:2 (9 October 1943): 9–11.

Girrand, Jane. "Scenes." *Penthouse,* 24:4 (December 1992): 24.

Gittler, Ian. *Pornstar.* New York: Simon and Schuster, 1999.

Glamour Girls of 1943. Melbourne, FL: Space Coast Software, 1994.

Goedde, Steve Diet. *The Beauty of Fetish.* Zurich: Édition Stemmle, 1998.

Goldin, Nan. *I'll Be Your Mirror.* New York: Whitney Museum of Art, 1996.

———. *The Other Side.* New York: Scalo, 1993.

Goldin, Nan, Marvin Heifernan, Mark Holborn, and Suzanne Fletcher. *The Ballad of Sexual Dependency.* New York: Aperture, 1986.

Goldsmith, Arthur. *The Nude in Photography.* Chicago: Playboy Press, 1975.

Goldstein, Richard. "The Taboo Artist: Andres Serrano Goes for the XXX." *Village Voice,* 11 March 1997, pp. 50–51.

———. "Wall of Change." *Village Voice,* 26 November 1991, p. 52.

Goode, James N. *How to Create and Sell Amateur Erotic Videos and Photos: Cashing In on the Amateur Craze.* Nashville, TN: Ferret Press, 1988.

Goude, Jean-Paul. *Jungle Fever.* New York: Xavier Mareau, 1981.

Gowland, Peter. *Peter Gowland's Glamour Camera.* New York: Fawcett, 1959.

————. *The Secrets of Photographing Women.* New York: Crown, 1981.

Grace, Della. *Love Bites.* London: Éditions Aubrey Walter, 1991; Boston: Alyson Press, 1991.

Graham, Judd. *The Porno 20s.* San Diego: Greenleaf Classics, 1971.

Gray, Mitchell, and Mary Kennedy. *The Lingerie Book.* New York: St. Martin's, 1980.

Greer, Germaine. "What Do We Want from Male Pin-Ups?" *Nova,* October 1973, 51–55.

Griffin, Susan. *Pornography and Silence: Culture's Revenge against Nature.* New York: Harper, 1982.

Griffon, Jules. *The Golden Years: Masterpieces of the Erotic Postcard.* Panorama, CA: Helios Press, 1978.

Grimes, William. "Lurid! Licentious! Collectible! The Flip Side of the 1940's and 50's." *New York Times,* 25 July 1994, p. B3.

Gross, Larry, John Stuart Katz, and Jay Ruby, eds. *Image Ethics: The Moral Rights of Subjects in Photographs, Film, and Television.* New York: Oxford University Press, 1988.

Gross, Michael. "Lingerie Catalogues: Changing Images." *New York Times,* 26 April 1987, p. 61.

Grover, Jan Zita. "Dykes in Context: Some Problems in Minority Representation." *The Contest of Meaning: Critical Histories of Photography,* ed. Richard Bolton. Cambridge: MIT Press, 1989, pp. 162–203.

Grumley, Michael, and Ed Gallucci. *Hard Corps: Studies in Leather and Sadomasochism.* New York: Dutton, 1977.

Hagen, Charles. "Photography View: Seeing 'Olympia' Afresh." *New York Times,* 4 August 1991, pp. H5, H6.

Halpert, Peter H. "Fantasy Buys." *American Photo,* 6:5 (September 1995): 27–28.

Hammond, Paul. *French Undressing: Naughty Postcards from 1900 to 1920.* London: Jupiter Books, 1976.

Haralovich, Mary Beth. "Film Advertising, the Film Industry and the Pin-Up: The Industry's Accommodations to Social Forces in the 1940s." *Current Research in Film: Audiences, Economics, and Law,* ed. Bruce A. Austin. 4 vols. Norwood, NJ: Ablex, 1985, I, 127–164.

Hedgecoe, John. *John Hedgecoe's Workbook of Nudes and Glamour.* Newton, MA: Focal Press, 1994.

Henry, Alice. "Images of Lesbian Sexuality [an interview with Tee Corinne]." *Off Our Backs,* 13 (April 1983): 10–12.

Henry, Buck. "The Betty Boom." *Playboy,* 39:12 (December 1992): 122–129, 239–242.

Hess, Thomas B. "Pinup and Icon." *Woman as Sex Object: Studies in Erotic Art, 1730–1970,* ed. Thomas B. Hess and Linda Nochlin. New York: Newsweek, 1972, pp. 222–237.

Hicks, Roger. *Techniques of Pin-Up Photography.* Secaucus, NJ: Chartwell, 1982.

Hillgardner, Bill. *Physique.* New York: Wehman Brothers, n.d. (1940s).

"History of Pin-Ups." *Playboy Video Magazine: Volume 10.* Los Angeles: Playboy Video, 1989.

Hoddeson, Bob. *The Porn People: A First-Person Documentary Report.* Watertown, MA: American Publishing Co., 1974.

Holt, Tonie, and Valmai Holt. *Picture Postcards of the Golden Age: A Collector's Guide.* London: MacGibbon and Kee, 1971.

Honscheidt, W., and Uwe Scheid. *Wheels and Curves: Erotic Photographs of the Twenties.* Berlin: Benedikt Taschen, 1995.

Howard, Justice. "PornARTraphy." *Gauntlet*, 14 (1997): 48–54.

Howe, Graham. "Outerbridge: From Cubism to Fetishism." *Artforum*, 15:10 (Summer 1977): 51–55.

Huhn, Michael. *Photos.* London: Éditions Aubrey Walter, 1992.

Hurrell, George. *Hurrell's Hollywood Portraits: The Chapman Collection*, ed. Mark A. Vieira. New York: Harry Abrams, 1997.

Jackson, Denis C. *The Price and Identification Guide to Marilyn Monroe.* 2d ed. Sequim, WA: Privately printed, 1995.

Jakovsky, Anatole, and Carl Lauterbach. *Post Card Album, and Also a Cultural History.* New York: Universe, 1961.

Jay, Bill. "The Erotic Dawn of Photography." *The Image.* London: Baroque Press, 1972, pp. 40–46.

JEB [Joan E. Biren]. *Eye to Eye: Portraits of Lesbians.* Washington, DC: Glad Hag Books, 1979.

Jenkins, Christie. *A Woman Looks at Men's Buns.* New York: Perigee, 1980.

Jones, Jeanette. *Walk on the Wild Side.* New York: Barricade Books, 1995.

Julien, Isaac, and Kobena Mercer. "True Confessions: A Discourse on Images of Black Male Sexuality." *Male Order: Unwrapping Masculinity*, ed. Rowena Chapman and Jonathan Rutherford. London: Lawrence Wishart, 1988, pp. 131–141.

Jullian, Philippe. *Le Nu 1900.* Paris: Barret/Trésors de la Photographie, 1976.

Jussim, Estelle. *Slave to Beauty: The Eccentric Life and Controversial Career of F. Holland Day, Photographer, Publisher, Aesthete.* Boston: Godine, 1981.

Kallan, Richard A., and Robert D. Brooks. "Playmate of the Month: Naked but Nice." *Journal of Popular Culture*, 8 (1974): 328–336.

Kalmus, Yvonne, Rikki Ripp, and Cheryl Wiesenfeld, eds. *Women See Men.* New York: McGraw-Hill, 1977.

Kelley, Tom. "Marilyn Monroe." *"Golden Dreams" Calendar.* Melrose Park, CA: John Baumgarth Co., 1953.

Kelly, Jain, ed. *Nude: Theory.* New York: Lustrum Press, 1979.

Kent, Sarah. "The Erotic Male Nude." *Women's Images of Men*, ed. Sarah Kent and Jacqueline Morreau. London: Pandora, 1990, pp. 75–105.

Kern, Richard. *New York Girls.* Cologne: Benedikt Taschen, 1997.

Kernes, Mark. "Adult Industry Ogles T & A at Glamourcon II." *Adult Video News*, 9:6 (May 1994): 16.

Kidder, Clark, and Madison Daniels, eds. *Marilyn Monroe unCovers.* Edmonton, Alberta: Quon Editions, 1994.

Kimmelman, Michael. "The Body as Provocateur and Victim." *New York Times*, national ed., 2 September 1990, p. H25.

———. "Peering into Peepholes and Finding Politics: Pornography or Feminist Bullying?" *New York Times*, national ed., 21 July 1991, pp. 2:1, 29.

Kipnis, Laura. "She-Male Fantasies and the Aesthetics of Pornography." *Dirty Looks:*

Women, Pornography, Power, ed. Pamela Church Gibson and Roma Gibson. London: British Film Institute, 1993, pp. 124–143.

Kirstel, M. Richard. *Pas De Deux*. New York: Grove Press, 1969.

Kiss and Tell. *Drawing the Line: Lesbian Sexual Politics on the Wall (Kiss and Tell)*. Vancouver, Canada: Press Gang Press, 1991.

Kiss and Tell [Blackbridge, Persimmon, Lizard Jones, and Susan Stewart]. *Her Tongue on My Theory: Images, Essays and Fantasies*. Vancouver: Press Gang Publishers, 1994; East Haven, CT: InBook Publishing, 1994.

Klaw, Irving. *Betty Page in Bondage*. Nos. 1–5. New York: Mutrix, 1960/1961.

———. *Irving Klaw. "The Pin-up King" Catalogs*. New York: Irving Klaw, 1950s.

Klein, Bonnie Sherr. *Not a Love Story*. Toronto: National Film Board of Canada, 1982.

Klein, Kelly, with an Introduction by Anne Rice. *Under World*. New York: Knopf, 1995.

Kloster, Doris. *Doris Kloster: Photographs*. Berlin: Benedikt Taschen Verlag, 1995.

———. *Forms of Desire*. New York: St. Martin's, 1997.

———. *Thirty Postcards*. Berlin: Benedikt Taschen Verlag, 1995.

Kobal, John. *Gods and Goddesses of the Movies*. New York: Crescent, 1973.

———. *Hollywood Glamour Portraits: 145 Photos of Stars 1926–1949*. New York: Dover, 1976.

———. *People Will Talk*. New York: Knopf, 1985.

Koetzle, Michael. *One Thousand Nudes from the Uwe Scheid Collection*. Berlin: Benedikt Taschen, 1995.

Koetzle, Michael, and Uwe Scheid, eds. *Feu d'Amour: Seductive Smoke*. Berlin: Benedikt Taschen Verlag, 1994.

Köhler, Michael. *Ansichten vom Körper: Das Aktphoto 1840–1987*. Schaffhausen: Stemmle, 1986; rev. ed. *The Body Exposed: 150 Years of the Nude in Photography*. Zurich: Edition Stemmle, 1995.

Köhler, Michael, and Gisela Barche, eds. *Das Aktfoto: Ansichten vom Körper im fotografischen Zeitalter: Ästhetik—Geschichte—Ideologie*. Munich: C. J. Bucher/ Stadtmuseum, 1985.

Kozloff, Max. *Now Becoming Then: Photographs by Duane Michaels*. Altadena, CA: Twin Palms, 1990.

Kraus, Rosalind, and Jane Livingston, with an essay by Dawn Ades. *L'Amour fou: Photography and Surrealism*. New York: Abbeville Press, 1985.

Kraus, Rosalind, and Norman Bryson. *Cindy Sherman: 1975–1993*. New York: Rizzoli, 1993.

Kroll, Eric. *Beauty Parade*. Cologne: Benedikt Taschen, 1997.

———. *Fetish Girls*. Berlin: Benedikt Taschen, 1994.

———. *Sex Objects: An American Photodocumentary*. Danbury, NH: Addison House, 1977.

Kronhausen, Eberhard, and Phyllis Kronhausen. *The Sex People: Erotic Performers and Their Brave New Worlds*. Chicago: Playboy Press, 1975.

Kyrou, Ado. *L'Age d'or de la carte postale*. Paris: André Balland, 1966.

Lacey, Peter. *The History of the Nude in Photography*. New York: Bantam, 1964.

———. *Nude Photography: The Art and Technique of Nine Modern Masters*. New York: Amphoto, 1985.

Lacy, Madison S., and Don Morgan, eds. *Leg Art: Sixty Years of Hollywood Cheesecake*. New York: Citadel, 1981; rpt. *Hollywood Cheesecake: Sixty Years of America's Favorite Pinups*. New York: Citadel, 1983.

Lalli, Joe, with an Afterword by Paul Cadmus. *Fun? Game: Male Models Revealed.* New York: Universe, 1998.

Laner, Mary Riege. "Make-Believe Mistresses: Photo-Essay Models in the Candy-Sex Magazines." *Sociological Symposium,* 15 (1976): 81–98.

Lau, Grace. "Confessions of a Complete Scopophiliac." *Dirty Looks: Women, Pornography, Power,* ed. Pamela Church Gibson and Roma Gibson. London: British Film Institute, 1993, pp. 192–206.

———. *Grace Lau: A Retrospective: Adults in Wonderland.* New York: Serpent's Tail, 1997.

Lebeck, Robert. *Busen, Strapzen, Spitzhoschen.* Dortmund: Harenberg Kommunication, 1982.

———. *Die Erotische Postkarte.* Frankfurt: Edition Stemmle, 1989.

———. *Kehr Seiten.* Dortmund: Harenberg Kommunication, 1980.

———. *The Kiss.* London: St. Martin's, 1981.

———. *Playgirls of Yesteryear.* New York: St. Martin's, 1981; also pub. as *Playgirls von Damals.* Dortmund: Harenberg Kommunication, 1980.

Leddick, David. *Naked Men: Pioneering Male Nudes, 1935–1955.* New York: Universe, 1997.

Lederer, Laura. "Then and Now: An Interview with a Former Pornography Model." *Take Back the Night: Women on Pornography,* ed. Laura Lederer. New York: William Morrow, 1980, pp. 57–70.

Leslie, Charles. *Wilhelm Von Gloeden, Photographer.* New York: Soho Photographic Publishers, 1977.

Lewinski, Jorge. *The Naked and the Nude: A History of the Nude in Photographs 1839 to the Present.* New York: Harmony, 1987.

"Lingerie." Special issue of *American Photo,* 6:5 (September 1995).

Louville, François de. *The Male Nude: A Modern View,* ed. Edward Lucie-Smith. New York: Rizzoli, 1985; Oxford: Phaidon, 1985.

Lowry, Thomas P. *The Story the Soldiers Wouldn't Tell: Sex in the Civil War.* Mechanicsburg, PA: Stackpole Books, 1994.

Lucie-Smith, Edward. *The Body: Images of the Nude.* London: Thames and Hudson, 1981.

Ludwig, Heinrich. "Die Erotik im Film." *Die Erotik in der Photographie,* ed. Erich Wulffen et al. Vienna: Verlag für Kulturforschung, 1931, pp. 233–253.

Lutz, Catherine A., and Jane L. Collins. *Reading National Geographic.* Chicago: University of Chicago Press, 1993.

Lyon, Elisabeth. "Unspeakable Images, Unspeakable Bodies." *Camera Obscura,* 24 (September 1990): 168–193.

MacCambridge, Michael. *The Franchise: A History of Sports Illustrated Magazine.* New York: Hyperion, 1997.

Machado, George. *Masculine.* New York: Crown, 1995.

Madonna, with photographs by Steven Meisel and art by Fabien Baron. *Sex,* ed. Glenn O'Brien. New York: Warner, 1992.

Mailer, Norman. *Marilyn.* New York: Grosset and Dunlap, 1973.

Der Mann in der Photographie. 4 Vols. Zurich: Der Kreis, 1942–1962.

Mannisto, Glen. "1950s Male Nude Photography." *New Art Examiner,* 19:9 (May 1992): 35–36.

Mapplethorpe, Robert. *Altars.* New York: Random House, 1994.

————. *Black Book*. New York: St. Martin's, 1986.

————. *Black Males*. Amsterdam: Galerie Jurka, 1980.

————, with an Introduction by Arthur Danto. *Mapplethorpe*. New York: Random House, 1992.

Marshall, Richard. *Robert Mapplethorpe*. New York: Whitney Museum of American Art/ Little, Brown, 1988.

Marshe, Surrey. *The Girl in the Centerfold: The Uninhibited Memoirs of Miss January*. New York: Delacorte, 1969.

Masterpieces of Erotic Photography. London: Aurum Press, 1977.

Mavor, Carol. *Pleasures Taken: Performances of Sexuality and Loss in Victorian Photographs*. Durham, NC: Duke University Press, 1995.

McBride, Will. *I, Will McBride*. Berlin: Konemann, 1998.

Meadows, Robert. *A Private Anthropological Cabinet of 500 Authentic Racial-Esoteric Photographs and Illustrations*. New York: Falstaff Press, 1934.

Meehan, Thomas. "We Like to Find a Late-Maturing Girl." *Audience*, 1:1 (January 1971): 28–43.

Meiselas, Susan. *Carnival Strippers*. New York: Farrar, Straus, and Giroux, 1979.

Mendes, Peter. "Victorian Erotic Photography." *Creative Camera*, 118 (April 1974): 122–129.

Mercer, Kobena. "Imaging the Black Man's Sex." *Photography/Politics: Two*, ed. Pat Holland, Jo Spence, and Simon Watney. London: Comedia/Methuen, 1987, pp. 61–69.

————. "Just Looking for Trouble: Robert Mapplethorpe and Fantasies of Race." *Sex Exposed: Sexuality and the Pornography Debate*, ed. Lynne Segal and Mary McIntosh. New Brunswick, NJ: Rutgers University Press, 1993, pp. 92–110.

————. "Reading Racial Fetishism: The Photographs of Robert Mapplethorpe." *Fetishism as Cultural Discourse*, ed. Emily Apter and William Pietz. Ithaca, NY: Cornell University Press, 1993, pp. 307–329.

————. "Skin Head Sex Thing: Racial Difference and the Homoerotic Imaginary." *How Do I Look?: Queer Film and Video*, ed. Bad Object-Choices. Seattle: Bay Press, 1991, pp. 169–222.

Merodack, Robert. *Mignones, Mignonettes*. Paris: Dominique Leroy, 1982.

Metz, Christian. "Photography and Fetish." *October*, 34 (1985): 81–90.

Meyer, Russ. *The Glamour Camera of Russ Meyer*. New York: Whitestone, 1958.

Meyerowitz, Joanne. "Women, Cheesecake, and Borderline Material: Responses to Girlie Pictures in the Mid-Twentieth Century United States." *Journal of Women's History*, 8:3 (Fall 1996): 9–35.

Michaels, Duane. *Homage to Cavafy: Ten Poems by Constantine Cavafy: Ten Photographs by Duane Michaels*. Danbury, NH: Addison House, 1978.

————. *The Nature of Desire*. Altadena, CA: Twelvetrees Press, [1986?].

Mills, Jerry, and Dwight Russ. "Hard-On Art: A History of Physique Art from the Forbidden 40s to the Explicit 80s." *In Touch*, 31 (1977): 60–69.

Milton, John, ed. *Smut from the Past: Vol. 2*. New York: Milky Way Productions, 1974.

Minkkinen, Arno, ed. *New American Nudes: Recent Trends and Attitudes*. New York: Morgan and Morgan, 1981.

Monk, Philip, ed. *The American Trip: Larry Clark, Nan Goldin, Cady Noland, Richard Prince: 2 February–8 April 1996, the Power Plant*. Toronto: The Power Plant, 1996.

Montel, Alfred de. *Cartes Postales Pornographiques de la Belle Epoque.* Paris: Le Club du Livre Secret, 1982.

———. *Journal Intime Illustre d'Alfred de Montel.* Paris: Editions de Nohan, 1980.

Moreck, Curt [Konrad Hammerling]. *Das Gesicht.* Vol. I of *Die Fünf Sinne,* ed. Bernhard A. Bauer. 5 vols. Vienna: Verlag für Kulturforschung, 1929.

Morey, Craig. *Studio Nudes.* Emeryville, CA: Morey Photo, 1993.

Morgan, Stuart. *Robert Mapplethorpe, 1970–1983.* London: ICA, 1983.

Morris, Willie. "The Wild One: Betty Page, the First Naked Woman in America." *Esquire,* August 1994, pp. 68–69.

Morrison, Paul. "Coffee Table Sex: Robert Mapplethorpe and the Sadomasochism of Everyday Life." *Genders,* 11 (Fall 1991): 17–36.

Morrisroe, Patricia. *Mapplethorpe: A Biography.* New York: Random House, 1995.

Morrocchi, Riccardo, and Stefano Piselli, eds. *The Golden Age of Exotic Gals: Sultry Strippers and Fetish Models.* Florence, Italy: Glittering Images/edizione d'essai, 1992.

[Morrocchi, Riccardo, et al.] *Diva Obsexion.* 12 vols. Florence, Italy: Glittering Images, 1992.

Musick, Michael. "Spirited and Spicy Scenes." *Civil War Times Illustrated,* 12 (January 1973): 26.

Muybridge, Eadweard. *Muybridge's Complete Animal and Human Locomotion.* 3 vols. New York: Dover Publications, 1979.

Myers, George, Jr. "Writers Express Love in All Ways." *The Columbus [Ohio] Dispatch,* 14 February 1993, p. 9C.

Nazarieff, Serge. *Early Erotic Photography.* Berlin: Benedikt Taschen Verlag, 1994.

———. *Jeus de Dames Cruelles: Photographies 1850–1960.* Berlin: TACO, 1988.

———. *The Stereoscopic Nude, 1850–1930.* Trilingual ed. Berlin: Benedikt Taschen Verlag, 1990.

Nelson, Edward J. *Yesterday's Porno: A Pictorial History of Early Stag Photographs.* 2 vols. New York: Nostalgia Classics, 1972.

Néret, Gilles. *1000 Dessous: A History of Lingerie.* Berlin: Benedikt Taschen, 1998.

Neumaier, Diane, ed. *Reframings: New American Feminist Photographies.* Philadelphia: Temple University Press, 1995.

Nørgaard, Erik. *With Love: The Erotic Postcard.* London: MacGibbon and Kee, 1969; rpt. *With Love to You: A History of the Erotic Postcard.* New York: Potter, 1969.

Nørgaard, Erik, and Michael Schiff. *In Liebe Dein: Sexpostkarten aus Grossvaters Pornokiste.* Munich: Lichtenberg Verlag, 1970.

Nude 1900: A Look at French Postcards. Dobbs Ferry, NY: Morgan and Morgan, 1978.

Nude 1925: A Look at French Postcards. Dobbs Ferry, NY: Morgan and Morgan, 1978.

Nudes of Yesteryear. New York: Eros Books, 1966.

Orwell, George. "The Art of Donald McGill." *Dickens, Dali and Others.* New York: Harcourt Brace Jovanovich, 1946, pp. 124–139.

Ouellette, William, and Barbara Jones Ouellette. *Erotic Postcards.* New York: Excalibur, 1977.

Ovenden, Graham, and Peter Mendes. *Victorian Erotic Photography.* London: Academy Editions, 1974.

Paine, Wingate. *Mirror of Venus.* New York: Ridge Press, 1971.

Painful Memories. New York: Diana, 1983.

Perkins, Michael, ed. *Smut from the Past: Vol. 1.* New York: Milky Way Productions, 1974.

Perrone, Jeff. "Duane Michaels: The Self as Apparition." *Artforum*, 15:5 (January 1977): 22–27.

Petit Catalogue des Fetichismes. Paris: Le Club Livre Secret, 1980.

Petronius [Joyce Greller]. *Tool Box Scandals.* New York: Cestrum Nocturum, 1971.

Phillips, Donna-Lee, and Lew Thomas, eds. *Eros and Photography: An Exploration of Sexual Imagery and Photographic Practice.* San Francisco: Camerawork/NFS Press, 1977.

The Pirelli Calendar, 1964–1997. New York: Rizzoli, 1997.

Pirelli Tire Company. *Heavenly Bodies: The Complete Pirelli Calendar Book.* New York: Harmony, 1975.

Piselli, Stefano, Riccardo Morrocchi, and Marco Giovannini, eds. *Betty Page: Volume I: The Glamorous Betty Page: Volume II: Dedicated to Betty Page.* [Milan?]: Esthetique Fetish and Bizarre, 1990.

Plant, Bud. *Bud Plant's Incredible Catalog.* P.O. Box 1689, Grass Valley, CA 95945, current.

Platt Lynes, George. *Photographs 1931–1955,* comp. Jack Woody. Altadena, CA: Twelvetrees Press, 1980.

Playboy. "Thirty Memorable Years: Three Decades of the Best, the Brightest, the Most Beautiful Women to Grace These Pages." *Playboy*, 31:1 (January 1984): 96–109.

Posing: Inspired by Three Stories. Produced by Suzy Beugen. Los Angeles: An Alta Loma/Republic Pictures Television/Gillian Production, 1989.

Potter, J. K. *Horripilations: The Art of J. K. Potter.* New York: Overlook Press, 1995.

———. "Potter." *Future Sex*, 7 (July–September 1994): 45–49.

Pultz, John, ed. *The Body and the Lens: Photography 1839 to the Present.* New York: Harry Abrams, 1995.

Quality Paperback Book Club. *Mixed-Media Catalog* (October 1995). Camp Hill, PA 17012.

"Questionable Subjects for Photography." *Photographic News*, I (26 November 1858): 135–136.

Raffaelli, Ron. *Desire.* New York: Diverse Industries, 1976.

———. *Raffaelli's Passion: An Erotic Portfolio.* Chatsworth, CA: Chatsworth Press, 1989.

———. *Rapture: Thirteen Erotic Fantasies.* New York: Grove Press, 1975.

Randall, Suze. *Suze.* London: Talmy Franklin, 1977.

Read, Michael. "The Life and Times of Raoul Gradvohl." *See: A Journal of Visual Culture*, 2:2 (1996): 18–25.

Renay, Liz. *My First 2,000 Men.* Fort Lee, NJ: Barricade Books, 1992.

Reynolds, Edward. *Der Flagellantismus in der Photographie.* 2 vols. London: Hippocrates Press, 1933.

Richardson, Herbert. "Playboy Playmates." *Nun, Witch, Playmate: The Americanization of Sex.* New York: Harper and Row, 1971, pp. 83–93.

Ritts, Herb. *Duo: Photographs of Bob Paris and Rod Jackson.* Altadena, CA: Twin Palms Press, 1991.

Rival, André. *Self-Images: 100 Women.* Zurich: Edition Stemmle, 1995.

Roberts, Nickie. *The Front Line: Women in the Sex Industry Speak.* London: Grafton Books, 1986.

Rodgerson, Gillian. "Lesbian Erotic Explorations." *Sex Exposed: Sexuality and the Pornography Debate*, ed. Lynne Segal and Mary McIntosh. New Brunswick, NJ: Rutgers University Press, 1993, pp. 275–279.

Rose, Al. *Storyville, New Orleans: Being an Authentic, Illustrated Account of the Notorious Red-Light District*. University: University of Alabama Press, 1974.

Rosen, Michael A. *Sexual Art: Photographs That Test the Limits*. San Francisco: Shaynew Press, 1994.

———. *A Sexual Magic: The S-M Photographs*. San Francisco: Shaynew Press, 1986.

———. *Sexual Portraits: Photographs of Radical Sexuality*. San Francisco: Shaynew Press, 1990.

Rothstein, Edward. "New Milieu for Monroe: Some Like It Operatic." *New York Times*, 8 October 1993, p. B3.

Rowberry, John W. *Gay Video: A Guide to Erotica*. San Francisco: G. S. Press, 1986.

Russell, Anne M. "Sexual Devolution: Naughty Pictures Never Die, They Just Fade Away." *American Photographer*, 19 (September 1987): 16.

Samaras, Lucas. *Samaras: The Photographs of Lucas Samaras*. New York: Aperture/ Farrar, Straus, and Giroux, 1987.

———. *Samaras Album: Autointerview, Autobiography, Autopolaroid*. New York: Whitney Museum, 1971.

———. *Sittings 8 × 10: 1979–1980*. New York: Pace Gallery, 1980.

Sansone, Tony. *Rhythm*. New York: Sansone, 1935.

Sargeant, Winthrop. "The Cult of the Love Goddess in America." *Life*, 10 November 1947, pp. 81–96.

Schapiro, Bob. "Betty Page Update." *Playboy*, 40:3 (March 1993): 32, 159.

Scheid, Uwe. *Das Erotische Imago: der Akt in frühen Photographien*. Dortmund, Germany: Harenberg, 1984.

———. *Das Erotische Imago II: das Aktphoto von 1900 bis heute*. Dortmund, Germany: Harenberg, 1985.

———. *Freudinnen: Bilder der Zärtlichkeit: Der Doppelakt in frühen Photographien*. Dortmund, Germany: Harenberg, 1987.

Schidrowitz, Leo, ed. *Sittengeschichte der Kulturwelt und ihrer Entwicklung in Einzeldarstellungen*. 10 vols. and supplement to vol. 2. Vienna/Leipzig: Verlag für Kulturforschung, 1926–30. I: *Sittengeschichte des Intimen: Bett, Korsett, Hemd, Hose, Bad, Abtritt, Die Geschichte und Entwicklung der intimen Gebrauchsgegenstände* (1926); II: *Sittengeschichte des Lasters: die Kulturepochen und ihre Leidenschaften* (1927), and *Erganzungsband* (1927); III: *Sittengeschichte von Paris; die Grosstadt, ihe Sitten und ihre Unsittlichkeit* (1926); IV: *Sittengeschichte des Proletariats; des Weg vom Leibes- zum Maschinensklaven, die sittliche Stellung und Haltung des Proletariats* (1926); V: *Sittengeschichte des Theaters, Ein Darstellung des Theaters, seiner Entwicklung und Stellung in zwei Jahrhunderten* (1926); VI: *Sittengeschichte der Liebkosung und Strafe. Die Zärtlichkeitsworte, Gesten und Handlungen der Kulturmenschheit und ihr Gegenpol der Strenge* (1928); VII: *Sittengeschichte des Geheimen und Verbotenen. Eine Darstellung der geheimen und verborgen gehaltenen Leidenschaften der Menschheit, die Einstellung der Staatsgewalt zum Geschlechtsleben der Gesellschaft* (1930); VIII: *Sittengeschichte des Hafens und der Reise, Eine Beleuchtung des erotischen Lebens in der Hafenstadt, im Hotel, im Reisevehikel. Die Sexualität des Kulturmenschen während des Reisens in fremden Milieu* (1927): IX: *Sittengeschichte*

der Revolution. Sittenlockerung und Sittenverfall, Moralgesetze und sexualethis-
che Neuorientierung in Zeiten staatlicher Zersetzung und revolutionären Um-
sturzes (1930); X: *Sittengeschichte des Intimsten. Intime Toilette, Mode und*
Kosmetik im Dienst und Erotik (1929).

Schmidt, Diane. *Chicago Exhibition.* Los Angeles: Melrose, 1985.

Schone, Mark. "Centerfolds Emeritus." *New York Times Magazine,* 20 July 1997, p. 12.

Schor, Mira. "From Liberation to Lack." *Heresies,* 6:4 (1989): 15–21.

Schreiber, Martin. *Madonna Nudes 1979.* Berlin: Benedikt Taschen Verlag, 1994.

The Secret Museum of Anthropology. New York: American Anthropological Society,
[1935].

Sensual Images, ed. PIE Books Staff. Carson, CA: Books Nippon, 1994.

Seufert, Reinhart. *Porno-Photographics.* Los Angeles: Argyle, 1968.

Siebenand, Paul Alcuin. *The Beginnings of Gay Cinema in Los Angeles: The Industry
and the Audience.* Ann Arbor, MI: UMI Press, 1980.

Silke, James. *Betty Page: Queen of Hearts.* Grass Valley, CA: Dark Horse/Bud Plant
Comic Art, 1992.

"Sluts and Goddesses." *Real Sex: 1,* produced and directed by Patti Kaplan. New York:
Home Box Office, 1991.

Smalls, James. "Public Face, Private Thoughts: Fetish, Interracialism, and the Homoerotic
in Some Photographs by Carl Van Vechten." *Sex Positives? The Cultural Politics
of Dissident Sexualities,* ed. Thomas Foster, Carol Siegel, and Ellen E. Berry.
New York: New York University Press, 1997, pp. 144–193.

Smith, Howard. "Ruckus Aroused: The Male Nude Taboo." *Village Voice,* 8 October
1979, p. 21.

Smith, J. Frederick. *Sappho: The Art of Loving Women.* New York: Chelsea House, 1975.

———. *Sappho by the Sea.* New York: Belvedere, 1976.

Soares, M. G., ed. *Butch/Femme.* New York: Crown, 1995.

Sokolowski, Thomas. *The Sailor 1930–45: The Image of an American Demigod.* Norfolk,
VA: Chrysler Museum, 1983.

Solomon-Godeau, Abigail. "The Legs of the Countess." *October,* 39 (Winter 1986): 65–
108; rpt. *Fetishism as Cultural Discourse,* ed. Emily Apter and William Pietz.
Ithaca, NY: Cornell University Press, 1993, pp. 266–306.

Sontag, Susan. "The Pornographic Imagination [1962]." *Styles of Radical Will.* New
York: Delta Books, 1969, pp. 35–73.

Sprague, William Edwin. *Sex, Pornography and the Law.* San Diego: Academy Press,
1970.

Sprinkle, Annie [Ellen Steinberg]. *Annie Sprinkle's Post Modern Pin-Ups Playing Cards:
Pleasure Activist Playing Cards.* New York: Gates of Heck, 1995.

———. *Post Porn Modernist.* Amsterdam: Art Unlimited, 1991.

———. *XXXOOO: Love and Kisses from Annie Sprinkle.* 2 vols. New York: Gates of
Heck, 1997.

Staggers, Rundu L. *Body and Soul: Black Erotica by Rundu.* New York: Crown, 1998.

Stein, Ralph. *The Pin-Up from 1852 to Today.* Chicago: Playboy Press, 1974; rpt. New
York: Crescent, 1984.

Steinberg, David, ed. *Erotic by Nature: A Celebration of Life, of Love, and of Our
Wonderful Bodies.* Berkeley, CA: Shakti Press, 1988.

Steinem, Gloria, and George Barris. *Marilyn/Norma Jean.* New York: Holt, 1986.

"Stephanie's Secret." *Playboy,* 40:2 (February 1993): 71–77.

Sternberg, Jacques. *Pin Up*. New York: St. Martin's, 1974.

Stevens, Dave. *Just Teasing: The Dave Stevens Poster Book*. Kansas City, MO: Ursus Imprints, 1992.

Stoctay, G. G. *America's Erotic Past: 1868–1940*. San Diego: Greenleaf Classics, 1973.

———. *The Illustrated Collector's Price Guide to Erotica*. San Diego: Greenleaf Classics, 1972.

Stratz, C. H. *Die Rassenschönheit des Weibes*. Stuttgart: Ferdinand Enke Verlag, 1911, 1922.

———. *Die Schönheit des weiblichen Körpers*. Stuttgart: Ferdinand Enke Verlag, 1898, 1910.

Sullivan, Constance. *Nude Photographs, 1850–1980*. New York: Harper and Row, 1980.

Sullivan, Steve. *Va Va Voom! Bombshells, Pinups, Sexpots, and Glamour Girls*. Los Angeles: General Publishing, 1995.

Talese, Gay. *Thy Neighbor's Wife*. New York: Doubleday, 1980.

Taylor, Stacey. "Bud Plant's Incredible Catalog." *Gallery*, 22:8 (August 1994): 36.

Thelen, Friedrich. *Das Verhalten der Flagellanten in Realität und Phantasie*. Hamburg: Hans Lassen, 1963.

Tomkins, Calvin. "Madonna's Anticlimax." *New Yorker*, 26 October 1992, pp. 38–39.

Tress, Arthur. *Facing Up*. New York: St. Martin's, 1980.

Truitt, Warren. *Textures*. London: Éditions Aubrey Walter, 1991.

Turbeville, Deborah, et al. *Women on Women*. New York: A and W Publishers, 1979.

Udovich, Mimi, Kate Tentler, Vince Aletti, and Simon Frith. "In Defense of *Sex*." *Village Voice*, 24 November 1992, pp. 22, 25–31.

Updike, John. "The Nude Marilyn." *Playboy*, 44:1 (January 1997): 68–83.

Van Rensselaer, Mrs. John King. *The Devil's Picture Books: A History of Playing Cards*. New York: Dodd, Mead, 1893.

Vance, Carole S. "The Pleasures of Looking: The Attorney General's Commission on Pornography versus Visual Images." *The Critical Image: Essays on Contemporary Photography*, ed. Carol Squires. Seattle: Bay Press, 1990, pp. 38–58.

Vasta Collection. Body Cello, P.O. Box 910531, Sorrento Valley, CA 92191

Venticinque, Mario. *Boudoir Photography: The Fantasy Exposed*. New York: Amphoto, 1986.

Volkmann, Roy. *Two Women in Love*. New York: Strawberry Hill, 1976.

Von Gloeden, Wilhelm. *Photographs of the Classic Male Nude*. New York: Camera Graphic Press, 1977.

Wagner, Geoffrey. *Parade of Pleasure: A Study of Popular Iconography in the U.S.A.* London: Verschoyle, 1954.

Wakerman, Elyce. *Air Powered: The Art of the Air Brush*. New York: Random House, 1979.

Waldberg, Patrick. *Eros Modern Style*. Paris: J. J. Pauvert, 1964; rpt. *Eros in La Belle Epoch*. New York: Grove Press, 1969.

Walters, Margaret. *The Male Nude*. London: Paddington Press, 1978.

Walters, Thomas. *Nudes of the 20s and 30s*. New York: St. Martin's, 1976.

Waugh, Tom. *Hard to Imagine: Gay Male Eroticism in Photography and Film from Their Beginnings to Stonewall*. New York: Columbia University Press, 1997.

———. "A Heritage of Pornography." *Body Politic*, 90 (1983): 29–33.

———. "Photography, Passion, and Power." *Body Politic*, 101 (1984): 29–33.

———. "The Third Body: Patterns in the Construction of the Subject in Gay Male

Narrative Film." *Queer Looks: Perspectives on Lesbian and Gay Film and Video*, ed. Martha Gever, Pritibha Parmar, and John Greyson. New York: Routledge, 1993, pp. 141–161.

Webb, Peter. *The Erotic Arts*. Boston: New York Graphic Society, 1975; rev. ed. New York; Farrar, Straus, and Giroux, 1983.

Weber, Bruce. *Bear Pond*. Boston: Little Bear Press/Little, Brown, 1990.

Weiermair, Peter. *The Hidden Image*. Cambridge: MIT Press, 1988.

———. *Male Nudes by Women*. Zurich: Edition Stemmle, 1995.

———, ed. *The Male Nude: A Male View*. Zurich: Edition Stemmle, 1995.

Weston, Edward. *Edward Weston Nudes*. New York: Aperture, 1977.

Wexler, Irving. "King Pin-Up." *High Society*, 3:7 (December 1978): 52–54, 79–81.

Wexler, Neil. "A Pocket Full of Pin-Ups." *Gallery*, February 1994, pp. 112–114, 116.

White, Edmund. "Tripping the Light Fantastic: Joyce Baronio on 42nd Street." *Village Voice*, 6 August 1979, pp. 35, 37.

White, Minor. *Minor White: Rites and Passages*. New York: Aperture, 1978.

———, ed. *Be/ing without Clothes*. New York: Aperture, 1970.

Whitman, Don. *Mountain Men: The Male Photography of Don Whitman*, with text by David Chapman. East Haven, CT: InBook/GMP Publishers U.K., 1991.

Wick, Rainer. *Die Erotische Daguerreotypie: Sammlung Uwe Scheid*. Weingarten, Germany: Kunstverlag Weingarten GmbH, 1989.

Williams, Linda. "Corporealized Observers: Visual Pornographies and the 'Carnal Density of Vision.' " *Fugitive Images: From Photography to Video*, ed. Patrice Petro. Bloomington: Indiana University Press, 1994, pp. 3–41.

———. *Hard Core: Power, Pleasure, and the "Frenzy of the Visible."* Berkeley: University of California Press, 1989.

Willie, John [J.A.S. Coutts]. *John Willie: The Art of Sophisticated Bondage, 1946–1961*. Florence, Italy: Glittering Images, 1989.

———. *Photographies de John Willie*. Paris: Futuropolis, 1985.

Willoughby, Martin. *A History of Postcards*. Secaucus, NJ: Wellfleet, 1995.

Wilson, Colin, and Piero Rimaldi. *L'Amour: The Ways of Love*. New York: Crown, 1970.

Witkin, Joel-Peter. *Forty Photographs*. San Francisco: San Francisco Museum of Modern Art, 1985.

———. *Gods of Heaven and Earth*. Altadena, CA: Twelvetrees Press, 1989.

———. *Harm's Way: Lust and Madness, Murder and Mayhem*. Altadena, CA: Twin Palms, 1993.

Woodman, Francesca. *Francesca Woodman*, ed. Hervé Chandès. New York: Scalo, 1998.

Woody, Jack, ed. *Collaboration: The Photographs of Paul Cadmus, Margaret French, and Jared French*. Santa Fe: Twelvetrees Press, 1992.

Wortley, Richard. *Pin-ups Progress: An Illustrated History of the Immodest Art*. London: Panther, 1971.

Wulffen, Erich, Erich Stenger, et al. *Die Erotik in der Photographie*. 3 vols. Vienna: Verlag fur Kulturforschung, 1931.

Wykes, Alan. *Saucy Seaside Postcards: An Illustrated Disquisition*. London: Jupiter, 1977.

Yeager, Bunny. *Betty Page Confidential*. New York: St. Martin's, 1994.

———. *Bunny's Honeys*. Berlin: Benedikt Taschen Verlag, 1995.

———. *How I Photograph Myself*. New York: A. S. Barnes, 1964.

————. *100 Girls: New Concepts in Glamour Photography.* New York: A. S. Barnes, 1967.

————. *Thirty Postcards.* Berlin: Benedikt Taschen Verlag, 1995.

Yulsman, Jerry. *Oh, Copenhagen!* New York: Lancer, 1971.

Zone, Ray, ed. *Betty Page, Captured Jungle Girl.* Los Angeles: Three-D Zone, 1990.

————. *The Betty Page 3-D Picture Book.* Los Angeles: Three-D Zone, 1989.

13

Motion Pictures and Videotapes

THEORETICAL APPROACHES TO FILM EROTICISM AND PORNOGRAPHY

Theories of representation in cinema and television have blossomed during four decades of growth for university departments of film, media, and cultural studies. During that same period, mainstream and pornographic cinema has become steadily more explicit and, thanks to videotape, widely available. Academics deconstruct cinematic representations in order to understand the role of the body, the nature of seeing, the cultural determinants of gaze, the place and response of audiences, the pleasures and dangers of fantasy, and so on, all of which have relevance for the study of pornography. Still largely taboo in both academic and popular communities are more basic questions: Is sexual arousal reprehensible, merely acceptable, or a highly desirable goal of cinema? Is a given film actually sexually stimulating? To whom? What are the mechanisms by which arousal is accomplished?

Readers should also note that quantitative studies of "pornographic" films often base their conclusions on extremely small samples and proceed from assumptions that are highly questionable. Pornographic films range across a fantastically large sexual landscape signposted here and there by genre and class markers. Of the thousands of films available, only a dozen or so figure in a typical study; usually these are unnamed, and there may be no attempt to demonstrate that they are pornographic in the first place, let alone to distinguish between individual films or genres. Most studies purporting to examine violence in pornography, for instance, are based not on hard-core films depicting actual intercourse but on mainstream exploitation, horror, or slasher films, genres that some Americans do not think of as pornographic at all. Moreover, because theories of representation that reduce sexuality to power relationships are often scarcely concealed attacks on producers, consumers, or institutions, the arguments can be meretricious. Still others assume at the outset that people who enjoy sexual images are psychologically deficient, a premise that may indicate far more about the pathology of the researcher than the alleged behavior that he or she is examining. Those warnings notwithstanding, the swirl of theory (and methodology) can be fascinating.

One school holds that the motion picture itself came about as the consequence of pornographic impulses. In "Style and Medium in Moving Pictures," perhaps the most famous single essay on the origins of film, the distinguished art historian Erwin Panofsky suggests that the roots of cinema reach down through folklore to pornography, by which he meant that screen images gratify basic voyeurism. Though in general agreement, Andre Bazin says in "Marginal Notes on Eroticism in the Cinema" that the private imperatives of real sex do conflict with the film's imaginative demands. Trendy postmodernists erase Panofsky's distinctions altogether: Frederic Jameson's *Signatures of the Visible* maintains that "the visual is *essentially* pornographic." Pornographic movies, Jameson suggests, are "only the potentiation of films in general, which ask us to stare at the world as though it were a naked body" (1). David James attempts to apply Jameson's theories in a jargon-ridden essay called "Hardcore: Cultural Resistance in the Postmodern." Similarly, in "Photography and Fetish," Christian Metz observes that film can deal with fetishism, while photographs themselves can become fetishes because of the more discrete artifactuality of the latter.

Feminist critics have appropriated Panofsky in their insistence that the origins of the cinema lie in the masculine exploitation of women. Noting the predilection of both Thomas Edison and Georges Méliès for training primitive cameras on beautiful women, Annette Michelson maintains in "On the Eve of the Future: The Reasonable Facsimile and the Philosophical Toy" that the female body was "the very site of cinema's invention" and that the motion picture is "marked in the very moment of its invention by the inscription of desire" (20). In *Hard Core: Power, Pleasure, and the Frenzy of the Visible*, Linda Williams marks that moment as Eadweard Muybridge's chronographic motion studies, in which she sees a masculine technology already inclined to fetishize woman's body, a cinema immediately energized by "the greater sexuality already encoded in the woman's body" (37). Why she should pick that particular sequence out of the dozen-plus *volumes* of images Muybridge published of men, women, animals, and so on is unclear, but the notion that cinematic and photographic representations draw power from the attempt to control the enormous, chaotic, and ultimately untamable sexuality of women is not only fashionable but also persuasive.

Such theoretical scenarios can be amusingly double-edged in the hands of less capable critics than Michelson and Williams. Some antiporn feminists attempt to celebrate the enormous potential of the female while simultaneously asserting that she is victimized by any attempt to capture her essence. In any case, pornography has revitalized and polarized women's film studies; if porn did not exist, then critics would have to invent it. Although many observers find a good deal of feminist criticism of porn ideologically motivated, misleading, misinformed, and downright silly (as is doubtless the case with criticism by any group with an ax to grind), they can easily find a good deal more that is exciting, provocative, insightful, and sparkling. Early feminist film criticism dealt primarily with the roles assigned to women in mainstream cinema. Pioneering feminist studies of the Hollywood product free from the postmodernist jargon more popular now are Marjorie Rosen's *Popcorn Venus: Women, Movies, and the American Dream*, Molly Haskell's *From Reverence to Rape: The Treatment of Women in the Movies*, and Joan Mellen's *Women and Their Sexuality in the New Film*. Patricia Erens has collected some excellent essays in *Sexual Strategems: The World of Women in Film*.

Gender studies have also expanded to include the treatment of masculinity in cinema. The essays in *Screening the Male: Exploring Masculinities in Hollywood Cinema*, edited by Steven Cohan and Ina Rae Hark, consider masculinity as spectacle in mainstream film. Peter Lehman, in *Running Scared: Masculinity and the Representation of the Male Body*, views the construction of masculinity in terms of syndromes of victimization formerly applied to women. Lehman believes that the display of the male body, especially in the nude, evokes a fear that cannot be reduced to anxiety about penis size. Michael Malone, on the other hand, concentrates on macho images in *Heroes of Eros: Male Sexuality in the Movies*. Richard Dyer says in "Male Sexuality in the Media," a chapter of his *The Matter of Images: Essays on Representations*, that some gay and feminist art and some sectors of vital popular culture are sources "of a sexuality that is not nasty and brutish, silly and pathetic, but varied, sensuous, langorous, warm and welcome" (121), as opposed to less welcome qualities in representations associated with heterosexual males.

Traces of the social, political, and economic forces that shape rarely explain the power of the images themselves; the force of taboo, because it grows out of irrational elements in the psyche, cannot so easily be discounted. Amos Vogel's *Film as a Subversive Art* makes the point most clearly; Vogel sees the evolution of film as a movement from "taboo to freedom" (11), and his discussion of the ways in which artistic violations of taboo can benefit a culture by transforming its institutions is without peer. Annette Kuhn's *The Power of the Image: Essays on Representation and Sexuality* deals with pornographic cinema as a form of "lawless seeing," a variation on theories usually called the "male gaze." Kuhn's take here is more interesting than most, however, because unlike cookie-cutter versions of the male gaze theory, she characterizes this "seeing" as anarchistic rather than hegemonic, though she acknowledges that it is often foreign to women audiences (see **The "Male Gaze": Visuality and Pornography** in Chapter 6). Kuhn's equally astute "The Body and Cinema," a provocative essay on cinematic representations of the body, deals with an inescapable paradox, that cultural repression of sexual images calls them into being: "What censorship both prohibits and produces is most especially that category of representations named the 'obscene' " (59). In other words, porn and antiporn are inextricably related as a fundamental dichotomy. Kuhn's earlier *Women's Pictures: Feminism and Cinema* is less successful because it conflates Lacanian reader-text analysis with a predictable Marxist characterization of cinema as a commodification of the female, though it contains an excellent chapter on the ways in which pornography codes female presence ("The Body in the Machine" [109–128]).

Peter Michelson's *Speaking the Unspeakable: A Poetics of Obscenity*, a revision of his famous *The Aesthetics of Pornography* (which had little to say about film), contains a chapter entitled "Unspeakable Spectacle, the Movies" (233–274). It traces explicitness from the avant-garde American cinema (especially films by Stan Brakhage) to modern porn features and into mainstream films by Bertolucci, Oshima, and Wertmuller. Michelson observes that high and low forms treat "subversive" pornographic material differently and that "obscene spectacle has an unpredictable detonation point": "Thus an art film carefully manipulates obscene spectacle, deploying it in a controlling ecology of images, situations, nuances. Where the smut film turns eroticism loose, swats its hindquarters and lets it run, the art film mounts it, spurs it here, reins it in there, disciplines and directs it through a course. In smut, obscenity may run proud and free, or buck or fart, or simply stop and graze, and the viewer responds according to his or her inclination. The effect of the art film depends on the tension between the rider's discipline and obscenity's natural energy" (240). Andrew Sarris's *Politics and Cinema*, which views film as an important medium for dramatizing political concerns, discounts the function of pornography as political statement, though he allows that it may have subversive value. For that matter, Sarris rejects the notion that hard-core movies represent a more authentic expression of eroticism than mainstream examples, if only because the former suffer from insufficient plotting and technical values. The chapter on pornography in *Politics and Cinema* nevertheless covers some of the better-known porn films of the 1970s.

Contributors to *Perspectives on Pornography: Sexuality in Film and Literature*, edited by Gary Day and Clive Bloom, employ as critical tools "feminism, post-structuralism, Marxism, Lacanism, psychoanalysis, and film theory"; most of these patronizing approaches shoulder aside eroticism in order to be clever. A case in point is Anthony Crabbe's "Feature-Length Sex Films," which speculates that men watch such films "for relief from their anxieties about attaining sexual satisfaction" (65); readers not aware that psychological inadequacy has ever been a prerequisite for enjoyment of sexual material may be impatient with such theories. Ulf Sondell's *Den pornografisha filmen som symptom på ett sambällstillstånd* advances the theory that pornographic films express a late capitalism that exercises control over individuals (à la Marcuse) by permitting rather than repressing hedonism. In this respect, says the author, pornographic films are not much different from other media; the argument is directed chiefly at technology, which Sondell thinks renders sexual expression "anti-human." Taste, obviously, is crucial to one's assessment of pornographic films. Richard Gehr's "Comin' at Ya" insists that porn films are "more enjoyable than, say, the average made-for-TV movie." By contrast, Vincent Canby's " 'Dirty Movies' Are a Bore" typifies the classic liberal response to porn, delivered as a yawn by a leading film critic of decades past.

HISTORIES AND COMMENTARIES ON SEX IN MAINSTREAM CINEMA

Most histories of sex in the mainstream cinema are compilations of stills interlaced with text of no particular insight into eroticism, though some make excursions into different genres. Useful information can be found in *Sex in the Movies* by Sam Frank; *A Pictorial History of Sex in the Movies* by Jeremy Pascall and Clyde Jeavons; *Sex on the Screen: Eroticism in Film* by Gérard Lenne; *Caught in the Act: Sex and Eroticism in the Movies* by David Shipman; *A Pictorial History of Sex in Films* by Parker Tyler; and *Sex in the Movies: The Celluloid Sacrifice* by Alexander Walker. *Erotica for the Millions: Love in the Movies* by Ove Brusendorff and Poul Henningsen, while global in reach, is also superficial. Maitland McDonagh's *The Fifty Most Erotic Films of All Time*, nicely illustrated, discusses mainstream examples from *Gilda* and *La Dolce Vita* to *Wide Sargasso Sea*. The coverage of film in Peter Webb's otherwise splendid *The Erotic Arts* is too brief to be of much utility.

More substantial histories include *L'Erotisme au Cinéma* by Guiseppe Lo Duca, whose idiosyncratic account is out-of-date although still valuable because it covers American as well as European eroticism; *Amour-Erotisme au Cinéma* by Ado Kyrou, an anecdotal, personal chronicle by a producer-director long involved in the film industry; volume V of *Mimus Eroticus* by Arthur Maria Rabenalt, who was Jean Renoir's cameraman; *Aesthetik des erotischen Kinos: Eine Einfuhrung in die Mythologie, Geschichte und Theorie des erotischen Films* by Georg Sesslen and Claudius Weil, a historian and a journalist, respectively; and *Sexuality in the Movies* by Thomas R. Atkins, better known for his work with erotic literature. "The History of Sex in Cinema," by Arthur Knight and Hollis Alpert, nineteen articles on (chiefly) American films running in *Playboy* from April 1965 to January 1969, is extremely well researched; the chapter called "The Stag Film" appears in the November 1967 issue. *Playboy* still runs authoritative annual articles on "Sex in Cinema" in November and "The Year in Sex" in February, both of which take notice of developments in pornographic genres. Installments from the 1970s were reprinted in annually dated paperbacks called *Playboy's Sex in Cinema*, each of them edited by Knight and Alpert. "Cinema Sex, from *The Kiss* to *Deep Throat*," an essay by Richard Corliss, is brief but direct. *Playboy* has also produced a loopy documentary survey of sex in cinema, highlighted by comment from David Friedman, Andrea Dworkin, Donald Wildmon, and Russ Meyer, among others, and released it as *The Story of X: 100 Years of Adult Film and Its Stars.*

Much of what passes for history focuses on cinematic nudity, scandal, and folklore. The occasional clandestine circulation of footage of nude scenes, excised but not always destroyed before early (1920–1930) films were released, gave rise to myths that male and female movie stars began their careers in stag films. During the same period, Hollywood studios such as MGM routinely shot nude or seminude photographs of male and female stars for archival and European advertising purposes; a dozen or so are reproduced in German texts such as the *Bilderlexicon der Erotik* and in Heinrich Ludwig's chapter, "Die Erotik im Film," for *Die Erotik in der Photographie* by Erich Wulffen et al. *Érotisme au Cinéma: Almanach 1964* is a collection of revealing shots and outtakes of actresses, including some Americans, compiled by Pierre Scudéry and Paul Scudéry. Similar pictures are the stuff of Raymond Lee's *A Pictorial History of Hollywood Nudity*, which features actors and actresses in dishabille; Michael Milner's *Sex on Celluloid*, which is both sketchy and dated; and Bill George's *Drive-In Madness: The Jiggle Movies*, which emphasizes the appeal of bouncing breasts. Periodicals like *Celebrity Skin* and its successor *Celebrity Sleuth* pack pages with nude stars. For more serious considerations of nudity and its equation with sexuality, researchers should consult *Cut: The Unseen Cinema* by Baxter Philips, who provides historical and social context, and the dated, but highly readable, *Original Skin: Nudity and Sex in Cinema and Theatre* by Gillian Hanson, who investigates the artistic, philosophical, and ideological reasons behind displays.

Richard Dyer speculates on frissons of celebrity flesh in *Heavenly Bodies: Film Stars and Society*, which advances Marilyn Monroe and Paul Robeson as important stereotypes of female and black sexuality and dilates on Judy Garland as a magnet for homosexuals. *The Image Makers: Sixty Years of Hollywood Glamour*, by Paul Trent, examines the techniques with which studios and publicists sexualized stars. Marybeth Hamilton's *"When I'm Bad I'm Better": Mae West, Sex, and American Entertainment* is an excellent social history spanning the eighty years of West's life, during which time she functioned as an American sexual icon. West deliberately parodied sex, exaggerating her physicality and mocking her own "seductiveness," and in that respect originated a self-reflexivity essential to both soft- and hard-core pornographic films today. *Fifteen Sex Queens on Sex: By the World's Most Desired Women* contains unremarkable conversations with mainstream actresses, most of them without a clue as to what engenders desire. Similar clichés are offset by footage of cleavage and curves in Buz Kohan's ABC broadcast *Sixty Years of Seduction.*

Though formatted as a filmography, James L. Limbacher's *Sexuality in World Cinema* contains essays on many aspects of the subject. Browsing the two volumes garners unusual information on cinematic sex before the 1980s. *Eros in the Cinema* and *Sexual Alienation in the Cinema*, Raymond Durgnat's readings of mainstream films of the 1950s, 1960s, and 1970s, employ Freudian and Marxist analysis. The most astute chapters in Parker Tyler's *Sex Psyche Etcetera in the Film* graph the libidos of Bergman and Fellini and marvel at U.S. reception of Vilgot Sjoman's *I Am Curious (Yellow)* (1968). Images of prostitutes always triggered special treatment in Hollywood, says Lea Jacobs, whose *The Wages of Sin: Censorship and the Fallen Woman Film, 1928–1942* deals with whores, nonvirgins, and "ruined" women in mainstream films, where they were presented as alternately reprehensible and fascinating. As agents of cultural stability, motion pictures quickly developed stereotypes and strategies for controlling unseemly female desires by relegating transgressive characters to the ranks of "bad" women, says Janet Staiger in *Bad Women: Regulating Sexuality in Early American Cinema*.

The most obvious taboos, however, have concerned representations of gays and lesbians. One could always depend on some prominent American condemning as pornographic any Hollywood product depicting homosexuality—despite the absence of any real candor or explicitness—as David Galloway makes clear in "Up Yours Tonto! Or, Growing Up Queer in America," which looks briefly at screen examples. Suzanna Andrews' "She's Bare. He's Covered. Is There a Problem?" comments on the double standard regarding nudity in mainstream films, where full frontal nudity for women actresses is commonplace but still unusual for male actors. Andrews notes that audiences do seem to be warming toward penises, however. According to some critics, homophobia explains the recoil from visible penises, while others cite male fears of increased vulnerability or point to the practice of shielding symbols of authority from public view in order to enhance their power by shrouding them in mystery. Still others cleave to aesthetic preferences, saying that Western cultures have traditionally worshiped female bodies for their beauty while rejecting penises as ugly and, more recently, as carriers of infection. In this regard, Richard Meyer offers a Mulvey-like reading of "Rock Hudson's Body," in which he examines the sexuality of the star's images for gays and heterosexuals from Hudson's early career to his death from AIDS.

Homosexuality on mainstream screens is the subject of Richard Dyer's *Gays and Film*. The second edition (1984) includes Dyer's three essays on camp. Dyer's *Now You See It: Studies on Lesbian and Gay Film* deals to a greater extent with pornographic examples and is perhaps the best single general work on homosexuality in films. Another recent, comprehensive, and lively text is *Queer Looks: Perspectives on Lesbian and Gay Film and Video*, edited by Martha Gever, Pratibha Parmar, and John Greyson, a group of essays on gay and lesbian artists in pursuit of an explicit homosexual aesthetic; the perspective is "queer theoretical" and multicultural. Just as politically correct are the essays in *How Do I Look? Queer Film and Video*, edited by a group calling themselves Bad Object Choices (Terri Cafaro, Jean Carlomusto, Douglas Crimp, Martha

Gever, Tom Kalin, and Jeff Nuokawa); if the essays vary sharply in quality, all are fascinating. The last three volumes listed here are mandatory for the study of gay and lesbian presence in film.

Vito Russo's *The Celluloid Closet: Homosexuality in the Movies* and Parker Tyler's *Screening the Sexes: Homosexuality in the Movies*, both dated, have been justly honored for breaking paths. Russo's survey is organized chronologically and thematically, Tyler's somewhat more idiosyncratically. Boze Hadleigh's *The Lavender Screen: The Gay and Lesbian Films, Their Stars, Makers, Characters, and Critics* is a lightweight, but entertaining, history of homosexual themes, characters, and images. Hadleigh interviews Edith Head, Sandy Dennis, Marjorie Main, Nancy Kulp, Barbara Stanwyck, and five other lesbian or bisexual women for *Hollywood Lesbians*. Two special issues of the journal *Jump Cut* are helpful: number 16 (1977), on gays and film, and number 24/25 (March 1981), on lesbianism in the cinema. As might be expected, gay and lesbian critics are best on the construction of homosexual characters and with the forms of discourse that cinema invents to treat homosexual subjects and themes. Tom Waugh's "The Third Body: Patterns in the Construction of the Subject in Gay Male Narrative Film" isolates gay stereotypes (e.g., artist, intellectual, and queen) and provides an excellent filmography of these and other stock characters. Among his several essays on black gay men, Kobena Mercer's "Dark and Lovely Too: Black Gay Men in Independent Film" centers on Marlon Riggs' *Tongues Untied* (1989) in its explication of "Black Queer culture politics"; Mercer, too, identifies stereotypes. Similarly, Jack Goldsby examines a 1990 film about Harlem drag queens and "vogueing" in "Queens of Language: *Paris Is Burning*." The term *vogueing* has come to prominence because it raises an important gender issue: must gays imitate women in order to establish a sexual identity of their own? In one of the few essays to consider other ethnicities in porn films, Richard Fung's "Looking for My Penis: The Eroticized Asian in Gay Video Porn" observes that Asian men seem always to be buggered by whites in Western videos, rather than the reverse, a practice that would seem to symbolize and extend patterns of neocolonialism.

Mandy Merck's *Perversions: Deviant Readings* comments on narrative strategies in texts, photos, and cinema. Chris Straayer's *Deviant Eyes/Deviant Bodies: Sexual Re-Orientations in Film and Video* adds substantially to our understanding of gender representations, as does Tom Waugh's *Hard to Imagine: Gay Male Eroticism in Photography and Film from Their Beginnings to Stonewall*; these two works offer substantial outlines and revisions of theoretical approaches to gay film pornography. Some of the essays in two volumes by Teresa de Lauretis, *Feminist Studies/Critical Studies* and *Technologies of Gender: Essays on Theory, Film, and Fiction*, also deal with lesbian representation in film. In the latter volume, de Lauretis says that the female subject is trapped in a heterosexual context, "at the same time inside and outside the ideology of gender, and conscious of being so, conscious of that pull, that division, that double vision" (298). Stefanie Hetze's *Happy-End für Wen? Kino und lesbische*

Frauen notes that lesbian representation, even where candid, inevitably leads to plot denouements in which heterosexual values prevail. Bonnie Zimmerman's thesis in "Lesbian Vampires" is that the most common lesbian film stereotype is that of the sexual predator. Andrea Weiss adds another stereotype in *Vampires and Violets: Lesbians in the Cinema*; Weiss finds that lesbians are most apt to be represented as either stealthy aggressors or shrinking, passive figures in mainstream cinema. "Lesbianism in the Movies," one chapter of Joan Mellen's *Women and Their Sexuality in the New Film*, also deals with common misrepresentations. Implausible imagery has reinforced the lesbian's sense of isolation, of separateness from family structures and social conventions, says Judith Mayne in *The Woman at the Keyhole*, which argues for a reinvented cinematic sensibility. Essays by Chris Cagle, Linda Dittmar, Lynda Goldstein, Marc Siegel, Chris Straayer, and Thomas Waugh, among others, collected in *Between the Sheets, in the Streets: Queer, Lesbian, Gay Documentary*, edited by Chris Holmlund and Cynthia Fuchs, consider the phenomenon of documentaries on homosexuality, some of them explicit, and their effects on audiences and the culture.

AVANT-GARDE FILMS: HIGH PORN

Beyond the realm of the mainstream legitimate cinema are genres sometimes deemed pornographic. Most of these can easily be distinguished from the *hardcore* film, once called a *stag* or *fuck film*, whose graphic depiction of intercourse endows it with a kind of purity or authenticity. One type that often does include explicit scenes and sometimes actual sex is the serious avant-garde movie, sometimes called the *underground, subversive,* or *alternative* film and less often *high porn* (as opposed to *low*, the usually anonymous, scruffy stag footage that has always lurked beneath the cinematic surface). Linda Williams' *Figure of Desire: A Theory and Analysis of Surrealist Film* develops discussion of Luis Bunuel into a treatise on sexual images in the surreal films often favored by the avant-garde, while Robert Benayoun's *Erotique du Surréalisme* seeks out weird and imaginative twists on the erotic among landmarks of this modernist school. Easily the best overall theoretical survey of nonmainstream film is Amos Vogel's *Film as a Subversive Art*, whose title is self-explanatory; the sections on purposive nudity, rebellious eroticism, and provocative homosexuality are superb. Parker Tyler's *Underground Film: A Critical History* discusses experimentation with pornographic themes and images by the avant-garde, especially with the voyeurism that, to a degree, animates all underground films. Tyler's *Sex Psyche Etcetera in the Film*, while largely concerned with mainstream directors, devotes a chapter to Andy Warhol.

Sheldon Renan captures the erotic excitement swirling around Warhol, Stan Brakhage, the Kuchar Brothers, Stan VanDerBeek, Kenneth Anger, and others in *An Introduction to the American Underground Film*. P. Adams Sitney's extraordinarily thorough *Visionary Film: The American Avant-Garde* views the eroticism of underground cinema as simply one of many cultural sensibilities to emerge in experimental cinema of the last decades. Informative also is Jonas Mekas' *Movie Journal: The Rise of a New American Cinema, 1959–1971*, which fashions his reviews of experimental and avant-garde films into a chronicle of controversy. "Experimental Films" (part 15 of Knight and Alpert's "The History of Sex in Cinema" in *Playboy*, 14 [April 1967]) links American exemplars Stan Brakhage and the Kuchar brothers with predecessors Man Ray and Maya Deren. Jack Stevensen interviews the Kuchar brothers (and John Waters) on their work and intentions for *Desperate Visions: Camp America*. The second half of Raymond Durgnat's *Sexual Alienation in the Cinema* studies underground auteurs, some of them American. Scott MacDonald devotes several pages of *Avant-Garde Film: Motion Studies* to sexual themes and images.

Patricia Mellencamp has written the only full-length feminist critique of the American avant-garde film in *Indiscretions: Avant-Garde Film, Video, and Feminism*, which covers the work of Land, Frampton, Jacobs, Connor, Nelson, Snow, Rainer, and Potter, with some attention to videos by Smith, Wegman, and Condit. Mellencamp uses theories by Foucault, Deleuze, and Guattari to elevate marginal genres to greater significance for gender studies. *Cinema Underground Oggi: A Cura di Sirio Luginbühl*, principally an annotated chronology of international underground cinema, provides dates and information on American performers and directors like Jack Smith, Kenneth Anger, Andy Warhol, Gregory Markopoulos, Bruce Baille, and Stan Brakhage, as well as comment on the explicit films shot in the United States by John Lennon and Yoko Ono; it is generously illustrated. Lennon and Ono discuss the rationales of *Bottom, Erection, Rape*, and other shorts in "Our Films." Walter Gutman, head of a foundation that funded films by George Kuchar, Carolee Schneemann, Andy Warhol, and others, humorously recalls shooting and editing in "My Pioneer Days in Underground Movies." Mark Finch talks with one of the Kuchar brothers on avant-garde moviemaking, his gayness, and other matters of sexual representation in "George Kuchar: Half the Story." Kuchar's candor is refreshing, especially when he admits, "I don't have the best taste in the world. Sometimes my taste is a little off kilter" (85). K. Carroll's "An Interview with Fred Baker" allows Baker to talk about the script of *Events*, a film notorious in the 1970s for glimpses of genitals.

Of the many studies of Warhol's explicit films, the essays in Michael O'Pray's *Andy Warhol: Film Factory* are best on examples like *Blowjob*, while Adriano Apra and Enzo Ungari provide the most accurate filmography of Warhol's work in this vein, including some films now lost, in *Il cinema di Andy Warhol*. In *Stargazer: The Life, World, and Films of Andy Warhol*, Stephen Koch evaluates the films in the context of Warhol's career and rarified subculture. Margia Kramer's *Andy Warhol et al: The FBI File on Andy Warhol* reproduces the hilarious official summaries of Warhol's *Lonesome Cowboys* as the FBI snooped on its production and distribution while trying to decide whether to prosecute. Grove Press published the script of Warhol's *Blue Movie: A Film. The Films of Paul*

Morrisey, by Maurice Yacowar, follows Warhol's principal collaborator as he moves away to direct on his own. Richard Dyer's *Now You See It: Studies on Lesbian and Gay Film* contains extended criticism on Warhol and other explicit underground homosexual filmmakers. Attached to the first edition of Dyer's *Gays and Film* (1980) is Caroline Sheldon's splendid appendix, "The Criminal Element: Male and Female Homosexuality in Pornographic and *Avantgarde* Film," which describes the gay and lesbian character as subversive and the films themselves as forms of "outlaw" discourse.

Homosexual themes and images are parsed by Jerry Tartaglia in "The Gay Sensibility in American Avant-Garde Film." Susan Sontag wrote "A Feast for Open Eyes," a review of *Flaming Creatures* by Jack Smith, the most celebrated gay avant-garde director, when the film was seized in New York; it remains definitive. Regarding Smith's vision, says Sontag in a rubric often quoted, "there are some elements of life—above all, sexual pleasure—about which it isn't necessary to have [an ideological or gendered] position" (375). When *Flaming Creatures* was exhibited in a retrospective at the 1991 New York Film festival, J. Hoberman reviewed the history of its censorship in "The Big Heat," recalling Strom Thurmond's attempt to show it on the floor of the Senate to forestall the confirmation of Abe Fortas as chief justice (on the grounds that Fortas' liberality had fostered circulation of such films). The impact of Smith's film derived from a profusion of moving penises when showing them was still taboo; Hoberman fears that "the initial shock of *Flaming Creatures* can never be recaptured" (72). Hoberman and Ed Leffingwell have edited Smith's own modest work into a volume called *Wait for me at the Bottom of the Pool: The Writings of Jack Smith*. Leffingwell, Carole Kismaric, and Marvin Heiferman have also collected essays on the filmmaker who seemed never to finish anything in *Flaming Creature: Jack Smith, His Amazing Life and Times*. Two good articles on Kenneth Anger, perhaps the most flamboyant of American underground auteurs, are John Calendo's "Kenneth Anger Rising" and Michael Wade's "Kenneth Anger: Personal Traditions and Satanic Pride," both of which consider the themes of *Scorpio Rising, Inauguration of the Pleasure Dome*, and *Fireworks. The Unauthorized Biography of Kenneth Anger*, by Bill Landis, critiques the man's career. The 1974 edition of P. Adams Sitney's *Visionary Film* contains a fine chapter on Gregory Markopoulos. Juan A. Suárez discusses Warhol, Smith, Anger, and many other filmmakers in *Bike Boys, Drag Queens, and Superstars: Avant-Garde, Mass Culture, and Gay Identities in the 1960s Underground Cinema*. Jack Sargeant's treatment of Jack Smith, William Burroughs, and Jonas Mekas in *Naked Lens: An Illustrated History of Beat Cinema* complements Suárez's.

Sources of information on contemporary gay underground producers and directors can be found in *Now You See It: Studies on Lesbian and Gay Film*, by Dyer, in *How Do I Look? Queer Film and Video*, edited by Bad Object Choices, and in *What Are You Looking At? Queer Sex, Style and Cinema*, by Paul Burston. Creating a homosexual perspective different from dominant heterosexual visions would appear to be the common goal of avant-garde gay and lesbian film artists today. Just how difficult this can be is the subject of Chris Straayer's "The Hypothetical Lesbian Heroine: *Voyage en Douce* and *Entre Nous*," which draws on two French films. B. Ruby Rich points out that dominance can also be a matter of race in "When Difference Is (More than) Skin Deep," which contrasts avant-garde African American and Latina lesbian cinema with more common American examples. Age can also affect lesbian sensibilities, admits Yvonne Rainer. In "Working Round the L-Word," Rainer discusses her career as an avant-garde dancer but concentrates primarily on her film, *Privilege*. Though now in her fifties, she thinks that she can empathize with younger lesbians. Moreover, she says: "I don't think one has to be a lesbian to make a film about lesbians. The question arises: How—let alone why—should one speak the struggles of those with whom one does not have precisely the same things at stake?" (16). Liz Kotz praises the ambiguity of selected films as germane to "ongoing discussions of lesbian subjectivity, feminist media, and political complexity and effectiveness" (100) in "An Unrequited Desire for the Sublime: Looking at Lesbian Representation across the Works of Abigail Child, Cecilia Dougherty, and Su Friedrich." Staking out fresh ground is the intent behind Jerry Tartaglia's film homage to Jean Genet. In "*Ecce Homo*: On Making Personal Gay Cinema," Tartaglia says his goal is "to explore glimpses of the gay 'window on the world' which doesn't fit neatly into an assimilationist framework" (203), that is, to present erotic aspects of this perspective. John Greyson discusses his film, *Urinal* (1988), which deals with entrapment of homosexuals in public washrooms in Ontario, in "Security Blankets: Sex, Video and the Police." In "A Queer Sensation," B. Ruby Rich rejoices at the showing at the Museum of Modern Art and other film festivals of important "queer" films like Jarman's *Edward II*, Lynd's *R.S.V.P.*, Araki's *The Living End*, and Kalin's *Swoon*.

In "Missionary Positions," Amos Vogel discusses films produced by the National Sex Forum (originally sponsored by the Methodist Glide Foundation), now called the Institute for Advanced Study of Sexuality. These include Laird Sutton's *Self-Loving* (1976), on women and masturbation; Lisa Croft's *Desert Pie* (1977), a hard-core cartoon of forty to fifty human figures copulating; *Give It a Try* (1978), footage on a quadraplegic and his able-bodied wife; Sutton's *Titles Available* (1972), a sound track of spoken porn titles; James Broughton's *Hermes Bird* (1977), sequences of a penis gradually swelling to erection; Dirk Kortz's *Words of Love* (1977), shots of penises over a sound track on which a woman describes them pornographically and obscenely; and Suzan Pitt's *Asparagus* (1974–1978), scenes both erotic and scatalogical. Dirk Kortz talks about his own work in "Eroticism vs Porn by an Ex-Practitioner." James Broughton, the most elegantly whimsical filmmaker to work in erotica, talks about his craft in an interview with Robert Peters for *Gay Sunshine Interviews II*. Broughton's own wonderfully entertaining memoirs, *Making Light of It*, describe the pleasures and perils of shooting erotica. HBO's *Real Sex: 5*, in a segment called

"Doctor/Director," looks at the work of Frank Sommers, M.D., founder of a Nobel Prize–winning nuclear peace organization who is also a noted sex therapist; he has been making explicit educational videotapes since 1978. Amy Taubin and John D. Thomas interview producers of highly explicit sex education videotapes at the Sinclair Institute of Chapel Hill, North Carolina, for "Softcore Sex Ed."

The remarkable Juliet Bashore has made the stark semidocumentary *Kamikaze Hearts* about the world of "lesbian junkie-porn stars," a close look at Sharon Mitchell, one of the most enduring porn stars (usually credited as Miss Sharon Mitchell) and Tina (Tigr) Mennett, who play themselves. Perhaps the most interesting avant-garde film to grapple with pornography as a subject is Bette Gordon's *Variety*, scripted by Kathy Acker. Gordon's own essay (with photos by Nan Goldin), entitled *"Variety*: The Pleasure in Looking," asserts that pornography is "one more place to investigate how sexuality is constructed" (194). Linda Dubler's review of *Variety* observes that Gordon's heroine, a ticket-seller at a 42d Street porn theater, becomes a detective and a voyeur. For the character, says Dubler, "the fantasy of pornography serves as a liberating means to selfhood and power" (27). In a dialogue published as "Look Back/Talk Back," Gordon and Karyn Kay agree that "[o]ur work isn't about pornography *per se*. It's about transgression. We're interested in transgressive behavior, breaking the rules—following someone, talking dirty on the phone, murdering people. Pornographic fantasies are all part of representing female characters who don't play by the rules" (99).

Performance artists have also brought feminist ideas to avant-garde film. Liz Kotz's "Interrogating the Boundaries of Women's Art: New Work in Video by Four Women" discusses work by Leslie Singer, Azian Nurudin, Cecilia Doughtery, and Valerie Soe, some of whom use nudity and sexual imagery to shock audiences into attention. Kotz's "Striptease East and West: Sexual Representation in Documentary Film" studies variations between Indian and American striptease, as the latter is represented in Caitlin Manning's *Stripped Bare: A Look at Erotic Entertainers* (1988) and Carol Leigh's (Scarlot Harlot's) *Live Girls Nude* (1989) videos. Carolee Schneemann writes about trying to translate explicit performance onto celluloid in *More than Meat Joy: Complete Performance Works and Selected Writings*. Scott Poulson-Bryant reviews "Dick," a fifteen-minute video (Island Visual Arts/Bananas Video, 1991) made for women by Jo Menell. It features the voices of women discussing penises while Polaroids of 1,000 penises flash on the screen; the idea is to objectify male parts as routinely as men reify women's. Peter Lehman devotes one chapter of *Running Scared: Masculinity and the Representation of the Male Body* to *Dick Talk* (1986), a videotape shot at the Houston Center for Photography. Here five women talk about penises, fellatio, and related subjects. Maureen Nappi discusses the artistic and educational intent behind "Clit Tapes," her May 1976 public video installation at the Grey Gallery of New York University in which five television sets displayed tapes of women masturbating.

In "Two Interviews: Demystifying the Female Body: Anne Severson's *Near the Big Chakra* [1972] and Yvonne Rainer's *Privilege* [1990]," Scott MacDonald interviews Severson, whose film presents successive close-ups of thirty-seven vaginas, and Rainer, whose film explores voyeurism. Barriers between documentaries and performance movies, between feminist antisex tapes and feminist erotica, are highly porous, especially since some of the filmmakers constantly cross back and forth. Male artists, of course, experiment, too: Ela Troyano's article on "Ken Jacobs' Film Performance" explains how playwright Jacobs uses a French stag film of the 1920s called *Cherries* as the backdrop for live performance onstage. J. Hoberman's "XCXHXEXRXRXIXEXSX" follows the evolution of the Jacobs piece, now a two-hour film version of his earlier performance event, featuring the recut French stag synthesized with actors performing in the foreground. Those assuming that underground genres became defunct in the 1990s should look at *Film Threat* and *Film Threat Video Guide*, quarterlies devoted to exploring the sensibilities of deliberately offensive, often sexually explicit movies and videos made by alternative producers like Lydia Lunch, Eric Kroll, and Richard Kern.

EXPLOITATION FILMS

Somewhere between mainstream cinema and hard-core pornography are "exploitation" movies, a large category of often sexually oriented, frequently violent, but invariably soft-core films. In recent years the category has assumed importance because exploitation films—rather than hard-core films, whose levels of violence are low—are the ones cited by virtually all social scientists engaged in examining connections between pornography and antisocial behavior.

Eric Schaefer's *Bold! Daring! Shocking! True!: A History of Exploitation Films, 1919–1959* is now the most authoritative single source on the various exploitation genres, replete with names, dates, and anecdotes. Kenneth Turan and Stephen F. Zito's *Sinema: American Pornographic Films and the People Who Make Them* traces older exploitation melodramas and modern hard-core features. It is much better informed on the soft-core variety and remains a good source on the "forty thieves," a group of sleazy producer/distributors led by Kroger Babb and Louis Sonney; these flourished by promising explicitness but offering only tease. Another serviceable history is Mike Quarles' *Down and Dirty: Hollywood's Exploitation Filmmakers and Their Movies*, which covers producers like Fred Olin Ray (who made his first feature for $298), Russ Meyer, John Waters, Andy Milligan, Doris Wishman, and many others. Quarles points out the "innovations" in *Marijuana—Weed with Roots in Hell, The Immoral Mr. Teas, The Texas Chainsaw Massacre, Nude on the Moon,* and other exploitation reels. Richard Meyers' *For One Week Only: The World of Exploitation Films* is a brief history of scandal movies, from white slavery shockers of the 1920s to birth control and miscegenation themes in the 1930s and 1940s. "Exploitation Films," a special issue of *Film History*, ranges across 1930s jungle films, biker films, and blaxploitation. In "Of Hygiene and Hollywood: Origins of the Exploitation Film," Eric Schaefer finds the roots of such genres in the pseudomedical films popular in the teens and 1920s, especially those that dealt with marriage techniques and venereal disease. Of special interest are his comments on Kroger Babb's *Mom and Dad*, which offered prurient homilies on such subjects. Still further back go Oliver Pilat and Jo Ranson, who offer glimpses of the penny arcade films with titles like *Artists and Models* and *Cleo, Queen of the Harem* that were popular in amusement parks of the teens and 1920s in *Sodom by the Sea: An Affectionate History of Coney Island.*

The first two parts of Knight and Alpert's "History of Sex in Cinema" unearthed early exploitation films; part 16 covers the proliferation of films capitalizing on nudity in the 1960s. Jimmy McDonough's "Sexposed" outlines formulas in productions whose low budgets were essential to the twitting of authority and convention. More thorough is *Incredibly Strange Films*, edited by Andrea Juno and V. Vale; sections provide important analyses of many exploitation categories: Biker, Juvenile Delinquency, Beach Party, LSD, Women in Prison, Mondo, Industrial Jeopardy, and so on. Chapters deal with Herschell Gordon Lewis, Ted V. Mikels, Russ Meyer, Joe Sarno, David F. Friedman, and Doris Wishman, among many others. Scholars will find the book's biographies, filmographies, and genre studies essential. Not in the same league but still useful is *Kings of the Bs: Working within the Hollywood System, an Anthology of Film History and Criticism*, edited by Todd McCarthy and Charles Fynn, who include material on directors one would hardly call masters of exploitation. In *The Sleaze Merchants*, John McCarty gathers essays on Ed Wood, Sam Katzman, Jim Wynorski, David Friedman, Jess Franco, F. O. Ray, and other directors. Maitland McDonagh covers Fred Olen Ray, Paul Bartel, Sam Raimi, Zalman King, Wes Craven, Andy Sidaris, and others in *Filmmaking on the Fringe: The Good, the Bad, and the Deviant.* Two glossy texts, heavy on illustrations laced with historical information, are *Bizarre Sinema! Wildest Sexiest Weirdest Sleaziest Films: Sexploitation Filmmakers, Masters of the Nudie-Cutie, Ghoulie, Roughie and Kinky*, by Riccardo Morrocchi, Stefano Piselli, and James Elliot Singer, and *Grindhouse: The Forbidden World of "Adults Only" Cinema*, by Eddie Muller and Daniel Faris.

In the first installment of David Chute's two-part interview with David F. Friedman, "Wages of Sin" and "Wages of Sin: II," the filmmaker sketches the evolution of the exploitation film (which he describes as a "con-game") in references to stalwarts such as Kroger Babb and Herschel Gordon Lewis; in the second, Friedman recalls his work of the 1960s, especially on *Ilsa, She Wolf of the SS* (1974), a film celebrated for its scruffiness, and predicts that hard-core films will ultimately destroy the exploitation genre. Friedman's own *A Youth in Babylon: Confessions of a Trash-Film King* recalls days on sets along with the battles, swindles, and high jinks of "the forty thieves" in the heyday of the exploitation film and thus amplifies and supplements the coverage of Turan and Zito. He has promised a second volume of autobiography and anecdotes; the first is essential to an understanding of the sexploitation industry. Daniel Krogh and John McCarty appraise the films of one of Friedman's colleagues in *The Amazing Herschel Gordon Lewis and His World of Exploitation Films*. Jimmy McDonough's "The Ormonds" details the almost forgotten careers of Ron and June Ormond, producers of sleaze movies (*Untamed Mistress, Girl from Tobacco Row, Parisienne Creations*, etc.) for four decades. Marshall Blonsky revisits an avant-garde auteur in "Joe Sarno, the Dismemberer." David Konow's *Schlock-o-Rama: The Films of Al Adamson* celebrates a filmmaker whose virtually total lack of talent endears him to fans. Rudolph Grey's *Nightmare of Ecstacy: The Life and Art of Edward D. Wood, Jr.* critiques another shlockmeister, the transvestite director/producer of *Glen or Glenda* and other exploitation classics. Tim Burton has directed *Ed Wood* (1994), a mainstream biography starring Johnny Depp as Wood, yet another example of the cultural cycle by which marginal art makes its way toward the center. Mark Carducci's documentary, *The Ed Wood Story: The Plan 9 Companion* (1992), covers Wood's forays into esoteric sexuality and tells readers more than they want to know about Wood's *Plan Nine from Outer Space*, a film that has probably appeared on more "worst movies ever made" lists than any other.

The two volumes of *Shock Express: The Essential Guide to Exploitation Cinema*, edited by Stefan Jaworzyn, critique movies past and present and venture occasionally into hard-core genres. Soft-core porn, breast fetishes, and strange censors are the subjects of Andrew Dowdy's *Movies Are Better than Ever: Wide-Screen Memories of the Fifties*. Kit Parker Films has edited footage from exploitation films into a serviceable history called *Sex and Buttered Popcorn*, complete with interviews with David F. Friedman, Don Sonney (son of pioneer Louis Sonney), Kroger Babb's widow, Mildred, and other exploitation veterans. Kroger Babb's understanding of audiences was precise, says Friedman, noting that Babb made *Mom and Dad* (1944) for about $40,000 but marketed it so skillfully that it generated about $90 million, at admission prices of only thirty-five to fifty cents. Host Ned Beatty emphasizes the "moral messages" carried by virtually all exploitation films, even the nudist types such as Brian Foy's *Elysia* (1933). Most amusing is the discussion of the "square-up reel." This was usually a nudie like *Hollywood Script Girl* (late 1920s) that would be shown to audiences after the exploitation film to "square-up with their expectations" that they were actually going to see something titillating; without the bare nipples and fannies on the additional reel they would be disappointed by the solemn regular feature.

Gerald Peary offers a study of a well-known female exploitation filmmaker in "Stephanie Rothman: R-Rated Feminist" with particular reference to the director's *The Student Nurses* (1970), *It's a Bikini World* (1966), *The Velvet Vampire* (1971), and *Working Girls* (1974). Rothman herself comments on her career in Tony Williams' "Feminism, Fantasy and Violence: An Interview with Stephanie Rothman." Rothman says that she deliberately shows naked males as well as naked females, so that the latter do not seem overly objectified.

I know as a woman that women are interested in the bodies of attractive men and have long wanted to see them on screen although it's only recently that it has occurred. Also, I think it's highly unfair just to do that [present only nude females] to women. It's a reflection of the inequitable distribution of power in our society. When a person is nude they [sic] are vulnerable. To have a dressed person with a nude one is to tell you immediately who is the vulnerable one. When both people are nude I don't think there's that kind of objectification and reduction into making one just a piece of flesh. You're not making the same kind of statement. But I don't want to do to men what I feel has been done to women. It's not my intention to get some revenge in that regard. If I have to do some scenes of nudity I want to establish a precedent which may be more humane for both. (87–88)

"Doris Wishman: Queen of Exploitation" interviews the elderly Doris Wishman, director of twenty-four films, and visits the set of her latest nudie. In 1997 the Whitney Museum of Art held a festival of her films, a circumstance noted by Michael J. Bowen in "Embodiment and Realization: The Many Film-Bodies of Doris Wishman," an article on how Wishman's films reflect her sense of the body as she grows older.

The most notorious of all female exploitation filmmakers, of course, is Roberta Findlay, whose 1971 film *Slaughterhouse* was released under the title *Snuff* by its distributor, who engineered a publicity campaign designed to persuade the public that its featured performer had been actually murdered during the course of the filming. Unwittingly co-opted, feminist groups picketed exhibitions in major cities, thus ensuring the financial success of what is surely one of the stupidest films ever made. Frenzied searches and huge awards offered by the FBI and the Adult Film Association failed then and since to turn up any authentic snuff films, but the alleged existence of such films, that is, those in which women are literally killed as the climax of a sexual act, remains an urban American myth cherished by antiporn feminists. Avedon Carol's "Snuff: Believing the Worst" chronicles the spread of the false belief that "snuff" films freely circulate and diagnoses the pathologies that keep the myth alive. Eithne Johnson and Eric Schaefer point out that *Snuff* was the second stage in a cultural progression that began with Laura Mulvey's attempt to indict patriarchy by redefining looking itself as an act of male oppression. *Snuff* is historically important, Johnson and Schaefer say in "Soft Core/Hard Core: *Snuff* as a Crisis in Meaning," because it seemed to reinforce the contention that the male gaze is lethal. Unaware or unwilling to concede that the film was a hoax, antisex feminist groups continued for years to use the film to advance agendas: "*Snuff* and the mythic snuff film were deployed to shift the definition of pornography—from sexual representation to a literal inscription of male dominance over women" (56). Theorists of social construction could hardly find a more egregious example of the fabrication of sexual anathemas.

Gerald Peary's article "Woman in Porn: How Young Roberta Findlay Grew Up and Made *Snuff*" reviews the history behind the successful hoax and comments on Findlay's hardcore *Angel Number 9* (1975). What makes the article important, however, is Findlay's own comparison of hard-core porn films and opera, perhaps the most succinct theoretical statement ever made about the construction—or deconstruction, since pornography has always "deconstructed" itself—of pornographic scenarios. According to Findlay, "You have the opera story, but then everything stops when the soprano has to sing. It's the same thing in sex films. The story goes on, then it stops, then they have to screw" (32). Of the vast number of articles on the *Snuff* hoax, Molly Haskell's "The Night Porno Films Turned Me Off" is still worth reading, although Johnson and Schaefer and Carol list many other contemporary accounts. Yaron Svoray, a former Israeli policeman, has written *Gods of Death*, a book in which he claims to have watched a snuff film with actor Robert DeNiro, but he provides no documentation.

According to Gene Ross' "Sexploitation Films: The 60s Sexplosion!!!" written for the trade magazine *Adult Video News*, renewed interest in the genre has led to increased transfer of older soft-core films to videocassette. *Adult Video News* regularly charts the robust market for old and new sexploitation features. In "Exploitation Films and Feminism," Pam Cook applies a Marxist critique to soft-core films. Wayne A. Losano's "The Sex Genre: Traditional and Modern Variations on the Flesh Film" surveys soft-core film genres in terms of conventional American sexual taboos. "Jail Birds, among Others," by Mike Wilkins, looks at the "women-in-gangs/prison" exploitation films, speculates on the fascination of "celebrity tit," and reviews the economics of the genre, observing that from 1977 through 1979, producers turned out only thirty sexploitation movies per year but that cable and other markets have led to a resurgence. *Soft-Core: A Content Analysis of Legally Available Pornography in Great Britain 1968–1990 and the Implications of Aggressive Research*, compiled by W. Thompson, J. Annettes, and others, surveys movies quaintly described as devoted to "recreation rather than education." So does David McGillivray's *Doing Rude Things: The History of the British Sex Film, 1957–1981*, on an exclusively soft-core comic genre, of relevance here because of occasional exhibition in the United States.

Femme Fatales, a popular film journal, revels in pictures and stories about B-movie stars such as Dona Speir, Patricia Tallman, Blaire Baron, Dee Wallace Stone, and others whose topless scenes in second-tier legitimate films have drawn followings of fans; each issue includes profiles and interviews, retrospectives of celebrated scenes, and critiques of genres. "B-Movie Bimbos" sandwiches the commentary of Joe Bob Briggs [John Bloom] among nude photos of reigning queens such as Bobbie Breese, Linnea Quigley, and Becky LeBeau, all of whom boast beautiful busts. The title of Briggs' "Joe Bob Briggs' Guilty Pleasures: The 10 Top Drive-In Movies to Get Nookie By" is self-explanatory. Briggs has expanded some of these comments into *Joe Bob Goes to the Drive-In*. Briggs himself, an often embattled critic, is the subject of "The Life and Times of Joe Bob Briggs, So Far," a humorous, but revealing, profile by Calvin Trillin;

the trash-film reviewer lost his job with the *Dallas Times-Herald* because of his unwillingness to expunge words such as "hooters" from his columns. Among Briggs' current enterprises is a newsletter of films replete with nipples and mayhem called *We Are the Weird*. Though not primarily concerned with the erotic films sometimes associated with drive-ins, Kerry Segrave discusses community concerns with morality and the distribution of trashy films in *Drive-In Theaters: A History from Their Inception in 1933*. Obviously regarding himself as heir to a trash film tradition, John Waters writes about X-rated films, especially those of Russ Meyer, in contrast to his own movies in *Shock Value: A Tasteful Book about Bad Taste*. Waters' *Trash Trio*, a collection of three of his screenplays, also contains his remarks on "trash" as a cultural category.

Perhaps because Russ Meyer's films are so close to self-parody, probably because their mix of violence and sex earned him entrée into mainstream cinema, and certainly because they focus on mammoth breasts, Meyer has received more critical attention than other exploitation filmmakers. Richard Schickel's "Porn and Man at Yale" dilates on the ironies of holding a Russ Meyer Film Festival at Yale University. Raymond Durgnat's "An Evening with Meyer and Masoch: Aspects of *Vixen* and *Venus in Furs*" explores the stylized cruelty of Meyer's work. Stan Berkowitz's "Russ Meyer: Sex, Violence and Drugs—All in Good Fun" deals with elements favored by the director most closely identified with soft-core films in America. Meyer's modest nudie *The Immoral Mr. Teas* (1959) caused a furor unequaled until the release of Damiano's hard-core *Deep Throat* (1972). Of the many reviews by cultural critics, "A Night with Mr. Teas," in which Leslie Fiedler reflected on a version censored by the state of New York, described the scenario as funny, sad, and significant. "Russ Meyer, King of the Nudies," by critic Roger Ebert, who wrote the script for Meyer's *Beyond the Valley of the Dolls*, praises the director's comic genius. Ebert's "The Immoral Mr. Meyer" is a more mature reassessment that views the director as more pro-female than previously assumed. Juno and Vale's *Incredibly Strange Films* contains an interview generous with career details and an excellent capsule biography, as does Turan and Zito's *Sinema*. One of Meyer's favorite actresses is the subject of Dannis Peary's "From Vixen to Vindication: Erica Gavin Interviewed," in which Gavin speaks of her experience working for directors as diverse as Meyer and Jonathan Demme: "[Meyer's] *Vixen* is really a put-down of women. It says that all women want is sex, that they're never satisfied, that they'll go anywhere to find it. It shows that women have no loyalty, nor sensitivity or sexual relationships" (24). In "Preposterous Sex Dimensions, and Russ Meyer's Hang-ups," Addison Verrill isolates the elements of the director's appeal:

The Meyer staple has always been the casting of melon-breasted women whose shameless cavortings drive square-jawed men (on screen) to lust and violence. It's the most basic of adolescent sex fantasies and Meyer's audience for pix like "Lorna" and "Vixen" and "Cherry, Harry & Raquel" have always been male adolescents of all ages. With

"Up," however, Meyer makes use of male frontal nudity for the first time and, he says, the ladies are flocking in. Meyer's "Up" men seem as preposterously endowed as his women, and though they don't get as much screen time, they are taking some of the edge off the standard femme criticism of Meyer as a chauvinist porker.

The elegance of Radley Metzger's eroticism appealed to audiences a bit more sophisticated than those for Meyer's work, at least until Metzger began shooting hard-core films under the name Henry Paris. Richard Corliss' "Radley Metzger: Aristocrat of the Erotic" interviews the director and discusses his soft-core films, which employ psychologically driven plots, well-costumed performers, tensely revealed nudity, and upscale sets highlighted by designer furniture and satin sheets. Don Graham examines the ontology of a 1970 Metzger film in "Commentary/*The Lickerish Quartet*," while Linda Williams deals briefly with *The Punishment of Anne* (1979) in "Power, Pleasure, and Perversion: Sadomasochistic Film Pornography" and with *The Opening of Misty Beethoven* (1975), his most celebrated hard-core film, in her *Hard Core: Power, Pleasure, and the Frenzy of the Visible*.

The bimonthly *Psychotronic Video* runs critical articles on exploitation, retrospectives on celebrated trash films, and news of current variations within the genre. Exploitation films still flourish because audiences are constant, but also because they are a reasonably democratic form, easily shot, and, thanks to direct-to-video release, easily distributed. In "Queen City Monster-Maker," Aaron Epple interviews Mike Fox, a Cincinnati maker of soft-core "nudie" movies; Fox considers himself a "small-town storyteller" who appeals to audiences for goofy, self-parodic B-films. The *New York Times* recently devoted two full *pages* to Andy Sedaris, the doyen of the topless adventure story. In that article, "Working the Angles in Low-Budget Paradise," author Peter M. Nichols marveled at Sedaris' carefully developed niche appeal in American and European markets. Nichols' piece is perhaps the best cultural indicator of the altered regard for contemporary exploitation movies.

FILM CONTENT: VIOLENCE AND SEX

Unlike hard-core producers, exploitation filmmakers often associate sex and violence, and most emphasize aggression more than skin or sensuality. Violence, as battle and fight scenes, murder, car chases, bruality, or just plain mayhem, has traditionally functioned as kinesis in motion pictures and television. In volume III of his *A History of Broadcasting in the United States*, Erik Barnouw notes that when motion picture theaters became established, "films used the violent climax because they, and only they, could do so. Physical combat was always impractical in theater, seldom going beyond a ritual ballet. Radio could only offer a few seconds of sound-effects clatter and grunts. Only film could make use of what has been called the 'pornography of violence' " (82). To a lesser degree, the same might be said of sex; motion pictures are far more successful at representing sexuality than the theater because of the former's greater control. John Fraser's *Violence in the Arts*, an exploration of the kinetic and metaphysical aspects of artistic aggression, leans heavily on film examples, though not necessarily pornographic ones; Fraser is preparing a book on violent soft-core genres. Michael Leach thinks that Americans too readily accept knee-jerk linkages between sex and violence; he condemns the syndrome in *I Know It When I See It: Pornography, Violence, and Public Sensitivity*. Gershon Legman has provided the best explanation in *Love and Death: A Study in Censorship*: Whenever a society suppresses representations of sexuality, the imagery of violence increases. According to Legman, violence serves as surrogate for sex, and the degree of violence serves as an index to the culture's sexual pathologies. Images of people making love are healthy, he says, while images of aggression indicate a fear of sexuality.

One category of the exploitation film is the "slasher film," also known as the "splatter film" (because of the blood), which mixes the macabre and the sexual, though rarely to the same degree that, say, a vampire movie does. Popularity has fostered handbooks such as those by John McCarty: *Splatter Movies: Breaking the Last Taboo of the Screen* and the two-volume *John McCarty's Official Splatter Movie Guide*. Shelley Kay's "Confessions of a Splatter Girl—Part I" recounts her experience of acting in a slasher film. "Tromatized," by Bill Landis, profiles Troma, a company specializing in splatter films like *Bloodsucking Freaks, Toxic Avenger*, and *Splatter U*; "Respect Finds a Movie Studio Built on Shock and Schlock," by William Grimes, notes that popular culture scholars are interested in Troma's splatter comedies. William Castle's *Step Right Up! I'm Gonna Scare the Pants Off America* offers recollections by a trash filmmaker who successfully blended horror and sexual come-ons in his advertisements. Wheeler Dixon's "In Defense of Roger Corman" points out that Corman's studios not only nurtured many mainstream directors and actors but also helped to shape suspense and sex genres. D. B. Polan's "Eros and Syphilization: The Contemporary Horror Film" glances back at the hygiene genres that combined sex and fright as progenitors of horror and slasher films that also trade on erotic terror. Several journals deal exclusively with mergers of sex and horror in low-budget and underground films. *Film Threat* and *Film Threat Video Guide* cover independent Super-8 film and video producers, while *Ecco: The World of Bizarre Video* runs articles on vintage and recent exploitation films on videotape. Typical of the latter is an interview with the actor Bill Rogers, who has appeared in many titillating trash films, entitled "Bill Rogers: A Man of Taste [of Blood!]." Another zine, *Highball*, also caters to aficionados of horrific and fantastic exploitation; the articles are weird. The best chapters in *Eros in the Mind's Eye: Sexuality and the Fantastic in Art and Film*, edited by Donald Palumbo, deal with eroticism in *Rocky Horror Picture Show* and *Alien*; the bibliography on sex and fantasy is splendid. The essays in *Necromicon: Book One: The Journal of Horror and Erotic Cinema*, edited by Andy Black, dote on sexual motifs in monster, evil scientist, and vampire films. Bill George's *Eroticism in the Fantasy Cinema* is a quite serviceable, similar examination. *Immoral Tales: European Sex and Horror Movies, 1956–1984*, by Cathal Tohill and Pete Tombs, contrasts American and Continental examples and contains a lot of fugitive information about the latter.

The "slasher film," sometimes incorrectly called the "women in danger" film, has achieved notoriety as the basis for many recent pornography studies indicating that males who watch them become desensitized to violence directed at women. Examples of mainstream formulas are films like *Halloween, Friday the 13th, Nightmare on Elm Street*, and their various sequels and clones. A typical plot involves a teenage rite of passage that suddenly erupts in carnage as a madman begins stalking victims in the neighborhood. The killer is at his most deadly when his prey are distracted by sex, which is invariably rendered as mild soft-core. It is important to note that many Americans have never thought of such films as pornographic, that is, intended to sexually arouse, and would be puzzled to hear them so described. Nor are such viewers excessively naive: audiences have always taken pleasure in being momentarily frightened.

Stephen Koch, one of the first critics to call slasher films pornographic, set the tone for others in "Fashions in Pornography: Murder as Cinematic Chic." Patricia Erens' "*The Seduction*: The Pornographic Impulse in Slasher Films" theorizes that the increase in soft-core violence aimed at women parallels the increase in feminist challenges to male supremacy, a thesis without much support. The many studies of slasher films are sometimes contradictory, depending on the methodologies wielded by different researchers, the difficulty of controlling for variables (the kinds and degree of nudity, the comic or solemn aspects of the simulated sex, the kinds of aggression and the genders and ages of victims, the psychology of the characters and the viewers, the level of caricature in the presentation of violence, the cultural context, and so on), the assumptions implicit in the selection of films and audiences, and the specific coding system for registering incidents of violence. Among the central assumptions of early studies were that women constituted by far the greater number of victims of brutal attackers in the films and that the women were innocent targets of male killers whose testosterone had peaked gratuitously. These premises became articles of faith among some sociologists and some feminist antiporn critics. Both now appear to be false.

The problem with so many theories, according to "Gender and Survival vs. Death in Slasher Films: A Content Analysis," for which the sociologists Gloria Cowan and M. O'Brien conducted an analysis of fifty-six slasher films, is that there is rough equivalence in the number of male and female victims. In a similar study of thirty-eight examples, reported in "Sex, Violence, and Victimization in Slasher Film," Fred Molitor and Barry S. Sapolsky conclude that sex and violence are *not* often linked in slasher films and that, on average, male characters suffer violence more often than females, though females suffer for longer periods. Finally, James B. Weaver directly challenges the assumptions of Linz, Donnerstein, and Penrod, who hold that such films may have deleterious social effects (see **Pornography and Violence** and **Pornography and Acceptance of Rape Myths** in chapter 19) by looking at what actually happens in the films. Weaver's "Are 'Slasher' Horror Films Sexually Violent? A Content Analysis" concludes that the levels of violence in these films are not predominantly sexual and are not directed at one sex or gender more than any other.

According to Mary Beth Oliver in "Contributions of Sexual Portrayals to Viewers' Responses to Graphic Horror," the combination of sexual situations and horrific violence directed at either gender increases the viewers' enjoyment, especially among male subjects and those who scored higher on scales of sexual permissiveness, in large part because the combination makes the scenes seem more frightening to the subjects. The evidence most damaging to the early studies is that marshaled in the massive British survey by W. Thompson, J. Annettes, and their team of researchers. Their *Soft-Core: A Content Analysis of Legally Available Pornography in Great Britain 1968–1990 and the Implications of Aggressive Research* insists that violence in the slasher film overtakes the foolish characters, that is, those who deliberately ignore menace—especially by having intercourse at a time when other people are being killed around them. Such disregard for danger resembles standard plot devices that call for the foolhardy heroine to don a nightie and creep down dungeon steps to investigate a noise when she knows that vampires are multiplying at an exponential rate. Thompson et al. theorize that the effect of soft-core films may actually be to diminish violence among viewers. The British report thus echoes the thesis of David J. Hogan's *Dark Romance: Sexuality in the Horror Film*: that horror, slasher, and other frightening films actually carry antisex messages, since scenes of promiscuity usually end in catastrophe. Say Thompson et al.: if violence occurs as punishment for stupidity, then it is hardly surprising that audiences should appear "desensitized" to it. Probably the best single article on the subgenre is Carol J. Clover's "Her Body, Himself: Gender in the Slasher Film," which became the basis for Clover's *Men, Women, and Chain Saws*. Clover finds that most slasher films end with the "turning" of a female victim; she defends herself by becoming masculinized and destroying her attacker. The heroine thus appeals to male audiences because of her will to survive—*not* because she has been sexually victimized. Recent books to explore the sexual complexities of horror films include *Recreational Terror: Women and the Pleasures of Horror Film Viewing*, by Isabel Pinedo; *The Dread of Difference: Gender and the Horror Film*, edited by Barry Grant; and *Trash Aesthetics*, edited by Deborah Cartmell, I. Q. Hunter, Heidi Kaye, and Imelda Whelehan.

Major problems with analyses of pornographic genres are that researchers rarely identify the films they examine, use only small samples (fewer than thirty, say, for an industry that turns out thousands a year), or elide distinctions between hard-core scenarios, where the incidence of violence is extremely low, and soft-core, where the rate is extremely high. T. S. Palys concludes in "Testing the Common Wisdom: The Social Content of Video Pornography" that mainstream films contain more violence than hard-core porn, though there is some aggression in the latter. His study surveyed fifty-eight "mature" (R-rated, or soft-core) films and eighty-nine hard-core films made between 1979 and 1983; he found that there was more violence in the soft-core category than the hard-core during those years, though neither was significant since violent content decreased over-all. Stephen Prince analyzes some thirty full-length porn films popular between 1972 and 1985 in "Power and Pain: Content Analysis and the Ideology of Por-nography." He decides, among other things, that while power relationships in which males dominate females are common, males are even more likely to be objectified. Moreover, men and women are equally sexually active in these sce-narios and enjoy equal opportunities for pleasure. The ways in which men and women code sex and violence for research purposes probably explain the dif-ferent conclusions of Gloria Cowan, Carole Lee, Danielle Levy, and Debra Syn-der. (If a male slaps a female on the buttocks, however lightly, most viewers would code the blow as threatening, perhaps downright menacing, even if the behavior were clearly part of a consensual S/M scenario. But if a male engaged in rear-entry intercourse grips a female's breasts to steady himself, should his grasp be coded as aggressive? Some call penetration of any sort aggressive, and some would so designate the rear-entry position itself, because the female may be kneeling or merely facing away from her partner.) Indeed, in "Dominance and Inequality in X-Rated Videocassettes," Cowan et al. note that men code sexual acts differently than women.

Their analysis of forty-five films is rendered a little odd by the naive "dis-covery" that the examples contain activities like vaginal, oral, and anal inter-course, masturbation, and so on. The women researchers coded half of the films as concerned with domination and exploitation and found that women were more likely to be dominated (these were not S/M or B/D films); they thus assert that the incidence of violence in their sample was high, but in terms that clearly suggest the levels are nowhere near the degrees of violence exhibited by main-stream and nonpornographic films. "The Question of a Sexuality of Abuse in Pornographic Films," another study by Prince conducted with Paul Messaris, is a content analysis of twenty-nine films (1972–1985) designated as pornographic without any indication as to whether they are of the soft- or hard-core genres. The two found that the incidence of violence in all of them is fairly low but that when there is aggression, males direct it against females.

In conducting their study for the British Home Office, Dennis Howitt and Guy Cumberbatch examined a great many American films. Their *Pornography: Impact and Influences* points out that violence in hard-core pornographic films is quite low; they also cite a study in which the number of violent images in randomly selected films fluctuated between 3.3 and 4.7 percent and another that discovered very few bondage and S/M scenes. Only 7 percent of the total num-ber of scenes depicted women as submissive, and only 9 percent depicted men as submissive (5–8). Ni Yang and Daniel Linz also assert that R-rated movies contain more sexual violence—and nonsexual violence—against women than do X-rated videos. These conclusions are based on a random sample of ninety

R-, X-, and XXX-rated films, with scenes coded by two males and two females, as conducted by Yang and Linz for "Movie Ratings and the Content of Adult Videos: The Sex-Violence Ratio." The sexual violence in a soft-X and an R-rated film differed little, say Yang and Linz, but was higher in both than in the triple-X types. In the latter category, the hard-core films, sexual violence accounted for 4.73 percent of content, and nonsexual violence for another 4.73, as against the R-rated type, where sexual violence accounted for 3.27 percent of content, and nonsexual violence for 35 percent. One prominent exception to average practice is the multimillion-dollar epic *Caligula*, produced by Bob Guccione, publisher of *Penthouse*, and starring an expensive cast ranging from Malcolm McDowell and Helen Mirren to Peter O'Toole and Sir John Gielgud. The original emphasis of the film was gore; Guiccione himself later edited in hard-core sex scenes that jar the continuity. *Penthouse* tried to generate an audience by printing stills from the film, and Piernico Solinas' *Ultimate Porno* provides an illustrated running commentary on the shooting of the script.

The debate will, of course, spiral on. In his report on a meeting of sex researchers in California in 1985, "Violence and Women: Researchers Condemn R-Rated Films as Worse Offenders than Pornographic Movies," David G. Savage pointed out that scholars agreed that mainstream films were far more violent than pornographic ones. The dissent came from Catharine MacKinnon, who maintains that sex and violence should always be equated; as she put it, "the distinction between sex and violence is a false one" (6). Given that assumption, any representation of heterosexual sex, even the most "normal," however gently, lovingly, or romantically depicted, would be an expression of violence and would still promote injustice to women. In any case, the widespread conflation of sex and violence among researchers helps to explain the contradictory and untrustworthy findings of so many studies.

When Brian De Palma released the R-rated *Dressed to Kill* (1984), its resemblance to the slasher film generated controversy. Marcia Pally's interview with De Palma, " 'Double' Trouble," clarifies his intentions and records his bewilderment at the furor. A different reading is that of Cathy Griggers, who identifies the pornographic elements as parodic in De Palma's *Body Double* (1984) and in David Lynch's *Blue Velvet* (1986) in "Bearing the Sign in Struggle: Pornography, Parody, and Mainstream Cinema." *Dressed to Kill* inspired news columns and magazine sections, most notably, "The Porn Debates," a symposium in *Vogue.* "Dressed to Kill," a series of statements on violence and sexuality by David Denby, Alan M. Dershowitz, Edward Donnerstein, Daniel Linz, Al Goldstein, Dorchen Leidholdt, Neil M. Malamuth, Jan Lindstrom, Janella Miller, Marcia Pally, Thomas Radecki, Margo St. James, Lois P. Sheinfeld, and Ann Snitow ran as a special section in *Film Comment.* In his remarks, Radecki pointed out that the National Coalition on Television Violence reports significantly higher violent content in PG- and R-rated films than in X-rated movies.

Such data lead to an interesting question, as Joseph Slade has framed it in "Violence in the Hard-Core Pornographic Film: A Historical Survey." For most of their history, hard-core pornographic films have been absolutely illegal. Stag films were distributed clandestinely, always to small groups meeting in secret. That being the case, such films were free to include any kind of content, presumably the more outrageous the better; adding violence would not have made them more illegal. In fact, however, for decades the hard-core filmmakers in this country and abroad steadfastly rejected violence. Rape is not a common theme, and levels of any kind of violence in hard-core porn—even today—are far below those in legitimate, mainstream films. The question Slade asks is, Why has there been so little violence? The answers seem to be, first, that sex itself has been far more taboo than violence and more than satisfying in itself and, second, that many Americans do, in fact, draw sharp distinctions between sex and violence and decline to conflate them. In a massive study undertaken as a Ph.D. dissertation, "Comparative Quantitative Analysis of the Similarities and Differences in Female- versus Male-Directed/Produced/Written Commercial Sex Films and Videos (1980–1990)," Patti Britton found that "fewer than 1 percent of pseudoviolent or coercive acts were portrayed overall, with a mean designation of 0.55 such acts for the female directors and 0.75 for the male directors."

Such distinctions are usually lost in the welter of argument. Probably the most notorious skirmish in memory was Bonnie Sherr Klein's *Not a Love Story*, a 1982 production of the National Film Board of Canada. The film's attack on pornography centers on a stripper who has her consciousness raised through encounters with various antiporn feminists. Extremely explicit, *Not a Love Story* is the definitive example of an antiporn genre that mirrors its target in both explicitness and reductiveness. Antiporn feminists and political conservatives (fundamentalists generally considered it too graphic) found it convincing, while other groups, including many feminists, found it shallow, misleading, and even dangerous. The most widely reprinted assessment is B. Ruby Rich's "Anti-Porn: Soft Issue, Hard World," in which Rich notes that the movie is slick, manipulative, but important and also observes that antiporn is a cul-de-sac for women, because hyperbolic diatribes constitute a genre indistinguishable from traditionally pornographic ones. Rich suggests that women create alternative discourses of sexuality. Suspicious of the speed with which media embraced the antiporn movement, Rich protests that "the campaign against pornography is a massive displacement of outrage that ought to be directed at a far wider sphere of oppression. Just as the film narrows the hunt down to sinners, villains, and victims, so too does the antipornography movement leave out too much in its quasi-religious attack on the Antichrist" (18). *Not a Love Story* is replete with mythology, including the story, apparently made up out of whole cloth, that the Nazis flooded Poland with pornography to soften the country's citizens for invasion.

FETISH FILMS

Radical feminists attack sadomasochism (see **Sadomasochism** in Chapter 10 for extended discussion) as being particularly demeaning to women. Statistically, however, filmed (and performed) S/M scenarios in which males are punished, dominated, or otherwise subordinated by women far outnumber those in which the roles are reversed. The majority of bondage and discipline and sadomasochistic films—the differences have to do with degrees of "punishment" and the solemnity of self-consciousness—do *not* include actual sex, which appears to be secondary to the pleasures of postures, costumes, and paraphernalia. In "Merlin of the Movies," Robert J. Stoller interviews a man and three women who have made half a dozen S/M videotapes together. The activities are consensual and heavily ritualized: displays of pierced body parts, mud-wrestling, bondage, and light "torments." "Of Human Bondage" documents the activities of Ona (herself a veteran star and producer of hard-core films) and Frank Zee, who make specialty videos of consensual bondage and "an exchange of power." Katrien Jacobs examines the sadomasochistic lesbian films of Maria Beatty in " 'The Lady of Little Death': Illuminated Encounters and Erotic Duties in the Life and Art of Maria Beatty"; Jacobs' is perhaps the boldest approach to the subject. Worth noting for their historical perspectives are Jean Streff's *Le Masochisme au Cinéma*, an examination of masochism in legitimate and pornographic cinema, and George de Coulteray's *Le Sadisme au Cinéma*, a survey of mainstream films where sadism has historically been more prevalent than in the pornographic genres. Both focus on cultural and psychological significance of specific images.

S/M aside, reflections on actual behavior in porn films vary widely. Horace Freeland Judson's "Skindeep: How to Watch a Pornographic Movie" identifies motifs and expresses hope that filmmakers will strive for more "erotic realism," though it is never quite clear what "realism" means. What people usually mean is depiction of *their* favorite fantasies, which can be romantic or raw. The increased incidence of heterosexual anal intercourse in the late 1970s, a trend that has risen steadily since, is the subject of Joseph Slade's "Recent Trends in Pornographic Films"; the article suggests that filmmakers must constantly violate taboos to attract audiences. Sociologists tend to list what they call "paraphilias," that is, addictive deviations, in terms not much different from the legalese employed in obscenity trials. For example, P. E. Dietz and B. Evans find that fetishes and "deviation" are staples of various genres in "Pornographic Imagery and the Prevalence of Paraphilia" (they note that S/M scenarios occur in few films, and that leather, rubber, and boots represent only 2 percent or less of the fetishes). L. T. Garcia and L. Milano conclude that fellatio is far more prevalent than cunnilingus in hard-core videotapes in "A Content Analysis of Erotic Videos." Such studies can be unintentionally amusing because they rely on pedantic quantification and thus resemble the obsessions of those individuals who testify before commissions as to the surface area of flesh revealed in a given medium. Since the latter method is to count each naked woman, then multiply by two breasts, the point is frequently lost in the arithmetic.

Fetish films and videocassettes often do not contain intercourse. (See **Fetishes** in Chapter 9.) Two videotape compilations of short bondage reels of the 1940s and 1950s, featuring Bettie Page and other popular models, are marketed as the *Classic Films of Irving Klaw: Volumes I and II.* Klaw's striptease and lingerie fetishes are discussed in *Incredibly Strange Films*, edited by Andrea Juno and V. Vale; Page's bondage and striptease films are covered in *The Betty Pages Annual.* The Page striptease films *Teasearama* and *Varietease* can be purchased from Something Weird Films (see **Films and Videotapes** in Chapter 4). Eric Kroll, who owns one of the world's largest collections of fetish material, has shot a homage to Klaw called *Girls from Girdleville* (1992); Home Box Office covered the shooting of the film, in which models parade in girdles, brassieres, and panties, as a segment of the channel's *Real Sex: 6.* Rowdy Yates reviewed the film in "Girls from Girdleville" to observe that its stylized classicism should appeal to nostalgia buffs and fetish freaks alike. Kroll has also released *Eric Kroll's The Fetish Tapes*, a four-cassette compilation of women in raised skirts, vintage panties, latex, corsets, leather boots and leggings, stiletto heels, and strap-on dildos; some are depicted shaving their pubic hair, tugging on the rings embedded in their nipples and navels, or employing kinky appliances. Though better shot than most, with deliberate attention to iconography, Kroll's tapes are typical of hundreds aimed at niche markets. Sylvia Plachy and James Ridgeway interview Carter Stevens, maker of fetish films (enemas, feet, and so on) in *Red Light: Inside the Sex Industry.* "Male Order Fantasies" visits the studios of Bob and Dave of Diane Peerless Productions, makers of fetish films to order since 1959. The two men tell many anecdotes of customers with special tastes. Ariel Hart, a writer of porn films, visits the set of Fred Lincoln, a maker of enema, bondage, and other products for Bizarre Films in "Bizarre Days."

Issues of *Adult Video News* review fetish films old and new. Typical is "Alternative Sexuality and the Video Retailer" in which Sam Masters lists tapes ranging from bondage and infantilism to large-breasted models and offers advice on marketing them on rental shelves. Striptease shorts, most of which rarely revealed a bare nipple and few of which exposed pubic hair, were staples of penny arcades and fairgrounds during the 1940s and 1950s. Their number is beyond counting, though many are available from mail-order houses specializing in vintage films. Various filmmakers have marketed historical compilations; the most famous is Alex de Renzy's omnibus *The History of the Blue Movie* (1971), which provides some commentary to go with a mix of soft- and hard-core examples. Several companies have transferred vintage stags and smoker films, arcade nudes and stripper films, peep-show loops, teasers, and other ancient footage from original prints (see **Films and Videotapes** in Chapter 4).

Scholars wishing to study fetish content need only look at examples, but they can find indicators in the reviews in *Adult Video News*, older magazines such as *Adult Cinema Review, Blue Movie Expose*, and *Cinema Blue*, and current ones such as *Hustler Erotic Video Guide, Video Xcitement, Gay Video Guide* (quarterly), and *Manshots* (bimonthly). The extreme range of fetishes offered is evident in any of the mail-order specialty catalog pages now included in most men's magazines. During the 1970s, *Variety* routinely reviewed porn features; the plot summaries are accurate and useful. The various guides to films (see **Films and Videotapes** in Chapter 4) break out listings by specific performers, specific directors, and specific behaviors. The autobiographies of performers listed elsewhere sometimes specify what they and their colleagues like or do not like to do on camera and what directors ask them to do. Some of the content studies in volume III (especially section IV) of the *Technical Reports of the Commission on Obscenity and Pornography* make for interesting reading, though some now seem pretty dated. Worth looking at also are some of those in the *Report* of the Attorney General's Commission, especially pp. 387–424. In both cases, the assumptions of the researchers often offer as much insight as the reported data.

THE "CUM SHOT"

If violence or aggression in pornography represents one pole of attention, then a fetish for orgasm stands at the other extreme. Richard Dyer's "Male Sexuality in the Media," a chapter of his *The Matter of Images: Essays on Representations*, observes that the word *climax* is common to both sex and narrative. "In both, the climax is at once what sex and story aim at and also the signal that the sex and the story are over. The placing of the women and the men in the stories ensures that a heterosexual model is reasserted, in which women represent what male sexuality is ostensibly there for. Women are the goal or the reward, they are the occasion of male sexuality—and yet they play no active part in it. The man drives himself, or his penis drives him; it is he who 'reaches' the climax" (120). At the same time, says Dyer, these conventions restrict males also: "What is perhaps more surprising is that these images should, by and large, be so unattractive, so straight and narrow, so dreary. Men too are fixed in place by this imagery, and if theirs is a place of superiority it is nonetheless a cramped, sordid, compulsive little place with its hard-edged contours and one-off climaxes" (121). How mainstream films handle depictions of climax is the subject of "Hollywood Orgasm" by Mattie Oliver, who speculates on what is likely to appeal to women: "The sex act doesn't have much going for it in the way of plot" (51), she says, and orgasms on the mainstream screen are unreal. By contrast, male orgasms in hard-core pornographic films are extremely graphic and visible. Stag films began to display ejaculation shortly before World War II; afterward the practice became nearly universal, thanks, in part, to new lenses and film stock that could capture fleeting spurts and, in part, to the rise of *mise-en-scène* narratives that displaced comic plots with landscapes of the body. By some accounts (those of veteran performers, for instance), ejaculation outside the body remain standard even when lenses could register orgasms on faces because actresses in the 1960s and 1970s did not trust birth control methods. More than one actress of the period has told Joseph Slade (for *Shades of Blue*) that they considered ejaculation inside inconsiderate if not rude. In any case, flying sperm became iconographic.

Cindy Patton's important essay, "Speaking Out: Teaching In" observes that critics have devoted too little space to discovering the meaning that viewers attach to specific acts such as the "cum shot," that is, ejaculation visible because the male withdraws in order to spurt semen into space or onto his partner's body or face. Patton notes that cum shots "enhance the illusion of control over ejaculation" (381) but notes also that heterosexual men rarely imitate the behavior they see in films in their own sexual lives, despite lots of anecdotal testimony to the contrary. "Clearly," says Patton, "few heterosexual men engage in this practice in real life. The men in porn are paid to *control* their orgasm, their sexuality, not for their partner in the film but for the viewer; the mimetic aspects of porn are surely contingent on the hermeneutic of viewers" (379). In "Male Gay Porn," Richard Dyer deplores the prevalence of the cum shot in gay films because it represents the "ideology of the visible" and reinforces a narrative that "is never organized around the desire to be fucked, but around the desire to ejaculate" (228). Male ejaculation has been a running theme in porn criticism since *The Other Victorians*, in which Steven Marcus underlined the economic associations of "spending," the nineteenth-century term for orgasm, as if semen were a precious fluid that could be depleted. Other terms include "splash shot," "spunk shot," "pearl necklace" (pooling the semen in the hollow of the partner's neck, so that it overflows on each side), and "juice shot." Linda Williams, noting that the cum shot today is also often called the "money shot," links it to Marcus' capitalist metaphor in her *Hard Core: Power, Pleasure, and the Frenzy of the Visible* and also in "Fetishism and Hard Core: Marx, Freud, and the 'Money Shot.' " Williams thinks of ejaculation as a leitmotif similar to those that punctuate musical comedy, a genre she thinks resembles the hard-core film. Although Williams' thesis tends to reduce porn films to a single heterosexual genre, *Hard Core* is remarkable because the author actually engages the subject instead of pontificating from a distance and because she insists that feminists must learn to reevaluate sexual expression.

The late Brendan Gill decided that the cum shot is a dramatic device signaling closure for that part of the narrative. Gill wrote "Blue Notes," an unsurpassed essay on the beginnings of commercial porn in the late 1960s and early 1970s. Openly fascinated by what he sees, Gill points out that detractors sneer at porn films because the sex isn't "the real thing." That argument, Gill says, assumes that everyone knows what the real thing is, whereas he cheerfully admits that he does not. As a drama critic with an eye for climaxes, he registers the inequity that results from the inherent difficulty in doing justice to female orgasm, especially when oral sex is involved. Performed properly, cunnilingus remains invisible to the film audience, whereas fellatio results in the arcing ejaculation: "Simply as theatre," says Gill, "cunnilingus isn't a patch on fellatio, and it is difficult to see what even the most ardent women's lib maker of blue movies can do about it" (11).

Gill's wordplay on *real* is lost on commentators who explain the ubiquity of the cum shot as evidence that the sex is "real." An actress who made four porn films before fear of AIDS drove her to quit scoffed at this idea. Speaking to Joseph Slade for his forthcoming *Shades of Blue*, she said that cum shots are merely one rhythmic element in the structure of a sex scene. American film-makers are adopting European rhythms, she thinks; the latter stress oral, vaginal, and anal intercourse, which usually occurs in an ascending dramatic order. In theory, anal intercourse ought to represent the climax, in "a sort of dead end," she puns, "since there's no place left to stick the dick," but in fact, she knows, the cum shot is still mandatory. "It's silly to say that the sex has to be proved," she laughs, "when I'm twisting my head to keep hair out of my face just so the camera can see I have a real dick in my mouth, or I'm holding my cheeks apart so the camera can see that he's *really* in my pussy or my ass." She thinks the cum shot is an emblem of desire for the female characters in the movie. "It's what we're supposed to lust after," she says, "all the rest is just dick-handling," a task she laughingly compares to baton-twirling. The ejaculation rounds off the scene by signaling closure: "The guy comes, and we lick it up, or rub it around on our face and tits like it's the greatest thing since aloe cream. The only problem is that I could never figure out whether I was supposed to look full or hungry for more." To these meanings, she says, the threat of AIDS has injected sinister implications that may perversely enhance the appeal of the cum shot, as if the performers were deliberately courting death by "playing around with toxic waste." "You could probably fuck every professional in the business, and be safer than going home with just one guy from a bar," the actress said, pointing out that actors are careful because filmed intercourse is their bread and butter. Even so, she thinks, "there comes a point when you start to worry." (Several performers have tested positive for HIV.)

The filmmaker Candida Royalle thinks the cum shot does subordinate the female's satisfaction to the male's. Describing her intent in founding Femme Productions in "Porn in the USA," Royalle says that when she began, "I was so fed up with seeing the cum shot in every movie—in a context that didn't support women's pleasure—that I decided to have no cum shots in my films" (29). In "Candida Royalle," a documentary on Royalle's videos, the director says that she eschews "cum shots" on the grounds that they are unappealing, stupid, and of little interest to female viewers. In her films, men "are very respectful of women." Royalle aims at an equity that includes lots of cunnilin-gus, as if she were taking up Gill's challenge; her heroines writhe about as their partners minister to labia. Eithne Johnson's "Excess and Ecstasy: Constructing Female Pleasure in Porn Movies," which uses Royalle's films as exemplars, observes that women's porn emphasizes mutuality: "If the conventional 'money' shot favors a close-up of the ejaculating penis, usually placed against a woman's face or genitals, the female orgasmic image in women's porn is depicted typically in a medium-long or a long shot. In this way, the cause-effect relationship between the two performers is privileged rather than fragmented, as in the 'money' shot, or displaced onto the feminized text-body, as in conventional porn" (41). Lisa Katzman's visit to Royalle's studio, reported in "The Women of Porn: They're Not in It for the Moneyshot," plays up efforts by feminist porn producers to devalue ejaculation: "Liberating porn from the omnipresent money shot, they are giving sex to the whole body and are reimagining the industry . . . by expanding porn's lexicon and articulating the eroticism of mutual pleasure. . . . They are broadening the continuum of desire" (33).

To such arguments, Bernice Faust responds in *Women, Sex and Pornography: A Controversial Study* that cum shots embody the logic of desire:

Since ejaculating into blank space is not much fun, ejaculating over a person who responds with enjoyment sustains a lighthearted mood as well as a degree of realism. This occurs in both homosexual and heterosexual pornography, so that ejaculation cannot be interpreted as an expression of contempt for women only. Logically, if sex is natural and wholesome and semen is as healthy as sweat, there is no reason to interpret ejaculation as a hostile gesture. Healthy semen is not like feces, which may smell offensive, dirty the sheets, and carry germs. Some women and men enjoy the silky feel of fresh semen, some enjoy the smell and some find it excites the imagination. (18)

It would be odd if semen were not one of our culture's principal fetishes, given our collective fondness for oral sex, though the latter has rarely been the subject of serious investigation. The only real mystery, perhaps, is why males are not more attracted to female secretions and do not devote equal time to orally coaxing orgasm from their female partners. Not exploiting the dramatic possibilities of ejaculation in a sex film would be tantamount to not exploiting the kinetic properties of car chases in adventure films.

In reviewing feminist antiporn ordinances, Lisa Duggan, Nan D. Hunter, and Carole S. Vance study the content analysis of *Deep Throat* made by Catharine MacKinnon in support of the Minneapolis and Indianapolis antiporn legislation in "False Promises: Feminist Antipornography Legislation." MacKinnon claimed that Linda Lovelace's role in that film was to serve as a "receptacle" for "male genitalia and ejaculate." Duggan, Hunter, and Vance believe that other viewers see a quite different movie, in which the heroine is "shown as both actively seeking her own pleasure and as trying to please men." The authors note that the Minneapolis ordinance assumes that "heterosexual sex itself is sexist; that women do not engage in it of their own volition; and that behavior pleasurable to men is necessarily repugnant to women. In some contexts, for example, the representation of fellatio and multiple partners can be sexist, but are we willing to concede that they always are?" (77–78). Scruffy and mean-spirited films can be more clearly one-sided in their sexism, of course. In "Let Me Tell Ya 'bout Suffering," Rhonda Nettles describes the content of *Let Me Tell Ya 'bout White Chicks* (Dark Brothers, VCA, 1984), a film in which a woman engages in oral, vaginal, and anal sex with two men. Nettles says that at one point, when the sex is vigorous, the woman starts to cry. "I don't care what anybody says. That woman was suffering. On those few seconds of videotape, all of the pain, shame, and degradation she felt in those moments, with her jaw all numb and exhausted and her asshole all stretched and pummeled, was written on her face in bright, flashing neon" (69). Nettles thinks that an industry that promotes that kind of degradation should not be permitted to exist.

One's own sexuality shapes attitudes toward filmed sex, says Cindy Patton in "The Cum Shot: Three Takes on Lesbian and Gay Sexuality." Patton observes that despite the different orientations between gay and lesbian representations, lesbians who like explicit lesbian porn also like explicit gay porn, a predilection that, in turn, suggests that more communication is possible than was previously thought. Says Patton in "Speaking Out: Teaching In":

There has been virtually no interest in the meanings viewers make of porn (quantitative analysis has related exposure to attitudes rather than discovering phenomenologically what interpretive modes viewers produce. In part because of cultural disinterest, until recently, in the rigorous study of popular culture, pornography was located on the outside edge of such culture. But, equally important, the idea that porn has no narrative or aesthetic pleasure beyond mere "getting off" has suggested the wrong criteria for evaluation of decoding skills or differences. (378)

ORGASMS AND GENDER INEQUITIES

Different decoding goes on. Scott MacDonald's well-known "Confessions of a Feminist Porn Watcher" argues that heterosexual men are drawn to porn films out of a simple curiosity about other men's penises and because they can watch them without being assumed to be homosexual. In his portentous "Pornographic Space: The Other Place," Dennis Giles speaks of pornographic boundaries, giving preference to the metaphysics of the vagina: "The interior space she encloses (identified as the woman *in essence*) is an *invisible space* . . . [that] cannot be possessed by visual knowledge. In order to emphasize its separation from the *known* space of the pornographic film, I call this central interior the Other place." Giles' point is that the real focus of the porn film is woman; men are at most penises, devoid of personality and individuality. Unfortunately, Giles seems at times to speak as a pediatrician of the sort who intones that "boys may be fancy on the outside, but girls are fancy on the *inside*." (Some filmmakers seem to have taken Giles' remarks about the female's interior space to heart. Several commercial films now feature microscopic cameras inserted into the vagina during intercourse to dispel these alleged mysteries. The audience can watch the vagina walls change color or see the rush of semen at climax.) Xavier Mendik's "From 'Trick' to 'Prick' " deals with gendered spectatorship of porn films.

Such reflections lead inevitably to the question of who identifies with whom in porn scenarios: do heterosexual males watching an "insatiable" female on-screen identify with her rampant sexuality, or do they instead identify with the male performer simply because they both have penises or perhaps because the performer has a penis to envy? Various other commentators, from Joseph Slade in "Pornographic Theatres off Times Square," to Linda Williams in *Hard-Core*, have tried to sort out this question. The question hardly interests all critics, of course, since many modern theories of porn reify individuals into simple polarities of oppression and victimization and turn their sexuality into social fictions, so that penises, vaginas, and sperm become lost in narratives of power. When penises become phalluses, the former can be ignored; that way one can avoid embarrassing words, distance one's self from the vulgar physicality of sweat and discharge, and construct entirely different fantasies out of hyperdiscourse.

Brendan Gill's challenge nonetheless resonates. Filmmakers are not insensitive to the political aspects of ejaculation and the disparities it symbolizes. The alleged inequity that the ability to ejaculate confers has led to a demand for females who can also ejaculate, a talent that has boosted the careers of "rainwomen" like Nikki Charm, Fallon, and Sarah Jane Hamilton (aka Victoria Secret), all of whom can spurt liquids for Olympian distances. Fatale Films, a lesbian production house, now distributes Fanny Fatale's videotape, *How to Female Ejaculate*, in which coaches instruct students in liquid gender equity. Interestingly, the session seems "socially constructed" with a vengeance; the model clearly mimics the fraternity house "circle-jerk." Advocates insist that women can train themselves to ejaculate liquid that is not urine from a reservoir separate from the urethra, but this is a matter of some dispute. Desmond Heath, in "An Investigation into the Origins of a Copious Vaginal Discharge during Intercourse: 'Enough to Wet the Bed—"That" Is Not Urine,' " and J. Lowndes Sevely and J. W. Bennett, in "Concerning Female Ejaculation and the Female Prostate," review the conflicting claims to conclude that denial turns on the semantics of the term *semen*; Sevely and Bennett conclude "that women can ejaculate, and that the female prostatic fluid discharged through the urethra is a component of female sexual fluids that contribute to erotic pleasure" (1).

In any case, porn films seem to be forcing the phenomenon, which has mild relevance for gender studies. The most politicized defense is that of Shannon Bell, who provides a good list of articles on the subject. In "Feminist Ejaculations," Bell asserts that producing a copious flow not only represents a legitimate exploration of feminine sexuality but is also a step toward greater equity. Construed as "feminist voice" or "discourse," female ejaculation validates the feminist theories of writers like Luce Irigaray and Julia Kristeva; the discharge, which Bell thinks can become copious with practice, thus becomes a species of supremely postmodern achievement. Bell appends a fascinating photograph of herself in midlaunch. In the absence of female performers acquiring this skill in large numbers, however, hard-core directors must struggle to convince audiences that female performers are having a good time.

They compensate with the sounds of orgasm, usually rendered as ecstatic female gasps and cries. In view of the stag film's deliberately remaining silent for almost six decades, studies of the relationship of sound and image in pornographic films are unsurprisingly few. For "Gender Differences in the Interpretations and Reactions to Viewing Pornographic Vignettes," Peter S. Gardos alters the sound tracks of cum-shot sequences to find that aggressive audio narratives cause males and females to regard the ejaculations as degrading, but silence or sounds of pleasure or acceptance result in much more positive responses. By contrast, Stephen Heath's "Body, Voice" observes that images of the body rather than spoken dialogue dominate in pornographic (and mainstream) cinema. Joseph Slade discusses the "voluptuousness of silence" in stag films in "The Pornographic Film Market and Pornographic Formulas" and notes that the appearance of the feature-length film in the late 1960s brought sound tracks to hard-core with ambivalent results. Cindy Patton's "Hegemony and Orgasm—Or the Instability of Heterosexual Pornography" deals with lesbians and lesbian scenes in heterosexual porn and also reflects on the difficulty of demonstrating female orgasm visually, which means that the sound of a woman's ecstasy has to persuade and rarely does. In "Faking It: Comment on Face-Work in Pornography," Dean MacCannell takes a Goffman-like approach to the counterfeiting of orgasm through distorted faces in pornographic frames. Eithne Johnson's "Sound and the Textuality of Female Orgasms" explains how sound and image combine in hard-core pornographic films to capture female orgasm, something difficult to illustrate convincingly. Pornographic films themselves, which are nothing if not self-reflexive, frequently make similar points. The quasi-documentary (and dopey) porn film *Boobs, Butts, and Bloopers* (1990), for instance, is one of several such efforts to demonstrate how facial expressions matched with groans of release are shot in reverse angle *after* acts of intercourse take place.

HARD-CORE GENRES

(For extensive bibliographies and guides to hard-core genres, see **Films and Videotapes** in chapter 4, especially *Adam Black Video Illustrated, Adam Film World, Adult Video News, Hustler Erotic Video Guide, Gay Video Guide, Manshots, Video Xcitement*, and *XXX Gay Video Showcase*.)

For most Americans, the "pornographic film" is the hard-core, triple-X reel or videocassette depicting actual sex or, at the very least, fetishistic activity clearly intended to arouse. Hard-core features are the descendants of the stag film, the first of which appeared in the United States no later than 1912, a genre shot first in 35mm, then 16mm and 8mm film widths to accommodate small, portable projectors. Because they were illegal, they were shot and distributed clandestinely, and that fact, more than any other, has made it difficult for historians to trace their evolution. Its outlaw status made the stag the purest of pornographic motion picture forms: a cinema of deliberate transgression. As the stag mutated into the triple-X videocassette, some of its authenticity was lost.

Aside from Eugene Slabaugh (see **Major Research Collections** in chapter

7), the principal authorities on pornographic films before 1945 are Kurt Moreck, the pen name of Konrad Hammerling, a sexologist at the Institute for Scientific Sexual Knowledge in Vienna during the 1920s; Ado Kyrou, a French film producer and historian; Frank Hoffmann, an American anthropologist and folklore specialist; and Joseph Slade, a historian of communication technologies. Moreck's major work, *Sittengeschichte des Kinos* (A Moral History of the Cinema), places stag films in the context of early cinema. Moreck was fascinated by traffic in stags as they moved around the world. Moreck's "Rosario, Der Steppenhafen" pinpoints an early source as Rosario, the brothel district of Buenos Aires. Moreck's *Das Gesicht*, a study of visual eroticism, covers stereoscopic porn and very early films, while his "Der pornographische Film" sketches the formulas that emerged in the 1920s. Ado Kyrou's "D'un Certain Cinéma Clandestin" is the single most important article on classic stags because it dates and identifies several dozen films (some from the great Gugitz collection, with interpolations from the Michel Simon collection, both of which have been since dispersed) by nationality and sometimes by producers and performers; these are preponderantly European, although Kyrou provides summaries of important American examples. Frank Hoffmann explores folkloristic motifs in stag films in the Kinsey Archives in "Prolegomena to a Study of Traditional Elements in the Erotic Film" and in *Analytical Survey of Anglo-American Traditional Erotica*. Both provide plot synopses and comment, historical references, and thematic analysis. Hoffmann was the first American scholar to speak knowledgeably on the subject. Joseph Slade's forthcoming history of the hard-core film, *Shades of Blue: A History of the Clandestine Film*, devotes several chapters to the evolution of the stag genre in Europe and America. Articles with a historical bent by Slade include "The Pornographic Film Market and Pornographic Formulas," which deals with genres and economics; "Pornographic Theatres off Times Square," which discusses audiences and tastes; "Recent Trends in Pornographic Films," which examines taboos; and "Violence in the Hard-Core Pornographic Film: A Historical Survey," which analyzes the lack of aggression in hard-core genres.

Also important are Stéphane Bourgoin, whose "Petite Histoire du Film Erotique Americain" deals with the 1920s and 1930s, although the article mistakenly attributes the animated film *Buried Treasure* (1922?) to Gregory LaCava (it was actually a collective work by most of the major cartoonists of the 1920s, shot as a birthday gift for Windsor McCay, creator of "Gertie the Dinosaur"). Relevant here is Joseph Slade's "Bernard Natan: France's Legendary Pornographer," which contrasts the early stags of several countries. *Lust und Elend: Das erotische Kino*, edited by Karola Gramann, Gertrud Koch, et al., collects historical, theoretical, mostly feminist essays on erotic films, some of them American. One of these, Gertrud Koch's "The Body's Shadow Realm," draws on Moreck and on Kurt Tucholsky, a Weimar journalist interested in porn films, for a historical sketch of early German stags. Heinrich Ludwig's "Die Erotik im Film" examines dealer catalogs of the teens and 1920s in order to reproduce scenarios of European and American stags. As always, the magisterial *Bilder-*

lexicon der Erotik is a reliable source; volumes III through VI contain snippets on early film eroticism.

Di Lauro and Rabkin's *Dirty Movies* follows the evolution of the stag film in an illustrated volume of little analysis; its filmography of stags merges the shelflists of the Kinsey Erotic Film Archives and the Hugh Hefner collection. Stag producers often shot stills and movies at the same time in order to take advantage of the photo market; some stills appear in Edward J. Nelson's two-volume *Yesterday's Porno: A Pictorial History of Early Stag Photographs*. The two volumes of *Smut from the Past*, the first edited by Michael Perkins, the second by John Milton, also contain stills from stag films mixed in with single shots from photo sets, but without captions identifying them as such. *Sinema*, by Turan and Zito, is weak on stags but excellent on the history of the "exploitation" and "nudie" types. *Der pornographische Film*, a history by Georg Sesslen, compares French and German pioneers with their American counterparts. Despite sketchiness, Robert Rimmer's historical comment in *The X-Rated Videotape Guide* is more or less accurate. Linda Williams' splendid *Hard Core: Power, Pleasure, and the Frenzy of the Visible*, which deconstructs contemporary films, rapidly glosses the stag genre. Richard Arlen's *Sex and Pornography in the Movies* is a cheesy history, as are Martin A. Grove and William S. Ruben's *The Celluloid Love Feast: The Story of Erotic Movies*, Marv Strick and Robert I. Lethe's *The Sexy Cinema*, Roger Blake's *The Porno Movies*, and the anonymously published *The Erotic Screen: A Probing Study of Sex in the Adult Cinema*, all of which sensationalize soft-core and late-1960s hard-core movies. Although subject to the same caveat, Richard Wortley's *Erotic Movies* is more helpful. Two general, but out-of-print, histories of sex in the United States, *The Sex Industry*, by George Paul Csicsery, and *Our National Passion: 200 Years of Sex in America*, by Sally Banes, Sheldon Frank, and Tem Horowitz, contain chapters on porn films and performers.

In 1970 and 1972 the Dutch porn magazine *Suck* sponsored "Wet Dreams" film festivals in Amsterdam. Entries from around the world are chronicled in stills with some commentary in *Wet Dreams: Films and Adventures*, edited by William Levy. In his article on the first of these events, "Sex Marathon," Colin MacInnes notices a fact "peculiar to sex films—if you don't like the performers, you don't like the film at all; whereas in a straight film, if the acting is good, you put up with a star who may not be your personal favorite" (990). The sudden popularity of *Deep Throat* and *Behind the Green Door* elevated movie porn to quasi respectability and gave porn performers—females, anyway—more than fifteen minutes of fame, as was noted by Bruce Williamson in "Porno-Chic." The explosion of hard-core led *Film Journal* and *Take One* to run special issues in 1972 and 1973, respectively. Parker Tyler reflects on the increasing candor in marginal films and on the ontological differences between hard- and soft-core sex in "Do They or Don't They? Why It Matters So Much." J. Morthland's "Porn Films: An In-Depth Report" is the best and most comprehensive survey of popular early porn features.

"L'Erotisme en Question," a special issue of *Cinema D'Aujourd'Hui* (1975–1976), contains several essays on the debate in the French National Assembly on the influx of American porn. Barthélemy Amengual comments on the relationship between pornography and physical reality; Georges-Albert Astre analyzes the social functions of pornography (subversive, liberating, demystifying, and secularizing); Richard Carroll comments on Puritanism and transgression as manifest in porn in New York; and Evelyne Lowins reviews Damiano's *The Devil in Miss Jones* (1972). In *Érotisme et cinéma: Themes et variations*, edited by Daniel Serceau, Gérard Leblanc's "Le cul loin du ciel: Essai sur le genre pornographique" provides an excellent discussion of the mechanics and formulas of porn genres. One of the few French porn films exported to the United States was *Exhibition*; it premiered at the Lincoln Center Film Festival in 1975. In "Le film pornographique n'est pas un genre," the director of *Exhibition*, Jean-François Davy, rejects the categorization of porn genres as trashy; Davy maintains that porn can be a legitimate element of cinema, especially in the documentary format in which he works. Didier Saillac's *X Vidéo Guide* offers additional comparisons between American and French products. The articles in "Censorship and Pornography," a special issue of *Continuum*, are concerned chiefly with cinema of the Pacific Rim, especially Australia, but base all comparisons on American products.

The tabloid *Screw* runs annual guides to adult films and videos. Typical is the 23 July 1979 issue (no. 542) on the output of the previous twelve months, including the since-suppressed *Never a Tender Moment* (Mitchell Brothers). William Rotsler's *Contemporary Erotic Cinema*, a journalistic approach to porn movies, is superficial, as are most such "investigations," but it does provide interviews with directors (the Mitchell Brothers, Lowell Pickett, and David Friedman), actors (Johnnie Keyes and John Holmes), and actresses (Emily Smith and Marilyn Chambers). David Chute's "Tumescent Market for One-Armed Videophiles" discusses Ann Perry as a producer (*Count the Ways*) and distributor (*Randy the Electric Lady*) and notes that hard-core features such as *Deep Throat* (1972) and *The Opening of Misty Beethoven* (1976) had been transferred to video formats and were driving the VCR industry.

GAY AND LESBIAN HARD-CORE

Conservatives have traditionally anathematized gay porn as godless and animalistic. Gay hard-core movies have come under attack more recently by antiporn feminists, who hold that all males are aggressive, that the depiction of an erect penis symbolizes the weapon used to oppress women, and that homosexual sex embodies the same patterns of power as heterosexual sex. Tom Waugh's "Men's Pornography: Gay versus Straight" compares straight and gay hard-core in terms of narrative and formulaic conventions; at the essay's center are elaborate tables of similarities and differences. Waugh argues against Kathleen Barry's claim that "homosexual pornography acts out the same dominant and subordinate roles of heterosexual pornography" by asserting that "unlike straight male porn, gay porn does not directly and systematically replicate the heterosexist patriarchical order in its relations of production, exhibition, consumption, or representation" (34). On the other hand, Waugh does observe that gay porn can be "a potential regressive force, valorizing sexism, looks-ism, sizeism, racism, ageism, and so on, as well as violent behaviors" (33). Waugh compares Curt McDowell's *Loads* (1986) to Barbara Hammer's lesbian films as political statements. Richard Dyer finds subversive value in gay pornography; visual depictions of gay sex strike at dominant American mind-sets. In "Male Gay Porn," he insists that pornography has an unsettling effect despite its commodification; since all messages must be delivered through commercial channels, Dyer does not think pornography has been more compromised than other messages.

Because audiences for early stag films were fraternity houses and American Legion posts, macho groups easily embarrassed by gay subjects, most pioneer producers did not make homosexual reels. Rare gay stags made before World War II are the subject of Tom Waugh's "A Heritage of Pornography: On the Gay Film Collection of the Kinsey Institute," which discusses content and circulation. Another Waugh essay, "Gay Erotic Cinema in the Postwar Era," prefigures his magnum opus, a full-scale history of gay pornographic images, *Hard to Imagine: Gay Male Eroticism in Photography and Film from Their Beginnings to Stonewall.* (The 1991 Third Annual New York International Festival of Lesbian and Gay Film featured *Hard to Imagine: Illicit Homoerotic Film and Photography 1850–1969,* a compilation film about which I have been able to learn little else save for the similarity of its title to Waugh's.) Excellent historical investigation informs Paul Alcuin Siebenand's *The Beginnings of Gay Cinema in Los Angeles: The Industry and the Audience,* which highlights studios that specialized in photographs of male models, dancers, and bodybuilders in the 1940s and 1950s. In *Gay Video: A Guide to Erotica,* John Rowberry notes that the output of the Athletic Model Guild of Los Angeles, a studio discussed by Siebenand, has been transferred to videotape. By 1985, according to Rowberry, these numbered fifteen volumes of wrestling, eighteen volumes of spanking, and thirty volumes of short subjects. AMG is historically important for challenging in court the notion that a representation of nudity in and of itself was "obscene." Richard Goldstein profiles Vince Migliore, owner of Gay Pleasures on Hudson Street in Manhattan, in "The Little Shop of Hornies." Migliore is an authority on gay photos and film and the styles and fashions of various periods of gay porn. *XXX Gay Video Showcase* is the leading monthly of the gay industry, although *Adult Video News* routinely publishes gay supplements.

Jim Martin's "Out of the Closets and into the Bijous" highlights Fred Halstead's *Sex Garage, L.A. Plays Itself,* and *Truck It* and Wakefield Poole's *Boys in the Sand* and *Bijou.* Clarke Taylor also talks about Poole and Halstead in "Male Eros Goes to the Movies." In "All Male Cast: Gay Films on Videocassette," Vito Russo admits that too much porn is terrible but offers limited praise for films by Halstead, Poole, and Joe Gage. John Greyson covers current trends in homosexual porn in "Gay Video: The Present Context." Dave Babbitt traces the prevalence of toilet scenes to roots in periods when gays made contact chiefly in men's rooms in "Glory Holes in Gay Film Erotica." Matias Viegener writes on gay fanzines and punk porno films in "The Only Haircut That Makes Sense Anymore." Most useful is John R. Burger's *One-Handed Histories: The Eroto-Politics of Gay Male Video Pornography*. Burger says that gay video serves "popular memory" in two ways: "first, as an object of study, it can be read by both gays and nongays alike, as a cultural document. Second, as a dimension of political practice, it abets the reshaping, reformulation, and rethinking of gay male culture and its role in society. In short, pornography makes gay men visible. . . . it is also about much more than that" (4). Cindy Patton's "Safe Sex and the Pornographic Vernacular" insists that porn should champion safe sex. Richard Fung's "Shortcomings: Questions about Pornography as Pedagogy," on the effectiveness of explicit safe-sex videos and films, centers on Asian American examples. Catherine Saalfield's "On the Make: Activist Video Collectives" reports on gay and lesbian film groups making explicit films and videotapes for educational and ideological purposes, especially those committed to better information on AIDS.

Andrea Weiss, herself a filmmaker, critiques the work of Barbara Hammer in "*Women I Love* and *Double Strength*: Lesbian Cinema and Romantic Love." Jacqueline Zita explores Hammer's *Women I Love* (1978) and *Dyketactics* (1974) in "Films of Barbara Hammer: Counter-Currencies of a Lesbian Iconography." Talking about her films in an essay of her own, Hammer says in "The Politics of Abstraction" that she found conventional cinema unable to deal with lesbian concerns and sometimes chose nonrepresentational images because she thinks abstraction permits "multiple references" and "perceptual insights": "There is not a feminism but feminisms, not a lesbian cinema but lesbian cinemas, and there is not abstraction but multiple manifestations of abstraction" (75). "Femme Experimentale," edited by Kate Haug, contains essays, bibliographies, and filmographies on, and interviews with, Carolee Schneemann, Barbara Hammer, and Chick Strand. Each pioneered the explicit depiction of women's sexuality on-screen. Mary T. Conway's "Spectatorship in Lesbian Porn: The Woman's Woman's Film" finds in lesbian hard-core challenges to the "male gaze" thesis.

Lisa LaBia's "Fatale Attraction: Or How My Porno Dream Came True" is an amusing account of the shooting of Fatale Video's production of *Suburban Dykes* (1990), in which LaBia enjoyed sex with some of her favorite stars. Cherry Smyth reviews recent lesbian productions, including some from Fatale Video, in "The Pleasure Threshold: Looking at Lesbian Pornography in Film." Smyth hopes that the genre will mature past old formulas; her implication is that there are too many dildos. Susie Bright, "the Pauline Kael of porn," lectures regularly to lesbian groups on the pleasures of eroticism. Bright tells Canadian interviewer H. J. Kirchhoff in "In Person: 'I'm Constantly Surprised at the Fan

Mail' " that Canadian authorities have forbidden her to bring into the country the two films she uses to supplement her lectures, *All Girl Action: Thirty Years of Lesbian Erotic Images in Cinema* and *How to Read a Dirty Movie*. Comprehensive and up-to-date analyses of films about lesbians are to be found in Tamsin Wilton's *Immortal Invisible: Lesbians and the Moving Image*; the contributors cover Andrea Weiss, Greta Schiller, Monica Treut and other directors, discuss mainstream and independent productions, and reflect on quotidian questions of representation.

FEMALE PERFORMERS

Porn stars have become low-rent celebrities on afternoon television talk shows. The appearance of Tom Byron and Julia Parton on an "Adult Video" segment of the *Joan Rivers Show* in 1991 is typical. Parton, a cousin of the country singer, is publisher of *High Society* magazine and an occasional hardcore performer. She and Byron discussed the falling wages ($3,000 per sex scene for women in 1984 versus $1,000 in 1991; both figures suspect) occasioned by proliferation of videotapes. They also counted the pluses of the porn industry, which include freedom: "No one ever tells you that you have to do anything you don't want to do" in the business, said Parton.

Long before *Geraldo*, however, Juanita Slusher, a Dallas stripper who took the stage name Candy Barr, achieved lasting notoriety. In "Candy Barr in Time and Space," Stephen Schneck explores the elements (her youth and unwillingness to perform oral sex) that made her stag film of the 1950s, *Smart Alec*, so iconographic. Gary Cartwright reviews the stripper's life and career in an interview/article, "Candy: Taking the Wrapper off a Texas Legend"; he does not ask about the rumor that Barr's leading man in the film was Gary Crosby (son of Bing), who was one of gangster Mickey Cohen's rivals for her affections. "Candy Barr" covers Barr's friendship with impresario Jack Ruby and her recollections of making *Smart Alec*. *Screw* published stills from what it claims is Barr's "other" stag film in its "Smut from the Past" column of 23 July 1979 (22); they would appear to be from the two striptease reels she did make. George Csicsery's *The Sex Industry* mentions *Smart Alec* and later hard-core films of the 1960s. (For more on Barr, see **Period Histories of Erotic/Pornographic Photographs** in Chapter 12.)

Screw routinely interviews major performers: issues during the 1970s spotlighted Helen Madigan, Andrea True, Merle Michaels, Vanessa Del Rio, and Georgina Spelvin. *Screw*'s Manhattan cable show, *Midnight Blue*, profiles "superstars": the 20 June 1991 edition interviews Holly Ryder and Teri Weigel. Weigel says that she moved from *Playboy* centerfold to soft-core films and then to hard-core, because it was only a matter of "sticking [the penis] in," because "the people [in hard-core] were nicer," and because she enjoyed the sex. Each issue of *Adam Film World* interviews a popular star also. Sarah Harris mentions early feature-film performers in *The Puritan Jungle: America's Sexual Under-*

ground; Laura Carter and Cathy Stevens offer breezy accounts of careers on- and off-screen in *The Porno Girls*; William Rotsler interviews Linda Lovelace and Rene Bond in *Girls Who Do Stag Movies*. "Interview with a Pornographic Film Star," in which Bond talks to Winston Hill, foregrounds Bond's skill at fellatio, a renown (unjustly) eclipsed by Linda Lovelace's. John Bowers interviews actors, actresses, and directors of the late 1960s and early 1970s in "The Porn Is Green"; "The Porno Girls" focuses on Linda Wong and Mary Rexroth, daughter of poet Kenneth. Kenneth Turan and Stephen F. Zito talk to Rexroth, Marilyn Chambers, and other early hard-core women pioneers in *Sinema: American Pornographic Films and the People Who Make Them*. Rexroth remembers directors so inexperienced that they thought that the amateur performers they recruited should not be amateurs when it came to sex: " 'They discovered if you just took two people off the street, it was kind of a 50–50 chance you'd come out with a film,' she said. 'The star system arose because some people not only knew how to couple well, but could also communicate their sexuality to an audience' " (113).

The Kronhausens discuss female stars of the 1970s in *The Sex People: Erotic Performers and Their Brave New Worlds*, as do "The New Girls of Porn" (1977) and "Pinkskin Review," which offer illustrated biographies of popular stars. Jack Curry's interviews with Annette Haven, Veronica Hart, and Seka give substance to "X-Rated Aphrodites." Haven, noting that she accepted a part in Blake Edwards' mainstream film *10*, turned down one in *The Howling*: "These guys say they want to take me out of [the porn] business. But I don't want to leave it" (22). Hart, perhaps the most talented woman ever to appear in hard-core, describes her journey from sex show performer doing live intercourse in front of a storefront audience to a $1,000-a-day porn star; she says that her training as an actress gives her an edge over other performers (24). Curry notes that "as with most X-travagant celebrities, Seka's speech is sprinkled with the sort of street talk in which 50 percent of the vocabulary rhymes with 'duck' " (25). Henri Rode's *Les Stars du Cinéma Erotique* critiques the styles of performers and directors, many of them American; some information is based on interviews. "Brigitte Bares It All," a nude pictorial (photos by Earl Miller) of Brigitte Maier, interviews an actress even more celebrated than Linda Lovelace for her proficiency at anal intercourse. Maier says she prefers working in European films by Lasse Braun because she is taken more seriously by Continental directors: "Americans can't seem to separate an enthusiastic porn actress from a prostitute" (55). That is a complaint voiced also in "Girls in Pornography," for which James Wolcott interviewed several women.

In addition to generating miles of newsprint on "deep throating"—for which she suppressed her gag reflex in order to engulf the entire length of a penis (a practice now standard in the industry)—Linda Lovelace published her own how-to manual of oral and anal techniques called *Inside Linda Lovelace*. *Playboy* covered her bid for legitimate stardom in "Linda Lovelace for President." When she later said that she had been exploited, Lovelace became a symbol for feminists like Gloria Steinem, whose "The Real Linda Lovelace" casts her as a victim objectified for male gratification. Two reviews of Lovelace's *Ordeal* illustrate the range of critical response. Steinem's "Linda Lovelace's 'Ordeal' " sympathizes with the actress' claim that her husband forced her into performing in scuzzy loops and *Deep Throat*. Aryeh Neier's "Linda Lovelace's 'Ordeal': Memoirs of a Woman's Displeasure" compares Lovelace's memoir with *Pamela*, the Victorian novel in which the heroine's virtue was outraged. Neier suggests that fictional tropes replicated in Lovelace's book reveal something about the ways in which reaction to pornography is socially constructed. Neier finds telling the circumstance that *Ordeal*'s coauthor, Mike McGrady, engineered a hoax, the porn novel (and later movie) *Naked Came the Stranger* (1969), which was written as a lark by two dozen *Newsday* reporters. Perhaps the most interesting comment on *Ordeal* is Candida Royalle's observation in "Porn in the USA" that the book is primarily a story of domestic abuse (a specialized genre), not a tale of the porn industry at all; indeed, Royalle thinks that porn actually helped Lovelace escape from her husband by elevating her to public notice as a star (25). Lovelace's third book, *Out of Bondage*, is also highly critical of the porn industry.

The term "porno-chic" was coined to indicate the phenomenal social interest in *Deep Throat*. Carolyn See's *Blue Money* draws on interviews with Lovelace, Marvin Miller, the porn publisher, Matt Cimber, a producer of blue movies, Jim Holland, the porn historian, and Burton Marks, the attorney for many pornographers, for an excellent contextualization of *Deep Throat*. Richard Smith's *Getting into Deep Throat* maps the film's impact in the climate of the time, though researchers will want to canvas the journalism of 1972; every major magazine and newspaper took note. Of the vast number of articles, perhaps the most enduring is "*Deep Throat*: Hard to Swallow," in which Ellen Willis hopes someone will make an erotic movie about *her* fantasies for a change.

Complementing Lovelace's memoirs are largely self-serving autobiographies by first-generation stars such as Tina Russell's *Porno Star* and the "Ivory Snow Girl's" *Marilyn Chambers: My Story*. Gregg Kilday's "Inside Marilyn Chambers" typifies many interviews during the late 1970s and early 1980s, when the actress was making *Insatiable*, polishing a Las Vegas act, and trying to break into legitimate cinema. Chambers figures prominently in David McCumber's *Rated-X: The Mitchell Brothers, a True Story of Sex, Money, and Death* and in John Hubner's *Bottom Feeders: From Free Love to Hard Core—The Rise and Fall of Counterculture Heroes Jim and Artie Mitchell*, as do other performers in Mitchell films and theaters. Annette Fuentes and Margaret Schrage's "Interview with Veronica Hart, Gloria Leonard, Kelly Nichols, Candida Royalle, Annie Sprinkle, and Veronica Vera: Deep inside Porn Stars" elicits frankness on drawbacks and perks of working in porn films. The performers, insistent that no one forced them to do anything, nonetheless complain about "lack of foreplay," lack of realism, and implicit racism against black and Hispanic women. Conscious of constituting a "first generation of porn stars" whose experience has been neither bad nor good, they acknowledge that the industry has "had a great impact on [their] lives" (43).

Sprinkle and Vera are now performance artists. In "Looking beneath the Surface: Deep inside Porn Stars," a largely disapproving review of the *Deep inside Porn Stars* performance at New York's Franklin Furnace (1984), Arlene Raven listens to Sprinkle and Vera speak of explicit acts as forms of consciousness-raising for audiences. The event was organized by porn director Candida Royalle to theatricalize experiences in the porn industry. In Linda Montano's "Summer Saint Camp 1987," with companion pieces called "Our Week at Sister Rosita's Summer Saint Camp," a story by Vera and a "scrapbook" by Sprinkle, the two actresses refer to themselves as "Sex National Treasures" and also "feminist/ activist porn stars" as they conduct a feminist-porn workshop in Kingston, New York. They emphasize sexual freedom for women. Vera's articulate testimony before the Meese Commission is charmingly reported by Marianne Macy in *Working Sex: An Odyssey into Our Cultural Underworld*, which also includes comment by Royalle, Sprinkle, Gloria Leonard, Amber Lynne, and other performers. According to Sylvia Plachy and James Ridgeway's *Red Light: Inside the Sex Industry*, Vera, always a pioneer, now runs a school for transvestites (116ff). Sprinkle's *Post Porn Modernist* reprises her career and its rationale from her days as a hooker, to her current celebrity as a performance artist. *Angry Women*, edited by Andrea Juno and V. Vale, contains a chapter on Sprinkle, whose real name is Ellen Steinberg; she has written and directed several films and published more than 300 articles, not to mention editing small magazines like *The Sprinkle Report: A Newsletter of Piss Art*. Sprinkle's performance artistry has attracted considerable attention. Chris Straayer's "The Seduction of Boundaries: Feminist Fluidity in Annie Sprinkle's Art/Education/Sex" and Linda Williams' "A Provoking Agent: The Pornography and Performance Art of Annie Sprinkle" examine Sprinkle's claims that her performances "deconstruct" and demystify sex. For some, self-conscious performers such as Sprinkle push porn films toward avant-garde genres. (For Sprinkle as photographer, see **Models and Techniques** and **Vending Machine Cards, Cigarette Cards, and Trading Cards** in Chapter 12.)

Somewhat different in detail and perspective is Louis Marvin's *The New Goddesses. Kay Parker, Sheri St. Clair, Mai Lin, Nina Hartley, Jeannie Pepper, Juliet Anderson Talk to Louis Marvin About Their Lifestyles, Personal Sex Life and Why They Enjoy Acting in Porno Films*, whose title is an accurate summary of conversations with actresses who say with some qualifications that they like the sex, the money, and the working conditions available in the industry. In *Burning Desires: Sex in America: A Report from the Field*, Steve Chapple and David Talbot converse with Nina Hartley, Annie Sprinkle, Missy Manners [Elisa Florez], and Veronica Vera. Hartley, a highly skilled, athletic performer with a sense of humor, the veteran of hundreds of heterosexual and lesbian films and a columnist for alternative newspapers, is brightly articulate on pornography. "I'm in pornography because it's an extension of my personal belief system"

(158), she tells interviewer Chip Rowe for "Nina Hartley Is the Smartest Woman in Porn." Hartley's "Confessions of a Feminist Porno Star" asserts that the magna cum laude nursing graduate from San Francisco State and radical feminist chooses her roles and tries to advance the cause of feminine sexuality through virtuoso performances. Hartley says that performing is gratifying for several reasons: "First, it provides a physically and psychically safe environment for me to live out my exhibitionistic fantasies. Secondly, it provides a surprisingly flexible and supportive arena for me to grow in as a *performer*, both sexually and non-sexually. Thirdly, it provides me with erotic material that I like to watch for my own pleasure. Finally, the medium allows me to explore the theme of celebrating a positive female sexuality—a sexuality that has heretofore been denied us" (142).

Hartley's remarks appear in *Sex Work: Writings by Women in the Sex Industry*, edited by Frédérique Delacoste and Priscilla Alexander, which also contains an interview entitled "Making Movies" with a pseudonymous "Jane Smith," who made "skin-flicks" but refused to perform intercourse. Smith maintains that she was exploited as "raw material" for a male industry, though her experiences in the industry "were not brutal or degrading" (140). By contrast, Seph Weene, a stripper and porn actress, acknowledges in "Venus" the power over men she feels in explicit performance. A good companion volume is Rachel Silver's *The Girl in Scarlet Heels: Women in the Sex Business Speak Out*. Although based primarily on interviews with British sex workers, the mixture of positive and negative responses is similar. Some actresses and prostitutes are bitter over exploitation and victimization, but others believe that their occupations liberate them, give them autonomy, allow them to feel self-respect, and often give them pleasure. In "Surviving Commercial Sexual Exploitation," Evelina Giobbe, a former prostitute, recounts how she was forced by her pimp to make porn loop films and how she thinks prostitution and pornography are inextricably connected in the abuses of women they perpetuate. Catherine Roman's *Bang for a Buck* is a pseudonymous autobiographical account of a woman working in North American sex industries, including porn films. A London-based stripper, Nickie Roberts, has collected transatlantic memoirs by strippers, porn stars, and prostitutes in *The Front Line: Women in the Sex Industry Speak;* the responses are equivocal.

Tuppy Owens recalls her role in Lasse Braun's *Sensations* in "Sex on My Mind": "I was a hopeless actress, hated having the camera on me, didn't like being told how to perform, detested not being able to move freely or I'd be out of focus. Well, you don't know till you try" (118). Celebrated as a global sexual doyenne, Owens has starred in porn movies, organized massive, semipublic orgies, and generally hurled herself against whatever sexual boundaries she could find. She is also author of *The Safer Sex Maniac's Bible*, compendium of country-by-country erotic information that includes listings and descriptions of films and videos. In *Porn Gold: Inside the Pornography Business*, probably the best contemporary investigation of the industry, David Hebditch and Nick Anning talk with Viper, the ex-marine famous for her pierced nipples and full-length body tattoo in the shape of a snake whose head is her vagina. "Meet Missy, Republican Porn Star" profiles Missy Manners, aka Elisa Florez, the former aide to Senator Orrin Hatch turned star of *Behind the Green Door: The Sequel* (1986); Manners describes herself as "a freedom fucker" and "the Pat Robertson of porn" because of her campaign for safe sex. Robert J. Stoller's posthumously published *Porn: Myths for the Twentieth Century* deals at book-length with performers of both sexes, as does his *Coming Attractions: The Making of an X-Rated Video*, coauthored with I. S. Levine.

Jami Bernard's "There's Life after Porn" reports on cult star Vanessa Del Rio, who left the industry to become a bodybuilder after being jailed for drug possession. Typical of *Adult Video News* interviews with popular performers are "Sunset Thomas," in which the actress sketches for Mark Kernes her career as model, trophy girl at the Daytona Speedway, R-rated movie player, and hard-core star, and "Kelly O'Dell," in which O'Dell laughs at her initial effort to introduce her coworkers to safe sex, described by interviewer Jackie L. Watt as "the day [O'Dell] discovered why men do *not* put pure non-oxynol 9 directly on their dicks—its effects are akin to novocaine" (132). Quasi-documentary "confessions" of female stars string together sex scenes featuring the performer in question, but a few serve also as vehicles for reflection. Two examples are *Deep inside Annie Sprinkle* (Video-X-Pix, 1982) and *Deep inside Shanna McCullough* (Video-X-Pix, 1992); in both the actresses speak intelligently of their intentions, their careers in the industry, their personal sexual histories and preferences, and their takes on various subjects. More conventional is the PBS-produced *Death of a Porn Queen*, a somewhat sensationalized story of Colleen Applegate, aka Shauna Grant, a porn star of uncommon freshness who killed herself in midcareer. Peter Wilkinson writes in "Dream Girl" about the personal and public life of Shannon Wilsey, better known as superstar Savannah, who also committed suicide, presumably in the belief that she was being displaced by women more nubile than herself; Wilkinson reviews Savannah's earlier incarnation as a celebrated rock star groupie as well.

MALE PERFORMERS

Again, *Screw* is a good source of information on veterans: Jack Wrangler (in issue 696), Harry Reems (710), and John Leslie (689) are only a few. *Adult Video News* runs frequent interviews with performers, especially those who have been in the business a long time or who have moved into the ranks of directors and producers. *Adult Film World* directories of heterosexual and gay films are also useful, as are Jim Holliday's historical anthologies, whose sound tracks provide personal and professional details about performers (see **Films and Videotapes** in chapter 4). *Batteries Not Included*, a zine edited and published by Richard Freeman, frequently contains interviews with porn stars as well as comment on the industry.

Male stars comment on their roles less often than women, who are the real celebrities and preferred guests on talk shows, but occasionally the ordinarily silent will speak. The title of Paul Phillips' " 'I Enjoy Making Porno Films'— An X-rated Star Speaks Out" conveys his message. In *The Porn People*, Bob Hoddeson interviews William Rotsler, an actor-director, as well as producers and distributors. Rotsler's own *Superstud: The Hard Life of Male Stag Film Stars* deals with male performers like Jaime Gillis and John C. Holmes; the archness of the title replicates the book's tone. The most informative piece on the most notorious of male stars is "Conversation with John C. Holmes," where he admits to his female interviewer that he is ambivalent about ejaculating on the faces of his costars. *Sinema*, the book by Turan and Zito, also carries an excellent interview. After Holmes died of AIDS, the tabloid television show *A Current Affair* ran a story called "Requiem for a Superstud" on his alleged involvement in a California murder case and reviewed a career during which his enormous penis earned him up to $20,000 a week, much of which he squandered on drugs. Hollywood offered its own accolade in the form of *Boogie Nights*, a somewhat patronizing *cinéma a clef* for which director Marc Ahlberg fictionalized Holmes' career. The success of the film, in turn, inspired articles such as Craig Vetter's "The Real Dirk Diggler," which reprised Holmes' life more accurately.

Candida Royalle tells Marianne Macy in *Working Sex: An Odyssey into Our Cultural Underworld* that women enjoyed working with Holmes not so much because of his huge penis, though many were eager for the experience, as for his skill and pleasure in cunnilingus (50). Marc Stevens' *Ten and a Half* and Harry Reems' *Here Comes Harry Reems!* are as much self-promotional as autobiographical. In 1991 Steve Dogherty and Dirk Mathison discovered that after failing to achieve a career on the legitimate stage, Reems retired from the porn business, found religion, and become a respectable Utah real estate agent, a story they call "Born Again Porn Star." Peter North has reflected on porn and his place in it in *Penetrating Insights*. He attributes his prodigious ejaculations (which earned him the nickname "beercan") to control, diet, and exercise. Jerry Butler's *Raw Talent: The Adult Film Industry as Seen by Its Most Popular Male Star* is the best exposé of the industry by a performer because of the star's confession that he got into the business for the money but stayed because of the attention and his need to perform. The year the book was published, Butler told an audience on the *Sally Jessy Raphael Show* that he was stupid to stay in the business as long as he had, given the increased danger of AIDS.

Jack Wrangler's *The Jack Wrangler Story: What's a Nice Boy like You Doing in a Business like This?*, the autobiography of a gay porn star written with Carl Johnes, holds interest because of his relationship with the singer Margaret Whiting. Richard Dyer's *Now You See It: Studies on Lesbian and Gay Film* occasionally refers to stars like Bobby Kendall of *Pink Narcissus*. *Sinema* devotes several pages to Pat Rocco, a pioneer performer in gay hard-core. Dave Kinnick talks with many performers in *Sorry I Asked: Intimate Interviews with Gay*

Porn's Rank and File; their experiences in the industry, as one might expect, are diverse, and some are cautionary. Probably the most famous of gay stars are Jeff Stryker—whose interview by Kevin Koffler elicits information about working conditions and his personal life—and the late Joey Stefano, whose career is covered by Charles Isherwood in *Wonder Bread and Ecstasy: The Life and Death of Joey Stefano*. The "tell-all" autobiography of "Spunk" O'Hara, another gay porn star, is entitled *Autopornography: A Memoir of Life in the Lust Lane*. *XXX Gay Video Showcase*, a monthly, frequently runs interviews with popular gay stars; as always with such sources, scholars should beware of hype.

In one of his interviews with a veteran male star for *Porn: Myths for the Twentieth Century*, Robert J. Stoller hears: "You're not fucking for yourself, you're fucking for the world. The world doesn't want to see you have fun. They want to see themselves have fun through you. And if it takes four hours to shoot your sex scenes, that's how long it's going to take for you to have their fun. We are nothing more than an extension and machine of their minds" (97). Despite the recent publication of Stoller's book, the material is dated, the result of interviews conducted over several years. In a second, posthumously published volume, *Coming Attractions: The Making of an X-Rated Video*, written with I. S. Levine, Stoller again examines sex-oriented businesses, sexual fantasies, and erotic films, with the narrative centered on the making of *Stairway to Paradise*, a romantic hard-core video directed by veteran performer Sharon Kane for VCA Platinum (Levine was the assistant director). The text includes interviews with Bill Margold, Nina Hartley, Kane, Porsche Lynn, and Jim Holliday (a film historian and director). In talking with them, Stoller hopes to confirm his belief that anger, cruelty, humiliation, and the desire for revenge may be components of a hostility that he thinks drives eroticism, though the evidence, at least as presented here, is equivocal. Steve Chapple and David Talbot talk to performers such as Richard Pacheco in *Burning Desires: Sex in America: A Report from the Field*.

The best thing about William Margold's *Sexual Stamina: The Secret of the Male Sex Star* is the title; it is a scruffy book about life on the set, larded with stills from various hard-core movies, including some of Margold's own. In an essay on the value of a penis, a question raised by the case of John Wayne Bobbitt (whose wife cut his off), Bruce Handy asks, "What's It Worth to You?" Handy cites agent Jim South, who says that his most successful male porn stars can earn $100,000 a year, and actor William Margold, who says that $50,000 to $75,000 is a more realistic figure. The last estimate assumes that the performer has the ability to complete two sex scenes per day for three to five days a week—" 'truly a gift,' Margold added, 'that very few men will attain.' " In "The Penis Page," a regular feature for *Penthouse*, Mark Christopher reveals some of the strategies used by male porn stars to maintain erections. Christopher notes that salaries work out to between $250 to $500 per ejaculation; he also quotes William Margold to the effect that "the physical pleasure is minimal, but the mental pressure is phenomenal." Chris Heath's "A Hard Man Is Good to Find" profiles T. T. Boy, Alex Sanders, and Peter North, all of whom are celebrated for maintaining erections. Susan Faludi argues in "The Money Shot," an article occasioned by the suicide of Cal Jammer, that the male performers are disposable; the female performers garner most of the rewards. Faludi interviews stalwarts such as T. T. Boy, Nick East, Tony Montana, and Jeff Stryker. "Body for Rent: A Journey through the Ruins of the Porno-Chic Empire," written by Bill Landis, who starred in porn films during the 1980s under the name "Bobby Spector," is a disillusioned account of the business. Landis depicts himself as a drug-hazed hustler exploited by sleazy producers and asks: "Is the fucking you get worth the fucking you get?" (36).

PRODUCERS AND DIRECTORS OF HARD-CORE PORN FILMS

For makers of stag films, see Slade's forthcoming *Shades of Blue*, a history of the hard-core film, with particular reference to porn filmmakers such as Bernard Natan of France and Alexander von Kollowrat of Austria. Unlike those prominent European professionals, few Americans of any stature made stag films. With the advent of hard-core features in the 1970s, pornographers emerged as entrepreneurs. In "Bill Osco, Boy King of L.A.," a bemused *Variety* marked Osco's success with Graffiti Productions, which made *Mona* and *Hollywood Blue* (the former was the first hard-core feature to be distributed nationally) and his plans for General National, his distribution company. John Bowers interviews pioneer director Alex De Renzy in "The Porn Is Green." Gerard Damiano, who made *Deep Throat* (1972) with $25,000 he borrowed from Mafia connections, talks to Kenneth Turan and Stephen F. Zito in *Sinema: American Pornographic Films and the People Who Make Them*. Despite sensationalism, *The Celluloid Love-Feast: The Story of Erotic Movies*, by Martin A. Grove and William S. Ruben, provides information on Bill Osco, Alex De Renzy, Russ Meyer, and Radley Metzger and on production companies like Sherpix and porn theaters in New York and San Francisco; a bibliography of reviews of early films is valuable. Interviewed by Ernest Peter Cohen, Fred Halstead says that he wants to arouse his audiences by remaining true to his own fantasies. Another classic gay director, Wakefield Poole, speaks of his sensibilities to Jack Fritscher.

Ronan O'Casey's "Getting It Up for a Porn Movie" recounts the day-to-day shooting of *The Double Exposure of Holly* (1976), directed by Bob Gill. During the 1970s, *Variety* routinely ran articles on porn markets and leading directors. Typical is "U.S. Porn Producer Goes O'Seas for Fresh Faces, More Natural Attitudes," on director Jonas Middleton's shooting of *Through the Looking Glass* (1976). Joseph Slade discusses various directors of the mid-1970s, including Middleton, in "The Pornographic Film Market and Pornographic Formulas." Steve Chapple and David Talbot interviewed the Dark Brothers, David Friedman, and the Mitchell Brothers for *Burning Desires: Sex in America: A*

Report from the Field. Of these the Mitchells have drawn the most attention, first for transforming the Ivory Snow Girl (Marilyn Chambers) into a different sort of American icon and then for a falling out in a dispute that led to Jim Mitchell's killing his brother Artie. Al Goldstein's "Citizen Cain and Abel" speculates on the enmity that grew from the success of *Behind the Green Door* (1972), as do the two book-length studies of the Mitchells by Hubner and McCumber. David Hebditch and Nick Anning's *Porn Gold: Inside the Pornography Business* contains interviews with directors Henri Pachard, Bill Margold, and Gerard Damiano. Jeremy Stone's "Interview with an Erotic Outlaw Auteur" elicits interesting reflections on artistic styles, life on the set, favorite fetishes, and personal goals from Rinse Dream, much-praised director of *Cafe Flesh* (1982) and *Nightdreams* (1990). Chi Chi LaRue's memoir *Making It Big: Sex Stars, Porn Films, and Me*, written with John Erich, offers an insider's view of the gay film industry by the director of more than 100, with tips on shooting, capsule biographies of important performers, and reflections on cinematic eroticism.

In *Coming Attractions: The Making of an X-Rated Video*, Robert J. Stoller and I. S. Levine foreground Sharon Kane, director of *Stairway to Paradise*, a romantic, hard-core video for VCA Platinum. Stoller and Levine investigate backgrounds and motivations of the participants, discuss legal and moral aspects of the industry, and comment on the mechanics and aesthetics of the genre. Anthony Petkovich interviews a number of actresses, directors, and camerapeople, and recounts his experiences visiting the set of videos such as *The World's Biggest Gang Bang* in *The X Factory: Inside the American Hardcore Industry*. Several subjects of Juno and Vale's *Angry Women* write, direct, or perform in hard-core; extensive interviews elicit articulate responses from Susie Bright, Lydia Lunch, Linda Montano, and Annie Sprinkle, to which are appended lists of their films and publications. In *Herotica: A Collection of Women's Erotic Fiction*, Susie Bright complains that because most porn films are made by males, "women are exasperated but well-practiced in 'taking what I can get and making the best of it.' This has been the theme song of women's sexual repression. . . . When women have taken a hand in the production of erotica, the results have been underpublicized and thwarted in distribution, but tremendously rewarding" (2–3). Bright praises hard-core by Candida Royalle and Chris Cassidy. Opinions pro and con are the substance of *Peril or Pleasure?: Feminist Produced Pornography*; on-camera participants include Susie Bright, Annie Sprinkle, Evelina Kane of Women Against Pornography, and Candida Royalle. They ask whether women can construct an eroticism of their own by entering the burgeoning homevideo porn market or whether they are simply playing into the hands of the enemy. In *Rate It X*, a less contentious documentary by Lucy Winer and Paula Koenigsberg, the camera visits a male clothing store, an erotic bakery, and other places where sexual fantasies take shape.

"Women's Porn?" reports on the "Female Influence on Erotic Films" panel at the Third Women and Movies Conference; the discussion centers on former star and magazine publisher Gloria Leonard, who maintains that the influence has been larger than some think. Candida Royalle, Gloria Leonard, and Lee Rothermund are the principal examples in "Debbie Directs Dallas: Video Erotica Made by Women for Women," by Jodie Gould. These three, says Gould, aim at elegant, romantic, soft-focus (but not necessarily soft-core) explicitness. In "Porn in the USA," Candida Royalle observes: "It's important to point out that the movies tend to look as bad as they do because it is an industry that is kept in the gutter by the stigma" (24). "There's . . . an asumption that if you are performing sex for a living, it detracts from your personal and sexual life. When I was in front of the camera I never felt that it interfered with my personal life at all" (26). "As a director, I find that good erotic performers are people who can lose themselves in the sex while staying in character" (26). Royalle also observes that "it is hard to spend any real money on porn movies, because everyone else is making them and selling them so cheap, just to make a buck" (30). Don Vaughn's "An Interview with Candida Royalle" also elicits information about her intentions and the content of her films. In David Flint's *Babylon Blue: An Illustrated History of Adult Cinema*, Veronica Hart speaks of her career as a performer (aka Randee Styles) turned producer (for director Michael Ninn) under the name Jane Hamilton, and her recent efforts at directing veterans such as Ginger Lynn (*Torn*, VCA, 1999) and Marilyn Chambers (*Still Insatiable*, VCA, 1999). Once she left stripping and performing, Hart acted in 30 R-rated features, worked for Playboy and other cable channels, wrote phone sex messages, and produced large numbers of hard-core videos. She thinks of herself as "lucky": "I think ours is a business of mutual exploitation. I'm sure it exists somewhere, but everybody knows what's going on, what the fee is, what you get paid for . . . and that's why I think, you don't see a lot of X-rated actresses transferring over into the R-rated business, because the R-rated business is much more difficult (138)." Hamilton/Hart is clearly proud of the videos she has herself directed; just as clearly, she has enjoyed her work: "I'm a Christian, and actually a pretty religious person. . . . Most of my friends are in this business, and they're pretty much good people and down to earth" (145).

Andrew Sarris is not impressed with differences between male and female producers and directors. Sarris' "Tapping into the Porn Pipeline," a review of *Femme* and *Urban Heat*, directed by R. Lauren Niemi for Candida Royalle's Femme Productions, thinks that feminist porn is just as tiresome as more conventional types; Sarris laments the lack of tease and characterizes the films as "more on the order of performance than narrative." In "Women and Pornography: Combat in the Video Zone," Jean Callahan covers directors such as Stephanie Rothman, Gail Palmer, Suze Randall, and Svetlana. Callahan says that women audiences prefer to know more about the performers they see, while male viewers prefer to see the sex itself. In an important essay, "Hard Corps: A New Generation of People of Color Penetrates Porn's Mainstream," Donald Suggs notes that because pornography legitimates desire, Afro-Americans, Hispanics, and Asians are staking out ground in porn cinema, partly to participate in profits, partly to advance their sexuality toward a central social consciousness. A better indicator of shifting genres is *Adam Black Video Illustrated*, a bi-monthly review of porn videos aimed at Afro-Americans. For "Words That Arouse: An Interview with Cathy Tavel" Don Vaughan talks with a prolific writer of porn movies, chiefly for Vivid Video, and her notions of what is sexy and what isn't.

For information on currently popular directors, the scholar must consult *Adult Film World* and *Adult Video News*. Both regularly review, interview, or comment on the work of warhorses such as Anthony Spinelli, Andrew Blake, Michael Ninn, and Candida Royalle. Mandy Merck devotes a chapter (217–235) in *Perversions: Deviant Readings* to Jerry Douglas, director of *More of a Man* (1990), a gay film Merck thinks fuses "sex and story." Most industry editors regard Alex de Renzy as the ur-master and will stop the presses to review a new film by him. Only slightly lower in the pantheon are John Leslie, a famous performer turned virtuoso director, John Stagliano, a director of enormous self-reflexivity who participates in the action, and Bruce Seven, who has built a career on specialty films on bondage and discipline, lesbian encounters, and various fetishes. Joseph Slade's "Flesh Need Not Be Mute" critiques the videos of John Leslie (John Nuzzo), one of the leading directors of the 1990s. As is the case with film and videotape of any sort, such porn directors bring different shooting styles, methods of dressing sets and performers, casting preferences, atmospheres, dialogues, and cutting to their scripts. When recognition of those variations becomes widespread, then porn films will have truly moved into the mainstream.

That may happen sooner, when historians begin to chronicle the rise of the major film/video producer/distributors, especially the larger companies (e.g., VCA, Vivid, Evil Angel) as they evolve from sleazy origins into marketing powerhouses. In that regard, their histories will parallel those of the major Hollywood corporations bent on dominating global markets.

AMATEUR FILMS AND VIDEOS

After the 1920s, when stag films were shot by entrepreneurs on the margins of the legitimate industry, hard-core moviemaking belonged to amateurs. That changed only in the 1960s, when hard-core moved back to the 35mm screen, a shift that required professional expertise. With the advent of cheap, high-resolution video cameras in the 1980s, porn mutated once again into a demotic form. Amateurs now shoot vast numbers of homemade cassettes, some of which circulate on the margins of culture (thus replicating an ancient pattern) among gay, lesbian, and heterosexual groups for their own amusement, but some of which enter commercial distribution and move toward the mainstream. Amateurs shoot videotapes because they enjoy the self-reflexivity and voyeurism implicit in preserving their sexual activity with mates or neighbors. Anastasia Toufexis' "Sex Lives and Videotape: More and More Couples Are Making Do-It-Yourself

Erotic Films" concentrates on couples' recording their lovemaking for personal gratification in the privacy of their homes. Despite the adherence of most amateur performers to genre tropes, the averageness and the alleged "realism" of their couplings, in turn, clearly appeal to other Americans. As Manohla Dargis observes in "Bush League: Homemade Porn, Playing Soon at a Bedroom near You," "what sells amateur porn is not fantasy bodies and fantastical situations, not Nina Hartly [*sic*] or a clitoris fluttering in the throat, but the idea that the people you watch include the attractive woman waiting for a bus, the less than attractive delivery man, your colleagues, friends, and relations. In essence, the folks right next door, people like you and me, electronically fused in a community of sexual emancipation" (49). Making amateur erotic films is not without dangers, as the actor Rob Lowe discovered, a circumstance covered by Elvis Mitchell in "Sex, Lowe, and Videotape."

Noting the explosive growth of amateur films in "New Adult Videos, Starring the Couple across the Street," Michael de Courcy Hinds talked to participants and examined markets. One of his sources was a Kentucky attorney who has made a couple of dozen films because she enjoys sex with other men and originally had her encounters videotaped so that her busy, but supportive, husband could watch; the enthusiasm she brought to those scenes led to national distribution of her tapes. "Mary Lou," the screen name of the thirty-seven-year-old lawyer, was featured on the October 1990 cover of *Amateur Video* magazine. Some amateur women have parlayed their home tapes into lucrative careers in the professional industry. D. Keith Mano's "I'm Ready for My Come Shot Now, Dear" provides tips and caveats for average citizens who wish to film themselves in intercourse.

In fact, a surprising number of how-to guides dispense advice. Kevin Campbell's *Video Sex: Create Erotic and Romantic Home Videos with Your Camcorder* points out that participating in a video shoot with people one trusts allows many people to act out fantasies. Dean Kuipers' "Sex, Home, and Videotape" is also informative and useful, though written from a masculine perspective. James Goode's two books are aimed at amateurs who want wider exposure. The first, *How to Create and Sell Amateur Erotic Videos and Photos: Cashing In on the Amateur Craze*, provides technical advice on production and helpful hints and also gives addresses of distributors. The second, *Directory of Amateur Erotica: Where to Buy and Sell Productions by Talented Amateurs*, educates those who wish to buy, sell or trade films and videotapes produced by amateurs. Al Goldstein, something of an expert on pornography, hails amateur videos as a refreshing change from normal fare; his "Making Your Own Erotic Video" discusses distributors, participants, and audiences. Once a useful manual, *The Film Maker's Guide to Pornography*, by Steven Ziplow, has been rendered more or less obsolete by sophisticated video technology but would still be helpful to amateurs concerned about lighting, camera angles, costumes, and lubricants. Major porn film guides regularly review heterosexual, lesbian, and gay amateur films and videos. One has just spun off a separate magazine, *Adam Presents*

Amateur Porn, to provide coverage of amateur and "pro-am" (i.e., amateurs engaged with professionals) genres. Amateur videos now account for 30 percent of the adult video rental market (*Adam X-Rated Movie Handbook 1993–94*, 11: 19 [September 1993]: 73), and professional directors such as Carter Stevens complain that amateurs have destroyed the market for quality erotica (Plachy and Ridgeway, *Red Light*, 45). And so the cycle of film pornography—if not exactly a folk art, then often the handiwork of amateurs—comes full circle.

REFERENCES

Adam Black Video Illustrated. Los Angeles: Knight Publishing, 1995–.
Adam Film World and Adult Video Guide. Los Angeles: Knight Publishing, 1968–, monthly.
Adam Film World Directory of Adult Films. Los Angeles: Knight Publishing, annual.
Adam Film World Directory of Gay Adult Video. Los Angeles: Knight Publishing, annual.
Adam Presents Amateur Porn. Los Angeles: Knight Publishing, 1993–.
Adam X-Rated Movie Handbook. Los Angeles: Knight Publishing, 1982–, annual.
Adult Cinema Review, New York, 1981–1988.
"Adult Video." *The Joan Rivers Show*. NBC, 9 May 1991.
Adult Video News. Upper Darby, PA, 1983–1996; Van Nuys, CA, 1996–.
Ahlberg, Marc, dir. *Boogie Nights*. Los Angeles: New Line Cinema/Home Video, 1997.
Amateur Video. Los Angeles, 1977–.
Andrews, Suzanna. "She's Bare. He's Covered. Is There a Problem?" *New York Times*, 1 November 1992, pp. 13–14.
Apra, Adriano, and Enzo Ungari. *Il cinema di Andy Warhol*. Rome: Arcana, 1972.
Arlen, Richard. *Sex and Pornography in the Movies*. Beverly Hills, CA: Valiant, 1971.
Atkins, Thomas R., ed. *Sexuality in the Movies*. New York: Da Capo, 1984.
Attorney General's Commission. *Attorney General's Commission on Pornography: Final Report*. 2 vols. Washington, DC: Government Printing Office, 1986.
Austin, Bruce A., ed. *Current Research in Film: Audiences, Economics, and Law*. 4 vols. Norwood, NJ: Ablex, 1985.
Babbitt, Dave. "Glory Holes in Gay Film Erotica." *Manshots*, April 1992, pp. 10–17.
Bad Object Choices [Terri Cafaro, Jean Carlomusto, Douglas Crimp, Martha Gever, Tom Kalin, and Jeff Nuokawa], eds. *How Do I Look? Queer Film and Video*. Seattle: Bay Press, 1991.
Banes, Sally, Sheldon Frank, and Tem Horowitz. *Our National Passion: 200 Years of Sex in America*. Chicago: Follett, 1976.
Barnouw, Erik. *A History of Broadcasting in the United States*. 3 vols. New York: Oxford University Press, 1970.
Bashore, Juliet. *Kamikaze Hearts*. Los Angeles: Facets Video, 1986.
Bazin, Andre. "Marginal Notes on Eroticism in the Cinema." *What Is Cinema?*, ed. Hugh Gray. 2 vols. Berkeley: University of California Press, 1971, II: 169–175.
Bell, Shannon. "Feminist Ejaculations." *The Hysterical Male*, ed. Arthur Kroker and Marilouise Kroker. New York: New World Perspectives, 1991, pp. 155–169.
Benayoun, Robert. *Erotique du Surréalisme*. Paris: Pauvert, 1965.
Berkowitz, Stan. "Russ Meyer: Sex, Violence and Drugs—All in Good Fun." *Film Comment*, 9:1 (January–February 1973): 46–51.

Bernard, Jami. "There's Life after Porn." *New York Post*, 6 October 1987, p. 31.

The Betty Pages Annual and *The Betty Pages Annual: Book 2*. New York: Black Cat Books, 1991, 1994.

Bilderlexicon der Erotik, Ein bibliographisches und biographisches Nachschlagewerk, eine Kunst- und Literaturgeschichte für die Gebiete der erotischen Belletristik . . . von der Antike zur Gegenwart. 6 vols. Vienna and Hamburg: Verlag für Kulturforschung, 1928–31, 1963. Edited by Leo Schidrowitz: I: *Kulturgeschichte*; II: *Literatur und Kunst*; III: *Sexualwissenschaft*; IV: *Ergänzungsband*. Edited by Armand Mergen: V and VI: *Sexualforschung: Stichwort und Bild*.

"Bill Osco, Boy King of L.A." *Variety*, 30 December 1970, p. 8.

"Bill Rogers: A Man of Taste [of Blood!]" *Ecco: The World of Bizarre Video*, 19 (Fall/ Winter 1993): 25–34.

Black, Andy, ed. *Necromicon: Book One: The Journal of Horror and Erotic Cinema*. London: Creation Books, 1996.

Blake, Roger. *The Porno Movies*. Cleveland, OH: Century, 1970.

Blonsky, Marshall. "Joe Sarno, the Dismemberer." *Artforum*, 12:6 (March 1974): 60–64.

Blue Movie Exposé. New York, 1981–1985.

Bond, Rene, and Winston Hill. "Interview with a Pornographic Film Star." *Sexual Deviance and Sexual Deviants*, ed. Erich Goode and Richard Troiden. New York: Morrow, 1974, pp. 68–72.

Boobs, Butts, and Bloopers. Los Angeles: Hollywood Video, 1990.

Bourgoin, Stéphane. "Petite Histoire du Film Erotique Americain." *Télécine*, 195 (January 1975): 10–15.

Bowen, Michael J. "Embodiment and Realization: The Many Film-Bodies of Doris Wishman." *Wide Angle*, 19:3 (1997): 64–90.

Bowers, John. "The Porn Is Green." *Playboy*, 18:7 (July 1971): 78–83, 182–183, 185–188.

Briggs, Joe Bob [John Bloom]. "B-Movie Bimbos." *Playboy*, 36:7 (July 1989): 130–139, 158, 160.

———. "Joe Bob Briggs' Guilty Pleasures: The 10 Top Drive-In Movies to Get Nookie By." *Film Comment*, 22:4 (July–August 1986): 70–73.

———. *Joe Bob Goes to the Drive-In*. New York: Delacorte, 1986.

———. *We Are the Weird*. P.O. Box 2002, Dallas, TX 75221.

Bright, Susie. "Introduction." *Herotica: A Collection of Women's Erotic Fiction*, ed. Susie Bright. Burlingame, CA: Down There Press, 1988.

"Brigitte Bares It All." *Penthouse*, 5:7 (July 1974): 49–55.

Britton, Patti. "Comparative Quantitative Analysis of the Similarities and Differences in Female- versus Male-Directed/Produced/Written Commercial Sex Films and Videos (1980–1990)." Ph.D dissertation, Institute for Advanced Study of Sexuality, San Francisco, 1993.

Broughton, James. [Interview by Robert Peters.] *Gay Sunshine Interviews II*, ed. Winston Leyland. San Francisco: Gay Sunshine Press, 1982, n.p.

———. *Making Light of It*. San Francisco: City Lights, 1977, 1992.

Brusendorff, Ove, and Poul Henningsen. *Erotik for Millioner: Karligheden I Filmen*. Copenhagen: Thaning and Appel, 1957. Trans. as *Erotica for the Millions: Love in the Movies*. Los Angeles: Book Mart, 1960.

Burger, John R. *One-Handed Histories: The Eroto-Politics of Gay Male Video Pornography*. New York: Harrington Park Press/Haworth Press, 1995.

Burston, Paul. *What Are You Looking At? Queer Sex, Style and Cinema.* New York: Cassell, 1995.

Burton, Tim, dir. *Ed Wood.* Los Angeles: Columbia Tri-Star, 1994.

Butler, Jerry. "Sally Jessy Raphael Show." American Broadcasting Network, 22 May 1989.

Butler, Jerry, with Robert Rimmer and Catherine Tavel. *Raw Talent: The Adult Film Industry as Seen by Its Most Popular Male Star.* Buffalo, NY: Prometheus Books, 1989.

Calendo, John. "Kenneth Anger Rising." *Oui,* 5:10 (October 1976): 59–60, 113–114, 116–117.

Callahan, Jean. "Women and Pornography: Combat in the Video Zone." *American Film,* 8 (March 1982): 62–63.

Campbell, Kevin. *Video Sex: Create Erotic and Romantic Home Videos with Your Camcorder.* Amherst, NY: Amherst Media, 1994.

Canby, Vincent. " 'Dirty Movies' Are a Bore." *New York Times,* 7 June 1970, p. C1.

"Candida Royalle." *Real Sex: 1.* Produced and directed by Patti Kaplan. New York: Home Box Office, 1990.

"Candy Barr [interview]." *Oui,* 5:6 (June 1976): 81–84, 110–113.

Carducci, Mark, dir. *The Ed Wood Story: The Plan 9 Companion.* Los Angeles: MPI, 1992.

Carol, Avedon. "Snuff: Believing the Worst." *Bad Girls and Dirty Pictures: The Challenge to Reclaim Feminism,* ed. Alison Assiter and Avedon Carol. Boulder, CO: Pluto Press, 1993, pp. 126–130.

Carroll, K. "An Interview with Fred Baker." *Evergreen Review,* 79 (June 1970): 39–43, 77–78.

Carter, Laura, and Cathy Stevens. *The Porno Girls.* New York: Ace Books, 1974.

Cartmell, Deborah, I. Q. Hunter, Heidi Kaye, and Imelda Whelehan, eds. *Trash Aesthetics.* Chicago: Pluto Press, 1997.

Cartwright, Gary. "Candy: Taking the Wrapper off a Texas Legend." *Texas Monthly,* 4 (December 1976): 99–103, 188–192.

Castle, William. *Step Right Up! I'm Gonna Scare the Pants Off America.* Mahwah, NJ: Pharos Books, 1992.

"Censorship and Pornography." Special issue of *Continuum: Journal of Media and Cultural Studies,* 12:1 (April 1998).

Chambers, Marilyn. *Marilyn Chambers: My Story.* New York: Warner Books, 1975.

Chapple, Steve, and David Talbot. *Burning Desires: Sex in America: A Report from the Field.* New York: Signet, 1990.

Christopher, Mark. "The Penis Page." *Penthouse,* 25:6 (February 1994): 118.

Chute, David. "Tumescent Market for One-Armed Videophiles." *Film Comment,* 17:5 (September–October 1981): 66, 68.

———. "Wages of Sin" and "Wages of Sin: II." *Film Comment,* 22:4 (July–August 1986): 32–39, 42, 48; and 22:5 (September–October 1986): 56–61.

Cinema Blue. New York, 1980–1985.

Cinema Underground Oggi: A Cura di Sirio Luginbühl. Padova: Mastrogiacomo Editori, 1972.

Clover, Carol J. "Her Body, Himself: Gender in the Slasher Film." *Representations,* 20 (Fall 1987): 187–228.

———. *Men, Women, and Chain Saws.* Princeton, NJ: Princeton University Press, 1992.

Cohan, Steven, and Ina Rae Hark, eds. *Screening the Male: Exploring Masculinities in Hollywood Cinema*. New York: Routledge, 1993.

"Conversation with John C. Holmes [interview]." *Oui*, 4 (July 1975): 66–68, 80, 82, 114–115.

Conway, Mary T. "Spectatorship in Lesbian Porn: The Woman's Woman's Film." *Wide Angle*, 19:3 (1997): 91–113.

Cook, Pam. "Exploitation Films and Feminism." *Screen*, 17:2 (Summer 1976): 122–127.

Corliss, Richard. "Cinema Sex, from *The Kiss* to *Deep Throat*." *Film Comment*, 9:1 (January–February 1973): 4–5.

———. "Radley Metzger: Aristocrat of the Erotic." *Film Comment*, 9:1 (January–February 1973): 18–29.

Coulteray, George de. *Le Sadisme au Cinéma*. Paris: Le Terrain Vague, n.d.

Cowan, Gloria, Carole Lee, Danielle Levy, and Debra Synder. "Dominance and Inequality in X-Rated Videocassettes." *Psychology of Women Quarterly*, 12 (1988): 299–311.

Cowan, Gloria, and M. O'Brien. "Gender and Survival vs. Death in Slasher Films: A Content Analysis." *Sex Roles*, 23 (1990): 187–196.

Crabbe, Anthony. "Feature-Length Sex Films." *Perspectives on Pornography: Sexuality in Film and Literature*, ed. Gary Day and Clive Bloom. New York: St. Martin's, 1988, pp. 44–65.

Csicsery, George Paul. *The Sex Industry*. New York: New American Library, 1973.

Curry, Jack. "X-Rated Aphrodites." *Home Video*, 3:1 (January 1982): 21–26.

Dargis, Manohla. "Bush League: Homemade Porn, Playing Soon at a Bedroom near You." *Village Voice*, 3 September 1991, p. 49.

Davy, Jean-François. "Le film pornographique n'est pas un genre." *Art Press*, 22 (January–February 1976): 11.

Day, Gary, and Clive Bloom, eds. *Perspectives on Pornography: Sexuality in Film and Literature*. New York: St. Martin's, 1988.

de Renzy, Alex, dir. *The History of the Blue Movie*. Los Angeles: California Video, 1971.

de Lauretis, Teresa, ed. *Feminist Studies/Critical Studies*. Bloomington: Indiana University Press, 1986.

Deep inside Annie Sprinkle. Los Angeles: Vid-X-Pix, 1982.

Deep inside Shanna McCullough. Los Angeles: Vid-X-Pix, 1992.

Delacoste, Frédérique, and Priscilla Alexander, eds. *Sex Work: Writings by Women in the Sex Industry*. Pittsburgh: Cleis Press, 1987.

———. *Technologies of Gender: Essays on Theory, Film, and Fiction*. Bloomington: Indiana University Press, 1987.

Di Lauro, Al, and Gerald Rabkin. *Dirty Movies: An Illustrated History of the Stag Film, 1915–1970*. New York: Chelsea House, 1976.

Dietz, P. E., and B. Evans. "Pornographic Imagery and the Prevalence of Paraphilia." *American Journal of Psychiatry*, 139 (1982): 1493–1495.

Dixon, Wheeler. "In Defense of Roger Corman." *Velvet Light Trap*, 16 (Fall 1976): 11–14.

"Doctor/Director." *Real Sex: 5*. Produced and directed by Patti Kaplan. New York: Home Box Office, 1991.

Dogherty, Steve, and Dirk Mathison. "Born Again Porn Star." *People*, 35:18 (13 May 1991): 83–84.

"Doris Wishman: Queen of Exploitation." *Real Sex: 21*. Produced and directed by Patti Kaplan. New York: HBO, 1998.

Dowdy, Andrew. *Movies Are Better than Ever: Wide-Screen Memories of the Fifties*. New York: Morrow, 1973.

"Dressed to Kill." Special section on the pornography debate. *Film Comment*, 20 (November–December 1984), 30–49.

Dubler, Linda. *"Variety." Film Quarterly*, 38 (Fall 1984): 24–28.

Duggan, Lisa, Nan D. Hunter, and Carole S. Vance. "False Promises: Feminist Antipornography Legislation." *Caught Looking: Feminism, Pornography, and Censorship*, by the Feminist Anti-Censorship Task Force. New York: Caught Looking, 1986, pp. 72–84.

Durgnat, Raymond. *Eros in the Cinema*. London: Calder and Boyars, 1966.

———. "An Evening with Meyer and Masoch: Aspects of *Vixen* and *Venus in Furs*." *Film Comment*, 9:1 (January–February 1973): 52–61.

———. *Sexual Alienation in the Cinema*. London: Studio Vista, 1974.

Dyer, Richard. *Heavenly Bodies: Film Stars and Society*. New York: St. Martin's, 1986.

———. "Male Gay Porn." *Jump Cut*, 30 (March 1985): 227–229; rpt. as "Coming to Terms." *Out There: Marginalization and Contemporary Culture*, ed. Russell Ferguson et al. Cambridge: MIT Press, 1990, pp. 289–298; rpt. *Only Entertainment*. New York: Routledge, 1992, pp. 121–134.

———. *The Matter of Images: Essays on Representations*. New York: Routledge, 1993.

———. *Now You See It: Studies on Lesbian and Gay Film*. New York: Routledge, 1990.

———, ed. *Gays and Film*. London: British Film Institute, 1980; rev. ed. New York: New York Zoetrope, 1984.

Ebert, Roger. "The Immoral Mr. Meyer." *Playboy*, 42:6 (June 1995): 88–93.

———. "Russ Meyer, King of the Nudies." *Film Comment*, 9:1 (January–February 1973): 34–45.

Ecco: The World of Bizarre Video. Washington, DC 20035: Box 65742, 1991–.

Epple, Aaron. "Queen City Monster-Maker." *(Cincinnati, OH) City Beat*, 30 October–5 November 1997, pp. 35–36.

Erens, Patricia. *"The Seduction*: The Pornographic Impulse in Slasher Films." *Jump Cut*, 32 (April 1986): 52–55.

———, ed. *Sexual Stratagems: The World of Women in Film*. New York: Horizon Press, 1979.

The Erotic Screen: A Probing Study of Sex in the Adult Cinema. Los Angeles: Private Collectors, 1969.

"Exploitation Films." Special issue of *Film History*, 6:3 (1994).

Faludi, Susan. "The Money Shot." *The New Yorker*, 30 October 1995, pp. 64–70, 72–76, 78–82, 84–87.

Fatale, Fanny. *How to Female Ejaculate*. San Francisco: Fatale Video/Blush Entertainment, 1992.

Faust, Bernice. *Women, Sex and Pornography: A Controversial Study*. New York: Macmillan, 1980.

Femme Fatales. Forest Park, IL, 1992–.

Fiedler, Leslie. "A Night with Mr. Teas." *The Collected Essays of Leslie Fiedler*. 2 vols. New York: Stein and Day, 1971.

Fifteen Sex Queens on Sex: By the World's Most Desired Women. Chicago: Novel Books, 1964.

Film Journal, 2:1 (September 1972). Special issue on explicit sex in movies.

Film Threat (Los Angeles, 1990–) and *Film Threat Video Guide* (Los Angeles, 1991–).

Finch, Mark. "George Kuchar: Half the Story." *Queer Looks: Perspectives on Lesbian and Gay Film and Video*, ed. Martha Gever, Pratibha Parmar, and John Greyson. New York: Routledge, 1993, pp. 76–85.

Flint, David. *Babylon Blue: An Illustrated History of Adult Cinema*. London: Creation Books, 1999.

Frank, Sam. *Sex in the Movies*. Secaucus, NJ: Citadel Press, 1986.

Fraser, John. *Violence in the Arts*. New York: Cambridge University Press, 1974.

Freeman, Richard, ed. *Batteries Not Included*. Yellow Springs, OH, 1995–.

Friedman, David, with Don De Nevi. *A Youth in Babylon: Confessions of a Trash-Film King*. Buffalo, NY: Prometheus Books, 1990.

Fuentes, Annette, and Margaret Schrage. "Interview with Veronica Hart, Gloria Leonard, Kelly Nichols, Candida Royalle, Annie Sprinkle, and Veronica Vera: Deep inside Porn Stars." *Jump Cut*, 32 (April 1986): 41–43.

Fung, Richard. "Looking for My Penis: The Eroticized Asian in Gay Video Porn." *How Do I Look?: Queer Film and Video*, ed. Bad Object Choices. Seattle: Bay Press, 1991, pp. 145–160.

———. "Shortcomings: Questions about Pornography as Pedagogy." *Queer Looks: Perspectives on Lesbian and Gay Film and Video*, ed. Martha Gever, Pratibha Parmar, and John Greyson. New York: Routledge, 1993, pp. 355–367.

Galloway, David. "Up Yours Tonto! Or, Growing Up Queer in America." *The Sex Industry*, ed. George Csicsery. New York: NAL, 1973, pp. 208–218.

Garcia, L. T., and L. Milano. "A Content Analysis of Erotic Videos." *Journal of Psychology and Human Sexuality*, 3:2 (1990): 95–103.

Gardos, Peter Sandor. "Gender Differences in the Interpretations and Reactions to Viewing Pornographic Vignettes." Ph.D. dissertation, University of Connecticut, 1995.

Gay Video Guide. Los Angeles, 1997–.

Gehr, Richard. "Comin' at Ya." In "Voice Film Special: Reel Sex." *Village Voice*, 4 December 1990, pp. 9, 25.

George, Bill. *Drive-In Madness: The Jiggle Movies*. Pittsburgh: Imagine, 1990.

———. *Eroticism in the Fantasy Cinema*. Pittsburgh: Imagine, 1984.

Gever, Martha, Pratibha Parmar, and John Greyson, eds. *Queer Looks: Perspectives on Lesbian and Gay Film and Video*. New York: Routledge, 1993.

Gibbs, Wolcott. "The Peepshow Season in Retrospect." *New Yorker*, 5:31 (21 September 1929): 25–26.

Giles, Dennis. "Pornographic Space: The Other Place." "Film: Historical-Theoretical Speculations." *The 1977 Film Studies Annual, Part II*, ed. Ben Lawton and Janet Staiger. Pleasantville, NY: Redgrave/Docent, 1977, pp. 52–65.

Gill, Brendan. "Blue Notes." *Film Comment*, 9:1 (January–February 1973): 6–11.

Giobbe, Evelina. "Surviving Commercial Sexual Exploitation." *Gender, Race and Class in Media: A Text-Reader*, ed. Gail Dines and Jean M. Humez. Thousand Oaks, CA: Sage, 1995, pp. 314–318.

"Girls from Girdleville." Real Sex: 6. Produced and directed by Patti Kaplan. New York: Home Box Office, 1993.

Goldstein, Al. "Citizen Cain and Abel." *Penthouse*, 23:2 (October 1991): 52–61, 120.

———. "Making Your Own Erotic Video." *Penthouse*, 24:7 (March 1993): 91, 110, 124, 126.

Goldstein, Richard. "The Little Shop of Hornies." *Village Voice*, 31 December 1996, pp. 44–46.

Goldsby, Jack. "Queens of Language: *Paris Is Burning*." *Queer Looks: Perspectives on Lesbian and Gay Film and Video*, ed. Martha Gever, Pratibha Parmar, and John Greyson. New York: Routledge, 1993, pp. 108–115.

Goode, James N., ed. *Directory of Amateur Erotica: Where to Buy and Sell Productions by Talented Amateurs*. Nashville, TN: Ferret Press, 1988.

———. *How to Create and Sell Amateur Erotic Videos and Photos: Cashing In on the Amateur Craze*. Nashville, TN: Ferret Press, 1988.

Gordon, Bette, with photos by Nan Goldin. "*Variety*: The Pleasure in Looking." *Pleasure and Danger: Exploring Female Sexuality*, ed. Carole S. Vance. Boston: Routledge and Kegan Paul, 1984, 189–203.

Gordon, Bette, and Karyn Kay. "Look Back/Talk Back." *Dirty Looks: Women, Pornography, Power*, ed. Pamela Church Gibson and Roma Gibson. London: British Film Institute, 1993, pp. 90–100.

Gordon, George N. *Erotic Communications: Studies in Sex, Sin and Censorship*. New York: Hastings House, 1980.

Gould, Jodie. "Debbie Directs Dallas: Video Erotica Made by Women for Women." *Elle*, 7:8 (April 1992): 144, 148, 150.

Graham, Don. "Commentary/*The Lickerish Quartet*." *Picture This: Films Chosen by Artists*, ed. Steve Gallagher. Buffalo, NY: Hallwalls, 1987, pp. 58–62.

Gramann, Karola, Gertrud Koch, et al. *Lust und Elend: Das erotische Kino*. Munich: Bücher C. J. Verlag, 1981.

Grant, Barry Keith, ed. *The Dread of Difference: Gender and the Horror Film*. Austin: University of Texas Press, 1996.

Grey, Rudolph. *Nightmare of Ecstasy: The Life and Art of Edward D. Wood, Jr*. Portland, OR: Feral House, 1992.

Greyson, John. "Gay Video: The Present Context." *Jump Cut*, 30 (March 1985): 36–38.

———. "Security Blankets: Sex, Video and the Police." *Queer Looks: Perspectives on Lesbian and Gay Film and Video*, ed. Martha Gever, Pratibha Parmar, and John Greyson. New York: Routledge, 1993, pp. 383–394.

Griggers, Cathy. "Bearing the Sign in Struggle: Pornography, Parody, and Mainstream Cinema." *American Journal of Semiotics*, 6:4 (1989): 95–107.

Grimes, William. "Respect Finds a Movie Studio Built on Shock and Schlock." *New York Times*, 20 July 1992, pp. B1–2.

Grove, Martin A., and William S. Ruben. *The Celluloid Love Feast: The Story of Erotic Movies*. New York: Lancer, 1971.

Gutman, Walter. "My Pioneer Days in Underground Movies." *Penthouse*, 1 (August 1970): 26–28, 30–31, 88.

Hadleigh, Boze. *Hollywood Lesbians*. New York: Barricade, 1995.

———. *The Lavender Screen: The Gay and Lesbian Films, Their Stars, Makers, Characters, and Critics*. New York: Citadel Press, 1993.

Halstead, Fred. [Interview by Ernest Peter Cohen.] *Gay Activist*, April 1972, pp. 11, 21–22.

Hamilton, Marybeth. *"When I'm Bad I'm Better": Mae West, Sex, and American Entertainment*. New York: Harper, 1994.

Hammer, Barbara. "The Politics of Abstraction." *Queer Looks: Perspectives on Lesbian and Gay Film and Video*, ed. Martha Gever, Pratibha Parmar, and John Greyson. New York: Routledge, 1993, pp. 70–75.

Handy, Bruce. "What's It Worth to You?" *New York Times Magazine*, 13 February 1994, p. 82.

Hansen, Christian, Catherine Needham, and Bill Nichols. "Skin Flicks: Pornography, Ethnography, and the Discourses of Power." *Discourse: Journal for Theoretical Studies in Media and Culture*, 11:2 (Spring–Summer 1989): 65–79.

Hanson, Gillian. *Original Skin: Nudity and Sex in Cinema and Theatre.* London: Stacey, 1970.

Harris, Sarah. *The Puritan Jungle: America's Sexual Underground.* London: Mayflower, 1970.

Hart, Ariel. "Bizarre Days." *Gauntlet*, 15 (1998): 46–48.

Hartley, Nina. "Confessions of a Feminist Porno Star." *Sex Work: Writings by Women in the Sex Industry*, ed. Frédérique Delacoste and Priscilla Alexander. Pittsburgh: Cleis Press, 1987, pp. 142–144.

Haskell, Molly. *From Reverence to Rape: The Treatment of Women in the Movies.* New York: Holt, Rinehart, and Winston, 1974.

———. "The Night Porno Films Turned Me Off." *New York*, 29 March 1976, pp. 56, 58, 60.

Haug, Kate, ed. "Femme Experimentale." Special issue of *Wide Angle*, 20:1 (January 1998).

Heath, Chris. "A Hard Man Is Good to Find." *Details*, September 1996, pp. 96–97, 100, 102, 104, 108, 110, 112, 270–271.

Heath, Desmond. "An Investigation into the Origins of a Copious Vaginal Discharge During Intercourse: 'Enough to Wet the Bed—"That" Is Not Urine.' " *Journal of Sex Research*, 20:2 (May 1984): 194–215.

Heath, Stephen. "Body, Voice." *Questions of Cinema.* Bloomington: Indiana University Press, 1981, 176–193.

Hebditch, David, and Nick Anning. *Porn Gold: Inside the Pornography Business.* London: Faber and Faber, 1988.

Hetze, Stefanie. *Happy-End für Wen? Kino und lesbische Frauen.* Frankfurt am Main: Tende, 1986.

Highball. Kronos Publications, PO Box 67, Oberlin, OH 44074–0067.

Hinds, Michael de Courcy. "New Adult Videos, Starring the Couple across the Street." *New York Times*, national ed., 22 March 1991, B1, B5.

Hoberman, J. "The Big Heat." *Village Voice*, 1 November 1991, pp. 61, 72.

———. "XCXHXEXRXRXIXEXSX." *Village Voice*, 19 January 1993, p. 47.

Hoddeson, Bob. *The Porn People: A First-Person Documentary Report.* Watertown, MA: American Publishing Co., 1974.

Hoffmann, Frank. *Analytical Survey of Anglo-American Traditional Erotica.* Bowling Green, OH: Bowling Green University Press, 1973.

———. "Prolegomena to a Study of Traditional Elements in the Erotic Film." *Journal of American Folklore*, 78 (April/June 1965): 143–148.

Hogan, David. J. *Dark Romance: Sexuality in the Horror Film.* Jefferson, NC: McFarland, 1986.

Holmlund, Chris, and Cynthia Fuchs, eds. *Between the Sheets, in the Streets: Queer, Lesbian, Gay Documentary.* Minneapolis: University of Minnesota Press, 1997.

Howitt, Dennis, and Guy Cumberbatch. *Pornography: Impact and Influences*. London: Home Office Research and Planning Unit, 1990.

Hubner, John. *Bottom Feeders: From Free Love to Hard Core—The Rise and Fall of Counterculture Heroes Jim and Artie Mitchell*. New York: Doubleday, 1993.

Hustler Erotic Video Guide. Mount Morris, IL, 1993–.

Isherwood, Charles. *Wonder Bread and Ecstasy: The Life and Death of Joey Stefano*. Boston: Alyson, 1996.

Jacobs, Katrien. " 'The Lady of Little Death': Illuminated Encounters and Erotic Duties in the Life and Art of Maria Beatty." *Wide Angle*, 19:3 (1997): 13–40.

Jacobs, Lea. *The Wages of Sin: Censorship and the Fallen Woman Film, 1928–1942*. Madison: University of Wisconsin Press, 1991.

James, David. "Hardcore: Cultural Resistance in the Postmodern." *Film Quarterly*, 42:2 (Winter 1988/1989): 31–39.

Jameson, Frederic. *Signatures of the Visible*. New York: Routledge, 1990.

Jaworzyn, Stefan, ed. *Shock Express: The Essential Guide to Exploitation Cinema*. Vols. I and II. London: Titan Books, 1992, 1994.

Johnson, Eithne. "Excess and Ecstasy: Constructing Female Pleasure in Porn Movies." *Velvet Light Trap*, 32 (Fall 1993): 30–49.

———. "Sound and the Textuality of Female Orgasms." Paper delivered at the 13th Ohio University Film Conference, Athens, Ohio, 8 November 1991.

Johnson, Eithne, and Eric Schaefer. "Soft Core/Hard Core: *Snuff* as a Crisis in Meaning." *Journal of Film and Video*, 45:2–3 (Summer–Fall 1993): 40–59.

Judson, Horace Freeland. "Skindeep: How to Watch a Pornographic Movie." *Harper's*, 250 (February 1975): 42–49.

Jump Cut, 16 (1977): Special Issue on Gays and Film; 24/25 (1981): Special Double Issue on Lesbians and Film.

Juno, Andrea, and V. Vale, eds. *Angry Women*. San Francisco: RE/Search, 1991.

———. *Incredibly Strange Films*. San Francisco: RE/Search, 1986.

Katzman, Lisa. "The Women of Porn: They're Not in It for the Moneyshot." *Village Voice*, 24 August 1993, pp. 31–33.

Kay, Shelley. "Confessions of a Splatter Girl—Part I." *Filmnews*, 17:9 (1987): 20.

Kernes, Mark. "Sunset Thomas." *Adult Video News*, 8:6 (May 1993): 134.

Kilday, Gregg. "Inside Marilyn Chambers." *Home Video*, 2:1 (January 1981): 24–27.

Kinnick, Dave. *Sorry I Asked: Intimate Interviews with Gay Porn's Rank and File*. New York: Badboy, 1993.

Kirchhoff, H. J. "In Person: 'I'm Constantly Surprised at the Fan Mail.' " *(Toronto) The Globe and Mail*, 8 November 1991, p. C5.

Kit Parker Films. *Sex and Buttered Popcorn*, hosted by Ned Beatty. Monterey, CA: Kit Parker Films/Main Street Movies, 1989.

Klaw, Irving. *Classic Films of Irving Klaw: Volumes I and II*. London: London Enterprises, 1984.

Klein, Bonnie Sherr. *Not a Love Story*. Toronto: National Film Board of Canada, 1982.

Knight, Arthur, and Hollis Alpert. "The History of Sex in Cinema." *Playboy*, 19 articles running from April 1965 to January 1969; the chapter called "The Stag Film" appears in the November 1967 issue.

———. *Sex in Cinema*. Chicago: Playboy Press, 1971–1974?

Koch, Gertrud. "The Body's Shadow Realm," trans. Jan-Christopher Horak. *Jump Cut*, 35 (April 1990): 17–29; rpt. *Dirty Looks: Women, Pornography, Power*, ed. Pamela Church Gibson and Roma Gibson. London: British Film Institute, 1993, pp. 22–45.

Koch, Stephen. "Fashions in Pornography: Murder as Cinematic Chic." *Harper's*, 253 (November 1976): 108–109.

———. *Stargazer: The Life, World, and Films of Andy Warhol*. Rev. and updated ed. New York: Marion Boyars, 1991.

Kohan, Buz. *Sixty Years of Seduction*. A Rastar Television Production, an ABC Special Presentation, 1980. Producers, Scott Garen, John Brice; Director, Jeff Margolis; writer, Buz Kohan. Script in Popular Culture Archives, Bowling Green State University Library, Bowling Green, OH.

Konow, David. *Schlock-o-Rama: The Films of Al Adamson*. Los Angeles: Lone Eagle, 1998.

Kortz, Dirk. "Eroticism vs Porn by an Ex-Practitioner." *Take One*, 4:5 (May–June 1973): 28–29.

Kotz, Liz. "Interrogating the Boundaries of Women's Art: New Work in Video by Four Women." *High Performance*, 12:4 (Winter 1989): 36–41.

———. "Striptease East and West: Sexual Representation in Documentary Film." *Framework*, 38/39 (1992): 47–63.

———. "An Unrequited Desire for the Sublime: Looking at Lesbian Representation across the Works of Abigail Child, Cecilia Dougherty, and Su Friedrich." *Queer Looks: Perspectives on Lesbian and Gay Film and Video*, ed. Martha Gever, Pratibha Parmar, and John Greyson. New York: Routledge, 1993, pp. 86–102.

Kramer, Margia. *Andy Warhol et al: The FBI File on Andy Warhol*. New York: UnSub Press, 1988.

Krogh, Daniel, and John McCarty. *The Amazing Herschel Gordon Lewis and His World of Exploitation Films*. Albany, NY: Fantaco Enterprises, 1983.

Kroll, Eric. *Eric Kroll's The Fetish Tapes*. 4 vols. San Francisco: Eric Kroll Photography, 1994.

Kronhausen, Eberhard, and Phyllis Kronhausen. *The Sex People: Erotic Performers and Their Brave New Worlds*. Chicago: Playboy Press, 1975.

Kuhn, Annette. "The Body and Cinema." *Wide Angle*, 11:4 (October 1989): 52–60.

———. *Cinema, Censorship, and Sexuality 1909–1925*. London: Routledge, 1988.

———. *The Power of the Image: Essays on Representation and Sexuality*. Boston: Routledge and Kegan Paul, 1985.

———. *Women's Pictures: Feminism and Cinema*. London: Routledge and Kegan Paul, 1982.

Kuipers, Dean. "Sex, Home, and Videotape." *Playboy*, 42:11 (November 1995): 114–116, 126, 154–156.

Kyrou, Ado. *Amour-Erotisme au Cinéma*. Paris: Eric Losfeld, 1966.

———. "D'un Certain Cinéma Clandestin." *Positif: Revue de Cinéma*, 61/62/63 (June/July/August 1964): 205–23.

LaBia, Lisa [Lisa Palac]. "Fatale Attraction: Or How My Porno Dream Came True." *On Our Backs*, 7:3 (January–February 1991): 15, 23–27, 38–39.

Landis, Bill. "Tromatized." *Film Comment*, 22:4 (July–August 1986): 77–80.

———. *The Unauthorized Biography of Kenneth Anger*. New York: Harper Perennial, 1996.

Landis, Bill, with Michelle Clifford. "Body for Rent: A Journey through the Ruins of the Porno-Chic Empire." *Village Voice*, 12 December 1995, pp. 31–36.

LaRue, Chi Chi [Paciotti, Larry], with John Erich. *Making It Big: Sex Stars, Porn Films, and Me*. Los Angeles: Alyson Books, 1997.

Leach, Michael. *I Know It When I See It: Pornography, Violence, and Public Sensitivity*. Philadelphia: Westminster Press, 1975.

Leblanc, Gérard. "Le cul loin du ciel: Essai sur le genre pornographique." *Érotisme et cinéma: Themes et variations*, ed. Daniel Serceau. Paris: Atlas L'Herminier, 1986, pp. 125–146.

Lee, Raymond. *A Pictorial History of Hollywood Nudity*. Chicago: Camerarts, 1964; aka *A Pictorial History of Hollywood Sex*. Los Angeles: RNS Publications, Winter 1965 issue.

Leffingwell, Edward, Carole Kismaric, and Marvin Heiferman, eds. *Flaming Creature: Jack Smith, His Amazing Life and Times*. New York: PS 1/Serpent's Tail, 1997.

Legman, Gershon. *Love and Death: A Study in Censorship*. New York: Breaking Point, 1949.

Lehman, Peter. *Running Scared: Masculinity and the Representation of the Male Body*. Philadelphia: Temple University Press, 1993.

Lenne, Gérard. *Sex on the Screen: Eroticism in Film*, trans. D. Jacobs. New York: St. Martin's, 1985.

Lennon, John, and Yoko Ono. "Our Films." *Filmmakers' Newsletter*, 6:8 (June 1973): 21–24.

"L'Erotisme en Question." Special issue of *Cinema D'Aujourd'Hui*, 4 (Winter 1975–1976).

Levy, William, ed. *Wet Dreams: Films and Adventures*. Amsterdam: Joy Publications, 1973.

Limbacher, James L. *Sexuality in World Cinema*. 2 vols. Metuchen, NJ: Scarecrow Press, 1983.

"Linda Lovelace for President." *Playboy*, 22 (February 1975): 76–83, 166.

Lo Duca, Guiseppe. *L'Erotisme au Cinéma*. 3 vols. and supplement. Paris: Pauvert, 1957, 1960, 1962, 1968.

Losano, Wayne A. "The Sex Genre: Traditional and Modern Variations on the Flesh Film." *Sexuality in the Movies*, ed. Thomas R. Atkins. New York: Da Capo, 1984, 132–144.

Lovelace, Linda. *Inside Linda Lovelace*. Los Angeles: Pinnacle, 1973.

———. *Out of Bondage*. Secaucus, NJ: Lyle Stuart, 1986.

Lovelace, Linda, with Mike Brady. *Ordeal*. New York: Citadel, 1980.

Ludwig, Heinrich. "Die Erotik im Film." *Die Erotik in der Photographie*, ed. Erich Wulffen et al. Vienna: Verlag für Kulturforschung, 1931, pp. 233–253.

MacCannell, Dean. "Faking It: Comment on Face-Work in Pornography." *American Journal of Semiotics*, 6:4 (1989): 153–174.

MacDonald, Scott. *Avant-Garde Film: Motion Studies*. Cambridge, England: Cambridge University Press, 1993.

———. "Confessions of a Feminist Porn Watcher." *Film Quarterly*, 36:3 (Spring 1983): 10–17.

———. "Two Interviews: Demystifying the Female Body: Anne Severson's *Near the Big Chakra* [1972] and Yvonne Rainer's *Privilege* [1990]." *Film Comment*, 45: 1 (Fall 1991): 18–32.

MacInnes, Colin. "Sex Marathon." *New Society*, 16 (3 December 1970): 989–991.

Macy, Marianne. *Working Sex: An Odyssey into Our Cultural Underworld.* New York: Carroll and Graf, 1996.

"Male Order Fantasies." *Real Sex: 19.* Produced and directed by Patti Kaplan. New York: HBO, 1998.

Malone, Michael. *Heroes of Eros: Male Sexuality in the Movies.* New York: Dutton, 1979.

Mano, D. Keith. "I'm Ready for My Come Shot Now, Dear." *Playboy,* 43:8 (August 1996): 81–82, 143–144.

Manshots—FirstHand Publications. Teaneck, NJ, 1995–.

Marcus, Steven. *The Other Victorians.* New York: Basic Books, 1965.

Margold, William. *Sexual Stamina: The Secret of the Male Sex Star.* San Diego: Greenleaf Publishers, 1973.

Martin, Jim. "Out of the Closets and into the Bijous." *Take One,* 4:5 (May–June 1973): 30.

Marvin, Louis. *The New Goddesses: Kay Parker, Sheri St. Clair, Mai Lin, Nina Hartley, Jeannie Pepper, Juliet Anderson Talk to Louis Marvin about Their Lifestyles, Personal Sex Life and Why They Enjoy Acting in Porno Films.* Malibu, CA: AF Press, 1987.

Masters, Sam. "Alternative Sexuality and the Video Retailer. *Adult Video News,* 8:12 (November 1993): 60, 62.

Mayne, Judith. *The Woman at the Keyhole.* Bloomington: Indiana University Press, 1990.

McCarthy, Todd, and Charles Fynn, eds. *Kings of the Bs: Working within the Hollywood System, an Anthology of Film History and Criticism.* New York: Dutton, 1975.

McCarty, John. *John McCarty's Official Splatter Movie Guide.* Volumes I and II. New York: St. Martin's, 1989, 1992.

———. *Splatter Movies: Breaking the Last Taboo of the Screen.* New York: St. Martin's, 1984.

———, ed. *The Sleaze Merchants: Adventures in Exploitation Filmmaking.* New York: St. Martin's, 1995.

McCumber, David. *Rated-X: The Mitchell Brothers, a True Story of Sex, Money, and Death.* New York: Simon and Schuster, 1992.

McDonagh, Maitland. *The Fifty Most Erotic Films of All Time.* Secaucus, NJ: Citadel/Carol Publishing Group, 1995.

———. *Filmmaking on the Fringe: The Good, the Bad, and the Deviant.* New York: Citadel, 1995.

McDonough, Jimmy. "The Ormonds." *Filmfax: The Magazine of Unusual Film & Television,* No. 27 (June/July 1991): 40–49; No. 28 (August/September 1991): 37–41.

———. "Sexposed." *Film Comment,* 22:4 (July–August 1986): 53–61.

McGillivray, David. *Doing Rude Things: The History of the British Sex Film, 1957–1981.* London: Sun Tavern Fields, 1992.

"Meet Missy, Republican Porn Star." *Playboy,* 34 (January 1987): 125–129, 178–180.

Mekas, Jonas. *Movie Journal: The Rise of a New American Cinema, 1959–1971.* New York: Collier, 1972.

Mellen, Joan. *Women and Their Sexuality in the New Film.* New York: Horizon Press, 1973.

Mellencamp, Patricia. *Indiscretions: Avant-Garde Film, Video, and Feminism.* Bloomington: Indiana University Press, 1990.

Mendik, Xavier. "From 'Trick' to 'Prick.' " *Necromicon: Book One: The Journal of Horror and Erotic Cinema*, ed. Andy Black. London: Creation Books, 1996, pp. 102–108.

Mercer, Kobena. "Dark and Lovely Too: Black Gay Men in Independent Film." *Queer Looks: Perspectives on Lesbian and Gay Film and Video*, ed. Martha Gever, Pratibha Parmar, and John Greyson. New York: Routledge, 1993, pp. 238–256.

Merck, Mandy. *Perversions: Deviant Readings*. New York: Routledge, 1993.

Metz, Christian. "Photography and Fetish." *October*, 34 (1985): 81–90.

Meyer, Richard. "Rock Hudson's Body." *Inside/Out: Lesbian Theories, Gay Theories*, ed. Diana Fuss. New York: Routledge, 1991, pp. 259–288.

Meyers, Richard. *For One Week Only: The World of Exploitation Films*. Piscataway, NJ: New Century, 1982.

Michelson, Annette. "On the Eve of the Future: The Reasonable Facsimile and the Philosophical Toy." *October*, 29 (1984): 3–22.

Michelson, Peter. *Speaking the Unspeakable: A Poetics of Obscenity*. Albany: State University of New York Press, 1993; rev. and enl. of *The Aesthetics of Pornography*. New York: Herder and Herder, 1971.

Midnight Blue. New York: Milky Way Productions, Channel J, Manhattan Teleprompter Cable, 1983–1990; Channel 35, 1990–.

Milner, Michael. *Sex on Celluloid*. New York: McFadden, 1964.

Milton, John, ed. *Smut from the Past: Vol. 2*. New York: Milky Way Productions, 1974.

Mitchell, Elvis. "Sex, Lowe, and Videotape." *Village Voice*, 4 July 1989, p. 59.

Molitor, Fred, and Barry S. Sapolsky. "Sex, Violence, and Victimization in Slasher Films." *Journal of Broadcasting and Electronic Media*, 37:2 (Spring 1993): 233–242.

Montano, Linda. "Summer Saint Camp 1987, with Annie Sprinkle and Veronica Vera," *TDR*, 33:1 (Spring 1989): 94–103, and "Our Week at Sister Rosita's Summer Saint Camp," 104–119.

Moreck, Curt [Konrad Hammerling]. *Das Gesicht*. Vol. I of *Die Fünf Sinne*, ed. Bernhard A. Bauer. 5 vols. Vienna: Verlag für Kulturforschung, 1929.

———. "Der pornographische Film." *Sittengeschichte Das Geheimen und Verboten*. Vol. VII of *Sittengeschichte der Kulturwelt und ihrer Entwicklung in Einzeldarstellungen*, ed. Leo Schidrowitz. 10 vols. and supplement to vol. II. Vienna: Verlag für Kulturforschung, 1930, pp. 155–170.

———. "Rosario, Der Steppenhafen." *Sittengeschichte des Hafens und der Reise*. Vol. VIII of *Sittengeschichte der Kulturwelt und ihrer Entwicklung in Einzeldarstellungen*, ed. Leo Schidrowitz. 10 vols. and supplement to vol. II. Vienna: Verlag für Kulturforschung, 1930, pp. 79–88.

———. *Sittengeschichte des Kinos*. Dresden: Paul Aretz, 1926.

Morrocchi, Riccardo, Stefano Piselli, and James Elliot Singer. *Bizarre Sinema! Wildest Sexiest Weirdest Sleaziest Films: Sexploitation Filmmakers, Masters of the Nudie-Cutie, Ghoulie, Roughie and Kinky*. Florence, Italy: Glittering Images/edizione d'essai, 1995.

Morthland, J. "Porn Films: An In-Depth Report." *Take One*, 4:4 (March–April 1973): 11–17.

Muller, Eddie, and Daniel Faris. *Grindhouse: The Forbidden World of "Adults Only" Cinema*. New York: St. Martin's, 1996.

Nappi, Maureen. "Clit Tapes." *Heresies*, 4:4 (issue 16: Film/Video; 1983): 24–25.

Neier, Aryeh. "Linda Lovelace's 'Ordeal': Memoirs of a Woman's Displeasure." *Images of Women in American Popular Culture*, ed. Angela G. Dorenkamp, John F. McClymer, Mary E. Moynihan, and Arlene C. Vadum. San Diego: Harcourt Brace Jovanovich, 1985, pp. 162–167.

Nelson, Edward J. *Yesterday's Porno: A Pictorial History of Early Stag Photographs.* 2 vols. New York: Nostalgia Classics, 1972.

Nettles, Rhonda. "Let Me Tell Ya 'bout Suffering." *Gauntlet: Exploring the Limits of Free Expression*, 5 (1993): 69–70.

"The New Girls of Porn." *Playboy*, 24:7 (July 1977): 133–144, 196, 198–199.

Nichols, Peter M. "Working the Angles in Low-Budget Paradise." *New York Times*, 3 August 1997, sec. 2, pp. 11, 20.

North, Peter. *Penetrating Insights*. Los Angeles: Privately printed, 1992.

O'Casey, Ronan. "Getting It Up for a Porn Movie." *Playboy*, 24:3 (March 1977): 123, 128, 156, 158, 161.

"Of Human Bondage." *Real Sex: 5*. Produced and directed by Patti Kaplan. New York: Home Box Office, 1991.

O'Hara, Scott "Spunk." *Autopornography: A Memoir of Life in the Lust Lane*. Binghamton, NY: Haworth Press, 1998.

Oliver, Mary Beth. "Contributions of Sexual Portrayals to Viewers' Responses to Graphic Horror." *Journal of Broadcasting and Electronic Media*, 38:1 (Winter 1994): 1–17.

Oliver, Mattie. "Hollywood Orgasm." *Playboy*, 41:7 (July 1994): 50–51.

O'Pray, Michael, ed. *Andy Warhol: Film Factory*. London: British Film Institute, 1989.

Owens, Tuppy. *The Safer Sex Maniac's Bible*. London: Miss Tuppy Owens, Box 4ZB, London WIA 4ZB, 1992.

———. "Sex on My Mind." *Bad Girls and Dirty Pictures: The Challenge to Reclaim Feminism*, ed. Alison Assiter and Avedon Carol. Boulder, CO: Pluto Press, 1993, 112–125.

Pally, Marcia. " 'Double' Trouble." *Film Comment*, 20:5 (September–October 1984): 1–17.

Palumbo, Donald, ed. *Eros in the Mind's Eye: Sexuality and the Fantastic in Art and Film*. Westport, CT: Greenwood Press, 1986.

Palys, Ted S. "Testing the Common Wisdom: The Social Content of Video Pornography." *Canadian Psychology*, 27 (1986): 22–35.

Panofsky, Erwin. "Style and Medium in the Motion Pictures" [1934]. *Film Theory and Criticism*, ed. Gerald Mast and Marshall Cohen. 2d ed. New York: Oxford University Press, 1979, pp. 243–263.

Pascall, Jeremy, and Clyde Jeavons. *A Pictorial History of Sex in the Movies*. London: Hamlyn, 1975.

Patton, Cindy. "The Cum Shot: Three Takes on Lesbian and Gay Sexuality." *Out/Look* 1:3 (Fall 1988): 72–76.

———. "Hegemony and Orgasm—Or the Instability of Heterosexual Pornography." *Screen*, 30:1/2 (Winter/Spring 1989): 100–112.

———. "Safe Sex and the Pornographic Vernacular." *How Do I Look? Queer Film and Video*, ed. Terri Cafaro et al. Seattle: Bay Press, 1991, pp. 31–63.

———. "Speaking Out: Teaching In." *Inside/Out: Lesbian Theories, Gay Theories*, ed. Diana Fuss. New York: Routledge, 1991, pp. 373–386.

Peary, Dannis. "From Vixen to Vindication: Erica Gavin Interviewed." *Velvet Light Trap*, 16 (Fall 1976): 2–27.

Peary, Gerald. "Stephanie Rothman: R-Rated Feminist." *Women and the Cinema*, ed. Gerald Peary and Karyn Kay. New York: Dutton, 1977, pp. 179–192.

———. "Woman in Porn: How Young Roberta Findlay Grew Up and Made *Snuff*." *Take One*, 9 (September 1978): 28–33.

Penthouse. New York, 1966–.

Peril or Pleasure?: Feminist Produced Pornography. San Francisco: Torrice Productions, 1993.

Perkins, Michael, ed. *Smut from the Past: Vol. 1*. New York: Milky Way Productions, 1974.

Petkovich, Anthony. *The X Factory: Inside the American Hardcore Industry*. Manchester, U.K.: Headpress, 1997.

Philips, Baxter. *Cut: The Unseen Cinema*. New York: Bounty Books, 1975.

Phillips, Paul. " 'I Enjoy Making Porno Films'—An X-rated Star Speaks Out." *Sexology*, 41:9 (April 1975): 29–34.

Pilat, Oliver, and Jo Ranson. *Sodom by the Sea: An Affectionate History of Coney Island*. Garden City, NY Doubleday, Doran, 1941.

Pinedo, Isabel Christina. *Recreational Terror: Women and the Pleasures of Horror Film Viewing*. Albany: State University Press of New York, 1997.

"Pinkskin Review." *Club*, 3:1 (February 1977): 27–35.

Plachy, Sylvia, and James Ridgeway. *Red Light: Inside the Sex Industry*. New York: Powerhouse Books, 1996.

Playboy. Chicago, 1953–.

Polan, D. B. "Eros and Syphilization: The Contemporary Horror Film." *Planks of Reason: Essays on the Horror Film*, ed. B. K. Grant. Metuchen, NJ: Scarecrow Press, 1984, pp. 201–211.

Poole, Wakefield. [Interview by Jack Fritscher.] *Drummer*, No. 27 (1978): 14–22.

"The Porn Debates." *Vogue*, 175 (September 1985): 678–681, 749–752.

"The Porno Girls." *Playboy*, 18:10 (October 1971): 138–148, 248–249.

Poulson-Bryant, Scott. "Dick." *Village Voice*, 20 August 1991, pp. 48–49.

President's Commission on Obscenity and Pornography. *Report of the Commission on Obscenity and Pornography*. Washington, DC: Government Printing Office, 1970.

———. *Technical Reports*. 9 vols. Washington, DC: Government Printing Office, 1971–1972.

Prince, Stephen. "Power and Pain: Content Analysis and the Ideology of Pornography." *Journal of Film and Video*, 42:2 (Summer 1990): 31–41.

Prince, Stephen, and Paul Messaris. "The Question of a Sexuality of Abuse in Pornographic Films." *Communication and Culture: Language, Performance, Technology, and Media*, ed. Sari Thomas and William A. Evans. Norwood, NJ: Ablex, 1990, pp. 281–284.

Psychotronic Video. Narrowsburg, NY, 1994–.

Public Broadcasting System. *Death of a Porn Queen*. PBS/Frontline, 1987.

Quarles, Mike. *Down and Dirty: Hollywood's Exploitation Filmmakers and Their Movies*. Jefferson, NC: McFarland, 1993.

Rabenalt, Arthur Maria. *Mimus Eroticus*. 5 vols. Hamburg: Verlag für Kulturforschung, 1965–1967. I: *Die erotische Schauszenik in der antiken Welt* (1965); II: *Das Venusische Schauspiel im Mittelalter und in der Renaissance* Part I (1965); III:

Das Venusische Schauspiel im Mittelalter und in der Renaissance Part II (1965); IV: *Beitrage zur Sittengeschichte der erotischen Szenik im Zwanzigsten Jahrhundert* Part I (1965); V: *Beitrage zur Sittengeschichte der erotischen Szenik im Zwanzigsten Jahrhundert* Part II (1967).

Rainer, Yvonne. "Working Round the L-Word." *Queer Looks: Perspectives on Lesbian and Gay Film and Video*, ed. Martha Gever, Pratibha Parmar, and John Greyson. New York: Routledge, 1993, pp. 12–20.

Raven, Arlene. "Looking beneath the Surface: Deep inside Porn Stars." *High Performance*, 7:4 (Issue 28, 1984): 24–27, 90–91.

Reems, Harry. *Here Comes Harry Reems!* New York: Pinnacle Books, 1975.

Renan, Sheldon. *An Introduction to the American Underground Film*. New York: Dutton, 1967.

"Requiem for a Superstud." *A Current Affair*. Fox Television, 1988.

Rich, B. Ruby. "Anti-Porn: Soft Issue, Hard World." *Village Voice*, 20 July 1982, 1, 16, 18, 30; rpt. *Films for Women*, ed. Charlotte Brunsdon. London: British Film Institute, 1986, 31–43; rpt. *Perspectives on Pornography: Sexuality in Film and Literature*, ed. Gary Day and Clive Bloom. New York: St. Martin's, 1988, pp. 101–112.

———. "A Queer Sensation." *Village Voice*, 4 March 1994, pp. 41–44.

———. "When Difference Is (More than) Skin Deep." *Queer Looks: Perspectives on Lesbian and Gay Film and Video*, ed. Martha Gever, Pratibha Parmar, and John Greyson. New York: Routledge, 1993, pp. 318–339.

Rimmer, Robert H. *The X-Rated Videotape Guide*. New York: Arlington House, 1984; rev. ed. New York: Crown, 1986; rpt. Buffalo, NY: Prometheus Books, 1988.

Roberts, Nickie. *The Front Line: Women in the Sex Industry Speak*. London: Grafton Books, 1986.

Rode, Henri. *Les Stars du Cinéma Erotique*. Paris: PAC, 1976.

Roman, Catherine. *Bang for a Buck*. Toronto: Somerset House, 1989; aka *Foreplay: The Memoirs of a Wanton Young Woman*. New York: Random House, 1989.

Rosen, Marjorie. *Popcorn Venus: Women, Movies, and the American Dream*. New York: Coward, McCann, and Geoghegan, 1973.

Ross, Gene. "Sexploitation Films: The 60s Sexplosion!!!" *Adult Video News*, 2:1 (March 1987): 82–84, 86.

Rotsler, William. *Contemporary Erotic Cinema*. New York: Penthouse/Ballantine, 1973.

———. *Girls Who Do Stag Movies*. Los Angeles: Holloway House, 1973.

———. *Superstud: The Hard Life of Male Stag Film Stars*. Los Angeles: Melrose Square, 1973.

Rowberry, John W. *Gay Video: A Guide to Erotica*. San Francisco: G. S. Press, 1986.

Rowe, Chip. "Nina Hartley Is the Smartest Woman in Porn." *Playboy*, 45:9 (September 1998): 116–118, 157–158.

Royalle, Candida. "Porn in the USA." *Social Text*, 11:4 (Winter 1993): 23–32.

Russell, Tina. *Porno Star*. New York: Lancer Books, 1973.

Russo, Vito. "All Male Cast: Gay Films on Videocassette." *Home Video*, 3:1 (January 1982): 29.

———. *The Celluloid Closet: Homosexuality in the Movies*, rev. ed. New York: Harper and Row, 1987.

Saalfield, Catherine. "On the Make: Activist Video Collectives." *Queer Looks: Perspectives on Lesbian and Gay Film and Video*, ed. Martha Gever, Pratibha Parmar, and John Greyson. New York: Routledge, 1993, pp. 21–37.

Saillac, Didier. *X Vidéo Guide*. Paris: Éditions Paramaribo, 1991.

Sargeant, Jack. *Naked Lens: An Illustrated History of Beat Cinema*. London: Creation Books, 1997.

Sarris, Andrew. *Politics and Cinema*. New York: Columbia University Press, 1978.

———. "Tapping into the Porn Pipeline." *Village Voice*, 3 December 1985, p. 21.

Savage, David G. "Violence and Women: Researchers Condemn R-Rated Films as Worse Offenders than Pornographic Movies." *Los Angeles Times*, 1 June 1985, sec. 2, pp. 1, 6.

Schaefer, Eric. *Bold! Daring! Shocking! True!: A History of Exploitation Films, 1919–1959*. Ph.D. dissertation, University of Texas at Austin, 1994; Durham, NC: Duke University Press, 1999.

———. "Of Hygiene and Hollywood: Origins of the Exploitation Film." *Velvet Light Trap* 30 (1992): 34–47.

Schickel, Richard. "Porn and Man at Yale." *Harper's*, 241 (July 1970): 34–38.

Schidrowitz, Leo, ed. *Sittengeschichte der Kulturwelt und ihrer Entwicklung in Einzeldarstellungen*. 10 vols. and supplement to vol. 2. Vienna/Leipzig: Verlag für Kulturforschung, 1926–30. I: *Sittengeschichte des Intimen: Bett, Korsett, Hemd, Hose, Bad, Abtritt. Die Geschichte und Entwicklung der intimen Gebrauchsgegenstände* (1926); II: *Sittengeschichte des Lasters: die Kulturepochen und ihre Leidenschaften* (1927), and *Ergänzungsband* (1927); III: *Sittengeschichte von Paris; die Grosstadt, ihe Sitten und ihre Unsittlichkeit* (1926); IV: *Sittengeschichte des Proletariats: des Weg vom Leibes- zum Maschinensklaven, die sittliche Stellung und Haltung des Proletariats* (1926); V: *Sittengeschichte des Theaters, Ein Darstellung des Theaters, seiner Entwicklung und Stellung in zwei Jahrhunderten* (1926); VI: *Sittengeschichte der Liebkosung und Strafe. Die Zärtlichkeitsworte, Gesten und Handlungen der Kulturmenschheit und ihr Gegenpol der Strenge* (1928); VII: *Sittengeschichte des Geheimen und Verbotenen, Eine Darstellung der geheimen und verborgen gehaltenen Leidenschaften der Menschheit, die Einstellung der Staatsgewalt zum Geschlechtsleben der Gesellschaft* (1930); VIII: *Sittengeschichte des Hafens und der Reise, Eine Beleuchtung des erotischen Lebens in der Hafenstadt, im Hotel, im Reisevehikel. Die Sexualität des Kulturmenschen während des Reisens in fremden Milieu* (1927); IX: *Sittengeschichte der Revolution, Sittenlockerung und Sittenverfall, Moralgesetze und sexualethische Neuorientierung in Zeiten staatlicher Zersetzung und revolutionären Umsturzes* (1930); X: *Sittengeschichte des Intimsten. Intime Toilette, Mode und Kosmetik im Dienst und Erotik* (1929).

Schneck, Stephen. "Candy Barr in Time and Space." *Ramparts*, 6 (15 June 1968): 53–58.

Schneemann, Carolee. *More than Meat Joy: Complete Performance Works and Selected Writings*. New Paltz, NY: McPherson/Documentext, 1979.

Screen. The Sexual Subject: A Screen Reader in Sexuality. London: Routledge, 1992.

Screw. New York, 1969–.

Scudéry, Pierre, and Paul Scudéry. *Érotisme au Cinéma: Almanach 1964*. Paris: Juilliard, 1964.

See, Carolyn. *Blue Money: Pornography and the Pornographers*. New York: David McKay, 1974.

Segrave, Kerry. *Drive-In Theaters: A History from Their Inception in 1933*. Jefferson, NC: McFarland, 1992.

Serceau, Daniel, ed. *Érotisme et cinéma: Themes et variations*. Paris: Atlas L'Herminier, 1986.

Sesslen, Georg. *Der pornographische Film*. Frankfurt am Main: Ullstein, 1990.

Sesslen, Georg, and Claudius Weil. *Aesthetik des erotischen Kinos: Eine Einfuhrung in die Mythologie, Geschichte und Theorie des erotischen Films*. Munich: Roloff und Sesslen, 1978.

Sevely, J. Lowndes, and J. W. Bennett. "Concerning Female Ejaculation and the Female Prostate." *Journal of Sex Research*, 14:1 (February 1978): 1–20.

Sheldon, Caroline. "The Criminal Element: Male and Female Homosexuality in Pornographic and *Avantgarde* Film." *Gays and Film*, ed. Richard Dyer. London: British Film Institute, 1980, pp. 8–11.

Shipman, David. *Caught in the Act: Sex and Eroticism in the Movies*. London: Elm Tree Books, 1985.

Siebenand, Paul Alcuin. *The Beginnings of Gay Cinema in Los Angeles: The Industry and the Audience*. Ann Arbor, MI: UMI Press, 1980.

Silver, Rachel. *The Girl in Scarlet Heels: Women in the Sex Business Speak Out*. N. Pomfret, VT: Trafalgar Square, 1994.

Sitney, P. Adams. *Visionary Film*. New York: Oxford University Press, 1974; 2d ed., 1979.

Slade, Joseph W. "Bernard Natan: France's Legendary Pornographer." *Journal of Film and Video*, 45:2/3 (Summer–Fall 1993): 72–90.

———. "Flesh Need Not Be Mute: The Pornographic Videos of John Leslie." *Wide Angle*, 19:3 (1997): 114–148.

———. "The Pornographic Film Market and Pornographic Formulas." *Journal of Popular Film*, 6 (1978): 168–186; rpt. *Movies as Artifacts: Cultural Criticism of Popular Film*, ed. Michael Marsden, John Nachbar, and Sam Grogg. Chicago: Nelson-Hall, 1982, pp. 145–160.

———. "Pornographic Theaters off Times Square," *Transaction*, 9 (November–December 1971): 35–43, 79; rpt. *Reflections*, 7:6 (1972): 27–47; *The Sexual Scene*, ed. John H. Gagnon and William Simon, 2d ed. New Brunswick, NJ: Transaction/ Dutton, 1973, pp. 263–289; *The Pornography Controversy*, ed. Ray C. Rist. New Brunswick, NJ: Transaction/Dutton, 1975, pp. 119–139.

———. "Recent Trends in Pornographic Films." *Society*, 12 (September/October 1975): 77–84; rpt. *Film in Society*, ed. Arthur Asa Berger. New Brunswick, NJ: Transaction/Dutton, 1980, pp. 121–135.

———. *Shades of Blue: A History of the Clandestine Film*. Forthcoming.

———. "Violence in the Hard-Core Pornographic Film: A Historical Survey." *Journal of Communication*, 34:3 (Summer 1984): 148–63.

Smith, Jack. *Wait for Me at the Bottom of the Pool: The Writings of Jack Smith*, ed. J. Hoberman and Ed Leffingwell. New York: High Risk/Serpent's Tail, 1997.

"Smith, Jane." "Making Movies." *Sex Work: Writings by Women in the Sex Industry*, ed. Frédérique Delacoste and Priscilla Alexander. Pittsburgh: Cleis Press, 1987, pp. 135–141.

Smith, Richard. *Getting into Deep Throat*. Chicago: Playboy Press, 1973.

Smyth, Cherry. "The Pleasure Threshold: Looking at Lesbian Pornography in Film." *Feminist Review*, 34 (Spring 1990): 152–159.

Solinas, Piernico. *Ultimate Porno*. New York: Eyecontact, 1981.

Sondell, Ulf. *Den pornografisha filmen som symptom på ett sambällstillstånd.* Göteborg, Sweden: Sociological Institute, University of Göteborg, 1977.

Sontag, Susan. "A Feast for Open Eyes." *Nation,* 198 (13 April 1964): 374–376.

Sprinkle, Annie [Ellen Steinberg]. *Post Porn Modernist.* Amsterdam: Art Unlimited, 1991.

Staiger, Janet. *Bad Women: Regulating Sexuality in Early American Cinema.* Minneapolis: University of Minnesota Press, 1995.

Steinem, Gloria. "Linda Lovelace's 'Ordeal.' " *Images of Women in American Popular Culture,* ed. Angela G. Dorenkamp, John F. McClymer, Mary E. Moynihan, and Arlene C. Vadum. San Diego: Harcourt Brace Jovanovich, 1985, pp. 155–161.

———. "The Real Linda Lovelace." *Outrageous Acts and Everyday Rebellions.* New York: Holt, Rinehart, and Winston, 1983, pp. 243–252.

Stevens, Marc. *Ten and a Half.* New York: Kensington, 1975.

Stevensen, Jack. *Desperate Visions: Camp America.* San Francisco: Creation Books, 1996.

Stoller, Robert J. "Merlin of the Movies." *Pain and Passion: A Psychoanalyst Explores the World of S and M.* New York: Plenum Press, 1991, pp. 241–251.

———. *Porn: Myths for the Twentieth Century.* New Haven, CT: Yale University Press, 1991.

Stoller, Robert J., and I. S. Levine. *Coming Attractions: The Making of an X-Rated Video.* New Haven, CT: Yale University Press, 1993.

Stone, Jeremy. "Interview with an Erotic Outlaw Auteur." *Adam Film World Guide,* 5: 12 (June 1991): 24, 34.

The Story of X: 100 Years of Adult Film and Its Stars. Los Angeles: Playboy Entertainment/Calliope Film, 1998.

Straayer, Chris. *Deviant Eyes/Deviant Bodies: Sexual Re-Orientations in Film and Video.* New York: Columbia University Press, 1996.

———. "The Hypothetical Lesbian Heroine: *Voyage en Douce* and *Entre Nous.*" *Jump Cut,* 35 (April 1990): 50–57.

———. "The Seduction of Boundaries: Feminist Fluidity in Annie Sprinkle's Art/Education/Sex." *Dirty Looks: Women, Pornography, Power,* ed. Pamela Church Gibson and Roma Gibson. London: BFI Publishing, 1993, pp. 156–175.

Streff, Jean. *Le Masochisme au Cinéma.* [Paris]: Éditions Henri Veyrier, 1978.

Strick, Marv, and Robert I. Lethe. *The Sexy Cinema.* Los Angeles: Shelburne, 1975.

Stryker, Jeff. [Interview by Kevin Koffler.] *The Advocate,* 12 September 1989, pp. 26–30.

Studlar, Gaylyn. "The Perils of Pleasure: Fan Magazine Discourse as Women's Commodified Culture in the 1920s." *Wide Angle,* 13:1 (January 1991): 6–33.

Suárez, Juan A. *Bike Boys, Drag Queens, and Superstars: Avant-Garde, Mass Culture, and Gay Identities in the 1960s Underground Cinema.* Bloomington: Indiana University Press, 1996.

Suggs, Donald. "Hard Corps: A New Generation of People of Color Penetrates Porn's Mainstream." *Village Voice,* 21 October 1997, pp. 39–40.

Svoray, Yaron, with Thomas Hughes. *Gods of Death.* New York: Simon and Schuster, 1997.

Take One. "Porn Symposium," a special issue. 4:5 (May–June 1973): 28–30.

Tartaglia, Jerry. "*Ecce Homo*: On Making Personal Gay Cinema." *Queer Looks: Per-*

spectives on Lesbian and Gay Film and Video, ed. Martha Gever, Pratibha Parmar, and John Greyson. New York: Routledge, 1993, pp. 204–207.

———. "The Gay Sensibility in American Avant-Garde Film." *Millennium Film Journal*, 4/5 (1979): 53–58.

Taubin, Amy, and John D. Thomas. "Softcore Sex Ed." *Village Voice*, 28 July 1998, p. 49.

Taylor, Clarke. "Male Eros Goes to the Movies." *Club*, 2:10 (December 1976): 52–54, 56.

Thompson, W., J. Annettes, et al. *Soft-Core: A Content Analysis of Legally Available Pornography in Great Britain 1968–1990 and the Implications of Aggressive Research*. Reading, England: Reading University Press, 1990.

Tohill, Cathal, and Pete Tombs. *Immoral Tales: European Sex and Horror Movies, 1956–1984*. New York: St. Martin's, 1994.

Toufexis, Anastasia. "Sex Lives and Videotape: More and More Couples Are Making Do-It-Yourself Erotic Films." *Time*, 29 October 1990, pp. 104–105.

Trent, Paul. *The Image Makers: Sixty Years of Hollywood Glamour*. New York: McGraw-Hill, 1972.

Trillin, Calvin. "The Life and Times of Joe Bob Briggs, So Far." *New Yorker*, 22 (7 December 1986): 73–88.

Troyano, Ela. "Ken Jacobs' Film Performance." *The Drama Review*, 25:1 (March 1981): 95–100.

Turan, Kenneth, and Stephen F. Zito. *Sinema: American Pornographic Films and the People Who Make Them*. New York: Praeger, 1974.

Tyler, Parker. "Do They or Don't They? Why It Matters So Much." *Evergreen Review*, 78 (May 1970): 25–27, 68–71.

———. *A Pictorial History of Sex in Films*. Secaucus, NJ: Citadel, 1974.

———. *Screening the Sexes: Homosexuality in the Movies*. New York: Holt, Rinehart, and Winston, 1972.

———. *Sex Psyche Etcetera in the Film*. New York: Horizon, 1969.

———. *Underground Film: A Critical History*. New York: Grove Press, 1969.

"U.S. Porn Producer Goes O'Seas for Fresh Faces, More Natural Attitudes." *Variety*, 4 November 1976, p. 23.

Variety. Los Angeles, 1922–.

Vaughn, Don. "An Interview with Candida Royalle." *Gauntlet: Exploring the Limits of Free Expression*, 5 (1993): 99–107.

———. "Words That Arouse: An Interview with Cathy Tavel." *Gauntlet*, 14 (1997): 41–47.

Verrill, Addison. "Preposterous Sex Dimensions, and Russ Meyer's Hang-ups." *Variety*, 10 November 1976, p. 27.

Vetter, Craig. "The Real Dirk Diggler." *Playboy*, 120–122, 124, 163, 166.

Video Xcitement. Fraser, MI, 1993–.

Viegener, Matias. "The Only Haircut That Makes Sense Anymore." *Queer Looks: Perspectives on Lesbian and Gay Film and Video*, ed. Martha Gever, Pratibha Parmar, and John Greyson. New York: Routledge, 1993, pp. 116–133.

Village Voice. New York, 1947–.

Vogel, Amos. *Film as a Subversive Art*. New York: Random House, 1974.

———. "Missionary Positions." *Film Comment*, 18:3 (May–June 1982): 73–75.

Wade, Michael. "Kenneth Anger: Personal Traditions and Satanic Pride." *Body Politic*, (April 1982): 29–32.

Walker, Alexander. *The Celluloid Sacrifice*. London: Michael Joseph, 1966; rpt. *Sex in the Movies: The Celluloid Sacrifice*. Baltimore: Pelican, 1968.

Warhol, Andy. *Blue Movie: A Film*. New York: Grove, 1970.

Waters, John. *Shock Value: A Tasteful Book about Bad Taste*. New York: Dell, 1981.

———. *Trash Trio*. New York: Vintage, 1988.

Watt, Jackie L. "Kelly O'Dell." *Adult Video News*, 8:6 (May 1993): 132, 134.

Waugh, Tom. "Gay Erotic Cinema in the Postwar Era." *CineAction*, 10 (October 1987): 65–72.

———. *Hard to Imagine: Gay Male Eroticism in Photography and Film from Their Beginnings to Stonewall*. New York: Columbia University Press, 1997.

———. "A Heritage of Pornography: On the Gay Film Collection of the Kinsey Institute." *Body Politic*, 90 (1983): 29–33.

———. "Men's Pornography: Gay versus Straight." *Jump Cut*, 30 (March 1985): 30–36; rpt. *The Problem of Pornography*, ed. Susan Dwyer. Belmont, CA: Wadsworth, 1995.

———. "The Third Body: Patterns in the Construction of the Subject in Gay Male Narrative Film." *Queer Looks: Perspectives on Lesbian and Gay Film and Video*, ed. Martha Gever, Pratibha Parmar, and John Greyson. New York: Routledge, 1993, pp. 141–161.

Weaver, James B. "Are 'Slasher' Horror Films Sexually Violent? A Content Analysis." *Journal of Broadcasting and Electronic Media*, 35:3 (Summer 1991): 385–392.

Webb, Peter. *The Erotic Arts*. New York: Farrar, Giroux, 1984.

Weene, Seph. "Venus." *Heresies* [Sex issue], 12 (1981): 36–38.

Weiss, Andrea. *Vampires and Violets: Lesbians in the Cinema*. London: Jonathan Cape, 1992.

———. *"Women I Love* and *Double Strength*: Lesbian Cinema and Romantic Love." *Jump Cut*, 24/25 (March 1981): 30.

Wilkins, Mike. "Jail Birds, among Others." *Film Comment*, 22:4 (July–August 1986): 63–69.

Wilkinson, Peter. "Dream Girl." *Rolling Stone*, 20 October 1994, pp. 73–80, 158.

Williams, Linda. "Fetishism and Hard Core: Marx, Freud, and the 'Money Shot.' " *For Adult Users Only: The Dilemma of Violent Pornography*, ed. Susan Gubar and Joan Hoff. Bloomington: Indiana University Press, 1989, pp. 198–217.

———. *Figure of Desire: A Theory and Analysis of Surrealist Film*. Urbana: University of Illinois Press, 1981.

———. *Hard Core: Power, Pleasure, and the Frenzy of the Visible*. Berkeley: University of California Press, 1989.

———. "Power, Pleasure, and Perversion: Sadomasochistic Film Pornography." *Representations*, 27 (Summer 1989): 37–65.

———. "A Provoking Agent: The Pornography and Performance Art of Annie Sprinkle." *Social Text*, 37 (Winter 1993): 117–133.

Williams, Tony. "Feminism, Fantasy and Violence: An Interview with Stephanie Rothman." *Journal of Popular Film and Television*, 9:2 (Summer 1981): 84–90.

Williamson, Bruce. "Porno-Chic." *Playboy*, 20:8 (August 1973): 132–41.

Willis, Ellen. *"Deep Throat*: Hard to Swallow." *Sexuality in the Movies*, ed. Thomas R. Atkins. New York: Da Capo, 1984, pp. 216–220.

Wilton, Tamsin, ed. *Immortal Invisible: Lesbians and the Moving Image*. New York: Routledge, 1995.

Winer, Lucy, and Paula Koenigsberg. *Rate It X*. New York: International Video, 1985.

Wolcott, James. "Girls in Pornography." *Village Voice*, 7 March 1977, pp. 36–37.

"Women's Porn?" *Off Our Backs*, 13 (April 1983): 5, 12.

Wortley, Richard. *Erotic Movies*. New York: Crescent Books, 1975.

Wrangler, Jack, and Carl Johnes. *The Jack Wrangler Story: What's a Nice Boy like You Doing in a Business like This?* New York: St. Martin's, 1984.

XXX Gay Video Showcase. Los Angeles: Knight Publishing, 1990–.

Yacowar, Maurice. *The Films of Paul Morrisey*. New York: Cambridge University Press, 1993.

Yang, Ni, and Daniel Linz. "Movie Ratings and the Content of Adult Videos: The Sex-Violence Ratio." *Journal of Communication*, 40 (Spring 1990): 28–42.

Yates, Rowdy. "Girls from Girdleville." *Film Threat Video Guide*, No. 5 (1992): 35.

Zimmerman, Bonnie. "Lesbian Vampires." *Jump Cut*, 24/25 (March 1981): 23–24.

Ziplow, Steven. *The Film Maker's Guide to Pornography*. New York: Drake, 1977.

Zita, Jacqueline. "Films of Barbara Hammer: Counter-Currencies of a Lesbian Iconography." *Jump Cut*, 24/25 (March 1981): 26–30.

14

Electronic Media

RADIO AND TELEVISION BROADCASTING

Legal issues aside (see **Broadcasting** in Chapter 20) there is little to say about eroticism on radio—because there isn't much. A book often referred to by people who have never read it is Lorenzo Milam's *Sex and Broadcasting: A Handbook on Starting a Radio Station for the Community*, which has gone through several editions. Despite the title, it has virtually nothing to do with sex of any kind in broadcasting. People in the radio industry worry far more about language, since it does not have to be obscene, merely "indecent," to be proscribed. *Expletives Deleted*, a videotape, discusses swearwords and other offensive expressions; its radio and television clips demonstrate the difficulties broadcasters face in striving for blandness. Moreover, any foray into candor will raise warning flags in the trade journals *Broadcasting and Cable, Cable World*, and *Electronic Media*.

John C. Carlin's historical essay, "The Rise and Fall of Topless Radio," reviews the limited candor on broadcast radio with specific reference to the Sonderling Broadcasting case and the FCC's move against WGLD-FM of Oak Park, Illinois, in 1973. Another article on the same period is "Touchiest Topic on Radio Now: Talk about Sex." Fred Powledge's article on the New York station, "Switched-On Radio: WBAI," is an admiring sketch of an experiment in broadcast freedom. Powledge reviews WBAI's history as a member of the Pacifica Foundation network, which began as KPZA in Berkeley in 1949 and linked up with KPFK in Los Angeles in 1959. Powledge quotes Pacifica's policy: "Our approach to broadcasting is permissive, bold, and naive, because we feel that these attributes hold the secrets of growth and wisdom" (26). Matthew Lasar's *Pacifica Radio: The Rise of an Alternative Network* sheds more light on Pacifica's censorship problems.

More recent comment includes Lisa Collier Cool's "Voices of America," which looks at the audiences for the increasing number of radio talk shows that push against limits of taste, and Howard Kurtz's *Hot Air: All Talk, All the Time*, which studies performer/pundits, some of them disturbing. Another general text, with chapters on foul-mouthed hosts, is Peter Laufer's *Inside Talk Radio: America's Voices or Just Hot Air?* Barry Farber thinks that such shows pressure more conventional programs into candor they do not want in "Why Clean Talk Show Hosts on Radio Are Losing the Battle to Vulgarians."

The most notorious of contemporary, foul-mouthed radio personalities is, of course, Howard Stern, whose antics, most notably his 1994 candidacy for governor of New York State, ensure a steady stream of comment. One of the first articles to notice Stern's booming listenership was David Wild's "Who Is Howard Stern and Why Is He Saying All Those Terrible Things on the Radio?" Then at WXRK in New York, Stern was building an audience around topics ranging from heterosexual intercourse to sodomy. Stern's broadcasts contain something to offend almost everyone; he will advocate lifting the ban on homosexuals in the armed forces, then immediately tell a gay joke. Marvin Kitman's "Howard Stern's Small Penis . . ." profiles the famous "shock jock." Fines levied against Infinity Broadcasting for carrying Stern's program by the FCC occasioned an outpouring of articles, of which Jonathan Alter's "The New Vulgarity" is representative. Richard Zoglin's "Shock Jock" grants Stern status as a serious cultural critic. Zoglin and other commentators point out that Stern avoids obscene words but employs narratives that the FCC has nonetheless ruled "indecent," a much looser term. A best-seller in 1993, Stern's autobiography, *Private Parts*, is perhaps a better indicator of his enormous popularity. The 1997 movie version of the book, directed by Betty Thomas, transforms Stern's life and career into the familiar tropes of the American success story, redolent with family values, and may thus serve as another reminder of the cultural dynamic that propels marginal expression into the mainstream. Stern has also branched into television and published a second book, *Miss America*, on his narcissistic high jinks. Jeremy Lipschultz's *Broadcast Indecency: F.C.C. Regulation and the First Amendment* includes a chapter called "The Social Construction of Howard Stern," an account of the collusion among performer, audience, and regulatory agency that extruded the commercial phenomenon that Stern has become. Marshall Fine's "Playboy Interview: Howard Stern" is probably the most literate encounter with the man.

As the principal storytelling medium of our time, television is constantly under attack. Don E. Wildmon catalogs the pernicious moral effects of broadcasting on youth and family values in *The Home Invaders*. Television exposes children to advocates of homosexuality, abortion, promiscuity, humanism, pornography, and assorted other evils, according to *The Responsible Parent's Guide to TV: A Noted Expert Looks at Television's Role in Changing Our Children's Values*, by Colonel V. Doner. Somewhat more thoughtful essays constitute *Where Do You Draw the Line? An Exploration into Media Violence, Pornog-*

raphy, and Censorship, edited by Victor B. Cline. Mary L. Coakley finds most television programs wanting in *Rated X: The Moral Case against TV*. One of the best-known groups, Morality in Media, publishes a *Newsletter* listing programs it finds objectionable and details strategies for combating them. By contrast, the National Council of Churches of Christ readily concedes that the First Amendment does and should protect most forms of expression in *Violence and Sexual Violence in Film, Television, Cable and Home Video* and merely urges media industries to exercise discrimination and taste. Ironically, says James Ledbetter in "Press Clips: Hardcore Hotel," the satellite-delivered Christian Broadcast Network's (CBN) *The 700 Hundred Club* ran fare such as a videotape in which Paula Jones alleges that President Clinton "pulled out his penis and asked her to 'kiss it' "; other segments use explicit language of exactly the sort the CBN ordinarily decries. Political hatreds, Ledbetter implies, have a lot to do with one's definition of pornography. (The cutoff date for material surveyed in this *Guide* is the fall of 1998, just as the Clinton-Lewinsky scandal began to blossom into a pornographic discourse the likes of which have never been heard on American broadcast media.)

Penises presidential or otherwise are an important subtext in broadcasting, or so says Paul Krassner in "Dicks in the Media." Krassner compares media practices of the past, when one Harry Shearson was fired from an FM radio station in 1972 for saying the word *penis*, to the present, when the actual and imagined lengths of Supreme Court justice Clarence Thomas' penis were alluded to on national television during his confirmation hearings. The word is still a kind of litmus test of permissible speech. Even as Phil Donahue, Oprah Winfrey, and David Letterman feature penis jokes and penis lore on television shows, the FCC in October 1991 fined three radio stations for carrying a segment of the *Howard Stern Show* during which the host made a joke about penis size. Cynics have observed that the real reason behind the media swirl around the Bobbitt case (1994), in which wife, Lorena, cut off the organ of husband, John, was that it gave broadcasters a genuine excuse to say the word *penis* on the air. Paula Yoo observes in "Tales from the Backside" that, since 1973, television programmers have used the word *ass* as many times as possible during prime time; it gets an easy laugh.

"Almost Obscene," a chapter of Jonathan Price's classic *The Best Thing on TV: Commercials*, looks at suggestiveness in television ads. Price quotes Jerry Della Femina, founder of one of the better-known agencies, who says, "There's not enough sex in commercials." Della Femina insists that censors prefer obscenity to sexuality. The television censor, says Della Femina, is "so carefully looking for the double entendre that he can't find the single entendre. They absolutely do not see sex in advertising if it's blatant; but if you should try to do something else, they can find sex. They can find sex in a garage mechanic talking about shock absorbers. But let somebody say, 'Flick my Bic'—this is beautifully obscene—everyone nods their heads and lets that go, because it's obvious that Bic and prick and stroke, well, we know you can't possibly mean that, that would be obscene, you wouldn't come near me with that type of commercial. So the secret of success with censors is to be more obscene" (35–36). The Della Femina riff on toilet-bowl cleaners that follows this passage is priceless.

Sex American Style: An Illustrated Romp through the Golden Age of Heterosexuality (97–108), by Jack Boulware, lists dozens of prime-time programs (e.g., *Three's Company, Blansky's Beauties, Cher, Match Game, Police Woman, Sugar Time, Wonder Woman, Charlie's Angels, Turn-On, Laugh In*) and late-night shows (e.g., *Saturday Night Live, Playboy after Dark*) whose skimpy costumes, double-entendre dialogue, sniggering plotlines, and sexual curiosity rolled back the limits of the permissible during the raucous 1960s and experimental 1970s. Other popular treatments of suggestive or candid programming during these and more recent decades include Craig Nelson's *Bad TV: The Very Best of the Very Worst*, whose title is its thesis. In "Sex in Primetime Television: 1979–1989," a notable example of academic bean-counting, Barry S. Sapolsky and Joseph O. Tabarlet conclude that the depiction of sex has not declined over the decade indicated in the title of their article. They observe that, despite AIDS, network television seems unconcerned with unsafe sex or poor contraception. Not surprisingly, the study finds that white male characters most often initiate sex between unmarried partners on the average show. Such studies rarely designate images on television *as* characters; the unspoken research assumption hidden in the quantification is that audiences cannot tell the difference between fiction and reality.

Each year the researchers watch a week or so of programming, count the number of kisses, hugs, and acts of implied or depicted intercourse, categorize them by gender and marital status of the participants, then break them down by time period and network. In 1989, for example, ABC led the pack in frequency of "noncriminal" acts of kissing. In the late 1980s the Planned Parenthood Federation commissioned a Louis Harris survey released as *Sexual Material on American Television during the 1987–88 Season*. Harris' analysis of 129 videotaped programs and ads clocked sexual events per hour; afternoon television contained the highest frequency, with roughly one and a half times the number of evening shows, though actual intercourse was the subject more often in the evening. As the federation suspected, broadcasters made few attempts to counter the sexual allusions with references to educational materials on sex, birth control, or sexually transmitted diseases.

Conservative laypersons count differently. Richard Viguerie, a supporter of Donald Wildmon's campaign to boycott advertisers, uses much larger numbers in *The New Right: We're Ready to Lead*. According to Viguerie, who looked at the fall lineup for the three years 1977 through 1979, virtually all the sex represented on television took place without benefit of marriage. He believes that the average viewer will annually encounter more than 10,000 sexually suggestive remarks or allusions and that revealing scenes, that is, those exposing too much skin, occur another 7,000 times per year. Viguerie calls such programming "pornography," though many Americans would call it just a sign of the times. John J. O'Connor faults some programming for its sniggering presentation in "For a Date (Wink) or a Tease (Smirk), Try Late-Night TV," an essay on leering date-shows like *Studs, Personals*, and *A Perfect Score*. Mimi White believes that television guides Americans through anxiety and crisis. Her *Tele-Advising: Therapeutic Discourse in American Television* considers television shows from *Good Sex!* to *Home Shopping Club* in terms of the advice they dispense to audiences and consumers.

Keith Howes' *Broadcasting It!* is an encyclopedia of homosexuality in radio and television on British broadcasting from 1933 to 1993. Howes includes many American programs among the capsule reviews of some 700 plays, films, documentaries, light entertainment, news features, serials, and series, with entries for producers, directors, and actors supplemented with sections on language, themes, and topics, and other data. Some PBS affiliates refused to carry *Tongues Untied*, a POV (Point of View) documentary on black gays, and those which did were sometimes criticized, as a PBS newsletter notes in "Archbishop Blasts Airing of Documentary." Kobena Mercer reflects on the "Black Queer culture politics" in Marlon Riggs' *Tongues Untied* (1989) in "Dark and Lovely Too: Black Gay Men in Independent Film." On the occasion of PBS' broadcast of the teledramatization of his *Tales of the City*, Armistead Maupin observed in "A Line That Commercial TV Won't Cross" that commercial stations are still not ready for nudity and same-sex kissing. The second series of *Tales of the City*, no more graphic in its depiction of gay lifestyles than the first, was turned down by PBS, presumably because of worries about conservative attack. Sasha Torres identifies circumlocutions and stereotypes in "Television/Feminism: Heartbeat and Prime Time Lesbianism." Torres, Richard Dyer, Larry Gross, Edward Allwood, Lisa Henderson, and other communication scholars speak in the documentary *Off the Straight and Narrow: Lesbians, Gays, Bisexuals, and Television*, an unusually intelligent study of cultural attitudes toward gender minorities in images, plots, and coverage to be found on American television today. While here unconcerned with eroticism, their reflections help to explain the persistence of stereotypes.

NYPD Blue may serve as an example of network shows that have engendered controversy in the last decade. In "The Thin Blue Line," an article on ABC's weekly morality play *NYPD Blue*, Craig Stoltz looks at the reasons that Americans for Responsible Television pressure advertisers not to support it. The conservatives see immorality, crime, and nudity (though it is tame in the extreme) that are unsuitable for children. For the network, however, the show is a bid to recapture an adult audience: "Sophisticated drama appealing to adults has largely migrated to cable or simply disappeared. By trying to protect kids, it appears, the networks risk throwing out the adults with the bath water" (4). Stoltz quotes Sherry Stringfield, who plays "Laura Kelly" on *NYPD Blue*, who detects hypocrisy in audiences that tolerate heavy breathing on afternoon soap operas but bridle at prime-time adult themes: "As Blake [on daytime television's *Guiding*

Light], I slept my way through an entire family of men. No one ever called to complain" (5). Robert S. Hanczor's "Articulation Theory and Public Controversy: Taking Sides over *NYPD Blue*" says that support and opposition to that program fall into ideological divisions based on clusters of social and political attitudes, with "liberals" and their allies as advocates of candor and "conservatives" and their allies on the attack. Hanczor's bibliography, which lists many newspaper editorials on both sides, suggests the power of a program to polarize debate over sexual representations. One could as easily work up a bibliography of comment pro and con on any controversial program, say *Married with Children*, that would be less about the program than the state of opinion at the time.

SOAP OPERAS

Actress Sherry Stringfield's remark recalls that sector of the broadcast day always set aside for the sexually explicit. About a dozen television soap operas (so called because of their original sponsorship as radio shows by companies such as Procter & Gamble) run daily in the United States, attracting more than 25 million viewers, the majority of them women. In "The New Woman Finds Her Place on the Small Screen," John J. O'Connor has observed that "television has almost entirely co-opted what used to be called the 'woman's movie,' " an incisive remark that is aimed more at the made-for-television movie than at soap operas, although both deal sentimentally with perversions or diseases of the week. The soap *The Young and the Restless*, for instance, features young Adonises stripping down to Calvin Klein underwear, but most manifestations of the genre revolve around once-taboo subjects such as incest, rape, extramarital affairs, bizarre sexual practices, pregnancy, safe sex, and teenage sex, all set in a narrative of romance, anguish, and travail. As a consequence, station owners routinely refer to soap operas as "porn for women," and the genre has received considerable attention, primarily from feminist critics.

The most comprehensive history of soap operas, with a wealth of information on the economic and industrial factors that have shaped them, is Robert Allen's *Speaking of Soap Operas*. Good, lively surveys, with no particular emphasis on eroticism, include Robert La Guardia's *The Wonderful World of TV Soap Operas*, Madeleine Edmondson and David Rounds' *From Mary Noble to Mary Hartman: The Complete Soap Opera Book*, and Marilyn J. Matelski's *The Soap Opera Evolution: America's Enduring Romance with Daytime Drama*. The first two are somewhat dated now, but all three provide period information. For a behind-the-scenes look at the shooting of soap operas, Dan Wakefield's *All Her Children* is excellent. "Soap Operas: Sex and Suffering in the Afternoon," a *Time* story of 1976, highlights popular writers, producers, and actors. Two solid general works, both of which speak of soap operas, are Horace Newcomb's *Television: The Most Popular Art*, which argues that soap operas have always been on the cutting edge of innovative television, and John Fiske's *Television Culture*, whose chapters on "Gendered Television" deal with programs aimed

specifically at women or men. Fiske acknowledges the pornographic characteristics of the genre but casts it in terms of the fashionable academic theory that
male pornographic fantasies are impoverished while female fantasies are richer
because they are differently contextualized. Fiske observes: "The response to
the male 'hunk' is a fantasy that appears very similar to the masculine pornographic fantasy, involving a fantasized identification with a sex object of the
opposite sex, but there are crucial differences. The sexuality of the 'hunk' is not
always confined to his body, but is often contextualized into his relationships
and interpersonal style. Similarly, the erotic turn-on of the love scenes is consistently described as resulting from the representation of a relationship, not the
body of an individual" (186).

Robert Allen's "On Reading Soaps: A Semiotic Primer" examines the formulaic "texts" of afternoon television. Some of the other essays in the volume
in which Allen's essay appears are worth reading also; this is *Regarding Television: Critical Approaches—An Anthology*, edited by E. Ann Kaplan. M. E.
Brown lists generic formulas and discusses the sexual politics of soaps as positive factors for women in *Soap Opera and Women's Talk: The Pleasure of
Resistance*. Brown thinks that soaps empower women by creating social networks of discourse about femininity and womanhood. Sandy Flitterman-Lewis
speculates on the significance of endless cycles of marriage and divorce—and
remarriage—as fantasy elements in "All's Well That Doesn't End—Soap Operas and the Marriage Motif." Marriage is also one of several persistent themes
in soaps identified by Kathryn Weibel in *Mirror Mirror: Images of Women
Reflected in Popular Culture*. Some themes are more powerful than others, says
Laura Stempel Mumford. Her "Plotting Paternity: Looking for Dad in the Daytime Soaps" points out that the soap opera's obsession with attributions of paternity—a common plot device is the discovery that a child was actually fathered
by a surprise dad—suggests the subversive nature of fantasies. The surprises
destabilize sexuality, says Mumford, in a way that implicitly underscores the
power of women to control reproduction. Mumford's *Love and Ideology in the
Afternoon: Soap Opera, Women and Television Genre* argues, however, that
the agendas of most soap operas reinforce cultural patterns of male dominance,
racism, classism, and heterosexism and in doing so offer considerable pleasure
even to feminists who decry the patterns. Tania Modleski's *Loving with a Vengeance: Mass-Produced Fantasies for Women*, probably the best single study
of sexual fantasies in the genre, also covers themes and focuses on character
types like the female villain in soap operas. Modleski thinks that one of the
most important aspects of the form is its open-endedness, a type of narrative
she thinks lends itself to female sensibilities. Soap operas resist "closure," sometimes hyperrealistically, with dead characters coming back to life, new relationships forming on the ashes of old ones, and desire that never quits.

In *No End to Her: Soap Opera and the Female Subject*, Martha Nochinson
says that to call soap operas porn is to misrepresent a fascinating and vibrant
genre. While soap operas are about women and desire, she says, what makes

them interesting is their function as a narrative of identity for women viewers. Other critics are quite comfortable with the notion that soaps are erotic forms of discourse specifically tailored to female expectations and fantasies. "Getting Down to Specifics about Sex on Television," a now-dated report by D. K. Johnson and K. Satow, surveyed Americans in 1978: 78 percent of women and 64 percent of men said that there was too much sex on television, but a majority of those women who thought there was excess also claimed to enjoy soap operas. Johnson and Satow conclude that women object to explicit sex, not the subtler, though still seamy, varieties.

"Sex on the Soap Operas: Patterns of Intimacy," a 1981 study by Dennis Lowery, Gail Love, and Malcolm Kirby, actually ranked shows in terms of sexual encounters. *General Hospital* came in first, having been clocked at sixteen acts of intimacy per hour. The sexiness disturbed the authors, who feared that soaps promoted a distorted view of "fornication and adultery" by eschewing moral didacticism. A follow-up (1989) study by Lowery and David E. Towles, "Soap Opera Portrayals of Sex, Contraception, and Sexually Transmitted Diseases," concluded that sexual content from 1980 to 1987 had increased (a modest .8 per hour) and that soap operas had still not evolved socially responsible messages for dealing with issues such as teen pregnancy and sexually transmitted diseases. Less moralizing is "Sex on the Soap Operas: Afternoon Delight," by Bradley S. Greenberg, Robert Abelman, and Kimberly Neuendorf, who also graphed the genre's fondness for intercourse. Five years later, a follow-up study by Greenberg and C. Stanley, M. Siemicki, C. Heeter, A. Soderman, and R. Linsangen, published as *Sex Content on Soaps and Primetime Television Series Most Viewed by Adolescents*, found that the number of intimate sexual acts, as measured in three television series, had increased significantly in that short period in both afternoon and prime-time programming. Greenberg and Rick W. Busselle find increasing rates of sexual activity (6.6 episodes per hour) in five of the leading soap operas, results reported in *Soap Operas and Sexual Activity* in 1994. In "Soap Operas and Sexual Activity: A Decade Later," Greenberg and Busselle revisit five of the soaps studied in their 1985 survey to discover that sexual activity had increased yet again, especially in the category of "long, passionate kisses." By contrast, Beth Olsen's analysis of 105 hours of soaps from 1989 to 1990 in "Sex and the Soaps: A Comparative Content Analysis of Health Issues" concluded that occurrences of sexual behavior were lower than previous studies indicated, though the incidence of sex between characters married to each other had increased, as had information about AIDS and safe sex. The bibliographies in each of these studies will lead the scholar to many more quantitative studies of sudsy representations on the afternoon screen.

Both Ien Ang's *Watching Dallas: Soap Opera and the Melodramatic Imagination* and Sue Brower's "TV 'Trash' and 'Treasure': Marketing *Dallas* and *Cagney and Lacey*" deal with the audience dynamics and sexual politics of prime-time soap operas. C. Lee Harrington and Denise D. Bielby conduct interviews with viewers, venturing as well into fan clubs, the followers of cyber versions of soaps, and other subcultural clusterings in *Soap Fans*. Several contributors to *Staying Tuned: Contemporary Soap Opera Criticism*, edited by Suzanne Frentz, examine hyperactive sexual behavior in soap operas in an effort to determine whether women view these serials any differently than men. That males are increasingly fond of soap operas seems clear, though Stuart Miller points out in "Fox 'Roc' 'n' Rolls in Male Demos" that while statisticians can keep easy track of women viewers, male audiences for anything except sports are unpredictable. In "P. & G. Is Seeking to Revive Soaps: Shaking Up TV Serials as Audiences Dwindle," Dana Canedy reports that Procter & Gamble, owner of *As the World Turns, Another World*, and *Guiding Light*, was trying to find the right blend of titillation and narrative that would increase viewership in the late 1990s. Worth consulting also are *Soap Opera Weekly*, a supermarket tabloid (typical article: "Hardline: Do the Soaps Practice Safe Sex?") and *Soap Opera Digest*, which summarizes eleven shows each week. Finally, the humorist Russell Baker's "Paradise for Pentagon" offers a tongue-in-cheek account of how television soap operas functioned as pornographic counterweights to the orgy of war coverage during the Persian Gulf conflict.

TELEVISION TALK SHOWS AND TABLOIDS

The influence of pornographic genres of discourse on the popular arts is clear where radio and television are concerned. In recent years, radio raconteurs like Howard Stern have pushed against the limits of broadcast candor, as have the celebrities who host sensational television programs. According to Annie Ample's *The Bare Facts: My Life as a Stripper* (130), Robin Leach lived for some years with Gloria Leonard, the porn star turned publisher of *High Society*, the men's magazine, and host of *The Gloria Leonard Show*, a New York cable porn program. Leach's enormously popular syndicated series, *Lifestyles of the Rich and Famous*, and its several spin-offs depend almost entirely on that confluence of prurience and envy that fuels the appetite for sexual representation. Typical is "Supermodel," the 5 January 1994 segment of *Lifestyles of the Rich and Famous*, peopled by photographers like Newton and Scavullo and models like Vendela, Claudia Schiffer, Naomi Campbell, and Cindy Crawford. The stock-in-trade of Raphael, Donahue, and Oprah is, of course, the sexuality, the more weird the better, of the freaks who parade across their afternoon television talk show sets. Strippers like Ample, actors and actresses from pornographic films, and ordinary Americans with a wide assortment of sexual problems and fetishes appear regularly on "sleaze" shows, as broadcast professionals refer to the talk shows and tabloid formats.

A good introduction to the television talk show is *All Talk: The Talkshow in Media Culture*, Wayne Munson's analysis of a format invented specifically for television. Munson discusses trash staples (e.g., *Geraldo*), tabloid and celebrity shows, talk programs, and call-in interview shows on both radio and television from a postmodernist perspective. Gloria Jean Masciarotte's "C'mon Girl: Oprah

Winfrey and the Discourse of Feminine Talk" credits Oprah with the coinvention of what Masciarotte believes is a distinctly feminine form; the article contrasts the lurid and graphic elements of the sexual discourse on Winfrey's show with those of other programs. A similar approach informs Shannon Bell's "Ejaculatory Television: The Talk Show and the Postmodern Subject." Bell, who studies stripping and other forms of sexual expression, discusses her participation on *The Shirley Show*, a Canadian talk show modeled on American versions, in a session devoted to "Women Making Pornography for Women." Bell thinks such programs offer women new insight into the role of sexuality in modern life.

Many critics consider programs like *Geraldo, Oprah, Hard Copy, Inside Edition, Confessions of Crime*, and *Current Affair*—not an exhaustive list—pornographic. Aware of that reputation, *Geraldo*'s producers announced new standards of taste for 1991. They abandoned planned shows on bestiality and necrophilia and canceled an already taped program on large penises; the uncharacteristic surge of virtue was the subject of Mark Mehler's "Geraldo: In Control . . . with an Edge." This halfhearted effort to sanitize a notorious program was somewhat offset by publication of Geraldo Rivera's autobiography, *Exposing Myself* (written with Daniel Paisner), in which the host brags about celebrities he seduced before and after their appearance on his show. Patricia J. Priest speculates on the motives that drive people who reveal their personal scandals on *Public Intimacies: Talk Show Participants and Tell-All TV*. Finding freaks is no problem, observes J. Max Robins in "Talkshow Producers Find Dial-a-Dilemma": the Donahues and Geraldos can draw on the National Talk Show Registry, a commercial "database of 2,000 Hollywood hookers, UFO [unidentified flying object] kidnap victims, transsexuals and the like," which for a fee furnishes bizarre guests. Bradley S. Greenberg and Sandi Smith led a team of researchers in analyzing sexual content on shows hosted by Phil Donahue, Gordon Elliott, Jenny Jones, Ricki Lake, Maury Povich, Sally Jessy Raphael, Geraldo Rivera, Jerry Springer, Rolanda Watts, Montel Williams, Oprah Winfrey, and the Spanish-language show *Christina*. Their *The Content of Television Talk Shows: Topics, Guests and Interactions* concluded that dating and sexual activity were discussed in about a third of the programs. They break out many other topics as well and buttress their findings with statistics. The bold thesis of Joshua Gamson's *Freaks Talk Back: Tabloid Talk Shows and Sexual Nonconformity* is that shows such as Jerry Springer's actually function to alter social attitudes toward deviant, marginal, or alternative sexual lifestyles. Springer, a former mayor of Cincinnati turned talk-show host, became notorious in the late 1990s as the unwitting star of a secretly filmed sex videotape and as the producer of a profitable line of videos full of graphic outtakes (nude dancers, obscene language) from the television show. *Esquire* ran his picture on the cover of the January 1999 issue as the new arbiter of American taste. When John Brady asked for a self-description in "Playboy Interview: Jerry Springer," Springer replied: "My show isn't a talk show. There's no talking. There's just yelling, cursing and throwing whatever's at hand" (64).

Tabloid shock programs, which can be distinguished from talk shows by their ersatz journalistic style, occupy a particular discursive niche on television, one whose subversive intent and effect are similar to those of older pornographic forms, says Kevin Glynn in "Tabloid Television's Transgressive Aesthetics: *A Current Affair* and the 'Shows That Taste Forgot.' " Critic Harry F. Waters condemns tabloids as lowbrow in "Trash TV," while television executive Van Gordon Sauter justifies their choice of subject matter as a response to genuine demand in "In Defense of Tabloid TV." Although he can hardly be said to defend the format, drama critic Walter Goodman's " 'Tabloid' Charge Rocks Network News" suggests that those who criticize them seem to be addicted to them: "The phenomenon of large numbers of people protesting against programs that even larger numbers of people apparently enjoy opens up the interesting question of whether many of those who proclaim their aversion to television violence keep watching." The larger issue for Goodman is the degree to which the financial success of tabloid shows encourages respectable news programs to imitate them. Richard Zoglin chronicles attempts by tabloids like *Hard Copy, A Current Affair, Inside Edition, American Journal*, and *Dateline NBC* to attain respectability for themselves by trumpeting their journalistic virtues in "Easing the Sleaze." David Rensin interviews the host of *A Current Affair*, who speaks of what he sees as a need for exposé television, in "Twenty Questions: Maury Povich." Not surprisingly, Povich places his show in an American muckraking tradition.

In "Tabloid TV: First Class Ratings But Second-Class Ad Rates," J. Max Robins notes that many Americans believe that "the content [of tabloid shows] is no further from the toilet bowl than a Phil Donahue or a Sally Jessy Raphael" and that this widespread perception makes it difficult for the producers to attract major advertisers. The best single article on the economics of broadcast tabloid journalism is Dana Kennedy's "Scandal Inc." Kennedy lists the "spin doctors of scandal"—the lawyers, producers, and reporters who make the deals—and charts the huge amounts of money involved. The article quotes Eric Naiburg, the Long Island attorney best known for representing Amy Fisher, on how the process works: "There's big dollars at stake. I know all the producers, all the talk shows, and all the tabloid shows. I can pick up the phone and broker deals. One attorney [for] a 17-year-old girl [who had been] propositioned by a well-known DA [district attorney] with a foot fetish calls me and says she's been contacted by the tabloids. I said, 'What are they offering you?' And she said, 'Five thousand dollars.' I said, 'It's sweeps month. You're going to do better.' Twenty minutes later, I had the girl $20,000" (20).

Almost as provocative is *Tabloid Truth: The Michael Jackson Scandal*, a PBS documentary centered on Michael Jackson's alleged sexual abuse of a youngster but really about the lucrative mechanics of scandal television. In surveying the combination of money and mayhem, the antics of brokers, agents, reporters, and producers, the scramble for ratings, the social imperatives, and the sheer hype of the industry, the documentary worries about the effects of media sensationalism on justice: "When every story is bought and sold, then we'll never know the truth." Mark Kernes goes further in "Adult Video News to the Media: Shove It." Kernes, the managing editor of *Adult Video News*, the industry trade journal, says that the magazine routinely provides statistics to journalists but notes that tabloid television shows like *Hard Copy* and *48 Hours* routinely twist information and construct a different kind of pornography out of false tropes about sex and violence. Tabloid stories, Kernes says, always seem to conclude with references to serial killer Ted Bundy and his allegations that pornography caused him to murder, an association now thoroughly discredited. The title of Brenda You's "The Hypocrisy in the Media's Criticism of Talk TV" is self-explanatory. Vicki Abt and Mel Seesholz in "The Shameless World of Phil, Sally, and Oprah: Television Talk Shows and the Deconstructioning of Society" suggest that while talk shows may desensitize audiences to deviant behavior, the effect may be offset by the notion of sharing problems as a form of therapy. For those seeking compilations of footage, including the never-broadcast scenes from the *Jenny Jones Show* that led to the death of a gay man, the HBO documentary *Talked to Death: Have TV Talk Shows Gone Too Far?* offers interviews with hosts, attorneys, guests, and producers in an investigation of manipulation and merchandising.

CABLE TELEVISION

In *Inside HBO: The Billion Dollar War between HBO, Hollywood and the Home Video Revolution*, George Mair expounds on the corporate thinking that led HBO to offer adult fare on cable systems. The competitive strategy recalls that of Hollywood in the 1950s, which successfully pulled audiences away from television by offering them mature themes and nudity they could not see on the small screen. Millions of Americans subscribe to premium cable services such as HBO and Showtime to receive movies and programs that network censors would never pass. Still others sign up for Spice and Playboy, two of the services offering soft-core porn. In the United States, leased-channels in major cities carry programs such as *Midnight Blue* and *The Robin Byrd Show*, both in New York, and *The Barbara Dare Show* in Los Angeles. These feature nudity, simulated sex, film clips, interviews, and features involving sex and lots of ads for escort services, topless bars, and so on. Major hotel chains offer satellite-delivered adult movies on a pay-per-view basis as balm for weary travellers. Penny Stallings covers many of these, though her *Forbidden Channels: The Truth They Hide from TV Guide* (1991) is doubtless already behind the times. Warren Berger reports on the policy shift of a cable network's shift toward seamy, scandalous programming in "That's E! for Entertainment (and Erotica?)"; E! programming "teases" by electronically obscuring the images of nipples, buttocks, and genitals of their nude subjects (just as CBS does for the televised *Howard Stern Show*). James Sterngold profiles Sheila Nevins, vice president and head of HBO's documentary division, in "HBO Programmer Likes to Kindle Both Heat and Light." Nevins is the force behind such shows as *Shock Video* and *Real Sex*, about which she says "We're all divided somewhere between our brains and our groins."

Mimi Udovitch's "Virtual Verité" reviews *Voyeurvision*, a program on Channel J (leased-access) of Manhattan Cable in New York, in which callers discuss fantasies with the semiclothed hostess, who also operates a 900-number service during and after the show. Udovich compares the program with other cable shows like Robin Byrd's. *Playboy* ran "Video Vamp," an illustrated article on Lynn Muscarella, hostess of "Voyeurvision." The program now appears on European cable systems as well. In "Short Takes: Around the Block," Rose Rubin Rivera reports on Dr. Susan Block's raunchy California cable show, in which the merry widow–clad hostess lounges on a bed and talks with callers on erotic subjects. HBO has run two video versions of Block's show as *Radio Sex: Off the Dial.*

The Gay Cable Network, in operation on Channel J (Manhattan) for more than ten years, carries weekly gay soap operas, erotic movie reviews, and other subjects of interest to gays. Jean Callahan analyzes serious attempts by women to work within soft-core formats on cable television in "Women and Pornography: Combat in the Video Zone." Callahan thinks that women viewers prefer to know more about the people they see engaged in sex, a crucial element in the examples of the artists she mentions, while male viewers prefer just to see the sex itself. In any case, cable seems a good medium for erotica, Callahan thinks, and cites Emily Armstrong's series called *Girl Porn*. The first video installment, *Boys' Backs*, depicts young men taking off their shirts; the author finds it amazingly erotic. Karen Jaehne, who draws on her experience as a film scheduler for a late-night cable show in "Confessions of a Feminist Porn Programmer," says that it is possible to schedule films that give more emphasis to women's pleasure and that it is important to realize that some female members of an audience will enjoy scenes (e.g., hard thrusting) that are not politically sanctioned. Jaehne thinks directors of soft-core want to reach women audiences. Amelia Simpson's *Xuxa: The Mega-Marketing of Gender, Race, and Modernity* analyzes a television show seen by millions in Latin America and (through satellite-served Spanish cable networks) the United States. Xuxa, a former *Playboy* centerfold and soft-core porn star, cavorts sensually in fishnet stockings, hot pants, and go-go boots on a Brazilian children's program whose representations of sensuality, a sort of Barbie-doll pitch, are disturbing to some critics.

MUSIC TELEVISION

MTV, or Music Television, a format popular with the young, has become a staple on cable and satellite channels, much to the dismay of those who consider much of it pornographic. Bob Larson's *Larson's Book of Rock*, for example, regards contemporary rock music and MTV as pornographic in much the same way that earlier generations routinely spoke of jazz as obscene. The ubiquity of

MTV has led critics to speculate on its eroticism, particularly the portrayal of women. The Parents' Music Resource Center has produced *Rising to the Challenge*, a videotape attacking contemporary music videos from an essentially fundamentalist religious perspective. Taking issue with *Rising to the Challenge* and with *Dreamworlds: Desire/Sex/Power in Rock Video*, a similar tape produced by Sut Jhally of the University of Massachusetts for his media classes, Jon Pareles wrote "Sex, Lies and the Trouble with Videotapes" to accuse both producers of distorting the images and messages of rock music. The deadpan pomposity of Jhally's videotape, aimed at undergraduates, provokes laughter even among feminists who agree with the thesis that women are abused by Music Television, but the second version, *Dreamworlds II*, is less doctrinaire and much smoother. Both tapes illustrate the pleasures as well as the perils of a methodology best described as gathering images to make a point.

Holly Brubach's "Rock-and-Roll Vaudeville" remains a useful essay on sexual roles in Music Television. To no one's surprise, Steven A. Seidman's study, "An Investigation of Sex-Role Stereotyping in Music Videos," finds that women performers wear fewer clothes than do male counterparts and that males are depicted as adventurous, aggressive, violent, and victimized, while females are shown as affectionate, dependent, nurturing, and fearful. The mix of sexual images and aggression in Music Television is the subject of "Guns, Sex and Rock and Roll" by Barry L. Sherman and Joseph R. Dominick. Sherman and Dominick conclude in "Violence and Sex in Music Videos: TV and Rock 'n' Roll" that men are portrayed more attractively than women, with significant erotic implications. Zillmann and Mundorf decide in "Image Effects in the Appreciation of Video Rock" that sexual and violent images apparently enhance the pleasure of audiences. Different viewers react quite differently, the authors say; all other things being equal, those who enjoy sexuality find their appreciation increased, while those who find the images disturbing are less prone to like the music. The single best volume on the subject is E. Ann Kaplan's *Rocking around the Clock: Music Television, Post Modernism and Consumer Culture*, an excellent treatment of Music Television in a larger context, with close attention to corporate models of eroticism.

Lisa A. Lewis thinks that women lyricists encode messages challenging male dominance in "Female Address on Music Television: Being Discovered." She uses as examples Madonna, Cyndi Lauper, Sheena Easton, and Karen Wheeler. In her *Gender Politics and MTV: Voicing the Difference*, Lewis attempts to refute the widespread belief that MTV presents only negative images of women by focusing on the careers and lyrics of Pat Benatar, Cyndi Lauper, Tina Turner, and Madonna as performers who advance their own sexual agendas through their music. Agreeing is Sally Stockbridge, who notes the subversiveness of female performance in "Rock Video: Pleasure and Resistance": on one hand, the lyrics appear to demean women, while, on the other, they appear to empower. Jane E. Brown and Laurie Schulze maintain in "The Effects of Race, Gender, and Fandom on Audience Interpretations of Madonna's Music Videos" that those three factors help audiences decide whether Madonna's music videos are pornographic or not (gender might determine response to the star's lingerie, for instance). Susan McClary's *Feminine Endings: Music, Gender, and Sexuality* deconstructs lyrics and performance, while the essayists in *Television and Women's Culture: The Politics of the Popular*, edited by Mary E. Brown, range across rock video, soap operas, fantasies, and the female gaze. Assertions of sexuality are crucial to the appeal of rock singers such as Patti Smith, Janis Joplin, Deborah Harry, and the Go-Gos, Ariel Swartley noted a decade ago in "Girls! Live! On Stage!" Liz Evans interviews Tori Amos, Kim Gordon, Delores O'Riordan, Björk, and many other performers for *Women, Sex and Rock 'n' Roll in Their Own Words*. For *Girls! Girls! Girls! Essays on Women and Music*, Sarah Cooper has gathered essays on women as producers, performers, and fans of music of all sorts, with occasional references to sexual themes. Robin Roberts' *Ladies First: Women in Music Video*, an examination of the ways in which women use Music TV to express their own sexuality, comes with a videotape of popular performers.

AUDIO RECORDINGS

Bawdy songs have an ancient pedigree, and commercial recordings of them abound. A randomly chosen catalog, the *Time Warner and Sony Sound Exchange* (New York, 1994) advertises the following on page 66 under the heading "Naughty Nostalgia": *Copulatin' Blues* (blues and jazz of the 1920s and 1930s), *Raunchy Business: Hot Nuts and Lollypops* (adult themes), *Risque Rhythm* (rhythm and blues), *Listen to the Banned* ("blue" songs of the 1920s and 1930s, including Mae West's "A Guy What Takes His Time" and Sophie Tucker's "He Hadn't Up Till Yesterday"), and *Rusty Warren: Knockers Up/ Songs for Sinners* (lounge humor). To these one can add the contents of cassette racks at truck stops, which feature raunchy music or ribald monologues with titles making a play on the word *Fudpucker*. C. Eddie Palmer classes off-color recordings and suggestive lyrics with other marginal forms as folklore in "Filthy Funnies, Blue Comics, and Raunchy Records: Dirty Jokes and Obscene Language as Public Entertainment." The late Gershon Legman promised in his "Erotic Folksongs and Ballads: An International Bibliography" to publish a discography of bawdy songs, but could not finish it. (See also **Folklore and Obscenity: Rhymes, Songs, Ballads, and Stories** in Chapter 15.)

Music, perhaps the most sensuous of all the arts, has long represented love and sexuality as a matter of course, and any number of philosophers and composers (from Plato to Nietzsche and from Wagner to Ned Rorem) have mused upon erotic rhythms and motifs. For those who wish a broad view, *Psychological Monographs: General and Applied* devoted a special issue to "Personality Functions of Symbolic Sexual Arousal to Music," by Michael A. Wallach and Carol Greenberg, who investigated the psychological and physiological aspects of music's sexual appeal. As a more pertinent reference here, the two volumes of

Incredibly Strange Music, edited by Andrea Juno and V. Vale, contain chapter after chapter on bizarre music, including the sexually oriented, and its performers; most of the aphrodisiac, seductive, and gender-bending categories are illustrated by American examples. Sometimes, modern associations can charge classical music with erotic connotations, as in the case of Ravel's *Bolero*, which, as adapted for the sound track of the Blake Edwards film *10*, now seems permanently linked with Bo Derek's lush curves. Where pornographic issues are concerned, however, discussion runs to lyrics, and the most controversial have been those of rock and roll.

Explicit Lyrics

To some Americans, rock music is dangerous because they think young people might be driven to immorality by explicit lyrics. Worse, allege some, the musicians are often evil, drug-crazed adherents of satanism; their mission is to secularize America and destroy the country's faith in God. Don Peters, Steve Peters, and Cher Merrill assert that rock musicians encode subliminal sexual messages in their lyrics that are detectable if the listener plays the records backward in *Rock's Hidden Persuader: The Truth about Backmasking*. Jacob Aranza's *Backward Masking Unmasked: Backward Satanic Messages of Rock Exposed* and *More Rock, Country and Backward Masking Unmasked* maintain that satanic codes show up in both rock and country recordings that can be reversed by teenagers in the know. Eric Barger's extremely ambitious *From Rock to Rock: The Music of Darkness Exposed!* ranks some 1,500 rock artists and groups on scales of sex and satanism. Godless forces do, indeed, shape the sexual content of rock 'n' roll, say Jeff Godwin in *The Devil's Disciples: The Truth about Rock* and Arthur Lyons in *Satan Wants You: The Cult of Devil Worship in America*. Taking a somewhat different tack, David A. Noebel in *The Marxist Minstrels: A Communist Subversion of Music*, one of several similarly titled books by the same author, discovers that the source of America's infection is communism masquerading as sex/porn; he identifies the Beatles as agents of the Kremlin. The examples here, and they are only a few of those available, constitute an antiporn genre charged with religious and political paranoia; rock stars are portrayed in this literature sometimes as unwitting dupes, sometimes as aggressive promoters of secularism, satanism, humanism, or communism, whose nefarious goals are advanced by pornographic lyrics that corrupt American youth—pretty much as fluoridated water was alleged to sap American morality back in the 1950s. Jerry Falwell aims at similar targets in "Music."

Closer to the mainstream are critiques such as Tipper Gore's *Raising PG Kids in an X-Rated Society*, a homily by the founder of the Parents' Music Resource Center and crusader against sex and violence in popular music. Steve Chapple and David Talbot profile Gore (then campaigning with her husband for the presidential nomination) in *Burning Desires: Sex in America: A Report from the Field*. To Chapple and Talbot, Ms. Gore reacts against rock because, as she herself admits, she was turned on by lyrics herself as a teenager but thinks it inappropriate for adolescents to be exposed to perversity in recordings today. Gore insists that she is not in favor of censorship, only self-policing by the industry. Noting that rock in the 1980s had become considerably less "tumescent" in the 1980s, the journalists observe archly that "this is what made Tipper's crusade so ironic. For the most part, rock in the late 1980s was a limp thing. Dominated by aging stars with flagging libidos and newcomers who were extremely wary of sex or strangely disinterested in it, rock came to reflect the antisex sentiments of the culture at large . . ." (62). Martha Bayles' *Hole in Our Soul: The Loss of Beauty and Meaning in American Popular Music* is an aesthetic critique. While Bayles graphs the decline of American popular music into perversity, decadence, and obscenity, she maintains that the industry should market better stuff more aggressively, not censor the trash that can be driven out by competition. Bayles believes that the essential vitality of American forms such as jazz will eventually reshape music and move it beyond travesty.

The most trenchant response to the critics of explicit lyrics comes from musicians who insist that lyrics are so submerged in the music that children cannot understand the words behind the driving beat. In *Media/Impact*, a standard college media text, Shirley Biagi (chapter 7) cites a 1987 study by UCLA psychologist Patricia Greenfield published in the *Journal of Early Adolescence*. Greenfield and her colleagues played Bruce Springsteen's "Born in the USA" to groups of fourth, eighth, and twelfth graders. Sixty percent of the entire sample did not comprehend the meaning of the song; only 30 percent of the eighth graders and only 40 percent of the twelfth graders accurately interpreted its theme, and hardly any of the fourth graders "got it" at all. Similarly, in a Los Angeles Times News Service piece, "Rock Lyrics: Who's Listening?" Randy Lewis reports on research by California State University's Lorraine Prinsky (sociology) and Jill Rosenbaum (criminal justice), who indicate that teenagers use rock mostly for background noise; the overwhelming majority do not understand the lyrics at all, do not know whether they speak of sex or drugs or satanism, in fact, seem not even to have a clue about them, a finding that undermines theories of causality. Prinsky and Rosenbaum also reject the concept of subliminal effects, confident that research data weigh against the possibility of unconscious influence. Dave Marsh blends hilarity and astute social comment in *Louie Louie: The History and Mythology of the World's Most Famous Rock 'n' Roll Song*, an account of the FBI's *two-year* attempt to demonstrate that the lyrics to the song were obscene. By the end of Marsh's book, it is clear that there is no song so stupid that it will not attract an even stupider censor.

Three essays from the 1980s take up sexist lyrics and aggressive themes in rock 'n' roll and contextualize them in terms of the rise of feminism: Chapter 1 ("Beatlemania: Girls Just Want to Have Fun") of *Re-Making Love: The Feminization of Sex*, by Barbara Ehrenreich, Elizabeth Hess, and Gloria Jacobs; "I'm Black and Blue from the Rolling Stones and I'm Not Sure How I Feel about It: Pornography and the Feminist Imagination," by Kate Ellis; "I'd Rather Feel

Bad than Feel Anything at All: Rock and Roll, Pleasure and Power," by L. Grossberg. All three stress ambiguity and avoid dogma. Camille Paglia uses running comparisons between rock musicians and romantic writers as carriers of decadent energy in *Sexual Personae: Art and Decadence from Nefertiti to Emily Dickinson*. Comments Paglia: "Rock music is normally a darkly daemonic mode. The Rolling Stones, the greatest rock band, are heirs of stormy Coleridge. But rock has an Apollonian daylight side as well, a combination of sun and speed: the Beach Boys" (358). Newspaper indexes of the 1970s document protests beyond counting against the Rolling Stones, Elvis Presley, Public Enemy, the Sex Pistols, Digital Underground, the Doors, Janis Joplin, and many, many others. Typical is A. Peck's "Stones Lyric Protest" for the magazine *Rolling Stone*, on a group aggrieved by a song. For many critics, of course, the lyrics were a form of understandable rebellion, part of the sexual revolution begun in the 1960s, a view adopted by Robert A. Rosenstone in " 'The Times They Are a-Changin': The Music of Protest." The late Frank Zappa actually thought that the roots of discontent lay in the previous decade and pinpointed some examples, including the predictable references to Elvis, in "Fifties Teenagers and '50s Rock." Probably the most astute theorist of rock's rebellious sexuality, Zappa was credited by Jon Pareles with enormous influence in "Musical Maverick Frank Zappa Had Impact Far beyond Rock." Zappa thought that a legitimate function of music is to shock, to arouse, and even to offend in order to make people think but that most of the time it did none of these things. In his autobiographical *The Real Frank Zappa Book*, written with Peter Occhiogrosso, Zappa recalled the censorship problems he and his bands encountered.

With its usual vulgarity, *Screw* highlighted the most outrageous performers in 1975 in a special issue titled "Rock and Raunch." The *Los Angeles Free Press*, another tabloid, ran Jay Ehler's series called "Cock Rock" for six issues in 1974. More recent articles indicate that explicit lyrics still flourish. Ipeleng Kgositsile's "Whose Pussy Is This?" discusses the ways Mary J. Blige's erotic lyrics fuse rhythm and blues and hip-hop. Ann Marlowe's "Inside Every Pussy There's a Little Dick" examines the lyrics of the group called Type O Negative. Carol Cooper's "Digital Underground" says that Humpty Hump, the group's lead singer, "is the poet laureate of smut." In "Blue Notes: A Look at the Time-Honored Relationship between Sex and Music," Lisa Palac takes the long view of eroticism in modern popular music, solicits remarks from rock musicians on the sexual content of their lyrics, asks about the kind of erotica they like, and suggests that music will continue to push against conventional morality in the future. Palac's "Plant One on Me: Plugging into Rock's Erotic Influence" is an account of her adolescent fascination with musician Bud Plant, which she extrapolates into the power of rock to stimulate auditors.

Analyses of lyrics uncover sexual themes. James R. Huffman and Julie L. Huffman focus on songs dealing with love between older and younger partners in "Sexism and Cultural Lag: The Rise of the Jailbait Song, 1955–1985," to which they append a splendid discography. Infidelity is a major theme, say

C. R. Chandler, H. Paul Chalfant, and Craig P. Chalfant in their historical and critical "Cheaters Sometimes Win: Sexual Infidelity in Country Music." Larry M. Lance and Christina Y. Berry pinpoint the 1970s as the most heated decade in "Has There Been a Sexual Revolution?: An Analysis of Human Sexuality Messages in Popular Music, 1968–1977," for which they investigated rock and roll songs on the charts in *Billboard* magazine for those years. In *Running Scared: Masculinity and the Representation of the Male Body*, Peter Lehman discusses the performer Roy Orbison and his association with a weird masculine sensibility in modern music. More recently, various underground luminaries offer their favorites, some of which are innocuous, some not, in "Aural Sex: The Top Ten Fuck Songs." Jim Holliday ranks the sound tracks of feature-length hard-core films in "The Top 30 Adult Tunes Countdown." The CD *Sex-O-Rama: Music from Classic Adult Films* contains themes from a dozen classic porn films such as *Behind the Green Door* and *Debbie Does Dallas*.

The most comprehensive volume on rap, *Rap on Rap: Straight-Up Talk on Hip-Hop Culture*, edited by Adam Sexton, gathers several dozen essays pro and con on lewd lyrics, significant censorship issues, the cultural dynamics of hip-hop, and the impact of rap on the music industry. John J. O'Connor's "Smut or Social Chronicle? MTV Debates Gangsta Rap" reviews *Gangsta Rap*, an MTV documentary on the musical form, with comment by performers, advocates, and critics. Now that Lawrence A. Stanley has published *Rap: The Lyrics: The Words to Rap's Greatest Hits*, readers can perhaps answer O'Connor's question for themselves. In "Are We Confused Yet?: Making Sense of Censorship," Ernest Hardy points out that while rap is frequently charged with encouraging the abuse of women, Salt-N-Pepa, a female rap group, also uses sexist lyrics. Similarly, says Imani Perry in "It's My Thang and I'll Swing It the Way That I Feel!: Sexuality and Black Women Rappers," when black women lay claim to their bodies in rap music, they do so in order to achieve empowerment. Lisa Anderson's "On the Record" quotes music personality Dick Clark, who maintains that music evolves in ways the culture cannot always comprehend: "There's a poster in my office. It says, 'Help save the youth of America. Don't buy Negro records.' That's the kind of posters we ran into in the early '60s, late '50s." Nowadays, says Clark, "If you don't like the lyrics to gangsta rap, then go clean up the urban neighborhoods and make their lives better." Mark Landler reports on the ironies of Time-Warner–owned *Time* running a cover story critical of Warner Music, which distributes gangsta rap music full of violence and sex, in "Time Warner, under Its Own Spotlight." The company sold one of its record divisions and changed music executives as a consequence of political attacks on its rap recordings.

Artists and Groupies

Randomly chosen commentaries nestle sexual folklore within interesting biographies. Ellis Amburn's *Pearl: The Obsessions and Passions of Janis Joplin* belongs to the Albert Goldman–style of celebrity biography, as does Peggy Caserta's *Going Down with Janis*, the latter a memoir of sex and drugs by one of Joplin's lovers. Both present Joplin as an erotomaniac whose career seemed a blur of pan-sexuality, booze, and raw lyrics sung at high volume. Alice Echols' *Scars of Sweet Paradise: The Life and Times of Janis Joplin* is a more balanced assessment. Chapter 16 of Bob Greene's *Billion Dollar Baby* recounts the 1973 tour of the Alice Cooper Band, during which porn movies ran continuously on the bus. Richard Cole, tour manager of Led Zeppelin from 1968 to 1980, recalls stories of debauchery and kinky high jinks with groupies on the road in *Stairway to Heaven: Led Zeppelin Uncensored*, written with Richard Trubo. Adam Sexton has gathered what is probably the best collection of popular and academic articles on another performer in *Desperately Seeking Madonna*. Given music critic Robert Christgau's determination to chronicle the lives and careers of weird and sexy musicians of this century, his forthcoming *Grown Up All Wrong: 75 Great Rock and Pop Artists from Vaudeville to Techno* should provide a great deal of information.

Ann Powers' essay on Pamela Des Barres' two books, "Pop View: That Girl by the Stage, and Why She's There," recalls the groupie's role as support, toy, and object. Powers thinks that the sexism is eroding, though Fox Television every now and then runs "documentaries" on girls who try to get backstage by pulling off their clothes. Des Barres' two works, *I'm with the Band: Confessions of a Groupie* (affairs with Jimmy Page, Mick Jagger, and Keith Moon) and *Take Another Little Piece of My Heart: A Groupie Grows Up*, are extraordinary chronicles of a sexist scene whose blandishments and disappointments the author learns to cast off. Groupies and musicians function symbiotically: the musicians need the groupies to validate their celebrity (and studios frequently encourage groupies), while the groupies sleep with the musicians as a way of sharing in the limelight. Noticing the dynamic years ago, *Rolling Stone* commissioned John Burks and Jerry Hopkins to write about the phenomenon in *Groupies and Other Girls: A Rolling Stone Special Report*. Jack Boulware's *Sex American Style: An Illustrated Romp through the Golden Age of Heterosexuality* (118–127) lists current groupie lore (and a list of favorite hangouts) and extends the circle of celebrities who sleep with these women to include athletes (Babe Ruth, Wilt Chamberlain, Joe Namath) and politicians (Wilbur Mills, Wayne Hays, Harry Byrd). (For the plaster casting of celebrity penises by groupies, see **Erotic/ Pornographic Objets d'Art** in Chapter 11.)

The autobiography of Marilyn Manson, *Marilyn Manson: The Long Hard Road Out of Hell*, written with Neil Strauss, explains the motivation of a performer who sometimes appears naked or in S/M garb and who routinely encounters attempts to suppress his concerts. "Kembra," an illustrated article by Michael Halsband on Kembra, former star of explicit films by Richard Kern, now lead singer for the Voluptuous Horror of Karen Black, an "industrial rock" group, discusses the performer's penchant for sewing up her vulva and appearing nude or bizarrely costumed onstage. "Ultimate Shock" reprises the career of recent suicide Wendy O. Williams, who began her career as a sex performer and rose to fame when promoter Rod Swenson built the Plasmatics, a rock group, around her. She sang in her signature outfit, a short skirt, a Mohawk haircut, and bare breasts with a strip of tape over each nipple. Peter Wilkinson's profile of the late Shannon Wilsey also traces her career as a famous rock groupie before she became Savannah, a porn film performer, in "Dream Girl." Wilkinson observes that fashion models typically signal their success iconographically by mating with rock stars; the number of such affairs and marriages is large enough to suggest deep affinities between clothing and music.

Clothing is an essential component of rock performances, a phenomenon explored by the essayists in Angela McRobbie's *Zoot Suits and Second Hand Dresses: An Anthology of Fashion and Music.* Mablen Jones highlights the plumage of male performers in *Getting It On: The Clothing of Rock 'n' Roll,* a book of photographs, while *Playboy* has run pictorials on female rockers who dress outrageously. Typical are "Oh, Wendy O.!," an illustrated article on Williams performing bare-breasted on stage, and Bruce Williamson's "Mondo Phoebe," an essay on Phoebe Légère, the singer featured in the film *Mondo New York* (1988), where she sports pubic hair accentuated by shorts pulled tight between her labia. Kurt Loder considers clothing, lyrics, stage presence, and the appeal to "teenage lust" as ingredients of rock stardom in *Bat Chain Puller: Rock and Roll in the Age of Celebrity.* Loder reminds his readers that rock 'n' roll, like jazz, takes its name from a synonym for intercourse. Sara McOustra's *Sex in Rock* presents candid snapshots of performers who promote their own sexuality, and *More Sex and Drugs and Rock 'n' Roll: Another Pictorial History of Sex and Drugs and Rock 'n' Roll* also interweaves portraits of rock musicians captured in erotic poses; the emphasis in both works is on sensationalism, decadence, and lurid subcultural themes.

Gendered Music

More straightforward considerations of sex and gender issues are the stuff of numerous critical works. Music is the principal thread of Greil Marcus' two histories of popular culture, *Lipstick Traces: A Secret History of the 20th Century* and *Mystery Train.* Both recapitulate the 1960s and 1970s as revolutionary periods suffused by creativity; both are dense with folklore and anecdotes, given texture by a critic sensitive to their nuance and significance. Simon Frith's *Performing Rites: On the Value of Popular Music* laments the decline of a robust and exuberant sexuality of music in the 1960s into the banal political correctness of rock in the present; it is a vibrant discussion of the potential in rock and roll. Just as ambitious is *The Sex Revolts: Gender, Rebellion, and Rock 'n' Roll,* by Simon Reynolds and Joy Press. Theirs is a Freudian and Lacanian analysis of rock 'n' roll's evocation of an infantile "oceanic bliss." According to the authors, rock began in rebellious misogyny but has mutated into less phallic obsessions, thanks chiefly to female rockers and gender-benders. Disco, metal and rap, college rock, Brazilian funk, and performers such as the Riot Grrls are the subjects of essays in *Microphone Fiends: Youth Music and Youth Culture*, edited by Tricia Rose and Andrew Ross, while sex, gender, and industrialization are the topics in *Sound and Vision: The Music Video Reader*, edited by Lawrence Grossberg, Simon Frith, and Andrew Goodwin. In an early essay, "Sex Rock Symbolism," Cris Hodenfield discusses the phallic power of rock performers. Simon Frith and Angela McRobbie extend those observations in "Rock and Sexuality" but also note possibilities other than reinforcement of sexism. Frith brings a sociological approach to *Sound Effects: Youth, Leisure, and the Politics of Rock 'n' Roll*, as does Deena Weinstein to *Heavy Metal: A Cultural Sociology*; the latter deals with heavy metal genres, sexual lyrics, and censorship. The anthology *Present Tense: Rock 'n' Roll and Culture*, edited by Anthony De-Curtis, contains several readings of sexuality and gender.

Gay and lesbian rock as subverter of gender assumptions is the subject of some of the essays in *Out in Culture: Gay, Lesbian, and Queer Essays on Popular Culture*, edited by Corey K. Creekmur and Alexander Doty, while lesbian rock as co-opted force is covered in *The Good, the Bad, and the Gorgeous: Popular Culture's Romance with Lesbianism*, edited by Diane Hamer and Belinda Budge. Lillian Faderman identifies lesbian undertones in jazz and blues of the 1920s and 1930s in her *Odd Girls and Twilight Lovers: A History of Lesbian Life in Twentieth-Century America*, as part of her larger discussion of music as a carrier of messages about lesbian longing. G. Marchetti's "Documenting Punk: A Subcultural Investigation" finds that cultural subversion is a driving force in punk rock, but Mary Ann Peacott and Pam Nicholas ask, "Where Are the Punk Dykes?" in an essay in *Rock against Sexism*, a zine entirely devoted to such questions. Tricia Henry credits punk rockers with anarchistic intent toward culture and sexual stereotypes in *Break All Rules: Punk Rock and the Meaning of a Style*. Among the punksters Angela McRobbie and J. Garber discuss in "Girls and Subcultures" are riot grrls, whose agenda is to forge an identity *from* stereotypes they have made their own by incorporating terms such as *slut, whore*, and *bitch* into their lyrics. Though defunct after eleven issues, the periodical *Search and Destroy* is still unequaled as a source of information on punk rock, but it was an early example of the proliferation of zines around musical styles. M. Goldberg examines some of these in "Rock and Roll Fanzines: A New Underground Press Flourishes." Many slick magazines regularly comment on erotic music; issue 7 of *Future Sex*, for example, reviews sexually oriented disks and tapes. Mainstream publications pale beside zines devoted to music subcultures, whose number is astonishing, as periodic glances at magazine racks in college bookstores will demonstrate.

K. Robert Schwarz discusses the gay and lesbian orientation of composers and how it affects music in "Composer's Closets Open for All to See." More illuminating yet are the essays in *Queering the Pitch: The New Gay and Lesbian Musicology*, edited by Philip Brett, Elizabeth Wood, and Gary Thomas, which bring contemporary cultural theories to bear on music oriented toward the margins. John Gill's melding of gossip and scholarship in *Queer Noises: Male and Female Homosexuality in Twentieth-Century Music* covers Benjamin Britten, Patti Smith, Boy George, Madonna, and other figures in gay pop, jazz, rock, and classical music. Wayne Studer's *Rock on the Wild Side: Gay Male Images in Popular Music of the Rock Era* analyzes the lyrics of some 200 songs dealing with gays and transvestites. Richard Smith's *Other Voices: A History of Homosexuality and Popular Music*, a volume on homoeroticism and androgyny in various genres, traces the music of Johnnie Ray, Liberace, the Kinks, Little Richard, and others. Smith's *Seduced and Abandoned: Essays on Gay Men and Popular Music* features gendered critiques, with chapters such as "Cock Rock: The Secret History of the Penis in Pop." *Man Enough to Be Woman: The Autobiography of Jayne County*, a memoir by the transsexual rock 'n' roll performer, delves into the gay and punk subcultures of rock today.

Any number of Americans are experimenting with explicit recordings. One of the more interesting cassettes is *Master/Slave Relationship: Being Led Around by the Tongue*, music for consensual S/M recorded by performance artist Debbie Jaffe. Chapters on Diamanda Galás, Lydia Lunch, and Kathy Acker in *Angry Women*, edited by Andrea Juno and V. Vale, highlight those artists' musical forays. Juno herself covers Kathleen Hanna, June Millington, Joan Jett, Chrissie Hynde, and others in the two volumes of her *Angry Women in Rock*. In "Viva La Pussy: Love, Sex, and Being Female with Ann Magnuson," Lisa Palac's interview with the recording artist (*Power of Pussy*), movie star (*The Hunger*), and multimedia performer, Magnuson observes: "Pornography never addresses the real desires of women. The only stuff I ever like is written; very rarely have I seen anything filmed or photographed that gets me excited" (27). Palac herself is one of the producers of *Cyborgasm*, a CD of "virtual audio" sounds of sex featuring Annie Sprinkle, Susie Bright, Mistress Kat, and other artists. In "Cyberspace," Palac describes its sixteen erotic tracks, some of which record actual intercourse. "Sex is eroticized repetition. Of course, doing the same thing over and over can lead to libido failure, but it's also a key ingredient for sexual arousal." Home Box Office sent a camera crew to record the making of the CD for a segment titled "Cyborgasm: The Making of an XXX-rated CD" on *Real Sex: 9*. Included are an interview with Palac and coproducer Ron Gompertz. Frank Di Constanzo also asked Palac about her intentions in "On the Beat: Aural Sex." "Except for the poems being read, I wanted it to sound real, be spontaneous and unscripted—with people who were comfortable about sex in front of a microphone," says Palac, who has aimed the disk as much at women as at men. Arthur Kroker's *Spasm—Virtual Reality, Android Music, Electric Flesh*, which celebrates gender and sexual variations, comes with a CD illustrating new trends. Trudi Rosenblum says in "Sex Audiobooks: Not What You Think" that audio versions of erotic fiction are enormously popular but that many chain stores will not handle them.

TELEPHONE SEX

Comparatively little has been published on commercial "phone sex" conversations directed to various genders. What there is tends to be comment by attorneys involved in the various battles over its regulation or by journalists keeping track of the legal intricacies (see **Censorship of Dial-a-Porn** in Chapter 20).

The roots of dial-a-porn reach back to the telephone sexual counseling popular during the liberal 1960s. Trained counselors, sometimes psychotherapists, operated services for gay or lesbian callers just discovering themselves, straights worried about venereal disease or contraception, or youngsters despairing of information from their parents. The range is evident in Isadora Alman's *Aural Sex and Verbal Intercourse*, a collection of transcripts of phone calls to the San Francisco Sex Information Service, with comment by Alman; dynamics vary from solemn to bantering. The Preterm Institute published a training manual for counselors called *Sex Counseling by Telephone*, and Vanda Wark has written a similar work called *The Sex Caller and the Telephone Counseling Center*, both of which offer helpful suggestions for dealing with anxious callers, responding to routine questions, and intervening in crises. The essays in *Talking to Strangers: Mediated Therapeutic Communication*, by Gary Gumpert and Sandra L. Fish, cover many topics, including radio talk shows dispensing sexual advice, to remote sex by telephone via 800/900 telephone exchanges.

Academic studies of pornographic telephone conversations include "Psychoticism, Previous Pornography Usage and the Effect of Dial-a-Porn Recordings on Male Listeners," in which Jack Glascock finds that psychosis is a factor in rape fantasies. In "A Content Analysis of 900 Numbers: Implications for Industry Regulation and Self-Regulation," Glascock and Robert LaRose discover that in 1992 only 6 percent of 900-exchange numbers were used for dial-a-porn messages; traffic had moved instead to the 800- or long distance numbers because of legal or policy considerations. Another article by Glascock and LaRose, "Dial-a-Porn Recordings: The Role of the Female Participant in Male Sexual Fantasies," reporting on a study based on content analysis of eighty-two dial-a-porn recordings (audiotext), said that the analysis found no violent themes such as rape or bondage. Where dominance did figure in the interchanges, it was exclusively female over male, as in traditional S/M scenarios.

Interviews with service providers confirm that last finding and provide other kinds of information. Since the people who answer the phones are paid well for what is, in effect, transient work, such jobs appeal to female college students, and the best place to find accounts of their experiences is in college newspapers. Typical is "1–900–Phone Sex," for which Hollie Landfried interviewed an Ohio State University student. The student makes sixteen dollars an hour plus commissions on lingerie, videos, and calendars she sells over the phone. Her duties include talking to callers about fantasies, moaning to simulate sexual excitement, and generally making explicit small talk. Her usual strategy is to listen to one caller's fantasies, then retell them to the next caller, who is presumably masturbating at the other end of the line. The student finds the work bizarre and complicated, but she is sympathetic toward her customers, who seem to her "desperate."

Andrea Simakis finds that those who provide the conversations actually cherish quite different, that is, conventionally romantic, fantasies in "Telephone Love: Real-Life Fantasies of the Fantasy Girls." Chapter 8 of *Burning Desires: Sex in America: A Report from the Field*, by Steve Chapple and David Talbot, includes an interview with Janet Taylor, a phone sex operator, who has identified patterns. Most callers, Taylor thinks, "have a precise list of ten things they want you to incorporate in their fantasy—and you sure as hell better do them, or they get very upset" (363). Other callers require careful handling to elicit their fantasies, and that, in turn, requires skill on the part of the operator, who has to learn to build the fantasy to a climax for them. Chapple and Talbot provide a brief history of the genre as well. Kathleen K.'s *Sweet Talkers* recounts successful fantasies and useful protocols by a veteran phone-sex hostess; it is probably the best single text for those seeking to know what actually goes on. Chapter 9 of Valerie Kelly's *How to Write Erotica*, entitled "Writing Telephone Sex Calls," outlines the protocols of scripting the audiotexts that services use to gratify callers. The degrees of illusion required in telephone sex are covered in *Dirty Talk: Diary of a Phone Sex "Mistress,"* by Gary Anthony (with Rockey Bennett), whose expertise at impersonating females makes his remarks about gender authoritative. *The Fantasy Factory: An Insider's View of the Phone Sex Industry*, by Amy Flowers, an ethnographic study of operators and, to a lesser extent of clients, offers insights from a scholar who worked in the industry.

Carrington McDuffie offers step-by-step instructions for novice callers in "A Gay Girl's Guide to Phone Sex," recalls masturbating while talking with a sex operator, and describes the sorts of fantasies the services offer and where they draw the line. Although a good deal of trial and error is necessary, says McDuffie, she thinks lesbian fantasy phone services are often rewarding experiences. On the other hand, Steve Abbott's "Dialing for Sex" recounts his frustrations in trying to dial a gay porn number; a friend suggests that "phone sex is safe but it's not healthy" (286), because it is exploitative and frequently interrupted. Ellis Hanson explores the erotic aspects of telephone sex for gays in "The Telephone and Its Queerness."

Richard Goldstein provides general information on the dialing phenomenon in "Dirty Dialing." John Speed's "Dial a Porn Star" identifies the many porn actresses who now operate 900 telephone talk services, most of which are advertised in men's magazines and at the beginning of hard-core videotapes. Allucqère Roseanne Stone speculates on the "presence" of the body in virtual reality, drawing parallels between computer-generated environments and telephone sex in "Virtual Systems." Stone notes that in "technosocial space," writing dominates, which implies radical revisions to the definition of bodies as social units and cultural figures. That observation could provide a rationale for Lynn

Darling's interview-article on the author of *The Fermata* and *Vox*, the latter a best-selling novel about dial-a-porn, entitled "The Highbrow Smut of Nicholson Baker." The argument has some relevance as well to the American release of a Dutch film produced and directed by Theo Van Gogh (grandson of the painter); *1–900* (1995) is a popularized story of telephone sex.

The scholar interested in tracking dial-a-porn services will probably have to start with ads in tabloid newspapers or men's magazines. Some multiline companies put out their own directories. Although the back pages of men's magazines, local and regional alternative papers, and dozens of other publications list numbers, such sources should be used with caution. Finally, Timothy Jay discusses a different kind of syndrome, the unsolicited obscene phone call, whose intent is aggression, in *Cursing in America: A Psycholinguistic Study of Dirty Language in the Courts, in the Movies, in the Schoolyards, and on the Streets*. Obscene phone calling—as opposed to the exchange of indecent fantasies—is usually classified as a psychiatric disorder and is beyond the focus of this chapter. Steven P. Schacht's "The Obscene Telephone Call: Heterosexual Instrumentalism and Male Dominance" examines the aggressive aspects of the practice in terms of cultural and ideological assumptions. For other sources, scholars should consult the "Bibliography on Obscene Phonecalls," compiled by the Kinsey Institute for Sex, Gender, and Reproduction.

DIGITALIZED PORNOGRAPHY

Almost from their inception, computers have been linked to pornography, partly because hackers are mostly male, prone to sublimate their sexuality by means of technology, and partly because pornography routinely drives new communication technologies. Some of the connections are superficial: David Gelernter named a powerful computer programming language Linda, after porn star Linda Lovelace.[1] Others linkages are more direct. As might be expected, the capacity of computers to function as erotic media is rapidly evolving as information highways are built, although sexual applications—digitized scans of photographs, QuickTime striptease movies, already followed by full-motion hard-core scenarios, racy e-mail on broadband, alt.sex.news and other bulletin boards on the Internet, chat rooms on networks—have been evident for some time. A basic introduction is *The Joy of Cybersex: An Underground Guide to Electronic Media* by Phillip Robinson and Nancy Tamosaitis, with Peter Spear and Virginia Soper. A disk of simple erotic games comes with the volume. Sections deal with the mechanics of plugging into the "universe of virtual sex" through modem connections to networks, review the adult bulletin board services available on different networks (state-by-state listing), and assess X-rated computer games, CD-ROMs, and other software. It is replete with suggestions on how to get the most out of e-mail interchanges, how to create personas of varying genders, and how to observe social protocols and on-line etiquette.

Computer Games and CD-ROMs

At the most primitive level are computer disk games designed to run on DOS-based or Macintosh personal computers. According to 1994 predictions by the Software Publishers' Association, says Dan Alaimo in "PCs Expect to Eclipse Game Machines," Americans should have been playing interactive games on at least 18 million personal computers by 1996, with erotic versions doing well. (The prediction was rendered moot by the rise of CD-ROM technology.) Thus far, most erotic types are primitive, like *Strip Poker II* (Art Work, Inc.), and *Strip Blackjack II* (I. O. Research). Story-oriented software features models with names like Passionate Patti and Virtual Valerie (the click of a mouse moves a dildo in and out of her vagina) rendered as crude images. According to Suzanne Stefanac's "Sex & the New Media," *Virtual Valerie* as of 1993 had "captured about 25 percent of the erotic sector [of the CD-ROM market], selling about 25,000 a year for a total of 100,000 units," but competitors were catching up (39). Greg Keizer's "Fast Forward: Power Plays" reviews new versions of *Leisure Suit Larry, Passionate Patti*, and *Sorcerers Get All the Girls*, while Michael D. Lemonick's "Erotic Electronic Encounters" covers the soft-core *Leisure Suit Larry* and hardcore fare such as *Sexxcapades* and *MacPlaymate*. The inventors of *Virtual Valerie* are interviewed on Home Box Office's *Real Sex: 6*; macho in tone, they wax fulsomely on the possibilities of technology. Enterprises like Starware Publishing, Magnetic Arts, and Sexxy Software sell programs like *M'Adam and Eve Erotica* for Macintosh computers and images that can be animated on IBM-PCs. A question on the Internet in 1994 brought responses indicating that the number of such games exceeded 100 but that they were already passé.

To the avant-garde hacker, older disks are now museum-grade artifacts made obsolete by high-volume, high-speed CD-ROMs. At the same time, the anachronism of the disk format lends itself to aesthetic purpose. Just as painters believe that they are more "serious" than photographers, artists can be more comfortable with less sophisticated technology. The difference in perspective appears in Kandy Arnold's "Deep Contact: Between Viewer and Voyeur," an article on Lynn Hershman, a San Francisco artist whose "Deep Contact: The Incomplete Sexual Fantasy Disk" has been exhibited in museums here and abroad. To most observers, however, the future belongs to CD-ROMs and Digital Video Disks (DVDs) offering full-motion video, which may eventually replace porn videocassettes and, beyond these artifacts, to the voluptuous potential of a limitless cyberspace itself.

Already many adult bookstores and videoshops are carrying CD-ROM and DVD versions of porn movies. In 1994 *Adult Video News*, the trade journal of the adult industry, introduced "CD-ROM and New Media" as a regular monthly department. The *Interactive Adult Movie Almanac* is an interactive CD-ROM loaded with 1,000 photos, 750 reviews of adult movies, 250 biographies of stars, and full-motion previews. When Dana Kennedy visited the Adult Video Exposition at the 1994 Las Vegas Consumer Electronics Show for "Flouting Convention," the most interesting areas were booths pushing interactive erotic CD-ROMs. "Porn is helping sell CD-ROM to the world, just the way it helped launch video and changed entertainment (27)," said Lawrence Miller of New Machine Publishing, a leading publisher of CD-ROM erotica. The booths were staffed by performers such as Lisa Lipps and Wendy Whoppers, who seem to enjoy their roles. "Is this [performing explicit sex on a medium] any more degrading than slave labor at McDonald's?," asked veteran actress Nina Hartley (28). According to Amy Harmon's "The 'Seedy' Side of CD-ROMs" (1995), fewer than 10 percent of the 6 million CD-ROMs sold in the United States are of the "adult" type, but that percentage has almost certainly increased since. In any case, scholars attempting to stay current should consult journals such as *Access* (itself only a few years old), which regularly review adult computer software.

The Internet

The most notable aspect of pornography on the Internet is the speed with which it has proliferated. For that reason, many of the sources listed here are intended as signposts to a period already slipping into technohistory. "The Road to the Global Village," a 1990 *Scientific American* article by Karen Wright, observed that the volume of pornography on the various American electronic networks did not come close to that on the Teletel network operated by France's Telecom, which featured a *messagerie* or chat line that has a subcategory called *"messagerie rose"* for erotic messages (88). Experts know that the volume of sexual messages on the American branches of the Internet is now much greater. Ideology and hyperbole being what they are, however, scholars must be very cautious. *Georgetown Law Review* unknowingly accepted a bogus study of pornography on the Internet by Martin Rimm, an undergraduate at Carnegie-Mellon University. Rimm's assertions in "Marketing Pornography on the Information Superhighway," among them that "83.5% of all images posted on the Usenet are pornographic," duped *Time* magazine, which featured the study in the cover article ("Cyberporn") as an "exclusive" for the 3 July 1995 issue; the piece was written by Philip Elmer-Dewitt. *Newsweek*, of course, countered with its own piece by Steven Levy, "No Place for Kids," which interviews on-line users, parents, and others, billing itself as a parent's guide to sex on the superhighway.

The same issue of *Georgetown Law Review* carried an article praising Rimm by antiporn activist Catharine MacKinnon, who had apparently vetted the study. The problem noted immediately by Internet experts, as Jeffrey Rosen points out in "Cheap Speech," a review-essay in the *New Yorker*, is that the actual figures are exponentially smaller. According to Rosen, "pornographic images represent only three per cent of all messages on the Usenet, a global network of discussion groups, and less than half of one per cent of all images on the Internet as a whole" (75). In the opinion of many experts, reports Thomas J. DeLoughry in "Researcher Who Studied On-Line Pornography Gets Invitation from Congress, Criticism from Scholars," Rimm's survey methodology seems not only flawed but fundamentally misconceived. Faced with that assessment, a polite designation for hoax, Congress withdrew its invitation to Rimm to testify in favor of the Communications Decency Act.

Major magazines have taken up the controversy, and, fortunately, most of them have checked more carefully than did *Time* in ballooning the Rimm study. Typical is *Newsweek*'s feature, by Charles Fleming, Barbara Kantrowitz, and Joshua Cooper Ramo. Their "Sex on the Info Highway" describes the Pleasure Dome in Virginia, the Windup BBS in New York, and NuPix in Denver, which are nodes that can access Throbnet, Swingnet, Studnet, and Kinknet. They cover Internet specialty services such as sex.bestiality, sex.bondage, and sex.fetish.feet, but note that the most popular is alt.sex.news, accessed by Usenet. Sexual explicitness in America On-Line "chat rooms" and in Text Sex on WELL (Whole Earth 'Lectronic Link) are the topics of "Lust Online," by Matthew Childs. Philip Elmer-Dewitt profiles Patricia DeLucchio, operator of the East Coast Eros conference board on the WELL, in "Orgies On-Line." The WELL, a computer conferencing system with chat rooms for discussion of sexual topics, can be modem-dialed direct. Mike Godwin's article, "alt.sex.academic.freedom," defends the right of news groups to explore prurient topics and dismisses the furor inspired by the Carnegie Mellon survey. Lawrence F. Haas reviews social, political, and technical impediments to regulating explicitness on the Net in "Public Access Information Networks (PAIN) and Pornography: Regulating the 'PAIN.' " The Cybersex Consortium has put together *The Perv's Guide to the Internet*, an instructional manual for those seeking sexual material.

E-mail and Communication in Cyberspace

Many Americans cruise the Internet from the on-ramps of Internet Service Providers (ISPs), using the conduits mostly for e-mail, which lends itself as easily to sexual talk as to business matters. For some, e-mail delivers fantasy on a scale never before possible, since people can adopt whatever personae they wish. Here a female paraplegic of sixty can take on the identity of a male psychotherapist in his forties and romance a blond temptress who is really a gay ad executive. Cybersex thus makes possible representation at levels and in modes never achieved before, allowing people to change gender, class, and ethnicity at will; as numerous writers have observed, such shape-shifting can be erotic in itself.

Part of the appeal of such exchanges would seem to be that the "sex" is *safe*. Mike Saenz, creator of *Virtual Valerie*, told Suzanne Stefanac in "Sex & the New Media" that virtual sex can teach safe sex through simulation (41). Brenda Laurel, of Interval Research, told Stefanac that e-mail exchanges also promote learning in a comfortable "environment": "We have a new representational world that allows people to construct representations of their own sexuality for each other. And these constructions are no longer bounded by the narrow vocabulary of real-world fashion and stereotypes. Teenagers, for instance, generally have a pretty narrow palette with which to express their sexuality. And yet we're starting to see opportunities with computer networks and to some extent interactive games, to construct flavors of one's sexual persona that aren't stereotypes, that escape these cages" (41).

Not specifically about sex groups but ethnographically fascinating is *Online Communities*, in which Starr R. Hiltz theorizes on the impulses that lead users to establish communication clusters and the attractions, conversations, and concerns that bind them. *Cyberspace: First Steps*, edited by Michael Benedikt, is a compendium of mostly sober estimates of various aspects of cyberspace, virtual reality, and information superhighways, with some reflections on erotic avenues. The best of the collection is Michael Heim's "The Erotic Ontology of Cyberspace," on voluptuous potential. Writing in *The War of Desire and Technology at the Close of the Machine Age*, Allucqère Roseanne Stone reflects on the presence of the body in "technosocial space," that is, in electronic environment that is everywhere and nowhere. If the body is not physically present at an Internet "site," what sort of eroticism is available? Stone says that communication technologies have become so sophisticated that they are literally reshaping erotic sensibilities, with prospects that are exciting. Claudia Springer's *Electronic Eros: Bodies and Desire in the Postindustrial Age* pursues similar themes. Metaphysical musings are also Gareth Branwyn's reason for writing "CompuSex: Erotica for Cybernauts." Cyberspace offers opportunities for performance art, say members of the Critical Art Ensemble, and "[c]omputer hackers and video pirates may be the avant-garde of performance" (216), in "Electronic Disturbances." Such pioneers are trying to escape the limitations of the body in their quest for erotic possibilities.

The title of Bruce M. Bowden's article, "How to Have an On-Line Affair— An Electronic, Endearing, and Erotic Experience," an e-mail exchange, is self-explanatory. Gerard Van der Leun's "This Is a Naked Lady" discusses sexual interchanges on computer networks and makes prognostications for the future. Sensual experiences on-line are also recalled by J. C. Herz in "Confessions of an Internet Junkie." Ad hoc groups carry on light discussion of sexual matters (e.g., jokes, erotic dialogue) continuously on electronic networks, that is, pathways such as BITNET and USENET that lace together to constitute the Internet. A *New York Times* editorial on "Sick Jokes" recently marveled at the speed with which off-color jokes now circulate by e-mail, in this case those having to do with the arrest of Pee Wee Herman (Paul Ruebens) for indecent exposure.

Erotic BBSs and Web Sites

Most notoriety has accrued to explicit bulletin boards reachable through dial-up on-line networks, which can link users around the globe. Norman Maidstone's "Freudian Chips" is an early article on what were then called "graffiti" networks for hackers to share sexual messages. These have since grown rapidly. Bulletin boards and databases hold erotic stories, pictures, jokes, videos, audio tracks, drawings, and so on, but they can also encapsulate serious comment. According to Suzanne Stefanac's "Sex & the New Media," the largest electronic private bulletin board, Event Horizons, with sixty-four lines and a customer base of 35,000, took in $3 million in 1992 (39). Eighty-five percent of the traffic occurred in the restricted, but soft-core access, adult areas. User groups, wider audiences, lurkers, and legalities are the subjects of "Sex with a Hard (Disk) On: Computer Bulletin Boards and Pornography," by Maureen Furness. *Future Sex* is essential for up-to-date information on electronic sex; the journal regularly reviews BBSs that specialize in sex as well as recordings that are particularly explicit. The publisher of *Future Sex*, Lisa Palac, is profiled by Michael Hirschorn as a missionary intent on bringing sex to the electronic masses in "The PC Porn Queen's Virtual Realities."

Literary critics have not yet begun to study the collective narratives generated on networks, but Katherine Silberger and Lauren Spencer have pointed the way in "Where Is the Lust?," an article on computer network pornography focused on "Cyberlust," an erotic fiction file started by a female student at the University of Massachusetts at Amherst. Many zines are now published electronically, and virtually all the established men's magazines now operate Web sites. "E-zines" are zines that exist in electronic form, on-line, often as downloadable files accessible through the Internet that connects distant conferencing systems. (See **Fanzines** and **Other Zines** in Chapter 17.) "Computer Goddesses, Not Computer Geeks," by Jeff Yang, discusses the visions of Lisa Palac of *Future Sex* magazine, cyberauthor Pat Cadigan, Stacy Horn of ECHO, VR visionary artist Brenda Laurel, and others such as Jaime Levy and Amy Bruckman.

Penthouse Online, operated by the magazine, provides e-mail service, bulletin boards with sexual confessions and fantasies, and photographs that can be downloaded by modem to a PC or MAC computer, using VGA/SVGA, 2400/9600 bps. The inauguration of this innovation was duly noted for *USA Today* readers by Kevin Maney in " 'Penthouse' Unveils Pet Computer Product," which also reports that the magazine itself is now available on interactive CD-ROM. Even the *New York Times* thought it an interesting development, so Deidre Carmody's interview, "New President at Penthouse Looks beyond Printed Page," revealed that electronic services will enable subscribers to communicate with Penthouse Pets or search the magazine's databases. Jack Olmsted says in "Playboy Opens WWW Emporium" that when *Playboy* opened its World Wide Web address, principally to sell Playboy products such as "Playboy Interviews," it logged 10,000 calls on the first day.

In "The Golden Age of Porn Online," Steve Silberman observes that the majority of triple-X images on the Net come from two or three vendors such as ZMaster in Florida and thus lack the diversity assumed by users and critics alike. Narratives, excerpts, and exchanges from e-mail, chat rooms, and other electronic pathways are the substance of *Torn Shapes of Desire: Internet Erotica* by Mary Anne Mohanraj. Pamela O'Connell examines Purve, a new Web site for women, and reviews other efforts by women to make erotic sites attractive to women in "Web Erotica Aims for New Female Customers." O'Connell also mentions *The Woman's Guide to Sex on the Web* by Anne Semans and Cathy Winks, and cites figures from Media Matrix, a research company, which says that 20 percent of women eighteen and older visit sex sites, as contrasted with 41 percent for males similarly aged. In "Putting the XX Back in XXX: With Estrogen-Powered Sex Sites Springing Up All over the Internet, Women Are Turning the Tables—and the Screws—on an Age-old Industry," Ingrid Hein observes that profit and opportunity are keys to proliferation of sex sites run by women, which are recognizable because of the pictures of pregnant women and greater sensuality. David Kushner points out that while most porn performers merely dabble in Web sites, some actresses have moved full-time into sites in "Debbie Does HTML." *Penthouse* ran "Take My Wife, Please—Over and Over," an article in which Gerard Van Der Leun profiles Jon David Messner, his wife, Cherie, and her sister Jill, a ménage à trois whose Web site (Horny-wife.com) has attracted phenomenal numbers of hits from viewers eager to see the photos of the three of them in intercourse. "This Is Sex?" asks James Gleick, aghast at the dumbness of Internet sites and the rubbish he finds there. (For listings of sex sites on the Internet, see **Electronic Media** in chapter 4, especially Brigman, Mason, Rose and Thomas, Tamosaitis, and Wildhack.)

Virtual Reality

In the future, say electronic enthusiasts, pornography will take an exponential step forward as the technology of "virtual reality," that is, an electronic environment that can be physically experienced by humans properly equipped with sensors, makes the representation of sex tactile and three-dimensional. The best single text on the subject is Howard Rheingold's *Virtual Reality*, which appraises the technology without hype. Rheingold coins the term "teledildonics" for representations of sex. He believes that electronic connection will serve as a sexual bridge between two humans at a distance rather than as a human-machine sexual experience, envisioning participants as covering themselves in a sort of giant condom equipped with transducers wired over long-distance fiber-optic networks for remote sex. A fascinating article called "Love Bites" reviews experiments by Kirk Woolford and Stahl Stensile, who are creating a CyberSM project, the first long-distance love machine, composed of cybersuits, modems, software, and computers that will convert electronic signals into tactile stimulation of erogenous zones.

Walter Lowe's "Adventures in Cyberspace" speculates on exotic "dick sleeves" and electronic dildos, as does Susie Bright's "Sex in the Computer Age," most of which is reproduced in her *Susie Bright's Sexual Reality: A*

Virtual Sex World Reader, whose essays cover subjects from the *Phil Donahue Show* to erotic exchanges in hyperspace. Perhaps the most interesting feature of such texts is the longing for improved sexual experience, for sexual transcendence made possible by getting beyond the limitations of the body. Even more futuristic is the "Virtual Sex" chapter of *Mondo 2000: A User's Guide to the New Edge*, although the predictions are grounded in technology available now. The editors discuss sensual sensors and Nick Herbert's concept, the "Pleasure Dome Project," inspired by the Italian porn actress and member of Parliament Ilona Staller. Alan Rifkin claims that "virtual reality is an extension of cave art" (32) in "Terminal Bliss," an article about a man who tries to digitalize his lover into a virtual reality clone.

Digitalized Sex and Culture

Some critics think that the openness of computer networks, so empowering, on one hand, can be menacing, on the other. In 1993 the Internet daily carried the messages of 15 million people and linked users to 30,000–40,000 computer bulletin boards, said Wayne T. Price in "Harassment Goes On-Line: Low-Tech Problem Hits PC Networks." There was also a surge in sexual images and discourse on the networks, some of which is disturbing to women in offices, where they receive the material without asking for it. Some of the messages, like obscene phone calls, are directed specifically to women. Anonymous networks seem to encourage the antisocial, agrees Peter H. Lewis in "Anarchy, a Threat on the Electronic Frontier?" Lewis' article is on the hucksters, pornographers, and "crackpots and sociopaths who seek to bully others with obscenities and threats" on the Usenet sector of the Internet. Lewis observes that the abusers and those who would police them both pose a threat to the democratic assumptions that have thus far governed the Usenet. Common sense is the key, Stephanie Brail tells women who want to go on-line in "The Price of Admission: Harassment and Free Speech in the Wild, Wild West": "Pornography is not harassment" (149); threats are. *Wired Women: Gender and New Realities in Cyberspace*, the book in which Brail's essay appears, is also worth reading. "If You Don't Love It, Leave It," advises Esther Dyson, who insists that smut and aggression on the Net are easy to avoid, with or without filters. Filters (blocking technologies) themselves are in their infancy, and their problems and efficacy are still in contention; a thorough review can be found in the essays collected by Monroe Price in *The V-Chip Debate: Content Filtering from Television to the Internet*.

Thomas J. DeLoughry's "Colleges Try to Devise Policies on Obscenity on Campus Networks" deals with the difficulties for librarians of providing access to the computerized catalogs of collections such as those of the Kinsey Institute but also the problems caused college administrators by the availability of erotica and sex-oriented bulletin boards like ALT.SEX on the Internet. (See also **Libraries and Pornography** in Chapter 7.) The problem is aggravated by the centrality of computer networks to modern higher education. Joe Abernathy's "The Texas Online Massacres" reminds readers that despite court decisions to the contrary, law enforcement agencies do not consider electronic mail and related network services to be protected by the First Amendment and that the FBI monitors erotica traffic on the America Online network, a national dial-up service similar to CompuServe. (See the section on **Censorship of Computers and the Internet** in chapter 20.)

Finally, it seems reasonable to assume that digitalization, new electronic technologies, and the commercial possibilities offered by the Internet will transform the ways in which Americans react to sexual representations. These forces will alter the production, distribution, and consumption of pornography in ways that we cannot yet anticipate. As this *Guide* goes to press, Julian Dibble covers the efforts by various porn producers, chiefly Vivid Video, to roll out interactive sex services in "The Body Electric."

NOTE

1. See "Yale Professor Badly Hurt by Mail Bomb," *New York Times*, 25 June 1993, pp. A1, A8. The usual reason given for the name is that the program could suck up data.

REFERENCES

Abbott, Steve. "Dialing for Sex." *Men Confront Pornography*, ed. Michael S. Kimmel. New York: Crown, 1990, pp. 285–287.

Abernathy, Joe. "The Texas Online Massacres." *Village Voice*, 26 January 1993, pp. 49–50.

Abt, Vicki, and Mel Seesholz. "The Shameless World of Phil, Sally, and Oprah: Television Talk Shows and the Deconstructioning of Society." *Journal of Popular Culture*, 28:1 (1994): 171–191.

Access. San Diego, 1994–.

Alaimo, Dan. "PCs Expect to Eclipse Game Machines." *Supermarket News,* 18 July 1994: 30.

Allen, Robert. "On Reading Soaps: A Semiotic Primer." *Regarding Television: Critical Approaches—An Anthology*, ed. E. Ann Kaplan. Los Angeles: American Film Institute, 1983, pp. 97–108.

———. *Speaking of Soap Operas*. Chapel Hill: University of North Carolina Press, 1985.

Alman, Isadora. *Aural Sex and Verbal Intercourse*. Burlingame, CA: Down There Press, 1984; aka *Sex Information: May I Help You?*

Alter, Jonathan. "The New Vulgarity." *USA Weekend*, 5–7 March 1993, pp. 4–5.

Amburn, Ellis. *Pearl: The Obsessions and Passions of Janis Joplin*. New York: Warner, 1992.

Ample, Annie. *The Bare Facts: My Life as a Stripper*. Toronto: Key Porter Books, 1988.

Anderson, Lisa. "On the Record." *Chicago Tribune*, 31 December 1995, sec. 2, p. 3.

Ang, Ien. *Watching Dallas: Soap Opera and the Melodramatic Imagination*, trans. Della Couling. London: Methuen, 1985.

Anthony, Gary, with Rockey Bennett. *Dirty Talk: Diary of a Phone Sex "Mistress."* Buffalo, NY: Prometheus Books, 1997.

Aranza, Jacob. *Backward Masking Unmasked: Backward Satanic Messages of Rock Exposed.* Lafayette, LA: Huntington House, 1983.

————. *More Rock, Country and Backward Masking Unmasked.* Lafayette, LA: Huntington House, 1985.

"Archbishop Blasts Airing of Documentary." *Current: The Public Telecommunications Newspaper,* 10:16 (9 September 1991): pp. 1, 4, 13.

Arnold, Kandy. "Deep Contact: Between Viewer and Voyeur." *New Media,* 3:4 (April 1993): 29.

"Aural Sex: The Top Ten Fuck Songs." *Taste of Latex,* 1:4 (Winter 1990–91): 14–15.

Baker, Russell. "Paradise for Pentagon." *New York Times,* national ed., 26 January 1991, p. 19.

Barger, Eric. *From Rock to Rock: The Music of Darkness Exposed!* Lafayette, LA: Huntington House, 1990.

Bayles, Martha. *Hole in Our Soul: The Loss of Beauty and Meaning in American Popular Music.* Chicago: University of Chicago Press, 1994.

Bell, Shannon. "Ejaculatory Television: The Talk Show and the Postmodern Subject." *Fuse,* 14: 5/6 (1991): 7–11.

Benedikt, Michael, ed. *Cyberspace: First Steps.* Cambridge: MIT Press, 1992.

Berger, Warren. "That's E! for Entertainment (and Erotica?)." *New York Times,* 26 June 1998, p. 27.

Biagi, Shirley. *Media/Impact: An Introduction to Mass Media.* Belmont, CA: Wadsworth, 1993.

Boulware, Jack. *Sex American Style: An Illustrated Romp through the Golden Age of Heterosexuality.* Venice, CA: Feral House, 1997.

Bowden, Bruce M. "How to Have an On-Line Affair—An Electronic, Endearing, and Erotic Experience." *Penthouse,* 25:6 (February 1994): 38.

Brady, John. "Playboy Interview: Jerry Springer." *Playboy,* 45:7 (July 1998): 63–64, 68, 70, 72, 149–153.

Brail, Stephanie. "The Price of Admission: Harassment and Free Speech in the Wild, Wild West." *Wired Women: Gender and New Realities in Cyberspace,* ed. Lynn Cherny and Elizabeth Reba Weise. Seattle: Bay Press, 1996, pp. 141–157.

Branwyn, Gareth. "Compu-Sex: Erotica for Cybernauts." *Flame Wars: The Discourse of Cyberculture,* ed. Mark Dery. Durham, NC: Duke University Press, 1994, pp. 223–235.

Brett, Philip, Elizabeth Wood, and Gary Thomas, eds. *Queering the Pitch: The New Gay and Lesbian Musicology.* New York: Routledge, 1994.

Bright, Susie. "Sex in the Computer Age." *Elle,* 7:6 (February 1992): 56, 58, 62.

————. *Susie Bright's Sexual Reality: A Virtual Sex World Reader.* Pittsburgh: Cleis Press, 1992.

Broadcasting [retitled in 1995 as *Broadcasting and Cable*]. Washington, DC, 1931–.

Brower, Sue. "TV 'Trash' and 'Treasure': Marketing *Dallas* and *Cagney and Lacey.*" *Wide Angle,* 11:1 (1989): 18–31.

Brown, Jane E., and Laurie Schulze. "The Effects of Race, Gender, and Fandom on Audience Interpretations of Madonna's Music Videos." *Journal of Communication,* 40:2 (1990): 88–102; rpt. *Gender, Race and Class in Media: A Text-Reader,* ed. Gail Dines and Jean M. Humez. Thousand Oaks, CA: Sage, 1995, pp. 508–517.

Brown, Mary E. *Soap Opera and Women's Talk: The Pleasure of Resistance.* Thousand Oaks, CA: Sage, 1994.

———, ed. *Television and Women's Culture: The Politics of the Popular.* Thousand Oaks, CA: Sage, 1994.

Brubach, Holly. "Rock-and-Roll Vaudeville." *Maincurrents in Mass Communications,* ed. Warren K. Agee, Philip H. Ault, and Edwin Emery. New York: Harper and Row, 1986, pp. 341–347.

Burks, John, and Jerry Hopkins. *Groupies and Other Girls: A Rolling Stone Special Report.* New York: Bantam, 1970.

Cable World: The News Magazine for Video, Voice and Data. Denver, 1988–.

Callahan, Jean. "Women and Pornography: Combat in the Video Zone." *American Film,* 8 (March 1982): 62–63.

Canedy, Dana. "P. & G. Is Seeking to Revive Soaps: Shaking Up TV Serials as Audiences Dwindle." *New York Times,* 11 March 1997, pp. C1, C4.

Carlin, John C. "The Rise and Fall of Topless Radio." *Journal of Communication,* 26:1 (Winter 1976): 31–37.

Carmody, Deidre. "New President at Penthouse Looks beyond Printed Page." *New York Times,* national ed., 2 December 1991, pp. C1, C8.

Caserta, Peggy, as told to Dan Knapp. *Going Down with Janis.* Secaucus, NJ: Lyle Stuart, 1973.

"CD-ROM and New Media." *Adult Video News,* 1994–.

Chandler, C. R., H. Paul Chalfant, and Craig P. Chalfant. "Cheaters Sometimes Win: Sexual Infidelity in Country Music." *Forbidden Fruits: Taboos and Tabooism in Culture,* ed. Ray B. Browne. Bowling Green, OH: Bowling Green State University Press, 1984, pp. 133–144.

Chapple, Steve, and David Talbot. *Burning Desires: Sex in America: A Report from the Field.* New York: Signet, 1990.

Childs, Matthew. "Lust Online." *Playboy,* 41:4 (April 1994): 94–96, 152–154.

Christgau, Robert. *Grown Up All Wrong: 75 Great Rock and Pop Artists from Vaudeville to Techno.* Cambridge: Harvard University Press, 1998.

Cline, Victor B., ed. *Where Do You Draw the Line? An Exploration into Media Violence, Pornography, and Censorship.* Provo, UT: Brigham Young University Press, 1975.

Coakley, Mary L. *Rated X: The Moral Case against TV.* New York: Arlington House, 1977.

Cole, Richard, with Richard Trubo. *Stairway to Heaven: Led Zeppelin Uncensored.* San Francisco: HarperCollins, 1992.

Cool, Lisa Collier. "Voices of America." *Penthouse,* 23:1 (September 1991): 85–86, 88–89, 176, 196, 225.

Cooper, Carol. "Digital Underground." *Village Voice,* 25 January 1994, p. 63.

Cooper, Sarah, ed. *Girls! Girls! Girls! Essays on Women and Music.* New York: Cassell, 1995.

County, Jayne. *Man Enough to Be Woman: The Autobiography of Jayne County.* New York: Serpent's Tail, 1996.

Creekmur, Corey K., and Alexander Doty, eds. *Out in Culture: Gay, Lesbian, and Queer Essays on Popular Culture.* Durham, NC: Duke University Press, 1995.

Critical Art Ensemble. "Electronic Disturbances." *The Last Sex: Feminism and Outlaw Bodies*, ed. Arthur Kroker and Marilouise Kroker. New York: St. Martin's, 1993, pp. 208–219.

Cybersex Consortium. *The Perv's Guide to the Internet*. New York: Masquerade, 1996.

Darling, Lynn. "The Highbrow Smut of Nicholson Baker." *Esquire* (February 1994): 76–80.

DeCurtis, Anthony, ed. *Present Tense: Rock 'n' Roll and Culture*. Durham, NC: Duke University Press, 1992.

DeLoughry, Thomas J. "Colleges Try to Devise Policies on Obscenity on Campus Networks." *Chronicle of Higher Education*, 27 January 1993, A27–29.

———. "Researcher Who Studied On-Line Pornography Gets Invitation from Congress, Criticism from Scholars." *Chronicle of Higher Education*, 21 July 1995, p. A19.

Des Barres, Pamela. *I'm with the Band: Confessions of a Groupie*. New York: Beech Tree Books, 1987.

———. *Take Another Little Piece of My Heart: A Groupie Grows Up*. New York: William Morrow, 1992.

Di Constanzo, Frank. "On the Beat: Aural Sex." *Gallery*, 22:3 (March 1994): 32.

Dibble, Julian. "The Body Electric." *Time Digital*, 12 April 1999, pp. 24–27.

Doner, Colonel V. *The Responsible Parent's Guide to TV: A Noted Expert Looks at Television's Role in Changing Our Children's Values*. Lafayette, LA: Huntington House, 1988.

Dyson, Esther. "If You Don't Love It, Leave It." *New York Times Magazine*, 16 July 1995, pp. 26, 28.

Echols, Alice. *Scars of Sweet Paradise: The Life and Times of Janis Joplin*. New York: Metropolitan Books/Henry Holt, 1999.

Edmondson, Madeleine, and David Rounds. *From Mary Noble to Mary Hartman: The Complete Soap Opera Book*. New York: Stein and Day, 1976.

Ehler, Jay. "Cock Rock." *Los Angeles Free Press*. Article spanning six issues, 15 February–15 March 1974.

Ehrenreich, Barbara, Elizabeth Hess, and Gloria Jacobs. *Re-Making Love: The Feminization of Sex*. Garden City, NY: Anchor/Doubleday, 1986.

Electronic Media. New York, 1981–.

Ellis, Kate. "I'm Black and Blue from the Rolling Stones and I'm Not Sure How I Feel about It: Pornography and the Feminist Imagination." *Socialist Review*, 14:3/4 (May–August 1984): 103–125.

Elmer-Dewitt, Philip. "Cyberporn." *Time*, 3 July 1995, pp. 38–45.

———. "Orgies On-Line." *Time*, 31 May 1993, p. 61.

Evans, Liz. *Women, Sex and Rock 'n' Roll in Their Own Words*. London: Pandora, 1994.

Expletives Deleted. Princeton: Films for the Humanities and Sciences, 1994.

Faderman, Lillian. *Odd Girls and Twilight Lovers: A History of Lesbian Life in Twentieth-Century America*. New York: Columbia University Press, 1991.

Falwell, Jerry. "Music." *Listen, America!* Garden City, NY: Doubleday, 1980, pp. 224–232.

Farber, Barry. "Why Clean Talk Show Hosts on Radio Are Losing the Battle to Vulgarians." *Television/Radio Age*, 25 January 1988, p. 77.

Fine, Marshall. "Playboy Interview: Howard Stern." *Playboy*, 41:4 (April 1994): 55–56, 58–60, 62–68, 158–160.

Fiske, John. *Television Culture*. New York: Routledge, 1987.

Fleming, Charles, Barbara Kantrowitz, and Joshua Cooper Ramo. "Sex on the Info High-
    way." *Newsweek*, 14 March 1994, pp. 62–63.
Flitterman-Lewis, Sandy. "All's Well That Doesn't End—Soap Operas and the Marriage
    Motif." *Camera Obscura*, 16 (1988): 119–127.
Flowers, Amy. *The Fantasy Factory: An Insider's View of the Phone Sex Industry.*
    Philadelphia: University of Pennsylvania Press, 1998.
FoneSecret Digest. Beverly Hills, CA, 1993–.
Frentz, Suzanne, ed. *Staying Tuned: Contemporary Soap Opera Criticism.* Bowling
    Green, OH: Bowling Green State University Popular Press, 1992.
Frith, Simon. *Performing Rites: On the Value of Popular Music.* Cambridge: Harvard
    University Press, 1996.
———. *Sound Effects: Youth, Leisure, and the Politics of Rock 'n' Roll.* New York:
    Pantheon, 1991.
Frith, Simon, and Angela McRobbie. "Rock and Sexuality." *Screen Education*, 29 (1978/
    1979): 3–19.
Furness, Maureen. "Sex with a Hard (Disk) On: Computer Bulletin Boards and Pornog-
    raphy." *Wide Angle*, 15:2 (1993): 19–37.
Future Sex. San Francisco, 1993–.
Gamson, Joshua. *Freaks Talk Back: Tabloid Talk Shows and Sexual Nonconformity.*
    Chicago: University of Chicago Press, 1998.
Gay Cable Network. Manhattan Cable Channel J. 32 Union Square East, New York City
    10003.
Gill, John. *Queer Noises: Male and Female Homosexuality in Twentieth-Century Music.*
    New York: Cassell, 1995.
Glascock, Jack. "Psychoticism, Previous Pornography Usage and the Effect of Dial-a-
    Porn Recordings on Male Listeners." A paper presented to the Broadcast Edu-
    cation Association, Las Vegas, April 1993.
Glascock, Jack, and Robert LaRose. "A Content Analysis of 900 Numbers: Implications
    for Industry Regulation and Self-Regulation." *Telecommunications Policy*, 16
    (1992): 147–155.
———. "Dial-a-Porn Recordings: The Role of the Female Participant in Male Sexual
    Fantasies." *Journal of Broadcasting & Electronic Media*, 37:3 (Summer 1993):
    313–324.
Gleick, James. "Fast Forward: This Is Sex?" *New York Times Magazine*, 11 June 1995,
    p. 26.
Glynn, Kevin. "Tabloid Television's Transgressive Aesthetics: *A Current Affair* and the
    'Shows That Taste Forgot.' " *Wide Angle*, 12:2 (April 1990): 23–44.
Godwin, Jeff. *The Devil's Disciples: The Truth about Rock.* Chino, CA: Chick
    Publications, 1986.
Godwin, Mike. "alt.sex.academic.freedom." *Wired* February 1995, p. 72.
Goldberg, M. "Rock and Roll Fanzines: A New Underground Press Flourishes." *Rolling
    Stone*, 418 (1986): 56–60.
Goldstein, Richard. "Dirty Dialing." *Village Voice*, 10 May 1988, p. 36.
Goodman, Walter. " 'Tabloid' Charge Rocks Network News." *New York Times*, 13 Feb-
    ruary 1994, p. H29.
Gore, Tipper. *Raising PG Kids in an X-Rated Society.* Nashville, TN: Abingdon, 1987.
Greenberg, Bradley S., Robert Abelman, and Kimberly Neuendorf. "Sex on the Soap

Operas: Afternoon Delight." *Journal of Communication*, 31:2 (Spring 1981): 83–89.

Greenberg, Bradley S., Jane D. Brown, and Nancy L. Buerkel-Rothfuss. *Media, Sex, and the Adolescent: Studies in TV and Adolescence.* Cresskill, NJ: Hampton Press, 1993.

Greenberg, Bradley S., and Rick W. Busselle. *Soap Operas and Sexual Activity.* Menlo Park, CA: Henry J. Kaiser Family Foundation, 1994.

———. "Soap Operas and Sexual Activity: A Decade Later." *Journal of Communication*, 46:4 (Autumn 1996): 153–160.

Greenberg, Bradley S., Sandi Smith, et al. *The Content of Television Talk Shows: Topics, Guests and Interactions.* Menlo Park, CA: Henry J. Kaiser Family Foundation, 1995.

Greenberg, Bradley S., and C. Stanley, M. Siemicki, C. Heeter, A. Soderman, and R. Linsangen. *Sex Content on Soaps and Primetime Television Series Most Viewed by Adolescents.* Project Cast Report 2. East Lansing: Department of Telecommunication, University of Michigan, 1986.

Greene, Bob. *Billion Dollar Baby.* New York: Atheneum, 1974.

Grossberg, L. "I'd Rather Feel Bad than Feel Anything at All: Rock and Roll, Pleasure and Power." *Enclitic*, 8:1/2 (1984): 94–111.

Grossberg, Lawrence, Simon Frith, and Andrew Goodwin, eds. *Sound and Vision: The Music Video Reader.* New York: Routledge, 1993.

Gumpert, Gary, and Sandra L. Fish. *Talking to Strangers: Mediated Therapeutic Communication.* Norwood, NJ: Ablex, 1990.

Haas, Lawrence F. "Public Access Information Networks (PAIN) and Pornography: Regulating the 'PAIN.' " D.P.A. dissertation, Golden Gate University, 1996.

Hamer, Diane, and Belinda Budge, eds. *The Good, the Bad, and the Gorgeous: Popular Culture's Romance with Lesbianism.* London: Pandora, 1994.

Halsband, Michael. "Kembra." *Penthouse*, 30:1 (September 1998): 139–147.

Hanczor, Robert S. "Articulation Theory and Public Controversy: Taking Sides over *NYPD Blue.*" *Critical Studies in Mass Communication*, 14:1 (March 1997): 1–30.

Handler, David. "Now the Playmates Move—But Will America Pay to Watch?" *TV Guide*, 25 June 1983, pp. 45–48.

Hanson, Ellis. "The Telephone and Its Queerness." *Crusing the Performative: Interventions into the Representation of Ethnicity, Nationality, and Sexuality*, ed. Sue-Ellen Case, Philip Brett, and Susan Leigh Foster. Bloomington: Indiana University Press, 1995, pp. 34–58.

Hardy, Ernest. "Are We Confused Yet?: Making Sense of Censorship." *Outweek*, 23 May 1990, pp. 68, 73.

Harmon, Amy. "The 'Seedy' Side of CD-ROMs." *Los Angeles Times*, 29 November 1995, p. A1.

Harrington, C. Lee, and Denise D. Bielby. *Soap Fans: Pursuing Pleasure and Making Meaning in Everyday Life.* Philadelphia: Temple University Press, 1995.

Harris, Louis, and Associates. *Sexual Material on American Television during the 1987–88 Season.* New York: Planned Parenthood Federation of America, 26 January 1988.

Heim, Michael. "The Erotic Ontology of Cyberspace." *Cyberspace: First Steps*, ed. Michael Benedikt. Cambridge: MIT Press, 1992, pp. 59–80.

Hein, Ingrid. "Putting the XX Back in XXX: With Estrogen-Powered Sex Sites Springing Up All over the Internet, Women Are Turning the Tables—and the Screws—on an Age-old Industry." *Toronto Hour*, 22–28 May 1997, pp. 12–13.

Henry, Tricia. *Break All Rules: Punk Rock and the Meaning of a Style*. Ann Arbor: UMI Research Press, 1989.

Herz, J. C. "Confessions of an Internet Junkie." *Playboy*, 41:7 (July 1994): 78–80, 168–171.

Hiltz, Starr R. *Online Communities*. Norwood, NJ: Ablex, 1984.

Hirschorn, Michael. "The PC Porn Queen's Virtual Realities." *Esquire*, June 1993, pp. 57–59.

Hodenfield, Cris. "Sex Rock Symbolism." *The New Eroticism: Theories, Vogues, Canons*, ed. Philip Nobile. New York: Random House, 1970, pp. 188–191.

Holliday, Jim. "The Top 30 Adult Tunes Countdown." *Only the Best*. Van Nuys, CA: Cal Vista, 1986, pp. 209–211.

Home Box Office. "Cyborgasm: The Making of an XXX-rated CD." *Real Sex: 9*. Produced and directed by Patti Kaplan. New York: HBO, 1994.

———. "Virtual Valerie." *Real Sex: 6*. Produced and directed by Patti Kaplan. New York: HBO, 1993.

Howes, Keith. *Broadcasting It!: An Encyclopedia of Homosexuality in Film, Radio and TV (UK 1923–1993)*. New York: Cassell/Mansell, 1993.

Huffman, James R., and Julie L. Huffman. "Sexism and Cultural Lag: The Rise of the Jailbait Song, 1955–1985." *Journal of Popular Culture*, 21:2 (Fall 1987): 65–83.

Interactive Adult Movie Almanac. Los Angeles: New Machine Publishing, 1994.

Jaehne, Karen. "Confessions of a Feminist Porn Programmer." *Film Quarterly*, 37:1 (Fall 1983): 9–16.

Jaffe, Debbie. *Master/Slave Relationship: Being Led Around by the Tongue*. San Francisco: Master/Slave Relationship, 1993.

Jay, Timothy. *Cursing in America: A Psycholinguistic Study of Dirty Language in the Courts, in the Movies, in the Schoolyards, and on the Streets*. Philadelphia: John Benjamins, 1992.

Jhally, Sut. *Dreamworlds: Desire/Sex/Power in Rock Video* and *Dreamworlds II*. Amherst, MA: Foundation for Media Education, 1990, 1995.

Johnson, D. K., and K. Satow. "Getting Down to Specifics about Sex on Television." *Broadcasting*, 22 May 1978, p. 24.

Jones, Mablen. *Getting It On: The Clothing of Rock 'n' Roll*. New York: Abbeville, 1987.

Juno, Andrea, ed. *Angry Women in Rock*. 2 vols. San Francisco: Juno Books, 1995, 1996.

Juno, Andrea, and V. Vale, eds. *Angry Women*. San Francisco: RE/Search, 1991.

———. *Incredibly Strange Music*. 2 vols. San Francisco: RE/Search, 1993, 1994.

K., Kathleen. *Sweet Talkers*. New York: Waite Group, 1995.

Kaplan, E. Ann. *Rocking around the Clock: Music Television, Post Modernism and Consumer Culture*. New York: Routledge, Chapman, and Hall, 1987.

———, ed. *Regarding Television: Critical Approaches—An Anthology*. Los Angeles: American Film Institute, 1983.

Keizer, Gregg. "Fast Forward: Power Plays." *Penthouse*, 22:8 (April, 1991): 16.

Kelly, Valerie. "Writing Telephone Sex Calls." *How to Write Erotica*. New York: Harmony Books, 1986, pp. 209–215.

Kennedy, Dana. "Flouting Convention." *Entertainment Weekly*, 1 January 1994, pp. 26–28.

―――. "Scandal Inc." *Entertainment Weekly*, 4 March 1994, pp. 18–24, 26–27, and cover.

Kernes, Mark. "Adult Video News to the Media: Shove It." *Gauntlet*, 5 (1993): 140–144.

Kgositsile, Ipeleng. "Whose Pussy Is This?" *Village Voice*, 10 November 1992, pp. 82–83.

Kinsey Institute for Sex, Gender, and Reproduction. "Bibliography on Obscene Phone-calls." Bloomington: Kinsey Institute for Sex, Gender, and Reproduction. Indiana University, current.

Kitman, Marvin. "Howard Stern's Small Penis . . ." *Penthouse*, 24:1 (September 1992): 82–84, 86, 88, 90–92, 94.

Krassner, Paul. "Dicks in the Media." *Penthouse*, 23:8 (April 1992): 52, 54, 57, 108, 110.

Kroker, Arthur, with music by Steve Gibson (CD included). *Spasm—Virtual Reality, Android Music, Electric Flesh*. New York: St. Martin's, 1994.

Kurtz, Howard. *Hot Air: All Talk, All the Time*. Boulder, CO: Westview Press, 1997.

Kushner, David. "Debbie Does HTML." *Village Voice*, 6 October 1998, p. 47.

La Guardia, Robert. *The Wonderful World of TV Soap Operas*. New York: Ballantine, 1974; rev. ed. *Soap World*. New York: Arbor House, 1983.

Lance, Larry M., and Christina Y. Berry. "Has There Been a Sexual Revolution?: An Analysis of Human Sexuality Messages in Popular Music, 1968–1977." *Journal of Popular Culture*, 15:3 (1982): 155–164.

Landfried, Hollie. "1–900-Phone-Sex." *Ohio State University Independent*. October 1995. P.O. Box 2111, Columbus, OH 43216.

Landler, Mark. "Time Warner, under Its Own Spotlight." *New York Times*, 12 June 1995, p. C5.

Larson, Bob. *Larson's Book of Rock*. Wheaton, IL: Tyndale, 1987.

Lasar, Matthew. *Pacifica Radio: The Rise of an Alternative Network*. Philadelphia: Temple University Press, 1999.

Laufer, Peter. *Inside Talk Radio: America's Voices or Just Hot Air?* New York: Carol/Birch Lane, 1995.

Ledbetter, James. "Press Clips: Hardcore Hotel." *Village Voice*, 17 May 1994, p. 9.

Legman, Gershon. "Erotic Folksongs and Ballads: An International Bibliography." *Journal of American Folklore*, 103 (October/December 1990): 417–501.

Lehman, Peter. *Running Scared: Masculinity and the Representation of the Male Body*. Philadelphia: Temple University Press, 1993.

Lemonick, Michael D. "Erotic Electronic Encounters." *Time*, 138:12 (23 September 1991): 72.

Levy, Steven. "No Place for Kids." *Newsweek*, 3 July 1995, pp. 46–50.

Lewis, Lisa A. "Female Address on Music Television: Being Discovered." *Jump Cut*, 35 (April 1990): 2–17.

―――. *Gender Politics and MTV: Voicing the Difference*. Philadelphia: Temple University Press, 1993.

Lewis, Peter H. "Anarchy, a Threat on the Electronic Frontier?" *New York Times*, 11 May 1994, p. C1.

Lewis, Randy. "Rock Lyrics: Who's Listening?" *Honolulu Advertiser*, 16 June 1986, p. B2.

Lipschultz, Jeremy H. *Broadcast Indecency: F.C.C. Regulation and the First Amendment.* Woburn, MA: Focal Press, 1996.

Loder, Kurt. *Bat Chain Puller: Rock and Roll in the Age of Celebrity.* New York: St. Martin's, 1991.

"Love Bites." *Details* (June 1994): 28.

Lowe, Walter, Jr. "Adventures in Cyberspace." *Playboy*, 39:4 (April 1992): 104, 124, 163–166.

Lowery, Dennis, Gail Love, and Malcolm Kirby. "Sex on the Soap Operas: Patterns of Intimacy." *Journal of Communication*, 31:2 (Spring, 1981): 90–96.

Lowery, Dennis, and David E. Towles. "Soap Opera Portrayals of Sex, Contraception, and Sexually Transmitted Diseases." *Journal of Communication*, 39:2 (1989): 76–83.

Lyons, Arthur. *Satan Wants You: The Cult of Devil Worship in America.* New York: Mysterious Press, 1989.

MacKinnon, Catharine A. "Vindication and Resistance: A Response to the Carnegie Mellon Study of Pornography in Cyberspace." *Georgetown Law Review*, 83 (June 1995): 1950–1970.

Magnetic Arts. *M'Adam and Eve Erotica.* Magnetic Arts, 6363 Christie St., Emeryville, CA 94608.

Maidstone, Norman. "Freudian Chips." *Screw*, 744, 6 June 1983, pp. 4–7.

Mair, George. *Inside HBO: The Billion Dollar War between HBO, Hollywood and the Home Video Revolution.* New York: Dodd, Mead, 1988.

Maney, Kevin. " 'Penthouse' Unveils Pet Computer Product." *USA Today*, 19 November 1993, p. 4B.

Manson, Marilyn [Brian Warner], with Neil Strauss. *Marilyn Manson: The Long Hard Road Out of Hell.* New York: Regan Books/HarperCollins, 1998.

Marchetti, G. "Documenting Punk: A Subcultural Investigation." *Film Reader*, 5 (1982): 269–284.

Marcus, Greil. *Lipstick Traces: A Secret History of the 20th Century.* Cambridge: Harvard University Press, 1990.

———. *Mystery Train.* New York: NAL, 1975.

Marlowe, Ann. "Inside Every Pussy There's a Little Dick." *Village Voice*, 25 June 1991, pp. 73, 76.

Marsh, Dave. *Louie Louie: The History and Mythology of the World's Most Famous Rock 'n' Roll Song: Including the Full Details of Its Torture and Persecution at the Hands of the Kingsmen, J. Edgar Hoover's F.B.I., and a Cast of Millions; and Introducing, for the First Time Anywhere, the Actual Dirty Lyrics.* New York: Hyperion, 1993.

Masciarotte, Gloria Jean. "C'mon Girl: Oprah Winfrey and the Discourse of Feminine Talk." *Genders*, 11 (Fall 1991): 81–110.

Matelski, Marilyn J. *The Soap Opera Evolution: America's Enduring Romance with Daytime Drama.* Jefferson, NC: McFarland, 1988.

Maupin, Armistead. "A Line That Commercial TV Won't Cross." *New York Times*, 9 January 1994, p. H29.

McClary, Susan. *Feminine Endings: Music, Gender, and Sexuality.* Minneapolis: University of Minnesota Press, 1991.

McDuffie, Carrington. "A Gay Girl's Guide to Phone Sex." *On Our Backs*, 7:3 (January–February 1991): 20–22, 44–45.

McOustra, Sara. *Sex in Rock*. New York: Crescent, 1983.

McRobbie, Angela, ed. *Zoot Suits and Second Hand Dresses: An Anthology of Fashion and Music*. Boston: Unwin, 1988.

McRobbie, Angela, and J. Garber. "Girls and Subcultures." *Resistance through Rituals*, ed. S. Hall and T. Jefferson. London: Unwin, 1976.

Mehler, Mark. "Geraldo: In Control . . . with an Edge." *Variety*, 26 August 1991, p. 70.

Mercer, Kobena. "Dark and Lovely Too: Black Gay Men in Independent Film." *Queer Looks: Perspectives on Lesbian and Gay Film and Video*, ed. Martha Gever, Pratibha Parmar, and John Greyson. New York: Routledge, 1993, pp. 238–256.

Milam, Lorenzo. *Sex and Broadcasting: A Handbook on Starting a Radio Station for the Community*. 3d ed. Los Gatos, CA: MHO and MHO Works, 1988.

Miller, Stuart. "Fox 'Roc' 'n' Rolls in Male Demos." *Variety*, 23 December 1991, p. 6.

Modleski, Tania. *Loving with a Vengeance: Mass-Produced Fantasies for Women*. New York: Methuen, 1984.

Mohanraj, Mary Anne, with photos by Tracy Lee. *Torn Shapes of Desire: Internet Erotica*. Philadelphia: Intangible Assets Manufacturing, 1996.

Morality in Media. *Newsletter*. New York, 1984–.

More Sex and Drugs and Rock 'n' Roll: Another Pictorial History of Sex and Drugs and Rock 'n' Roll. London: Bobcat, 1988.

Mumford, Laura Stempel. *Love and Ideology in the Afternoon: Soap Opera, Women and Television Genre*. Bloomington: Indiana University Press, 1995.

————. "Plotting Paternity: Looking for Dad in the Daytime Soaps." *Genders*, 12 (Winter 1991): 45–62.

Munson, Wayne. *All Talk: The Talkshow in Media Culture*. Philadelphia: Temple University Press, 1993.

"Music and Sex." Special issue of *Future Sex*, 7 (July–September 1994).

National Council of Churches of Christ in the U.S.A. *Violence and Sexual Violence in Film, Television, Cable and Home Video*. New York: National Council of Churches of Christ, 1985.

Nelson, Craig. *Bad TV: The Very Best of the Very Worst*. New York: Dell, 1995.

Newcomb, Horace. *TV: The Most Popular Art*. New York: Anchor, 1974.

Nochinson, Martha. *No End to Her: Soap Opera and the Female Subject*. Berkeley: University of California Press, 1992.

Noebel, David A. *The Marxist Minstrels: A Communist Subversion of Music*. Tulsa, OK: American Christian College Press, 1974.

O'Connell, Pamela Licalzi. "Web Erotica Aims for New Female Customers." *New York Times*, 13 August 1998, p. D6.

O'Connor, John J. "For a Date (Wink) or a Tease (Smirk), Try Late-Night TV." *New York Times*, 30 June 1992, pp. B1–2.

————. "The New Woman Finds Her Place on the Small Screen." *New York Times*, national ed., 4 November 1990, p. 33.

————. "Smut or Social Chronicle? MTV Debates Gangsta Rap." *New York Times*, 25 May 1994, p. B5.

Off the Straight and Narrow: Lesbians, Gays, Bisexuals, and Television. Northampton, MA: Media Education Foundation, 1998.

"Oh, Wendy O.!" *Playboy*, 33:10 (October 1986): 70, 178, 180.

Olmsted, Jack. "Playboy Opens WWW Emporium." *New Media*, 4:11 (November 1994): 58.

Olsen, Beth. "Sex and the Soaps: A Comparative Content Analysis of Health Issues." *Journalism Quarterly*, 71:4 (Winter 1994): 840–850.

Paglia, Camille. *Sexual Personae: Art and Decadence from Nefertiti to Emily Dickinson.* New York: Vintage, 1991.

Palac, Lisa. "Blue Notes: A Look at the Time-Honored Relationship between Sex and Music." *Future Sex*, 7 (July–September 1994): 22–26, 28–29.

———. "Cyberspace." *Penthouse*, 25:7 (March 1994): 20.

———. *Cyborgasm*. San Francisco: Algorithm, 1993.

———. "Plant One on Me: Plugging into Rock's Erotic Influence." *Future Sex*, 7 (July–September 1994): 6–7.

———. "Viva La Pussy: Love, Sex, and Being Female with Ann Magnuson." *Future Sex*, 6 (March–May 1994): 24–28.

Palmer, C. Eddie. "Filthy Funnies, Blue Comics, and Raunchy Records: Dirty Jokes and Obscene Language as Public Entertainment." *Sexual Deviancy in Social Context*, ed. Clifton D. Bryant. New York: New Viewpoints, 1977, pp. 82–101.

Pareles, Jon. "Musical Maverick Frank Zappa Had Impact Far beyond Rock." *Columbus (Ohio) Dispatch*, 7 December 1993, p. 11D.

———. "Sex, Lies and the Trouble with Videotapes." *New York Times*, 22 June 1991, pp. 31, 40.

Parents' Music Resource Center. *Rising to the Challenge*. Arlington, VA: PMRC, 1991.

Peacott, Mary Ann, and Pam Nicholas. "Where Are the Punk Dykes?" *Rock against Sexism*, 4 (1990/91). P.O. Box 390643, Cambridge, MA 02139.

Peck, A. "Stones Lyric Protest." *Rolling Stone*, 16 November 1978, p. 19.

Perry, Imani. "It's My Thang and I'll Swing It the Way That I Feel!: Sexuality and Black Women Rappers." *Gender, Race and Class in Media: A Text-Reader*, ed. Gail Dines and Jean M. Humez. Thousand Oaks, CA: Sage, 1995, pp. 524–530.

Peters, Don, and Steve Peters, with Cher Merrill. *Rock's Hidden Persuader: The Truth about Backmasking*. Minneapolis: Bethany House, 1985.

Powers, Ann. "Pop View: That Girl by the Stage, and Why She's There." *New York Times*, 20 December 1992, p. H30.

Powledge, Fred. "Switched-On Radio: WBAI." *Avant-Garde*, September 1968, pp. 25–29.

Price, Jonathan. "Almost Obscene." *The Best Thing on TV: Commercials*. New York: Penguin, 1978, pp. 35–43.

Price, Monroe E. *The V-Chip Debate: Content Filtering from Television to the Internet*. Mahwah, NJ. Lawrence Erlbaum Associates, 1998.

Price, Wayne T. "Harassment Goes On-Line: Low-Tech Problem Hits PC Networks." *USA Today*, 6 August 1993, pp. B1–B2.

Priest, Patricia J. *Public Intimacies: Talk Show Participants and Tell-All TV*. Cresskill, NJ: Hampton Press, 1995.

Radio Sex: Off the Dial. Produced and directed by Shari Cookson. New York: HBO/Dave Bell Associates, 1997.

Rensin, David. "Twenty Questions: Maury Povich." *Playboy*, 37:9 (September 1990): 140–141, 163–164.

Reynolds, Simon, and Joy Press. *The Sex Revolts: Gender, Rebellion, and Rock 'n' Roll*. Cambridge: Harvard University Press, 1995.

Rheingold, Howard. *Virtual Reality*. New York: Summit Books, 1991.

Rifkin, Alan. "Terminal Bliss." *Details* (June 1993): 30–32, 34, 36, 38.

Rimm, Martin. "Marketing Pornography on the Information Superhighway: A Survey of 917,410 Images, Descriptions, Short Stories, and Animations Downloaded 8.5 Million Times by Consumers in over 2,000 Cities in Forty Countries, Provinces, and Territories." *Georgetown Law Review*, 83 (June 1995): 1849–1958.

Rivera, Geraldo, with Daniel Paisner. *Exposing Myself*. New York: Bantam, 1991.

Rivera, Rose Rubin. "Short Takes: Around the Block." *Gallery*, 21:10 (October 1993): 25.

Roberts, Robin. *Ladies First: Women in Music Video*, packaged with a videotape. Jackson: University of Mississippi Press, 1996.

Robins, J. Max. "Tabloid TV: First Class Ratings but Second-Class Ad Rates." *Variety*, 20 January 1992, pp. 27, 34.

———. "Talkshow Producers Find Dial-a-Dilemma." *Variety*, 11–17 April 1994, pp. 45–46.

Robinson, Phillip, and Nancy Tamosaitis, with Peter Spear and Virginia Soper. *The Joy of Cybersex: An Underground Guide to Electronic Media*. (Includes a DOS-disk.) New York: Brady Books, 1993.

"Rock and Raunch." Special issue. *Screw*, 345 (13 October 1975).

Rose, Tricia, and Andrew Ross, eds. *Microphone Fiends: Youth Music and Youth Culture*. New York: Routledge, 1994.

Rosen, Jeffrey. "Cheap Speech." *New Yorker*, 7 August 1995, pp. 75–80.

Rosenblum, Trudi M. "Sex Audiobooks: Not What You Think." *Billboard*, 4 November 1995, pp. 74–75, 77.

Rosenstone, Robert A. "The Times They Are a-Changin': The Music of Protest." *Mass Media and Mass Man*, ed. Alan Casty. 2d ed. New York: Holt, Rinehart, and Winston, 1973, pp. 110–119.

Sapolsky, Barry S., and Joseph O. Tabarlet. "Sex in Primetime Television: 1979–1989." *Journal of Broadcasting and Electronic Media*, 35:4 (Fall 1991): 505–516.

Sauter, Van Gordon. "In Defense of Tabloid TV." *TV Guide*, 31–37 (5 August 1989): 4.

Schacht, Steven P. *"The Obscene Telephone Call: Heterosexual Instrumentalism and Male Dominance."* Ph.D. dissertation, Colorado State University, 1990.

Schwarz, K. Robert. "Composer's Closets Open for All to See." *New York Times*, 19 June 1994, sec. H, pp. 1, 24.

Search and Destroy. 11 issues. San Francisco: RE/Search, 1977–1978.

Seidman, Steven A. "An Investigation of Sex-Role Stereotyping in Music Videos." *Journal of Broadcasting and Electronic Media*, 36:2 (Spring 1992): 209–216.

Semans, Anne, and Cathy Winks. *The Woman's Guide to Sex on the Web*. New York: Harper/Collins, 1999.

Sex Counseling by Telephone. Cambridge, MA: Schenkman Publishing, 1976.

Sex-O-Rama: Music from Classic Adult Films. Oglio Records, P.O. Box 404, Redondo Beach, CA 90277.

Sexton, Adam, ed. *Desperately Seeking Madonna*. New York: Dell, 1993.

———. *Rap on Rap: Straight-Up Talk on Hip-Hop Culture*. New York: Dell, 1995.

Sexxy Software. 2880 Bergey Road, Hatfield, PA 19440.

Sherman, Barry L., and Joseph R. Dominick. "Guns, Sex and Rock and Roll." *Maincurrents in Mass Communications*, ed. Warren K. Agee, Philip H. Ault, and Edwin Emery. New York: Harper and Row, 1986, pp. 347–350.

———. "Violence and Sex in Music Videos: TV and Rock 'n' Roll." *Journal of Communication*, 36:1 (1986): 79–93.

"Sick Jokes." *New York Times*, national ed., 6 August 1991, p. A10.

Sierra On-Line. *Leisure Suit Larry in the Land of the Lounge Lizards*. Oakhurst, CA: Sierra On-Line, 1991.

Silberger, Katherine, and Lauren Spencer. "Where Is the Lust?" *Village Voice*, 3 April 1991, p. 6.

Silberman, Steve. "The Golden Age of Porn Online." *Wired News* (www.wired.com/news/news/culture/story/16175.html) (October 1998).

Simakis, Andrea. "Telephone Love: Real-Life Fantasies of the Fantasy Girls." *Village Voice*, 17 July 1990, pp. 35–36, 38–39.

Simpson, Amelia. *Xuxa: The Mega-Marketing of Gender, Race, and Modernity*. Philadelphia: Temple University Press, 1993.

Smith, Richard. *Other Voices: A History of Homosexuality and Popular Music*. New York: Cassell, 1998.

———. *Seduced and Abandoned: Essays on Gay Men and Popular Music*. New York: Cassell, 1995.

Soap Opera Digest. New York, 1987–.

Soap Opera Weekly. Los Angeles, 1989–.

"Soap Operas: Sex and Suffering in the Afternoon." *Time*, 12 January 1976, pp. 46–53.

Speed, John. "Dial a Porn Star." *Adam Film World Guide*, 5:10 (April 1991): 26, 34.

Springer, Claudia. *Electronic Eros: Bodies and Desire in the Postindustrial Age*. Austin: University of Texas Press, 1996.

Stallings, Penny. *Forbidden Channels: The Truth They Hide from TV Guide*. New York: HarperPerennial, 1991.

Stanley, Lawrence A. *Rap: The Lyrics: The Words to Rap's Greatest Hits*. New York: Penguin, 1992.

Starware Publishing Corporation. Erotic Computer Software (MAC and IBM-PC). P.O. Box 340203, Boca Raton, FL 33434.

Stefanac, Suzanne. "Sex & the New Media." *New Media*, 3:4 (April 1993): 38–45.

Stern, Howard. *Miss America*. New York: Regan Books/HarperCollins, 1995.

———. *Private Parts*. New York: Simon and Schuster, 1993.

Sterngold, James. "HBO Programmer Likes to Kindle Both Heat and Light." *New York Times*, 15 April 1998, p. B2.

Stockbridge, Sally. "Rock Video: Pleasure and Resistance." *Television and Women's Culture*, ed. Mary Ellen Brown. Newbridge Park, CA: Sage, 1990, pp. 102–113.

Stoltz, Craig. "The Thin Blue Line." *USA Weekend*, 18–20 February 1994, pp. 4–6.

Stone, Allucqère Roseanne. "Virtual Systems." *Incorporations*, ed. Jonathan Crary and Sanford Kwinter. New York: Zone 6 (MIT Press), 1992, pp. 609–621.

———. *The War of Desire and Technology at the Close of the Machine Age*. Cambridge: MIT Press, 1995.

Studer, Wayne. *Rock on the Wild Side: Gay Male Images in Popular Music of the Rock Era*. San Francisco: Leyland, 1994.

"Supermodel." *Lifestyles of the Rich and Famous*. Produced and directed by Robin Leach. New York: American Broadcasting Company/Almasini Productions, 5 January 1994.

Swartley, Ariel. "Girls! Live! On Stage!" *Mother Jones*, 7 (June 1982): 25–31.

Tabloid Truth: The Michael Jackson Scandal. Boston: Frontline: WGBH, Documentary Consortium, 1994.

Talked to Death: Have TV Talk Shows Gone Too Far? New York: HBO, 1998.

Tedford, Thomas L. "CensrSex Biblio: Comserve Database." University of North Carolina at Greensboro.

Thomas, Betty, director. *Private Parts*. Paramount, 1997.

Torres, Sasha. "Television/Feminism: Heartbeat and Prime Time Lesbianism." *The Lesbian and Gay Studies Reader*, ed. Henry Abelove, Michele Aina Barale, and David M. Halpern. New York: Routledge, 1993, pp. 176–185.

"Touchiest Topic on Radio Now: Talk about Sex," *Broadcasting*, 19 March 1973, p. 118.

Udovitch, Mimi. "Virtual Verité." *Village Voice*, 12 March 1991, pp. 45–46.

"Ultimate Shock." *People*, 27 April 1998, p. 132.

Van der Leun, Gerard. "Take My Wife, Please—Over and Over," *Penthouse*, 30:5 (January 1999): 171–173.

———. "This Is a Naked Lady." *Wired*, 1:1 (1993): 74, 109.

Van Gogh, Theo, producer and director. *1–900*. Amsterdam: Zeitgeist Films, 1995.

"Video Vamp." *Playboy*, 39:6 (June 1992): 78–83.

Viguerie, Richard. *The New Right: We're Ready to Lead*. Falls Church, VA: Viguerie Company, 1980.

"Virtual Sex." *Mondo 2000: A User's Guide to the New Edge*, ed. Rudy Rucker, R. U. Sirius, and Queen Mu. New York: HarperCollins, 1992, pp. 270–275.

Wakefield, Dan. *All Her Children*. New York: Doubleday, 1976.

Wallach, Michael A., and Carol Greenberg. "Personality Functions of Symbolic Sexual Arousal to Music." A special issue of *Psychological Monographs: General and Applied*, 74:7 (1960).

Wark, Vanda. *The Sex Caller and the Telephone Counseling Center*. Springfield, IL: Charles C. Thomas, 1984.

Waters, Harry F. "Trash TV." *Newsweek*, 14 November 1988, pp. 74–75.

Weibel, Kathryn. *Mirror Mirror: Images of Women Reflected in Popular Culture*. Garden City, NY: Anchor, 1977.

Weinstein, Deena. *Heavy Metal: A Cultural Sociology*. New York: Lexington Books, 1991.

The WELL (Whole Earth 'Lectronic Link). 415–332–6106.

White, Mimi. *Tele-Advising: Therapeutic Discourse in American Television*. Chapel Hill: University of North Carolina Press, 1992.

Wild, David. "Who Is Howard Stern and Why Is He Saying All Those Terrible Things on the Radio?" *Rolling Stone*, 14 June 1980, pp. 87–89.

Wildmon, Don E. *The Home Invaders*. Wheaton, IL: Victor Books, 1987.

Wilkinson, Peter. "Dream Girl." *Rolling Stone*, 20 October 1994, pp. 73–80, 158.

Williamson, Bruce. "Mondo Phoebe." *Playboy*, 35:6 (June 1988): 70–77, 132.

Wright, Karen. "The Road to the Global Village." *Scientific American*, 262 (March 1990): 83–94.

Yang, Jeff. "Computer Goddesses, Not Computer Geeks." *Mademoiselle*, October 1993, pp. 170–171.

Yoo, Paula. "Tales from the Backside." *People Weekly*, 45:13 (1 April 1996): 5.

You, Brenda. "The Hypocrisy in the Media's Criticism of Talk TV." *Editor & Publisher*, 128:18 (6 May 1995): 52–53.

Zappa, Frank [interviewed by Richard Blackburn]. "Fifties Teenagers and '50s Rock." *Evergreen Review*, 81 (August 1970): 43–46.

Zappa, Frank, with Peter Occhiogrosso. *The Real Frank Zappa Book.* New York: Poseidon Books, 1989.

Zillmann, D., and N. Mundorf. "Image Effects in the Appreciation of Video Rock." *Communication Research,* 14 (1987): 316–334.

Zoglin, Richard. "Easing the Sleaze." *Time,* 6 December 1993, pp. 7–74.

———. "Shock Jock." *Time,* 30 November 1992, pp. 72–73.